ENGLISH TEACHER'S GREAT BOOKS ACTIVITIES KIT

60 Ready-to-Use Activity Packets Featuring Classic, Popular & Current Literature

GARY ROBERT MUSCHLA

THE CENTER FOR APPLIED
RESEARCH IN EDUCATION
West Nyack, New York 10995

10 9 8 7 6 5 4 3

Library of Congress Cataloging-in-Publication Data

Muschla, Gary Robert.
    English teacher's great books activities kit : 60 ready-to-use
activity packets featuring classic, popular, and current literature
/   Gary Robert Muschla.
        p.   cm.
    ISBN 0–87628–854–9
        1. English literature—Study and teaching—Aids and devices.
2. Literature—Study and teaching—Aids and devices.   3. Activity
programs in education.   I. Title
PR35.M87   1994
820'.71'273—dc20   93–44779
                                                                           CIP

ISBN 0-87628-854-9

**THE CENTER FOR APPLIED RESEARCH
IN EDUCATION**
West Nyack, NY 10994

On the World Wide Web at http://www.phdirect.com

Printed in the United States of America

❧ *Dedication* ❧

As always, for Judy and Erin.

❋ *About the Author* ❋

Gary Robert Muschla received his B.A. and M.A.T. degrees from Trenton State College in New Jersey. He teaches at Appleby School in Spotswood, New Jersey, where he has specialized in the teaching of reading and writing, conducted writing workshops for teachers and students, and edited magazines of students' writing.

In addition to his 19 years as a classroom teacher, Mr. Muschla has been a successful freelance writer, editor, and ghostwriter. He is a member of the Authors Guild, the Authors League of America, the National Writers Club, and the Associated Business Writers of America.

Mr. Muschla has also authored three other resources for teachers: the *Writing Workshop Activities Kit: Ready-to-Use Worksheets and Enrichment Lessons for Grades 4-9* (The Center for Applied Research in Education, 1989), *The Writing Teacher's Book of Lists* (Prentice Hall, 1991), and the *Writing Workshop Survival Kit* (The Center for Applied Research in Education, 1993).

❊ *Acknowledgments* ❊

I'd like to thank John C. Orlick, my principal, for the support he has always given me. My appreciation also to Julia Rhodes, our district's language arts supervisor, and my colleagues, for their encouragement and help.

Special thanks go to my wife Judy for her work in choosing and arranging the artwork throughout this book.

I'd also like to thank Brian Blatz for his help in research, and for sharing his understanding and insight of literature.

My thanks to Donna Cooper, my typist, who somehow managed to keep the manuscript updated despite all the little (but nagging) revisions that I always seem to make right up until production.

I greatly appreciate the work and suggestions of Susan Kolwicz, my editor, who helped me to fashion this book into what I hope will be a useful resource for teachers. Thanks also to Zsuzsa Neff, my production editor, and Dee Coroneos my desktop editor, whose efforts resulted in a book design that is attractive and easy to use.

And finally, I'd like to thank my students whose enthusiasm, curiosity, and friendship over the years have been a wonderful source of inspiration.

❀ *About English Instruction* ❀

I like to argue that learning English is crucial to the overall success of any student. When a student understands the skills vital to reading and writing in the English language, he or she has acquired the ability to communicate—to express, share, and discuss ideas. Effective communication is essential to every other discipline.

While there are many ways to teach English, probably the best is through a linkage of reading and writing. The research clearly indicates that students who read well also write well, and students who enjoy writing usually are good readers. Reading and writing are the foundation of effective English instruction.

The research also indicates that students learn the skills of language best when the skills are taught in relationship and context. Literature, therefore, is an excellent tool for teaching English, because students learn the skills for language in their relationship to an entire story rather than in isolation on a drill sheet where there is little or no contextual meaning. Moreover, when you use literature to teach English, you are opening the world to your students, giving them the chance to glimpse new places, contemplate fresh ideas, and imagine things of which they had no previous inkling.

This resource provides you with the opportunity to teach English skills through exciting literature that covers various genres, themes, and cultures. Not only will you be teaching the skills for effective reading and writing, but you will be helping your students to experience the world. My best wishes to you as you begin.

❧ *How to Use This Resource* ❧

The *English Teacher's Great Books Activities Kit* is divided into two major parts. Part I offers classroom management strategies for the teaching of reading and writing that can help you make your teaching efficient and effective. Part II contains teaching suggestions and reading and writing activities for 60 novels (and plays), selected especially for their relevance and use in middle and high school English classes.

Part I contains Sections 1 through 3, and provides detailed information on topics such as management, setting up your classroom, organizing your reading and writing instruction for the whole class, groups, or individuals, building a classroom library, the writing process, and evaluation and grading. There is also information on whole language for teachers who are using this approach. These sections contain various reproducibles for both students and teachers. (You may prefer to make transparencies of some and use them on overhead projectors.) I suggest that you read through Part I first, and use the materials that best suit your needs and program.

Part II, Sections 4 through 6, contains materials for 60 novels (and plays), organized into three groups: grades 7-8, 9-10, and 11-12. Based on the specific needs and abilities of your students, however, the grade level designations may vary. The material for each novel includes information and teaching suggestions for you, a reproducible writing assignment, and reproducibles for questions, projects and activities for the students. There are also questions that extend into other subject areas.

You have several options for teaching the novels. The material for each novel is suitable for whole-class, group, or individual learning. All of the materials for students are reproducible. You may assign all of the questions or just some; you may form groups and assign each a different project. You may even work with another teacher. For example, as you teach the novel, students may work on the "Curriculum Connections" with a teacher from another discipline. If you select some of the novels for whole-class reading, you might provide students with a list of the remaining books and encourage them to read these titles individually. You can then make packets of the reproducibles available to your students to work on as they go along.

The more than 180 reproducibles throughout this resource contain numerous activities and projects. They will provide your students with a variety of interesting and challenging assignments for a broad range of literature, which will help make your teaching easier and more effective.

❧ Contents ❧

PART II. READY-TO-USE ACTIVITIES

❧ *Chart for Interdisciplinary Activities* ❧

While many of the activities in Part II touch upon other subject areas, the questions for each book appearing under "Curriculum Connections" are designed for interdisciplinary development. The following chart identifies specific questions for each book that can be easily used in other subject areas. In many cases, there is more than one question for each category marked.

Key: SS - Social Studies, Sci - Science, M - Math, A - the Arts, including music, dance, and artwork.

		SS	Sci	M	A
1.	*Homecoming*	x	x		
2.	*One Fat Summer*	x	x		x
3.	*Call It Courage*	x	x		x
4.	*The Outsiders*	x			
5.	*A Wizard of Earthsea*	x			x
6.	*Roll of Thunder, Hear My Cry*	x			x
7.	*The Chocolate War*	x			x
8.	*The Slave Dancer*	x			x
9.	*The Princess Bride*	x			x
10.	*Julie of the Wolves*	x	x		x
11.	*The Contender*	x			x
12.	*The Sword in the Stone*	x			x
13.	*The Upstairs Room*	x			x
14.	*The Pigman*		x	x	x
15.	*Sing Down the Moon*	x	x		x
16.	*I Will Call It Georgie's Blues*	x			x
17.	*Durango Street*	x			x
18.	*House of Stairs*		x		x
19.	*Home Before Dark*	x			
20.	*Farewell to Manzanar*		x		
21.	*A Separate Peace*	x			x
22.	*To Kill a Mockingbird*	x	x		
23.	*Animal Farm*	x			x
24.	*A Tale of Two Cities*	x			
25.	*Of Mice and Men*	x			x

		SS	Sci	M	A
26.	*I Know Why the Caged Bird Sings*	x			x
27.	*After the First Death*	x			x
28.	*Dicey's Song*	x		x	x
29.	*I Never Promised You a Rose Garden*		x		x
30.	*Flowers for Algernon*		x		x
31.	*Hiroshima*	x			x
32.	*The Miracle Worker* (play)		x		x
33.	*Dragonwings*	x	x		x
34.	*Running Loose*	x			x
35.	*Flowers in the Attic*	x	x	x	x
36.	*The Adventures of Huckleberry Finn*	x			x
37.	*Something Wicked This Way Comes*	x	x		x
38.	*The Pearl*	x	x		x
39.	*The Hitchhiker's Guide to the Galaxy*	x	x		x
40.	*Night*	x			x
41.	*Lord of the Flies*	x	x		
42.	*The Scarlet Letter*	x			x
43.	*All Quiet on the Western Front*	x			x
44.	*Wuthering Heights*	x			x
45.	*Brave New World*	x	x		x
46.	*Fahrenheit 451*	x			x
47.	*A Raisin in the Sun* (play)	x			x
48.	*Watership Down*		x		x
49.	*A Little Love*	x			x
50.	*Dune*		x	x	x
51.	*Gone with the Wind*	x			x
52.	*Native Son*	x			x
53.	*Jane Eyre*	x			x
54.	*Dinner at the Homesick Restaurant*	x	x		
55.	*Slaughterhouse-Five*	x	x		x
56.	*One Flew Over the Cuckoo's Nest*	x	x		
57.	*The House on Mango Street*	x			x
58.	*Fallen Angels*	x			x
59.	*Hamlet* (play)	x			
60.	*Memory*	x	x		x

PART I

MANAGING YOUR ENGLISH CLASSES

❧ 1 ❧

An Overview

There are many kinds of English classes. Whether it is called a traditional class, literature-based program, or whole language, each one reflects the philosophy and personality of its teacher. You should develop your classes in a way that meets your needs and the needs of your students. While individual English classes may differ, all share many common components. See the "Elements of Effective English Classes," which follows.

In a well-run English class, students use language even as they learn language. In the typical class, reading is taught through the use of various types of literature. Writing is done for meaningful purposes, frequently on self-selected topics. The connection between reading and writing is a strong one and becomes one of the interweaving threads of the class.

Effective English classes are filled with activity. There is much cooperation, collaboration, and sharing. Students learn language by observing others using it well, and also by using it themselves. The classes are busy places where students work alone, interact with each other, and confer individually and in groups with the teacher. An entire class may listen to you present a mini-lesson, and then break into groups to discuss a novel that the students are reading. Depending on how you organize your classes, all students may be reading the same novel or they may be reading different novels. Small groups of students may be reading a particular novel. In writing, students may be working on a variety of different topics. Some of these topics may grow out of their reading, while others may be separate topics that the students want to write about. Some students may be writing material for a class publication. Successful English classes offer almost limitless possibilities for learning.

Of course, classroom rules, routines, and standards of behavior must be set and maintained. Methods of evaluation must be determined to insure that course requirements are met. You must decide on how you will run your classes, based on district guidelines and your objectives and expectations.

As their teacher, you will provide the environment where your students can become immersed in all aspects of language. Through the effective management of your classroom, you will offer your students the wonder and power of language in context and meaning.

ELEMENTS OF EFFECTIVE ENGLISH CLASSES

Although English classes may differ because of the personality of the teacher and the particular needs of students, all effective English classes share many of the following:

- ❊ Language is respected and celebrated.
- ❊ Language skills are taught in context.
- ❊ Literature is used meaningfully.
- ❊ A variety of reading materials is available.
- ❊ Various types of reading and writing are studied.
- ❊ Students have some choice in what they read.
- ❊ Students are encouraged to generate their own topics for writing.
- ❊ Writing is purposeful and on meaningful topics.
- ❊ Writing is treated as a process of stages—prewriting, drafting, revising, editing, and publishing (sharing).
- ❊ Students assume responsibility for their learning.
- ❊ Cooperation and collaboration are encouraged.
- ❊ Language is used as a tool for learning even as it is being learned.
- ❊ Students and teachers become partners in learning.
- ❊ Students understand how they will be evaluated.
- ❊ Evaluation is consistent.
- ❊ Goals and objectives are made clear to students.
- ❊ Sufficient time is allotted for learning.
- ❊ Striving toward excellence is required.

The Whole Language Class

No definition can accurately describe whole language. Nor is there a specific program or step-by-step methodology that can be labeled whole language. Rather, whole language is an approach to instruction that focuses on the teaching of language skills *in context.* Instead of breaking language learning down into isolated skills that fit neatly into a day's lesson, the whole language teacher presents language "whole" in real and relevant relationships. Most good English teachers do that no matter what type of program they teach.

At the core of the whole language movement is the belief, based on research and observation, that language is learned more effectively when it is meaningful and functional. Quite simply, students learn to read best by reading, and they learn to write best by writing. Few English teachers would disagree.

Because the whole language class is nontraditional in its structure, should you decide to teach in this manner, you will assume new roles. See "The Role of the Whole Language Teacher." No longer will you be a mere provider of information who lectures, leads discussions, and assigns homework on isolated skills in English texts or workbooks, but instead you'll be the manager of learning in your classroom. Much of your teaching will be via mini-lessons. You will work with the whole class, small groups, and individuals. The greatest amount of class time will be spent on reading and writing. You will model many of the skills your students will encounter.

As a whole language teacher, you will become a facilitator and resource. Instead of "spoon-feeding" facts in small, bite-sized pieces, you will guide your students as they discover language for themselves. By presenting students with a setting in which they find meaningful uses for language, you will be offering them the opportunity for learning.

During the class you circulate, meet with students, and maintain an orderly environment. Your tasks will be many and varied. Based on how you structure your class, you might speak with individuals about the novels they are reading, or meet with small groups. You might ask probing questions of a student to help him see the author's purpose in a story, or you might listen to a student share her ideas for a piece of writing. From there you might sit in on a literature response group and model the appropriate behavior. For many teachers, their whole language classes become workshops for students in which the opportunities for learning and individual growth are boundless.

Using Mini-Lessons in Your Classes

An effective way to teach concepts and skills in any English class is to use mini-lessons. Since the major portion of class time should be spent allowing students to read, write, and confer, mini-lessons offer an efficient way of teaching specific language skills, techniques, and strategies. They provide a time at the beginning of the period when the class comes together as an entire group.

Mini-lessons also can be used with small groups. If you find that some students in your class are having trouble with a particular skill—for instance, an author's choice of point of view in a novel—you might offer a mini-lesson to just these students. It makes no sense to spend the valuable class time of other students on a skill they have already mastered.

THE ROLE OF THE WHOLE LANGUAGE TEACHER

The role of the whole language teacher is a varied one. Each day you may do any or all of the following:

* Guide a literature response group.
* Affirm students' efforts in identifying a story's theme.
* Help a student select a book to read.
* Encourage a reluctant reader to read.
* Share your impressions of a good book with students.
* Answer students' questions.
* Ask students questions.
* Help a student find a topic for writing.
* Remind students of class rules and routines.
* Maintain an orderly learning environment.
* Plan with students the publication of a class magazine.
* Help a student writing on a word processor.
* Help a student create an idea cluster for writing.
* Train parent volunteers to help maintain book inventories.
* Confer with students about writing.
* Offer revision strategies to a student.
* Order books to build a class library.
* Meet with peer groups to confer about writing.
* Help students focus topics for research papers.
* Teach a mini-lesson on a specific writing skill.
* Teach a mini-lesson on a reading strategy.
* Read a favorite piece of poetry to the class.
* Read a passage of a favorite book to the class.
* Read a piece of your own writing to the class.
* Listen to a student explain how he or she will open a story.
* Plan an interdisciplinary thematic unit with other teachers.

The typical mini-lesson takes less than ten minutes, and should focus on one skill. A mini-lesson might share a reading strategy, point out the use of imagery in novels, discuss a particular genre, or demonstrate a specific writing skill. As you get to know your students and come to see their strengths and weaknesses, you will likely design mini-lessons for their needs.

While the information shared through some mini-lessons will be used right away, for example, the theme of a particular novel, others, like how to use italics in writing, may not be used until students need that specific skill. You will find that once a mini-lesson is presented, you will refer to it as necessary when you confer with students. As the year progresses, the information shared through mini-lessons will build an impressive wealth of knowledge about language.

The best English classes are those built on the way people actually learn language. When a young child first begins to talk, he or she uses language to communicate. The child doesn't acquire the skills of language in isolated parts, but rather in the context of communication in order to express needs. The use and learning of language is meaningful. Effective English teachers recognize that natural process and seek to continue it in the classroom.

❧ 2 ❧

Managing Your English Classes

Effective management in any English class begins with a basic understanding of how language is learned. Language is learned best through reading, writing, speaking, and listening. Even as the need for language increases, learning and language development is individual. Everyone learns the skills and use of English in his or her own time. All babies don't utter "da-da" when they're the same age; but all babies eventually learn to talk. (By two or three most exasperated parents feel their kids talk too much.) Focus your program on the individual as much as possible. Allow each of your students to start at his or her own level and progress from there.

A successful English class is a place of vigorous ideas. As you develop your routines and methods, work hard to make your classes forums where students feel comfortable and confident to express their thoughts. Insure that opinions are respected and valued, and efforts toward excellence are supported and applauded by all.

Since the purpose of language is communication, which transcends all fields of learning, always be ready to bring other subjects and disciplines into your classes. Look to link up with math teachers, the arts, sciences and social studies. Working with teachers across the curriculum on interdisciplinary projects enhances the importance of language in the eyes of students and shows them that language is vital to communication and understanding.

Developing Your Curriculum

In today's English classes teachers and students often have the chance to make decisions about and plan their curriculums. The degree to which you do this, of course, depends on your personal tastes as well as the requirements of your department. When it comes to determining what kinds of topics to study, consider seeking the input of your students. The advantage of this is clear. When students help select topics for study, they gain a measure of ownership in the learning process. They will likely be more interested in studying topics they suggested, and this makes your classroom management easier.

There are several ways to obtain student suggestions for topics. Probably the most direct is to brainstorm ideas with the class. At the beginning of the school year, explain to your students that you would like their suggestions for topics to study. As they offer ideas, write them on an overhead projector or the board. A class of 25 can quickly generate several possible topics. After compiling the topics, eliminate those that you feel could not be developed into solid units, and allow students to vote from among the rest. You might want to let them vote the next day, for this will give you some time to reflect on the topics.

Another method of gathering students' ideas for topics is to ask students for their input by way of a questionnaire. See "A Questionnaire of Student Interests," which is included in this section. Distribute copies of the questionnaire and ask students to complete it. Afterward, as you review the information, look for some common interests or trends. (It's not necessary to tabulate the responses for each question.) As trends emerge—for example, the same books or movies keep coming up—note them. This will give you clues to the interests of your students. If you have several classes, note the trends and interests for each, and then compare them. You can then write a list of several possible topics. You might distribute this list to students and let them pick their top three choices. From that list you should be able to identify good topics. To reduce the workload, have students compile the information. You might even work with the math teacher on this and have students graph the results. Using computers for the graphics is a way to include yet another discipline.

In addition to having students select topics, gather topics from teachers of other content areas. You can do this at department meetings, informally in the teacher's room, or leave a brief note in teachers' mail boxes. Obtaining topic suggestions from teachers of other subjects will help you to develop a list of interdisciplinary selections.

The key to selecting any topic is that it provides a rich language experience. Topics may be developed into units that run two to three weeks; thus you will cover several topics throughout the year. See "Possible Topics for a Core Curriculum," which is included here. The list of topics provided offers opportunities to study various human conditions, issues and genres. If you were studying science fiction, for example, you might have your class read *Dune* by Herbert, and then have students select another science fiction book to read individually. A writing activity could be class book reviews. If you were doing a unit on plays, you might have students read Shakespeare's *Romeo and Juliet* or perhaps a modern play. A culminating activity might be to encourage students to form groups and write and perform their own plays. If you were doing a theme-based unit on minority authors, you might assign *Native Son* by Wright and then have students research the racial problems that affect the United States. You could organize debate teams and examine the causes of our problems and their possible solutions. Such units are a marvelous way for students to learn language even as they are using it.

Building a Positive Climate

A successful English class is distinctive in its emphasis on language learning. The physical arrangement of the classroom and the atmosphere within it help to create a positive climate. Although secondary teachers often are not able to control much about their classroom setting—especially if they have a different room for each section—there is much they can do about the atmosphere of their classes. See "Promoting a Positive Atmosphere," which follows.

Before students can be expected to do well in any class, they must clearly understand its goals and objectives. The tone you establish on the first day of school can do much to set the climate of your classes. Try to handle all the preliminaries as soon as possible and get your students into routines.

NAME _____ DATE_____ SECTION _____

A QUESTIONNAIRE OF STUDENT INTERESTS

To help me make this class meaningful to you, I'd like to know some of your interests, especially in reading and writing. Please answer the following questions.

1. What is your favorite book? _____

2. What are your favorite types of books? _____

    _____

3. What is your favorite TV show? _____

    _____

4. What is your favorite movie? _____

    _____

5. Do you like to write? _____ If yes, what types of writing do you like to do (stories, articles,

    poems, etc.)? _____

    _____

    _____

6. Name three things you like to do. _____

    _____

7. Name three things you dislike doing. _____

    _____

8. Name three things you would like to find out more about. _____

    _____

9. Name three things you worry about. _____

    _____

POSSIBLE TOPICS FOR A CORE CURRICULUM

— *UNIT THEMES* —

Relationships

Nature

Struggle for Life

Poetry
 Types
 Individual Authors

Challenges

True Stories

The Newspaper

The Environment

Minority Authors

Survival

Competition

Modern Essays

Breaking Away

Winning/Losing

Growing Up/Coming of Age

War

Strivings of Minorities

Strange and True

Values

Change

Heroes/Heroines

Sports

Short Stories

The Future

Women Authors

Conflict

Beyond Reality

The Classics

Exploring

Dilemmas

— *GENRES* —

Mystery, Suspense, Detective

Romance

Realistic Fiction

Biographies

Autobiographies

Comedy, Humor

Historical

Adventure

Westerns

Science Fiction and Fantasy

Mythology, Folklore

Plays

Horror

Screenplays

PROMOTING A POSITIVE ATMOSPHERE

There are many things you can do to promote a positive atmosphere in your classes. Here are just a few:

- Encourage the use of language by providing a variety of purposeful language experiences. Remember that language is best learned by using language.

- Encourage independence. Encourage students to "do" for themselves—choose books to read, find writing topics, revise and edit their own writing, learn the new skills necessary to get through difficult material.

- Establish and maintain effective routines.

- Create a class which is an open forum for sharing ideas.

- Set standards for completing work. Make sure that students clearly understand course requirements.

- Set clear standards for behavior.

- Encourage cooperation and sharing.

- Maintain a belief that all students in your class can learn. Express this belief to students frequently through your words and actions.

- Encourage students to assume responsibility for their learning.

- Model the behaviors you want your students to adopt. Read, draft, write, and edit yourself in class, and show students how you use language in your professional life.

- Accept that learning is individual. Students will arrive in your class with different skills and will progress at different rates.

- Adopt teaching methods whereby you build on the strengths of a student even while correcting weaknesses.

© 1994 by The Center for Applied Research in Education

First, explain to your students that they will be taking part in an English class in which they will learn reading and writing in meaningful ways. You should also discuss how the class will be organized, for example, how much class time will be spent on reading, on writing, whether students will work individually, in groups, or a combination of both. You might also wish to discuss class rules and behavior. If you find it helpful, distribute copies of or project "Student Responsibilities," which follows. After that describe your schedule—for example, which days you will be meeting for reading and writing—and also explain your grading system and course requirements. (See "Evaluation" later in this section for information on grading and evaluating reading and writing.)

The first day is the time to start building a positive atmosphere. Remember that even after having established routines, you'll need to remind students of procedures and appropriate behavior. Effective modeling is essential. You should frequently model suitable behavior in various activities, for example, by sitting in and sharing with groups. Students take cues from their teachers, and your modeling can make it easier for them to understand the behaviors you expect. The time period for students to become familiar and comfortable with the class might take a week or two to several weeks.

Once you have established effective routines, remain consistent. It is in classes with predictable, steady patterns that learning flourishes.

Setting Up the Room

If you are one of those fortunate secondary teachers who has his or her own room throughout the day, you can do wonderful things to make it a learning center. Even if you must share a room, or travel throughout the day, you still can do some of the suggestions that follow.

No matter what type of room you have, it should be set up so that students can read, write, confer, and work cooperatively. You might arrange one corner for partner conferences, and another as a reference section, or set up a part of the room to house writer's supplies. If you have computers or word processors, you might set them against the back or side wall, leaving the rest of the room for whole-class, group, and individual work. If your classroom is very small, or you can't section it off, you might have students confer in the hallway, just outside the door. (Before doing this, however, check with your principal about your school's policy and regulations. Some districts, for example, require that students always be supervised by a teacher when in class. A hallway, even if it is just beyond the door, might not be acceptable.)

Ideally, you should replace desks with tables, which are more conducive to group activities; however, it's easy to cluster four desks to make a table. For large group activities, have your students form their chairs and desks into a U-shape or semi-circle. Such arrangements break down barriers and promote a sense of belonging.

Any English class needs language materials. Try to fill your classes with as many books, magazines, newspapers, posters, and examples of print as possible. Utilize bulletin boards to highlight items about language, as well as to display the work of your students. In particular, highlight things like the "Book of the Week," and the "Author of the Week" (which might be a professional or a student). If you run out of space in the room, use hallway displays.

STUDENT RESPONSIBILITIES

You can help make this English class a successful and exciting learning environment by assuming the following responsibilities and attitudes:

* Recognize the importance of learning language; respect and celebrate language.
* Use language even as you learn language.
* Understand that language is our means of communication, and is important to every class, not just this one.
* Come to class each day ready to read and write.
* Accept the responsibility of choosing books to read.
* Accept the responsibility of selecting meaningful topics to write about.
* Do your best to learn the skills of language.
* Accept the responsibility of completing work on time.
* Support your peers in the learning process, just as they support you.
* Work with your peers in the learning of reading and writing skills and strategies.
* Try new techniques, methods, and strategies in the learning of reading and writing skills.
* Behave appropriately.
* Take pride in your work and produce the best you can.
* Grow as a reader, writer, and individual.

To reduce your workload, encourage students to be responsible for bulletin boards and

displays. Not only does this give you more time to work directly with students on language skills, but it gives students a sense of ownership and commitment to the class. You can assign volunteers or appoint committees of students to organize bulletin board ideas such as "Top Science Fiction Authors," "Novel of the Week," and "Favorite Books."

While some environments are more easily changed than others, virtually any physical plan can be made to work. It is your outlook, attitude, and efforts that create a climate for learning.

Organizing Your Day

Planning and scheduling are crucial to smooth-running English classes. Unlike many elementary schools where teachers are self-contained or team teach in blocks, either of which offers great flexibility, the set time frames of most of the upper grades present restrictions. However, careful planning can overcome most obstacles.

First, it might be possible to schedule English classes in longer time periods. In many middle schools, for example, reading and English are taught in separate classes. Scheduling such classes back-to-back, or even setting up an environment where the reading and English teachers team teach, can result in tremendous flexibility.

If your classes are set in chunks of 45 to 50 minutes, you can still teach reading and writing effectively. You might, for example, alternate reading and writing workshops in two-week time frames. For two weeks, schedule reading, and then for two weeks do writing. You can easily carry over many of the ideas and concepts covered in reading to the writing that follows it. For example, if you have just covered plays in reading, students could write plays during writing. You will find, however, that many students will naturally write even as they read.

Another method is to do writing three days a week—Monday, Tuesday, and Thursday—and reading on Wednesday and Friday. At less than three meetings per week, it will be hard to sustain interest in writing except for the most motivated students. Moreover, most students find it easier to read a novel at home than it is to write. I prefer this schedule because it offers the advantage of easily linking reading and writing. See "A Sample Schedule" and "A Sample Lesson Plan," both of which follow.

If you prefer more individualization, you can do both reading and writing daily. At any given time, some students will be reading and some will be writing. Students work on their own projects and progress at their own paces.

Providing a Supply of Reading Materials

Essential to any successful English class are reading materials. You might utilize your school library, a classroom library, a public library, or all three. Students need to be able to choose from a variety of fiction and nonfiction books, magazines and newspapers. Various genres and subjects should be included.

A SAMPLE SCHEDULE

Writing:
(Based on a workshop model. Total time, 50 minutes.)

Students enter class and pick up writing folders. (2 minutes to get settled)

Mini-lesson. (8 minutes)

Students write in journals or continue writing works-in-progress, confer with other students or teacher, generate ideas, revise, edit. (25 minutes)

Peer response groups. Students break into prearranged groups, share works-in-progress, and respond to each other's writing. Or a few students share their work with the entire class. (15 minutes)

Students deposit writing folders and leave.

Reading:
(Class is literature-based. Total time, 50 minutes.)

Students enter class and get settled. (2 minutes)

Teacher shares a passage taken from the last assignment and notes the powerful imagery. (10 minutes)

Students break into groups to share journal responses on their last reading, compare and discuss ideas. (15 minutes)

Students read individually, write answers to specific questions in their reading journals, or confer with teacher about their reading. (20 minutes)

Teacher gives the next assignment, including additional questions to be answered in reading journals. (3 minutes)

Students leave.

Note: Times are estimates and can be changed to fit various plans.

A SAMPLE LESSON PLAN

The following lesson plan is based on a schedule in which writing workshop meets three times per week, and reading meets twice. (Note—the reading assignments used for this sample can be found on Activity Packet 2-5 in Part II of this book.)

Monday: Writing Workshop

Mini-lesson: Writing leads. Discussion of the importance of leads. Sharing of examples of leads.

Procedure: Students write in journals and on works-in-progress.

Closure: Peer response groups.

Tuesday: Writing Workshop

Mini-lesson: Writing conclusions for nonfiction. Discussion of the elements of conclusions. Share two examples.

Procedure: Students write in journals and on works-in-progress.

Closure: Peer response groups.

Wednesday: Reading

Mini-lesson: The characterization of George and Lennie in *Of Mice and Men.*

Procedure: Students meet to share and discuss answers in their reading journals. Students will then continue reading novels.

Closure: Assignment, read chapters 1 and 2, and answer questions 1 and 2 on Activity Packet.

Thursday: Writing Workshop

Mini-lesson: Cutting clutter; listing of several "cluttered" phrases on overhead projector.

Procedure: Students write in journals and on works-in-progress.

Closure: Two volunteers read a script for a radio commercial they co-authored.

Friday: Reading

Mini-lesson: Steinbeck's use of foreshadowing.

Procedure: Students meet to share and discuss answers in their reading journals. Students then continue reading novels.

Closure: Assignment, read chapters 3 and 4, and answer questions 3 and 4 on Activity Packet.

Along with providing access to plenty of reading materials for your students, encourage them to borrow books from public libraries and buy their own from local bookstores. Also suggest that they build their own libraries at home. I still have books I read in junior high in my home library. A good book remains a good book.

Utilizing Your School Library

Most middle and high school libraries can service the requirements of English classes, if the librarians know what you need. You should discuss with your librarian how you would like to utilize the school library.

Ideally, the library will be available when you have your classes. To allow students access, you might arrange to send five or six at a time at the beginning of the period to select books. To reduce confusion of who goes when, assign five or six students to go each Monday, an equal number on Tuesday, Wednesday, and so on. A class of 25 to 30 students can easily be serviced in this way. Since students know when they go, they can plan on it. You can give the librarian a list so that she knows who to expect. If your librarian requires passes, let students sign up at the beginning of the period as they walk in. If the library is not open every day during your classes, you might send larger groups and encourage students to go on their free periods or after school.

Insist that students always come to class with at least one book to read. Even if they are reading a novel with the whole class, I require students to have an extra book in case they have free time and want a change of pace.

When I discuss the use of the library with students, I remind them that they are going there to find books, not to gossip or kill time. Browsing for books is fine, but wasting time is not. If I find students spending too much time, I set time limits of 10 to 15 minutes for them to return. You might also enlist the librarian's help in this. Anyone wasting time gets sent back. The message will get across.

Rather than sending students to the library in groups, you might conduct class in the library once every two weeks (of course this depends on the media director's schedule). Meeting in the library will give students ample time to select, return, renew books, and browse. An advantage to this option is that you will be there to help them.

Working closely with the librarian will help her to obtain books to support your teaching. When your students are reading science fiction, for example, your librarian might be able to reserve various appropriate titles. Most librarians will do this if you give them advance notice. To help your librarian help you, explain the needs of your classes, share book lists with her, and inform her of the kinds of books your students prefer. Most librarians are happy to order materials that they know will be used.

Utilizing Public Libraries

If your school library is small or you have only limited access to it, encourage your students to use public libraries. Contact the librarian and let him know that your students will be using the public library to support their studies. You might also tell the librarian what types of books your students like and will be using. Try to work with the head librarian, or at least a person who has the authority to handle your requests. After you establish contact with such a person, continue to work with him or her. This will prevent your requests from becoming lost in channels.

When suggesting to students that they use the public libraries, emphasize the importance of library courtesy. Students should obtain their own library cards. They should treat books with care and return them on time. When in the library, students should be quiet and not disturb others.

Many public libraries will permit you to sign out multiple copies of books for your program if you check with them first. Explain that you are teaching a literature-based English program. Some librarians will be happy to work with you and stock multiple copies of many paperback books you'll be using. When you talk with the librarian, be sure to have a list of book suggestions. If the librarian is unfamiliar with your program, explain the underlying principles and how the library can support your teaching efforts.

Building Your Own Library

Because the use of books is so important to students in English classes, it is helpful to have a classroom library. If you have your own classroom, or share a room with another teacher, you can easily build a classroom library. Even if you don't have your own room, you might be able to build a small library in a spare room, or add your books to the school's library, perhaps stocking them in a separate section.

There are many ways to obtain books. First, try to have the administration provide money to purchase books for your library. If you can't build a classroom library, suggest (and push) to have money allocated to the school librarian so that he or she can purchase the books you'll need.

To raise additional funds, consider organizing bake sales, car washes, and other promotions. Have your students write the advertisements and promotional flyers.

The local PTA can also be a source of funds. Many PTAs give grants to school programs for the purchase of supplies and materials. Few things are as worthy as the purchase of books.

Mail-order book clubs are another avenue through which you can obtain books. Many of these companies offer bonus points, based on the amount of books students buy. The bonus points can frequently be cashed in to obtain books for the class.

If you like to browse through garage sales, rummage sales, used book shops and similar places, you will often find books that are in surprisingly good condition. You might have to plop down your own money, but many schools have petty cash accounts from which teachers are reimbursed for personal purchases of classroom materials. Before buying like this, however, check with your principal to make sure your school has petty cash available and that you will be reimbursed. If you are not reimbursed, but still want to buy books, save any receipts and record the purchases on your income taxes. They're deductible.

Parents, private citizens, and community organizations can be additional sources of used reading materials. Don't hesitate to ask parents and district residents to donate old books. Sometimes doctors and dentists will provide old magazines. Advertise for old books and magazines in school publications, PTA newsletters, and flyers to parents. Encourage students to write the material. Talk up your need for books every chance you get, mentioning it at back-to-school night and parent-teacher conferences. You'll be surprised at how many people will help.

Despite your best efforts at obtaining books, seldom will there be enough money to buy all that you want. If budgets are tight—which they usually are—buy single copies of many books rather than many copies of a few books. Quality and variety should be your objectives in the building of a classroom library.

Choosing Books

Since the funds for book purchases are probably as scarce in your school as they are in mine, you must select your books carefully. Before buying any books, make a list of some that you feel are especially appropriate to your classes. Check with colleagues, language arts supervisors, and librarians. Consult book lists and identify books you feel should be purchased. Aim for books that will satisfy a variety of interests and abilities. For further suggestions on choosing books, consult the "Book Buying Checklist," which follows.

Maintaining the Inventory of Your Books

If you have your own classroom, or share a room with another teacher, it's relatively easy to house a classroom library. It becomes more complicated with several people sharing a room, especially if all are not English teachers. If you travel among many rooms, you'll need to rely on the school library, or house your books in a separate storage area.

If you rely on the school library, your students will follow the library's procedures for obtaining books. However, if you keep books for your students, you will need a simple and efficient system for students to check them out. It is worthwhile to invest in the time it takes to keep a stock of your own books; what can be easier than a student getting a book from a shelf in your room?

If you build a class library, however, management will be a major concern. Most importantly, you'll need to maintain a record of your inventory. I use a Book Inventory Sheet, which is a lined sheet of paper with the words *Author, Title, Number of Copies,* and the *Condition* of the books written across the top. Always tag your books by writing or rubber stamping your name and the book number in the inside cover. This helps you in recording and maintaining your inventory.

When I first began building my library, I simply made a running list of titles according to author. As my stock of books grew, and I began to acquire several books by the same authors, I began using a separate sheet for each author, and kept it in alphabetical order. That soon became tedious, however, and it wasn't long before I transferred my inventory to a computer disk. Now, as new books are acquired, they are simply added to the file which is periodically updated. Virtually any word processing program can be used to set up a file containing the information of the book inventory sheet.

If you keep your inventory on a computer disk, I suggest that you maintain backup copies of the disk, as well as printouts. Power outages, electrical surges, and spilled coffee can ruin a disk, destroying all records of your inventory. I'm in the habit of upgrading the backup every time I enter new books. I save the file on one disk, and then save it on the copy.

BOOK BUYING CHECKLIST

Before purchasing books for your classes, ask yourself the following questions:

1. Have I considered the abilities of my students?

2. Have I considered literature that is interesting, yet challenging?

3. Am I providing a variety of literature for my students?

4. Have I selected both fiction and nonfiction titles?

5. Have I selected literature that depicts males and females in various lifestyles and roles?

6. Have I selected books that avoid stereotyped characters?

7. Have I considered the sensitivities of my students, particularly those of different ethnic groups, and chosen books that relate to them?

8. Have I provided literature that offers a rich experience in reading?

9. Have I selected literature that contains strong themes?

10. Have I selected literature that includes some "classics"?

BOOK SIGN-OUT SHEET

Name	Title & Copy #	Signed Out	Returned

Although computers can be a great help in keeping lists of inventory, they are not practical for class sign-out records of books. In this case, it's easier to simply keep a "Book Sign-Out Sheet," which is included. Keeping a separate sheet for each class simplifies record-keeping. Students write their name, the title of the book, when they signed it out, and when they returned it on the sheet. You can keep the sheet on a clipboard on your desk and students can sign out the books themselves.

If you share books with other teachers, it's helpful to have teachers sign out books just like students. Maintaining a record of who has what eliminates the problem of not being able to find a book when you need it. A copy of a sign-out sheet for teachers should be kept in a safe but accessible place with the books. A desk drawer or file cabinet can serve this purpose.

Housing books on shelves should be kept simple. Storing books alphabetically by the author's last name makes it easy to find and replace titles.

Keeping Your Books in Good Repair

Along with maintaining an updated inventory, it's vital to keep your books in good repair. Paperbacks (or even hardcovers) will not last long if steps aren't taken to prevent and fix damage. Remind your students of some simple "don'ts" and one important "do" when using classroom or library books:

- Don't bend covers.
- Don't dogear pages.
- Don't spill food or drinks on books.
- Don't write on or in books.
- Do treat books like a treasure.

I always repeat this to my classes. It may sound a little corny, but it emphasizes the point and I'm convinced it reduces damage. Listing these points on a wall chart is also helpful.

Book repair should be an ongoing enterprise. Most book covers can be repaired and reinforced with transparent tape. A two-inch wide roll is good because it can be used to strengthen book spines as well as covers. Rolls of tape and applicators can be obtained at any office supply store. You might also be able to order them through general supplies. Your school librarian probably has some, too.

I find it's easier to repair books as needed rather than put them on the side and wait to repair a few dozen at once. I keep tape handy and fix books as necessary. I also encourage students to tape torn covers or weak spines. While book repair is ongoing in my classes, at the end of the year every book is checked and those needing repairs are fixed. During the last week of school, I'll have student volunteers help me in this.

Along with student volunteers, you should consider using adult volunteers. Many parents, grandparents, and senior citizens are willing to help in the schools. Adults can help record inventory, repair books, make sure books are returned to the shelves, and even help students select books. The presence of adult volunteers also helps to reduce discipline problems and time wasting. If you have a volunteer program in your school, utilize it; if you don't have one, try to set one up. A letter to parents will get you started.

When enlisting the aid of adults, take some time after school or during a free period to meet with your volunteers and explain what they are to do. Set up a schedule. If they are coming in just to update your inventory and repair books, perhaps an hour per week will be sufficient. If your volunteers will be helping students to select books, or checking to see if books are in the right place on the shelf, more time may be needed. Never have volunteers come in and not have anything for them to do.

Student volunteers can be quite helpful, too. Reliable students can help you keep track of your inventory and repair books during free periods or after school.

Occasionally, books will be lost or damaged beyond repair. When this happens, students should pay for the book. Books that are lost or irreparably damaged should be replaced as soon as possible. Make it a point to maintain your library. Even better, keep expanding it.

Managing Your Time

Since teachers never have enough time, effective time management is crucial. The more time you spend on non-teaching tasks, the less time you will have to spend with students.

To utilize time advantageously, organize routines and activities with efficiency in mind. Once routines are established, stick with them. Changing routines can be disruptive to students, and the time necessary to learn new routines is lost. When students understand the class's procedures, the day runs smoother. For example, when students know that they have writing workshop on Mondays, Tuesdays, and Thursdays, they will come to class on those days with their materials and prepared to write. Having reading when writing is scheduled will only cause confusion.

The handing in of assignments after due dates also disrupts efficiency. When you give assignments, be sure that students know when they are due. Suggest that they write assignments down in a notebook or assignment pad. For long-range assignments, remind students often of the due date. When students are late with the completion of assignments, there should be consequences. Some teachers simply count the assignment as a zero while others may schedule detention. Determine consequences based on how you wish to work with your class, but once set, you should discuss the importance of completing assignments and explain what happens when work is not done. Trying to track down students with late assignments can become a frustrating drain of your time.

Some teachers get bogged down with special projects and activities. The production of class magazines is a good example. The teacher announces the deadline for the magazine and begins collecting material. Unfortunately, some students who promise articles don't finish them, or the pieces are handed in but they need additional work. The deadline comes and goes and the magazine doesn't come out on time. The teacher is frustrated and the students are disappointed. Eventually the magazine gets produced, but instead of people being satisfied with it, they are simply relieved the job is done.

In planning any long-term project like a magazine, give yourself enough lead time. Set a deadline for students to hand in work, but leave enough time for the pieces to be revised.

Organize committees of students to help with the editing and proofreading. Remind students often of the deadline and work with those who might need extra help. As material is handed in, have it edited and revised. Don't wait for pieces to pile up and then a few nights before the deadline try to tackle them all at once. Break the work down into manageable parts. (For more information on producing a class magazine, see "Class Magazines" in the next section.)

Approach grading in the same way. Staggering the workload makes it easier. Rather than taking a hundred papers home over the weekend to read, take a few each night. Trying to read a tote-bag full in one sitting will only discourage you; further, you'll wind up rushing and lose objectivity.

The way you organize and manage group work can also result in time wasted, or time saved. If you intend to organize groups, it's usually better to set them up before class. Doing it with the students wastes class time. Prior to class list the names of group members on file cards, then during class simply call out the names. While it's beneficial to change groups periodically, avoid doing so too often. Established groups usually work more efficiently than new ones.

Collaboration can also aid efficiency in your class. In writing, encourage students to work with an editing partner. The editors read each other's work and offer suggestions for revision before the piece is submitted to you. Not only do students learn by sharing ideas about writing, but by middle and high school, students can often catch errors in mechanics on each other's papers. This frees you to concentrate more on the overall piece.

A well-run English class involves students in the class's routines and procedures. Design your classes so that class time is spent on learning.

The importance of sound management to your classes can't be overemphasized. Frequently, when people walk into a successful English class for the first time, they are impressed at how smoothly the class functions. Students are busy at various tasks, noise is purposeful, and the interest in language learning is evident. What's not usually seen is the strong management skills of the teacher. Yet it is those very skills that are responsible for the success of the class.

❋ 3 ❋

Reading, Writing, and Evaluation

There is a strong connection between reading and writing. Readers remain interested in what they are reading because of an author's ideas and skills. Since authors want their material to be read, they use their writing skills to express their ideas and keep their readers hooked. An English class built around these points permits students a wonderful opportunity to explore the bonds between good reading and writing.

Reading in Your English Class

No matter which reading model you use in your class—whole class guided reading, small group guided reading, paired reading, or individualized reading—your primary purpose is to develop competent, independent readers.

Because of the emphasis on reading in your class, you will find that many students read more than one book at the same time—the book that is assigned and a book of their own. To record their impressions of books they read individually, have your students answer some or all of the questions on the student "Book Completion Summary" sheet, which is provided. The questions may be answered on a separate sheet of paper or in literature response logs. Obviously, the sheet is meant to serve only as a guide, as not all of the questions are appropriate for every book. For example, question number 7, about characters, won't apply to nonfiction; I instruct my students to skip questions that aren't relevant. Since the questions are open-ended, you can easily determine whether a student read and understood a particular book, even if you are unfamiliar with that title.

Literature Discussion Groups

Literature discussion groups (also called response groups) provide students with the opportunity to share reactions about their reading. Ideally, the literature discussion group is heterogeneous and small, about 5 to 6 students. In the discussion group, students use their own experiences and knowledge to draw conclusions, analyze and synthesize ideas, and share opinions.

In the beginning of the year, it is likely that you will need to work closely with your groups. You will provide guidance and model appropriate behavior. You might wish to distribute copies of "Literature Discussion Group Guidelines," which is included. It highlights important characteristics of effective discussion groups.

BOOK COMPLETION SUMMARY

Answer the following questions.

1. Write the title of the book, the author's name, the publisher, place of publication, and copyright date.

2. Briefly describe what the book is about.

3. Describe the author's style. Give an example. Was it appropriate for the book? Why or why not?

4. Describe the setting.

5. What did you find most interesting about the book? Why?

6. What part of the book did you find the least interesting? Why?

7. Who was the most interesting character? Why?

8. What was the conflict in the story?

9. What did you learn from this book?

10. Did the book keep you interested? Why or why not?

11. Would you like to read another book by this author? Why or why not?

12. Would you recommend this book to others? Why or why not?

LITERATURE DISCUSSION GROUP GUIDELINES

You will be meeting in a literature discussion group this year where you will share your ideas and opinions about reading. The following suggestions will help your group work smoothly.

1. Remember that the purpose of the literature discussion group is to share reactions to and opinions about the reading.

2. Always be polite and considerate.

3. It's not necessary to raise your hand to be recognized, but don't call out and don't interrupt the speaker.

4. Speak clearly and back up your statements with facts. Cite pages and examples from the text to support your ideas.

5. Make your positions clear. Try starting your comments with phrases like—

   * I believe that . . .
   * I don't believe that . . .
   * I agree with that because . . .
   * I disagree with that because . . .
   * I don't see your point . . .
   * I'd like to add . . .
   * I'm not clear about what you're saying . . .

6. Be willing to give the floor to others.

7. Remember that everyone is entitled to his or her opinion. You may not agree, but you must be willing to let others offer their ideas.

8. Keep an open mind to new ideas. Don't dismiss the ideas of others without first reflecting on them.

9. Remember that everyone should get a chance to speak.

10. If you don't understand what someone said, ask for clarification. There are probably others who don't understand either.

As students become familiar with the discussion groups' routines, you should slip more to the background. You might appoint group leaders who take the responsibility for starting the discussion and making sure that everyone contributes. I like to appoint leaders for one-week intervals. This gives the group leaders time to gain some experience on the task, but also ensures that eventually everybody gets a chance. You'll find that students relish this opportunity of "taking your place." As students assume more responsibility for conducting the group discussions, you are freed to circulate and sit in on various groups. This is an excellent management strategy, for it allows you to monitor student behavior, evaluate individual efforts, and guide the discussions when necessary.

At the end of the discussion time, you might want to summarize the major points. This is particularly appropriate when the entire class is reading the same book and is on the same chapter. You can summarize for the whole class at once. If the groups are reading different books, you might designate the leader to summarize the points that were covered. In this case, designate a secretary, or recorder, to take notes during the discussion.

It takes time for students to become proficient at literature discussion groups, especially if they have never done them before. However, as they gain confidence, the discussions will go beyond the mere facts of the story to a thorough reflection and analysis of storylines, development, and themes.

Literature Response Logs

To ensure that students come to their discussion groups prepared, require them to keep literature response logs (also known as literature logs, reading logs, reading journals, literature journals, and probably a half-dozen other names I haven't heard of). Spiral notebooks, three-ring binders, or booklets can be used for students to record their thoughts and impressions of what they read, as well as answer questions you or others might pose. Require students to date their entries and number their notebooks, 1, 2, 3, etc. By the end of the year students may have several, which, together, will comprise an extensive collection of their reactions to literature.

The logs can be used in various ways. You might present students with a question to answer during their reading, ask them to respond to a particular scene in a story, examine a character's actions or motivations, or reflect upon the theme. You might simply assign an activity packet from Part II of this book, and instruct students to answer the questions as they read the book. I usually ask students to record at least one thing in the reading that impressed them, for example, the author's style, the action, setting, dialogue, imagery, or the emotional impact. What impressed them most might even be that the story bogged down and they began to lose interest. That's fine, as long as they support their opinions. I encourage students to note the page number and paragraphs of sections that support their views so that they can direct group members to specific examples.

Writing in Your English Class

While you can build your writing program around various models, you should teach the writing process, which focuses on the way real authors actually work. The writing process is composed of at least five stages: prewriting, drafting, revising, editing, and publishing.

Although each stage is characterized by different activities, the lines between them are fluid and authors easily move back and forth through the stages as necessary. If your students are unfamiliar with the writing process, you may wish to distribute copies of the "Stages of the Writing Process," which follows.

Writing for Authentic Purposes

Students, as well as professional authors, write best about subjects and topics that they find meaningful. Encourage your students to select topics of their own, as well as topics that naturally grow out of their reading experiences. Reading can be a powerful motivator for writing, as students react to the ideas they encounter in literature.

Your classroom should be a place where students can experiment with various kinds of writing. Some suggestions are provided in "Types of Writing," which I copy and distribute to my students. It emphasizes that they need not limit themselves to just essays and stories—which for some students are the only kinds of writing they've ever done in school.

Writing Journals

Writing journals are a fine way to promote writing in your class. Kept in a spiral notebook or booklet, journals become storage sites for an author's ideas, reflections, questions, and dreams. Entries may explore topics, or be simple musings. Not only do journals help build the habit of writing, but they provide the opportunity for students to experiment with written expression.

Before students start writing in journals, you should lay down the ground rules. Will journals be shared? If yes, with whom? Will you look at the journals? If you do, will they be used in evaluation? Once the rules are set, they should be maintained throughout the year.

While I encourage students to write about personal thoughts, I instruct them to turn down the pages of entries they don't want me to read. However, I also warn them that if I read something in a journal that indicates someone is in trouble, I am obligated to report it.

Writing journals frequently become a record of a student's writing experiences throughout the year. As such, they chronicle the growth of your students.

Writing Folders

I encourage students to keep their writing in folders. Only *writing* is to be kept in the writing folders, and I require students to bring them to class each day. This way works-in-progress are always handy.

Some teachers, particularly those who have their own rooms, prefer to keep writing folders in the classroom. This eliminates the problem of lost pieces and forgotten folders. If you have your own classroom, or can safely store folders in the room in which you meet, keep the folders of each class in a separate box or milk crate to prevent them from being spread around. (Permit students to keep their journals so that they may write in them at home.) Alphabetizing the folders makes retrieval easier, and storing them near the door enables students to pick up their folders on their way into class. This saves the time of passing them out. If you find it necessary to have the folders passed out, ask for two or three volunteers to do it. Assigning volunteers on a weekly basis eliminates the need of picking different people each day. Likewise, you can have students collect the folders at the end of class.

STAGES OF THE WRITING PROCESS

Writing is composed of at least five stages. Authors move back and forth through the stages as they develop their pieces.

- ❋ *Prewriting* is the stage in which an author decides on her topic, purpose, and audience. She generates ideas, gathers information, analyzes and organizes the information, and considers what form her writing should take.

- ❋ *Drafting* is the writing of a piece. During drafting the author often writes, then pauses to read what he has written. He may then rewrite some of the work, or find that he needs to go back to the prewriting stage to change some of the original ideas.

- ❋ *Revising* comes after drafting. The word "revising" means "re-seeing." Authors read through their work carefully, adding, deleting, and rewriting. If changes are major, they might return to drafting or even to prewriting.

- ❋ *Editing* is the stage in which the writing is prepared for publishing or sharing. Final corrections to mechanics are made and the piece is put in its finished form, either printed via computer or typewriter, or written neatly in longhand. If the author finds that more rewriting is needed, she can switch back to revising, drafting, or even prewriting.

- ❋ *Publishing* is the final stage of the writing process. It is the time the piece is shared. For students this includes simple sharing with teachers, peers, parents, or the public. It may also include publication in school newspapers or newsletters, as well as local, regional, or national magazines and newspapers.

TYPES OF WRITING

There are many types of writing you can do in your class. Throughout the year, try as many of the following as you can.

advertisements

advice columns

allegories

anecdotes

anthologies

articles

autobiographies

awards

ballads

biographies

book reviews

books

brochures

comic strips

diaries

editorials

essays

fables

fiction (adventure, fantasy, historical, horror, mystery, romance, science fiction)

folk tales

greeting cards

how-to articles

informational articles

jokes

journals

letters (apology, thanks, business, complaint, congratulations, friendly, job application, to the editor)

movie reviews

myths

newspaper articles

plays

poetry—all kinds

posters

puzzles

quizzes

radio scripts

recipes

reports

research papers

résumés

song lyrics

speeches

sports articles

surveys

tall tales

TV scripts

yearbooks

Publishing the Work of Your Students

All authors need an audience. They need others to react to their writing. If your students know that their writing will be published, they will write better than if the writing is only something to be turned in for a grade.

Publishing refers to all the ways writing is shared—from reading a piece aloud to a partner, group, or class, to displays on bulletin boards and actual publication in magazines. Because it is so important, publishing should be an ongoing activity in your classes. See "Ways to Share Student Writing," which follows.

Class magazines are a high-profile way to share the writing of students. With access to computers and desktop publishing software, you can easily produce impressive magazines. The simplest class magazines, however, may be collections of works written neatly in longhand and produced on a photocopier. I usually produce both kinds of magazines. The important thing is that students see their work published. See "Guidelines for Producing Class Magazines," which follows.

Evaluating Reading and Writing

Several methods of evaluation are appropriate for English classes. Whichever methods you choose, evaluation should be based on authentic language experiences, should be consistent, and should be understood by both students and parents. Following are some of the more common evaluation strategies.

Logging

Keeping a daily record for each student in several classes each day, in which you enter letters, numbers, or checks and minuses in a grade book can become tedious at best and overwhelming at the worst. Instead, consider maintaining a log, or annotated list, of student accomplishments.

You might permit students to keep their own logs, and maintain a running account of what they do each day. You'll find that most students are quite honest. For those who "fudge," casually checking what they're doing each day can foster honesty. Allowing students to record their progress relieves you of the burden of daily record-keeping.

If you prefer, you can keep the log. Make the process a part of your class routines. As you circulate around the class, carry a clipboard or three-ring binder with individual student log sheets. (Each log sheet needs only the student's name and section. Remember to date each entry.) As you observe what students are doing, take notes, but avoid writing too much. Following is a sample log entry:

Date: 10/14
    Spent period reading independently. Worked well with discussion group.

Date: 10/15
    Worked on draft of essay, "Violence in Schools." Conferred with me about
    the lead.

WAYS TO SHARE STUDENT WRITING

Following are some ways students can share, or publish, their work:

- ❈ Reading a piece to a partner
- ❈ Reading a piece to a peer group
- ❈ Reading a piece to a class
- ❈ Displaying writing on class bulletin boards
- ❈ Displaying writing on hallway exhibits
- ❈ Reading a piece at special events or programs
- ❈ Publishing writing in class or school magazines or newspapers
- ❈ Publishing writing in district or PTA newsletters
- ❈ Reading a piece to students of other grades
- ❈ Producing anthologies of student writing
- ❈ Displaying student writing in the school library
- ❈ Photocopying pieces and distributing them to other students
- ❈ Submitting writing to local newspapers (See if a local paper is willing to run a "Students' Corner" and have your students write for it.)
- ❈ Submitting writing to magazines that publish student writing (A good list can be found in *Market Guide for Young Writers, 3rd Edition* by Kathy Henderson, Writer's Digest Books, 1507 Dana Ave., Cincinnati, OH 45207. You might also consult *Writer's Market,* Writer's Digest Books, at the same address. Both books can be found at many libraries.)

GUIDELINES FOR PRODUCING CLASS MAGAZINES

It's not that hard to produce class magazines of your students' writings. The following guide makes it even easier.

* Decide what type of magazine it will be. Will it contain only fiction? Only nonfiction? Only poetry? Or will it contain all three? If it is to be fiction, will it focus on one type of genre (for example, fantasy)?

* Decide on standards. How long will pieces be? Especially decide on what is unacceptable (for example, gory murders). Caution students that pieces must be original. Discuss plagiarism.

* Set your deadline for material well in advance of your publication date. As students hand in material, read it and have them revise ahead of time. Don't wait until the last week and hand back a dozen pieces for revision. You'll never get them all back in time.

* Store finished pieces in a separate folder. If students from more than one class are contributing to the magazine, store each class's work in a separate folder. This makes it easier to find particular pieces.

* Have students enter as much of the magazine as possible into computers. Working on computers makes revision easier. Good printers also produce sharp letters, which reproduce well on photocopiers. Desktop publishing software can produce high-quality magazines, and the software isn't that hard to use.

* Ask for parent volunteers to help in typing. Sending a letter home in advance helps to line up volunteers early. Whenever you send something home for typing by a parent, be sure that you provide adequate instructions of how you want the material set on the page. A copy of a page from a previous magazine is helpful.

* If you use artwork, stick with line drawings. Elaborate illustrations won't reproduce well on the typical photocopier. Have students do illustrations on separate sheets of paper, then cut them out and paste or use white tape to attach them to the page. Drawing directly on the printed page risks making a mistake and having to do the entire page over.

* For titles, subtitles, and page numbers, use transfer letters or stencils. (Of course, if you have access to desktop publishing, the software can do all this for you.) Use light, blue-lined graph paper to help position letters.

* Before printing have student proofreaders carefully check every page. Impress on students that the magazine should be error-free (at least as far as humanly possible). Working on a class magazine helps to teach students the importance of quality work.

* Print your magazine on a photocopier. If your school has a print shop, see if the printing classes can produce your magazine. You'll get a great-looking magazine, and the print shop students will have the chance to work on a meaningful project.

(Class magazines can also be produced on duplicators, but then all of the pieces will need to be put on ditto masters.)

❋ Print on both sides of each page. Not only does this save paper, but it improves the appearance of the magazine.

❋ To make the job of putting the magazine together, do it in parts. Do the first eight pages, then the next eight, and so on.

❋ Print enough copies of the magazine for students, as well as the principal, school library, and other interested parties.

To reduce the amount of writing, use phrases, abbreviations for procedures and activities (r. for reading, w. for writing, d. for draft, etc.), and be specific. If you find that it is too difficult to observe each student every day, focus on five or six in each class today and others tomorrow. The information contained in the logs can help you to follow student progress, zero in on weaknesses, and set objectives. You'll find that over time logging builds a fine profile of your students.

Portfolios

In recent years portfolios of student work have become popular tools of evaluation. A portfolio is a collection of a student's work, showing that skills have been mastered and class objectives have been met. Portfolios also enable students to see and reflect on their own growth, and can provide the basis of goal-setting.

The work is usually stored in a large folder or portfolio. You may select the work to be stored, based on specific criteria, or permit students to select work that they feel best demonstrates achievement. Over the length of the year, the portfolios become an excellent vehicle for showing student growth.

Students may also be enlisted in portfolio evaluation. Working in pairs or small groups, students may offer opinions on each other's portfolios, what they feel are strengths and weaknesses, and suggest what the portfolio owner could work on next.

Reviewing Logs and Journals

Periodically, I review literature response logs and writing journals. Monitoring the logs and journals enables me to follow the daily activities of students. While I may comment on their work, I don't red-pen or grade logs or journals. I'm concerned that if I did students would take fewer risks. They would pay more attention to mechanics, and write what they thought I wanted to see. They'd be writing for the grade instead of genuinely reflecting on their ideas.

Grading

No matter what type of program you have, it's likely you'll still have to grade your students. Many grading systems can be used.

To determine reading grades, you might test students on the various novels they read. Grades can be calculated on a percentage basis. You might also assign a specific percentage to the satisfactory completion of daily activities.

Writing can be graded according to various elements or pieces. Here's a breakdown I like to use:

Focus—20 percent
> The topic is clearly defined; all ideas and details relate to the topic.

Content—25 percent
> The piece contains fresh ideas. Main ideas are logically developed and supported with details.

Organization—25 percent
> The piece is developed logically from the opening to the conclusion. There is a clear progression of thought. The piece is unified.

Style—15 percent
> The author's tone and voice are appropriate for the topic.

Mechanics—15 percent
> The piece exhibits correct punctuation, grammar, and spelling.

Another system of grading that works well is the point system. You assign certain points for particular activities. Reading a novel and completing its accompanying activities might have a value of 10 points, completing a piece of writing satisfactorily might be worth 10 more, and completing a group project might be 15. During a marking period, the points are added up and at the end are converted into a grade.

Similar to the point system is the minimum plus. In this grading system, certain activities must be completed satisfactorily to achieve a specific grade. The base might be a "C", and additional work would raise that to a "B" and then an "A." This may or may not be used in conjunction with student contracts.

The success of your classes will depend in large part on your management skills. Classes in which students know the procedures, know what is expected of them, and are encouraged to do their best will be far more successful than those where students are unsure of the classroom routines and objectives.

PART II

READY-TO-USE ACTIVITIES

Ready-to-Use Activities

The following activities for novels are arranged in three sections—for grades *7-8, 9-10,* and *11-12.* Depending on the abilities of your students, however, you may find some of the books are useful in other grades.

The activities are reproducible and support whole-class, group, or individual reading. You may have your students record their answers in reading logs or notebooks, ask them to hand in answers daily, or turn in all the written work upon completion of the novel.

Each set of activities has three parts: (1) a "Writing Connection," which is a specific writing assignment that grows out of the reading, (2) a page of "Questions to Consider" that focuses on comprehension and interpretation, and (3) a page of "Projects and Activities to Consider" and "Curriculum Connections" that offers the students an assortment of challenging assignments for both individual and group work. (Activities under "Curriculum Connections" are coded for subject areas: SS for Social Studies, Sci for Science, M for Mathematics, and A for the Arts.)

Of course it is not necessary to assign all of the work contained on the reproducibles. You may, for example, instruct students to answer all of the items on the "Questions" page, but give them a choice of projects and activities and curriculum connections. You can eliminate some questions by simply having students cross the number of the question out on their sheet. The reproducibles make it easy for you to assign work to go along with the reading, and follow the progress of your students.

4

Novels for Grades 7-8

1. *Homecoming* - Voigt
2. *One Fat Summer* - Lipsyte
3. *Call It Courage* - Sperry
4. *The Outsiders* - Hinton
5. *A Wizard of Earthsea* - Le Guin
6. *Roll of Thunder, Hear My Cry* - Taylor
7. *The Chocolate War* - Cormier
8. *The Slave Dancer* - Fox
9. *The Princess Bride* - Goldman
10. *Julie of the Wolves* - George
11. *The Contender* - Lipsyte
12. *The Sword in the Stone* - White
13. *The Upstairs Room* - Reiss
14. *The Pigman* - Zindel
15. *Sing Down the Moon* - O'Dell
16. *I Will Call It Georgie's Blues* - Newton
17. *Durango Street* - Bonham
18. *House of Stairs* - Sleator
19. *Home Before Dark* - Bridges
20. *Farewell to Manzanar* - Wakatsuki Houston and Houston

1. *Homecoming* by Cynthia Voigt *(Ballantine Books, 1981)*

Synopsis

Dicey Tillerman and her three younger siblings—James, Maybeth and Sammy—are abandoned in a Connecticut mall parking lot by their mother, who later is deemed mentally ill. They do not know their father or any other family; they have only the address of a great aunt. They set off on foot to cross Connecticut toward her house, and must survive with hardly any cash and no supplies. When they arrive they find that the aunt is dead, and they are taken in by her daughter, Eunice, a religious fanatic. It isn't long before they run away from her to find their grandmother, whom they have never met, in Southern Maryland. Along the way they meet many people. Dicey becomes more resourceful as their leader, and each of the children grows and emerges as a distinct personality. They find their grandmother, Abigail, a bitter recluse who refuses to accept them. By making themselves useful to Abigail, the children win her affection and she invites them to stay with her.

Ideas and Concepts to Highlight

1. Discuss the importance of parents to their children. Parents help their children to acquire the skills and understanding necessary to survive in the world.

2. Note how Dicey must assume the role of father and mother to her younger siblings.

3. Emphasize the many decisions that the children must make on their journey from Connecticut to Maryland. (This can be set up on a class or individual student chart with information filled in as students read the novel.)

4. Point out how the children grow and change because of their experiences.

Writing Connection: "How People Change Because of Their Experiences"

This topic lends itself well to the essay form. Explain the essay to your students. Note that most essays follow a structure of introduction, where the main point is offered; the body, which explains and supports the main idea with details; and the conclusion, which usually adds a final idea to support the argument. This activity can be done individually or as a small group exercise for part of the class period. If you wish to have students work independently, instruct them to complete Worksheet 1-1 to generate and organize ideas, and then write their essays. If you wish to use this assignment as a group activity, instruct students to finish the worksheet individually, and then meet in small groups to discuss and share their ideas before writing.

1-1. HOW PEOPLE CHANGE BECAUSE OF THEIR EXPERIENCES

Directions: Write an essay explaining how experiences can change people. Use examples from your own life or examples from others. Writing down ideas and notes under the appropriate sections will help you to organize your essay.

Opening: _____

_____

_____

_____

_____

Body: _____

_____

_____

_____

_____

_____

_____

_____

_____

_____

_____

Conclusion: _____

_____

_____

_____

1-2. QUESTIONS TO CONSIDER FOR
HOMECOMING

1. Dicey confides to James that she was proud of Sammy for stealing food, yet she acted angry toward him. Why did she do this?

2. After the children were left on their own, Dicey assumed the role of parent over the other children, especially the two younger ones. For example, when necessary, she would console, discipline, and nurture them. Discuss Dicey's role as a mother and father figure for the two younger children. Use specific examples from the story.

3. List five values that Dicey holds, then list five that she tries to impart to the others. Is there much overlap? Discuss the saying "practice what you preach," and how parents do or do not follow their own advice.

4. Compare Stewart, Eunice, Father Joseph, Will and Abigail as moral influences and disciplinarians. How did each of them affect Dicey and the other children?

5. Dicey's "family" is quite different from many American families. In what ways does Dicey's "family" compare and contrast with the idea of the typical American family? Cite specific examples from the story in your answer.

6. Explain Dicey's reasoning at the New York bus station when she is buying tickets to Delaware and tells James, "Two and two is not the same as four."

7. Given the sharp characterizations the author draws for each of the children (and disregarding their uncertain futures), in what careers could each of them excel? What types of arts or sports? Keep in mind the kind of mind-set, mental preparation, discipline and self-control that each of these might require.

8. Suppose you were Dicey. How would you have managed to get the younger children to a new home? What would you have done differently? How would you have disciplined the children? What social services would you have sought out? How would you have traveled? Is there any way Dicey could have been more successful? Why or why not?

1-3. PROJECTS AND ACTIVITIES TO CONSIDER FOR HOMECOMING

1. During the story, Sammy grows from a "problem child" to a strong and cooperative boy. Describe some events that helped him to change. Use a chart like the one below to organize your ideas.

Events	Changes
1.	
2.	
3.	

2. Many novels are adapted into movies. Working in a small group, select a section of the book and write a screenplay for it. Produce and videotape your screenplay. (A good source for screenplay formats is *The Elements of Screenwriting: A Guide for Film and Television Writers* by Irwin R. Blacker, New York, MacMillan, 1986.)

3. In a small group, develop dialogue for a scene. Select various sections of the book. Then have them act out the scene.

4. Create an oral report, a panel, or small group discussion on catatonia, their mother's illness. Is it hereditary? Is there any treatment for it? Is there any chance for their mother's recovery? If their mother were to recover, what might then happen to Dicey and the children?

Curriculum Connections:

1. Why wouldn't Dicey hitchhike? Obtain a map of the Eastern United States and trace each trip, from Peewauket all the way to Crisfield. How many miles is it? How long would it take you to walk the distance at a steady pace? (SS)

2. Imagine you are planning the trip from Connecticut to Maryland. Consult the *New York Times* or your local newspaper, and follow the weather patterns for several days over the areas through which you will be traveling. Chart the patterns. Also consult an encyclopedia for geographical features, noting the important ones that you will need to take into account during your trip. How and when would you plan a trip from one destination to another? Prepare a short report about your trip. (SS or Sci)

2. *One Fat Summer* by Robert Lipsyte
(HarperCollins, 1977)

Synopsis

Bobby Marks is 14 and spending the summer at the family home on Rumson Lake, populated mostly by vacationing families, but with its share of generations-old local clans. At more than 200 pounds, Bobby is insecure and dreading the summer because more of his body will be exposed. His friend Joanie, also insecure because of her big nose, persuades Bobby to take a job keeping grounds for the stern Dr. Kahn. Bobby's parents are not very supportive, and, not wanting to be put down by his father, Bobby lies about the job. Bobby works hard, but is harassed by Willie Rumson, a local who worked for Dr. Kahn last summer and hates Bobby, who he feels stole his job. Bobby is eventually kidnapped by Rumson and his friends and left naked on an island. While there, he chides himself for always being put down and abused. One of the gang members retrieves Bobby, but his resolve is solidified. After a few weeks he loses considerable weight, and finally is cornered by Rumson toting a shotgun. They fight and Bobby topples him off a dock into the water and holds him under water until Rumson nearly drowns. Bobby learns much about manhood, self-confidence and getting along with others during his eventful summer.

Ideas and Concepts to Highlight

1. Discuss the insecurities and physical awkwardness that adolescents feel. Encourage dialogue about how children can keep from getting emotionally troubled by taunting.

2. Discuss the benefits of summer jobs in terms of physical and material gain and personal growth. Talk about interview techniques when someone is applying for a job.

3. Marital tension is present in the story, seen through Bobby's eyes. Talk about its effects on Bobby and adolescent behavior in general.

Writing Connection: "The Makeover"

Bobby feels badly about his weight. In the story, he becomes determined to lose weight, and he does. Most people would like to change themselves in some way, if they could.

For this writing assignment, ask your students to imagine that they, or a character they create, can change their personality or physical makeup. What would they change, and why would they change? Instruct them to complete Worksheet 2-1, and then write about "The Makeover" in an essay or story.

2-1. THE MAKEOVER

Directions: Few people feel that they are perfect. Most, if given the chance, would change themselves. Imagine that you, or a character you create, could change some thing(s) about your body or personality. Answer the questions below and then write an essay or story about these changes.

1. What would you change about your personality? _____

    _____

    _____

    _____

2. Why would you make these changes? _____

    _____

    _____

    _____

3. What would you change about your body? _____

    _____

    _____

    _____

4. Why would you make these changes? _____

    _____

    _____

    _____

5. Describe the type of person you would become because of these changes. _____

    _____

    _____

    _____

© 1994 by The Center for Applied Research in Education

2-2. QUESTIONS TO CONSIDER FOR
ONE FAT SUMMER

1. Bobby speculates that he and Joanie are best friends because of their physical detractions. Do you agree? What else draws them together? Compare their characters.

2. Define "defense mechanisms" and point out Bobby's and Joanie's. In the early chapters, when musing to himself, why does Bobby strike down people like Pete who are nice to him?

3. Explain the tension between Bobby and his father. Why is their relationship the way it is? In your opinion, how might they resolve it?

4. Define self-esteem. Compare Joanie's deliberate transformation with Bobby's naturally evolved emotional one. Which accomplishes more in terms of boosting self-esteem? What are their effects?

5. Discuss Bobby's relationship with Michelle. Trace its evolution, and write a few paragraphs about how you think their relationship will be in adulthood.

6. Bobby seems to lack positive role models in the story. Name some men whom you think Bobby would benefit from knowing. Consider both celebrities and people you know personally. Support your answer in the context of Bobby's story.

7. What is your opinion of Bobby at the beginning of the story? What is it at the end? How has it changed?

8. By the end of the story, Bobby has changed more than in just losing weight. Explain how else he has changed.

2-3. PROJECTS AND ACTIVITIES TO CONSIDER FOR
ONE FAT SUMMER

1. In your group, discuss what types of summer jobs are available to students of your age. What are some jobs you'd like? What would you earn, and what kind of personal growth could you derive from it? Make a list of the jobs your group discusses, the qualifications (if any) that are required, and the type of pay you could expect to receive. Share your list with other groups.

2. Bobby's imagination is quite vivid, especially while he is working. Use your imagination to "see" a favorite place, activity, or item and write a physical description of it. Try to make your writing as detailed and vivid as you can by including your senses: sight, sound, touch, smell, and taste.

3. Imagine that you were a close friend of Bobby. What type of advice could you give him about his problems with Rumson? Write a conversation you would have with Bobby.

4. Research articles and books on divorce. Organize and conduct a panel discussion on the pros and cons of divorce, particularly the effects on the people involved.

Curriculum Connections:

1. Research weight-loss programs from books, magazine articles, and broadcast media. Prepare a short report on your findings. Pretend you are Bobby's dietitian, and include recommendations for him in your report. (Sci)

2. Weight-loss is often achieved better when the person also begins an exercise program. Imagine that you are a trainer and that Bobby has asked you to design an exercise program for him. Consult the necessary references and create an exercise plan for Bobby. (Sci)

3. Obtain copies of some of the recordings Bobby likes and listen to them. What do you think of them? What do they say about Bobby's personality? Expand your answer to include what you think your own choice of music says about you. (A)

4. Obtain a map of a popular recreational area similar to Bobby's summer home. Draw a map of Rumson Lake and the vicinity, using Bobby's description as a guide. Include landmarks, paths and roads like the map you read about. (SS)

3. *Call It Courage* by Armstrong Sperry
(Macmillan, 1940)

Synopsis

Mafatu, a Polynesian boy whose father calls him Stout Heart, fears the sea. When he is very young, he and his mother are caught on the sea during a great storm. Although she manages to save her son, Mafatu's mother dies. From then on Mafatu's haunting dreams make him avoid the sea until his people brand him as a coward: Mafatu, the Boy Who Was Afraid. No longer able to bear the scorn of his people, Mafatu leaves his home island in his canoe with only his small dog and pet albatross. A storm strands him alone on a volcanic island that he comes to find out is a sacred place to the eaters-of-men. While on the island Mafatu survives several tests of courage, including an escape from the savages who would kill him. When he finally returns home, he is truly Mafatu, the Stout Heart.

Ideas and Concepts to Highlight

1. Locate Polynesia on a map. Emphasize that it is made up of numerous islands scattered throughout the central and south Pacific.

2. Discuss that the story is based on a legend. Note the importance of legends to people.

3. Note that, being island dwellers, Polynesians find the sea vital to their survival.

4. Mention that throughout the story, Mafatu wants to make his father proud of him. Along with this, however, he also wants to be proud of himself.

Writing Connection: "Fear!"

Mafatu was known as the *Boy Who Was Afraid*. He not only struggled with the scorn of others, but he had to cope with his fearfulness as well. Discuss the issue of fear with your students, and note that everyone is afraid of something.

For this writing assignment, ask your students to consider their fears, and write about them. They may pick a fear from the past which they overcame, or one that still bothers them. Worksheet 3-1 can be used for a prewriting activity.

NAME _____ **DATE** _____ **SECTION** _____

3-1. FEAR!

Directions: Everyone has fears. Mafatu, for example, was afraid of the sea. Explore your fears through writing. Answer the questions to help clarify and organize your ideas.

1. List some of your fears: _____

_____

_____

2. Which one bothers you the most? _____

_____Why? _____

_____

3. How have you tried to overcome it? _____

_____

_____

4. Have you been successful in overcoming your fear? _____

If you haven't, what will you try to do next to overcome it? _____

_____

_____

5. Who can you go to for help in overcoming it? _____

_____

How might this person be able to help you? _____

_____

_____

_____

3-2. QUESTIONS TO CONSIDER FOR
CALL IT COURAGE

1. Mafatu's father was Tavana Nui, Great Chief of the island Hikueru. Do you think that because his father was a chief, Mafatu was expected to be braver than other boys? Why or why not? Do parents usually have expectations for their children? Give some examples. Are parents' expectations good or bad for their children? Explain.

2. In what ways did the Polynesians rely on the sea? How did this reliance on the sea increase the scorn his people had for Mafatu?

3. Why did Mafatu leave Hikueru? What did he hope to do? Was he right in leaving? Why or why not?

4. When Mafatu dove into the water to fight the shark, he did so to save his dog. Do you think Mafatu thought about what he was doing? Or did he just react to save his dog? Do you think that heroes think about what they are doing, or do they just react to a situation? Explain.

5. How did Mafatu feel when he realized the eaters-of-men had come? Did he have any other choice except trying to get away from the island? Explain.

6. On his return home, in deep despair, Mafatu suddenly rages at Moana, the Sea God. He remembered always being afraid of Moana, but now he says, "I am not afraid of you! Destroy me—but I laugh at you. Do you hear? I laugh!" Why was this declaration important to Mafatu? What finally happened?

7. Do you think that Mafatu's triumph over his fear had a lasting effect on his character? Explain.

3-3. PROJECTS AND ACTIVITIES TO CONSIDER FOR *CALL IT COURAGE*

1. This story is based on a legend. What is a legend? Give some examples of other legends you know. Why are legends important and valued by people? Are legends as important to people today as they were in the past? Explain.

2. Mafatu wants to impress his father with his courage. Think of a time you wanted to impress someone. Who was it? When was it? How did you want to impress this person? What happened?

3. Write a poem celebrating Mafatu's victory over his fear.

4. Organize a debate over the statement: A person isn't born with courage; courage is an effort of will. Conduct the debate in front of the class and let the class decide who won.

Curriculum Connections:

1. Hikueru is a barrier reef. Describe what a barrier reef is. Consult references if necessary. (SS)

2. Mafatu becomes stranded on a volcanic island. What is a volcanic island? How is it different than a barrier island? Why is the soil of volcanic islands so rich? Consult references if necessary. (SS or Sci)

3. Based on a description of Mafatu's sailing canoe, draw or make a model. (A)

4. Research Polynesia. Give its location. Where did the people originally come from? Describe the traditions, customs, and livelihood of the islands. Based on your research, design a model that represents some aspect of Polynesian life, for example, a mask, hut, village, model of an island, a figurine, etc. (SS or A)

5. On his return home, Mafatu looked for constellations to guide him. Throughout history, sailors have relied on the stars to guide them. In the northern hemisphere the most familiar guiding star is Polaris, the North Star. Why? What makes the North Star unique among stars? Will Polaris always be the North Star? Consult references and write a brief report. (Sci)

4. *The Outsiders* by S.E. Hinton
(Viking, 1967)

Synopsis

Ponyboy Curtis lives in the urban Southwest with his older brothers Sodapop and Darry. They are the Greasers, members of a gang with four other teenagers, who are in constant conflict with the upper class, known as the Socs (Socials). Pony and another gang member, Johnny, are jumped by a group of Socs and Johnny kills one of them with a knife. Johnny and Pony hide in an abandoned church, which catches fire while kids wandering away from a field trip are trapped inside. Johnny and Pony save the youngsters, but Johnny is hurt and dies shortly after. Pony, only fourteen, grows up significantly during and after the killing.

Ideas and Concepts to Highlight

1. Note that this story is written in the first person. Explain that this point-of-view (POV) makes it seem as if Ponyboy is speaking directly to the reader. This POV is limited, however. The narrator can only relate those things Ponyboy has experienced or found out about in some way.

2. Discuss gangs and why people, especially teenagers, might belong to them. What does a gang provide its members? Expand the discussion to include peer pressure.

3. This book was written about the urban Southwest of the 1960s. That culture resulted in various pressures on teenagers. Discuss what some of these pressures were. Have students point out the similarities of today's pressures. What might be some solutions?

4. Discuss the differences between the Socs and Greasers, especially their values and actions. Also note their appearance versus the reality.

Writing Connection: "Why Gangs Are Bad (or Good)"

Explain that editorials, sometimes called persuasive writing, opinion pieces, or personal essays, express an author's opinion about a topic and usually try to convince readers to adopt the same position. Many newspapers contain editorials written by both staff and ordinary readers. Most editorials follow a simple structure of opening, which contains a strong statement about the problem, a body, which offers facts and examples to support the author's position, and a conclusion, in which the author suggests what should be done and often calls on the reader to take action. Distributing copies of Worksheet 4-1 will help students to formulate ideas for their editorials.

4-1. *WHY GANGS ARE BAD (OR GOOD)*

Directions: Teenage gangs are a problem in many American cities and suburbs. Consider your feelings about gangs. Are they good? Bad? What do they offer young people? Is there any other way of providing the same "opportunities" to young people? Write an editorial about teenage gangs. Use this worksheet to organize your thoughts and list some ideas for your editorial before starting to write.

Why Gangs Are Good	**Why Gangs Are Bad**

Alternatives to gangs: _____

_____

_____

_____

_____

_____

_____

_____

4-2. QUESTIONS TO CONSIDER FOR
THE OUTSIDERS

1. Why do the two groups, the Socs and Greasers, fight? What do they hope to accomplish?

2. Why did Darry pressure Ponyboy to get good grades? Do you think Darry was right to do this? Why or why not?

3. Describe the relationship between Johnny and Dallas. Why does Johnny look up to Dallas? Why does Dallas care so much for Johnny?

4. Why does Cherry Valance get along with Ponyboy?

5. What are some of the problems the Socs have? What are some of the problems the Greasers have? What do you think these problems arise from?

6. How is Ponyboy different at the end of the story than he was at the beginning?

7. Ponyboy describes other members of his gang as having "too much energy, too much feeling with no way to blow it off." What could the gang have done instead of fighting, drag racing, and shoplifting?

8. The story is written in the first person. It has a distinctive style and voice. Does it sound like it is written by a fourteen-year-old? Why or why not? Is the "voice" appropriate for this story? Why or why not? If the story was written in an adult's voice, how would the story be affected? Would it be as believable? Why or why not?

9. Does Johnny's act of heroism fit his character? Why or why not? What might he have done if Socs were trapped in a life-threatening situation?

10. What might have been S.E. Hinton's purpose in writing this story? Support your answer with examples from the story.

4-3. PROJECTS AND ACTIVITIES TO CONSIDER FOR _THE OUTSIDERS_

1. Check a newspaper and find some articles about racial tensions. Compare the newspaper articles with the gang fights in the story. Prepare an oral presentation that describes some similarities and differences.

2. Imagine a court scene in which you are a lawyer defending a still-living Johnny Cade. What do you think the charge would be? How would you plan your defense? Working with your group, prepare a court scene. Determine roles for Johnny, witnesses, the prosecutor, defense attorney, judge, and jury. Write a script and act out the courtroom drama. Let the jury decide the case.

3. Write a poem, either rhyming or non-rhyming, from Pony's point of view about his feelings after Johnny's death.

4. Ponyboy says that "Nobody would write editorials praising Dally." Imagine that you are the exception. Write an editorial describing what you think were Dally's greatest qualities and achievements in the story.

Curriculum Connections:

1. This story was written about the urban Southwest in the 1960s. How does the culture of that time and place differ with yours today? How is it the same? Do teenagers still have the same kinds of problems? How do teenagers cope today? (SS)

2. Consult a reference and list the other major geographical areas that the United States can be divided into. Could this story have taken place in a city in one of those areas? Explain. (SS)

3. Consult references and list some "traditional" American values. Which, if any, of these values are held by the Greasers? Why might someone hold values that are different from the majority? (SS)

5. *A Wizard of Earthsea* by Ursula K. Le Guin
(Parnassus Press, 1962)

Synopsis

Earthsea is a group of island kingdoms at a time when wizards and magic were common in the world. As a young boy, Sparrowhawk learns simple magic from his witch-aunt. After defending his village against invaders, he becomes an apprentice to a master wizard. Impatient to learn more about the powers of magic, Sparrowhawk goes to a famous school for wizards. He learns quickly, but his pride makes him want even greater power. In attempting to summon the dead—a most dangerous spell—he unleashes a terrible evil. Regretful over what he has done, Sparrowhawk starts on a quest to hunt down the evil shadow in a journey that takes him across much of Earthsea. When Sparrowhawk at last finds the shadow, he finds himself as well.

Ideas and Concepts to Highlight

1. Point out that this story is a fantasy. While there are many types of fantasies, magic and the supernatural are essential to the plot. Most fantasy stories also have a quest of some sort.

2. Discuss magic. Primitive people often believed in magic as a way to gain control over their world, which was often unpredictable and frightening. Extend the discussion to magic today. Do people still believe in magic?

3. Talk about pride. Focus on how pride can be a positive thing and how it can be destructive.

4. Explain what an archipelago is. On a map, identify some archipelagos. (The islands in the Aegean Sea are a good example.)

5. Note that when Ogion advised Sparrowhawk to become the hunter it was just another way of saying face your problems.

Writing Connection: "A Fantastic Tale"

Fantasy is a genre in which stories contain magic. Fantasies can be set in any time or place. Many, like *A Wizard of Earthsea,* are set in mythical or magical kingdoms where societies are primitive. A good example of heroic fantasy are stories about Conan the Barbarian, while an example of a modern fantasy is *It's a Wonderful Life,* the movie starring Jimmy Stewart that airs during every Christmas season.

Instruct your students to write a fantasy. It can be either heroic or modern. Completing Worksheet 5-1 will help them organize their ideas.

5-1. A FANTASTIC TALE

Directions: *A Wizard of Earthsea* is an example of a fantasy. Fantasies are stories in which magic plays an important role. Write a fantasy of your own. It can be set in ancient or modern times, in a world of your design. Complete this worksheet to develop your ideas.

Setting

When my story takes place: _____

Where my story takes place: _____

Brief description of the setting: _____

_____

_____

Main Characters (Use the back if you need more space.)

1. Name: _____ Age: _____

Characteristics: _____

_____

2. Name: _____ Age: _____

Characteristics: _____

_____

Plot

1. What is the quest of the characters?_____

_____

_____

2. What is the major conflict in the story? _____

_____

_____

5-2. QUESTIONS TO CONSIDER FOR
A WIZARD OF EARTHSEA

1. After Sparrowhawk saves his village, Ogion offers to make him his apprentice. What is an apprentice? Why did he do this?

2. In Chapter 2 Ogion says, "Have you never thought how danger must surround power as shadow does light?" What does he mean? How might this be a warning to Sparrowhawk?

3. Why did Sparrowhawk become impatient with Ogion's teaching? Do you think Ogion was right in letting Sparrowhawk go to the school at Roke? Why or why not?

4. Why do you think Jasper makes Sparrowhawk feel foolish? How does Sparrowhawk feel about Jasper? Why does he feel this way?

5. Sparrowhawk had great pride in his magic-working. What is pride? How did his pride lead him to challenge Jasper to a sorcerer's duel? What happened? How did Sparrowhawk feel after the duel?

6. Why did the people of Earthsea hide their true names from all but their most trusted friends and relatives? Why did Vetch give Sparrowhawk his true name? What was so significant about this?

7. When Sparrowhawk returned to Ogion, his former master advised him to no longer run but to "hunt the hunter." What did he mean by this? Do you think his advice was sound? Why or why not? If you were giving a friend similar advice about a problem, how might you word it?

8. When Sparrowhawk finally confronts the shadow, he and it said the same word. What was it? Le Guin wrote: "Light and darkness met, and joined, and were one." What does this mean? What, or who, was the shadow?

5-3. PROJECTS AND ACTIVITIES TO CONSIDER FOR
A WIZARD OF EARTHSEA

1. Sparrowhawk was born with the ability to do magic. Give some examples of people you know who you believe were born with certain abilities. Do they have to practice their talents? Why?

2. Magic plays a prominent role in the story. Write a brief report about what magic is and why some people believe in it. Consult reference books.

3. What was sunreturn? What day of the year is it on our calendar? Why do you think sunreturn was so important to the people of Earthsea? Why do we mark such days as the beginning of spring, summer, autumn, and winter on our calendars today?

4. Either individually or with a partner or small group, write the lyrics of a song praising Sparrowhawk's ultimate victory. If you play an instrument, set the lyrics to music and perform the song for your class.

Curriculum Connections:

1. In Chapter 3 the Master Hand explains that the "world is in balance, in Equilibrium. A Wizard's power of Changing and Summoning can shake the balance of the world." What does he mean? Apply this to ecology and the concept of "balance of nature." Explain how nature is in balance. (Sci)

2. An archipelago is a large group of islands. How might living in such islands affect the way a people develop? (Hint: Think in terms of language, customs, traditions, trade, etc.) (SS)

3. Study a world map and list examples of archipelagos. (SS)

4. In the story, people sang songs of glory, great deeds, and celebrations. What do people sing of today? Give some examples. (A)

© 1994 by The Center for Applied Research in Education

6. *Roll of Thunder, Hear My Cry* by Mildred Taylor
(Bantam Books, 1976)

Synopsis

An African-American girl living in rural Mississippi during the 1930s, Cassie Logan and her family are owners of rich agricultural land coveted by their white neighbors. Strong and protected from most prejudice, Cassie becomes incensed when her school is given discarded books from the state and she is forced to kowtow to a white girl. Her parents, angry that a white grocery is extorting black families for their crops, decide to boycott and begin driving to a store in Vicksburg, taking orders for other black families. The well-connected grocery owners, upset by the boycott, attack Mr. Logan on the road and his wagon rolls over on him and breaks his leg. Cassie's brother Stacey's troublemaker friend T.J. gets mixed up with the lawless sons of the store owners; they break into a gun shop and assault its owner, who later dies. The white townspeople converge on T.J.'s home and mean to lynch him, but are stopped by a fire that breaks out and threatens a wealthy white man's land. The fire, supposedly caused by lightning, is actually set by Mr. Logan to stop the townspeople. T.J. is then arrested by the sheriff and taken away. As the story progresses, Cassie comes to understand the trials of African-Americans.

Ideas and Concepts to Highlight

1. Review the transitional period between the Emancipation Proclamation in 1865 and the Civil Rights Act of 1964, especially in terms of whites' treatment of blacks. Note the major milestones in that period, such as blacks' role in the World Wars, the Industrial Revolution, Reconstruction, and the 1963 march on Washington, D.C. A good source of information for this is *The African American Experience in U.S. History* (Globe Book Company, 1992), which is written at a middle school reading level.

2. Compare blacks' place in American culture during Cassie's day with modern times. Encourage the class to express their views about what has changed and what has not changed.

3. Discuss symbolism. Explain how people and events can function as metaphors for larger themes that occur frequently in other novels and everyday life.

4. Discuss self-respect and how most black people were forced to swallow their pride regularly. Elicit discussion on the importance of self-image and how its obstruction can affect people.

Writing Connection: "The Melting Pot—Is It What We Want?"

The United States is often referred to as a "melting pot" in which people of various cultures and races have come together to build America and share in the American dream. Whereas in the past most immigrant groups suffered discrimination but were assimilated in time, blacks have had difficulty achieving true equal rights and equal economic opportunities. Reasons given for this vary. Some people feel that because of their skin color blacks have not been able to "blend in" and join the mainstream. Others feel that their past slavery remains an obstacle, an invisible barrier. Also, many individuals today reject the value of the "melting pot," preferring a term like "mosaic" that recognizes the persistence of unique cultural identities.

Instruct your students to examine this issue through their writing. Encourage them to consult references and then write an essay examining the concept of the melting pot. After students complete Worksheet 6-1 you might suggest that they meet in groups and discuss their ideas before writing.

6-1. THE MELTING POT—IS IT WHAT WE WANT?

Directions: The United States is often described as a "melting pot." While many people would agree with that statement, others would not. Consult the necessary references to answer the questions below, and then write an essay about the American melting pot.

1. What is the concept of the American Melting Pot?_____

_____

_____

_____

_____

2. Do you think all cultural groups would agree with the concept of the melting pot? _____

Why or why not? _____

_____

_____

_____

_____

3. Do you agree with the concept of the melting pot? _____

Why or why not? _____

_____

_____

_____

4. What might make the melting pot better? _____

_____

_____

_____

_____

6-2. QUESTIONS TO CONSIDER FOR
ROLL OF THUNDER, HEAR MY CRY

1. Taylor uses strong and precise character descriptions throughout the story. Discuss how her characterization adds to the story's realism. Give some specific examples.

2. Describe the Mississippi of the 1930s where this story takes place. Compare it to your home. How is it alike? How is it different? Consider the physical area as well as the relationships between people.

3. Describe Cassie's reaction when she learns that the books her school received had been discarded by the state. How would you feel in that situation? What would you do about it? Explain.

4. Which character in the book is most like you? Why? Select a scene from the novel and write about what you would have done and said in that character's place.

5. When they learn that a white grocery is extorting blacks for their crops, Cassie's parents become angry and decide to boycott the grocery. Do you think they did the right thing? Why or why not? What else could they have done? Explain.

6. Describe your feelings about the Logans' continuous rejection of Jeremy Simms. Are they justified? How would you treat him if you were in their situation?

7. Discuss some of the symbolism in the book, such as T.J., the fire, Stacey's new coat and the thunder. What do they represent? What other symbols could you add to the story?

8. Cassie changes much throughout the story in her understanding of African-Americans' position in Mississippi in the 1930s. How did her opinions and feelings change from the beginning of the story? Give specific events that affected her the most.

6-3. PROJECTS AND ACTIVITIES TO CONSIDER FOR
<u>ROLL OF THUNDER, HEAR MY CRY</u>

1. Imagine that you are a modern-day Cassie. You go to a store or restaurant and are told that you will not be served and that you cannot buy anything. You are told to leave. How would you feel? Write an essay about your feelings over such an incident and share it with the members of your group.

2. Write a short poem similar to "Roll of Thunder" at the beginning of Chapter 11. Choose any character and write it in the spirit of that person's feelings.

3. Imagine that you are an attorney representing Cassie and her family. You intend to sue the local school system for not providing Cassie and the students at her school an education equal to that of surrounding white schools. What would your arguments be? Around what points would you build your case? Working with a group, write the court scene showing how this drama would be played out. Act the scene for the class.

Curriculum Connections:

1. Research the types of employment available to unskilled blacks in the 1930s. Compare the types of jobs open to them in the past to the types of jobs available now. Also compare incomes for blacks of the past with blacks today. Compare the income of blacks with the income of whites. Give your opinion on how much, or how little, economic conditions for blacks have changed. Include graphs with your report. (SS)

2. What was the period of Reconstruction? How did it affect race relations and the geography and government of the United States? Consult the necessary references and write a brief report. (SS)

3. Make a "family tree" for Cassie, including all the characters related to her who are mentioned in the story. Discuss the importance to Cassie of her family "roots." (SS or A)

4. Read newspapers and magazines that contain national news and cut out articles that involve the African-American experience. Write a few sentences about any trends or connections you discover. Make a collage of the articles and pictures, using your words as a caption. (A)

7. *The Chocolate War* by Robert Cormier
(Dell Publishing, 1974)

Synopsis

Jerry Renault, a freshman quarterback, attends the private Trinity School, which is engineering a large fund-raising chocolate sale. The school's assistant headmaster, Brother Leon, is desperate to raise cash and seeks the backing of The Vigils, a gang of upperclassmen who thrive on intimidation and serve at the pleasure of Archie Costello, an icy senior with little concern for anything except power. The Vigils assign Jerry to reject selling the chocolates for 10 days, but after that time he continues to defy both Brother Leon and The Vigils. He becomes a sort of folk hero, but his refusal is a threat to Archie, The Vigils (who decide to thwart him by selling all the chocolates except Jerry's 50), and the school. After threats and a beating, The Vigils force Jerry to box the school's most vicious street fighter, Emile Janza, in a match governed entirely by students who pay a dollar for the right to call a punch in the ring. The Vigils, on the verge of collapse, are rejuvenated through the fight and the support of Brother Leon.

Ideas and Concepts to Highlight

1. Discuss the power of fear, intimidation and blackmail.

2. Discuss the themes of victimization and "lost innocence."

3. Peer pressure, though the term is never used, plays a significant role in the story. Discuss some of its negative effects, as well as the concepts of individuality and self-respect.

4. Review the concepts of tone and rising tension, and their use in the story. Consider the book's theater-like format, including rising and falling action, climax and denouement.

5. Discuss shifting points of view, and how seeing through the eyes of each character makes the story more engrossing.

Writing Connection: "A Modern-Day Hero"

In *The Chocolate War,* after defying both Brother Leon and The Vigils, Jerry becomes a hero to many of the students. For this writing assignment instruct your students to write about someone they admire and look up to. Completing Worksheet 7-1 will help them to organize their thoughts.

7-1. A MODERN-DAY HERO

Directions: After he stood up to Brother Leon and The Vigils, Jerry became a hero to some of the students. Answer the questions below and write about someone you look up to and admire.

1. Who is the person you admire? _____

_____

2. What qualities do you admire in this person?_____

_____

_____

_____

_____

3. Do others admire this person?_____ If yes, in your opinion, is it for the same reasons? _____ Explain. _____

_____

_____

_____

_____

4. What is this person's most important accomplishments?_____

_____

_____

_____

_____

7-2. QUESTIONS TO CONSIDER FOR
THE CHOCOLATE WAR

1. Who do you think is the most fascinating character in the book? Why? Which one is most like you? Elaborate on why you think so.

2. Many characters in the book are dishonest and deceitful. Do you think this is representative of the people you know? Could a "Chocolate War" happen in your school? Why or why not?

3. Where do you think Jerry gets his strength to resist? What events in his life contribute to his resolve? Create some of the missing background in Jerry's past to support your answer.

4. Why do you think the Brothers ignored The Vigils and their pranks?

5. If a gang like The Vigils was in your school, how might they affect it? Would they have much influence? Would school authorities be able to stop them? How would you feel about them?

6. Consider what effect these events will have on Jerry as an adult. What kind of man do you think he will become? Explain.

7. Define the term "fatal flaw." What is Archie's? How might Carter, Obie and the others topple him?

8. Were you satisfied with the ending? How else could you conclude the action?

9. The story's action is told from a third-person omniscient point of view. Why do you think the author shifts points of view? How would the novel be different if it were told only from Jerry's point of view?

10. How has the story affected your view of peer pressure? Explain The Goobers' feeling that something was "evil" at Trinity.

© 1994 by The Center for Applied Research in Education

7-3. PROJECTS AND ACTIVITIES TO CONSIDER FOR
THE CHOCOLATE WAR

1. Obtain a book of poems. Select three that you think Jerry would like. Support your choices.

2. Write a prologue scene in the hospital between Jerry and his father, or between Jerry and Brother Leon.

3. Construct a character sketch of Archie Costello. Use examples from the book to support your ideas.

4. Picture Archie in a situation where he chooses the black ball; select any prank and write the scene as if Archie had to perform it. Try to imagine what techniques he would employ, whom he would ask for help and what would be going through his mind.

5. Select a worthy cause—money for a class trip?—and organize and carry out a fund-raiser. Your fund-raiser might be something as simple as a bake sale or a used book sale. If you are daring, you might conduct a candy sale or similar project.

6. List each act of intimidation inflicted on Jerry by the various characters. Taken together, how do they make you feel? Pretend you are Jerry reading this list, and you have been told you would experience them in the next few weeks. What would you do to prevent them, given your resources?

Curriculum Connections:

1. Imagine that the fund-raiser in the story was successful with big sales. Create a chart that records the sales. Include columns for total units, units sold, costs, summaries, etc. (SS and A)

2. Compare The Vigils, who thrive on mental intimidation, to a gang that asserts or defends itself through violence. Consider the tactics of each. Which is more convincing to you? More frightening? Which one would you rather belong to, if forced to choose? Consult references if necessary. (SS)

8. *The Slave Dancer* by Paula Fox
(Dell Publishing, 1973)

Synopsis

Jessie Bollier, a 13-year-old poor white boy living in 1840s New Orleans, is kidnapped by pirates and forced to sail on a slave ship to Africa. Talented at playing the fife, Jessie's main function as a crew hand is to "dance the slaves," so that they will move about on deck and prevent their muscles from atrophying. Although the crew is generally a cruel lot, a few befriend the boy and show him how to avoid trouble with Captain Cawthorne, first mate Nicholas Spark, and the treacherous Benjamin Stout. The ship sails to Africa and picks up a cargo of Africans. After three diseased and famine-riddled months at sea, the ship is overtaken by American law enforcers and flees into a storm, dumping slaves and other evidence in the ocean as it goes. Jessie and one young slave about his own age hide in the hold in the ship's belly, and when the ship is wrecked in the storm, only they survive. They swim to shore in Mississippi, and are taken in by Daniel, an aged black man hiding from captivity in the woods. The two boys, though they cannot communicate, become friends. The young African boy is smuggled to the north, while Jessie returns to his family. The experience has a lasting impression on Jessie, who never again can listen to music.

Ideas and Concepts to Highlight

1. *The Slave Dancer* was written by a woman, yet it is told from a boy's point of view. Discuss the concept of taking on such a challenge in writing, and how young writers might adopt a point of view so different from their own.

2. Slavery as an institution makes up a significant piece of American history, well-explored in literature and nonfiction and highly charged with emotion. Compare some of the history and lore with modern-day situations. Bring history to life by noting how some of today's news stories may be the stuff of future novels.

3. Jessie, as a 13-year-old, feels many emotions that are typical of children his age. Encourage students to imagine modern situations comparable to Jessie's plight, and predict how they would react.

4. Discuss slavery as an immoral act that benefited people like Cawthorne, who considered it his "God-given trade." Compare it to current world events, in which great evils may be committed by people who believe staunchly in their cause for political or religious reasons or personal gain.

Writing Connection: "Abduction"

Instruct your students to imagine that they, or someone they know, is abducted. They might review Jessie's feelings in the story when he was abducted and taken aboard the ship. Completing Worksheet 8-1 first will help students clarify their thoughts for writing. Upon the completion of the writing, consider having students share their stories in small groups.

8-1. ABDUCTION

Directions: Imagine that you are abducted. Write a story about this chilling event. Answer the questions below to help you generate ideas.

1. Who abducts you?_____

2. Where are you abducted? _____

3. How are you abducted? _____

_____

_____

_____

_____

4. Why are you abducted? _____

_____

_____

_____

_____

5. What happens while you are abducted? _____

_____

_____

_____

_____

6. How do you escape? _____

_____

_____

_____

_____

© 1994 by The Center for Applied Research in Education

8-2. QUESTIONS TO CONSIDER FOR THE SLAVE DANCER

1. Jessie, at the outset of the story, is disrespectful toward Aunt Agatha and feels scorn for her. How would you feel toward a woman like her? What do Jessie's thoughts and actions toward his aunt say about his character before his ordeal?

2. Trace the evolution of Jessie's feelings toward Benjamin Stout. Describe some of the foreshadowing in the story that warns Jessie of Stout's true character. Was Jessie justified in his initial assessment?

3. Compare the egg-stealing incident and the resulting punishment to a crime of theft today. Do you think modern punishments are more likely to stop people from committing crimes than old-time consequences? Why or why not?

4. Explore Stout's character. Is he the same as or different from the other men? Compare Stout to Purvis. How are they alike? How are they different?

5. Explain the crew's lack of remorse for the treatment of the slaves. Why do they feel they are superior? How might they feel threatened and defensive?

6. Jessie at one point says he hates the slaves. Explore this complicated emotion. Why does he feel this way? Where do you think his anger truly comes from?

7. Midway through the story, Ned emerges as one of the more moral characters. Why did he continue to work on a slave ship? Do you think he is any less to blame because he is not as harsh as the others and claims to dislike all men? Why or why not?

8-3. PROJECTS AND ACTIVITIES TO CONSIDER FOR
THE SLAVE DANCER

1. Consider Daniel's complex emotions, as a black man, as he releases Ras. Compare it to what he feels toward Jessie, a white boy. Write the final scene of that chapter from Daniel's point of view.

2. Trace the development of Jessie's feelings toward blacks throughout the major events in the story. How is his attitude different in the end? Write an essay about how people's positive experiences with other races promote tolerance. Support your thoughts with concrete examples—from newspapers, television, magazines, movies or personal experience.

3. Ras and Jessie are unable to communicate verbally, yet play together in harmony. Imagine yourself on a vacation in an unfamiliar place and meeting someone who cannot speak your language. Create a short story about the experience.

4. Compare Jessie's distasteful "job" to an experience you have had, where you had to do something you didn't like or knew was wrong. If you cannot think of such an experience, create one. Pay particular attention to your feelings about it, and the pressures you experienced.

Curriculum Connections:

1. Research the Emancipation Proclamation of 1865, and the Civil Rights Act of 1964. What are the major achievements of each? Which was a greater step toward racial equality? Support your argument with factual examples of blacks' place in society at either time. (SS)

2. Research and report on diseases that plagued crew members and Africans on the slave ships. Detail the symptoms and suffering. What types of treatments and medicines are available today for these diseases? (Sci)

3. There are many situations in history that were accepted in their time but are considered wrong now. Indentured servants were common during colonial days. What was an indentured servant? (Consult references if necessary.) How was an indentured servant different than a slave? Why in your opinion are there no openly indentured servants today? (SS)

9. *The Princess Bride* by William Goldman (Ballantine Books, 1974)

Synopsis

This story is a fast-moving spoof of the standard fairy tale. Buttercup, the most beautiful woman in the world, loves Westley, a farm boy, who is very handsome. When Westley sails to America to make his fortune so that he and Buttercup can have a fine future together, he is captured by the Dread Pirate Roberts. Fearing Westley dead, Buttercup vows never to love again. When Prince Humperdinck proposes marriage to Buttercup, she tells him that she can never love him. The Prince is unconcerned by that, however, for he plans to kill her anyway and blame her death on a rival kingdom. He arranges to have Buttercup kidnapped before the wedding, but Westley, who has survived and has assumed the identity of the Dread Pirate Roberts, saves her by defeating her kidnappers: Inigo, a master swordsman; Fezzik, a giant; and Vizzini, a Sicilian. Humperdinck captures Westley and Buttercup and decides to marry Buttercup after all, and then strangle her. He has Westley tortured and killed (so he thinks), but Inigo and Fezzik recover Westley's body and take him to a wizard who brings him back to life. Inigo needs Westley to help him find Count Rugen, who killed Inigo's father and who Inigo has vowed to kill in turn. In the end, Inigo kills the Count and Westley saves Buttercup.

Ideas and Concepts to Highlight

1. Discuss the elements of the classic fairy tale—the theme of good and evil, a beautiful princess and her handsome hero, the triumph of good over evil. Note how this story is a spoof.

2. Discuss Goldman's authorial intrusions. Why does he do this? Does it enhance the story?

3. Point out how Goldman describes the characters in physical detail, and keeps returning to the concept of beauty. Buttercup, for example, is the most beautiful woman in the world. Discuss the idea of beauty and handsomeness in American culture.

4. Note the writing style. It is light and fast. The dialogue is sharp, witty, and has a modern sound to it. How does this affect the story?

Writing Connection: "Beauty"

Throughout the story Goldman seems to be poking gentle fun at the idea of beauty. Discuss with your students the importance of beauty in contemporary American society. Consider the media, entertainment, and cosmetics industries. Is beauty really that important?

Instruct your students to complete Worksheet 9-1, and then write either an essay or story showing how beauty plays a major part in American culture today.

9-1. BEAUTY

Directions: Beauty (and handsomeness) seems to be very important in American culture. Just think about TV, the movies, and fashion models. But is it *really* that important? Answer the questions on the worksheet and then write an essay or a story about beauty.

1. Is beauty important?_____ If yes, why? If no, why not?_____

_____

_____

_____

2. What makes someone beautiful? _____

_____

_____

_____

_____

3. Why might feeling beautiful, attractive, or "trendy" be important to people? _____

_____

_____

_____

_____

4. Which do you feel is more important in a person—appearance or personality? _____
Explain. _____

_____

_____

_____

_____

© 1994 by The Center for Applied Research in Education

9-2. QUESTIONS TO CONSIDER FOR
THE PRINCESS BRIDE

1. When did Buttercup decide she loved Westley? How did she come to realize this? What was Westley's reaction to her telling him that she loved him? Why do you think he reacted the way he did?

2. Why did Westley decide to go to America? What happened on his voyage? What was Buttercup's reaction when she heard?

3. Goldman uses an unusual format in which he interrupts the story at key points. Do his intrusions add to the story? Do they detract from it? Why? What might Goldman's reason for doing this be?

4. Buttercup tells Prince Humperdinck that she cannot love him. But then she agrees to marry him. Why?

5. Why did Inigo become a swordsman? What was his purpose in seeking the six-fingered man? How skilled a swordsman was he? Give some examples. What happened when Inigo couldn't find the six-fingered man? What does this say about his character?

6. What happened when Inigo dueled the man in black? How did Inigo handle his defeat?

7. Why did the Prince plan to kill Buttercup?

8. Describe Count Rugen's character. What did he like to do? Why?

9. Westley was able to withstand his torture by "taking his brain away." What does that mean? Is it possible for anyone to do that? Explain.

10. After he realized who the man in black was, Inigo decided it was necessary to save him. Why did he do this?

11. In the climax, Goldman keeps noting the time, in a type of countdown. Why do you think he did this? Explain.

9-3. PROJECTS AND ACTIVITIES TO CONSIDER FOR
THE PRINCESS BRIDE

1. Why do you think Goldman provided such detailed physical descriptions of the characters? Choose one of the main characters and write a paragraph describing him or her in detail.

2. The dialogue of the story is snappy and witty. How does it add to the story? Take a scene and rewrite it with a formal dialogue that fits in more with the setting of the story. How does a formal dialogue change the story?

3. Assume that Prince Humperdinck immediately begins hunting Westley, Buttercup, Inigo, and Fezzik. Write a new ending to the story.

4. Watch the movie, *The Princess Bride* (Twentieth Century Fox). How are the novel and movie version of the story alike? How are they different? Write a movie review of the film.

5. The Dread Pirate Roberts was unlike most pirates. Read *Captain Blood* by Rafael Sabatini (Grosset, 1922) and write a book review. Share the review with other members of your class.

Curriculum Connections:

1. Goldman gives little thought to real history. List several examples of how he bends history to fit the needs of his story. For example, he notes in one place that the story happens "before Europe," but then, when Westley announces that he is sailing to America, says, "This was just after America..." (SS)

2. Throughout history royal marriages were often arranged for political reasons. Consult references and find some examples where royalty married, not for love, but for politics. Compile your notes and present a brief oral report to your class or group. (SS)

3. Pick a favorite scene of the book and create a comic strip of it. Change the dialogue if necessary to fit your comic strip. (A)

© 1994 by The Center for Applied Research in Education

10. *Julie of the Wolves* by Jean Craighead George *(Harper and Row, 1972)*

Synopsis

When Miyax (Julie), a 13-year-old Eskimo girl, can no longer tolerate her life with her husband, Daniel, she feels that she has no choice but to leave. Leaving, though, means crossing the tundra. Taking only essentials that she needs to survive, she begins walking, her destination being her pen pal's home in San Francisco. Despite her knowledge of the Arctic (which she obtained from her father whom she believes is dead), Miyax soon learns that the tundra is more vast and dangerous than she had thought. She becomes lost and runs out of food. Her only hope of survival is to gain the acceptance of a nearby pack of wolves. Through great effort in learning their ways, she wins their confidence and they come to view her as one of their own. She develops a close kinship with the wolves, who share their food with her and help her to make her way across the tundra. As she does, she realizes much about civilization and the world of the far north. When she finally finds her father alive, he has changed much and Miyax understands that the old world of the Eskimo is gone.

Ideas and Concepts to Highlight

1. Discuss the world of the Eskimo and how it has changed in recent years. Note how Miyax tried to cling unsuccessfully to the old ways.

2. Locate the Arctic Circle on a map, and especially Barrow and the North Slope of Alaska. This area is a major oil-producing region; discuss how the coming of such technology would likely affect the lives of the Eskimo.

3. Note the climate and terrain of the tundra.

4. Emphasize the environmental overtones of the book, particularly how the animals and plants exist in a "balance of nature."

5. Point out the structure of the book, that it opens with Miyax lost on the tundra, then details her time up to leaving Daniel, and concludes with her finding her father whom she thought was dead.

Writing Connection: "Surviving in the Wilderness"

Miyax was alone on the tundra where she survived on her resourcefulness and the help of a wolf pack. For this writing assignment, ask your students to imagine that with a parent or an older sibling, they will be going on a two-week survival trek to a wilderness area of their choice. How would they plan for this journey? What would they take?

Instruct your students to complete Worksheet 10-1 and write a story of how they would survive in the wilderness.

10-1. SURVIVING IN THE WILDERNESS

Directions: Imagine that you and a parent or older brother or sister are going on a two-week survival trip. Could you do it? Answer the questions below and write a story about your imaginary experience.

1. Where would you go on your wilderness survival trip? _____

    _____ Why? _____

    _____

2. Who would go with you? _____

    _____

3. Describe the area you are going to. _____

    _____

    _____

4. What items or materials will you need to survive? _____

    _____

    _____

5. How will you get to this place? _____

    _____

    _____

6. Where will you stay once you arrive? _____

    _____

7. How will you spend your days? _____

    _____

    _____

© 1994 by The Center for Applied Research in Education

10-2. QUESTIONS TO CONSIDER FOR
JULIE OF THE WOLVES

1. Why did Miyax believe that the wolves might help her get food? How did she hope to communicate with them? Think of some of the animals you know. Do they have certain actions that tell you how they are feeling? Give some examples in your explanation.

2. Why was Miyax alone on the tundra? How had she gotten lost? Do you think her attempt to cross the tundra alone was a wise one? Explain.

3. Throughout her ordeal on the tundra, Miyax recalls much of Kapugen's advice. At one point she recalls he said: "Change your ways when fear seizes, for it usually means you are doing something wrong." What did he mean? Explain how you could apply that advice to your own life.

4. What did Miyax learn from Amy? Why was having Amy as a pen pal important to her?

5. Why did Miyax agree to marry Daniel even though she was only 13 years old? Can you imagine being married at 13? Explain.

6. How did the hunters' killing of Amaroq change Miyax's thinking about civilization? How did this experience change Miyax?

7. What was Miyax's impression of Daniel? Was she right in leaving him and attempting to cross the tundra? What else could she have done?

8. When Miyax is reunited with Kapugen in Kangik, what does she find? How has Kapugen changed? How did Miyax feel about him?

9. At the conclusion of the story after Miyax buries Tornait in the snow, she said: "...the hour of the wolf and the Eskimo is over." What did she mean?

10-3. PROJECTS AND ACTIVITIES TO CONSIDER FOR
JULIE OF THE WOLVES

1. Miyax learned several ways that wolves communicate. For example, upon rising from sleep, they wagged their tails in greeting of each other. Observe a pet, or a bird, squirrel or other animal around your home, and record its actions and their possible meanings. Share your notes with the members of your group.

2. To pass the time and loneliness, Miyax invented rhymes about the tundra. Write your own rhyme about your own environment.

3. Describe the order of the wolf pack. Amaroq, for example, was the leader. Who was next? What position did Jello occupy? What position did the pups occupy? Which pup was the most important? Design a chart to display the order.

4. Miyax's knowledge of the tundra was impressive. Working with a group, compile a list of how she used her knowledge to survive. An example—she dug out a hole in the frozen ground and used it as a refrigerator. Share your list with other groups.

Curriculum Connections:

1. After Kapu brought Miyax a caribou leg, she cut it up and cooked it. As it cooked, she felt inspired to dance. Create your idea of Miyax's dance. (A)

2. Identify the areas wolves currently inhabit in North America. Once they were found on much of the continent. Why have their numbers declined? Consult references and write a brief report. (Sci)

3. When wolves hunt a herd of caribou, they single out the oldest, slowest, or weakest. How might this be good for the herd? Explain. (Sci)

4. Describe the climate and terrain of the tundra. What kinds of animals and what types of vegetation would you find there? Consult the necessary references. (Sci)

5. Life on the tundra is bound in cycles, particularly that of predator and prey. Give several examples of predator-prey relationships found on the tundra. Consult references if necessary. (Sci)

6. The Arctic is known as the "land of the midnight sun." What does this mean? When does night begin and how long does it last? Consult references if necessary. (Sci)

11. *The Contender* by Robert Lipsyte
(Harper Keypoint, 1987)

Synopsis

Albert Brooks seems to be going nowhere. A high-school dropout, he works at a dead-end job in a small grocery store. His friends don't have jobs and are slowly drifting into drug use and theft. They try to pull him in with them, but Albert resists. A vague something in Albert wants more. He begins going to Donatelli's gym where he starts training as a boxer. Mr. Donatelli, who has trained champions, tells him straight out "Nothing's promised to you," but Albert accepts the challenge. As he continues his training, he learns that it is not the win that is important, but that it is what's inside a person that really counts.

Ideas and Concepts to Highlight

1. Discuss the setting, which may be unfamiliar to students who don't live in a major city.

2. The book offers conflicting opinions of blacks toward whites. For example, Hollis blames whites for the condition of blacks, while Uncle Wilson and Jeff see the world changing into a place where there are many opportunities for blacks. Note the effects of these opinions on Albert and how he balances them with his own experiences.

3. Note that being a "Contender" represents more than just the boxing ring; it represents life as well.

4. Point out how Albert changes after he begins training. The training strengthens his self-esteem which in turn influences his outlook on life.

Writing Connection: "The Expert"

Through training, Albert becomes a good boxer. Ask your students about some of the things they do well. Some might take dance lessons, others might be good athletes, while still others may have artistic talent. Discuss what it takes to become really "good" at something.

For this writing assignment, instruct your students to think of something they do well. Either in the form of a personal narrative or a story, they are to write about being an expert. Completing Worksheet 11-1 will help them get started.

11-1. THE EXPERT

Directions: Think about something you do well. It might be a hobby, a sport, a craft, dancing, or other activity. Answer the questions below. Then write either a personal narrative or story about "The Expert."

1. What are you an expert in? _____
   _____
   _____
   _____

2. How did you become an expert? _____
   _____
   _____
   _____

3. Why do you like this activity? _____
   _____
   _____
   _____
   _____

4. Do you plan to pursue this activity as you get older? Why or why not? _____
   _____
   _____
   _____

5. What advice could you give to others who are just starting this activity? _____
   _____
   _____
   _____

11-2. QUESTIONS TO CONSIDER FOR
THE CONTENDER

1. Why did Albert refuse to go with his friends to rob Epsteins' grocery store? How did he feel about not going? How did he feel after he found out that James had been caught by the police? Why did Albert care so much about James?

2. On the Monday after the attempted robbery, when Albert returned to work, the Epsteins no longer trusted him. Do you think they were being fair to him? Why or why not? How important is trust between people? Explain.

3. When Albert first met Donatelli, the trainer said to him: "Nothing's promised to you." What did he mean?

4. After he watched the fight at the Garden, Albert was confronted by Major and Hollis, who wanted him to disconnect the burglar alarm at Epsteins' grocery. When Albert refused, Major threatened him with a knife. What happened? Why is Albert's action significant? What does this tell you about his character? Explain.

5. Why did Albert accept Major's invitation to go to the clubhouse again? What happened when Albert met James? Why do you think Albert stayed when he knew he shouldn't because he was in training?

6. After the incident with Major and the stolen car, Albert tells himself that he "ain't gonna be a boxer anyway." Why does he say this? Do you think he really means it? Why or why not?

7. The title of the story, *The Contender,* has an obvious meaning of boxers "contending" in the ring. But it also can be applied to life. Explain. What does a person need to be a contender?

8. After his first fight, Aunt Pearl tells Albert how, when she was a young woman, she was offered a contract to sing in a stage show. Because she was only seventeen, her mother had to sign for her, but her mother refused. Why did Pearl tell Albert this? What was Albert's reaction?

9. Why did Albert fight once more? How did the fight with Hubbard turn out? Why did Albert stay in the ring so long, even when he was getting beaten?

11-3. PROJECTS AND ACTIVITIES TO CONSIDER FOR THE CONTENDER

1. Why do many of the blacks in the story distrust whites? Does this view mirror our society? What programs, actions, or laws might help to bring blacks and whites into greater understanding and harmony? Consult the necessary references and organize a panel to discuss this issue.

2. Imagine that you are a sports writer. Choose one of Albert's fights and write a sports article about it.

3. Create a scene in which Albert is able to steer James away from drugs before James becomes addicted. Write the dialogue and act it out with the help of your classmates.

4. What happened with Albert's fight with Barnes? Why did Donatelli want Albert to quit after the fight? Do you think Donatelli was right? Why or why not? Discuss this in your group. List reasons pro and con.

5. James turned to drugs. Why do you think he did this? Research how and where people who are addicted to drugs can get help. Create a poster or pamphlet with this information and share it with your class.

Curriculum Connections:

1. Study the Civil Rights Movement. Compare the general conditions for blacks in this country before the Civil Rights Act of 1964 with now. Have conditions improved since then? How? In what ways? Give some examples. (SS)

2. Many people tried to influence Albert in the story. Create a chart and record how people tried to influence Albert. Include Major, Hollis, James, Aunt Pearl, Henry, Uncle Wilson, and Mr. Donatelli. (Feel free to include some of the other characters as well.) Who do you think was the biggest influence on him? Explain. (SS or A)

© 1994 by The Center for Applied Research in Education

12. *The Sword in the Stone* by T.H. White
(Putnam, 1939)

Synopsis

Wart is destined to be King Arthur, but before he can assume his role as England's king he must be educated. Although Sir Ector provides Wart and Kay, his own son, with the necessary learning of the day, he realizes it is not enough and he wishes to find a tutor. Not long after that, Merlyn, a magician, arrives. Merlyn's purpose (unknown to Wart, who is unaware of his destiny) is to educate Wart so that he will be an able ruler. To that end he provides an education built on magic and reality, in which he turns Wart into various animals, giving the boy the chance to gain valuable knowledge from different perspectives. When Kay is to become a knight, Wart is to be his squire. Although accepting his position, Wart nevertheless wishes that he could be a knight, too. He accompanies Kay and Sir Ector to London where Kay is to take part in a tournament. When Kay leaves his sword behind, Wart must find him another. The only one he can get is a sword stuck in an anvil at a church. It is the Sword in the Stone that only the new king of England can pull out. Not realizing the sword's significance, Wart pulls it from the anvil.

Ideas and Concepts to Highlight

1. Explain castle life of Medieval England. Emphasize how White uses vivid detail to paint a realistic setting.

2. Point out the blending of magic and reality in the story.

3. Explain personification and note some of the many examples of it.

4. Discuss the differences between Kay and Wart, and note how Wart grows in understanding and knowledge throughout the story.

Writing Connection: "A Humanlike Acquaintance"

Personification is a literary device by which the author gives human qualities to non-human things or ideas. Giving objects and animals human traits can add a rich element to fiction.

For this assignment, instruct your students to imagine that something in their house or yard suddenly assumes human qualities. Students are to write a short story about their suddenly humanlike acquaintance. Completing Worksheet 12-1 will help them to generate ideas.

12-1. A HUMANLIKE ACQUAINTANCE

Directions: Personification is a literary technique authors use to give human qualities to non-human things or ideas. Talking animals, an evil tree whose branches grab unsuspecting hikers, and a thinking, feeling river are all examples of personification.

Imagine that something in your home or yard suddenly takes on human qualities. Complete the worksheet and write a brief story about your new acquaintance.

1. What "thing" did you select to be personified? _____

   _____

   _____

2. How did it assume human qualities? _____

   _____

   _____

3. What does it do once it has human qualities? _____

   _____

   _____

   _____

4. What would your parents or friends probably say about it? _____

   _____

   _____

   _____

5. Does it return to normal? _____   If yes, how? _____

   _____

   _____   If no, what happens next? _____

   _____

   _____

© 1994 by The Center for Applied Research in Education

12-2. QUESTIONS TO CONSIDER FOR
THE SWORD IN THE STONE

1. What was Kay's reaction when he and Wart lost Cully? What was Wart's reaction? What do their reactions tell you about their characters?

2. Describe how Wart's education is different from yours. Give some examples. Merlyn says, "Education is experience." Explain what he meant.

3. Choose one of the animals that is personified in the story and describe his character. What did Wart learn from this character?

4. Kay became jealous of Merlyn's attention to Wart and said, "Merlyn does everything for you, but he never does anything for me." How did Wart feel about this? What did he do? Describe what happened when the boys went on their "adventure."

5. There is much humor in the story. What character did you find most amusing? Why? What scene did you find most amusing? Why? Would the story have been as interesting without the humor? Why or why not?

6. As Kay and Wart grew up, Kay no longer cared to associate with Wart. Why?

7. How did Wart feel about Kay becoming a knight? Why did Wart refer to himself as Cinderella?

8. The first time Wart tried to pull the sword from the stone, what happened? How did he gain the strength to pull it out?

9. Do you think that Wart's education will help him to be a good king? Why or why not?

12-3. PROJECTS AND ACTIVITIES TO CONSIDER FOR
THE SWORD IN THE STONE

1. Imagine that you were a reporter at the time of the story. Write an article about the old king's death and the search for a new king who could pull the Sword from the Stone.

2. Based on the story, write a prediction of the type of king you would expect Arthur to be. Use examples from the story to back up your ideas.

3. The dialogue of the story is reminiscent of Medieval England. It also shows how language changes over the years. For example, many words that we use today were not known a few hundred years ago. Working with a group, generate a list of words that Wart would not be familiar with. Some examples—astronaut, computer, television. Share your list with other groups. Compile a class list and think of a title for it.

4. Read another book or account of King Arthur. A good suggestion: *A Connecticut Yankee in King Arthur's Court* by Mark Twain (Morrow, 1988). How does this book compare with *The Sword in the Stone?*

5. Working with a group of three or four students, create a storyboard showing Wart when he was changed into different animals. What did he learn from each? Share your findings with the class or your group.

Curriculum Connections:

1. Although much legend surrounds King Arthur, most historians agree that he was a real man. Consult reference books and present an oral report to the class on the real versus legendary King Arthur. (SS)

2. The time of knights is often referred to as the Age of Chivalry. What does this mean? Working with a group, consult references to learn about the Age of Chivalry. With another group, debate the question, "Was There Really an Age of Chivalry?" (SS)

3. When Arthur was king, the castle dominated much of English life. Consult references and write a report describing life at the typical castle. Include facts both about noblemen and women and commoners. (SS)

4. Using clay, create a model of a medieval castle. (A)

© 1994 by The Center for Applied Research in Education

13. <u>*The Upstairs Room*</u> *by Johanna Reiss*
(Thomas Y. Crowell Company, 1972)

Synopsis

World War II begins and Jews all across Europe are in danger. When the Germans attack Holland and occupy Winterswijk, the town where the de Leeuw family lives, Annie and her family are forced to separate and go into hiding. Eight-year-old Annie and her older sister, Sini, eventually come to stay with the Oostervelds, a farm family who keep the girls safe from the Germans, at considerable risk to themselves. Told from Annie's point of view, the story recounts the initial innocence she at first had about the war and the terror, anger, and sadness she felt during the long years in hiding. Her story also shows the courage, resourcefulness, and unbreakable spirit people can call upon when living through horrifying, life-threatening events.

Ideas and Concepts to Highlight

1. Provide background information on World War II. Although the causes of the war had their roots in the conclusion of World War I, World War II officially began in 1939 when Germany attacked Poland. In response, Britain and France declared war on Germany and the war spread rapidly. By the summer of 1940, Nazi Germany had overrun most of Western Europe. In 1941 the Germans attacked Russia, opening a second front. After Pearl Harbor, Germany, an ally of Japan, declared war on the United States. Just a few hours later, the U.S. declared war on Japan, Germany, and Italy, which was allied with Germany and Japan, together called the Axis Powers. The countries allied with the U.S. were called the Allies. The war finally ended in 1945, but only after millions of people had died, including an estimated six million Jews who were systematically murdered by the Nazis in what is now known as the Holocaust.

2. Explain that the story is written from Annie's point of view, that of a young girl. Note that throughout the story, Annie interjects her thoughts and feelings.

3. Emphasize that along with the barbarity of war there was also courage and kindness. Many people risked their own lives to save others.

4. Discuss propaganda and how countries use it during wartime.

Writing Connection: "Hatred"

The German persecution of the Jews underscores hatred on a worldwide scale. However, hatred, bias, and intolerance are found, unfortunately, just about everywhere. Your students are undoubtedly aware of this, and may have experienced prejudice themselves. For this writing, ask your students to consider why some people hate others. Ask students to complete Worksheet 13-1 first, then meet in groups to discuss their feelings before writing.

13-1. HATRED

Directions: Consider the issue of hatred. At the least, it might result in a nasty or hurtful remark to another person. At the worst, it can lead to violence. Answer the questions below and then write an essay detailing your views on the topic.

1. What can cause people to hate others? _____

_____

_____

_____

_____

2. Give some examples of hateful acts. _____

_____

_____

_____

_____

3. Have you or someone you know ever been a victim of a hateful act? _____If yes, how, when, and why? _____

_____

_____

_____

_____

4. What can be done to lessen hatred? _____

_____

_____

_____

_____

© 1994 by The Center for Applied Research in Education

13-2. QUESTIONS TO CONSIDER FOR
THE UPSTAIRS ROOM

1. Why didn't Annie's mother want to go to America? Do you think the reason she gave was the real reason? Explain.

2. Did the de Leeuw family believe they would be safe in their new home outside of Winterswijk? Did you think they would be safe? Explain.

3. Compare the attitudes of Annie's father and mother about the German occupation. Which one do you think had a better understanding of what was "really" happening? Explain.

4. Several people, at great personal risk, were willing to help Jews during the war—Reverend Zwaal, the Hanninks, the Oostervelds, for example. Explain why you think they would do this.

5. Johann Oosterveld listened to what he called "the real news" on the radio. What did he mean by that? When might the "news" not be the news?

6. Pick an adjective to describe each of the Oostervelds—Johann, Dientje, and Opoe. Why did Annie and Sini feel safe with them?

7. Johann often referred to himself as a "dumb farmer." Do you think he was being accurate in referring to himself like this? Why or why not?

8. When Johann went to hide out in Enschede, Dientje sent the girls back to the Hanninks. Why did she do this? How did Annie feel about this?

9. How do you think Annie felt about the Oostervelds? Explain.

10. How do you think Annie's experience might have affected her? What kinds of values might she hold as an adult because of her ordeal? Explain.

13-3. PROJECTS AND ACTIVITIES TO CONSIDER FOR THE UPSTAIRS ROOM

1. Research the term "propaganda." What is it? When is it used? When might propaganda be justified? Select an article from the newspaper and rewrite it as propaganda. Hint: An article about international conflict would be best for this.

2. Working with a group, research the causes of World War II. Organize a panel discussion of how the war might have been prevented. What should have been done? Did other countries such as Britain, France, and the United States have a right or responsibility to stop Hitler before he was strong enough to wage war?

3. Imagine that you are Annie, with the Oostervelds during the war. Write a letter to her father. What would she say?

4. Annie and Sini made up rhymes during their stay with the Oostervelds. Work with a partner and assume that you are in their situation. What kinds of rhymes would you make up? Share them with other groups.

5. Imagine that you had to remain hidden in your house every day with only the other members of the household knowing you were there. You had no TV, a radio that only offered news once a day, no books to read, no stereo, no games. Write a short description of how you would spend your days.

6. Write a tribute to the Oostervelds.

Curriculum Connections:

1. Research Kristallnacht. What was it? When and why did it happen? Describe what happened. Write a brief report. (SS)

2. Working with a partner or small group, create a timeline showing the major events of World War II. (SS)

3. Draw or create a model of one of Annie's and Sini's hiding places. (A)

4. Draw a map of Europe. Label the countries and major geographical features. Supply the names and dates of major battles, the dates of German occupation and subsequent liberation. (SS or A)

14. *The Pigman* by Paul Zindel
(Harper & Row, 1968)

Synopsis

John and Lorraine are two lonely high school students who entertain themselves and each other by making crank phone calls. One of Lorraine's calls, as she poses as a charity worker, is to Angelo Pignati, an old widower who invites them over. They meet him, to his delight, and he treats them with respect, interest and kindness—unlike anything they are used to in their unhappy homes. They go to the zoo with him and gradually spend much of their free afternoons at his home and let him buy them things. One evening, after a shopping spree, the three race around the house on new roller skates and the Pigman—so named as much for his collection of pig figurines as his name—suffers a heart attack. John and Lorraine look after the house during his hospital stay, and decide to throw a party. Dozens of young people show up, and they explore all corners of the Pigman's house. Fights break out, and during the melee the Pigman comes home in a taxi. John and Lorraine are arrested but the Pigman declines to press charges, feeling only disappointment and betrayal. In their remorse they ask him to meet them at the zoo. During the visit, the Pigman discovers that his favorite baboon, Bobo, died during his absence. The Pigman suffers another heart attack and dies at the zoo. The book's format alternates, and the story is recounted as a "memorial epic," one chapter written by John, the next by Lorraine, and so on.

Ideas and Concepts to Highlight

1. Review the unusual format of the book. Discuss its effectiveness in the first person, and note the differences in point of view between John and Lorraine.

2. Discuss growing up through experience, in the context of platonic boy-girl relationships.

3. Have students share some of their experiences with elderly people, specifically those who are not related to them.

4. Explore the idea of loneliness, and point out how John and Lorraine lessened the Pigman's loneliness.

Writing Connection: "When Boys and Girls Are Just Friends"

John and Lorraine had a platonic relationship, which is quite different from the typical teen boy-girl relationship that centers around dating. Instruct your students to explore the topic, "When Boys and Girls Are Just Friends" by completing Worksheet 14-1, and then write an essay on it. At the end of the writing, you might like to compile the class's essays in a book by the same title.

14-1. WHEN BOYS AND GIRLS ARE JUST FRIENDS

Directions: John and Lorraine were friends. They weren't dating and they weren't in love. How was their relationship different from the usual boy-girl relationship?

   Think about the pressures on boy-girl relationships. Answer the questions on the worksheet, and then write an essay on the topic.

1. Can teenage boys and girls be close friends? _____

Why or why not? _____

_____

_____

_____

2. How do boys and girls act toward each other when they are close friends? _____

_____

_____

3. How do they act toward each other when they are interested in dating? _____

_____

_____

4. Is there pressure on good friends to date each other? _____

Why or why not? _____

_____

5. If you have a close friend of the opposite sex, do you treat him or her differently than your same-sex friends? _____ If yes, how? If not, why not? _____

_____

_____

_____

_____

© 1994 by The Center for Applied Research in Education

14-2. QUESTIONS TO CONSIDER FOR
THE PIGMAN

1. What do you think draws John and Lorraine together? What draws them to the Pigman? Do you think that they like him as a friend, or do they "use" him to buy them things? What draws the Pigman to John and Lorraine? Who do you think values the relationship more—John and Lorraine or the Pigman? Explain.

2. What is an "alter ego"? How does the term apply to the book? Describe what your alter ego would be like.

3. Both John and Lorraine have unhappy family relationships. Do you think their portrayal of their parents is accurate? What might they do to help improve their family relationships? Explain and offer some examples.

4. Describe your feelings, as an observer, as you read about the events at the party. Compare them to John's and Lorraine's, who are participants.

5. John is an attention seeker, as is Lorraine to a lesser extent. Why do they do the provoking things they do? Are their purposes achieved or do they misfire? Explain. Think of some of the things you do for "effect" and write about why and how they make you feel.

6. What would you do if you met someone like the Pigman? Would you be friends with him? Would you let him buy you things? How would you treat him? If you did become friends with him, how would you react at his funeral?

7. Why do you think Zindel chose to alternate the format of this story, having John write a chapter, then Lorraine, and so on? Do you think that this was a wise choice? Why or why not? Could he have chosen a better format? Explain.

8. What is your opinion of John and Lorraine? Do you like them? Would you like to have either of them as friends? Why or why not?

14-3. PROJECTS AND ACTIVITIES TO CONSIDER FOR
THE PIGMAN

1. Create a chart that lists at least three values held by John, Lorraine, and the Pigman. Which ones, if any, do they share? What do their values say about each of them?

2. Read some magazine and newspaper advertising. Cut out a picture that resembles your mental representation of the Pigman. Discuss the amount of physical description in the novel, and explain whether or not you believe it is adequate.

3. Write and deliver a eulogy for the Pigman.

4. Notice the unusual tactic of shifting points of view. Select a few paragraphs and write them from the opposite point of view, keeping in mind the alternate character's style and values. Does the change in point of view change the impression on the reader? How?

5. Many elderly people live alone and consequently are lonely and isolated. Research what social agencies are available in your community to help the elderly. Imagine that you are a social worker and wish to inform the elderly about these organizations. Write a brochure explaining what organizations they can turn to for help and how they can be contacted.

Curriculum Connections:

1. Research heart attacks and present an oral report to your group or class. What are the major contributing factors? What can be done to reduce the risk of a heart attack? Do you think John and Lorraine considered the Pigman's age in their activities with him? If they had known about the risks, what would they have done differently? (Sci)

2. Go to a shopping center with a list of all the items the Pigman bought for John and Lorraine. Estimate how much he would have spent on them at your location. (Hint: Round off the prices.) How would you feel about a non-relative spending that much money on you? (M)

3. Recall the Pigman's game about the boatman. Whom or what do you think is most to blame for the Pigman's death? Be imaginative, and support your reasoning. Draw a diagram similar to the one he used, but fill in different names and situations as needed. (A)

© 1994 by The Center for Applied Research in Education

15. *Sing Down the Moon* by Scott O'Dell
(Houghton Mifflin, 1970)

Synopsis

Bright Morning is a young Navaho girl who lives with her family in a village in Canyon de Chelly. The peace and promise of that spring of 1864 is soon shattered for Bright Morning when she is captured by Spanish slavers and sold to a wealthy white woman. After she escapes and returns to her village, the village is destroyed by U.S. soldiers who force the Navahos to march to a reservation at Bosque Redondo. The conditions are terrible and many Navahos die. As she recounts her experiences, Bright Morning also tells the story of Tall Boy, the young warrior who is wounded as he helps her escape from slavery, and who eventually becomes her husband. Together, Bright Morning and Tall Boy escape from the reservation and start a new life for themselves. This story tells of the removal of an entire people from their land, breaking their hearts and spirits; but it also is a story of courage and hope.

Ideas and Concepts to Highlight

1. Note that Navaho country was centered in what is now northeastern Arizona.

2. Point out that the story is told in the first-person. O'Dell likely chose this point of view because of the immediacy it offers. It is as if Bright Morning is speaking directly to the reader.

3. Mention that this story is based on historical fact. In 1863 the U.S. army began destroying Navaho villages, crops, and livestock in an effort to remove the Indians from their lands. By early 1864 most Navahos began to surrender. This was followed by The Long Walk to a reservation near Fort Sumner. Many Navahos died because of the hard conditions.

4. Discuss how during a great tragedy as befell the Navahos, some people's spirits are broken and they give up, while others find inner strength which helps them to courageously face the hardest situations.

5. Explain that O'Dell uses much symbolism for dramatic impact. For example, the death of Meadow Flower comes during the spring. Spring is a time of rebirth, growth, and hope, yet the little girl died at that time.

Writing Connection: "A Report on the Navahos"

Sing Down the Moon is set in the American southwest in the 1860s. The story revolves around the Navaho Indians, whose culture and customs are likely to be unfamiliar to many students.

Instruct your students to research and write a report on some aspect of Navaho history, culture, or traditions. For example, some students may choose to write about the Long Walk, while others might concentrate on tribal customs or mythology. Remind students that their reports should have an introduction, body, and conclusion. Briefly discuss the 5 W's and How as a technique to ensure that they include pertinent information in their reports. Because a subject like the Navahos is so broad, Worksheet 15-1 is designed to help students choose and focus a topic before writing.

15-1. A REPORT ON THE NAVAHOS

Directions: The Navaho Indians of the 1860s lived in close harmony with their land and had many interesting customs and traditions. Choose an aspect of Navaho life and write a report on it. Complete the worksheet to find and focus a topic.

1.   List some possible topics for your report: _____

_____

_____

_____

_____

_____

2.   Which (if any) of the topics overlap each other? _____

_____

How? _____

_____

Which can be combined? _____

_____

_____

3.   Choose a topic and define it by answering the 5 W's and How. (Use another sheet if you need more room.)

   What is your topic about?_____

   When did it happen? _____

   Where did it happen?_____

   Who was involved? _____

   Why did it happen? _____

   How did it happen? _____

15-2. QUESTIONS TO CONSIDER FOR
SING DOWN THE MOON

1. The story is written in the first-person. Would the story be as powerful if O'Dell had used the third-person point of view? Why or why not?

2. How did Bright Morning feel about slavery? Compare her feelings about it with those of Rosita. Give some examples to support your views.

3. Describe the Womanhood Ceremony. What was its purpose? Describe a ceremony that we have today in modern American culture. What is its purpose?

4. When the Navahos deserted their village, they didn't think the soldiers would stay long. When did they realize that the soldiers weren't going to leave? What did the Navahos then decide to do? Why do you think the soldiers destroyed the village? Why didn't the Navahos of Bright Morning's village fight?

5. Tall Boy throws his lance at the soldiers but it falls short. This is symbolic of the weakness of the Navahos against the soldiers. Explain. Give another example of symbolism in the story and tell what it represents.

6. How did Tall Boy feel about his useless arm? Explain.

7. Throughout the story Bright Morning is shown to be intelligent, resourceful, and sensitive. Identify examples in the story that support each of these descriptive words.

8. Describe how Tall Boy's character changes after he lost the use of his arm. Give some examples.

9. Why does Bright Morning decide to leave the reservation at Bosque Redondo? Why do you think so few Navahos tried to leave?

10. At the end of the story, why did Bright Morning step on the toy willow spear that Tall Boy had made for their son? What does her action signify?

© 1994 by The Center for Applied Research in Education

15-3. PROJECTS AND ACTIVITIES TO CONSIDER FOR
SING DOWN THE MOON

1. The novel ends on a note of hope. If you had been writing this story and continued it, what would happen next?

2. Many Americans in the 1860s saw nothing wrong with forcibly removing Indians from their lands as the nation expanded westward. Such people believed that Americans had a right to take what resources they could. Others felt that such actions were wrong. Organize a debate and examine the issue.

3. Imagine that you were a reporter riding with the soldiers who rounded up the Navahos and marched them to Bosque Redondo. Write a newspaper account of the event.

4. Imagine that you were an 1860s public advocate, and the Navahos came to you to argue their case for leaving the Bosque Redondo and being able to return to their lands. Prepare a list of reasons why the Navahos should be allowed to go back to their lands. Write a scene in which you present your reasons to the Superintendent of the Reservation. With the help of classmates, act the scene out.

Curriculum Connections:

1. "Manifest Destiny" was a term used to justify the expansion of the United States across the continent. What does Manifest Destiny mean? How might the term have been used to justify the forcing of the Navahos off their lands? Consult references if necessary, and write a brief report. (SS)

2. Draw a map of Navaho country. Consult references. (SS)

3. Create an art object that represents some facet of Navaho life. (A)

4. Although the Navahos did not have any "hard" sciences, they knew much about nature and their world. Research the Navahos' understanding of nature and compare it to our modern understanding of nature. Present your findings orally to your group. (Sci)

16. *I Will Call It Georgie's Blues* by *Suzanne Newton*
(Viking, 1983)

Synopsis

Neal Sloan's father is a Baptist minister in a small southern town. His father tries to show his congregation that he and his family are stable, exemplary members of the community. This isn't so, however. Beneath the facade he shows his congregation, Neal's father is slowly losing control of himself, with terrible consequences for his family. Each of the family members tries coping with the father's excessive demands in his or her own way. Neal retreats from the family's conflict by secretly immersing himself in playing jazz. His sister, Aileen, rebels outright. She infuriates her father by failing her English class, which will prevent her from graduating, and by dating Pete Cauthin, a noted troublemaker. Neal's mother struggles with divided loyalties between her husband and her children. But it is Neal's younger brother, Georgie, who suffers the most. Quiet, unassuming, Georgie is often ignored by the others, except his father, who demands as much of Georgie as he does the others. Only when Georgie begins fantasizing that his parents are false (he believes his real parents were abducted) does Neal realize how serious the family's problems are. Even then, it takes Georgie losing his sanity and running away for the family to seek the help they need.

Ideas and Concepts to Highlight

1. Note that the story is told from Neal's point of view.

2. Discuss the idea of presenting a false facade to others, giving others the impression that you are something you are not. Neal's father, for example, presented himself to his congregation as a steady, compassionate man. Another example is Neal, who did not want others to know that he loved playing jazz on the piano.

3. Discuss the various ways the family members tried to cope with the father's excessive (or even abusive) demands. Neal retreated from confrontation, Aileen openly rebelled, Georgie imagined that his parents weren't real, and Neal's mother tried to remain loyal to her husband yet also protect her children.

Writing Connection: "The Real Me"

Much of the Sloan family's turmoil is rooted in people not being themselves.

Instruct your students to write an essay entitled "The Real Me." Ask them to describe in their writing the type of person they feel others see them as, and the type of person they really are. Suggest that students may keep their writings private if they wish and need not share them with other students. Completing Worksheet 16-1 can be helpful in organizing their thoughts.

NAME _____ DATE _____ SECTION _____

16-1. THE REAL ME

Directions: Neal Sloan did not want others to know about his jazz playing. By keeping that part of himself hidden, others were not able to know the "real" Neal. Think about how others view you. Do others see you as the person you really are? Complete the worksheet below and write about the real you.

1. Fill in the appropriate information in the boxes.

What People Think I Am	What I Think I Really Am

2. Are you, or aren't you, what you appear to be? Why or why not?_____

_____

_____

_____

_____

_____

_____

16-2. QUESTIONS TO CONSIDER FOR
I WILL CALL IT GEORGIE'S BLUES

1. When Neal tells Pete that "Preachers' kids aren't any different from anybody else," Pete answers, "Maybe not, but they're supposed to be." Do you agree with him? Explain. Think of some other jobs parents may have for which their kids might be expected to behave better than other kids. What are they? Why?

2. What is Neal's opinion of his father? How was his opinion different from the opinions of church members? Explain.

3. What is your impression of Neal? Describe him. Would you like to have him as a friend? Why or why not?

4. Why did Neal like and respect Mrs. Talbot?

5. Why didn't Neal want anyone to know about his jazz playing? Was he right in keeping it a secret? Explain. Why was his music so important to him?

6. When Neal refused to tell others about his jazz, Mrs. Talbot told him, "It takes so much less energy to live an honest life." What did she mean? Do you agree with her? Why or why not?

7. How did Neal's mother feel about being a preacher's wife? What was Neal's opinion of his mother at the beginning of the story? How did it change toward the end? Explain.

8. If you were Neal, how would you have reacted when Georgie told you that he didn't believe his mother and father were his real parents? What would you have done?

9. After Neal's fight with Pete, how did his father act in the principal's office? What does his behavior tell you about his deteriorating mental stability? Explain.

10. In talking with Mrs. Talbot, Neal says, "Everything is connected...Changing one piece means changing all the pieces." What does he mean? Give an example of how things are connected in your own life.

16-3. PROJECTS AND ACTIVITIES TO CONSIDER FOR *I WILL CALL IT GEORGIE'S BLUES*

1. At what point in the story did you realize that Georgie was very troubled? Discuss your opinion and reasons with the members of your group. List the different places. Did any of you agree? Discuss why not all of you chose the same place.

2. Write a scene in which Neal explains to his father and mother why he goes to Mrs. Talbot's. Think about how they would react before writing.

3. Listen to some jazz and compare it to one of your favorite kinds of music. How is it similar? How is it different?

4. Listen to the jazz of various musicians. Choose some songs that you feel Neal would have liked. Play the recordings for your group or class and explain why you feel that Neal would have liked the ones you chose.

5. Assume that the Sloans have entered counseling. Write a new ending to the story.

6. Imagine that you are Georgie. Write a letter to Neal telling him that you are planning to run away. Be sure to give your reasons.

7. Research and list the places family members might turn to for help if they are in trouble. In your opinion, what might be the best place to seek help? Why?

Curriculum Connections:

1. Research jazz in the United States. Describe jazz. How did jazz originate? Who are some of its greatest names? Write a brief report. (SS or A)

2. Research one of the great jazz musicians—Erroll Garner, Theo Monk, Charlie Parker, and Dizzy Gillespie are some possibilities. Present an oral presentation to the class and play some of his music. (SS or A)

3. If you play a musical instrument, compose a short piece that you feel Neal would write and title it "Georgie's Blues." If you're feeling brave, play it for the class or record it and play the recording. (A)

17. *Durango Street* by Frank Bonham
(Dell, 1965)

Synopsis

When Rufus Henry is released from the forestry camp detention home, he hopes to straighten out his life. He considers going back to school so that he can get a good job some-day. Although he realizes that his future depends on not joining a gang, joining one is the only way to stay alive in the neighborhood of Durango Street. It doesn't take long for him to have an altercation with the Gassers, one of the local gangs. For protection, Rufus joins the Moors and soon fights his way to be headman. At the same time, he contends with Alex Robbins, a social worker who tries to guide the Moors and Gassers away from their destructive lifestyles and into positive activities. Only when the Moors, with Alex's help, sponsor a neighborhood graduation dance, does Rufus start to see how he can be a positive factor in life.

Ideas and Concepts to Highlight

1. Discuss life in the inner cities where poverty, lack of educational and economic opportunities, and violence are ever-present. Try to avoid stereotypes as you do so. It is likely that many students living in suburban or rural areas will have trouble identifying with the setting, and base their knowledge of it on television and other media.

2. Discuss the protection a gang can provide its members.

3. Explain how poverty and lack of opportunities provide a setting for gangs like the Gassers and Moors.

Writing Connection: "Ten Years from Now"

Rufus Henry has potential. He is intelligent, possesses leadership qualities, and is a good athlete. If he returns to school and begins playing football again, in 10 years he might be a star. An individual's future is tied to his or her expectations. For example, the student who expects and desires to go to college usually does. The student who expects to one day work in his or her parent's business often takes it over when the parent retires.

Ask your students to imagine that it is 10 years from now. What will they be doing? What kind of person will they be? Completing Worksheet 17-1 will help them generate ideas for writing about their futures.

NAME _____ **DATE** _____ **SECTION** _____

17-1. TEN YEARS FROM NOW

Directions: Think about Rufus Henry. Based on his experiences and potential, what might he be doing 10 years after the last scene of *Durango Street?* Would he be successful in his life?

Now think about you. Imagine it is 10 years from today. What will you be doing? What kind of person will you be? Answer the questions below and then write about your future.

1. What will you be doing 10 years from today? _____

_____

_____

_____

2. Why will you be doing this? _____

_____

_____

_____

3. Will you need any special skills, training, or education? _____ How will you obtain these?

_____

_____

_____

4. Describe yourself 10 years from now. _____

_____

_____

_____

5. Will you be married? Will you have children? Describe your family. _____

_____

_____

_____

17-2. QUESTIONS TO CONSIDER FOR
DURANGO STREET

1. Why did Rufus feel that he had to join a gang? How did Mr. Travers feel about gangs? What was his warning to Rufus?

2. What was Rufus's mother's opinion of him? Did she give him much support? Support your answer with examples from the story. How did he feel about her?

3. Describe the setting around Durango Street. Would you like to live there? Why or why not?

4. Why was Rufus so desperate for Ernie Brown to be his father? Do you think Ernie was his father? Explain. Why was the scrapbook Rufus kept so important to him?

5. After Rufus's altercation with Simon Jones and the Gassers, why did he need to join the Moors? Why couldn't he simply have called the police? Explain.

6. How did a person get into and out of the Moors? Why didn't Rufus run when he was attacked?

7. When Alex Robbins studied the files on the Moors, what did he find out about them? What did Rufus think of Alex when he first met him? Do you think Rufus's assessment of Alex was an accurate one? Explain.

8. When Rufus first agreed to have the Moors sponsor the graduation dance, what was his reason? How did his feelings about the dance change? What might Rufus have learned about himself because of the dance?

9. What do you think Rufus will be doing ten years after the story ended? Write a brief scene showing him at that time.

© 1994 by The Center for Applied Research in Education

17-3. PROJECTS AND ACTIVITIES TO CONSIDER FOR <u>DURANGO STREET</u>

1. Ernie Brown was Rufus's hero. Discuss with your group what makes a hero. Create a list of heroes, and include a reason why each person on the list qualifies as a hero. Discuss how a hero can influence your life. Share your list with other groups.

2. Imagine that Rufus returns to school, becomes a football star and makes it to the NFL. Interview him about his past and what advice he can offer to young people. Write an imaginary interview. What would he say? With a partner playing the part of Rufus, act out the interview for the class.

3. Imagine that you are a news reporter covering the Durango Street area. Select an incident in the story (perhaps a fight between the Gassers and Moors) and write a news article about it.

4. Working with your group, brainstorm ways that trouble between the Gassers and Moors could be minimized. Make a list of possible activities the two gangs could participate in that would improve their relations. Organize a panel discussion consisting of the members of various groups and discuss the various suggestions. Which ones are the most realistic? Why?

5. Imagine a conversation between Alex and Rufus about Rufus's future. What advice would Alex likely have given him. Write a dialogue between the two.

6. Compare the gangs in *Durango Street* to the gangs in *The Outsiders* by S.E. Hinton. How are they alike? How are they different? How are they alike and different from gangs today that you have heard or read about? Consult other sources if necessary.

Curriculum Connections:

1. Create a scrapbook of a famous sports star, celebrity, or other newsworthy individual. Include articles, photos, etc. (A)

2. Based on the information in the book, draw a map of the area around Durango Street. (SS)

3. Design a poster advertising the graduation dance. Provide an illustration and include all pertinent information such as cost, dress, entertainment, and refreshments. (A)

18. *House of Stairs* by William Sleator
(Dutton, 1974)

Synopsis

In this science fiction story, five 16-year-old orphans—Peter, Lola, Blossom, Abigail, and Oliver—are brought to a place that has nothing but stairs, a mysterious food machine, and a toilet. The teens have very different personalities, and none has any idea why he or she was brought to the house of stairs. There is no way out. At first they try to get along and work together, especially in attempting to make the food machine work. They are unaware that the machine is used by researchers to condition them. Eventually, Lola figures out that the machine works best when they hurt each other in some way—verbally or physically. Refusing to allow themselves to be manipulated, Lola and Peter decide not to eat. They vow to starve instead. Blossom, Abigail, and Oliver, however, lack the will to do this and they continue to cause each other pain for their reward of food. Only when Lola and Peter are near death do the researchers stop the experiment. Afterward, Blossom, Abigail, and Oliver continue to show the effects of their conditioning. Lola and Peter are labeled misfits and are to be sent away to an island for misfits. That doesn't matter to them, though, because they know that they won.

Ideas and Concepts to Highlight

1. Note the mystery to the novel. The reader knows only as much about the house of stairs and why the teens are there as the teens do. This is a powerful technique for generating and sustaining suspense.

2. Note the point-of-view shifts. This allows the reader to experience the story from each character's perspective.

3. Discuss that food is a necessity for life. It is an excellent conditioning agent.

4. Explain behavioral conditioning and how the behavior of an organism, through the use of the appropriate stimuli, can be manipulated and shaped. You might want to talk about Ivan Pavlov and B.F. Skinner, both of whom did much work in behavioral psychology.

Writing Connection: "The Misfits"

At the end of the story Lola and Peter were to be sent to an island for misfits. Ask your students to imagine what will happen to Lola and Peter there and write a story about their experiences. Completing Worksheet 18-1 will help students to generate ideas. You might wish to let students discuss their ideas with a partner before writing to help them focus their ideas even more.

18-1. THE MISFITS

Directions: Imagine that Lola and Peter are sent to the island for misfits. Write a story about what happens to them there. Answer the questions below to generate ideas for your story.

1. Describe the island._____

_____

_____

_____

_____

2. Who do they find there?_____

3. What happens?_____

_____

_____

_____

_____

4. Do their experiences on the island change Lola or Peter? _____

If yes, how?_____

_____

_____

_____

5. Do they ever leave the island? _____ If yes, how? _____

Then what happens to them?_____

_____

_____

_____

© 1994 by The Center for Applied Research in Education

18-2. QUESTIONS TO CONSIDER FOR
HOUSE OF STAIRS

1. Describe the house of stairs. What was so unusual and frightening about it?

2. In what ways were the characters alike? How were they different?

3. In Chapter 9, when the teens heard the voice, each heard a different message. Speculate how that could be. Analyze each message and explain the meaning it had for the character who heard it.

4. Describe how the characters reacted to one another the longer they were trapped on the stairs. Why do you think they weren't able to get along better?

5. How did the machine shape the movements of the dance the characters did?

6. When did the characters realize what the machine really wanted them to do? How did each of them react to this understanding?

7. Why was Lola surprised when Peter came to her and told her that he didn't want to go along with what the machine wanted? Do you think each could have refused the machine alone? Or did they need each other? Explain.

8. How did Blossom, Abigail, and Oliver get food after Peter and Lola left? Why do you think they continued to act this way?

9. Do you feel that the machine could have made Blossom, Abigail, and Oliver act hatefully to each other if they were not inherently evil? Explain. Can anyone or anything make a "good" person act "bad"?

10. What was the purpose of the house of stairs? Did his five subjects give Dr. Lawrence the results he had expected? What was the purpose of Dr. Lawrence's research? Do you think he was justified in using the teens as "guinea pigs" without their consent? Explain.

© 1994 by The Center for Applied Research in Education

18-3. PROJECTS AND ACTIVITIES TO CONSIDER FOR
HOUSE OF STAIRS

1. If you had been included with the group in the house of stairs, how would you have acted? Would you have stayed with Blossom, Abigail, and Oliver, or would you have gone with Lola and Peter? Explain.

2 Research behavioral conditioning and discuss this question with your group: Can people be conditioned to do evil? Organize a debate with a group that feels differently than you do. Stage the debate for the class and let them vote on the winner.

3. Work with a partner and list at least three traits of each character. Which character do you like the most? Which one do you like the least? Why? Which one has the strongest personality? Which one has the weakest? Why? Which one grew the most because of the ordeal? Who deteriorated the most? Explain. Compare your conclusions with the conclusions of other groups.

4. Throughout the story, the characters reveal what society is like on the outside. For example, few diets contain meat, and there is mention of a past war. Review the book and, based upon such details, write a description of what you think the United States is like at this time. Would you like to live there? Why or why not?

5. With your group, discuss what the likely lasting effects of their experience in the house of stairs would be on each character. Use specific examples from the story to support your ideas.

Curriculum Connections:

1. Research behavioral conditioning. Write a short report on it. (Sci)

2. Select a major researcher of conditioning, such as B.F. Skinner or Ivan Pavlov. Research his contributions to the understanding of conditioning and present your findings orally to your group or the class. (Sci)

3. With four other students, create the dance that the characters did for the machine. (A)

4. Review some of M.C. Escher's drawings. Draw your own idea of what the house of stairs looked like. (A)

19. *Home Before Dark* by Sue Ellen Bridges
(Knopf, 1976)

Synopsis

For much of the first 14 years of her life Stella Willis lived out of her father's car as her family moved from one picking station to another. When her father finally takes his family to his boyhood home and they move into a small tenant house on her Uncle Newton's farm, Stella is thrilled. It is the first time she has ever had a real home and she views this as the start of a new life. She meets Toby, a boy her age whose friendship turns into love, and Rodney, an older boy who wants all her attention. Stella quickly learns that life, even when she lives in her own home, can be hard. Not only must she cope with the attentions of Toby and Rodney, but she struggles with her feelings over her mother's tragic death and her father's sudden remarriage. Unwilling to leave her "home" and move into her stepmother's house with her father and younger siblings, Stella stays in the tenant house alone. Only when she realizes that loving people is more important than loving things can she rejoin her family.

Ideas and Concepts to Highlight

1. Note that the story is told through multiple points of view. This enables the reader to experience the story through the eyes of the various characters.

2. Discuss how her early poverty helped to shape Stella's personality. Because of her past, her small house meant very much to her.

3. Explain what the lives of migrant workers are like, and how they move from place to place following the sowing and harvesting of crops. Discuss how difficult this type of life is on children, who are constantly uprooted as their family moves.

4. Discuss the value of relationships versus the possession of material things.

Writing Connection: "The Most Important Thing in My Life"

When Stella moved into the small tenant house, her "home" became one of the most valuable things in her life. After her mother died and her father began courting Maggie, Stella clung to her home because it offered her something tangible and steady, and for a while it was more important to her than her family.

Instruct your students to think about the thing (or person) that is most important to them. Ask them to complete Worksheet 19-1 and then write about this topic.

19-1. THE MOST IMPORTANT THING IN MY LIFE

Directions: Think about your life, and the things that mean the most to you. Answer the questions below and then write an essay on this topic.

1. What is most important in your life? _____

_____ Why? _____

_____

_____

_____

_____

_____

2. How would your life be different without this thing? _____

_____

_____

_____

_____

_____

_____

_____

3. Could something else take the place of this thing? _____

Explain. _____

_____

_____

_____

_____

_____

_____

19-2. QUESTIONS TO CONSIDER FOR
HOME BEFORE DARK

1. What was Stella's first impression of the tenant house her family was going to live in on Uncle Newton's farm? How did she feel about living in a real house? How did her mother feel about the house?

2. Why did Stella's mother want to leave the farm?

3. Compare Anne and Stella's mother, Mae. How were they alike? How were they different? Support your ideas with examples from the story.

4. In Chapter 7, Silas tells Toby that, "...what's fitting is for people like the Willises and the Biggers to be under the same bit of moonlight." What does he mean? Do you agree with him? Why or why not?

5. How did Mae's death affect Stella? How did it affect her father?

6. Why didn't Toby tell the police or his parents who gave him the beating? If you were Toby, would you have told? Why or why not?

7. How did Stella react to Toby's beating? How did her feelings about Rodney change? What does this tell you about Stella's character? Explain.

8. Why do you think Stella's father began courting Maggie so soon after his wife's death? Do you think he was in mourning long enough? Explain.

9. How did Stella react when her father told her that he was courting Maggie?

10. Why did Stella refuse to leave the tenant house after her father married Maggie and he and the other children moved in with her? Do you think Stella was being reasonable? Explain.

11. What did Stella finally learn from Maggie?

© 1994 by The Center for Applied Research in Education

19-3. PROJECTS AND ACTIVITIES TO CONSIDER FOR
HOME BEFORE DARK

1. Assume that Stella did not leave the tenant house. Write a new ending for the story.

2. List at least five adjectives that describe Rodney Biggers. What is your opinion of him? Based on his character revealed in the story, what type of man do you think he will grow up to be?

3. Suppose that Mae didn't die. How would that have changed the story? Discuss this question with your group, then create a list of possible changes in the story. Share and discuss your list with other groups. As a group select one of the changes and create a new scene for the story.

4. Imagine that you are Stella. Write about your feelings for the tenant house.

5. Imagine that Stella and Toby have graduated from high school. Do you think they would still be close at this time? Or would they have drifted apart? Consider their backgrounds and aspirations. Write a scene in which Toby says goodbye to Stella as he prepares to leave for college.

6. Consider the lives of migrant workers. If necessary, conduct research, then brainstorm with your group ways that the plight of migrant workers and their families might be improved. Organize a panel discussion of the topic.

7. Write a wedding announcement about James Earl and Maggie for the local paper in Montreet County.

Curriculum Connections:

1. Using maps, try to determine the state that Montreet County might be found in. Hint: Use clues from the story to help you. For example, tobacco grew in the area; there were hot summers, and cold winters. (SS)

2. Write a report about migrant workers. In what states are they found? What are the predominate ethnic groups that make up migrants? What are their wages? What laws have been written to protect them from being exploited? (SS)

125

20. *Farewell to Manzanar*
by Jeanne Wakatsuki Houston and James Houston
(San Francisco Book Co./Houghton Mifflin Co., 1973)

Synopsis

Jeanne Wakatsuki was seven years old when her family was forced out of their home in southern California and detained in the Manzanar internment camp. Manzanar was part of the U.S. government's attempt to maintain national security by imprisoning Japanese-Americans during World War II. Jeannie's large family endures many indignities, living in cramped quarters without privacy, and her father, Ko, is exiled to North Dakota for months while he is interrogated for disloyalty. Jeannie spends her formative years behind Manzanar's barbed wire. The camp evolves into a small city with stores, entertainment, services and schools. When the war ends, Jeannie and her family must return to a society from which they had grown apart, and the family itself breaks down from the extreme living conditions and community unrest. Jeannie, who grows up with low self-esteem and confused feelings that she somehow deserved to be detained in the camp, finally returns to the ruins of Manzanar 27 years later. She makes peace with her fears of rejection and racism, her buried anger at a government that imprisoned her, and her disappointment in her prideful, arrogant father. The book is a series of vignettes, some out of chronological order, combining her recollections of actual events with her adult feelings.

Ideas and Concepts to Highlight

1. Discuss the importance of family in Japanese culture, and the strain that living in an internment camp placed on the Wakatsukis.

2. Compare, in relative terms, the detention of Japanese-Americans with the Nazi death camps in Europe. Encourage discussions about patriotism and morality, and government's role in preserving security during wartime.

3. Discuss irony and its many manifestations in the book—that the children were actually afraid to leave the compound, that the Japanese-Americans interned were not even permitted to contribute to outside society, and so on. Encourage students to relate ironic situations from their own experiences to illustrate the meaning of the term.

4. Discuss the long-term psychological effects that a childhood experience can trigger, especially in terms of racism and rejection.

Writing Connection: "Manzanar—A Question of Rights"

Although at the time during war hysteria, the internment of Japanese Americans was supported by most of the country, the episode has since been questioned by many people on moral and judicial grounds. Essentially, the question comes to this: Is it acceptable for a free country to imprison a segment of its population (or an individual) that is deemed a threat, even though those individuals have done nothing wrong?

Pose that question to your students for this writing assignment. Instruct them to complete Worksheet 20-1 and then write an essay about their views.

NAME _____   DATE _____   SECTION _____

20-1. MANZANAR—A QUESTION OF RIGHTS

Directions: Manzanar symbolizes a time in American history when the rights of Japanese-Americans were suspended. Even though they had done nothing wrong, they were considered to be threats to security and were deprived of their basic rights as Americans. Supporters of internment camps justified the camps because of the war. If you were living during World War II, would you have been a supporter? Answer the following questions and then write an essay explaining your views.

1.   Fill in the boxes with the appropriate information.

Basic freedoms Americans enjoy	Which should be suspended during war? Why?	What might happen as a result?

2.   Would you "understand" having your freedoms denied for any reason?_____
Explain. _____

_____

_____

_____

3.   What alternatives did the U.S. government have to internment camps like Manzanar?

_____

_____

_____

20-2. QUESTIONS TO CONSIDER FOR FAREWELL TO MANZANAR

1. Jeannie maintains that the style of living in Manzanar caused her family structure to collapse. Give some examples of the major events that strained the family. What are some comparable situations today that can break down an existing family?

2. Describe Jeannie's feelings when she first arrived at Manzanar. How would you feel if you were suddenly forced into an internment camp as she was? Explain.

3. Describe Manzanar. In what ways is it like your community? How was it different?

4. Was Kiyo justified in punching his father to protect his mother? Compare the situation in the context of American versus Japanese culture. Does the event have differing significance from culture to culture? How?

5. Make a list of five values important to Japanese culture. How did the internment affect these values? Did the values change? If yes, how? If not, explain why.

6. What is irony? Discuss how it relates to Manzanar and the families' attempts to create normalcy in a virtual prison. Also, expound on the irony of the loyal Japanese-Americans being detained. Cite examples of ironic situations from the story.

7. Ko's pride is often his downfall. Trace some of his major failures. What are the effects on the family? How much is he to blame for the breakdown of its structure?

8. "What if" plays a significant role in Jeannie's childhood. Write five "what if" questions that she might wonder about, and answer them in the context of her experiences.

9. Jeannie's pilgrimage back to Manzanar helped her come to terms with her childhood. What does the term "pilgrimage" mean to you? How did Jeannie feel after her return to Manzanar? Was that trip important to her? Explain.

20-3. PROJECTS AND ACTIVITIES TO CONSIDER FOR *FAREWELL TO MANZANAR*

1. Manzanar functioned as a community on its own. Imagine that the inhabitants published a newspaper. Pretend you are a reporter, and interview classmates who pose as detainees. As a class, write news stories and create sections for the paper. Produce and distribute it, and discuss what effect a news organ might have had on the camp.

2. Write an essay about how *Farewell to Manzanar* changed your feelings toward World War II, and your own nationalism.

3. Watch the film *Hiroshima* or read the book (by John Hersey). Jeannie says that after the bombing, "internment camps were undeniably a thing of the past." Why? What did Hiroshima represent to Jeannie and to the Japanese culture?

4. Haiku is a poetic form of Japanese origin. Find out its format, then write two haikus from Jeannie's point of view regarding her experiences at Manzanar.

5. Imagine that the U.S. government did not detain Japanese-Americans in internment camps during the war. How would not having had experienced Manzanar changed Jeannie's life? Write a short biography of what this "different" life would have been like.

Curriculum Connections:

1. Research the current state of the laws applying to immigration into the U.S. from three countries of your choice. How are they different? Are they fair, in your opinion? Write a letter to a government official or to a newspaper expressing your views. (SS)

2. The author revisited Manzanar in 1972. Conduct some research to find out what currently stands on the spot where the camp was. Describe the climate, terrain, wildlife and any monuments or population. (SS)

3. During George Bush's presidency, Japanese-American survivors of the camps were compensated by the federal government. Obtain news, magazine, and/or broadcast reports or documentaries and research the feelings and opinions of the recipients of the compensation. Do you think they were adequately rewarded? Write an essay about the government response. Choose a specific angle and incorporate quotes from the survivors. (SS)

5

Novels for Grades 9-10

21. *A Separate Peace* - Knowles

22. *To Kill a Mockingbird* - Lee

23. *Animal Farm* - Orwell

24. *A Tale of Two Cities* - Dickens

25. *Of Mice and Men* - Steinbeck

26. *I Know Why the Caged Bird Sings* - Angelou

27. *After the First Death* - Cormier

28. *Dicey's Song* - Voigt

29. *I Never Promised You a Rose Garden* - Greenberg

30. *Flowers for Algernon* - Keyes

31. *Hiroshima* - Hersey

32. *The Miracle Worker* (play) - Gibson

33. *Dragonwings* - Yep

34. *Running Loose* - Crutcher

35. *Flowers in the Attic* - Andrews

36. *The Adventures of Huckleberry Finn* - Twain

37. *Something Wicked This Way Comes* - Bradbury

38. *The Pearl* - Steinbeck

39. *The Hitchhiker's Guide to the Galaxy* - Adams

40. *Night* - Wiesel

21. *A Separate Peace* by John Knowles
(Macmillan, 1960)

Synopsis

Gene Forrester returns to the Devon School 15 years after he graduated from it. He walks slowly through the campus, coming to a big tree by a river. At this point, Gene tells what happened when he attended the school during World War II. Although the Devon School tries to shield the boys from the war, the war is always lurking in the background. The boys realize that, at 16, they don't have much time before they will be fighting. Phineas, the best athlete in the school, is always devising games and challenges that symbolically represent the war. One of these is jumping from the big tree. Phineas considers Gene his best friend, and is always urging Gene to join him. However, Gene is not so sure of his feelings for Phineas, whom he both admires and envies. One night, as the boys are jumping off the tree, Phineas falls. Gene wonders if he jounced the branch to make Phineas lose his balance. Phineas breaks his leg and is crippled. Although Phineas does not blame Gene, Gene struggles with his uncertainty and guilt. The climax of the story occurs when other boys, led by Brinker Hadley, conduct a mock trial in which Gene is accused of causing Phineas's fall. Phineas ends the trial by erupting in anger. He rushes from the room and falls down the stairs. This fall leads to his death because some marrow from the broken bone escapes into his bloodstream and goes to his heart. After Phineas's death Gene is finally able to come to terms with the fear, jealousy, and guilt he feels.

Ideas and Concepts to Highlight

1. Note that the story is told in the first person. Gene returns to Devon School and tells the story of when he was a student there.

2. Discuss how this novel is a war story. Knowles makes continual reference to the war throughout the story.

3. Discuss the relationship between Phineas and Gene.

4. Point out that one of the major themes of the novel is how people must confront their own fears and hatreds and find their own separate peace.

5. Explain Knowles's view of the essential cause of wars—that wars are made "by something ignorant in the human heart."

Writing Connection: "My Own Separate Peace"

One of the major themes of this novel is an individual's search for personal peace, his or her attempts to reconcile internal conflicts. While not all conflicts are as dramatic as Gene's, everyone seeks his or her separate peace, often on a variety of issues.

Ask your students to think of a time they gained a separate peace and share the experience through their writing. (For students who may not have achieved a separate peace in some way, ask them to write about a separate peace they would like to achieve.) Instruct students to first complete Worksheet 21-1, which will help them to focus their ideas.

21-1. MY OWN SEPARATE PEACE

Directions: Everyone searches for his or her own separate peace. Answer the questions below and then write about a separate peace you've gained.

1. Describe the conflict that led to your separate peace. _____

    _____

    _____

    _____

    _____

2. How did you feel about the conflict?_____

    _____

    _____

    _____

3. Why was it important to resolve the conflict?_____

    _____

    _____

    _____

4. How did you resolve it?_____

    _____

    _____

    _____

5. How did achieving your separate peace change you? _____

    _____

    _____

    _____

    _____

© 1994 by The Center for Applied Research in Education

21-2. QUESTIONS TO CONSIDER FOR
A SEPARATE PEACE

1. Why do you think Knowles opened the story with Gene returning to the Devon School 15 years after he graduated?

2. Compare and contrast Gene and Phineas. What are the strongest traits of each? How does Phineas feel about Gene? How does Gene feel about Phineas? Of the two, which one do you like better? Why?

3. How does his fall from the tree affect Phineas? How does it affect Gene? Do you think Gene was responsible for Phineas's fall? Explain, citing examples from the story.

4. What did the fall from the tree symbolize for Phineas?

5. How does Gene react to Leper's enlisting in the ski troops? Later, what effect did Leper's telegram have on Gene? Why, in your opinion, couldn't Leper adjust to life in the army?

6. Why does Phineas claim that the war isn't real?

7. Describe the war trial that Brinker Hadley organizes. Why did Brinker do this? How did Gene feel about the trial? Why did Phineas react the way he did?

8. In your opinion, who was responsible for Phineas's second fall? Explain.

9. Do you think Phineas's death affected the type of man Gene became? Explain.

10. Why do you think Knowles titled this novel *A Separate Peace?*

11. *A Separate Peace* has been widely acclaimed as a great novel. Do you agree? Explain.

21-3. PROJECTS AND ACTIVITIES TO CONSIDER FOR
A SEPARATE PEACE

1. Write an essay explaining what you feel are John Knowles's feelings about human nature and war. Use examples from the story to support your ideas.

2. Working with a group, dramatize a scene from the book. (The trial organized by Brinker would be a good choice.) Feel free to improvise and expand the dialogue. Create a different ending for your scene, keeping in mind the personalities of the characters.

3. Read the book *Phineas* by John Knowles (Random House, 1968) which is a collection of six stories, including the one that *A Separate Peace* is based on. Compare the stories and Knowles's style, and present an oral report of your opinions to your group or class.

4. Phineas invented games in the story. Work with a partner and invent a game of your own. Write down its object and rules.

5. Imagine that you were a recruiter for the Devon School, and it was your job to convince young men to select the Devon School over others. Write a brochure in which you describe the benefits that the Devon School offers its students.

Curriculum Connections:

1. Create a time line of the major events of World War II. Consult the necessary references. (SS or A)

2. Research the causes of World War II. How did the war begin? Which were the major countries at war? How did the United States become involved in the war? How many people were killed? What were the monetary estimates of the total destruction? How did the war finally end? What were the results of the war? Write a report of your findings. (SS)

3. The Devon School was located in New England. Research that part of our country. What states make up New England? Describe New England's climate, geography, and economy. What influence did the Puritan religion have on New England? Does any of that influence remain today? Finally, why do you think Knowles located his story in New England? Write a report. (SS)

4. The inscription over the main door of the Devon School's First Building, where Phineas and Gene were taken to trial by Brinker Hadley, is "Here Boys Come to Be Made Men." How did those words apply specifically to Gene? Design a logo that includes these words. (A)

22. <u>To Kill a Mockingbird</u> by Harper Lee
(J.B. Lippincott Company, 1960)

Synopsis

Scout Finch, a young girl, tells this story that reveals the prejudice in a small Alabama town during the Great Depression. In the summer, Scout, her brother, Jem, and their friend, Dill, play on the street around Scout's home. A few houses down is the Radley house, a place of much superstition because of Boo Radley, a mysterious recluse. When Miss Maudie's house catches fire one night and everyone has to go outside because all of the nearby houses are made of wood, Boo slips a blanket around Scout's shoulders to protect her against the chill. Although Boo plays a major role later in the story, Scout's father, Atticus, is the central character. A lawyer, Atticus defends Tom Robinson, a black man accused of raping a white woman. Despite proving Tom innocent by showing that Bob Ewell, the girl's father, was responsible for her beating, Tom is still found guilty by the prejudiced jury. Furious at Atticus for making him appear a fool in court, Bob Ewell threatens Atticus. Later, Tom tries to escape from a prison farm and is killed; few people mourn him even though they know he was innocent. The story climaxes when Ewell tries to get back at Atticus by attacking Scout and Jem. He likely would have killed the children except that he is killed by Boo Radley. Scout and Jem grow up significantly throughout the story, learning to see prejudice for what it is, and judge people individually.

Ideas and Concepts to Highlight

1. Briefly explain the history of the South, and the changes brought by the Civil War.

2. Discuss prejudice and the place of African-Americans in the social order of the 1930s South, which is the setting of the story.

3. Note that Scout Finch narrates the story. She is a young girl and her point of view is limited by her age.

4. Point out how Lee, who comes from the South and is a relative of the Civil War general Robert E. Lee, captures the language and color of the setting.

Writing Connection: "Injustice"

A great injustice was done to Tom Robinson in *To Kill a Mockingbird*. Because he was a black man in the 1930s South, merely being accused of a crime by a white woman (despite its obvious falsehood in court) was enough for him to be convicted. Unfortunately, there are still many examples of injustice in our society.

For this assignment, ask your students to consider an injustice they perceive in society. (If you wish you can narrow the assignment to an injustice they perceive in their personal lives.) Instruct them to complete Worksheet 22-1, which will help them to generate ideas for their topic. Remind your students to include details to support their main ideas, and consult references if necessary.

NAME _____ DATE _____ SECTION _____

22-1. INJUSTICE

Directions: Tom Robinson suffered a great injustice in *To Kill a Mockingbird*. Think about an injustice you see in the world. Answer the questions below and then write about your feelings.

1. Describe the injustice you will write about. _____

_____

_____

_____

2. Why do you feel this event or problem is an injustice? _____

_____

_____

_____

3. How can this injustice be corrected? _____

_____

_____

_____

4. Will some people be unwilling or reluctant to correct this injustice? _____
Why? _____

_____

_____

_____

5. How can such people be persuaded to change? _____

_____

_____

_____

22-2. QUESTIONS TO CONSIDER FOR
TO KILL A MOCKINGBIRD

1. Why do you think Scout opened the novel by mentioning her brother's broken arm? Why did she then tell about Simon Finch and provide so much information about Maycomb?

2. Compare Scout and Jem. As the novel progresses, which one of them seems to understand more of what is happening? Explain.

3. How do the white townspeople react to Atticus defending Tom Robinson? What does Atticus tell Scout and Jem to do about the "talk" they will hear? How do you think Scout felt about the remarks others made about her father? Explain, citing examples from the story.

4. Describe Atticus Finch. What kind of man is he? How does Scout feel about him in the beginning of the story? How does she come to feel about him at the end? Offer examples from the story to support your answers.

5. After Mrs. Dubose's death, why did Atticus tell Scout that Mrs. Dubose was the bravest person he ever knew?

6. How did Scout feel about Aunt Alexandra coming to spend the summer with them? How did Atticus feel about Alexandra's pride with the family background? What does this tell you about Atticus? Explain.

7. Describe how Atticus defended Tom Robinson. Was his defense a sound one? Explain. Why was Tom Robinson found guilty?

8. How do Scout and Jem react to the trial? What lasting impression do you think the result had on them? Explain.

9. Why do you think Boo Radley saved Scout and Jem?

10. At the end of the story, why does Heck Tate insist that Bob Ewell fell on his own knife? Why does Atticus finally agree? How does Scout show that she understands their decision?

11. What is a mockingbird? How does a mockingbird symbolize Tom Robinson?

22-3. PROJECTS AND ACTIVITIES TO CONSIDER FOR TO KILL A MOCKINGBIRD

1. Write your own editorial about Tom Robinson's conviction and death.

2. This story is told from the point of view of a young girl. In that sense, it is limited by Scout's lack of experience. Working with a small group, discuss how using the POV of an older Scout, or a third person POV would have affected the story. Would the story have had as much impact? Why or why not? Appoint a recorder to write down your group's conclusions and then share them with other groups.

3. Form a panel and discuss this question: How is prejudice a major theme of the novel? Cite specific examples from the story in support of your ideas.

4. Work with a partner and try to determine who—Scout or Jem—changed more during the course of the novel. Write about your conclusion and share it with others.

5. Watch the movie *To Kill a Mockingbird*. How is the movie different from the novel? Which version of the story do you like better? Why? Write an essay comparing the two.

6. Imagine that you are Atticus Finch. Devise a different defense for Tom Robinson. Write the trial scenes over, using your new defense. Do you manage to convince the jury to find Tom not guilty? With the help of some classmates, dramatize your new trial.

Curriculum Connections:

1. Research the state of Alabama. What is its population? Describe its economy. What is its climate like? Compare the Alabama of today with the Alabama of the 1930s. Write a report of your findings. (SS)

2. Find out what a mockingbird is. Where is this bird found? Why is it called a mockingbird? Do you think *To Kill a Mockingbird* was a good title for this story? Explain. (Sci)

3. Consult newspaper and magazine articles written about the South. Based on your research, decide whether conditions for African-Americans have improved since the time of the novel. In your opinion, is there as much prejudice today as there was then? Present your conclusions to the class in an oral report. (SS)

23. *Animal Farm* by George Orwell
(Harcourt Brace Jovanovich, Inc., 1946)

Synopsis

Animal Farm is a political satire in which the characters and events mirror the rise of Communism in the Soviet Union. The story, set on a farm, begins with old Major, a prominent pig, sharing a dream with the other animals. He explains how humans oppress animals and urges the animals to revolution. Major dies three days later and the revolt comes shortly thereafter when Mr. Jones, the farmer, gets drunk and forgets to feed the animals and milk the cows. When the animals break into the feed bins, Jones tries to stop them, but they drive him, his wife, and the hired hands out. The animals, under the leadership of Napoleon and Snowball, two pigs, assume operation of the farm, now called Animal Farm. The pigs formulate *The Seven Commandments of Animalism,* which assert that "All animals are equal." In the weeks and months that follow, however, Napoleon and the rest of the pigs become pre-eminent. Napoleon forces Snowball off Animal Farm by claiming that Snowball is a traitor. Supported by the other pigs, and dogs he uses to ensure that his policies are carried out, Napoleon gradually becomes a totalitarian ruler, in effect, assuming Jones's old role. Most of the animals on Animal Farm work harder and have less to eat, but, because of skillful propaganda, believe they are better off than before.

Ideas and Concepts to Highlight

1. Explain that this story is often described as a fable. A fable is a story that uses animals to represent truths about human beings.

2. Point out that the story is one of literature's greatest political satires. Explain that a satire is a story that exposes human weakness or failings through irony or humor. Orwell satirizes Communism.

3. Note that this story is also quite ironic. Although the animals rebelled to gain freedom, they in fact only gained a new master.

4. Discuss the use of propaganda by leaders and governments.

5. Note Orwell's use of personification—the giving of human traits to nonhuman things (the animals).

Writing Connection: "Freedom"

The animals of Animal Farm were told that they had freedom. Of course, they had no freedom, but since they didn't remember what their condition was like under Farmer Jones they believed Squealer and the pigs. Instruct your students to consider the issue of freedom. What is it? Does it have any limitations? Do they feel that they enjoy freedom? After completing Worksheet 23-1 instruct them to write an essay about freedom.

NAME _____ **DATE** _____ **SECTION** _____

23-1. FREEDOM

Directions: Think about freedom. Consider your own experiences as well as what you have read and heard about this important topic. Answer the questions below and then write an essay detailing your thoughts about freedom.

1. What does freedom mean to you? _____

_____

_____

_____

2. Are there any limits to freedom?_____ If yes, what are they? If no, why aren't

there any limits? _____

_____

_____

3. Does everybody enjoy the same amount of freedom?_____

Explain and give examples. _____

_____

_____

4. What can be done to ensure that everyone enjoys the same amount of freedom?_____

_____

_____

_____

5. What, if any, is the relationship between freedom and power? Explain. _____

_____

_____

_____

_____

141

23-2. QUESTIONS TO CONSIDER FOR
ANIMAL FARM

1. In Chapter 1, why does old Major tell the animals they should rebel against humans? Give some of his reasons. What final advice does he give the animals?

2. Soon after the revolution the animals worked together. When did this begin to change? Which animals assumed command? How were they able to do this?

3. How did Squealer explain to the other animals why the pigs got the milk and the apples? If you were one of the other animals, how would you feel about his explanation? Explain.

4. Napoleon eventually became the leader of the animals. In what ways was his behavior like that of Jones? Give some examples.

5. Do you think Snowball was responsible for the windmill being knocked down? Do you think he was responsible for the other acts of mischief? Why do you think Napoleon claimed that Snowball was responsible?

6. How were the original Seven Commandments changed as time passed? Why were the changes made?

7. How did Napoleon rewrite the history of Animal Farm? Why did he do this?

8. The pigs used propaganda, with Squealer as their "spokes-pig," to convince the other animals that things were better than they really were. Give some examples of Squealer's effective use of propaganda.

9. What is the significance of Animal Farm's name being changed back to the Manor Farm? Explain.

10. At the conclusion of the story, the animals could not tell the difference between the men and the pigs. What do you think was Orwell's message here?

23-3. PROJECTS AND ACTIVITIES TO CONSIDER FOR ANIMAL FARM

1. Working with a partner or small group, consult newspapers, news magazines (such as *Time or U.S. News and World Report*), and TV newscasts, and list places around the world where political systems are being challenged. Find out the causes of the turmoil and the groups involved. After compiling your information present your information orally to the class.

2. Read some of Aesop's fables. Compare how Aesop used animals to convey morals and truths to the way Orwell did. Which in your opinion is more effective? Why? Share your opinion with your group.

3. The pigs use violence to bring about the new order of Animal Farm. They lead the fight against the humans and order the dogs to kill traitors. Organize a debate and examine this question: Is violence a necessary tool of leaders to establish and maintain order? Is such violence justified?

4. Working with your group, chart the pigs' rise to power. Identify the policies and decisions that ensured that the other animals would not challenge the pigs.

5. One of the major themes of *Animal Farm* is that power corrupts those who possess it. Explain how Orwell supports this idea throughout the story. (Hint: Think about Napoleon and the pigs.)

6. Irony is a situation in which someone expects one thing but gets the opposite. Working with a partner, list and describe as many examples of irony as you can. Share your list with others.

Curriculum Connections:

1. Napoleon, the Berkshire boar of the story, is often thought to be Napoleon Bonaparte, the French dictator. Research the historical Napoleon and compare him to Orwell's Napoleon. Write a brief report. (SS)

2. Research Communism and write a report. What type of political/economic system is it? Provide examples in your report. What countries currently adhere to a communist system? (SS)

3. Working with a partner, identify the major events in *Animal Farm* and find corresponding events of Communism in the Soviet Union. Create a flowchart showing how one event led to another. (SS or A)

4. Why did Communism in the Soviet Union collapse? Consult references and write a report. (SS)

5. Design a plaque that highlights the Seven Commandments of Animalism. (A)

24. *A Tale of Two Cities* by Charles Dickens
(Greenwich House, 1982)

Synopsis

Jarvis Lorry, accompanied by Lucie Manette, journeys from England to France in hopes of finding Lucie's father, Dr. Alexandre Manette, who has been jailed in the Bastille. They find the doctor in Paris. He has suffered greatly during his many years of imprisonment, and they return with him to London. Five years later, Lorry, Lucie, and Dr. Manette are called to testify at the trial of Charles Darnay, a Frenchman living in England who has been accused of treason. Although Lucie reluctantly provides evidence against him, he is acquitted because the evidence is circumstantial. Darnay and a lawyer at his trial, Sydney Carton, to whom Darnay bears a strong resemblance, both fall in love with Lucie. Because Carton is an alcoholic, Darnay wins Lucie's love and they are married. Carton, however, continues to love her and remains a friend. During this time, France is drifting toward revolution. The aristocracy oppresses the people who plan their vengeance. When Darnay's uncle, a cruel, heartless nobleman is assassinated, Darnay inherits his estate, but he renounces his claim, for he wants no part of the French nobility. The Revolution comes in 1789. In 1792, Darnay receives a plea for help from the family steward, who has been jailed. Darnay leaves for France, and is quickly jailed himself. Lucie, along with her daughter and Dr. Manette, go to France to help Darnay. Dr. Manette helps to get Darnay acquitted, but Darnay is arrested again. This time he is convicted and sentenced to death. Sydney Carton arrives in Paris and learns of Darnay's sentence. He works fast. Getting into the prison with the help of a spy he knows, Carton drugs Darnay and changes places with him. The resemblance between the two men ensures the success of his plan. Carton goes to the guillotine, and because of his sacrifice, Darnay, Lucie, their daughter, and Dr. Manette escape France and return safely to England.

Ideas and Concepts to Highlight

1. Note that the story is divided into three books, each dealing with a different period and focus, though all move forward to the climax.

2. Discuss the theme of resurrection that is woven throughout the novel. For example, when Carton sacrifices himself to save Darnay, Carton is symbolically reborn. Something good has come out of his wasteful life. Out of the destruction and death of the Revolution, a new society emerges.

3. Note Carton's pure love for Lucie, which enables him to make the greatest sacrifice to save her husband.

4. Provide background about the French Revolution. Begun in 1789, the country swiftly went over to mob rule. Unlike the American Revolution, which gave rise to a democratic republic, the French Revolution led to Napoleon.

Writing Connection: "A Great Sacrifice"

When Sydney Carton took Charles Darnay's place before the guillotine, Carton could offer no greater sacrifice. He gave his life because of his love for Lucie.

For this assignment, ask your students to write a story of their own in which a character sacrifices something. Have students complete Worksheet 24-1 to generate ideas.

24-1. A GREAT SACRIFICE

Directions: Sydney Carton sacrificed his life for his love of Lucie Darnay. Create a story in which your character(s) sacrifice something. While the sacrifice may not be as great as Carton's was, it should be significant enough to affect the story's climax. Answering the questions below will help you plot and organize your story.

1. What is the central conflict or problem of your story? _____

   _____

   _____

   _____

   _____

   _____

2. How do the characters solve (or fail to solve) the problem? _____

   _____

   _____

   _____

   _____

3. What sacrifice is made? _____

   _____

   _____

   _____

   _____

   _____

4. On a separate sheet of paper, list your main characters. Provide brief descriptions of their physical and personality traits.

24-2. QUESTIONS TO CONSIDER FOR
A TALE OF TWO CITIES

1. Why does Dickens open the novel with a description of the period?

2. What is the significance of the title of each book?

3. Describe Dr. Manette when Lucie and Mr. Lorry first see him. Why is he in this condition? What does this tell you about prison conditions of this time?

4. Compare Charles Darnay and Sydney Carton. How are they alike? How are they different? Which, in your opinion, is the stronger personality of the two? Why?

5. Why did Dr. Manette, when distressed, take up his cobbling?

6. Why did Charles Darnay return to France in 1792? Do you think his decision to go back was a wise one? Explain. What happened to him soon after he arrived?

7. How did Dr. Manette save Darnay at his first trial in France? Why was he able to influence the jury?

8. Why was Darnay arrested again? Why wasn't Dr. Manette able to save him this time?

9. As Carton contemplates how he can help Darnay, he walks through the streets with the biblical passage, "I am the resurrection and the life," repeating in his mind. What significance does this have in his decision to save Darnay?

10. "Liberty, Equality, Fraternity" was the motto of the French Revolution. What does it mean? In your opinion, did the Revolution live up to its motto? Explain.

24-3. PROJECTS AND ACTIVITIES TO CONSIDER FOR
A TALE OF TWO CITIES

1. Assume that Carton didn't change places with Darnay. Write a new ending for the story.

2. Throughout the story Dickens gives several characterizations of nobility. Write an essay explaining what you think were Dickens's opinions of the French and English aristocracy. Use examples from the story to support your ideas.

3. A motif is a recurring idea in a story. One of the most important motifs in *A Tale of Two Cities* is the idea of resurrection. Working with a partner, find several examples of resurrection, then list and share them with your classmates.

4. Research the causes of the French Revolution and the eventual course the Revolution took. Organize a panel and discuss this question: Could the great violence have been averted, or at least minimized?

5. View the movie version of *A Tale of Two Cities* and compare it to the book. Which one did you find more interesting? Why?

Curriculum Connections:

1. This novel was written during England's Victorian Age. What was the Victorian Age? How might have the beliefs, attitudes, and customs of that time influenced Dickens's writing? Consult the necessary references and write a brief report. (SS)

2. Locate London and France on a map. How far apart are they? During the time of the novel, how did people travel between the two cities? How do people travel between them today? (SS)

3. Research the Bastille. What was it? Why did French men and women hate it so? What did its storming signify? (SS)

4. Research the French monarchy at the time just prior to the Revolution. Louis XVI and his wife, Marie Antoinette, ruled. Write an essay on how their attitudes and actions helped bring about the Revolution. (SS)

5. Consulting the necessary references, create a time line of the major events of the French Revolution. (SS or A)

6. Consult references and find out what happened to France after the Revolution. Present an oral report to the class about your findings. (SS)

25. *Of Mice and Men* by John Steinbeck
(Viking, 1937)

Synopsis

George Milton and Lennie Small are walking to a farm where they hope to find work. They stop by a stream for the night. George takes away a dead mouse Lennie has accidentally killed. (Lennie, who is mentally handicapped, likes to pet soft things.) George then repeats their dream for the future in which they will one day work their own place. George also tells Lennie that he should return to this spot if he (Lennie) gets in trouble. The next day they obtain work. Curley, the boss's son, picks on Lennie, but George comes to Lennie's defense. George's concern for Lennie's welfare grows when Curley's wife comes to the bunkhouse. George immediately sees her as a "tramp." Later, angry about his wife, Curley takes his rage out on Lennie, punching him in the face. Lennie doesn't fight back until George tells him to, and then he crushes Curley's hand. A few days later, Lennie is in the barn playing with a puppy Slim gave to him. Lennie plays too roughly with it and kills it. When Curley's wife comes into the barn, she gets Lennie to tell her that he likes soft things. She lets him touch her hair. He strokes it, she becomes frightened, and he accidentally kills her. Afraid, Lennie runs to the stream. When the men find Curley's wife, they want revenge. Curley leads them, but George finds Lennie first. He shoots and kills Lennie to prevent the others from hurting him.

Ideas and Concepts to Highlight

1. Discuss the relationship between George and Lennie. You might also wish to discuss mental disabilities.

2. Note the many examples of foreshadowing. For example, Lennie's accidental killing of the mouse and the puppy foreshadow his killing of Curley's wife.

3. Note the poverty of migrant workers like George and Lennie of the 1930s. Compare their lives to the migrant workers of today.

Writing Connection: "A Mercy Killing"

George's killing of Lennie, from George's perspective, is an act of mercy. He believes that what would happen to Lennie if he were apprehended would be far worse than the merciful death George gave him. Lennie's last thought was of his and George's dream.

Ask your students to consider George's action in killing Lennie. Was he justified? After completing Worksheet 25-1 instruct your students to write an essay or story that examines this topic.

25-1. A MERCY KILLING

Directions: Think about George's killing of Lennie in *Of Mice and Men*. Was he right? Answer the questions below, then write an essay or story that explains your views.

1. Describe the relationship between George and Lennie. _____

_____

_____

_____

2. What crime did Lennie commit?_____ Why did he do it? _____

_____

_____

_____

3. What do you think would have happened to Lennie if he was apprehended?_____

_____

_____

_____

4. Why did George kill Lennie?_____

_____

_____

_____

_____

5. Was George justified to kill Lennie? _____ Explain. _____

_____

_____

_____

_____

© 1994 by The Center for Applied Research in Education

25-2. QUESTIONS TO CONSIDER FOR
OF MICE AND MEN

1. Describe the relationship between George and Lennie. What did Lennie get from their friendship? What did George get? How did their friendship separate them from the other farm hands?

2. Describe George's dream of the future for Lennie and himself. Do you think it was a realistic dream? Explain. Why was the dream so important to them? Why did Candy and Crooks want to share in the dream?

3. Give at least three examples of foreshadowing. How does Steinbeck's use of foreshadowing build suspense in the story?

4. Why did Candy finally agree to let Carlson shoot Candy's old dog? Do you agree with Carlson's reasons? Explain.

5. When Lennie first comes to Crooks's quarters, Crooks tells him to get out. Why does he then allow Lennie to come in? How are Lennie and Crooks alike?

6. Curley is described as being a "mean little man" who picks on bigger men to prove his manhood. Do you agree with that description? Explain.

7. Curley's wife often flirts with the other men. Why does she do this? What reasons does she offer?

8. Why did George shoot Lennie? Do you agree with what he did? Explain.

9. At the end of the novel Slim says to George, "You hadda, George. I swear you hadda." What does he mean?

25-3. PROJECTS AND ACTIVITIES TO CONSIDER FOR
OF MICE AND MEN

1. Assume that Lennie was caught and brought to trial. Write a scene, in the format of a play, of his trial. Working with a group, assume the parts of prosecutor, defense lawyer, judge, and witnesses. Other class members can be the jury. What would the outcome of the trial be?

2. Write a new ending for the story. George does not kill Lennie. Neither does Curley. What happens then?

3. Discuss with your group whether Lennie was responsible for his actions in killing Curley's wife. Appoint a recorder to write down the conclusions of your group—and your reasons—and share your results with others.

4. Lennie, George, Curley's wife, Curley, and Crooks, in his or her own way, are tragic characters. For which one do you have the most sympathy? Why? Write about your feelings in a short essay.

5. Watch one of the movie versions *Of Mice and Men* and compare it to the novel. Which in your opinion has the greater impact? Did the movie follow the story-line of the novel? How was it changed? Write a review of the movie for your classmates.

6. Imagine that George is arrested and goes to trial for the murder of Lennie. You were a worker on the farm and are called as a witness for the defense. What could you say to help George to be found innocent? Write a dialogue between you and the defense attorney. (This can be reversed. You can be a witness called by the prosecution. You would then be expected to support the state's case and help prove that George is guilty.)

Curriculum Connections:

1. Locate the Salinas River and Soledad on a map of California. Using an atlas or other reference, describe the topography and climate of the area. What types of crops are grown there? (SS)

2. Research the area around the Salinas River and Soledad. Compare the area of the 1930s when the novel is set to the area today. Include such things as population, crops, economic activity, and lifestyle. (SS)

3. Draw or sketch one of your favorite characters of the story. (A)

4. Research the conditions of migrant workers during the 1930s. In what ways, if any, have those conditions changed today? Write a brief report of your findings. (SS)

26. *I Know Why the Caged Bird Sings* by Maya Angelou
(Random House, 1969)

Synopsis

Marguerite Johnson, nicknamed Maya, is a product of a broken home and as a child is sent to live with her grandmother in Depression-era Arkansas. Her grandmother owns a large grocery and it is a solace for Maya to be a part of it. When she is seven, Maya and Bailey, her brother, are sent to St. Louis to live with their mother. While there, she is raped by her mother's boyfriend, and after his trial he is lynched. Her brooding is too much for the family to bear, and the two children are sent back to the grandmother in Arkansas, where Maya begins to realize how inferior blacks are considered to be. After Bailey witnesses the brutal treatment of a black corpse, their grandmother takes them to live in California. For a time Maya lives with her father in the south, then she joins her mother and Bailey in San Francisco. One summer during their teen years, she vacations with her father in the south, and has a fight with her father's girlfriend. She runs away and lives briefly in an abandoned junkyard with homeless children, then returns to San Francisco. She gets a job as the first black conductor on the city streetcars. During her first voluntary sexual experience she becomes pregnant, and gives birth to a son. Maya, always tall and feeling awkward, gains a sense of who she is and learns to make her way with the world instead of opposing it or shrinking from it.

Ideas and Concepts to Highlight

1. Discuss the importance of role models, and how they can affect a child's life and future.

2. Discuss the considerable interplay of poetry and prose in the book, recognizing Angelou's renowned poetic talent.

3. Recount the protagonist's ugly and beautiful growing-up experiences. Discuss how a person's adult character is formed by them.

4. Review autobiography as a narrative form, including such contexts as race relations, emotional development, and the difficulty of self-examination and exhuming painful memories.

Writing Connection: "Writing from the Heart"

Maya Angelou is an accomplished writer of poetry as well as prose. Her work examines many of the difficult issues of our time.

For this assignment, instruct your students to write a piece on a topic of their choice. Encourage them in the use of figurative language, such as similes and metaphors, and symbolism. Completing Worksheet 26-1 will help students with their ideas.

26-1. WRITING FROM THE HEART

Directions: Think of a topic that has great meaning to you. It might be a person, a place, an event, or an idea. Write about your feelings regarding this topic. Answer the questions below to organize your thoughts.

1. What is your topic?_____

_____

_____

2. Why is this topic meaningful to you?_____

_____

_____

_____

_____

3. Write two similes that might appear in your piece._____

_____

_____

_____

4. Write two metaphors about your topic that might appear in your piece. _____

_____

_____

_____

5. How might you represent your topic symbolically?_____

_____

_____

_____

_____

26-2. QUESTIONS TO CONSIDER FOR
I KNOW WHY THE CAGED BIRD SINGS

1. Compare the roles for black women in Maya's three societies: Stamps, St. Louis, and San Francisco. How was Maya affected by each?

2. What is a rite of passage? What are Maya's rites of passage, and how does each affect her?

3. At Maya's graduation, a white man "exposes" the black race, theorizing that black children's only role models were athletes. Was that true, or only Maya's interpretation? How are role models important for young people? Explain. Name at least one role model of yours. Why is this person a role model?

4. Choose three adults in Maya's life who you feel influenced her the most. Describe how each affected her.

5. Reread the anecdote at the end of Chapter 27. Write about another such anecdote if you have heard one. If not, create one. How do they make you feel?

6. In Chapter 28, Maya is delighted that Miss Kirwin treats teenagers with respect, stating parenthetically, "Adults usually believe that a show of honor diminishes their authority." Do you agree or disagree with this statement? Explain.

7. What do you think the book's title means? Why do you think Angelou chose it? Write three alternate titles.

8. Why do you think Angelou wrote this book? What was her purpose? Explain.

9. What, if any, effect did this book have on you? Explain.

26-3. PROJECTS AND ACTIVITIES TO CONSIDER FOR
I KNOW WHY THE CAGED BIRD SINGS

1. Maya Angelou, an accomplished poet, was featured during the inauguration festivities of President Bill Clinton. Find out what some of the President's favorite poems were. Why do you think he enjoyed them? How do you relate to them?

2. A "found poem" is a short, vividly described piece contained within prose that resembles a poem after only minor adjustments in punctuation and structure. "Find" a poem in the author's prose, and present it in verse form.

3. Read *Roll of Thunder, Hear My Cry* by Mildred Taylor and compare its protagonist, Cassie Logan, with Maya Johnson. Select a major conflict in each novel and reverse the two girls' places. How would each react in the other's situation? How are they alike and different? Who has the stronger voice, and why do you think so?

Curriculum Connections:

1. Using drafting tools and the author's descriptions, create an architect's design of the Store. (A)

2. Research the law in your state about rape. What is the punishment for a man raping a child like Mr. Freeman raped Maya? Why was his punishment so light? Would the sentence have been different if Maya were white? After compiling your research, debate this issue with the members of your group. (SS)

3. Research the emotional trauma victims usually suffer after rape. (Trauma can be especially serious in children.) Was Maya's withdrawal normal? Was her family justified in sending her back to Stamps? Do you think that situation turned out to be best? Support your answer from your research and the story itself. (SS)

4. Maya is struck by the racial diversity of San Francisco. Conduct some research to find out the city's racial and cultural makeup today. Then research the makeup of a large city near your home. How does your city compare with San Francisco? Include factors such as population, racial and ethnic diversity, and economies. Create a chart that compares the information. (SS or A)

© 1994 by The Center for Applied Research in Education

27. *After the First Death* by Robert Cormier
(Dell Publishing, 1979)

Synopsis

Miro and Artkin are terrorists from an unnamed foreign country. They hijack a bus full of children and its woman driver, drug them and demand that their demands be met. They kill two of the children during the standoff. One of the demands is the dismantling of a secret government agency. The head of that agency, General Mark Marchand, is also required by the terrorists to send his only son, Ben, as a goodwill token to the bus. The son is tortured and shot but released in the ensuing firestorm. Miro, who is only a teenager, escapes with the woman and kills her. A year later, Marchand visits his son at school. They talk briefly, and the boy has never quite recovered from the shock and feelings of betrayal. While Marchand visits teachers, Ben kills himself. The book begins with the school visit and is recounted. Although much of the story is told from Miro's point of view, the point of view is shared by Ben, Marchand, and the bus driver in alternating chapters.

Ideas and Concepts to Highlight

1. The novel is told from varying points of view. Discuss point of view as a literary technique, and explain how a single story can change significantly when point of view is altered.

2. Discuss terrorism as a continuous threat. Encourage students to relate their feelings about it, and how they believe authorities should confront the problem of terrorist acts.

3. Discuss the father-son relationship, and how it can be affected by the father's career.

Writing Connection: "Terrorism"

No country is safe from terrorism. Because of the violence they are willing to do, terrorists are rewarded with prime coverage on the evening news. Even if their acts don't achieve their demands, the publicity they receive is often worth the risks they take.

Discuss terrorism with your students and talk about recent terrorist acts. Note that one of the most frightening aspects of terrorism is that perpetrators can strike anywhere and inflict great destruction. Seldom are they concerned with the lives of innocent people.

Instruct your students to reflect on their feelings about terrorism and write an essay that details their views. Completing Worksheet 27-1 will help them to organize their thoughts.

27-1. TERRORISM

Directions: Terrorism can strike anywhere in the world. But what can be done about it? Answer the questions below and write an essay expressing your opinions.

1. What is terrorism? _____

_____

_____

_____

2. Give some examples of terrorism. _____

_____

_____

_____

3. Why might an individual or group commit a terrorist act? _____

_____

_____

_____

_____

_____

4. Can terrorism ever be justified? _____ Explain. _____

_____

_____

_____

5. How can society stop terrorism? _____

_____

_____

_____

27-2. QUESTIONS TO CONSIDER FOR AFTER THE FIRST DEATH

1. What are your feelings toward Miro? The author alternately portrays him as a savage terrorist and a seeming tragic figure. Cite examples from the book where you feel anger for him as well as sympathy. Why do you think Cormier portrays Miro as he does?

2. Which, if any, of Miro's demands were realistic? In your opinion, could he have taken less violent action to achieve his goals? Explain.

3. Ben's father reads Ben's "diary." How would you feel if your parent read yours? Compare your feelings to how you think Ben would react.

4. Why do you think Marchand risked his son's safety for the sake of the children on the bus? Why did Ben agree to go? Do you consider him to have been brave or foolish? Why?

5. Interpret, in your words, the dialogue in Part 11. What is really being said?

6. There are numerous stories in *After the First Death* being told almost independently of one another. Do you think the unusual techniques served the book well? Which story touched you the most? Why?

7. In your opinion, was there anything Marchand could have done to resolve the situation with less violence? Explain.

8. How could Miro justify his actions, especially the killing of children? Imagine you are Miro, and try to explain why he did what he did.

9. Were there any "winners" in this story? Explain.

27-3. PROJECTS AND ACTIVITIES TO CONSIDER FOR *AFTER THE FIRST DEATH*

1. Cut out some newspaper articles about recent international terrorist acts. Find enough information to form a portrait of America's policy towards terrorists. Support your conclusions with specific case examples.

2. In the *New York Times Book Review,* a newspaper, or magazine, find a book review that you think is particularly well-written. Using its format as a guide, write a book review of *After the First Death.* Avoid simply retelling the story; critique the plot, point of view, and style.

3. What is an "ode"? Find some examples of this literary form, and write one for a character in the book.

4. Interview an adult and find out how that person would react in the general's situation. Be careful to spell out all the details, and do not reveal the outcome of the book to your subject. Deliver an oral report on your findings to the class, without identifying the adult.

5. Many parents today monitor their children's growth and learning closely, similar to Ben's father. Even if their intentions are good, do you think it is wise? Write an essay contrasting the encouraging of children and "pushing" them.

6. Imagine you were a TV journalist at the scene of the hijacking and following drama. Write a script in which you interview Marchand, Miro, or Ben. With a classmate assuming the other role, act out your script for the class. Consider videotaping the scene.

Curriculum Connections:

1. Write down all the instances Miro mentions his "homeland." Using an almanac, encyclopedia or similar source, find a country that could be his homeland. Write a short report on the state of that country's relationship with the United States. (SS)

2. Draw a picture of Miro in his mask, using the description provided in the story. (A)

3. Research newspaper or recent magazines and make a list of various countries that support terrorism. Try to find out why countries, or groups, resort to and support terrorism. Write a brief report and share it with your group. (SS)

© 1994 by The Center for Applied Research in Education

28. *Dicey's Song* by Cynthia Voigt
(Ballantine Books, 1982)

Synopsis

In this sequel to Voigt's *Homecoming,* Dicey Tillerman and her three younger siblings, James, Maybeth and Sammy, are taken in by their estranged grandmother, Abigail, in Maryland. The children begin school and, since they are accustomed to total freedom, suffer some serious adjustment difficulties. Dicey, ferociously protective because she is the oldest, learns slowly how to make friends and adapt to a structured world. Their mother dies and Dicey and Abigail fly to Boston to have Liza cremated. They bring her back to Maryland, and the children are able to close the emptiness that they have felt since their mother abandoned them. Each child learns to carry on despite his or her impediments—James is arrogantly smart, Maybeth has a reading disability, and Sammy is a quick-tempered, unruly child—but as Abigail takes more interest in them the children flourish. At last Dicey is able to be a teenager instead of guarding her family like an adult.

Ideas and Concepts to Highlight

1. There is a strong theme of adolescent development in the story. Discuss the varying pace at which some young people grow up, especially runaways and abandoned children versus children in nurturing homes.

2. Discuss children taking on adult responsibilities and growing up too fast.

3. Point out how Dicey and Abigail both must let go of the past. Their strong pride alternately thwarts and supports them as they struggle to carry on and permit change.

4. Note that the novel's primary appeal is its strong characterization. Each person is drawn precisely and meticulously. Discuss the most distinguishing traits of each character.

5. Compare the story line with that of *Homecoming,* which contains more action as compared to this story's exploration of characters. Discuss the strengths and weaknesses of each.

Writing Connection: "A Major Responsibility"

Discuss with your students how Dicey assumed great responsibility in protecting the younger children. It is likely that your students, too, have responsibilities, although perhaps not as profound as Dicey's. Instruct your students to write about an important responsibility, task, or obligation they have. Completing Worksheet 28-1 is a helpful prewriting activity.

NAME ______________________ DATE __________ SECTION ______

28-1. A MAJOR RESPONSIBILITY

Directions: Dicey assumed great responsibility in taking care of the younger children. Think of some responsibilities that you have. Answer the questions below and write about one of your responsibilities.

1. My responsibility is ______________________

____

____

2. To fulfill this responsibility, my duties, tasks, etc., include: ______________________

____

____

____

____

____

3. How I feel about this responsibility: ______________________

____

____

____

____

____

4. This responsibility is important because ______________________

____

____

____

____

____

28-2. QUESTIONS TO CONSIDER FOR
DICEY'S SONG

1. Gram's emotions varied widely, from cold-hearted to great worry to affection. What does such a wide display of emotions say about her? How does it affect the children?

2. Why do you think Gram is reluctant to take charity? What values does she hold that make her this way?

3. Dicey is very cautious in making new friends. Why is she like this? Could you be friends with Dicey, knowing her background? What do you like and dislike about her?

4. William Faulkner was noted for naming his characters according to some symbol attached to their personality or situations. Discuss Voigt's choice of the surname Tillerman. Why did she choose it? Relate it to and explain Dicey's attachment to boats and the sea. Create a surname for yourself that incorporates something about you.

5. Dicey did not like home economics. Why does she rebel against it so quickly? Explain your opinion in terms of her masculine and feminine traits.

6. Dicey attains a great deal of respect from others. Why is this so? Why do people respect her aloofness?

7. Discuss "reaching out," as Gram defined it. Relate how Dicey reaches out to make friends. How does it affect her? Why did Gram urge her to do it?

8. Explain Mina's attraction to Dicey. Why does she try so hard to befriend her, when Dicey constantly resists her? How would you feel about someone pursuing your friendship the way Mina does with Dicey?

9. Define feminism. Compare Dicey's brand of feminism with Mina's, and with Gram's. Contrast the gender roles that each female faces, or has faced.

28-3. PROJECTS AND ACTIVITIES TO CONSIDER FOR DICEY'S SONG

1. Create a conversation between Gram and Dicey about her emerging sexuality, including what you believe to be Gram's moral beliefs about it. Why does Dicey resist these types of conversations? Why do you think most teenagers are uncomfortable discussing sexuality with adult relatives or authority figures?

2. Imagine you are Dicey's teacher. Construct a short conference about her attitude and study habits from the teacher's point of view. Have a classmate act as Dicey and act out the dialogue, incorporating what you and the classmate think their responses would be.

3. *Dicey's Song* won the Newbery Medal, given for excellence in juvenile novels. What do you think is the book's major strength? What criteria do you use to judge whether fiction is good or great? List them, and rank *Dicey's Song* in each category.

4. Write a short scene in which Dicey receives her first kiss, first from her point of view, then from Jeff's. Try to adopt Dicey's personality as you write, working through the moment as Cynthia Voigt would.

5. Write an obituary for Dicey's mother.

6. Write a scene in which any of the four children venture into the attic without permission. What would he or she find there? What would these items, which Gram has kept for so many years, say about Gram?

7. Imagine that Dicey is one of your classmates. What would she write in your yearbook?

Curriculum Connections:

1. Draw or sketch a boat that you think Dicey would like. (A)

2. Imagine that Dicey, who likes the sea, could take an all-expense-paid cruise around the world. As her travel agent, you are planning her trip. Where would you start from? Which countries and cities would you visit? When would you return? How many miles would you sail and how long, approximately, would the trip take? (SS and M)

29. *I Never Promised You a Rose Garden*
by Joanne Greenberg, as Hannah Green
(Holt, Rinehart, and Winston, 1964)

Synopsis

Sixteen-year-old Deborah Blau retreats from a reality she finds too hurtful into an imaginary world called Yr. It is in Yr that she hears voices that pull her farther into madness. Only after attempting suicide do her parents acknowledge Deborah's "problem" and seek help for her. When Deborah enters an institution for the mentally ill, she begins her journey back to reality. Under the compassionate and tireless counseling of Dr. Fried, an eminent psychiatrist, Deborah slowly starts to see that she created her imaginary world in response to the pressures of her real world. The book details the setbacks Deborah suffers, as well as her fragile victories. Along the way the reader shares vividly in Deborah's institutionalized life, coming to know many patients, whose only bond to each other is their insanity.

Ideas and Concepts to Highlight

1. Explain that schizophrenics have their own visions of reality. This is why it is so hard for them to cope in the real world.

2. Discuss schizophrenia, its potential causes and treatments. (Since this book was written, drug therapy has come to play an increasingly important role in treatment.)

3. Note the slow recovery and many setbacks many mentally ill patients suffer.

4. Point out the intrusions into Deborah's mind by the inhabitants of Yr. This author's technique underscores Deborah's fractured reality.

Writing Connection: "Walk in My Shoes"

Everyone has his or her own reality; no two people see the world in precisely the same way. This point is powerfully made by Deborah Blau. Even though the sane may not see things in the same way, they can at least agree on the general facts of the real world. Schizophrenics are deprived of this. How can anyone truly understand something he or she does not experience?

For this writing assignment, instruct your students to select someone they know well. They are to imagine being that person for a day and write a diary of their likely experiences, including their thoughts and feelings. To gain information about the individual's daily routine, it might be helpful for students to interview the person whose "shoes" they will assume. Completing Worksheet 29-1 will help students get started.

29-1. *WALK IN MY SHOES*

Directions: No two people can see or understand the world in the same way. Everyone has his or her own reality. But understanding others is necessary for people to get along.

Choose someone you know well and imagine what one of his or her days is like. Put yourself in this person's shoes. What does this person experience? How does he or she view life? Answer the questions below and then write a diary—a day in the life of your subject.

1. Whose "shoes" did you assume?_____

Why did you choose this person? _____

_____

_____

2. List the major events of his or her day. (You might wish to interview your subject for details.)

_____

_____

_____

_____

3. What part of the day does he or she like best? _____

Why? _____

_____

_____

_____

4. What part of the day does he or she like least?_____

Why? _____

_____

_____

_____

_____

© 1994 by The Center for Applied Research in Education

29-2. QUESTIONS TO CONSIDER FOR
I NEVER PROMISED YOU A ROSE GARDEN

1. Do you think that before she went to the hospital Deborah was aware that she was suffering from schizophrenia? Explain. If she was aware, why couldn't she help herself overcome her condition?

2. Describe Deborah's first meeting with Dr. Fried. What was her attitude at the beginning of the meeting? How had it changed by the end? Did the doctor give Deborah hope that she could get well? Explain.

3. How did Deborah's parents inform the rest of the family where Deborah was? Why were they so cautious in their telling? How did the members of the family react? Why do you think it was so difficult for the family members, especially her mother and father, to adjust to the fact that Deborah needed help? Explain.

4. Describe the Pit. How did Deborah behave in the real world after she had "fallen" into the Pit?

5. Why was Yr important to Deborah? Why did she have trouble letting it go?

6. Why did Deborah burn herself?

7. In Chapter 24, what is the significance of the dream?

8. When, in your opinion, did Deborah decide to keep living? Do you think it was her decision, or the voices of Yr? Explain.

9. Reflect on the title of the novel. Of what special significance do those words have for Deborah? Explain.

10. What did Deborah finally learn about herself through counseling?

© 1994 by The Center for Applied Research in Education

29-3. PROJECTS AND ACTIVITIES TO CONSIDER FOR
I NEVER PROMISED YOU A ROSE GARDEN

1. Work with a partner and examine in what ways, if any, Deborah's parents may have contributed to her illness. Create a list and back up your ideas with examples from the story. Then share your list with others.

2. Assume that both Deborah and Carla were released from the hospital. Also assume that they remain in touch with each other, periodically informing each other of their progress. Pretend you are Deborah and write a letter to Carla, telling her how you are doing.

3. Write a final scene to the book, showing Deborah being released and going home. As you develop the scene, be sure to keep in mind the personalities of the different characters, particularly Deborah's parents and sister.

4. Write a dialogue in which Deborah breaks off with the inhabitants of Yr. With classmates assuming the voices of Yr, read the dialogue aloud to the class.

5. If Deborah was a classmate of yours before she entered the hospital, do you think you could be good friends with her? Explain.

6. Deborah's world of Yr was so real to her that she even invented a language for it. Working with a partner, invent your own language for Yr. Create an alphabet, words, and grammatical system. Write some sentences in your invented language.

Curriculum Connections:

1. Sketch or draw Lactamaeon, Anterrabae, or Idat. (A)

2. Sketch, draw, or using clay, create your impression of Yr. (A)

3. Research schizophrenia. Write a report including its causes, symptoms, and treatments. What advances in treatment have been made since this book was written? (Sci)

4. Research other types of mental illness, their causes and treatments and present an oral report to your group or class. (Sci)

© 1994 by The Center for Applied Research in Education

30. *Flowers for Algernon* by Daniel Keyes
(Harcourt, 1966)

Synopsis

Charlie Gordon works at a bakery, has friends, seems happy, and is retarded. All this changes for him when he becomes the subject of an experiment that enhances intelligence. This novel is a series of progress reports, written by Charlie, that detail his experience. Before his operation, Charlie is capable of only cleaning toilets at the bakery. To determine if his intelligence is improving, his researchers test him against a mouse, named Algernon, whose intelligence has also been enhanced and who proves to be quite skilled at negotiating mazes. It is not long before Charlie's I.Q. begins to improve, and he is given a promotion at work. Soon his co-workers come to resent and fear him and his boss fires Charlie. As his intelligence increases more, Charlie realizes that he is becoming smarter than the researchers in charge of his experiment. Although he acquires the intellectual capacity of a genius, his emotions are much like those of an adolescent. He falls in love—or so he believes—with Alice, his teacher, but he is unable to achieve a satisfying relationship with her. Because no one is sure if the intelligence enhancement is permanent, Charlie begins working on the theory underlying his experiment. When Algernon starts showing signs of deterioration, Charlie becomes worried. Not long after that, he discovers that he, too, will deteriorate mentally. The final pages of the book show his deterioration, until he returns to his earlier level of retardation. He forgets all he had learned.

Ideas and Concepts to Highlight

1. Note that this book is written in the form of progress reports made by the main character, Charlie Gordon. Discuss how the reports reflect Charlie's intellectual capacity.

2. Discuss mental disabilities in general, and retardation specifically.

3. Note Charlie's relationships and his varying happiness.

4. Explain that this book is fiction. Researchers are, as yet, unable to conduct experiments that might enhance intelligence.

Writing Connection: "Improving Human Beings"

Charlie Gordon was the subject of an experiment to improve intelligence. At the time *Flowers for Algernon* was written, such experiments were impossible. However, with recent advances in understanding the human genetic code, the possibility of an "improved" human being might not be so far off. Already doctors are able to correct faulty genes in the treatment of some diseases. Some researchers predict that science will soon have the power to alter human genes before a baby is born. Parents will be able to pick the sex of their child, the color of its hair and eyes, its height, maybe even its I.Q. But should they? While few people would argue that using gene therapy to treat disease should be stopped, a controversy already exists over whether human traits should be manipulated.

Ask your students to reflect on this issue and write about their feelings in a story or essay. Encourage them to consult references if necessary to find out more about genes and gene therapy. Completing Worksheet 30-1 will help them to organize their thoughts.

30-1. IMPROVING HUMAN BEINGS

Directions: Researchers tried to improve Charlie Gordon's intelligence. In the future, such experiments might be possible. But are they right? Should science tamper with improving human beings? Answer the questions below and write a story or essay on this topic.

1. In what ways might humans be improved? _____

_____

_____

_____

_____

_____

2. Who would decide which individuals should be improved? _____

_____

3. What would happen if an individual, marked for improvement, didn't want to be "improved"?

_____

_____

_____

_____

_____

_____

4. How would you feel if someone in authority decided you needed to be improved? _____

_____

What would you do? _____

_____

_____

_____

_____

30-2. QUESTIONS TO CONSIDER FOR
FLOWERS FOR ALGERNON

1. How do the progress reports Charlie writes tell you what kind of man he is? Give examples from the story to support your ideas.

2. Why is Charlie selected for this experiment?

3. Charlie views the other workers at the bakery as his friends. Do you think they were his friends? Explain.

4. Why do you think Charlie's co-workers become frightened of him and resent him as he becomes smarter?

5. Describe Charlie's feelings when he discovers that Gimpy deliberately under-charged a customer. Why did he feel this way? How would you feel about such a situation? Do you agree with the way Charlie confronted Gimpy? Explain.

6. Though flashbacks, Charlie recalls many events of his youth. Describe his relationships with his mother, father, and sister. Why does he feel he has to see them when he is smarter? How does his meeting with each of them turn out? Do you think he expected the meetings to turn out the way they did? Explain.

7. How does Charlie react to his realization that he has become smarter than Alice? Smarter than his doctors? He becomes critical of Nemur and Strauss. Do you think he was accurate in his assessment of these men? Explain.

8. When do you think Charlie was happier—when he was working at the bakery before the experiment, or when he was a genius? Cite examples from the story to support your ideas.

9. Would you describe Charlie Gordon as a tragic character? Why or why not?

30-3. PROJECTS AND ACTIVITIES TO CONSIDER FOR FLOWERS FOR ALGERNON

1. Working with your group, discuss what society owes the mentally handicapped like Charlie Gordon. What should society provide for these individuals? Consider things such as education, training, jobs, and housing. Compile your ideas and present them to the class.

2. Imagine that you are Professor Nemur. After Charlie has reverted to his retarded state, write a letter to a colleague telling him about your experiment. Would you consider the experiment to have been a success? Think about Nemur's personality before writing.

3. Find out what facilities, programs, and institutions are available to the mentally handicapped in your area. Present your findings to the class in an oral report.

4. Work with a partner and speculate what might happen in the future if intelligence can be improved. Make a list of how society would be affected if such an opportunity became available to people. Share your list with others.

5. At the end of the story, Charlie was preparing to go to Warren. Imagine what his routine would be like. Write a scene describing it.

6. Although the researchers in Charlie's experiment took care of him, one must wonder if what they did was ethical. After all, they experimented with Charlie without really knowing what would happen to him. Work with a group and discuss the question of ethics in medical experiments—do doctors or researchers have the right to test experimental drugs or therapies on people if the test subjects might suffer adverse effects?

Curriculum Connections:

1. Charlie suffered from mental retardation. What does the term retardation mean? What are its causes? How can retarded persons be helped? Write about your findings in a report. (Sci)

2. What is a Rorschach test? How was it developed and what is its purpose? Consult the necessary references and share your findings with your group or class. If possible, provide some examples of Rorschach pictures. (Sci)

3. What does I.Q. mean? How is this measurement of intelligence arrived at? Do the experts on intelligence testing all agree on the validity of I.Q. tests? Write a short report on this topic. (Sci)

31. *Hiroshima* by John Hersey
(Alfred A. Knopf Inc., 1946, 1985)

Synopsis

Hiroshima follows the lives of six Japanese who survived the 1945 atomic bombing of the city that is the title of the book. The initial four chapters of the nonfiction book were written in 1946, and an additional chapter was added in 1985, briefly recounting each character's previous four decades. *Miss Toshiko Sasaki,* a clerk, had just sat down in her office when the bomb struck. For many hours she lay buried beneath a pile of books. Her leg was crushed. Finally, she was dragged out and left under a lean-to for days. When at last she was treated, her leg healed improperly and, despite several operations, she walked with a limp. Her fiancee abandoned her and she eventually became a nun, administering group homes. *Dr. Masakazu Fujii,* a wealthy physician, watched his house tumble into a river; he was trapped in tree branches while wearing only his underwear. After struggling free, he escaped to a friend's house in the north. Years later he drowned himself in alcohol and luxury, dying after spending nine years in a coma brought on by a suicide attempt. *Hatsuyo Nakamura,* a widowed seamstress, was caught in her home's rubble with her children, but managed to free them and escape to a relative's home. Impoverished, she suffered many years with radiation sickness, finally finding a job that accommodated her handicaps. She retired in 1966, moving into a pleasant old age. Jesuit *Father Wilhelm Kleinsorge,* later Father Takakura, was reading in his room. Upon impact he lost consciousness and later found himself wandering aimlessly through the home's gardens. Dedicated to service, Father Kleinsorge spent the next few weeks tirelessly ministering to the bomb victims. Despite his debilitating radiation illnesses, he continued similar ministry until his death in 1977. *Dr. Terufumi Sasaki* was in a hospital. He spent the next three days, as one of the only surviving medics in the area, treating thousands of patients with barely any supplies. He became a very wealthy physician in later years, only lightly affected by the bomb, but haunted by the mass cremations of unidentified bomb victims in the days following the blast. *Rev. Kiyoshi Tanimoto,* also barely affected physically, ministered to bomb victims immediately after the explosion, and spent the following decades lobbying for peace and the treatment of the disfigured. The responses of each *hibakusha*—bomb survivor—vary greatly and their lives curiously intertwine.

Ideas and Concepts to Highlight

1. Discuss the conflicting positions of civilians and military personnel, paying particular note to the fact that innocent civilians often "die for the cause" in war.

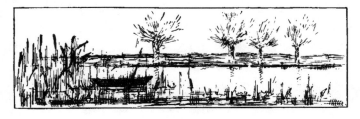

2. Discuss the author's style and how it evokes sympathy.

3. Discuss the ethics of the atomic bomb. Encourage students to express their views, and compare them to the characters in the book, who mostly avoided any moral discussion of it.

4. Compare the last chapter, which was added in 1985, to the first four. Discuss whether it adds to the book, by rounding out the lives of the characters, or detracts from it, by extending the drama to a 40-year versus a one-year reach.

Writing Connection: "The Controversy Over Nuclear Weapons"

Although at the time, during World War II, most Americans supported the dropping of the bomb, many people have since come to question the morality of using nuclear weapons. Such weapons, because of their great destructive power, can kill civilians on an unprecedented scale. Yet, the non-nuclear German bombing of Britain and the Allied bombing of many German cities also killed thousands of civilians.

For this assignment, instruct your students to reflect upon their thoughts about nuclear weapons. Are such weapons justifiable? Having students complete Worksheet 31-1 will help them to generate and organize their thoughts.

31-1. THE CONTROVERSY OVER NUCLEAR WEAPONS

Directions: The United States, along with several other countries, has a stockpile of nuclear weapons. While some people are convinced that nuclear weapons ensure the safety of the United States, others believe that all nuclear weapons—because of their great destructive force—should be dismantled. These people feel that nuclear weapons are immoral and their use can never be justified. Consider your thoughts about the controversy over nuclear weapons. Answer the questions below and write about your feelings in an essay.

1. Why were nuclear weapons designed? _____

_____

_____

2. What, if any, advantage(s) do nuclear weapons provide a country with? _____

_____

_____

3. What, if any, problem(s) do they give a country? _____

_____

_____

4. Should the United States, in its world leadership role, renounce and dismantle its nuclear

weapons?_____ Why or why not?_____

_____

_____

5. Was the United States right to drop an atom bomb on Hiroshima? _____ Why or why

not?_____

_____

_____

_____

_____

© 1994 by The Center for Applied Research in Education

31-2. QUESTIONS TO CONSIDER FOR
HIROSHIMA

1. Create a list of the major characteristics of each hibakusha. Which individuals, in your opinion, were the strongest personalities? Which were the weakest? For which did you have the most sympathy? Why?

2. How does the destruction of the bomb and its after-effects make you feel about America? Have your sentiments about patriotism changed? Explain.

3. Describe what you think Mr. Fukai was feeling as he protested Father Kleinsorge's valiant attempts to save him. Is there a psychological basis for his reaction? Explain.

4. List five "miraculous" occurrences or bizarre coincidences that spared lives or had other freak effects during the bomb blast or soon thereafter. Describe how you would explain such incredible events, either from a religious or scientific viewpoint.

5. Select one of the six survivors and recount, briefly, that person's experience. Now substitute yourself for that person. How would you have reacted differently?

6. Hersey wrote that "A surprising number of the people of Hiroshima remained more or less indifferent about the ethics of the bomb." Why is this so? How do you feel about it as an ethical issue?

7. How does "The Aftermath," which was added to *Hiroshima* in 1985, change your perceptions of the incident itself and the story? Does it enhance or detract from its drama? Explain.

8. Describe the unusually close relationship between Father Takakura and Yoshiki-san. Why was their relationship such a close one? Explain.

9. What do you think Hersey's purpose was in writing *Hiroshima?*

31-3. PROJECTS AND ACTIVITIES TO CONSIDER FOR HIROSHIMA

1. Obtain publications about Japanese culture and customs. Explain (a) why the people felt "honored" by the emperor's public announcement that the war was over, and (b) why "disposal of the dead...is a greater moral responsibility to the Japanese than adequate care of the living."

2. The first four chapters of *Hiroshima* were written in 1946. Conduct research and review what scientists and the medical community have since learned about radiation sickness. Were the author's observations accurate? What sicknesses can today's nuclear weapons cause, short of death?

3. Research the explanations given as to why the bomb was dropped on Hiroshima. Organize a debate and discuss the question: Was it necessary to drop the atomic bomb? Be sure to consider such issues as the war being prolonged, with thousands more American lives likely being lost in an assault on Japan, as well as American anger over Japan's attack on Pearl Harbor.

4. Compose an interview for one of the characters. Create 10 questions you would like to ask, and share them with the class. Have classmates take on the role of the interviewee and answer your questions as they think the hibakusha would.

5. Imagine that you were a newspaper editor during World War II. Taking into consideration the emotions and feelings of the times, write an editorial either in support of or in opposition to the use of the atomic bomb.

Curriculum Connections:

1. Using the book and other sources, construct a geographical map of Hiroshima. Show the center of the bomb's explosions, and where each of the six featured characters was situated at that moment. (SS or A)

2. What other countries were allied with Japan in World War II? Why do you think the bomb was not used on those countries? Conduct the necessary research and present your findings to your group. (SS)

3. Conduct research and make a time line, tracing the development of nuclear weapons, beginning during World War II and continuing to the present. Write a short report to accompany your diagram. (SS or A)

32. *The Miracle Worker* by William Gibson
(Atheneum, 1960)

Synopsis

This play opens with a doctor assuring Captain Keller and his wife, Kate, that their infant daughter, Helen, will recover from a serious fever. Soon after the doctor leaves, however, Kate realizes that Helen is deaf and blind. The play then moves to when Helen is about six years old. She is a wild, undisciplined child. Though they try, her parents are unable to help or control her. In desperation they hire a young woman, Annie Sullivan. From the moment Annie arrives, it is clear that she and Helen will be gripped in a great struggle. But Helen is not the only problem for Annie. Annie must also convince the Kellers, especially the Captain, that she, Annie, needs complete control of Helen if she is to reach the child. Annie is certain that language is the key to gaining access to Helen's mind, and she constantly spells the names of things on Helen's palm. Although Helen can spell them back on Annie's palm, the understanding that the words represent things eludes her. After spending two weeks together in the garden house, Helen finally obeys Annie, but when the time is up and they return to the family, Helen quickly reverts to her former behavior. The Kellers are indulgent, ready to fall back in their old pattern of behavior, but Annie doesn't let them. When Helen spills a water pitcher on Annie, Annie takes her out to refill it. She spells "water" into Helen's hand, and suddenly the miracle happens. Helen understands.

Ideas and Concepts to Highlight

1. Explain the format of a play. Most plays are built around four important parts.

    a) *Opening*—reveals the problem.

    b) *Plan*—the characters try to solve the problem and reach a goal.

    c) *Obstacles and Complications*—events and situations that block the characters from solving the problem.

    d) *Climax*—the characters solve (or fail to solve) the problem and reach (or fail to reach) their goal.

2. Note Helen's behavior before Annie's arrival. Discuss why she was allowed to act in so undisciplined a manner.

3. Emphasize the clashing of personalities throughout the play—Helen and Annie, the Captain and Annie, James and the Captain.

4. Discuss the disabilities of blindness and deafness.

Writing Connection: "The Challenge"

Helen Keller was faced with a great challenge—the struggle to manage in life despite the enormous handicaps of being deaf and blind. Everyone, however, has challenges.

For this assignment, instruct your students to consider a challenge they face and write about it. The challenge they might face is how to obtain good enough grades so that they can go on to a good college, how to excel at a sport, dance or similar activity, how to get along with a brother, sister or other family member, or how to cope with a personal disability. Having students complete Worksheet 32-1 will help them get started.

32-1. THE CHALLENGE

Directions: Helen Keller faced a great challenge in life. Think of a challenge you face. Answer the questions below and write about the challenge you must overcome.

1. What is your challenge? _____

_____

_____

_____

2. Why is overcoming this challenge important? _____

_____

_____

_____

3. How might you overcome it and be successful? _____

_____

_____

_____

_____

4. Who might help you? _____ How? _____

_____

_____

_____

5. What will you gain by overcoming your challenge? _____

_____

_____

_____

32-2. QUESTIONS TO CONSIDER FOR
THE MIRACLE WORKER

1. Before Annie's arrival, how did Helen's disabilities and behavior affect the Keller family? Be specific in discussing the Captain, Kate, and James.

2. Describe Annie Sullivan. What kind of young woman was she? Cite examples from the play to support your views.

3. Describe Captain Keller and Kate. Why do you think they had so much trouble in controlling Helen?

4. How do you think Annie's background, especially her memories of her younger brother Jimmie, influenced her behavior as an adult? Explain.

5. What are James's and Aunt Ev's roles in the story? Why do you think the author included them?

6. Why wouldn't Annie let Helen take food from her (Annie's) plate? Why was Annie's battle with Helen at the table so important?

7. Why was it necessary for Helen to be completely dependent on Annie during her learning? What was the Captain's reaction to Annie's demand of staying alone with Helen at the garden house? Why do you think he finally gave in?

8. When Helen and Annie returned from the garden house, why do you think Helen "tested" Annie and her parents at the table? What happened? In your opinion, was Annie right?

9. Why do you think "water," "wah, wah," was the first word Helen recognized?

10. The characters undergo profound changes by the end of the play. Explain how Helen, Annie, the Captain, and James changed.

32-3. PROJECTS AND ACTIVITIES TO CONSIDER FOR
THE MIRACLE WORKER

1. Research Helen Keller. Write a biographical sketch of this truly remarkable woman. Include her achievements and triumphs.

2. Write an additional scene to the play. What happens after Helen begins to understand words? Create a scene that shows how Annie continues to teach Helen. With the help of classmates, act out and dramatize your scene.

3. Toward the end of the play, Annie says to Kate, "We're born to use words..." With your group, discuss the importance of language. Brainstorm how different life would be without language. Appoint a recorder for your group to write down your ideas, and then discuss your ideas with the members of another group.

4. Research Annie Sullivan and present an oral report about her to your class. Include her background, education, and her accomplishments.

5. Before Annie came to the Keller house, Helen was wild and undisciplined. Her parents seemed unable to control her. Organize a panel to discuss this question: How important is parental discipline and guidance to children? Support your opinions with examples from the play as well as your own experiences.

6. Louis Braille created a method by which blind people can read. Research the Braille method. How does it work? Obtain a book or magazine written in Braille and see if you can read it through touch.

Curriculum Connections:

1. Research the cause of Helen Keller's blindness and deafness. Could her disabilities have been prevented using modern treatments and drugs? (Sci)

2. Annie suffered from trachoma. Research this affliction. What causes it? How can it be treated? (Sci)

3. Many researchers are concerned that listening to loud music too often might cause hearing loss or eventual deafness. Research this question and present your findings orally to your class or group. (Sci)

33. *Dragonwings* by Laurence Yep
(HarperTrophy, 1975)

Synopsis

When he is eight years old, Moon Shadow leaves China and his mother to sail for America to join his father, Windrider. Expecting to find mountains of gold, Moon Shadow is both surprised and awed by the real America. He is also fearful of the demons, the name given to Americans by the Tang, his people. Living with his father and other Tang in San Francisco's Chinatown, Moon Shadow settles into his new life. He works long hours helping his father, who he learns is a man of dreams and visions. Upon hearing that the Wright brothers built a flying machine, Windrider becomes determined to build one too. There is much work for the Tang men, however, and Windrider, even with Moon Shadow's help, can devote only his little spare time to his flying machine, which he calls Dragonwings. After fighting with Black Dog, who stole money from Moon Shadow to support his opium habit, Windrider takes Moon Shadow away from Chinatown. Moon Shadow now realizes that not all demons are evil. Their landlady, Miss Whitlaw and her niece, Robin, are kind, decent people who become friends with Windrider and Moon Shadow. Father and son continue to work on the flying machine, but their progress is interrupted by the great San Francisco earthquake. With Miss Whitlaw and Robin, Windrider and Moon Shadow help pull people from the destruction. As the city rebuilds, Windrider again begins work on Dragonwings. Finally, his flying machine is done and he flies; but the flight is short-lived and Windrider crashes, breaking his leg and some ribs. Knowing that he has flown is enough for him. Returning to Chinatown, Windrider makes plans to bring Moon Shadow's mother to America so that his family, at last, is together.

Ideas and Concepts to Highlight

MUSCH 45

1. Note that the story is written in the first person, with Moon Shadow as the narrator.

2. Discuss the Chinese customs and traditions that are shared with the reader.

3. Discuss the prejudice that the Chinese encountered.

4. Note that the late 19th and early 20th centuries were a time of great immigration. Discuss the reasons people from other countries come to America.

Writing Connection: "A New Land"

Moon Shadow's coming to the United States was an incredible journey filled with anticipation, excitement, and fear, for it meant going to live in a new land with different people and customs. Ask your students to think about what such experiences must have been like.

For this assignment, ask students to imagine that their family has decided to move to another country, where the language and customs are unfamiliar. How would your students manage in such a place? Instruct them to complete Worksheet 33-1 to organize their thoughts, and write a story about their move to a new land. Encourage them to consult reference books about their new country to find information about its customs and traditions.

NAME _____ DATE _____ SECTION _____

33-1. A NEW LAND

Directions: Imagine that you, like Moon Shadow, are to move to a new country with your family where you can't speak the language and are unfamiliar with the customs and traditions. What would this experience be like? Answer the questions below and then write a story about your new land.

1. To which country will you move? _____

2. Why will you move there? _____

    _____

    _____

    _____

3. Where will you live? _____

4. Where will you go to school? _____

5. How will you learn the language? _____

    _____

    _____

6. What customs will you need to know about?_____

    _____

    _____

    _____

7. How will you make friends? _____

    _____

8. What will you do in your spare time? _____

    _____

    _____

33-2. QUESTIONS TO CONSIDER FOR
DRAGONWINGS

1. Why did Moon Shadow's father go to America? Why didn't he take Moon Shadow and his mother?

2. Why did the Chinese refer to Americans as the "white demons"?

3. Describe Moon Shadow's vision of America. Compare the America he thought existed when he was in China with the America he found when he arrived here.

4. What is the significance of the story of the Dragon King that Windrider told Moon Shadow? Why did Moon Shadow feel as if he had found his true father?

5. Why did the Tang men wear a queue? What was the queue's original meaning? Why didn't many of the Tang men know what the queue really meant? If they did, do you think they would have continued to wear it? Explain.

6. How did Black Dog's opium addiction result in Windrider and Moon Shadow leaving the company?

7. What was Moon Shadow's impression of Miss Whitlaw? Why did he believe she had been a Tang woman in a former life?

8. Describe Moon Shadow's relationship with Miss Whitlaw and her niece Robin. What did he learn about "demons" from them?

9. Do you think that Windrider's decision to build a flying machine was a wise one? Explain.

10. Toward the end of the story, Moon Shadow says, "I had found my mountain of gold, and it had not been nuggets but people who made it up..." Explain what he means.

11. Describe Moonrider's flight with Dragonwings. What went wrong? Why didn't Windrider build another flying machine?

© 1994 by The Center for Applied Research in Education

33-3. PROJECTS AND ACTIVITIES TO CONSIDER FOR DRAGONWINGS

1. Every Tang can have several names—for example, a family and personal name, a name for when he comes of age, a nickname. Make a list of various names for yourself with reasons why you chose them.

2. Confucius was a Chinese philosopher who profoundly affected Chinese culture and tradition. Research his life and teachings, and write a report.

3. Black Dog was addicted to opium. Working with a partner, research the opium trade. What is opium? What effect does it have on the body? Why is it illegal today? Present your findings orally to your group.

4. Working with your group, review the story and list several examples of prejudice. Brainstorm and list reasons why Americans were biased against the Chinese immigrants. Then consider if Americans are less biased against immigrants today. Discuss your opinions and have your recorder present your conclusions to other groups.

5. What becomes of Moon Shadow after the story? Write a scene showing what happens to him in the future.

Curriculum Connections:

1. Consult references and research the great 1906 San Francisco Earthquake. Describe the destruction. Why is fire a danger in the aftermath of an earthquake? What causes earthquakes? Is science able to predict them? What are the chances of San Francisco experiencing a similar earthquake in the future? Write a report of your findings. (Sci)

2. Obtain some books on early aviation and study the diagrams and pictures. Draw or sketch what you believe Moonrider's Dragonwings looked like. (A)

3. The late 19th and early 20th centuries saw enormous immigration from Europe and China to the United States. Consult references and compare the immigration totals from 1890 to 1920 from the major European countries and China. Create a bar graph that represents your findings. Compare the immigration laws then to the laws now and write a brief report. (SS or A)

34. *Running Loose* by Chris Crutcher
(Dell, 1983)

Synopsis

Louie Banks is looking forward to playing football during his senior year in high school. He is a first-string receiver, and good friends with the team's star quarterback, Carter Sampson. When Louie begins dating Becky Sanders, one of the most popular girls in the school, he feels that life is great. And it is, until Coach Lednecky instructs the team to knock out an opposing player in an upcoming game. At first Louie doesn't believe it will happen, but when Boomer Cowens slams the player into the bench on the sidelines, Louie explodes. He demands of the referee to call a penalty against his own team, and confronts his coach. To Louie that kind of play isn't what football should be. For standing on his own principles, Louie is thrown off the team and ridiculed at school. Only his parents, Carter, and Becky support him. During this time, it is his growing feelings for Becky and hers for him that helps him to withstand the pressure. When Becky dies in a car accident, Louie's life is upended. Her death makes no sense to him and he questions God how such things can happen. When he comes to understand that life has its own set of random rules, Louie at last comes of age.

Ideas and Concepts to Highlight

1. Note that the story is written in the first person. Louie Banks is the narrator, and the story is written in a conversational tone as if Louie is speaking to the reader.

2. Discuss what it means to stand up for one's principles.

3. Point out Crutcher's excellent characterization and the sharp contrasts between many of the characters—for example, Carter and Boomer, Coach Lednecky and Coach Madison, Mr. Jasper and Norm.

Writing Connection: "Taking a Stand"

When Louie Banks confronted his coach about the cheap hit on Washington, he stood up for his principles even though it cost him his place on the football team and resulted in ridicule. It was a brave thing to do.

For this assignment, ask your students to think of a time they stood up for a principle. (If they didn't, ask them to think about a time that they wish they had or a situation in which they would like to.) Instruct them to complete Worksheet 34-1 and then write about taking a stand.

NAME _____ DATE _____ SECTION _____

34-1. TAKING A STAND

Directions: Louie Banks took a stand on principle that cost him his place on the football team and led to his being ridiculed by many of his classmates. Think about a time you or someone you know took a stand on principle. Answer the questions below and write about this event.

1. When did you (or another person) take a stand on principle? _____
_____
_____

2. Describe the event and why the stand was taken._____
_____
_____
_____
_____

3. Who was involved in the event?_____
_____
_____

4. What happened when you (or someone else) took a stand?_____
_____
_____
_____
_____

5. Looking back, was taking the stand the right decision? _____
Why or why not? _____
_____
_____
_____

34-2. QUESTIONS TO CONSIDER FOR
RUNNING LOOSE

1. Compare Carter and Boomer. How does Louie feel about each? Do you agree with his opinions? Explain.

2. Describe Louie's relationship with his parents. Use specific examples from the story to support your ideas.

3. Louie asks Becky why she was willing to spend time with him when she could've dated any guy in school, and she answers, "Because if I was an animal in these woods and I saw you, I'd come up to you." What did she mean? What does that tell you about Louie?

4. How does Louie feel about Coach Lednecky's orders to deliberately knock Washington out of the game? What happened during the game? How did Louie react? Do you agree or disagree with his reaction? Explain.

5. What was Becky's advice to Louie after the Washington incident? Do you agree with that advice? Explain.

6. Compare Carter's and Louie's views about Lednecky and his orders to hurt Washington. Who do you think had the more practical opinion? Why? With which one do you agree? Explain.

7. How did Becky's death affect Louie?

8. After Becky's funeral Dakota tells Louie that "...knowin' the rules" is what separates a man from a boy. What did he mean? What did Louie learn about life from Dakota's "checker" game?

9. Coach Madison helped Louie get on the track team because he believed that Louie needed activity to get his mind off Becky's death. Do you think keeping active can help someone cope with a tragedy? Explain.

10. Why did Louie smash the plaque that was put up for Becky? Was he justified in this action? Explain.

11. What did Louie learn about life during his senior year in high school? Use examples from the story to support your answer.

34-3. PROJECTS AND ACTIVITIES TO CONSIDER FOR RUNNING LOOSE

1. Imagine that Becky hadn't been killed. Write a scene to the story showing where Louie's and Becky's relationship would have gone.

2. What happens to Louie after high school? Write a scene showing what happens to him next.

3. Working with your group, brainstorm what Louie could have done to get back on the football team without compromising his principles. List possible solutions, discuss the merits of each, and share your list with the members of other groups. See if the class can come up with a solution.

4. Working with a partner, go through the book and identify the events that had a major impact on Louie. List the event and how it affected Louie. Share your list with others.

5. Imagine that you were a sports writer covering the game in which Boomer knocked Washington into the sidelines bench. Write an article about the game, especially noting Boomer's hit.

6. Write an obituary for Becky Sanders.

7. Work with a partner and identify the various conflicts in the story. Create a diagram that represents the conflicts. Share your diagram with others.

Curriculum Connections:

1. Design your own plaque for Becky Sanders. What would you write on it? (A)

2. Research the state of Idaho. Find out about its population, climate, and geography. Locate it on a map of the western United States. What states border it? Write a report and include a map. (SS)

3. Although baseball is often called America's favorite sport, football is king in the fall. Consult references and research the history of football. Trace its development and try to determine why so many boys and men play the game, and why so many fans enjoy watching it. Write a report of your findings. (SS)

35. *Flowers in the Attic* by V.C. Andrews
(Pocket Books, 1979)

Synopsis

Christopher, Cathy, and twins Cory and Carrie have been shut in the attic of a mansion while their mother, Corrine, tries to win back her wealthy father's blessing. Corrine disgraced her family with her marriage, and when her husband dies, Corrine is destitute. Her father does not know of the children, but her mother does, and she assumes the responsibility for feeding and disciplining them, and monitoring their behavior as everyone waits for the grandfather to die. Because she considers them evil spawn, the religious-fanatic grandmother punishes them through starvation, whippings and harassment. Corrine's visits to her children become less frequent as she re-enters genteel society, promising freedom but delivering only gifts and promises, shaming them with guilt as she swears she will set them free when the grandfather writes Corrine into his will and dies. The children learn ways to steal out of the room and rob the house of small amounts of money and treasures, which they hope to use for escape. After two years, Chris, planning a large and final robbery, overhears from servants that the grandfather is long dead and Corrine has remarried and moved away, but not before Chris and Cathy's burgeoning sexuality leads to intercourse. They learn that Cory's death toward the end of their imprisonment is from arsenic poisoning, covertly sprinkled on doughnuts delivered by their grandmother, and the three survivors flee bitterly from the house, Cathy plotting revenge.

Ideas and Concepts to Highlight

1. Melodrama plays a significant role in *Flowers in the Attic,* both in plot and diction. Speculate on whether the author intends it or if it is her natural writing style. Discuss it as a literary technique and its successful use in the novel.

2. Cathy, the novel's narrator, is aged 12 to 14, and the story is told as a flashback through her eyes. Discuss the use of this young narrator and encourage students to express opinions about it.

3. Discuss the need of children to grow up in environments where they interact with others and are free to go outdoors.

Writing Connection: "People's Needs"

In the story, the children were denied a normal life. Many of their needs were not met.

For this assignment, discuss with your students what the basic needs of human beings are. Obviously, things like food and water will be mentioned, but just as important are love, purpose, relationships, and the opportunity for personal growth. Ask your students to reflect on what they feel their needs are and then write an essay on the topic. Completing Worksheet 35-1 will help them to organize their thoughts.

NAME _____ **DATE** _____ **SECTION** _____

35-1. PEOPLE'S NEEDS

Directions: All people have basic needs. Consider your needs, and then think about the needs of others. It is likely that many of them will be the same. Answer the questions below and then write an essay about the needs of people.

1.

List basic needs beyond food, water, oxygen.	What may result if needs are not met?

2. Disregarding the needs for food, water, and oxygen, how would your life be affected if some of these other needs weren't met? _____

_____

_____

_____

_____

3. What can you do to ensure that your needs are met? _____

_____

_____

_____

_____

35-2. QUESTIONS TO CONSIDER FOR
FLOWERS IN THE ATTIC

1. Compare Corrine Foxworth to characters you see in soap operas or similar television shows or movies. Is she more realistic? Is her character more like someone created by Hollywood or someone you know? Explain.

2. Describe the grandmother. What kind of person was she? What allowed her to try to kill her own grandchildren?

3. At what point do you think the children stopped believing their mother? At what point did you stop believing her? Support your answer with examples you find in the story.

4. After she views the Christmas party, Cathy says she has to "make herself over...better and become like Chris—eternally cheerful." How difficult is that for Cathy? How hard is that for a person in general?

5. Discuss the moral question surrounding Chris and Cathy's experience. Do you hold them accountable for their sexual incidents? Explain.

6. Trace the relevant events that lead to Chris's sexual assault on his sister. Which do you think was most significant? What might have prevented the attack?

7. In what ways do you think the grandmother was vulnerable? Was there any way the children might have won her over? Could they have stopped her? Support your answer with examples from the book.

8. Were you satisfied with the climax and ending of the story? If yes, why? If not, how would you have changed the plot to improve it?

9. Would you recommend this book to a friend? Why or why not? If you were a parent, would you recommend it to your own child? Why or why not?

35-3. PROJECTS AND ACTIVITIES TO CONSIDER FOR
FLOWERS IN THE ATTIC

1. In 1987, *Flowers in the Attic* was released as a movie. The movie was not well received by the public. Pretend that it is being remade this year, and you are the casting director. Which actors and actresses would you hire for the film? Justify your selections.

2. How do you think the rape will affect Cathy later in life? Find statistics and sources of information about the effects of incest on which to base your predictions.

3. Conduct research and write a report on the respective ailments that you think killed Malcolm and Cory.

4. Working with your group, assume you are the children. Brainstorm ways that you might be able to gain freedom. Appoint a recorder to write down your ideas and then examine them more closely, identifying both the strengths and weaknesses of the plans. Share your lists with other groups.

5. Imagine that you were one of the children and it was possible to smuggle a note for help out of the house. What would you write? And how could you manage to get the note to someone who could in fact help you?

6. Suppose that the children's grandfather doesn't die, and they escape from the house. Write a scene of their escape.

Curriculum Connections:

1. Using the author's description and your own imagination, draw one of the paintings mentioned in Chapter Three. (A)

2. Use your imagination to create a mental picture of the bedroom and attic. Draft a floor plan for both, creating measurements and dimensions. (A or M)

3. Make a Foxworth family tree from the "Momma's Story" chapter. Research the legality of the so-called "evil marriage" between Corrine and Chris. (A or SS)

4. In the story, Cory dies because of arsenic poisoning. Consult references and find out more about arsenic. Although the element is poisonous, it also has other uses. Write a brief report of your findings. (Sci)

36. *The Adventures of Huckleberry Finn*
by Mark Twain, pseudonym for Samuel L. Clemens
(Grosset and Dunlap, 1948)

Synopsis

Huckleberry Finn, son of the town's drunk, lives with the Widow Douglas and Miss Watson, the widow's sister. He likes the widow, but doesn't enjoy her attempts to "civilize" him. When pap, Huck's father, returns to town, he wants Huck to live with him, mostly because he wants to get his hands on money that Huck is entitled to. (Huck shares $12,000 with Tom Sawyer. In Twain's *The Adventures of Tom Sawyer,* which was written earlier, Huck and Tom found the money in a robber's cave. The money was then put in trust for them.) Since Huck doesn't want to go with pap, his father catches him and takes him to a cabin where nobody can find him. Huck escapes, though, and hides out at Jackson's Island. A few days later Huck finds Jim, Miss Watson's slave. Jim tells Huck that he ran away because he was afraid that Miss Watson was going to sell him to a slave trader in New Orleans. Huck promises not to turn Jim in. They begin traveling down the river on a raft, hoping to get Jim to the free states. Along the way they have several adventures. They take up with two con-men, one of whom betrays Jim by telling a man that Jim is a runaway slave. When Huck learns that Jim has been captured, he and Tom Sawyer, who has joined him, plan an elaborate scheme to save Jim, finally freeing him. The story is episodic with many adventures, rich in the dialects of the times, and provides vivid details of life along the Mississippi before the Civil War.

Ideas and Concepts to Highlight

1. Note that the story is told in the first person, with Huck as the narrator. Emphasize that Twain used the dialects of the times and that he wrote the story as if Huck were actually speaking. (Some students may have trouble with the dialects.)

2. Discuss the setting. The story takes place in the South prior to the Civil War. The country was divided into slave and free states.

3. Explain that the novel is episodic. The plot consists of numerous events, each of which is a very short story by itself. (Critics often complain that Twain wandered with the plot and occasionally needed to rely on coincidence to make things work out. Although this may be valid in some cases, it doesn't diminish the story's appeal and many strengths.)

4. Emphasize the powerful contrasts that are found throughout the book, the most striking being the differences between Huck and Tom, and slavery and freedom.

5. Note Huck's basic goodness. Although he has faults, he is willing to go against his society to help Jim.

6. Point out Twain's use of irony, which he frequently employs to give his opinions on the behavior of people. A good example is Huck's belief in the values of his society. He has been taught that slavery is right, and feels that it is wrong for him to help Jim. Yet, he helps Jim anyway and accepts Jim as an individual.

Writing Connection: "The Continuing Adventures of Huckleberry Finn"

Huck is truly an interesting character. Uneducated, he is intelligent; a product of his times, he nevertheless is willing to break social customs (and laws) that he feels are wrong. Although he has a keen understanding of people, he doesn't always make the right decisions. One of his most unwavering traits, however, is his desire to avoid being "civilized." That's why at the end of the novel he intends to go to "Injun" territory.

For this assignment, instruct your students to imagine that Huck did indeed go to Injun territory. Keeping in mind his personality, students are to write of his continuing adventures. Have students complete Worksheet 36-1 to generate ideas.

36-1. THE CONTINUING ADVENTURES OF HUCKLEBERRY FINN

Directions: Imagine what Huck Finn's next adventure will be. Answer the questions below and write a story about what happens to Huck next.

1. Where does Huck go after Jim is freed? _____

    _____

2. Why does he go there? _____

    _____

    _____

    _____

3. How does he get there? _____

    _____

    _____

    _____

4. Who goes with him? _____

    _____

    _____

5. What happens when Huck arrives? _____

    _____

    _____

6. How does this new adventure affect or change Huck? _____

    _____

    _____

    _____

© 1994 by The Center for Applied Research in Education

36-2. QUESTIONS TO CONSIDER FOR *THE ADVENTURES OF HUCKLEBERRY FINN*

1. Describe Huck's feelings about living with the Widow Douglas and her sister, Miss Watson. Which one of the ladies does he like more? Why? What does he feel about their attempts to "civilize" him?

2. What kind of man was Huck's father? Use examples from the story to support your answer. How did Huck feel when his father returned to the village?

3. Why does pap forbid Huck to go to school? How would you react to pap's demand if you were Huck? Explain.

4. Why did Huck stage his own death?

5. When Huck finds Jim, he promises that he will not turn Jim in, even though Jim is a runaway slave. What does this tell you about Huck's character?

6. What did the river mean to Huck? Explain.

7. Huck quickly realizes that the Duke and Dauphin are con-men. What is a con-man? What does his ability to see these men for what they really are tell you about Huck? What does his decision not to confront them about their fraud tell you?

8. How was Jim betrayed? How did Huck react when he learned that Jim had been captured as a runaway slave? What did he decide to do?

9. The story contains several ironic episodes. Identify three and describe them. Explain why they are ironic.

10. Throughout the story, Huck rebels against civilization. At the end of the novel, has he become more "civilized"? Explain.

36-3. PROJECTS AND ACTIVITIES TO CONSIDER FOR *THE ADVENTURES OF HUCKLEBERRY FINN*

1. In many ways, Jim assumes the role of a father to Huck. Working with a partner, find examples of this. Share your findings with the members of your group.

2. Select a favorite scene of the book and, with classmates assuming the necessary roles, act it out, reading the dialogue. This will give you a feel for the flow of the dialects that were common during the time of the novel.

3. Research Mark Twain (Samuel L. Clemens). Write a biographical sketch and share it with the members of your group.

4. Read Twain's *The Adventures of Tom Sawyer*. Write a book review of it, comparing it to *The Adventures of Huckleberry Finn*.

Curriculum Connections:

1. Research slavery and write a report about it. In your report answer the following questions: Which were the slave states? Which were the free states? How was it determined that a new state would be free or slave? What reasons did slave states give for justifying their need for slaves? How was slavery one of the issues that led to the Civil War? (SS)

2. Research the dialects of American English and write a short report. What are the major dialects? How do dialects arise? (SS)

3. Make a model of the raft Huck and Jim used to float down the Mississippi River. (A)

4. Using an atlas or other reference, locate the Mississippi River. How long is it? What states does it border? Research the Mississippi of the 1830s (about the time the novel takes place) and compare how the river was used then to the way it is used today. Make an oral presentation of your findings to your group or class. (SS)

© 1994 by The Center for Applied Research in Education

37. <u>*Something Wicked This Way Comes*</u> *by Ray Bradbury* *(Simon and Schuster, 1962)*

Synopsis

When Cooger and Dark's carnival comes to town, Will Halloway and Jim Nightshade, two thirteen-year-old friends, are fascinated by it and they stumble on to a fantastic sight: hidden, they watch as Mr. Cooger rides the carnival's merry-go-round backward and becomes younger. When they try to warn Miss Foley, their 7th grade teacher, that the young Cooger is posing as her nephew, Cooger becomes suspicious that they know the secret of the merry-go-round. Later, he makes it seem that the boys are stealing Miss Foley's jewelry. Will and Jim run after Cooger and chase him to the merry-go-round. While Cooger is on it, moving forward in years, Jim and Will scuffle at the control, breaking it and causing Cooger to go around so many times that he becomes an old man. Mr. Dark, the illustrated man, so called because his body is covered with tattoos, now tries to capture the boys to protect the secret. Will's father tries to help the boys. Although Dark tempts Will's father with renewed youth, Mr. Halloway recognizes Dark's evil and finds a way to stop him and his carnival.

Ideas and Concepts to Highlight

1. Note that the story is told from multiple points of view. This allows Bradbury to share the thoughts and feelings of various characters with the reader.

MUSCH 49

2. Point out that the story begins with a prologue. Mention that a prologue often serves to pique the reader's interest with a promise that something dramatic will happen in the book. Direct students to the last sentence of the prologue.

3. Discuss the theme of good versus evil.

4. Emphasize the fantastic allure of the merry-go-round—the possibility of eternal youth.

Writing Connection: "Riding Cooger and Dark's Merry-Go-Round"

Ask your students to imagine that Cooger and Dark's carnival came to their town or city, and that they could ride the merry-go-round. They could become any age they wished. Instruct them to complete Worksheet 37-1, and then write a story about their adventure.

37-1. RIDING COOGER AND DARK'S MERRY-GO-ROUND

Directions: Imagine that you could take a ride on Cooger and Dark's merry-go-round. Answer the questions below and write a story about your adventure.

1. Would you ride backward or forward? _____

How many years would you go? _____ Why? _____

_____

_____

_____

2. How would you be changed?_____

_____

_____

_____

3. How might your family, friends, and home have changed?_____

_____

_____

_____

_____

4. What happens to you in your new age? _____

_____

_____

_____

5. Would you ride the merry-go-round back to your current age? _____ Why or why not?

_____

_____

_____

© 1994 by The Center for Applied Research in Education

37-2. QUESTIONS TO CONSIDER FOR
SOMETHING WICKED THIS WAY COMES

1. How does Bradbury use the lightning rod salesman to build early suspense in the story?

2. Describe Will's father. What type of man is he? Describe Will's relationship with his father. Use examples from the story to support your answer.

3. Compare and contrast Will and Jim. How are they alike? How are they different? Which one seems to be more adventurous? Which one is more cautious? Why do you think they are such good friends?

4. What special fascination did the merry-go-round hold for Jim? Did Will share this fascination? Explain.

5. Why do you think Bradbury chose a traveling carnival for the setting of evil?

6. What happened to Miss Foley?

7. What were the "autumn people"? Who did Mr. Halloway think Cooger and Dark were? Why did he consider them to be dangerous?

8. How did Dark tempt Mr. Halloway? Why was this the greatest temptation he could offer Mr. Halloway? Why did Mr. Halloway resist the temptation?

9. What did Mr. Halloway discover was the way to defeat the witch when she was trying to stop his heart? When he shot her with the wax bullet, what do you think really killed her? Explain.

10. How did Mr. Halloway finally defeat Dark? Why was evil, in the end, powerless against him?

11. What part of the book did you like the best? Why? What part did you like the least? Why?

37-3. PROJECTS AND ACTIVITIES TO CONSIDER FOR _SOMETHING WICKED THIS WAY COMES_

1. Think about a time you went to a carnival or circus. (One hopes it wasn't as frightful as the carnival of Cooger and Dark!) Write about your experience and share it with the members of your group.

2. Write a poem about the illustrated man.

3. Imagine that Mr. Halloway gave in to Dark's temptation of a ride on the merry-go-round. Write a story about how this would change Halloway's life.

4. Imagine that you were a reporter for the local newspaper in town. Write an article about the attractions one could see at Cooger and Dark's carnival.

5. Pretend that you are the barker at a side show at a carnival. Decide what type of show you'd be running. Write a sales pitch you would use to entice people to pay to see your show.

6. Watch the movie version of _Something Wicked This Way Comes_ and compare it to the novel. How is the movie different? Which, in your opinion, has the greater impact? Write a movie review and share it with the members of your group.

7. Read _The Illustrated Man_ by Ray Bradbury and write a review of the story.

Curriculum Connections:

1. Draw the illustrated man and some of the other characters of the carnival. (A)

2. Design an advertising poster for Cooger and Dark's Pandemonium Shadow Show. (A)

3. Science is rapidly unraveling the mystery of what makes people grow old. Working with a partner or small group, research aging. Find out the latest information on how scientists are trying to stop or turn back the biological clock. Present an oral report to the class. (Sci)

38. *The Pearl* by John Steinbeck
(Viking, 1947)

Synopsis

When Kino, a young Mexican fisherman, finds a pearl of great value—the "Pearl of the World"—his entire life is changed. He now has the means to pay the local doctor to treat his son for a scorpion bite (the doctor would not see the boy before this), Kino can afford the fee to marry his wife, Juana, in the church, and he will be able to provide his son with an education. All these dreams are quickly ruined, however. A man comes to steal the pearl in the night, and Kino fights him off. When Kino tries to sell his pearl to the pearl buyers, they offer him only a fraction of what the pearl is worth and he refuses to sell it. More men try to steal the pearl and Kino kills one of them. Knowing that he must leave the village, he and Juana take their son and set out, but they are followed by three men. Kino attacks them, but a stray bullet, fired by one of the men, kills his son. Kino and Juana return to the village, and Kino casts the pearl back into the sea.

Ideas and Concepts to Highlight

1. In the opening, Steinbeck describes the story as a parable. Explain that a parable is a simple story with a moral or lesson.

2. Discuss the symbolism in the story. The pearl, for example, represents material wealth and evil. Steinbeck seems to say that as one gains material riches he loses himself.

3. Discuss Mexico's rigid social structure that has come down from the Spanish colonization. The Spanish held positions of influence in government and business, while the mestizos and Indians occupied the lowest levels in the social order.

4. Note the theme of exploitation of the poor by the rich.

5. Locate La Paz, the setting of the story, on the Baja Peninsula.

Writing Connection: "Never Satisfied"

One of the themes of *The Pearl* is greed, that people are never satisfied with what they have. They always want more. In a prewriting activity, discuss this topic with your students. Then instruct them to complete Worksheet 38-1 and write about the subject. Encourage them to support their ideas with examples from the story as well as their own experiences.

38-1. NEVER SATISFIED

Directions: After Kino finds the "Pearl of the World," the greed of many people becomes clear. Even Kino refuses to get rid of the pearl when his wife begs him to. Do you feel that most people are never satisfied with what they have? Answer the questions below and write about your feelings.

1.   Give some examples (from the story or your own experiences) of people who *are* satisfied with what they have. _____

_____

_____

_____

_____

2.   Give some examples (from the story or your own experiences) of people who *are not* satisfied with what they have. _____

_____

_____

_____

_____

3.   In your opinion, are most people satisfied with what they have? _____
Explain. _____

_____

_____

_____

4.   What advice could you offer to those who are not satisfied? _____

_____

_____

_____

_____

© 1994 by The Center for Applied Research in Education

38-2. QUESTIONS TO CONSIDER FOR
THE PEARL

1. Describe Kino's life before he found the pearl. How did his life change after he found it? Give specific examples from the story.

2. Describe the townspeople's reaction to Kino finding the pearl. Why do you think the priest came? Why did the doctor come?

3. What were Kino's dreams? Given the reality of his position in the village, do you think his dreams were realistic? Explain.

4. Steinbeck writes: "From now on they (the neighbors) would watch Kino and Juana very closely to see whether riches turned their heads, as riches turn all people's heads." What does he mean by this? Do you agree or disagree? Why or why not?

5. What was Kino's opinion of the doctor? What was the doctor's opinion of villagers like Kino? How does Steinbeck use their opinions to show the rigid class structure of the village?

6. When Kino took his pearl to the pearl buyer, the man said, "This pearl is like fool's gold. . . . There is no market for such things." Was he being truthful? Why might he say this? How did Kino feel about his offer? What did he do? What would you have done if you were in Kino's place?

7. What did Steinbeck mean when he wrote that Kino "had lost one world and had not gained another"? Explain.

8. When he first found the pearl Juana was as happy as Kino was, but she soon began to view it differently than Kino. Describe their different opinions about the pearl. Who held the more accurate opinion of it? Why?

9. The pearl ends in tragedy. Given Kino's personality, is there anything he could have done to avert the sad ending? Explain.

10. What is the moral or lesson of the story? Explain, using examples from the story.

38-3. PROJECTS AND ACTIVITIES TO CONSIDER FOR
THE PEARL

1. Working with a partner, identify the major events of the story and show how they affected Kino's behavior. Create a chart and share your findings with your group.

2. *The Pearl* is often thought of as a parable. What is a parable? Relate it to another parable. How is it alike and different from the story of Kino and his pearl? Share your conclusions with your group.

3. Read *The Sea of Cortez* by Steinbeck and discuss with your group how his travels there helped him write *The Pearl*. Also discuss this question: Does an author need first-hand experience about a setting to write realistically about it?

4. What do you think happens to Kino and Juana after they return to the village? Write a final scene to the story. Especially consider how their experience with the pearl changed them.

5. Imagine you were a close friend of Kino. After learning that he had found the pearl, what advice would you have given him?

6. Working with a partner, identify several examples of symbolism in the story. List the symbol and what it represented. Compare your list with others.

Curriculum Connections:

1. Research the class structure in Mexico. Trace its development from the time of Spanish colonization. What efforts have been made to reduce the class structure? How successful have these efforts been? Write a brief report on your findings. (SS)

2. Write words to the "Song of the Family," or the "Song of Evil." (A)

3. Research how pearls are formed, and write a report. Illustrate your report. (Sci)

4. Consult an atlas or similar reference and study the climate of La Paz. What is its annual average rainfall? What is its annual average temperature? Create graphs that show its rainfall and temperature each month. Compare it to the climate of your own town or city. (Sci)

5. Based on the information of the story, create a map of Kino's village. (A)

39. *The Hitchhiker's Guide to the Galaxy* by Douglas Adams
(Harmony Books, 1979)

Synopsis

Arthur Dent is an unassuming Earthling buffoon whose house in England is about to be bulldozed for a freeway. Arthur does not know that Earth is about to be vaporized to make way for an intergalactic superhighway. His friend Ford Prefect, a hitchhiker from outer space who is researching Earth for his famous guide, rescues Arthur just before Earth is destroyed. They get away by grabbing a ride on the destroyers' spaceship. The marauding Vogons expel Arthur and Ford into space and they are picked up with a second to spare by Zaphod Beeblebrox, who is piloting the hijacked *Heart of Gold,* the premier method of space travel powered by the Infinite Improbability Drive. They arrive at Magrathea, a seemingly deserted planet that Beeblebrox is certain holds incredible wealth. The planet awakens after they arrive, and the galactic police that are pursuing Zaphod for stealing the *Heart of Gold* land on the planet. Arthur, Ford, Zaphod and his girlfriend Trillian, also an Earthling, escape and head for the Restaurant at the End of the Universe.

Ideas and Concepts to Highlight

1. Douglas Adams is a practitioner of a writing style that is kooky and playful, playing off the icons of contemporary culture. Discuss the relationship between technology and contemporary values and how technology can influence values.

2. Discuss comedic writing. Encourage students to explore humor in its many forms, and in their own writing.

3. Discuss science fiction as a genre, comparing it to other types of fiction. (Note that this book is a rare blend of comedy and science fiction.) Encourage students to share their favorite stories and authors.

4. Since many characters in the book are not Earthlings, they are described in great detail. Discuss the importance of character description, and encourage students to visualize such characters as Adams depicts them.

Writing Connection: "A Science Fiction Short Story"

Adams provides plenty of imaginative characters and situations in this book. For this writing assignment, ask your students to write their own science fiction story. Remind them that SF stories are technologically based and often have aliens. Good SF stories don't violate the physical laws of our universe, although futuristic devices allow characters far greater command over their realities than we currently have on Earth. Completing Worksheet 39-1 will help students to formulate their ideas for their stories.

39-1. A SCIENCE FICTION SHORT STORY

Directions: Science fiction is one of the most popular types of writing. Answer the questions below and write your own SF story.

1. Describe the world(s) on which your story will take place. _____

   _____

   _____

   _____

   _____

2. List your main characters. (On a separate sheet, write a detailed description of each.) ____

   _____

   _____

   _____

3. List some of the technological advances your SF world will have. _____

   _____

   _____

   _____

4. Describe the central conflict of your story. _____

   _____

   _____

   _____

   _____

© 1994 by The Center for Applied Research in Education

39-2. QUESTIONS TO CONSIDER FOR THE HITCHHIKER'S GUIDE TO THE GALAXY

1. What is Arthur's reaction when he learns that the Earth is about to be vaporized? How would you react if you suddenly found out that the Earth was to be vaporized?

2. The typical science fiction story has advanced technology. Describe some examples of advanced technology in this story.

3. Name a celebrity or someone you know who attracts attention, like Zaphod Beeblebrox, whose very livelihood is dependent on doing so. Compare their styles. What is your opinion of their behaviors? Explain.

4. Explain why you think Marvin the robot was so depressed.

5. Do you think Arthur Dent was a suitable companion for Ford? Why do you suppose Ford brought him along? Explain Arthur's role.

6. Explain the author's fixations with alcohol and digital watches.

7. What did you find most plausible in the story? Why? What did you find the least plausible? Why?

8. Who is the "main" character in the story? The protagonist? The antagonist? Why do you think so? If you could adjust the personality of any character, whom would it be?

9. Would you describe this story as a comedy? As science fiction? Why or why not? Use examples from the story to support your views.

39-3. PROJECTS AND ACTIVITIES TO CONSIDER FOR *THE HITCHHIKER'S GUIDE TO THE GALAXY*

1. Select another science fiction book, and compare the author's writing style with that of Douglas Adams in *The Hitchhiker's Guide to the Galaxy*.

2. Find 10 words that the author arbitrarily created for use in his book. Then invent five of your own, defining them. Write two paragraphs using all five, plus as many of the author's as you can.

3. Speculate for a few paragraphs how *you* think the Earth will end. Share your predictions with your group or class.

4. Write a stanza of Vogon poetry and illustrate it. (Work with your group to produce a volume of Vogon poems.)

5. Working with your group, create a new adventure for Arthur Dent. Appoint a recorder to write your story down and then share it with other groups.

6. Create a menu for The Restaurant at the End of the Universe.

7. Many people believe that the Earth is indeed doomed—not by invading Vogons, but by our own hand. What do you think is necessary to save the planet? Working with your group, discuss major pressing issues that you believe are necessary to preventing our self-destruction. As a group, write a letter to a newspaper or magazine editor expressing a collective viewpoint.

8. Obtain several editions of the comic strip "Calvin and Hobbes." Compare Bill Watterson's vivid imagination with the imagination of Douglas Adams. How are they similar? Where do you think such imaginations come from?

Curriculum Connections:

1. Design a new book jacket for *The Hitchhiker's Guide to the Galaxy*. (A)

2. Pretend you are a Magrathean designer of customized planets. Design a planet for Earthlings. Include all details, specifications, costs and time required. (A or Sci)

3. Magrathea was a legendary lost civilization. What are some similar legends on Earth? Research and report on one. (SS)

4. Research our Milky Way Galaxy. What does it consist of? How big is it? How did it form? What shape does it have? How many galaxies are there in space? Include the answers to these and similar questions in a report. (Sci)

40. *Night* by Elie Wiesel
(MacGibbon & Kee, 1960)

Synopsis

Eliezer Wiesel is a 12-year-old Hungarian Jew who yearns to become a mystic. He is learning from an older Jew until all foreign Jews are expelled from his town in 1941. When the old man returns months later, he tells stories of concentration camps and mass murders, but the townspeople remain complacent, expecting the Russian front to defeat the Nazis any day. The Germans, however, arrive in their town and within a few weeks they team with the Hungarian police and rob all the Jews of their possessions, cramming the people into ghettos. Soon they are deported, and after a horrific train ride, they arrive at Auschwitz, where Elie and his father are separated from his mother and sisters, and Elie sees the crematories for the first time. At that moment, he loses all faith in God. Elie and his father are sent to labor camps at Buna, where they survive for many months despite being surrounded by death. On numerous occasions they are nearly selected for death. As the Allied fronts advance, the German troops and their prisoners flee deeper into Germany, forcing a death march in the snow, first to Gleiwitz, then Buchenwald, where Elie's father finally dies after horrendous suffering. The prisoners at Buchenwald, aware that the American forces are near, revolt and scatter the German officers. That same day, the Americans arrive and liberate the camp. Elie survives, but sees himself in a mirror as a corpse.

Ideas and Concepts to Highlight

1. Discuss the death of Elie's religious faith, a focal point of many scholarly discussions of *Night,* and how religion is often the sole support of a person in great need.

2. Compare the Holocaust with other genocides, such as the "ethnic cleansing" in Bosnia, massacres of Native Americans, the slaughter of Kurds in Iraq or similar events in history. Discuss the long-term impact of such events.

3. Discuss the long-term effects of the Holocaust on individuals, and the varying ways in which survivors and their families deal with the experience in following years.

4. Mention the movement by Neo-Nazis in Europe and the United States, who promote the idea that the Holocaust never happened.

Writing Connection: "No More Holocausts"

Night is a chilling account of one of history's truly dark periods. Even while it was happening, many people refused to believe that it was. Afterward, people around the world vowed that it would never happen again. Unfortunately, one need only follow the news to see that hatred and brutality still exist in the world and the potential for new holocausts haunts us.

For this assignment, ask your students to reflect on the Holocaust and think how future holocausts can be prevented. Instruct students to complete Worksheet 40-1 and then write about this topic.

NAME _____ DATE _____ SECTION _____

40-1. NO MORE HOLOCAUSTS

Directions: The Holocaust was a terrible episode in history. Answer the questions below and then write an essay explaining how new holocausts can be prevented.

1. What caused the Holocaust? _____

_____

_____

_____

_____

2. What might have ended the Holocaust before so many people were killed? _____

_____

_____

_____

_____

_____

3. What can the United Nations, or other countries, do to prevent another holocaust?_____

_____

_____

_____

_____

_____

4. What, if anything, can individuals do? _____

_____

_____

_____

_____

_____

40-2. QUESTIONS TO CONSIDER FOR
NIGHT

1. Why do you think the townspeople remained complacent, despite the advance of the German army?

2. Suppose you were Elie. What would you take with you when you were exiled? Why? What would your feelings be?

3. Justify Elie's reaction when his father was struck savagely by Idek. Why did he act that way? How did you feel after reading that paragraph?

4. Why did Elie lie to Stein, his relative, about Stein's family? Do you think he was morally right in doing so? Explain.

5. Define the following: Talmud, cabbala, Gestapo, Kaddish, Aryan, and Palestine.

6. Why do you think the Jews were made to strip, and constantly pass through showers?

7. Explain the author's meaning when he says after the hanging of the youth from Warsaw that "the soup tasted excellent that evening," yet after the *pipel* was hanged, "the soup tasted of corpses." Why did he utilize this juxtaposition?

8. Contrast the crucifixion of Christ with the many deaths in concentration camps. Why do you think the author continuously employs this specific image? Are they comparable? Support your answer.

9. What is the significance of "night" in the novel? Cite examples from the story to support your answer.

10. What effect do you think his experience had on the author in his later life?

11. What enables people to survive such horrible experiences as the Holocaust? Where, in your opinion, do they find the strength to live through such ordeals?

40-3. PROJECTS AND ACTIVITIES TO CONSIDER FOR
NIGHT

1. What is the purpose of a foreword? Write a new one for *Night,* based on the perspectives of the 1990s. Has understanding of the Holocaust changed since the book was written?

2. Obtain clippings, and if possible, a videotaped documentary about the Holocaust Museum, which opened April, 1993 in Washington, D.C. Discuss in your group your reaction to this monument. Is it sufficient remembrance or do you feel that it opens new emotional wounds? Arrive at a consensus, organize a debate with another group, and try to convince them of your position.

3. Recall the march in the snow, as the Russian front advanced through Germany. Consult references about other famous forced marches. (A good example is the Cherokee Nation's "Trail of Tears.") Choose one and compare and contrast it to the march in the snow. Write an essay.

4. Locate a person who survived or is the child of a survivor of the Nazi concentration camps. Have the person speak to the class about the Holocaust, and discuss your reactions.

5. With your group, discuss the historical significance of the Holocaust and how it is often cited when the world averts its eyes to tragedy. Why does the Holocaust still evoke such strong emotions? Share your conclusions with the members of other groups.

6. Imagine that you were Elie, and you were able to write a letter and have it smuggled out of Auschwitz. What would you write to tell the world what was happening?

Curriculum Connections:

1. Working with your group, print, in large block letters, the three paragraphs that begin with "Never shall I forget that night," the most well-known excerpt from the story. Make a poster, using illustrative or creative lettering to exhibit the drama of the words. Then have a group member read the words aloud, and discuss the impact and meaning of these words. (A)

2. Research the Holocaust and try to answer the following question: In a supposedly "civilized" world, how could it have happened? (SS)

6

Novels for Grades 11-12

41. *Lord of the Flies* - Golding
42. *The Scarlet Letter* - Hawthorne
43. *All Quiet on the Western Front* - Remarque
44. *Wuthering Heights* - Brontë
45. *Brave New World* - Huxley
46. *Fahrenheit 451* - Bradbury
47. *A Raisin in the Sun* (play) - Hansberry
48. *Watership Down* - Adams
49. *A Little Love* - Hamilton
50. *Dune* - Herbert
51. *Gone with the Wind* - Mitchell
52. *Native Son* - Wright
53. *Jane Eyre* - Brontë
54. *Dinner at the Homesick Restaurant* - Tyler
55. *Slaughterhouse-Five* - Vonnegut
56. *One Flew Over the Cuckoo's Nest* - Kesey
57. *The House on Mango Street* - Cisneros
58. *Fallen Angels* - Myers
59. *Hamlet* (play) - Shakespeare
60. *Memory* - Mahy

41. *Lord of the Flies* by William Golding
(Coward-McCann, 1962)

Synopsis

During an atomic war, a group of boys are evacuated from England. When their plane is attacked, they are ejected in a passenger tube and land on a tropical island. Ralph and his companion Piggy soon find other boys, including a group led by Jack. Although Ralph is elected chief, he is unable to lead effectively, and soon he and Jack become rivals. The novel details a disintegration from order to chaos in which the boys return to a savage state. The darker side of human nature eventually dominates, resulting in two of the boys being killed by the others.

Ideas and Concepts to Highlight

1. Discuss the good and evil of human nature. Ask for students' opinions and feelings on what makes people "good." Do they believe that individuals can be both "good" and "evil"?

2. Discuss the question of innate good versus innate evil. Can anyone be truly either?

3. Emphasize the symbolism found in the novel. The conch represents authority; the fire represents hope, rescue and optimism; and the beastie represents the brutality in all human beings.

4. Note the significance of the title. The Lord of the Flies refers to Beelzebub, a prince of devils. In the novel, the Lord of the Flies is a fly-covered pig's head.

5. Discuss what happens when laws, regulations, and the conventions of society are removed.

Writing Connection: "Good Versus Evil"

A major theme of *Lord of the Flies* is good versus evil. Golding seems to be saying that without the constraints imposed on people by civilization, most people would do evil acts.

For this assignment, first lead a discussion about good and evil. Ask students to share their opinions, and then complete Worksheet 41-1, which will help them to clarify their thoughts further before writing an essay on the topic.

NAME _____ **DATE** _____ **SECTION** _____

41-1. GOOD VERSUS EVIL

Directions: One of the major themes of *Lord of the Flies* is good versus evil. Answer the questions below and then write an essay on this topic.

1. Can a person be born "good" or "evil," or does a person learn to be good or evil? _____
_____ Explain. _____

_____

_____

_____

2. Can a person be all good? Or all evil? _____
Explain. _____

_____

_____

3. Give an example of a good person you've read or heard about. _____
Why is this person good? _____

_____

_____

4. Give an example of an evil person you've read or heard about. _____
Why is this person evil? _____

_____

_____

5. Why might someone choose evil over good? _____

_____

_____

_____

_____

41-2. QUESTIONS TO CONSIDER FOR
LORD OF THE FLIES

1. Compare Ralph and Jack. Who is the better leader at the beginning of the story? Why? Who is the better leader at the end of the story? Is either one of them a good leader? Why or why not?

2. What is the conch? Why is it important?

3. How is the fire important to the boys being rescued? What might the fire, in the author's opinion, also represent?

4. In Chapter 5 during a meeting with the others, Ralph says, "Things are breaking up. I don't understand why. We began well; we were happy. And then—" What does he mean? What is happening? Why do you think this is happening?

5. The "beastie" throughout the story represents Golding's view that within all human beings is brutality. Do you agree with his assessment of people? Why or why not?

6. How does Jack change as the novel progresses? Give some examples. If the boys weren't rescued, what kind of person do you think Jack would have become in a few years?

7. The title of the story, *Lord of the Flies,* is a name for Beelzebub, a prince of devils. Why do you think Golding chose this for the title of his story?

8. At the end of Chapter 8, Simon has a conversation with the Lord of the Flies. What does the Lord of the Flies tell him? Does this foreshadow Simon's eventual death? How?

9. How did the British officer react when he first found Ralph? How did his attitude change when he began to realize what had happened on the island? Why did the boys begin to sob? Do you think he understood why the boys began to cry? Why or why not?

10. After completing the novel, has your opinion about the basic goodness or evil of people changed? Why or why not? If yes, in what ways?

41-3. PROJECTS AND ACTIVITIES TO CONSIDER FOR *LORD OF THE FLIES*

1. By the end of the novel, the boys have lost their civilization. Create a flow chart showing the events leading up to this. Why do you think this happened? Was it inevitable? What might they have done differently to stop their slide into savagery?

2. Authors often express their opinions or viewpoints about issues through their stories. Working with a group, research Golding's views in more depth. What do you think is Golding's likely opinion of the human race? Does he think that most people are inherently good? Bad? What do you think Golding would say is the reason most people act "good"? Organize a debate exploring Golding's views.

3. Imagine that you were marooned on a deserted island. What types of things would you need for survival? How would you manage to occupy your time? How would you overcome the loneliness? How would you feel if you were never rescued?

4. In the story, although Ralph was elected chief and assumed the role of "leader," he was unable to lead the boys effectively. Think of someone you feel is a good leader or role model. Write a biographical sketch of this person, focusing on the personal traits and accomplishments that make this individual a "real" leader. If necessary, consult reference books for background information.

Curriculum Connections:

1. Describe the island. Consult a resource on climates. What is the definition of a tropical island? Does the island the boys are on fit this definition? If yes, between what north and south latitude lines must it lie? Now study a world map. Which tropical islands are closest to England? Try to pinpoint the island the boys might have landed on. What island might it be? Why do you think this? (SS or Sci)

2. At the time this novel was written, nuclear war was a major worry for many people. The tensions between the United States and Soviet Union were often described as the Cold War. Research the Cold War. What was it? How did it begin? In your opinion, has it ended? Explain. Do many people worry about nuclear war today? What are some reasons for their attitudes? Present your findings in an oral report to your group. (SS)

3. When the boys hunted the pigs, they encircled the animals so that they would be easier to kill. Many animals—wolves are an example—hunt in groups or packs. Research the hunting strategies of wolves or other animals. Why do they hunt in packs? What advantage do they gain? How do they bring down their prey? How do these characteristics relate to human behavior? (Sci)

42. *The Scarlet Letter* by Nathaniel Hawthorne

Synopsis

Hester Prynne has committed adultery in Puritan Boston in the mid-seventeenth century. Brought out of prison with her infant daughter, and wearing an embroidered "A" which stands for adultery on her breast, she bears the ridicule of the townspeople. Although they demand to know the child's father, Hester refuses to tell them. Returned to prison, the baby becomes sick, and a doctor, who says his name is Roger Chillingworth, comes to treat her. Hester is frightened because Chillingworth is her husband, whom she hasn't seen in two years. He helps the baby, named Pearl, but demands to know the identity of the baby's father. When Hester refuses to tell him, he exacts a promise from her that she will not reveal his (Chillingworth's) true identity either. This is in exchange for his promise not to kill her lover if he is found out. Once Hester is released from prison, she moves to a small cottage where she raises Pearl. Meanwhile, Chillingworth comes to suspect Arthur Dimmesdale, a prominent young minister, as Pearl's father. Befriending Dimmesdale, Chillingworth begins a devious plan to psychologically "torture" the minister. Over time (the novel spans seven years) his plan works. Dimmesdale, who has never been able to admit his affair with Hester, becomes so distraught with guilt that his health begins to fail. Hester, on the other hand, has accepted her position and gains respect because of her willingness to help people. When she and Dimmesdale meet in the forest, she convinces him that their only hope is to leave Boston. He is afraid, but agrees when she promises to be his strength. Hester books passage on a ship which is to sail soon after Dimmesdale gives an important sermon. Although the sermon is one of his greatest, he is so weakened by his remorse and guilt that he struggles to the town's scaffold, where he confesses and dies.

Ideas and Concepts to Highlight

1. Note that "The Custom House. Introductory Sketch" is not essential to the novel. It has been suggested that Hawthorne added this extra material because he felt that the story was too short to be a novel. Still, the introduction provides valuable insight to Hawthorne's mind.

2. Point out the style, which is typical of writing at the time this story appeared in 1850.

3. Emphasize Hawthorne's use of symbolism—the "A," Pearl, the scaffold, and the forest are some of the more obvious.

4. Note Hawthorne's use of irony. For example, even as Dimmesdale struggles with his dark secret, his reputation as a minister grows.

5. Compare Puritan society with that of contemporary American society.

Writing Connection: "Breaking the Rules"

Hester Prynne broke an important rule of her society and paid a heavy price in ridicule and scorn. Although contemporary society is not Puritanical, there are laws and "unwritten" rules that, if broken, result in punishment.

Ask your students to create a character who breaks one of our society's laws or unwritten rules. What happens to this character? Is he or she, like Hester, eventually able to rise above the mistake? Instruct your students to complete Worksheet 42-1 and write a story about a character who breaks the rules. Note that answering the questions will provide a plot skeleton.

42-1. BREAKING THE RULES

Directions: Create a character who breaks one of society's laws or "unwritten" rules. Answer the questions below and then write a story of what happens to this character.

1. What is your character's name?_____

_____

2. Describe your character. _____

_____

_____

_____

_____

3. What rule does your character break? _____

_____

_____

4. Why does he or she break it? _____

_____

_____

_____

5. What consequences does your character experience?_____

_____

_____

6. How does your character cope with, or overcome, those consequences?_____

_____

_____

_____

© 1994 by The Center for Applied Research in Education

42-2. QUESTIONS TO CONSIDER FOR
THE SCARLET LETTER

1. Describe the scene as Hester, with Pearl, emerges from the prison. What symbol is Hester wearing? What does it mean? How does the crowd treat her? What does the crowd's reaction to Hester's "sin" tell you about Puritan society?

2. Why do you think Hester named her baby Pearl?

3. Who did Chillingworth blame for Hester having "...fallen into the pit..."—her, himself, or her lover? Explain.

4. Why does Hester go to the Governor's mansion? Why do you think she dressed Pearl in the scarlet dress? Describe what happened at the mansion. Why do you think Dimmesdale argues in favor of Hester and Pearl?

5. Once Chillingworth comes to suspect Dimmesdale as Hester's lover, what does he do to "torture" Dimmesdale? Use specific examples from the story to support your answer.

6. Over the years the townspeople's view of Hester slowly changes. Describe the change and the reasons for it.

7. Describe several ways that Dimmesdale's inner turmoil is reflected in his behavior and appearance. Why do you think he couldn't admit his guilt to the town?

8. While with Dimmesdale in the forest, Hester convinces him that they should leave Boston and live with Pearl like a family. Given their personalities and their situation, do you think this was a practical decision? Explain.

9. Explain how Dimmesdale triumphed on the scaffold when he confessed that he shared Hester's sin.

10. In your opinion, which of the characters was the most tragic and suffered the most? Use examples from the story to support your answer.

11. The story actually ends with the final scaffold scene. Why do you think Hawthorne included the "conclusion"?

42-3. *PROJECTS AND ACTIVITIES TO CONSIDER FOR THE SCARLET LETTER*

1. Working with your group, discuss Hawthorne's likely opinion of Puritan society. Identify specific examples from the story that support your views. Appoint a recorder to take notes. When the group reaches a consensus, choose one of the members to report your conclusions to the rest of the class.

2. Working with a partner, go through the story and identify several instances of irony. Write down why each is ironic and share your findings with others.

3. The four main characters—Hester, Chillingworth, Dimmesdale, and Pearl—change significantly throughout the story. Work with a partner and create a chart that shows these changes.

4. Analyze Hawthorne's writing style and technique. Include his use of metaphors, similes, and symbols. What do you think his purpose was in writing *The Scarlet Letter?*

5. Select one of the scenes of the story. With the members of your group, act it out. Use Hawthorne's dialogue to achieve realism.

6. Imagine that Hester, Dimmesdale, and Pearl had managed to get on that ship and leave Boston. Write a scene that represents their new life together.

7. Think about Chillingworth. Why did he torment Dimmesdale? Was Chillingworth evil, or was he insane? Write an essay that attempts to explain his behavior.

Curriculum Connections:

1. Consult references and research Boston of the mid-1600s. Include the city's population, commerce, religious groups, and government. How is Boston's past reflected in the city today? Write a report that shares your findings. (SS)

2. Research Puritanism. Who was the movement's founder? What were the beliefs of Puritans? What was the Puritan Ethic? Present your information orally to your group. (SS)

3. Using clay or a similar material, design the letter "A" that Hester was forced to wear. (A)

43. <u>*All Quiet on the Western Front*</u> by Erich Maria Remarque (Little, Brown and Company, 1987)

Synopsis

In this novel, which has been called the greatest war story ever written, Paul Baumer is a young man in the German army during World War I. Soon after coming to the front, Paul realizes the terror of trench warfare. Through his eyes, the reader witnesses the destruction not only of men's bodies, but of their spirits and hopes as well. Unlike the people at home, the soldiers at the front quickly lose their passion for battle, their instinct for survival overriding all else. As he survives the attack-retreat-attack-retreat fighting in the trenches, the horror of gas attacks, the chilling and insensitive treatment in the war hospitals, the lack of proper food and enough munitions, and his stabbing and killing of a French soldier who falls into the same shell-hole, Paul comes to question the reason for war. As one by one his friends are killed or maimed, he understands that his generation is a lost one—young men who have experienced such unspeakable horrors that their lives will be forever altered. Despite all this, Paul's character is strong enough to continue with his duty until near the end of the war, when he, too, is killed on a day that was "all quiet on the western front."

Ideas and Concepts to Highlight

1. Note that Paul, who is the lead character, is also the narrator of the story. The reader experiences the story through Paul's eyes.

2. Note the use of present tense. Most novels are written in the past tense—it is assumed that since the story is being told the action has already happened. Discuss how Remarque's use of the present tense makes the action seem more real to the reader, almost as if the reader is there.

3. Mention that Remarque used a variety of techniques in the story such as irony, symbolism, and impressionism. Discuss examples of each. Perhaps the greatest irony of all in the book is Paul's death on a "quiet" day at the front. A good example of symbolism is the earth, which is like a protective mother to the soldiers. Finally, Remarque's focusing on details throughout the story created for the reader an overall impression of the grim reality of the trenches and horror of the war.

4. Discuss the background of World War I. Several reasons contributed to the war: British and German rivalry in trade, the French desire for revenge because of the defeat the Germans had given them in 1870, and the Austrian and Russian competition to dominate southeastern Europe. Prior to the war, the nations of Europe had aligned themselves into two great alliances—the Triple Entente of Britain, France, and Russia, and the Triple Alliance of Germany, Austria-Hungary, and Italy. Tensions were high throughout the continent. The flashpoint was the assassination of Archduke Francis Ferdinand, the heir to the Hapsburg throne, and his wife in Sarajevo by a Serbian student in June of 1914. World War I was the first modern war, and it resulted in unprecedented destruction and death.

Writing Connection: "A Great Novel"

Some critics have called *All Quiet on the Western Front* the greatest war novel ever written. That is powerful praise. For this assignment, ask your students to share their opinions and impressions of the novel by writing a book review. Ask students to refer to *The New York Times* "Book Review" section that appears each Sunday for examples of reviews. Completing Worksheet 43-1 will help them to clarify their ideas.

43-1. A GREAT NOVEL

Directions: *All Quiet on the Western Front* has been called the greatest war novel ever written. What are your opinions and impressions of the story? Answer the questions below and then write a book review sharing your thoughts.

1. On a separate sheet of paper, describe the characterization of the story. Include Paul, Kat, and at least two other characters. Were Remarque's characters believable?

2. How did Remarque use realism in the story? (Give examples.) _____

_____

_____

_____

3. How did Remarque use techniques such as irony, symbolism, and impressionism? (Choose one and give examples.) _____

_____

_____

_____

4. What was Remarque's likely purpose in writing this story? _____

_____

Did he stray from his purpose? Explain. _____

_____

_____

_____

5. What is your opinion of the book? _____

_____

_____

_____

_____

43-2. QUESTIONS TO CONSIDER FOR ALL QUIET ON THE WESTERN FRONT

1. What is Paul's opinion of Muller scheming to get Kemmerich's boots? What does this tell you about the conditions of the German soldiers during the war?

2. What was Paul's training like under Corporal Himmelstoss? How did Paul feel about the corporal? How did that training prepare him for war in the trenches? Later, when Himmelstoss joins Paul and his company at the front, how do they treat him?

3. How does Paul describe the "consciousness of the front..."? How does that consciousness help him to survive?

4. Compare Paul's life as a student to his life in the war. How does the war change him? Cite examples from the story to support your answer.

5. Describe the horror of trench warfare that Paul experienced. According to Paul, how did a man survive that kind of fighting?

6. When Paul returns home on leave, he feels "a sense of strangeness." Why do you think he feels this way? Why does he find it difficult to talk about the war to his parents, especially his father? How are the opinions of the townspeople about the war different than Paul's?

7. Describe Paul's thoughts about the Russian prisoners he guards. He says, "A word of command has made these silent figures our enemies, a word of command might transform them into our friends." What does he mean?

8. How does his stabbing of Gerard Duval in the shell-hole affect Paul? When he gets back to his own lines, how do Kat and Albert help him overcome his feelings?

9. Toward the end of the war, did Paul feel there was any hope for himself? Did he feel there was any hope for the generation of young men who fought the war? Explain.

10. What do you think Remarque's purpose was in writing *All Quiet on the Western Front?*

© 1994 by The Center for Applied Research in Education

43-3. PROJECTS AND ACTIVITIES TO CONSIDER FOR _ALL QUIET ON THE WESTERN FRONT_

1. Poison gas was used for the first time during World War I. It was considered to be so hideous that nations refrained from using it during World War II out of fear of retaliation. Still, some countries have reportedly used it against minority populations. Research the use of poison gas in recent years. When was it used? By whom? Why? What action was taken by the rest of the world? Write a report of your findings. (Hint: Magazine articles will be a good source of information. Consult the _Reader's Guide to Periodical Literature._)

2. Remarque's writing has often been called impressionist. Impressionism is a literary style characterized by the use of powerful details and mental associations that evoke sensory impressions. Working with a partner, identify several examples of impressionism. Explain how the examples are indeed impressionistic and share your findings with others.

3. Remarque served in World War I, and was wounded five times. Discuss with your group how his experiences helped him write the story. Appoint a recorder to take notes, and then share your conclusions with the members of other groups.

4. Imagine that Paul wrote a letter to Gerard Duval's family. What would he say? Pretend you are Paul and write that letter.

5. Read Stephen Crane's _The Red Badge of Courage_ (New York: Harcourt, Brace & World, 1962). Compare it to _All Quiet on the Western Front_. Write a report that analyzes the characterization, style, action, and realism of the two books.

Curriculum Connections:

1. Research World War I. What were the causes of the war? Which countries were involved? What were the major battles, and how did they affect the course of the war? What finally led to the ending of the war? Write a report. Include maps. (SS)

2. World War I has been called the first "modern" war. Why is it referred to in that way? Write a report on the new weapons introduced during the war. (SS)

3. Create an illustration or model of the trenches that Paul described. (SS or A)

4. Paul mentions various diseases the soldiers suffered, including dysentery, typhus, and influenza. Research each of these. What were the disease's symptoms? What treatments are now available for it? (SS)

44. *Wuthering Heights* by Emily Brontë

Synopsis

Mr. Lockwood, a new tenant at Thrushcross Grange, visits his landlord, Heathcliff, at Wuthering Heights. Lockwood finds Heathcliff to be a dark, brooding man. Becoming curious about the residents of Wuthering Heights—so named because of the weather to which the house is subjected during storms—Lockwood asks his housekeeper, Nelly, about Heathcliff. Nelly, who has been a servant at the Grange and the Heights for years, takes over the narration of the story and tells Lockwood how Mr. Earnshaw, the owner of the Heights, returned home from a trip one day with an abandoned boy he named Heathcliff. Mr. Earnshaw was more pleased with Heathcliff than he was with his own son, Hindley. Upon Earnshaw's death, Hindley inherited Wuthering Heights and he treated Heathcliff harshly. He tried to keep Heathcliff away from his (Hindley's) sister, Catherine, but in spite of his efforts Heathcliff and Catherine come to share a strong and hopeless love. In time Catherine becomes friends with the children who live in Thrushcross Grange, Edgar and Isabella Linton. When Hindley's wife dies while giving birth to his son, Hareton, Hindley rapidly declines into alcoholism. His torment of Heathcliff increases until Heathcliff leaves Wuthering Heights. Three years later, Catherine marries Edgar Linton. Soon afterward, Heathcliff returns, well-dressed and wealthy. He stays at Wuthering Heights as a paying guest and soon has Hindley indebted to him. Heathcliff visits Catherine often. When Edgar orders him to stay away, Heathcliff elopes with Edgar's sister, Isabella. Catherine becomes sick over the hate between the two men, and she dies giving birth to a daughter, also named Catherine. Heathcliff is never able to forget his love for her. Because of his brutal treatment of Isabella, she runs away from him, but not before she becomes pregnant. When Hindley dies, Wuthering Heights falls into Heathcliff's hands because of Hindley's debts to him. Heathcliff's ultimate plan for revenge now takes shape: he wishes to unite the Grange and Heights. Some years later, after Isabella's death, Heathcliff manages to bring his own son, Linton, to Wuthering Heights. As Edgar approaches death, Heathcliff kidnaps Cathy and forces her into marriage with Linton. Thus, when Edgar dies, soon followed by Linton, Heathcliff, through Cathy, gains control of both properties. Mr. Lockwood then leaves the Grange. When he returns some time later, he finds that Heathcliff is dead and Cathy and Hareton have fallen in love. Nelly tells him that once his revenge was achieved, Heathcliff yearned more and more for his dead Catherine. He stopped eating and one day was found dead.

Ideas and Concepts to Highlight

1. Explain that *Wuthering Heights* has a framed structure. The story begins with Lockwood as the narrator, but then the narration switches to Nelly. At the end of the story, Lockwood again becomes the narrator. His narration frames the narration of Nelly.

2. Emphasize and discuss the complex relationships in the book.

3. Discuss Heathcliff's unrelenting anger and desire for revenge and how it touches everyone in the story.

4. Discuss the story as being both a mystery and a romance.

5. Note the powerful use of symbolism in the story. The wind in Lockwood's dream, for example, represents the power of nature and the passion of human beings.

Writing Connection: "Where You Come From"

Everyone is influenced by the way he or she was raised in his or her home. Although it is not always true that coming from a good home ensures that a person will be upstanding and honest, environment does affect behavior. In *Wuthering Heights* Heathcliff's unrelenting quest for vengeance arises from his mistreatment by Hindley, and Hareton's oafishness is a direct result of Heathcliff's refusal to allow the boy an education.

For this assignment, ask your students to consider the effect environment plays on the behavior of people. They should use personal experience as well as information they have gained through reading or the media. Instruct them to complete Worksheet 44-1 and then write an essay or story about this topic.

44-1. WHERE YOU COME FROM

Directions: The behavior of people is often influenced by their environment. Because of Hindley's mistreatment, Heathcliff set upon a course of revenge. Hareton turns out to be an oaf because Heathcliff denied the boy the opportunity of an education. Think about how the environment affects a person's behavior. Answer the questions below and then write an essay or story on this topic.

1. How has your environment influenced you? _____

_____

_____

_____

_____

_____

2. Give examples of how their environment has influenced other people you know. _____

_____

_____

_____

_____

3. Is it possible for people to overcome the influence of their environment?_____ If yes,

how? If not, why not? _____

_____

_____

_____

_____

_____

© 1994 by The Center for Applied Research in Education

44-2. QUESTIONS TO CONSIDER FOR
WUTHERING HEIGHTS

1. Why is Heathcliff's house named Wuthering Heights?

2. How does Heathcliff's past influence the man he has become? Cite examples from the story to support your answer.

3. What reason does Catherine give Nelly for marrying Edgar instead of Heathcliff? Do you agree with her? Explain.

4. After a three-year absence, Heathcliff returns to Wuthering Heights. Compare Heathcliff now to the person he was three years ago. How has he changed? How does Catherine react to his return? What is Edgar's reaction?

5. Why does Heathcliff marry Isabella? How does he justify his treatment of her to Nelly? How is Isabella's marriage much like Catherine's?

6. How does Heathcliff react to Catherine's death?

7. When he finds out that Isabella died and Edgar has brought Linton to Thrushcross Grange, Heathcliff sends Joseph to demand that Linton be brought to Wuthering Heights. Why does Heathcliff want the son he never saw?

8. Explain how Hareton's character was shaped by Heathcliff. Cite specific examples from the story to support your answer.

9. Upon Edgar's and Linton's deaths, how does Heathcliff manage to claim all of Thrushcross Grange?

10. As Lockwood returns to Wuthering Heights after having left, he notices the setting sun and rising moon. Explain what they symbolize.

11. In the story, Lockwood's narration frames the narration of Nelly. In your opinion, as each tells his or her part of the story, are they objective narrators? Explain.

12. Explain how revenge is one of the story's major themes.

44-3. PROJECTS AND ACTIVITIES TO CONSIDER FOR _WUTHERING HEIGHTS_

1. Throughout the story Brontë relied on foreshadowing to prepare the reader for coming events. Working with your group, identify several examples of foreshadowing. Create a list of your examples and decide what event each example hints at. Share your list with the members of other groups.

2. Conflict is the fuel of any story. Conflict sets the stage for action, allowing character to be revealed. Work with a partner and identify the major conflicts in the story. Create a chart, showing how the conflict affected the characters.

3. Heathcliff is an example of a dark hero. An extremely complex character, at times he seems to be a devil, yet he also inspires a certain amount of sympathy. Analyze the character of Heathcliff and discuss his traits in an essay.

4. The novel spans two generations. Working with your group, discuss how the first generation of characters influences the second. Cite specific examples from the story. Appoint a recorder to take notes and then share your conclusions with other groups.

5. Imagine that Lockwood and Cathy married. Keeping in mind their personalities, write a scene showing what their marriage would be like.

6. Watch the film version of _Wuthering Heights_ (1939), and compare it to the novel. Did the movie follow the novel closely? Why do you think some parts of the novel were left out? Which version did you like better, the movie or the novel? Why?

7. Read _The Complete Poems of Emily Brontë_ (New York: Columbia University Press, 1941, edited by C.W. Hatfield). Do any of the ideas in her poems appear in her novel? Explain.

Curriculum Connections:

1. Design a genealogical chart to delineate the various characters in the story. (A)

2. Locate northeastern England, which is the setting of the story. Describe its geography and climate. (SS)

45. *Brave New World* by Aldous Huxley
(Harper and Row, 1946)

Synopsis

As the Director of Hatcheries and Conditioning takes a group of students on a tour of a hatching and conditioning center, the reader sees how people are "produced" and "conditioned" in the World State of the future (about the year 2532). The Director explains how conditioning ensures that people will be happy in the job selected for them so that they will contribute to society. However, once in a while, the process breaks down. Bernard Marx is unhappy and dissatisfied, although he is not sure why. His friend, Helmholtz Watson, is too perfect, and likewise suffers a vague feeling of not fitting in. When Bernard, accompanied by Lenina Crowne, visits the Savage Reservation, he finds people who have not been conditioned. Bernard and Lenina meet John, whose mother, Linda, was conditioned but had a baby (no woman in the World State has babies!) and was sent to the Reservation. John is unlike anyone Bernard has ever met. Like the other Savages, he is an individual, but he also reads Shakespeare. Bernard and Lenina bring John and his mother back to London where John becomes an oddity. Known as the Savage, people wish to meet him. In the meantime, John helps Bernard and Helmholtz become aware of new ideas. Lenina falls in love with John, but the differences in their value systems keeps them apart. After John's mother dies, he realizes that the people of the World State are being controlled and he tries to warn them. They won't listen. Brought before a World Controller, it is decided that Bernard and Helmholtz are to be sent to an island while John is forced to remain. Unable to accept the World State, John hangs himself.

Ideas and Concepts to Highlight

1. Emphasize the theme of the story—while the advancement of science brings great benefits, it also brings dangers.

2. Note that the story is an example of science fiction, which Huxley used as a vehicle to express his ideas about where he felt society was heading.

3. Explain that Huxley took the title, *Brave New World,* from Shakespeare's play, *The Tempest.* One of the characters, Miranda, says, "How beauteous mankind is! O brave new world that has such people in it." Unwittingly, she says this of people who had plotted against her and her father. Miranda does not see the evil of the people she praises. Huxley felt that way about people who support the rapid advancement of science—they see only the good and not the potential problems.

4. Discuss the value system of the World State and compare it to our contemporary system of values.

Writing Connection: "The Advancement of Science"

One of Huxley's themes in *Brave New World* is that the advancement of science offers great benefits as well as dangers. For this writing assignment, ask your students to select an issue in science that supports Huxley's contention. Some possible topics include genetic engineering, machines that can extend the survival of terminally ill patients, and powerful medicines that can treat disease but may also result in potent side effects. Encourage students to consult references if necessary, and instruct them to complete Worksheet 45-1 and then write an essay about their topics.

NAME _____ **DATE** _____ **SECTION** _____

45-1. THE ADVANCEMENT OF SCIENCE

Directions: In Huxley's future World State, science has advanced to the point where people are controlled for the benefit of society. In Huxley's opinion, such advancement always has a price. Select a current issue or topic in science, answer the questions below, and then write about the benefits and dangers of your subject.

1. My topic is:_____

2. List the benefits and dangers of your topic.

Benefits	Dangers

3. How can the dangers be avoided or lessened? _____

_____

_____

_____

1. How does the World State make sure that its citizens conform to the ideas of the government? Give examples in your answer. Why is conformity so important to the World State?

2. Who is Ford? Why has he replaced God? What significance does this have for the people of the World State?

3. What is soma? Why do the people of the World State take it?

4. Why does Bernard Marx feel alone? What do he and Helmholtz Watson have in common?

5. Describe the Savage Reservation. How is it different from the rest of the World State? In your opinion, were the Savages really "uncivilized"? Explain.

6. Why is John different from the other Savages? How does he introduce Bernard and Helmholtz to new ideas?

7. Lenina and John fall in love. How does their relationship symbolize the differences between the values of the World State and the values of the Reservation?

8. It is the belief of Mustapha Mond, a World Controller, that people are unable or unwilling to act intelligently and reasonably, and that they prefer comfort and happiness to truth. Do you agree or disagree? Explain.

9. Which value system—that of the World State or the Savage Reservation—is most like yours? Why?

10. At the end of the story, John commits suicide. What do you think Huxley is saying by this act?

11. If you had a choice to live in the World State or the Reservation, which one would you choose? Why?

45-3. PROJECTS AND ACTIVITIES TO CONSIDER FOR *BRAVE NEW WORLD*

1. Work with a partner and create a chart showing the main groups of the inhabitants of the World State. Provide a description of their intelligence and the types of jobs the members of each group are likely to have.

2. Work with your group and discuss the ways that the World State has replaced God and taught a new set of values. List the ways the State makes certain that people conform and work to contribute to the betterment of society.

3. Huxley chose the names of his characters with care, using the names to imply ideas. For example, Ford refers to Henry Ford, who developed the assembly line method of production. Bernard Marx represents Karl Marx, Lenina Crowne represents Nikolai Lenin, and Benito Hoover is a combination of Benito Mussolini and Herbert Hoover. Consult references to find out who these people are, and explain why you think Huxley chose them to appear symbolically in his book.

4. Write an editorial in favor of or opposition to the World State.

5. Read *1984* by George Orwell, which also offers a view of what the future might be like. Compare it to *Brave New World,* and write an essay about your impressions.

6. Imagine that you are a "civilized" Savage in the World State. Write a dialogue in which you discuss with a World Controller why he should allow individuality in the World State. Upon completion, have a classmate take the part of the World Controller and together read the dialogue aloud to the rest of your group or class.

Curriculum Connections:

1. Design a banner showing the World State's motto of "Community, Identity, Stability." (A)

2. Research conditioning. Is it possible to condition a person to the degree that is practiced in the World State? Based upon your research, do you think it will be possible in the future? Write a short report about your findings. (Sci)

3. Choose one of the following men and write a report: Henry Ford, Nikolai Lenin, Karl Marx, Benito Mussolini or Herbert Hoover. Include the subject's accomplishments. Why do you think Huxley used him symbolically in his book? (SS)

46. *Fahrenheit 451* by Ray Bradbury
(Del Rey, 1953)

Synopsis

Guy Montag is a fireman. Not the kind we would recognize, though. In the future world of the story, buildings are fireproof and firemen burn books and the places where they are found. Montag enjoys his work until he meets Clarisse, a teenage girl who admits that she is "peculiar." Clarisse is an outcast of society because she is interested in life and rejects the meaningless existence people have come to accept. After speaking with Clarisse a few times, Montag begins to wonder about his life and question what he is doing. He admits that his life is without happiness. His relationship with his wife is empty, he sees people everywhere committing suicide and murder, and the world is at the edge of war, although he is not sure why. After the burning of a house in which an old woman dies with her books, Montag gets in touch with Faber, a man he once met, who still remembers what the world was like before books were banned. At first Faber is afraid of Montag, because he is a fireman, but when he realizes Montag's dilemma he lets him in and they talk. Montag learns how books were banned and learning was lost. Faber also tells him about people who live in the country and who still cherish books. When Montag falls under suspicion by his captain, Montag's own house is burned. He learns that his wife called in the alarm. Uncertain of his feelings, but sure that he can no longer accept his reality, Montag, rather than being taken prisoner, kills his captain and flees. Briefly he stops at Faber's house, and then makes his way to the country where he finds other "fugitives," men who are waiting for the chance to bring their knowledge of books back to society. The war starts and the city is destroyed. Perhaps out of the ruin will come their chance.

Ideas and Concepts to Highlight

1. Explain that this story is science fiction. Note that SF stories are usually set in the future with some form of high technology being important to the plot.

2. Explain and discuss censorship and its effects on society.

3. Note how history has been rewritten in the story.

Writing Connection: "Censorship"

Fahrenheit 451 is about censorship in the future. Although the United States is a free country, with freedom of the press guaranteed by the Constitution, censorship is always a threat when someone or some group wishes to suppress information. Discuss censorship with your students. Is censorship ever justified? For example, during wartime, is the government right in suppressing information that might protect its troops? What about the efforts of special interest groups to censor or ban books? Does any minority have the right to prevent people from reading a book because the "minority" objects to something in the book? Is one group's morality better, or higher, than another's? Are the ideas of censorship and freedom in opposition? Undoubtedly, these are difficult questions and you should encourage students to consult additional sources if necessary.

For this assignment, instruct your students to complete Worksheet 46-1 and then write an essay explaining their views about censorship.

46-1. CENSORSHIP

Directions: Guy Montag in his role of fireman was really practicing censorship. Despite the United States being a free country, censorship is often an issue. What are your feelings about this important issue? Answer the questions below and then write an essay about your views.

1. What is censorship? _____

_____

_____

_____

2. Is censorship limited to just books? _____ If no, what else can be censored?

_____

_____

_____

3. Give some examples of censorship. _____

_____

_____

_____

4. What might be the reasons for censorship? _____

_____

_____

_____

5. Can censorship ever be justified? _____ If yes, when? _____

_____

_____

_____

_____

© 1994 by The Center for Applied Research in Education

46-2. QUESTIONS TO CONSIDER FOR
FAHRENHEIT 451

1. Clarisse described herself as being "peculiar." Do you think Montag would agree with her? Why or why not? Would you agree? Explain, citing examples from the story.

2. Describe the relationship between Montag and his wife, Mildred. Why do you think they had so much trouble communicating?

3. Why was Montag unhappy? What do you think was missing in his life? Describe what happiness, over the course of life, means to you. Do you think that most people would agree with you? Why or why not?

4. Why, according to Beatty, was it necessary to burn books? How did society come to that point?

5. Why do you think that Bradbury selected the Bible as the book Montag took to Faber?

6. Faber said, "Those who don't build must burn. It's as old as history and juvenile delinquents." What did he mean? Do you agree with him? Explain.

7. What was Montag's and Faber's plan? When you first read about it, did you think it had a chance of being successful? Explain.

8. Faber spoke of himself as being a coward. Do you agree with his assessment of himself? Explain.

9. Why do you think Mildred turned in the alarm on Montag?

10. Describe how Montag changed throughout the story. Use examples to support your answer.

11. At the end of the story, did you feel that there is hope for Montag's world? Or did you feel that his society will merely continue as it is? Explain.

12. What do you think Bradbury's purpose was in writing this story? Explain.

46-3. PROJECTS AND ACTIVITIES TO CONSIDER FOR
FAHRENHEIT 451

1. Imagine that you are a friend of Guy Montag and that you could share a book with him. What book would you give him? Why? If you could share a poem with him, which one would it be? Why? Write a scene in which you explain to Montag your reasons for giving him these. Share your writing with the members of your group.

2. Write a scene that shows what happens after the war has ended. Has Faber or Mildred survived? Does Montag find them? What does Montag do about the books?

3. In the story, history has been rewritten. For example, firemen don't put out fires; they burn books. Working with a partner, review the story and list instances where history was rewritten. Include how history was changed, and why you believe it was changed. Share your results with your group.

4. Imagine that you were Montag. What books would be most important to you? Why?

5. Organize a debate on the issue of censorship and try to answer this question: Is censorship ever justified?

6. Work with your group and select ten books that you feel are the most important to the world. Which ones would they be? Create a chart, listing the books, and provide a reason why you chose each one.

Curriculum Connections:

1. Granger referred to the current world as a Dark Age. Consult references to learn about the Dark Ages in Europe. What were they? Why were they called the Dark Ages? How did they start and how long did they last? How did they finally end? Were they _really_ "dark"? Present your findings in an oral report to your group or class. (SS)

2. Research censorship in other countries. Who is responsible for the censorship? What is censored? Why? How does censorship affect the people's ability to understand the truth? Write a report of your findings. (SS)

3. Design an emblem for Montag's fire company. What would be written on it? (A)

© 1994 by The Center for Applied Research in Education

47. <u>*A Raisin in the Sun*</u> *by Lorraine Hansberry* *(Random House, 1966)*

Synopsis

The Youngers are an African-American family living in a small apartment on Chicago's Southside between World War II and the late 1950s. The family is headed by Lena, the mother. Her son Walter and his wife, Ruth, her daughter, Beneatha, and her grandson, Travis (the son of Walter and Ruth), make up the family. Walter is unhappy with his life because he can't get ahead, and his bitterness is straining his marriage. He tries talking his mother into giving him the insurance money ($10,000) she is to receive because of his father's death. He wants to invest it in a liquor store with two of his friends. He is convinced that this will be the opportunity he needs. His sister also wants the money to pursue her schooling; she hopes to become a doctor. When the check arrives, Lena refuses to give it to Walter, instead putting some of the money down on a house in a white section of town. Walter is furious. Seeing how much the money meant to him, Lena relents and tells him to put half of the remainder into an account for his sister's schooling and keep the rest for himself. Shortly thereafter, a Mr. Lindner, a man representing the white property owners, comes with an offer to buy the house from the Youngers. The whites don't want them moving into their neighborhood. Walter sends him away. After one of Walter's friends comes and tells him that the other friend stole the money they had invested for the liquor store—Walter admits that he used Beneatha's money as well as his own—he calls Lindner, hoping to make a deal. As upset as the rest of the family is over the money, they are more upset that Walter would sell out the family's pride. Realizing they are right, Walter sends Lindner away again and the family prepares to move to their new home.

Ideas and Concepts to Highlight

1. Note the setting of the play—somewhere between World War II and the present, which was 1959, the time when the play was first performed. Explain that the play is still relevant today.

2. Discuss employment opportunities for blacks as opposed to those for whites, and focus on good jobs as being a key to overcoming poverty.

3. Note the strong characterizations in the play.

4. Discuss the effects of prejudice in our society.

Writing Connection: "Prejudice"

The United States is composed of people of various races and ethnic origins. While much of our country's great strength grows out of the rich diversity of its people, that diversity is also a source of friction and hostility. Prejudice is a serious issue in America today.

For this writing assignment, ask your students to reflect on the differences of Americans—skin color, ethnicity, and religion, for example—and how these differences result in bias and hostility in some people. Conduct a class discussion on the topic to draw out students' feelings and opinions. Instruct students to complete Worksheet 47-1 and then write about this topic in the form of an essay or story.

NAME _____   DATE _____   SECTION _____

47-1. PREJUDICE

Directions: Consider the issue of prejudice, which is often a result of differences in skin color, ethnic origin, or religion. Answer the questions below and then write an essay or story that offers ideas of how we can overcome our differences.

1. List reasons why you feel differences in skin color, heritage, or religion make some people suspicious or hostile to others:

_____

_____

_____

_____

_____

2. Have you ever witnessed an act of bias?_____   If yes, describe it. If not, offer an example you have read or heard about or seen on TV.

_____

_____

_____

_____

3. What can government do to promote more understanding and mutual respect between people? _____

_____

_____

4. What can individuals do? _____

_____

_____

_____

_____

47-2. QUESTIONS TO CONSIDER FOR
A RAISIN IN THE SUN

1. Walter blamed much of his problem for not being able to get ahead on Ruth, claiming that she wasn't behind him and wouldn't build him up to help him. Do you think he was being fair to her in that accusation? Why or why not?

2. What is the cause of Walter's unhappiness? How does Lena feel about it? How does Ruth feel?

3. Walter believes that "money is life." Do you agree with him? Explain.

4. Why do you think Ruth considers abortion when she finds out that she is pregnant? If you were a close friend of hers, what would you advise her to do? Why?

5. Compare Beneatha's ideas of her black heritage with George's. In your opinion, who has the more practical view? Explain.

6. Why did Lena buy a house in Clybourne Park, a place where no blacks yet lived? How did the rest of the family react to this? Do you think they were over-reacting? Explain.

7. What was your reaction to Lindner's offer on behalf of the Clybourne Park Improvement Association? Do you think the Association was right in their fear of having a black family move in? Could such an offer be made today? Explain.

8. How did Walter plan to make up for the loss of the money? What did the others think of his plan? What did you think of it? In your opinion, what made him change his mind?

9. Why does the old plant mean so much to Lena?

10. At the end of the story, Lena says quietly to Ruth about Walter: "He finally come into his manhood today..." What did she mean? Do you agree with her? Explain.

© 1994 by The Center for Applied Research in Education

47-3. PROJECTS AND ACTIVITIES TO CONSIDER FOR
A RAISIN IN THE SUN

1. Write a descriptive sketch of each character. Include their desires and conflicts.

2. Work with your group and reflect on Walter's personality. Imagine he had been able to buy a liquor store. Would he have been successful as its owner? Discuss that question and come to a consensus. Have your recorder report your conclusions and reasons to the members of other groups.

3. Pick a scene that you found especially dramatic or moving. With classmates assuming the various roles, act the scene out. Perhaps you can videotape the scene.

4. Write a new act to the play, showing the Younger family moving into their house in Clybourne Park. With the help of classmates, act out this new material.

5. The book version of the play opens with a poem by Langston Hughes. Read other poems of Hughes. Which ones did you like the best? Why? Share your impressions with the members of your group.

6. View the movie version of *A Raisin in the Sun* and compare it to the play that you read. Which one, in your opinion, has greater impact? Why? Write a review that compares the two versions.

7. Organize a panel discussion on abortion. Should women have the unimpeded right to abortion? Or should abortion be limited or perhaps even banned? Panel members should research the topic to gain a solid command of the facts to balance against their opinions.

Curriculum Connections:

1. Trace the political gains made by blacks since the end of the Civil War. Create a time line that marks the most significant dates. Present your findings to the class in an oral report. (SS or A)

2. One of Walter's complaints in the play was his lack of a good job. Blacks, historically, have labored in lower paying jobs than whites in the U.S. Research the topic of blacks in the workforce and compare the occupations held by blacks to the occupations held by whites. Also compare the typical salaries. Write a report of your findings. Include graphs (bar graphs are good choices) comparing the jobs and salaries of blacks to whites. (SS or A)

48. *Watership Down* by Richard Adams
(Macmillan Publishing Company, 1972)

Synopsis

Hazel, Fiver, and Bigwig are three wild rabbits living securely in a comfortable but somewhat autocratic warren. Fiver, gifted with second sight, foresees the warren's destruction and persuades his brother Hazel, Bigwig, and several others to find a new home. After exhausting travels, they come to Watership Down and settle there. Later, two of the rabbits who stayed behind at the old warren find them and tell them that the warren was indeed destroyed by men. When the new dwellers, with Hazel as their leader, realize they have no females to breed with, they raid a nearby farm and collect three hutch rabbits, but they are unsure of their ability to breed and adapt to life in the wild. They travel many miles to Efrafa, a military-style warren run by the ruthless General Woundwort. Bigwig infiltrates their ranks and escapes with eight females, but Woundwort organizes a posse and attacks Hazel's warren. During the siege, Hazel and two other rabbits slip out to the farm and gnaw loose the rope that leashes a large dog. The dog pursues them back to the warren, and Woundwort's followers are caught above ground and destroyed. Hazel's leadership and willingness to risk his life continuously for his friends earn him the title of Chief Rabbit, and the Watership Down warren prospers.

Ideas and Concepts to Highlight

1. *Watership Down,* with its wide sweep and rich characterization, can be considered a modern epic. Discuss the novel as an epic, noting the major epic elements such as heroism, myth, oral tradition, predictions, fate versus free will, dramatic irony, and quest.

2. Discuss *Watership Down* as an allegory as well, and how it functions as an extended metaphor in which objects and characters symbolize or represent meanings beneath their visible surface. Metaphors may include such diverse areas as birth of civilization, triumph of good over evil, divine intercession, or actual historic events such as wars and politics.

3. Encourage scientific discussion about so-called "second sight."

4. Note the author's use of personification in the characterizing of the animals.

Writing Connection: "A Critic's Reaction"

Watership Down is a vast, sweeping work that people seem either to love or hate. For this assignment ask your students to assume that they are literary critics and that they have been asked to share their opinions about Adams's epic. Completing Worksheet 48-1 will help them to examine their thoughts.

NAME _____ **DATE** _____ **SECTION** _____

48-1. A CRITIC'S REACTION

Directions: Assume that you are a literary critic and that you have been asked to comment about *Watership Down.* What would you say? Answer the questions below and then write about your reaction to the novel.

1. In a sentence, tell what the novel is about: _____

    _____

    _____

    _____

2. What was Adams's purpose in writing this story?_____

    _____

    _____

    _____

3. Would you consider this story an epic?_____ Why or why not?_____

    _____

    _____

    _____

4. On another sheet, analyze the following:

    ❀ the characterization

    ❀ the author's style

    ❀ the author's use of techniques such as foreshadowing, symbolism, similes, metaphors, and personification

5. On a scale of 1 to 5 with 5 being highest, how would you rate this book?_____ Why?

    _____

    _____

    _____

48-2. QUESTIONS TO CONSIDER FOR
WATERSHIP DOWN

1. The rabbits seem to have trouble understanding concepts we humans take for granted such as numbers, floating objects, and shapes. Write down a few other such things that you believe the characters would have difficulty with, then write a dialogue in which one of the rabbits explains the concepts.

2. Recount the elements of foreshadowing in *Watership Down*. How do they enhance the story? Decide if any of the foreshadowing events could have led to some other occurrence and explain why you feel that way.

3. When do you think Hazel becomes Chief Rabbit? When does Hazel feel he is Chief Rabbit? What characteristics make him a good leader, and when does he exhibit them? Explain.

4. Most of the survivors of the Sandleford warren have a special talent or significance that they contribute to the new tribe. List each character and his contribution.

5. Explain Cowslip's hesitation in answering any question beginning with "Where?"

6. When they arrive at Watership Down, the rabbits number 12. What significance do you think the author attaches to that?

7. Note the author's technique of opening chapters with poems. Why does he do this? What is the effect? Select two or three of your favorites and explain why you like them.

8. Symbolism abounds in the book. What do you think the following represent? The Efrafan warren, Blackavar, Kehaar, the down itself, Fiver, the Black Rabbit of Inle, El-ahrairah, and the wires.

9. What sort of creature do you suppose King Darzin was? Support your answer with examples from the story.

10. In Chapter 43, Hazel-rah approaches Woundwort with reasonable terms for peace before hostilities erupt, and for a moment the general entertains the idea. Why did he turn the terms down and fight? What does his action tell you about his leadership? Explain.

© 1994 by The Center for Applied Research in Education

48-3. PROJECTS AND ACTIVITIES TO CONSIDER FOR WATERSHIP DOWN

1. Discuss precognition with your group. Consult references and try to reach a consensus on whether precognition is possible. Appoint a recorder to write down your conclusions and share them with the members of other groups.

2. Find a parable in the Bible, or a story in another religious book, that is similar to one of the legends told by the rabbits to explain their creation. Share the parable or story with the members of your group.

3. Why do you suppose Adams chose rabbits to be the focus of his epic? What other animals could be subjects for this kind of wide-sweeping story? Work with a partner and create an outline for another saga, selecting a different animal as the lead characters. Include an opening, body, rising and falling action, and conclusion. Write a few scenes of your story.

4. Find out the meaning of "Dea ex Machina," Chapter 48's title. What do you think the author's meaning was?

5. Name the events that each of the rabbits' myths explains. Then concoct another legend featuring El-ahrairah that the rabbits might utilize to explain a natural occurrence or attribute of themselves.

6. Write a poem from Fiver's point of view about any major event in the story.

7. Working with your group, identify and list what you feel are the major events of the book. Next, decide why each of the events you selected is significant to the story and how it adds to the story's epic nature. Share your results with other groups.

Curriculum Connections:

1. Draw a floor plan for the Honeycomb and the rest of the Watership Down warren. (A)

2. Consult references about rabbits and write a short report about the phenomenon of female rabbits reabsorbing young into their bodies. Find out if any other creatures can do this. What other such attributes are more or less unique to rabbits? (Sci)

49. *A Little Love* by Virginia Hamilton
(Philomel Books, 1984)

Synopsis

Sheema, a 17-year-old high school student who was raised by her Granmom and Granpop, desperately wants to find the father she has never met. She has never met her mother either, because she died while giving birth to Sheema. Aside from her grandparents, the only other person who loves Sheema is Forrest, her boyfriend. Forrest understands Sheema's hurt and wants to take care of her. That's why when she tells him that she has to find her father he is willing to help her. Although Sheema has tried in the past to get her grandparents to tell her about Cruzey, her father, who is a sign-painter, until she decides to find him they won't tell her much. Finally, Granmom explains to Sheema that Cruzey was never able to accept Sheema's mother's death during childbirth. Incapable of coping with it, he left and never returned. That he kept sending a monthly check to her grandparents to help them in raising her makes Sheema feel that he loves her. Although he has many mis-givings, Forrest agrees to take her in search of her father. Granmom is able to give them some clues where they might find Cruzey, but she doesn't have his address. Taking all the cash they have, and following one lead after another, Forrest and Sheema drive from Ohio through Kentucky and Tennessee, finally winding up in Georgia where Sheema meets her father. The meeting is not what she expects. Her father has remarried and it is clear that there is no place in his life for her. At first deeply hurt, Sheema is able to draw strength from the experience and pass from youth to adulthood.

Ideas and Concepts to Highlight

1. Discuss Sheema's powerful motivation for wanting to find her father.

2. Note the setting of the story, which takes place near Dayton, Ohio and moves through Kentucky, Tennessee, and Georgia.

3. Discuss the relationship between Sheema and her grandparents, and Sheema and Forrest. How did she draw support from each of them?

Writing Connection: "Love Is…"

Sheema was supported by the love of her grandparents and Forrest. However, she was also driven by the need for her father's love to find him, and was hurt when she did. Love, unquestionably, is a powerful force in anyone's life.

For this assignment, ask your students to reflect on love. Why do we need it? Or, do we really need it? Instruct them to complete Worksheet 49-1 and write about their opinions about love either in a story or essay.

NAME _____ **DATE** _____ **SECTION** _____

49-1. LOVE IS...

Directions: Love is one of the strongest of human emotions. It can drive us, sustain us, or make us miserable. Answer the questions below and then write a story or essay about what you think love is.

1. In your opinion, what is love? _____

_____

_____

_____

2. How can love motivate, or drive, a person to do something? _____

_____

_____

_____

3. How can love sustain, or support, a person? _____

_____

_____

_____

4. How can love hurt, or make a person miserable? _____

_____

_____

_____

5. Can a person live a full, satisfying life without love? _____ Why or why not?

_____

_____

_____

_____

49-2. QUESTIONS TO CONSIDER FOR
A LITTLE LOVE

1. Describe the joint. What type of students go there? How does Sheema feel about it?

2. Describe Sheema. How does she feel about herself?

3. Describe the relationship between Sheema and Forrest. What bound them to each other? Compare Sheema to Forrest. Who, in your opinion, was the more realistic of the two? Explain, using examples from the story.

4. Why did Sheema feel that she needed to find her father? How did Forrest feel about helping her? Why did he?

5. What did Sheema learn about her father from the album her grandmother gave her? Why do you think her grandparents didn't tell her the truth about her father and mother before? How did Sheema react to Granmom's telling her about her father?

6. After Granmom told Sheema about her father, she said: "Don't make a move, nothin ever even start to change. Movin is livin. Changin is life!" What did she mean? Do you agree with her? Explain.

7. When Sheema and Forrest left to search for her father, did you think they had a reasonable chance of finding him? Why or why not?

8. Describe the trip searching for Sheema's father. What problems did Sheema and Forrest encounter? How did they solve them?

9. Did finding her father turn out the way Sheema expected it would? Explain. How did the meeting change her?

10. What is your opinion of Cruzey?

© 1994 by The Center for Applied Research in Education

49-3. PROJECTS AND ACTIVITIES TO CONSIDER FOR
A LITTLE LOVE

1. Imagine that you are Sheema and you are planning a menu for your school cafeteria. What would your menu be? Keep in mind that it should be nutritious, varied, and tasty.

2. This story takes place before the ending of the Cold War and Sheema is concerned about "the bomb." Interview a parent, older brother or sister, or relative about the Cold War and worries about a nuclear war. Prepare a list of questions ahead of time so that your interview runs smoothly. (You might wish to do some background reading first.) After your interview, write an article based on your interview.

3. Discuss Cruzey with your group. Why did he leave Sheema? Can his action of leaving her be justified? Did his monthly checks for her welfare make up for his absence? What is your opinion of his action? Have a recorder keep notes of the discussion and then share your ideas with other groups.

4. Write a scene showing Forrest telling his father that he and Sheema plan to get married.

5. Predict what will happen to Sheema and Forrest in the future. Will they get married? Will they be happy together? In a short essay write what you think the future holds for them.

6. Plan a trip to a destination in another state or country. Where would you go? Why would you go there? What would you take with you? How far away is your destination? How would you get there? How long will the trip take? About how much money would you need for the trip? Write a short piece about your trip.

Curriculum Connections:

1. Create a sign advertising Sam's Garage, as you think Cruzey would do it. (A)

2. Using a map and referring to the story, trace the trip Sheema and Forrest made in search of her father. What cities and major towns did they pass? How many miles did they travel? Consult references and write brief descriptions of the states they drove through. (SS)

3. Work with a partner and write a song or lyric poem about Sheema's search for her father. Share it with other members of your class. (If you write a song, try setting it to music and performing it for the class.) (A)

50. *Dune* by Frank Herbert
(Chilton Book Company, 1965)

Synopsis

When Duke Leto Atreides is ordered to Arrakis, a dry, barren planet known as Dune, he knows that there will be trouble. Taking his entire House, which includes his consort Jessica, his son, Paul, and his advisors and troops, Leto assumes control with military efficiency. Jessica is a Bene Gesserit, a woman who has undergone ancient mental and physical training. Often referred to as a witch because of her special powers, Jessica has trained Paul in her wisdom, bestowing on him great powers that will one day serve him well. Leto takes various precautions in securing his position on Dune, because his rival, the Baron Harkonnen and his followers, have had control of Dune and are unwilling to give it up. Dune is the only place where melange, a spice prized for its geriatric qualities, is produced. Control of the spice trade is worth a fortune. Because of its great worth, all of the major Houses, including the Emperor, have a stake in its control, and the plot of this story is filled with intrigue, betrayal, and expedient political alliances. When Leto dies because of a Harkonnen plot that also destroys virtually all of House Atredies, Jessica and Paul escape to the desert where they are accepted into a band of Fremen, fierce desert dwellers who hate the Harkonnens. Awed by Paul, who they suspect is the Kwisatz Haderach, a male Bene Gesserit who has the ability to see the future, they become followers. Paul eventually becomes the leader of all the Fremen, whom he molds into an unstoppable force. In the final battle, Paul defeats the Harkonnens and the forces of the Emperor, clearing the way for an Atreides to gain the throne.

Ideas and Concepts to Highlight

1. Discuss the scope and breadth of this science fiction story. Herbert has created a world, Dune, populated it with a wide assortment of believable characters, and given it a history, religion, social and military order. He even includes appendices and a glossary.

2. Discuss the plot and the many conflicts, noting the many individuals vying for power and how they try to achieve it.

3. Discuss the possibility of a future for humankind as Herbert depicts it in the story. Will people ever colonize the stars? Will we meet other lifeforms?

4. Note the similarities between Dune and Earth's deserts.

Writing Connection: "Out Among the Stars"

In Frank Herbert's *Dune,* set far in the future, humankind has traveled to the stars and populated the galaxy. Discuss the possibility of interplanetary and interstellar travel in the future with your students. Ask them to speculate on what the future might be. Is it likely or unlikely that we will find other forms of life? What are the chances?

For this assignment, instruct your students to consider what the future of humankind will be. Will we go to the stars just like the explorers and colonists of the past came to the New World? Completing Worksheet 50-1 will help them to generate ideas. Suggest that students consult references if necessary.

NAME _____ **DATE** _____ **SECTION** _____

50-1. OUT AMONG THE STARS

Directions: Speculate on what humankind's far future will be. Will we reach and colonize the stars? What will life be like then? Answer the questions below and then write an essay of what you think our future will be.

1. Will people explore the planets of our solar system? _____ Why or why not? _____

_____

_____

_____

_____

2. Given the great distances to the stars, will people ever explore other star systems? _____
Why or why not? _____

_____

_____

_____

_____

3. Will humans ever encounter other forms of life? _____ Why or why not? _____

_____

_____

_____

_____

4. Describe what you think the distant future of humans will be._____

_____

_____

_____

_____

_____

50-2. QUESTIONS TO CONSIDER FOR
DUNE

1. Why did the Atreides go to Dune? What was so important about the planet? Why did Baron Harkonnen plan to destroy the Atreides?

2. How did Duke Leto react when he was informed that the Harkonnens intended to use the Lady Jessica against him?

3. Why did Dr. Yueh betray the Duke? Why wasn't he suspected of being a possible traitor?

4. After the Duke's death, what happened to Jessica and Paul? What happened to the Atreides' guards and supporters?

5. What changes occurred in Paul soon after his father's death? What do you think brought about the changes? Why do you think he was unable to grieve?

6. After he destroyed the Atreides, what was Baron Harkonnen's plan for Dune?

7. Why was the spice, melange, so valuable?

8. Why were the Fremen willing to accept Paul and Jessica? How did Paul win the respect and support of the Fremen?

9. After Paul passed the test of becoming a sandrider, many of the Fremen wanted him to challenge Stilgar for leadership. Why did Paul refuse? How did he manage to keep the loyalty of the Fremen?

10. What was the Kwisatz Haderach? How did Paul become the Kwisatz Haderach?

11. How did Paul plan to defeat the Baron and the Emperor in the final battle on Dune? Why was he so sure that he would be successful?

12. Describe the changes Paul underwent throughout the story, from being a 15-year-old boy to the leader of an entire planet with a claim to the Emperor's throne.

50-3. PROJECTS AND ACTIVITIES TO CONSIDER FOR <u>DUNE</u>

1. Who was your favorite character in the story? Write a short character sketch and then write a new scene in which your character plays a major role.

2. Read one or more of the other books in the Dune Chronicles (all written by Frank Herbert): *Dune Messiah, Children of Dune, God Emperor of Dune,* and *Chapterhouse Dune.* Write a short review of the one you like the best.

3. Watch the movie version of *Dune* (1984) and compare it to the novel. Which one do you like better? Why? Write an essay comparing the two versions of the story.

4. Imagine that you are Princess Irulan. Write a short biography of Paul-Muad'Dib.

5. Work with your group and discuss the characters of the story. Which of them, if any, was truly noble? Give reasons for your answers and share your conclusions with the members of other groups.

Curriculum Connections:

1. In the glossary of the book, Dune, Arrakis, is described as the third planet of Canopus. Consult a reference on stars and determine how far Canopus is from Earth. How many light-years? How many miles? Research the possibility of interstellar travel. What developments in spacecraft would be necessary before a trip like that could be attempted? (Sci or M)

2. Sketch a stillsuit, and label its various parts. (A)

3. Compose a lyric poem or song about Dune, as Gurney Halleck might have sung it. (A)

4. Research one of Earth's deserts and compare it to Dune. Describe the plant and animal life of the Earth desert. How do plants and animals adapt to an environment in which water is scarce? Write a brief report. (Sci)

5. Create a chart showing the House of Atreides with its supporters and allies. (A)

51. <u>*Gone with the Wind*</u> *by Margaret Mitchell* *(Macmillan Publishing Company, 1936)*

Synopsis

Scarlett O'Hara is the daughter of a wealthy planter in the South just before the Civil War. Scarlett is pretty, spoiled, and ruthless in her desires. When she can't have Ashley Wilkes for a husband because he marries Melanie Hamilton, Scarlett marries Charles Hamilton, Melly's brother. The war breaks out, and Charles dies of pneumonia. As the war continues and worsens, the South that Scarlett grew up in is destroyed. Many of the young men she knew are killed, her mother dies of typhoid, and her father loses his mind to grief. Although she manages to save Tara, her home, Scarlett comes to know hunger, fear, and bitterness. Throughout her ordeal, she continues to love Ashley, even though Rhett Butler, a dashing, arrogant gambler and blockade runner, has fallen in love with her. After the war, Scarlett struggles during Reconstruction. Unable to pay the taxes on Tara, she marries Frank Kennedy. Eventually, with the help of money borrowed from Rhett, Scarlett becomes a successful businesswomen. She still loves Ashley, but after Frank's death she gives in to Rhett's proposal of marriage. Although Rhett, who is wealthy because of his shrewd business dealings during the war, can give her everything, she doesn't recognize his love. Only later, after much tragedy that destroys their marriage, does Scarlett finally come to realize that she has truly loved Rhett all along. But it is too late.

Ideas and Concepts to Highlight

1. Discuss the pre-Civil War South and the causes of the war. Slavery, the dispute over state's rights, and economic factors all helped contribute to the war.

2. Note the effects of the war on the South, as well as the characters. Emphasize that the war resulted in the end of an entire way of life.

3. Discuss the strong characters in the story, and their conflicts.

4. Note that while the story takes place during the Civil War, its focus is on the relationships of the people and the effects of the war on them.

Writing Connection: "Scarlett and Rhett"

Margaret Mitchell created two of literature's most memorable characters in *Gone with the Wind*—Scarlett O'Hara and Rhett Butler. Both were complex individuals, finely detailed, who were in conflict with their world, their contemporaries, and each other. At times they were heroes, while at other times they were downright scoundrels. Fascinating in their own right, it is their love and hate of each other that supplies the flame of the story.

For this assignment, ask your students to analyze Scarlett and Rhett. Completing worksheet 51-1 will help them to organize their ideas.

NAME _____ **DATE** _____ **SECTION** _____

51-1. SCARLETT AND RHETT

Directions: Scarlett O'Hara and Rhett Butler are two of literature's most memorable characters. Their love and conflict is at the heart of *Gone with the Wind*. Answer the questions below and then write an analysis of these two complex people.

1. Describe Scarlett's personality. What are her strongest traits? What are her weakest? _____

   _____

   _____

   _____

   _____

   _____

   _____

2. Describe Rhett's personality. What are his strongest and weakest traits? _____

   _____

   _____

   _____

   _____

3. Which one do you believe is the stronger character? _____ Why? _____

   _____

   _____

   _____

   _____

4. Would the story have been as powerful if they had been changed in some way? Explain.

   _____

   _____

   _____

   _____

51-2. QUESTIONS TO CONSIDER FOR
GONE WITH THE WIND

1. Describe Scarlett at the beginning of the story. What is your opinion of her? Explain.

2. Why do you think that Scarlett can't accept Ashley's marrying Melanie? Why did Scarlett then marry Charles?

3. Gerald says to Scarlett: "Land is the only thing in the world that amounts to anything, for tis the only thing in this world that lasts..." What does he mean? Do you agree or disagree? Why?

4. Describe Rhett. What was Scarlett's first impression of him? What was your first impression of Rhett? Did your opinion of him change?

5. Describe how the war affected life in the South. What were some of the reasons the North eventually won?

6. Describe the relationship between Scarlett and Melanie. What was Scarlett's opinion of Melanie? What was Melanie's opinion of Scarlett? Of the two, which one did you like better? Why?

7. Why did Scarlett return to Tara? What did she find there? How had her father changed? How had Scarlett changed during the war?

8. Compare Tara before the war and after the war. What were some of the problems Scarlett faced at Tara? How did she solve them? Do you approve of her methods? Why or why not?

9. What was Rhett's opinion of Ashley? Do you agree with him? Why or why not?

10. Why do you think Rhett proposed marriage to Scarlett? Why did she accept? Given their personalities, what did you think their chances were for a successful marriage? Why? What eventually came between them?

11. At the end of the story, Scarlett is convinced that she has loved Rhett all along. Do you think she really did? Explain.

51-3. PROJECTS AND ACTIVITIES TO CONSIDER FOR GONE WITH THE WIND

1. One of the most interesting aspects of *Gone with the Wind* is the relationship between Scarlett and Rhett. There are many examples of irony in it, especially their dialogue. Working with a partner, go through the story and find several examples of irony. Share your findings with other members of your group.

2. Working with your group, discuss the characters of Scarlett and Rhett and how each was a rebel against their society. Use examples from the story to support your opinions. Appoint a recorder to write down your conclusions and share them with other groups.

3. Why do you think Margaret Mitchell chose *Gone with the Wind* for the title of her book? Write a short essay sharing your ideas.

4. There were many powerful scenes in the story. Choose your favorite and in an essay tell why you liked it.

Curriculum Connections:

1. Create a time line of the major events of the Civil War. (A or SS)

2. The Civil War was a defining point in American history. Work with your group and research the causes and results of the war. Organize a panel discussion on the war's effects on the United States. Seek to answer the question of how the war changed America. (SS)

3. Create a map of the Civil War South. Mark the states, major cities, and important battles. Be sure to include a legend. (SS or A)

4. Research the period of Reconstruction and the Carpetbaggers. Who were they? Why were they so hated by the former Confederates? Present your findings orally to your group or class. (SS)

5. Consult reference books and compare the economic differences between the North and South prior to and during the Civil War. Which side had more industrial capacity? Which had the greater population? In your opinion, how much of a factor was economic might in the winning of the war? Write a short report. (SS)

52. <u>*Native Son*</u> *by Richard Wright*
(Harper and Row, 1940)

Synopsis

Bigger Thomas is a young African-American man living in Chicago in the 1930s. Because of the white society, which Bigger feels is biased and hostile to blacks, he is filled with hatred, bitterness, and frustration. He has few values and shows his brutality by mercilessly beating his friend Gus. Offered a job as a chauffeur for the Daltons, a wealthy white family, Bigger reluctantly accepts. The Daltons proudly donate money to help blacks, but at the same time they own much of the ghetto in which blacks, including Bigger, live. The first day on his job, Bigger is supposed to drive Mary, the Daltons' daughter, to school, but instead she has Bigger pick up Jan Erlone, a Communist. Mary, a headstrong, rebellious girl, is also a Communist, and she and Jan speak to Bigger about wishing to be his friend. Jan gives him some material about Communism to read, and they insist that he join them while they eat at a black diner. Despite their apparent friendliness, Bigger remains suspicious of them. They wind up drinking and by the time Bigger drives Mary home, she is drunk. He helps her inside and to her room—a dangerous act for a black man at that time. When her mother (who is blind) comes to check on her, Bigger becomes frightened that Mary will say something. Trying to keep her quiet, he accidentally kills her. He disposes of Mary's body by burning it in the furnace, and then invents a story that diverts suspicion of Mary's disappearance to Jan. Hoping to trick the Daltons into thinking that Mary was kidnapped by Communists in an effort to raise money for their cause, Bigger sends a ransom note, but his plan abruptly ends when Mary's bones are discovered in the furnace. Desperate to escape, Bigger winds up killing his girlfriend, Bessie, but he is caught. Although Bigger still must undergo a trial, he knows that he will be found guilty and executed.

Ideas and Concepts to Highlight

1. Discuss the differences between the worlds of blacks and whites of 1930 Chicago. Talk about what changes, if any, have occurred in the relations between blacks and whites since then.

2. Note that one of the major motifs of the novel is fear. Bigger hates the white world, but he is also afraid of it. This prevailing fear is woven throughout the story.

3. Explain that the Daltons symbolize white society that feels it helps blacks, yet in fact profits from the very system that makes it difficult for blacks to get ahead.

4. Discuss Bigger's character. Given his personality and the conditions he lived in, did he have a fair chance in life?

Writing Connection: "Race in America"

One of Richard Wright's messages in *Native Son* is that white society is largely responsible for the conditions and plight of blacks. Discuss this view with your students. Is Wright accurate in his assessment? Is he being fair?

For this assignment, instruct your students to write an essay or short story showing what they believe is the condition of race relations between blacks and whites today. Completing Worksheet 52-1 will help students to generate ideas.

NAME _____ **DATE** _____ **SECTION** _____

52-1. RACE IN AMERICA

Directions: Race has always been a major issue in American society. Either through an essay or short story, express your views about race in the United States today. Answer the questions below before writing.

1. Describe Richard Wright's views of the relations between blacks and whites, as depicted in *Native Son.* _____

_____

_____

_____

_____

2. Would he feel the same way today?_____ Why or why not?_____

_____

_____

_____

3. Name some books, movies, or TV shows that fit your own view of race relations today, and explain how they support your views. _____

_____

_____

_____

_____

4. How can the relations between blacks and whites be improved?_____

_____

_____

_____

_____

52-2. QUESTIONS TO CONSIDER FOR
<u>NATIVE SON</u>

1. Describe Bigger Thomas. Why is he so bitter? How is he different from his brother, Buddy? Why do you think they look at their world differently?

2. Some people would consider Mr. and Mrs. Dalton to be hypocrites for donating money to help blacks, but at the same time owning much of the ghetto in which blacks live. What is a hypocrite? Do you agree that they are hypocrites? Explain.

3. Describe how fear is a major motif of the novel.

4. When they were talking about robbing Blum's store, Bigger called Gus yellow for hesitating, but Gus claimed that Bigger was yellow, too. What was his reason for saying this? Do you think he was right? Why or why not?

5. What was Bigger's impression of the Daltons when he first met them? Do you believe he viewed the job as chauffeur as an opportunity? Explain.

6. What was Bigger's impression of Mary Dalton and Jan Erlone? Why was he unable to trust them?

7. Why did Bigger kill Mary? How did he feel about it? How did the murder change Bigger's opinion of himself?

8. How did Bigger plan his story so that he would not be a suspect in Mary's disappearance? Why did he involve Bessie with his plan? Why did he kill Bessie?

9. Throughout his trial, did Bigger show any remorse? Did he show any feelings for Mary? For Bessie? Explain.

10. Why do you think Wright chose *Native Son* for the title of this book? What significance does the title have?

11. Do you feel that Bigger is a tragic character? Explain.

52-3. PROJECTS AND ACTIVITIES TO CONSIDER FOR *NATIVE SON*

1. Read Richard Wright's autobiography *Black Boy* (New York: Harper and Row, 1945). Compare it to *Native Son*. Do any of the same ideas and themes appear in both books? Explain.

2. Watch the movie version of *Native Son* (1986), and compare it to the novel. How are the two versions of the story alike? How are they different? Write about your impressions.

3. Working with a partner, compare the newspaper accounts in the book of the disappearance and murder of Mary Dalton with similar types of articles found in today's newspapers. (You might wish to consult the library for articles on file.) Based on your research, do you think that a modern-day Bigger would have been convicted of the same crime? Do you think he would have gotten the same sentence? Share your conclusions with others.

4. The author seems to be making the point that Bigger and his violence are a product of white society. Because of the conditions and circumstances of his life, which was forced upon him by white America, Bigger was doomed to do what he did. Discuss this idea with the members of your group, and then, working alone, write an essay expressing your feelings and opinions. Use examples from the story to support your views.

Curriculum Connections:

1. Research and trace black migration from the South to the North. Answer these questions: Why did blacks migrate? About how many blacks moved northward? Where did they eventually settle? What were the results of the migration? Write a report of your findings, and include a map or graphs to highlight your information. (SS or A)

2. Race and ethnic origin have always been factors in American society. Research the races and major ethnic groups in the United States today. Create a table and pie graph to illustrate the diversity of America's population. Find studies that project the numbers into the future. What will be the percentages of race and major ethnic groups then? Based on your results, what changes do you anticipate in American society in the future? Share your ideas in a brief report. (SS, M, or A)

3. Research the Communist Party in the United States. When was it founded? How many people belong to it? What does the party advocate? Why has it never become a major force in American politics? Write a report sharing your findings. (SS)

53. *Jane Eyre* by Charlotte Brontë

Synopsis

Jane Eyre is a 10-year-old orphan living with relatives, the Reeds—Mrs. Reed and her children, Eliza, Georgiana, and John. Jane is treated badly and is glad to be sent away to Lowood School. Although her adjustment at Lowood is hard, during the next several years she comes to love the school. It is here that she grows up. After eight years, Jane begins to realize that she would like to know more of the world. She leaves Lowood and becomes the teacher of a young girl, Adele, at Thornfield Hall. The little girl does well under Jane's tutelage, but Jane still feels something is missing, until the master of the house, Mr. Rochester, returns home. An abrupt, changeable man, Jane learns that he is sullen over past experiences, although she is unable to find out more. Despite his moods, Jane sees good, strong qualities in Mr. Rochester and falls in love with him. There is much mystery in Thornfield Hall, however. One of the ser-

Charlotte Brontë

vants is Grace Poole, a strange woman, who keeps to herself and whose duties remain obscure. Moreover, there are screams in the night and on one occasion a guest suffers a serious knife wound. None of these incidents are satisfactorily explained to Jane. When Jane learns that Mr. Rochester is planning to marry Blanche Ingram, a pretty but shallow woman, she is dejected. She sadly continues with her duties until she is summoned by the Reeds because Mrs. Reed is dying. Dutifully, Jane returns. On her deathbed Mrs. Reed tells Jane that her (Jane's) uncle had wanted to adopt her but that she (Mrs. Reed) wrote to him and told him that Jane was dead. Jane forgives her and helps settle Mrs. Reed's daughters after her death. Returning to Thornfield Hall, Mr. Rochester tells Jane that he is not going to marry Blanche and proposes to Jane. She is thrilled. When the wedding day comes, however, the marriage is stopped because it is revealed that Mr. Rochester already has a wife— a mad woman who is taken care of by Grace Poole. When asked by Mr. Rochester to marry him anyhow, Jane reluctantly declines. She leaves and stays with the Rivers' family. It is while she lives with the Rivers' that Jane receives an inheritance from her uncle. Although Jane receives a proposal of marriage from Mr. Rivers, she feels she must return to Thornfield Hall. When she does, she finds the house burnt down. Mr. Rochester's mad wife caused the fire that took her life. Mr. Rochester, himself, was severely injured, losing a hand and an eye. Jane goes to him immediately and finds that their love for each other is still strong.

Ideas and Concepts to Highlight

1. Note that the story is told by Jane as an adult. The years of her childhood are told in retrospect, and from an adult's viewpoint.

2. Point out Brontë's descriptive settings.

3. Note the symbolism, especially when Rochester proposes to Jane amid the gathering storm. The storm symbolizes the power and turmoil of their emotions.

4. Discuss Brontë's use of foreshadowing, especially her use of dreams.

Writing Connection: "The Brontës"

The Brontës—Charlotte, Branwell, Emily, and Anne—were a unique literary family. Although they lived relatively short and tragic lives, books by Charlotte and Emily became known and read around the world.

For this writing assignment, instruct your students to research and write about the Brontës. Worksheet 53-1 will help them gather information for a thorough report.

53-1. THE BRONTËS

Directions: Research and write a report about the Brontës. Answering the questions below will get you started in your research. Include footnotes and a bibliography.

1. Who were the Brontës? _____
_____

2. Where were they born? _____
Where did they grow up? _____
Who were their parents? _____
How did their parents influence their future accomplishments? _____
_____
_____
_____

3. How did their background and childhood experiences affect their writing? _____
_____
_____
_____

4. Of the Brontës, who, in your opinion, became the most accomplished author? _____
_____ Why? _____
_____

5. What was some of the critical reaction to the published works of the Brontës? _____
_____

6. What is your opinion of their works? _____
_____
_____

53-2. QUESTIONS TO CONSIDER FOR
JANE EYRE

1. Describe Jane's life with the Reed family. Cite examples from the story to support your answer. Why was she staying with them?

2. Describe Jane's experience at Lowood School during the eight years she stayed there. Use examples from the story to support your answer.

3. Why did Jane go to Thornfield Hall. Was she helpful to Adele? Explain. Was Jane happy at Thornfield? Explain. What did she feel was missing in her life?

4. What was Jane's initial opinion of Mr. Rochester? What was your opinion of him? How did Jane's opinion of him change? Did your opinion of him change? Explain.

5. How did Jane view Lady Blanche Ingram? Having fallen in love with Mr. Rochester, do you think Jane could be objective in her appraisal of Blanche? Explain.

6. Why did Jane return to Gateshead? What did she find there? How had Jane changed since she had left there eight years before? What did Mrs. Reed confess to Jane? What was Jane's reaction? What would your reaction be in a similar situation?

7. When Mr. Rochester proposed to Jane in the orchard, she doesn't believe him at first. Why not? What do you think Brontë was telling the reader, if anything, through the lightning splitting the horse-chestnut tree in two?

8. After the wedding was stopped, why do you think Jane didn't go with Mr. Rochester to his villa in France? Do you think her explanation was reasonable? Explain.

9. How did Jane react to St. John's proposal of marriage? Do you think she did the right thing? Why or why not?

10. What had happened to Thornfield Hall during Jane's absence? What did she do when she learned of Mr. Rochester's condition?

53-3. PROJECTS AND ACTIVITIES TO CONSIDER FOR *JANE EYRE*

1. In Chapter 12, Jane feels that women have a right to a full life, the same as men do. She seems to be calling for equal rights for women. Working with a partner, research the status of women's rights during the 1840s, which was about the time the novel was written. Compare women's rights then to women's rights today. Present an oral report of your findings.

2. Working with your group, identify instances of foreshadowing. Decide what coming action each pointed to. Discuss how Brontë's use of foreshadowing made her plot more believable. Share your findings with the members of other groups.

3. Brontë used excellent descriptive writing in the story. Pick one of your favorite scenes and write your own description of it.

4. Read *Wuthering Heights* by Emily Brontë. Heathcliff in that story and Mr. Rochester in *Jane Eyre* have much in common. Write an essay analyzing these two characters.

5. Sickness, especially tuberculosis, played a large role in Charlotte Brontë's life. How does this come out in the novel?

Curriculum Connections:

1. Draw or sketch a portrait of Jane, as you think Jane herself would do it. (A)

2. In the story, Georgiana Reed becomes a nun. Research the Catholic and Anglican Churches. At one time, they were the same. When did the split come? Why? How different are the two churches in outlook and beliefs? Have there been any attempts to reconcile? Write about your findings in a report. (SS)

3. The Brontës grew up in Yorkshire, England. What was Yorkshire like in the early 1800s? Describe its climate, economy, and population. How might have their upbringing in Yorkshire affected the stories the Brontës wrote? Write a short report. (SS)

54. *Dinner at the Homesick Restaurant* by Anne Tyler
(Ballantine Books, 1982)

Synopsis

Pearl Tull is dying. She is an old woman who had spent the best years of her life raising her three children—Cody, Ezra, and Jenny—after her husband, Beck Tull, left. Told from multiple viewpoints, the story examines the effects of Beck's abandonment. Pearl, working as a cashier at a small store and struggling to support her family, often takes her frustration and anger out on her children. Cody becomes a successful, hard-driving business consultant, Ezra comes to own a restaurant, and Jenny, on her third marriage by the time the story ends, becomes a pediatrician. The family seems unable to love. Cody steals Ezra's fiancee away from him, eventually marrying her more to spite his brother than out of love; Ezra is never able to form another loving relationship; and Jenny selects men more out of whim and convenience than emotion. Except for Ezra, who remains living at home with Pearl, Cody and Jenny have a strained relationship with their mother. This is especially true of Cody, who slips out of touch for long periods, blaming his work. The family's underlying conflicts are aptly shown through repeated scenes in Ezra's restaurant. Whenever there is a gathering and they sit down to a meal, someone always gets angry and they are never able to finish it. Only at the gathering after Pearl's funeral, with their father attending, does the family resolve to finish the meal.

Ideas and Concepts to Highlight

1. Note that the viewpoint characters change throughout the story. This gives readers the chance to see the family from various perspectives.

2. Point out that many parts of the story are told in flashbacks.

3. Discuss the relationships and conflicts of the family members, and how they cope with them.

Writing Connection: "Trouble in the Family"

In recent years much has been written about the American family being in trouble. In many ways the Tulls are a good example—the father abandons the family, the mother is forced to raise the children alone, and the children grow up into adults scarred by their childhood. In turn, each of the children, as an adult, has trouble building a stable family of his or her own.

Discuss the issue of the disintegrating American family and ask your students to write an essay detailing their views. Encourage them to base their essay on the story, other readings, and their own experiences. Completing Worksheet 54-1 will help them to uncover their thoughts and feelings about this difficult topic.

NAME _____ DATE _____ SECTION _____

54-1. TROUBLE IN THE FAMILY

Directions: According to many social observers, the American family is under assault these days. Some go so far as to say that the traditional family of a father, mother, and children is no longer the norm. Consider the issue of the breakdown of the American family, answer the questions below, and write an essay detailing your opinions.

1. Do all families fit the model of the traditional family?_____ Why or why not? _____

    _____

    _____

2. Give some examples of non-traditional families. _____

    _____

    _____

3. Can non-traditional families provide a loving, nurturing atmosphere for family members?

    _____ Why or why not? _____

    _____

    _____

4. Why do some families break down? _____

    _____

    _____

5. What are some results of broken families? _____

    _____

    _____

6. What, if anything, should be done to save the traditional family?_____

    _____

    _____

    _____

54-2. QUESTIONS TO CONSIDER FOR
DINNER AT THE HOMESICK RESTAURANT

1. How did Pearl react when Beck left her? Why do you think she acted like that? Do you think her reaction is common when a husband or wife leaves his or her family? Explain.

2. How did each of the children react to his or her father's abandonment? Cite examples from the story to support your answer.

3. Pearl hoped that she could lean on Cody for support after Beck left. Was Cody helpful to her? Explain.

4. How did Pearl react to the news that Ezra had become a partner in Scarlatti's restaurant? Pearl says, "I've never been the type to meddle." Do you agree? Explain.

5. Why did Jenny marry Harley? Did she really know him? How did her opinion of him change after they were married? How was Harley's treatment of Jenny similar to Pearl's treatment of Jenny?

6. Describe Ezra's relationship with Mrs. Scarlatti. Why do you think he liked working with her? Do you think that in some ways Mrs. Scarlatti took the place of Pearl? Explain.

7. What changes did Ezra make to the restaurant when Mrs. Scarlatti was sick in the hospital? Why did he make the changes? Do you think he was right to make them? Just before she died, Mrs. Scarlatti said to her nurse: "Tell Ezra to change the sign...it isn't Scarlatti's restaurant anymore." What did she mean?

8. Why did Cody steal Ruth away from Ezra? What is your opinion of his actions?

9. Describe Jenny's life with Joe and the children. Do you think they provided a nurturing environment in which children could grow up? Explain.

10. What is your opinion of Beck Tull? What was his reason for leaving his family? Do you feel he was justified in leaving, or was he simply being irresponsible? Explain.

© 1994 by The Center for Applied Research in Education

54-3. PROJECTS AND ACTIVITIES TO CONSIDER FOR DINNER AT THE HOMESICK RESTAURANT

1. Would you describe Pearl and her children as a loving, caring family? Write down your opinion and then share it with the members of your group. Group members should then discuss the various opinions and arrive at a consensus that their recorder can share with other groups.

2. How do you think Pearl's death will affect the members of her family? Finish the final scene at the Homesick Restaurant.

3. Write a skit that the Tulls might play, your own version of "The Mortgage Overdue." With classmates assuming the various roles, act the skit out for the rest of the class.

4. Anne Tyler reveals much about each character through the eyes of other characters. Work with a partner, review the story, and find at least three examples where she does this. Share your examples with other members of your group and discuss whether or not this is an effective way to characterize. What other ways did she reveal character?

5. Imagine that you are Jenny. Instead of Harley writing a letter of proposal to her, you are to write one to him. How would Jenny have worded such a letter?

6. Design a menu for the Homesick Restaurant as Ezra might have made one.

7. Which of Pearl's children—Cody, Ezra, or Jenny— do you feel you have the most in common with? Write a short essay explaining why.

Curriculum Connections:

1. At one point in the story, Pearl starts to mention that Becky, Jenny's daughter, suffers from anorexia nervosa. Research this condition and write a report on its causes, symptoms, and treatments. (Sci)

2. Research the city of Baltimore, the setting of the story. Compare the Baltimore of the 1940s (when the story began) to the Baltimore of today. Include facts about its population, ethnic and racial make-up, economy, and climate. Undoubtedly, you will find many changes have occurred to Baltimore over the years. What has caused these changes? Write a report of your findings. (SS)

55. *Slaughterhouse-Five* by Kurt Vonnegut, Jr.
(Dell Publishing Company, 1972)

Synopsis

Slaughterhouse-Five is an account of a fictitious war "hero," Billy Pilgrim, who, through escapism and fantasy, travels through time and space. In an attempt to "make sense" of his past, he hallucinates being kidnapped to the planet Tralfamadore as a specimen from Earth. While there he tries to come to terms with what he perceives as the absurdity of life. His time and space travels arise out of his deeply buried war experiences. During World War II he was a valet to a chaplain, was captured by the Germans, and survived the firebombing of Dresden which killed nearly twice as many people as the atomic bomb dropped on Hiroshima. As a POW he experienced many labor camps, including living in an abandoned slaughterhouse, until the Allies liberated him. After the war, he marries a rich woman, is set up as an optometrist in upstate New York, and has two children. Vonnegut's story is told in a roundabout, jumping style with no linear plot. Billy, as taught by the Tralfamadorians, is "unstuck in time," and his experiences are related in small segments that often do not connect right away.

Ideas and Concepts to Highlight

1. Note that Billy lives as much in reality as he does fantasy. His time and space travels arise from his need to understand the absurdity of war.

2. Encourage the class to identify imagery throughout the book, and discuss symbolism as a literary technique.

3. Note how Vonnegut uses names to suggest ideas. Pilgrim, for instance, suggests a person who seeks enlightenment or understanding. Roland Weary parallels Roland, one of Charlemagne's generals, in the *Song of Roland*. After battling the Saracens in Spain, Roland was given the charge of guarding the rear of the main army as it returned to France. When attacked by the Saracens, Roland, wanting to defeat the enemy himself, refused to call for reinforcements. His entire company was killed. Ilium, Billy Pilgrim's hometown, is the classical name for the ancient city of Troy.

4. Discuss Vonnegut's rambling, non-linear style, and how the novel itself is "unstuck in time." Is this an effective way to tell this story?

5. Encourage the class to share thoughts on Vonnegut's purpose for writing the book, and what this unusual novel achieves. Is this, in fact, an anti-war novel?

Writing Connection: "An Anti-War Novel?"

There are many themes in Kurt Vonnegut's *Slaughterhouse-Five*, three of the most important being good versus evil, war and its effects, and nationalism. As these themes recur throughout the novel, the reader must ask him- or herself why Vonnegut emphasizes them so much. Was his purpose in writing this story primarily to show the terrible effects of war, or was his purpose an indictment of the absurdity of war?

For this assignment, ask your students to consider the extent to which *Slaughterhouse-Five* is an anti-war novel. Instruct students to complete Worksheet 55-1, and write about their thoughts in the form of an essay. Having students then return to their groups to discuss their impressions before writing can help broaden their perspectives.

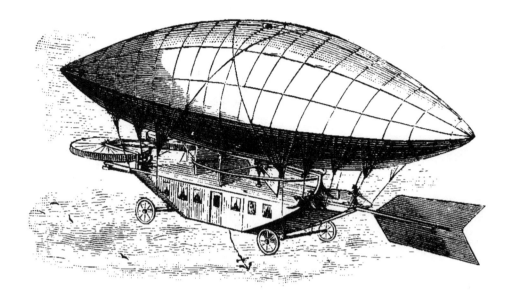

55-1. AN ANTI-WAR NOVEL?

Directions: Three of the most important themes in Kurt Vonnegut's *Slaughterhouse-Five* are good versus evil, war and its effects, and nationalism. Was he using these as a vehicle to protest the absurdity of war? Answer the questions below and then write an essay explaining your thoughts.

1. Give some examples of how Vonnegut brings out the theme of good versus evil. _____

_____

_____

_____

_____

2. List some ways that Vonnegut supports his theme of nationalism. _____

_____

_____

_____

_____

3. List some ways that Vonnegut shows the effects of war. _____

_____

_____

_____

_____

4. Do these themes support the opinion that the story is an anti-war novel? _____
Why or why not? _____

_____

_____

_____

_____

_____

55-2. QUESTIONS TO CONSIDER FOR
SLAUGHTERHOUSE-FIVE

1. Discuss the author's continuous use of "So it goes." What was his purpose? Why the repetition?

2. Define your understanding of Vonnegut's term "unstuck in time." Describe how Billy was "unstuck in time." Use examples from the story to support your answer.

3. What is the significance of the name "Billy Pilgrim"? Why do you suppose the author placed him in Ilium, New York?

4. In Chapter 2, the author writes that Billy's mother, "like so many Americans, was trying to construct a life that made sense from things she found in gift shops." What do you think this means? When you answer, be sure to take into account the kind of person Billy turned out to be.

5. In Chapter 4, what is the significance of Billy being able to see the war movie in reverse?

6. Record Vonnegut's many digressions and tangents in *Slaughterhouse-Five,* many of which end in death of some sort and the phrase "So it goes." What is the purpose of such tangents? What do they accomplish? Are they disruptive or essential? Support your answer with examples from the story.

7. Billy is portrayed as abnormally detached from reality. Why is he like this? Why does Vonnegut accentuate it so? Explain.

8. Describe Billy's stay on Tralfamadore. What provides the substance for Billy's fantasy life? Why do you think Billy needs this fantasy life? What is he really trying to find on Tralfamadore?

9. Decide whether Billy Pilgrim represents Everyman, the author himself, or somebody else. Support your conclusions with specific examples.

10. What is the "moral," or message, of *Slaughterhouse-Five?*

55-3. PROJECTS AND ACTIVITIES TO CONSIDER FOR
SLAUGHTERHOUSE-FIVE

1. Research other stories about people who say they were kidnapped by outer-space creatures. Share the stories with the members of your group or the whole class, and select the most believable. What makes some more believable than others? With your group, discuss the possibility of some of these stories actually being true.

2. Strong symbolism abounds in *Slaughterhouse-Five*. Working with your group, select several examples of symbolism. Discuss what each represents, then share your conclusions with the members of other groups.

3. The novel contains strong religious imagery. Work with a partner and find as many religious images and references as you can. Define them, and explain their use in context. Share your findings with the members of your group.

4. Create a plot for a Kilgore Trout novel.

Curriculum Connections:

1. Draw or sketch a representation of Billy's habitat on Tralfamadore. (A)

2. Consult the necessary references and write a report on the destruction of Dresden during World War II, highlighting the most significant events. In addition, try to answer these questions: Why was the attack ordered? How much destruction was caused? How many lives were lost? Were the military objectives gained? In your opinion, was the attack justified? Include a map detailing the attacks or the areas of heaviest damage. (SS)

3. Conduct research to find possible reasons why the Germans did not slaughter American captives the way they did Jews and other prisoners. Present an oral report to your group or class about your findings. (SS)

4. Research the concept of time. What is time? Is time travel a theoretical possibility? Write a short report. (Sci)

56. <u>One Flew Over the Cuckoo's Nest</u> by Ken Kesey (Viking Penguin, 1962)

Synopsis

To escape work on a prison farm, con man Randle P. McMurphy has himself committed to a mental hospital. The story is told by the Chief, a patient who hasn't spoken in years and is believed to be deaf and dumb. Once committed, McMurphy tries to change the routines of the hospital to suit himself. This puts him in conflict with Nurse Ratched, the Big Nurse, a former army nurse who maintains order through manipulations and fear. McMurphy, who symbolizes individuality (the Big Nurse represents society's need for conformity), quickly becomes a hero to the other patients. They draw strength from him and start to get better. Even the Chief begins speaking again. The Big Nurse, however, is unwilling to let her authority slip away and she is determined to "break" McMurphy. After fighting with an orderly, McMurphy is given shock treatment, but he still challenges the Big Nurse. Bribing the night attendant, McMurphy stages a party, inviting prostitutes he knows, one of the purposes being to help Billy, another patient, lose his virginity. The next morning, the Big Nurse is furious. Berating Billy, she threatens to tell his mother, a prospect that Billy can't face. Left alone for a few minutes, Billy takes a razor and kills himself. Now McMurphy is furious. He attacks the Big Nurse and tries to strangle her. McMurphy is stopped and taken away from the ward. When he returns, he has been lobotomized and is merely a vegetable. The Chief, unwilling to let the Big Nurse have the final victory, smothers McMurphy in the night. Having gained strength and courage from McMurphy, he is able to escape.

Ideas and Concepts to Highlight

1. Discuss how Kesey uses the mental hospital to represent society.

2. Note that by using a patient as the narrator, Kesey allows the reader to glimpse the hospital from the inside out. This sometimes gives the impression that the "inside" is saner than the outside world. Also point out that since the Chief is insane, his observations are thus tainted by his condition. Is he always objective?

3. Note that the conflict between McMurphy and Nurse Ratched symbolizes the battle between good and evil, and the individual against the authority of society that demands conformity.

4. Discuss the religious imagery throughout the story, particularly McMurphy being portrayed symbolically as Christ.

5. Note the strong conflict of male versus female. Many consider this novel to be misogynistic.

Writing Connection: "The Individual Versus Society"

In the story, Kesey uses the mental hospital as a setting for a showdown between the individual (McMurphy) and his need for "being what he is" and society (the Big Nurse) that demands conformity. Discuss the needs of individuals and the needs of society. Are they mutually exclusive? Or are there times they are convergent?

For this writing assignment, ask your students to write an essay or story that shares their feelings on the topic. Completing Worksheet 56-1 will help them to organize their thoughts.

56-1. THE INDIVIDUAL VERSUS SOCIETY

Directions: One of the themes of *One Flew Over the Cuckoo's Nest* is the conflict between individuals and their quest for freedom, and society, which often demands conformity. Answer the questions below and then write an essay or story that reflects your feelings about the topic.

1. List the major needs of individuals: _____

_____

_____

_____

_____

_____

2. List what society expects of individuals: _____

_____

_____

_____

_____

3. List needs of the individual that might be in conflict with the needs of society: _____

_____

_____

_____

_____

4. What might happen when needs are in conflict? _____

_____

_____

_____

_____

56-2. QUESTIONS TO CONSIDER FOR
ONE FLEW OVER THE CUCKOO'S NEST

1. How did McMurphy come to be admitted to the mental hospital? How did he treat the other patients? How did they react to him?

2. What is the conflict between McMurphy and the Big Nurse?

3. Describe a typical group meeting. What was the purpose of these meetings? Do you think they were helpful to the patients? Why or why not? What do you think the Big Nurse was really trying to do at the meetings?

4. Why do the patients think of themselves as rabbits? Does McMurphy feel that way? Explain.

5. Why did the Big Nurse argue against sending McMurphy to Disturbed? What do you think her real reason was?

6. After McMurphy realizes that he can be discharged only after the hospital staff, including Nurse Ratched, believes him to be ready to re-enter society, he stops challenging Nurse Ratched. How do the other patients react to his change in behavior? Why did Cheswick commit suicide? How does his death affect McMurphy?

7. How do the patients gain strength from McMurphy? What does McMurphy help the Chief to realize?

8. After the fishing trip, how does the Big Nurse get the others to turn against McMurphy? What do you think were her motives?

9. Why was McMurphy given the shock treatments? What did the Big Nurse hope to gain?

10. After Billy's suicide, why did McMurphy attack the Big Nurse? What happened to McMurphy because of this?

11. Why did the Chief kill McMurphy? Was he wrong or right to do this? Explain.

56-3. PROJECTS AND ACTIVITIES TO CONSIDER FOR ONE FLEW OVER THE CUCKOO'S NEST

1. Work with your group and discuss the characters of McMurphy and the Big Nurse. What drove them? Why, from the beginning of the story, was it inevitable that they would come into conflict? Why couldn't McMurphy back down? Why did Nurse Ratched force him to conform? In the end, was she successful? Answer the above questions during your discussion and then share your conclusions with the members of other groups.

2. Write a story showing the Chief's first days outside the hospital. Is he able to adapt to the outside world?

3. Kesey uses much religious imagery throughout the novel, especially in the final parts, and implies that McMurphy is like Christ in the mental hospital. Working with a partner, review the story and identify examples of religious imagery. Then, write an essay discussing the parallels between McMurphy and Christ. Is the parallel justified? Why or why not?

4. Who is your favorite character in the story? Write a new scene for the story in which your character plays a central part.

5. At the end of the novel, some readers feel that the Chief represents the "Noble Savage," a term often used in literature and the social sciences. Research the term and apply it to the Chief. Is he truly a "Noble Savage"?

Curriculum Connections:

1. The Chief is described as being a paranoid-schizophrenic. Research this condition. What are its causes, symptoms, and treatments? Is the condition curable, or at least controllable? Write a report. (Sci)

2. Along with their mental illness, Sefelt and Fredricks suffer from epilepsy. Research this disorder and write a report on its causes, symptoms, and treatments. (Sci)

3. This story was copywritten in 1962. Has the treatment of the mentally ill changed much since then? Consult the necessary references and present an oral report to your class about the treatment of mental illness today. Include some of the common conditions and treatments. Also include the ways patients receive treatment, for example, through institutionalization, out-patient clinics, or personal physicians. (SS or Sci)

57. <u>The House on Mango Street</u> by Sandra Cisneros
(Vintage Contemporaries, 1991)

Synopsis

Esperanza Cordero is growing up in a house on Mango Street in the Hispanic section of Chicago. Through a series of vignettes, she shares with the reader her feelings and thoughts about the oppressive street where hopelessness and hardship are staples. The reader learns about Esperanza's family, friends, and neighbors, their routines, sorrows, and joys. Throughout the book Esperanza's desire to one day leave Mango Street is unshakable. She draws her strength from this, even as she sees her neighbors and friends submit to the desolation of their reality. This short book is told with a simple, yet compelling prose that carries the reader from one vignette to another without the slightest pause.

Ideas and Concepts to Highlight

1. Note that the story is told in a series of vignettes. Although the vignettes may not at first seem to be related, they build to a whole that gives a detailed description of Mango Street and its effect on the people who live there.

2. Discuss the setting of Mango Street.

3. Discuss Esperanza's character as it is slowly revealed through the vignettes.

Writing Connection: "Esperanza and Me"

Esperanza has many of the same basic values and ambitions as other young people. For this writing assignment, ask your students to compare their goals and values to those of Esperanza. Completing Worksheet 57-1 will help your students to organize their thoughts.

57-1. ESPERANZA AND ME

Directions: How much do you have in common with Esperanza Cordero? Answer the questions below and then write an essay comparing yourself to Esperanza.

1. Complete the charts.

My Goals	Esperanza's Goals

My Values	Esperanza's Values

2. Ways Esperanza and I are alike:_____

_____

_____

_____

3. Ways Esperanza and I are different: _____

_____

_____

_____

57-2. QUESTIONS TO CONSIDER FOR
THE HOUSE ON MANGO STREET

1. Is the house on Mango Street the kind of house Esperanza always wanted? What kind of house does she want? Explain.

2. Describe Esperanza's neighborhood. Would you like to live there? Explain.

3. In "Those Who Don't," Esperanza says of her neighborhood, "All brown all around, we are safe." What does she mean? How does she feel about going into a neighborhood of another color?

4. Esperanza introduces the reader to many different characters on Mango Street. Do they have any common bonds? If yes, what are they? If no, why not?

5. Why are the Four Skinny Trees important to Esperanza?

6. In "Beautiful and Cruel" Esperanza says, "I have begun my own quiet war." What does she mean?

7. Of the three sisters, what did the sister with the marble hands mean when she told Esperanza that she (Esperanza) must remember to come back for the others? What does the circle refer to?

8. Throughout the story, Esperanza clings to her desire to leave Mango Street. Keeping her character in mind, do you think that one day she will leave? Explain.

9. Describe Esperanza. Do you believe her to be a keen observer of her world? Explain, using examples from the story.

10. In English, "Esperanza" means Hope. Does Esperanza's name fit her character? Explain.

11. This book has a distinct narrative structure. What effect did this structure have on you? Did it enhance or detract from the book? Explain.

© 1994 by The Center for Applied Research in Education

57-3. PROJECTS AND ACTIVITIES TO CONSIDER FOR THE HOUSE ON MANGO STREET

1. What do you predict for Esperanza's future? Write a short story showing what you think her future holds.

2. Read *Woman Hollering Creek* by Sandra Cisneros (Random House, 1991), which is a collection of short stories. Compare the stories to *The House on Mango Street* and note similarities and differences in the ideas and writing style. Write an essay comparing the two works.

3. Discuss with your group Cisneros's telling of her story in a series of vignettes. Was this format effective? Could she have told the story another way that might have improved it? Work toward a consensus and then have your recorder share your conclusions with the members of other groups.

4. Write a poem about Mango Street, as Esperanza might write one.

5. In "Bums in the Attic," Esperanza states that once she owns her own house, she will not forget where she came from, and that when passing bums ask if they can come in, she will offer them the attic and ask them to stay. Will she really do this? Or once she has a nice house away from Mango Street will she forget her past? Discuss these questions with your group. When you are done, your recorder should share your conclusions.

6. *The House on Mango Street* is unusual in its format. Imagine that you were telling a friend about this book. What would you say? Write down your impressions.

Curriculum Connections:

1. Hispanics—Americans of Spanish or Latin American descent—comprise a major ethnic group in the United States. Research this group. From what countries do they come? In which areas of the U.S. are Hispanic populations concentrated? How well are they able to enter the mainstream? Write a report of your findings. (SS)

2. American culture incorporates the customs and traditions of many of the large ethnic groups that have settled here. It has always been this way. Find out how the cultures of people from Spanish and Latin American descent have found a place in the overall culture of the United States. Consider things like food, language, and specific events. Create a chart that shows your findings. (SS or A)

58. *Fallen Angels* by Walter Dean Myers
(Scholastic Inc., 1988)

Synopsis

Richie Perry is a fresh-faced, African-American teenager from Harlem who enlists in the army because he is not sure what to do after high school. Sent to Vietnam in the late 1960s just prior to the Tet offensive, he and a small squad of men experience war for the first time almost immediately. These young men—Peewee, Brunner, Johnson, Lobel, Monaco and Walowick—become friends and comrades as they fight the Viet Cong and the North Vietnamese army village by village, through rice paddies, ambushes, and exploding children. Although many come from rough-and-tumble city life, they still have childlike fears and anguish. Richie is wounded in a firefight but heals well enough to return to combat. He is wounded more gravely a second time after finding his way back to his comrades when he and Peewee are lost. Also wounded, Peewee joins Richie on a plane back to the United States. Both are changed forever, redefining their values and their views about God, death and relationships.

Ideas and Concepts to Highlight

1. Discuss the Vietnam War and how it was different from any previous conflict involving Americans. Talk about things such as public opinion, the treatment of returning veterans, political posturing and propaganda, and fighting in the jungle.

2. Discuss the military experience, including boot camp, machismo, tensions between blacks and whites, death and dying, camaraderie, assignments (orders), and relationships with family.

3. Discuss the state of Communism today. Encourage the class to discuss what they think the Vietnam War accomplished, and if today's situations were affected by it.

4. Note Richie's coming of age, and the major events in his life that influence the man he will become. Have the class talk about these events in a group setting.

Writing Connection: "The Impact of the War on Richie Perry"

We all experience defining moments that can redirect the course of our lives. War, like other great events, unquestionably changes people.

For this writing assignment, ask your students to consider how the war changed Richie Perry. Ask them to compare the Richie before the war to the one after the war. How was he changed? Will the changes affect him throughout the rest of his life? Instruct your students to answer the questions on Worksheet 58-1 and then write an essay detailing their opinions.

NAME _____ **DATE** _____ **SECTION** _____

58-1. THE IMPACT OF THE WAR ON RICHIE PERRY

Directions: Without doubt, the war changed Richie Perry. Answer the questions below, and then in an essay write your opinions about how the war did in fact change him.

1. Describe Richie Perry in the boxes below.

Before the War	After the War

2. What was the biggest change in him? _____

_____

_____ What caused this change? _____

_____

_____

3. Will his war experiences affect him for the rest of his life? _____ Why or why not?

_____

_____

_____

_____

58-2. QUESTIONS TO CONSIDER FOR
FALLEN ANGELS

1. Richie describes himself as a "middle-of-the-road kind of guy." Do you agree with this assessment? Explain, using examples from the story to support your answer.

2. Did white soldiers have different war experiences than black soldiers? Using examples from the book, write about what you think were the differences, if any. What caused the differences?

3. What was a "pacification mission"? During a "pacification mission," Richie insists to Lobel, "I am not a killer." Why did he say this? What did he mean?

4. Describe the terrain that Richie fought in. What was difficult about fighting there?

5. Describe the enemy. Was it always clear who the enemy was? Explain. How did this affect the Americans?

6. Why did Richie feel so strongly about his younger brother? What character traits and experience did Richie have that intensified his emotions regarding his brother?

7. Why did Richie's mother write to Peewee? Write a diary entry for Mabel on the day she wrote the letter.

8. During a mission, Richie says to himself, "Would God think I was a hypocrite, praying every time I was scared?" What is your opinion?

9. Describe Captain Stewart. What effect did he have on the men under his command?

10. Write a short epilogue to the book, using Richie's first-person point of view.

11. What part of the book had the greatest impact for you? Explain.

58-3. *PROJECTS AND ACTIVITIES TO CONSIDER FOR FALLEN ANGELS*

1. Richie wrote to Lt. Carroll's wife about his death, and mentioned his bravery and leadership. Write a similar letter to Jenkins's mother, considering that he was a new private.

2. Describe, as Richie Perry did after Jenkins was caught in the trap, your first major experience with death.

3. Have a Vietnam War veteran speak to the class about his experiences. Then write an essay about your feelings before and after the presentation.

4. During most overseas conflicts that the United States has been involved in, it has been a popular custom for people to write to American soldiers whom they do not know. Write a letter to any of the characters in *Fallen Angels*.

5. Work with your group. From general reading, media proliferation, talking to others and the novel, what conclusions can you draw about the generation that fought (or did not fight) in the Vietnam War? How was it affected in the long run? What are its values? What is its legacy? What is its future?

Curriculum Connections:

1. What is the state of the U.S. armed forces today? Clip articles and photos and make a collage of news stories about them. Write about trends you find. How are the armed forces of today different from those of the Vietnam War? (SS or A)

2. Find articles and data from the Vietnam War era. Create a chart showing public opinion about American intervention in the conflict. Break out your data across age, region and ethnic lines. Contrast sentiment from the late 1960s with that near the end of the war. (SS or A)

3. Work with a partner and compare the Vietnam War with Desert Storm. Consult the necessary references and try to answer the following questions: What were the causes of each? How did the U.S. public react? How did public sentiment affect the war effort? What were the results of each war? Why were the results so different? Present your findings in the form of an oral report. Feel free to use charts and graphs to support your presentation. (SS)

59. *Hamlet* by William Shakespeare

Synopsis

A ghost with the likeness of the dead king of Denmark appears to guards at Elsinore Castle. The guards tell Prince Hamlet, who concludes that the ghost, who looks like his dead father, is a sign of trouble. Hamlet is despondent over his father's recent death and his mother Gertrude's hasty marriage to his Uncle Claudius, now King. Hamlet meets the ghost, who tells him that it is indeed the spirit of his father, and that Hamlet must avenge his murder by Claudius. Feigning madness, Hamlet makes his plans. Soon, however, he comes to question the ghost, and worries that it is the spirit of a demon sent to trick him. Although Claudius handles Hamlet with apparent consideration, the King is concerned about what Hamlet might do with the people's support. Polonius, Claudius's councillor, offers to have his

daughter, Ophelia, meet with Hamlet while the King and he secretly listen to the conversation in an effort to observe Hamlet. After hearing Hamlet's bitter discourse, the King becomes more convinced that Hamlet is a potential threat. When Hamlet instructs actors who perform a play to do it in a manner that implies Claudius's role in King Hamlet's death, Claudius orders Polonius to find out what he can about Hamlet's supposed madness. Polonius hides behind a wall hanging in Gertrude's room; when Hamlet goes there to speak to his mother, Hamlet becomes aware that someone is listening and he kills Polonius with a sword thrust. Certain now that Hamlet is dangerous, Claudius orders two members of the Court to take Hamlet to England where he will be killed. But Hamlet thwarts the plan and returns to Denmark, where Ophelia has killed herself in despondency over Hamlet's murder of her father Polonius. As soon as Claudius hears of this, he engages Laertes, Polonius's son, to challenge Hamlet to a duel

William Shakespeare

and through treachery kill him. It is decided that Laertes's rapier will not be blunted, and that Laertes will dip the tip in poison. Hamlet is challenged to a duel by Laertes. The duel takes place at Court, in front of Claudius and Gertrude. During the duel, Gertrude mistakenly drinks from a poisoned cup Claudius had meant for Hamlet (just in case Laertes didn't kill the Prince). In the meantime, Laertes wounds Hamlet with the poisoned rapier. The two scuffle and exchange rapiers, and Hamlet wounds Laertes. When his mother falls, she tells Hamlet that she has been poisoned and Hamlet kills Claudius. Laertes and Hamlet also die.

Ideas and Concepts to Highlight

1. Note the setting and time period. Explain that the play was written during the Renaissance, a time of revival in Europe during which the arts, literature, and learning flourished.

2. Discuss Hamlet's multifaceted character.

3. Emphasize the two major issues that lead to Hamlet's tragedy—Claudius murdering his father and then marrying his mother. Note how these issues underlie the conflict throughout the play.

4. Discuss the motif of revenge.

5. Discuss the difficulty Hamlet has in deciding what to do.

Writing Connection: "Prince Hamlet"

Hamlet is one of the most enigmatic characters in literature. Driven by his need for revenge, he decides to play the role of a madman, yet, after a while, the audience begins to wonder if in fact his grief and sorrow haven't truly made him insane. He lusts for revenge, but often wavers, not sure of what action to take. He is a tortured soul.

For this writing assignment, ask your students to consider what type of man Hamlet was, and then write an essay analyzing his character. Completing Worksheet 59-1 will help students to organize their thoughts.

59-1. PRINCE HAMLET

Directions: In many ways Hamlet is one of the most puzzling and tragic characters in literature. Answer the questions below and then write an essay analyzing his character.

1. List five facts about Hamlet's character. _____

_____

_____

_____

_____

_____

2. What was Hamlet's driving force in the play? _____

_____

_____

_____

3. Why didn't Hamlet kill Claudius at his first opportunity? _____

_____

_____

_____

4. Was Hamlet acting insane, or was he insane? _____ Explain. _____

_____

_____

_____

5. Given his character and his desire for revenge, was there any way for Hamlet to escape

tragedy? _____

_____

_____

© 1994 by The Center for Applied Research in Education

59-2. QUESTIONS TO CONSIDER FOR
HAMLET

1. What troubles Hamlet at the opening of the play?

2. When Horatio tells Hamlet about the apparition, who does Hamlet think it might be? What does he decide to do? What type of omen does Hamlet think the apparition is?

3. Describe Hamlet's meeting with the ghost. Who is the ghost? Why has it appeared? What does the ghost tell Hamlet to do? What might be some other reasons for the ghost appearing?

4. Why does Hamlet act as if he were mad? What does Polonius think the reason for the madness is? Do you agree with him? Why or why not?

5. How does Claudius react to the performance of _The Murder of Gonzago?_ Why? What does his reaction convince Hamlet of?

6. Describe Claudius and Gertrude. What does each think of Hamlet? How does each treat him? What does Hamlet think of them?

7. Why does Hamlet kill Polonius? How does Hamlet act after he finds out who he killed? What is your opinion of his actions?

8. How does Claudius feel about what he did to King Hamlet? As he is praying, Hamlet enters with his sword drawn. Why doesn't he kill Claudius?

9. Why does Claudius decide to send Hamlet to England? What does he plan for Hamlet upon Hamlet's arrival there? What happens instead?

10. How does Claudius hope to eliminate Hamlet during the Prince's duel with Laertes? Describe what happens during the duel.

11. Would you describe Hamlet as a tragic hero? Why or why not?

59-3. PROJECTS AND ACTIVITIES TO CONSIDER FOR
HAMLET

1. In Act III, Scene i, lines 56-89, Hamlet gives his famous soliloquy, "To be or not to be..." Interpret these lines and apply their meaning to our current era.

2. Imagine that Hamlet had followed his father to the throne instead of Claudius following King Hamlet. Would Hamlet have made a better king than Claudius? Which man had the better skills to be king? Write an essay.

3. Watch the movie version of _Hamlet_ (1990) starring Mel Gibson. Compare it to the play. Does it follow the action of the play closely? Write an essay and discuss the film's realism. Do you think the producers created a realistic setting? Did the actors and actresses present believable characters? What was your overall impression of the film?

4. Select a favorite scene of the play and, with the help of classmates, act it out. Try to read the dialogue as realistically as possible to capture the flavor of the times.

5. Read another of Shakespeare's plays and compare the lead character to Hamlet. (_Macbeth_ would be a good choice.) How are they similar? How are they different? Is there a possibility of either escaping destiny?

6. Claudius attains the Danish throne through deceit. Unlike some villains who clearly exhibit evil and have no redeeming qualities, Claudius is a man of various emotions. He is an intelligent and cautious man. At one point he even feels guilty for what he has done, but this doesn't stop him from plotting against Hamlet. Working with a partner, discuss Claudius's character and write a character sketch.

Curriculum Connections:

1. Research William Shakespeare. What kind of man was he? Include the major facts about his life. Did he really write all the plays attributed to him? Write a short biography. (SS)

2. Research the monarchies of Europe during the Renaissance. Concentrate on a few that interest you the most and answer the following questions in a report: Upon a king's death, how was succession decided? How did royal families retain power? What types of political alliances were formed and what were their purposes? What was meant by "divine right"? Did kings exercise absolute power during the Renaissance? (SS)

© 1994 by The Center for Applied Research in Education

60. <u>Memory</u> by Margaret Mahy
(J.M. Dent & Sons Ltd., 1987)

Synopsis

Jonny Dart, 19 years old and haunted by his sister's accidental death, tries one evening to find her best friend, Bonny, in an effort to cope with some of the memories. But during his wanderings through the city that night, he meets Sophie, a sufferer of Alzheimer's disease, and follows her to her squalid house. Jonny, feeling like an outcast himself, takes refuge with her, partially to escape trouble he had gotten into while searching for Bonny but also to sort out his painful past. Over the course of a few days he begins to take care of the amnesiac Sophie, who believes him to be a relative to whom she had once been attracted. People from his past appear in coincidences and he is forced to face the parts of his life that he has chosen to bury. As Sophie's guardian and friend, however, he realizes that he has responsibility to others beside himself, and his life takes on new meaning. He ends his brooding and is able to make peace with some of the abuse and fear he had sustained as a youngster.

Ideas and Concepts to Highlight

1. Discuss Alzheimer's disease, amnesia, and senility, and note how memory and a person's past create his or her present conditions. Have the class speculate on how losing memory could rearrange their personal world.

2. Discuss Jonny's coming of age as a man, and how maturity is more often attained through experience rather than simply the passage of time or the reaching of a certain age.

3. Have the class reflect on the welfare of the aged, and how they often require as much care and comfort as children but are less likely to receive it.

4. Discuss people's feeling of responsibility to suffering strangers, and how helping them can bring good feelings to the provider.

Writing Connection: "Being Old"

Jonny's experience with Sophie helped him to understand some of the problems of growing old. Aging is a hard concept for young people to understand—when you're young you feel that youth lasts forever.

For this writing assignment, ask your students to think about an older person they know. This may be a grandparent, older relative, or even a neighbor. What type of relationship do they have with this person? Do they understand him or her? Does this person understand them? How might any gaps in understanding be bridged? Instruct them to answer the questions on Worksheet 60-1, and then write about their experiences.

60-1. BEING OLD

Directions: Through his relationship with Sophie, Jonny came to understand many of the problems of old people. Think about your relationship with a special grandparent, old relative or neighbor. Answer the questions below and then write about this relationship.

1. What is the name of this person, and his or her relationship to you? _____

_____

2. On what things do the two of you agree? _____

_____

_____

_____

3. On what things do you disagree?_____

_____

_____

_____

4. Why do you see some things differently? _____

_____

_____

5. What do you value, or cherish, most about this person? _____

_____

_____

6. Is there any way you would want to improve your relationship with this person? _____
If yes, how?_____

_____

_____

© 1994 by The Center for Applied Research in Education

60-2. QUESTIONS TO CONSIDER FOR
MEMORY

1. Why do you think that Jonny had a difficult time associating with people? Which of his character traits are responsible? What prejudices did people hold against him? Were those feelings about him valid? Explain.

2. When Jonny first met Sophie, he said, "I'm glad to meet you at last. You could be a big help to me." What do you think he meant?

3. How is Jonny affected by meeting Sophie? What changes occur in him?

4. What is the significance of Marribel Road to Jonny?

5. In Chapter 9, Jonny wonders "whether or not one was entitled to turn away from the wheel of fortune because its magical accidents offered something one didn't want to get mixed up with." What did he mean by this? Do you agree with him? Why or why not?

6. Discuss the function of the song lyrics interspersed throughout the novel.

7. Define your understanding of Jonny's term, "pythoness."

8. Compare the characters of Jonny and Bonny in terms of their treatment of Sophie.

9. Jonny often second-guesses himself, recalling situations where he might have acted differently or said something else. Recall situations where you have had this self-doubt. Why does Jonny do it? Does he do it less as his character evolves? Support your answer.

10. Try to find a specific moment in the story where Jonny makes peace with his sister's death. Support your answer.

60-3. PROJECTS AND ACTIVITIES TO CONSIDER FOR __MEMORY__

1. Invite a person representing a support group for Alzheimer's caregivers to speak to the class. Write a report on the visit.

2. Work with your group and discuss this question: How do you think the story would have been different if Jonny had found Bonny Benedicta in the opening scene? After your discussion, work together to reorganize the story and then present it to the class in outline form.

3. Describe a situation in which you wanted to escape responsibility. What factors went into your decision? What were your feelings? Compare them to Jonny's.

4. Work with a partner and find out what social services are available through local government or non-profit organizations to people like Sophie. Make a chart, listing the pros and cons of the different services, then select one for Sophie. Explain your reasoning to your group.

5. In Chapter 14, Jonny imagines "what he might think if he were a social worker and someone like him turned up and told a strange tale of life with Sophie." Imagine that you are that social worker. What would you think if someone told you about Sophie and Jonny? Write about what your impressions would be.

Curriculum Connections:

1. Sketch Sophie's house, including the giant water tap jutting from its front. (A)

2. Research the Maori Land Treaty and the activism that Bonny's sister embraced. What is its current status? How do you feel about it? How does it compare with the Native American situation in North America? (SS)

3. *Memory* is set in New Zealand. Select another culture with which you are familiar. How would the story be different if set in that culture? Use examples from the culture's mores and norms. Consult the necessary references for accuracy, and write a brief report. (SS)

4. Sophie suffered from Alzheimer's disease. Research this disorder and find out its causes and treatments. As yet, there is no cure, but recent advances offer hope for limiting the disease's effects. What are these advances? Present your findings orally to the class. (Sci)

HOW TO DO JUST ABOUT ANYTHING

Your **A-Z guide** to **1,001** practical skills and household solutions

Reader's Digest

PUBLISHED BY THE READER'S DIGEST ASSOCIATION, INC.

LOND⟨ ⟩AL

boil an egg, **bandage** a leg, pack a **backpack** ... **As it says on the cover, this book will show you how to do just about anything.** And we mean *anything* – 1,001 things to look up in an emergency or to improve your home and garden, things to cook, make or play, and surprising things you didn't even realise you wanted to do. It's all here: the need-to-know and the fun, the modern and the traditional, the easy and the challenging, in clear words and helpful pictures. Dive into this ocean of information and discover how to ...

... drop an **anchor** ▪ identify **animal footprints** ▪ beat **aphids** ▪ set up an **aquarium** ▪ win an **argument** ▪ prepare an **artichoke** ▪ survive an **avalanche** ▪ make a **balloon animal** ▪ trim a **beard** ▪ choose **beef** cuts ▪ pour a **beer** ▪ make **blinis** ▪ build a **bonfire** ▪ tie a **bow tie** ▪ bake **bread** ▪ play **bridge** ▪ soothe **burns** ▪ sew on a **button** ▪ keep **cacti** alive ▪ decorate a **cake** ▪ reverse a **caravan** ▪ **carve** meat ▪ uncork **champagne** ▪ play **chess** ▪ use **chopsticks** ▪ open a **coconut** ▪ **complain** effectively ▪ make **compost** ▪ give **CPR** ▪ dress a **crab** ▪ relieve **cramp** ▪ follow **cricket** ▪ learn to **crochet** ▪ win at **croquet** ▪ do **cross-stitch** ▪ work out cryptic **crosswords** ▪ use **crutches** ▪ cook a **curry** ▪ dress a **cut** ▪ weave a **daisy chain** ▪ **darn** a sock ▪ impress on a **date** ▪ groom a **dog** ▪ **draw** a face ▪ interpret **dreams** ▪ build a **drystone** wall ▪ **dye** clothes ▪ calculate the date of **Easter** ▪ use **eBay** ▪ observe an **eclipse** safely ▪ separate an **egg** ■ do **embroidery** ■ **exfoliate** skin ■ shape **eyebrows** ■ **face-paint** a child ■ draw up a **family tree** ■ fly a **flag** ■ get a **flight** upgrade ■ kick a **football** ■ throw a **frisbee** ■ thaw out **frozen pipes** ■ cut **fuel** **consumption** ■ make **garnishes** ■ deal with a **gas leak** ■ look after **goldfish** ■ get to grips with **golf** ■ make great **gravy** ■ tune a **guitar** ■ clear **gutters** ■ cure a **hangover** ■ make a paper **hat** ■ deal with a **heart attack** ■ perform the **Heimlich manoeuvre** ■ stop **hiccups** ■ walk in **high heels** ■ hop the **hopscotch** ■ ride a **horse** ■ protect your **identity** ■ soothe **indigestion** ■ make a mark in an **interview** ■ send an **invitation** ■ unfreeze an **iPod** ■ make **jam** ■ remove lids from **jars** ■ beat **jet-lag** ■ do the **jive** ■ tell a **joke** ■ master **judo** moves ■ learn to **juggle** ■ prepare **kebabs** ■ fly a **kite** ■ get **knitting** ■ sharpen **knives** ■ tie **knots** ■ choose **lamb** cuts ■ lay a **lawn** ■ compose a **limerick** ■ apply **lipstick** ■ design a **logo** ■ do the **Macarena** ■ perform **magic tricks** ■ peel a **mango** ■ play **marbles** ■ make great **mash** ■ give a **massage** ■ choose a **mattress** ■ chair a **meeting** ■ treat **migraines** ■ win at **Monopoly** ■ create a **mosaic** ■ grow **mustard and cress** ■ paint **nails** ■ remember **names** ■ fold a **napkin** ■ thread a **needle** ■ stop a **nosebleed** ■ follow the **offside rule** ■ make an **omelette** ■ appreciate **opera** ■ care for **orchids** ■ open an **oyster** ■ fold a **paper plane** ▪ **park** a car ▪ choose a **password** ▪ lay garden **paving** ▪ take good **photos** ▪ play a **piano** tune ▪ learn **Pilates** ▪ create a **podcast** ▪ play **poker** ▪ choose **pork** cuts ▪ grow **potatoes** ▪ make a **presentation** ▪ take a **pulse** ▪ carve a **pumpkin** ▪ get out of **quicksand** ▪ dance the **quickstep** ▪ **quilt** a cover ▪ run a **quiz night** ▪ hold a **rabbit** ▪ cook perfect **rice** ▪ build a **rocket** ▪ read **Roman numerals** ▪ climb a **rope ladder** ▪ grow **roses** ▪ place **roulette** bets ▪ **row** a boat ▪ build a **sandcastle** ▪ rescue **sauces** ▪ win at **Scrabble** ▪ learn **semaphore** ▪ build a **shelter** ▪ fold a **shirt** ▪ lace **shoes** ▪ prune **shrubs** ▪ **skim** stones ▪ get a good night's **sleep** ▪ improvise a **sling** ▪ stop **smoking** ▪ build a **snowman** ▪ dig **soil** ▪ bake a **soufflé** ▪ remove **stains** ▪ cook the perfect **steak** ▪ combat **stress** ▪ pack a **suitcase** ▪ lay a **table** ▪ do the **tango** ▪ make a proper cup of **tea** ▪ understand **teenagers** ▪ grow **tomatoes** ▪ sharpen **tools** ▪ learn to **type** ▪ repair an **umbrella** ▪ digitise old **videos** ▪ grow **vines** ▪ know your **vitamins** ▪ conserve **water** ▪ paint a **watercolour** ▪ build a **website** ▪ control **weeds** ▪ store **wine** ▪ **wrap** up a gift ▪ try the **xylophone** ▪ learn **yoga** positions ▪ perform **yo-yo** tricks ▪ make a **Yorkshire** pudding ▪ repair a **zip** ▪ recognise signs of the **zodiac**

... plus hundreds and hundreds of other essential, and less than essential, skills and solutions old and new.

CONTENTS

A-Z of just about anything 6-373

build Aerobic exercise into your life

Regular, energetic exercise will make you stronger, leaner, fitter and healthier. Not only that, it can boost your self-confidence and even help to stave off depression.

30 minute workout Allow at least 2 hours after a heavy meal before exercise. Start with a 'dynamic' warm-up, such as 5 minutes of light jogging on the spot, and finish with 5-10 minutes of gentle stretching (see below). Wear appropriate clothing and invest in a pair of trainers with good tread and cushioning. A park or other public space with steps or a slope is the ideal location for a simple workout divided into 5 minute segments (see below).

make Address labels on your PC

Address labels are a great time-saver if you have to send letters out to lots of people – for a charity mailshot, say, or if you're doing your Christmas cards. Using Microsoft software, all the work is done via a blank Word document. Open a document, then go to the **Mailings** tab. From the 'Create' group, click on **Labels**. Follow the instructions to create a list of addresses for printing.

The labels themselves come in many sizes, each with its own code number. Word lists the most commonly used brands and sizes to format your document to fit.

✷ golden rules

MAKE ADDRESS LABELS
- Compile a list of addresses in Word or Excel before you start.
- Save details of any labels that you might need again.
- Run off a test sheet on plain paper before you print on your expensive labels.

1 **Walk briskly,** gradually increasing the pace and starting to use your arms.

2 **Power-walk** at a fast pace, pumping your arms like pistons.

3 **On the spot,** do star jumps or skip with a rope.

4 **Jog or power-walk,** remembering to breathe deeply and evenly.

5 **Run or jog** up a flight of steps or up a slope.

6 **Walk at leisure** to cool down, shaking out your arms and shoulders.

FINISHING OFF Stretch gently, focusing on your leg muscles to avoid injury. Stretch gently and progressively, leaning into the stretch as you find it more comfortable: don't bounce.

calf stretch

groin stretch

hamstring stretch

Find your routine You don't need to join a gym to take up aerobics. Any brisk exercise will do the job, provided it demands extra work from your heart and lungs. Aerobic training exercises the body's large muscles in the limbs, buttocks and chest. You should feel warm, perspire and breathe heavily, but still be able to hold a conversation on the move.

Choose exercises you enjoy: swim, cycle, even dance to get the blood pumping. Badminton, tennis, squash, rowing, hiking with a backpack – all are aerobic. Vary your routine, walking one day and swimming the next, for example, to focus alternately on the lower and upper body. Just 20 minutes of high-intensity exercise three times a week, or a moderate 30 minute workout five times a week, can make a real difference to your fitness. Or try interval training – alternating short bursts of intense exercise with long, more gentle periods – for example, walk or jog for 90 seconds, sprint for 30. It's super-effective and fun.

get the measure of Alcohol units

The idea that 'a drink' – a glass of wine, a half of beer, a nip of spirit – equates to a unit of alcohol is a common misconception. A 'unit' is 10ml (8g) of pure alcohol. The proportion of pure alcohol in a drink is expressed as 'alcohol by volume' (ABV).

Avoid free-pouring (always measure what you serve) and get to know your ABVs to stay within safe limits (men, no more than 3-4 units a day, women 2-3 units). Remember, just as not all drinks are created equal, some people have lower alcohol tolerance than others: know your own limits.

To determine the units in a drink, use this equation.
Units = volume (ml) x ABV (%) ÷ 1,000

Drink	Volume	ABV%	Units
LOW-ALCOHOL BEER, LAGER, CIDER	330ml	2	0.7
BEER, LAGER, CIDER	330ml	4-6	1.3-2
STRONG BEER, LAGER, CIDER	330ml	9	3
SPIRITS	25ml	40	1
WINE, CHAMPAGNE (small)	125ml	12-14	1.5-1.75
WINE, CHAMPAGNE (standard)	175ml	12-14	2.1-2.5
WINE, CHAMPAGNE (large)	250ml	12-14	3-3.5
SHERRY, PORT	50ml	20	1

get through Airport check-in quickly

Follow these tips to beat the queues and speed your way from the check-in desk to the departure gate.

Before you leave home, check in online if you can. Most airlines open this facility 24 hours before departure and some allow you to print out your boarding pass, too.

As soon as you reach the airport, go to a self-service kiosk (if there is one) and pick up your boarding pass if need be. Queues are usually shorter than at the check-in desk.

Travel with hand luggage only to avoid the queues at baggage check-in. Be sure that your bag is small enough: most airlines specify a maximum 56 x 45 x 25cm, including handles, wheels and pockets, but check your airline's own specific rules. Make sure you're aware of and follow any restrictions on objects or liquids that aren't allowed in the cabin.

When you get to security, empty your pockets of all metal objects and put them in your bag or jacket before you reach the scanner. If you have a laptop, take it out of its bag so that it can be seen.

A

cope in an Allergic emergency

Someone has been stung by a bee or eaten a peanut, triggering an extreme allergic reation (anaphylaxis). They may struggle for breath, be unable to speak or swallow, have a swollen face or limb, a rapidly spreading flush or rash (hives), a tight chest, feel weak or even collapse into unconsciousness. What can you do to help them?

Quick action
- Call an ambulance; tell the controller what's happening.
- Have the casualty sit down, upright.
- Does the person carry an autoinjector of adrenaline? If so, find it and use it.
- If you see a bee stinger, draw it at once (*see* BEE-STING).
- If the patient becomes very pale and their pulse falters, lie them down with their knees raised above heart level. If they become unconscious and you can't perform cardiopulmonary resuscitation (*see* CPR), call for someone who can.

follow American football

Territory is the name of the game in American football. Both teams set out to invade the enemy's half, looking to take the ball to the touchline.

A game begins with one team kicking the ball, which is about the size and shape of a rugby ball, deep into the opposition's half of the pitch.

The opposing team collects the ball, and is then allowed four attempts (downs) to advance 10 yards or more up the field with the ball. Each down ends when a pass is missed, or when a player with the ball is stopped by the other team or goes out of bounds.

If the attacking side succeeds in their advance, they win four more downs. If they fail, the opposing team wins possession and goes on the offensive. So the match proceeds in a series of short set pieces, each of which is more like a rally in tennis than, say, the open play of football.

There are long pauses, because when a team switches from 'defense' to 'offense', or vice versa, it brings on a group of players that specialises in that role. Points are scored much as in rugby: a 'touchdown' in the opposing endzone is worth six points, and a field goal (drop kick between the posts) is worth three.

drop and set an Anchor

Don't be tempted to simply throw your anchor over the side of the boat and drop all the anchor chain at once: it might get tangled in the scope (the anchor line) or anchor and then not catch properly on the bottom.

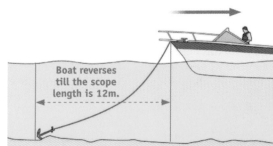

Boat reverses till the scope length is 12m.

3m

1 Approach where you want to anchor, facing into the wind. Estimate the depth of the water (3m in the example above), then pay out a length of scope equivalent to four times the depth for a chain anchor line and six times for a rope and chain combination. Secure the scope on the deck cleat.

2 Reverse the boat slowly or let it drift until you feel the anchor bite, then set it in place with a short burst of astern power. Allow a longer length of scope if the water is rough. Check that the scope is securely tied and hoist your anchor ball or use an anchor light to indicate you are at anchor.

identify Animal footprints

Wild animals leave a 'signature' behind them in sand, in snow, on wet soil or parched earth, as they walk, run, hop, scuttle and slither, and each one can be read when you know how. When studying an animal trail, think about what species are local to the terrain. In your own back garden that might be a fox, rabbit, mouse, vole or a tomcat on the prowl, while streams, forests, deserts, swamps, prairie, jungle, marsh and mountain will all yield different clues.

Within most landscapes there are wildlife hotspots in which many species congregate – near water, for example, or beneath a hedge. These provide rich pickings for the tracker, whether they are spotting out of curiosity or looking for signs that there are dangerous predators near by.

 DOGS, foxes and other canines leave triangular claw marks.

 CATS retract their claws when on the move.

Close to home, look for dog or cat prints. Dogs and cats walk on tiptoes, so only the central pad and the four toes leave an imprint. Many mysterious big-cat prints are traced back to dogs, who zigzag, while cats walk in a straight line. A fox track is like a dog's, but more compact, with the outer digits curving inwards. And while a dog will romp through mud, a fox will pick its way around the wet and dirt.

Hooved animals – horse, deer, sheep, cows and moose – also 'tiptoe'. Most recognisable is the print of a solid-hoofed horse, with its rounded fore hoof and more pointed hind. Cattle, like deer, are cloven-hoofed.

DEER are cloven-hooved and leave a distinctive print, like a heart split in two.

HORSE prints are deepest at the toe. They have heel bulbs and a triangular 'frog' in the centre of the sole.

A small print with four toes at the fore and five on the hind foot tells you that a rodent has passed by – a mouse, vole, chipmunk or squirrel, for example.

SQUIRREL

Rabbits' and hares' hind legs leave long, exaggerated prints, which, because of their leapfrog gait, appear in front of the front paws.

RABBIT

Count five toes on both front and (smaller) back feet, and you're on the trail of a raccoon (the prints look like tiny human hand and footprints), or a weasel or a member of its family – badger, mink, otter, skunk, beaver, opossum or even a bear. Unusually, an otter pad is almost round.

BADGERS have a large, kidney-shaped pad and visible claw marks.

BEAR prints are big, with significantly larger hind feet, and follow a drunken zigzag.

deal with Ants

If you find ants in your house, first follow the trail back to see if you can locate their nest. It's probably outside somewhere in soft or sandy soil, perhaps beneath some slabs.

Apply ant-killer to any large or busy holes. Boiling water poured repeatedly on the nest may also help to eliminate it.

Indoors, wipe up any ants you see with a soapy cloth; this will destroy the odour trails. Make sure your floors and surfaces are free of crumbs and other food debris.

Follow the ants back to their entry point into your house and seal it.

---

get rid of Aphids

Aphid infestations, which include greenfly and blackfly, build up quickly, so treat them fast.

If you garden organically, treat with pyrethrum insecticide, or try sprinkling leaves with wood ash or talc then hosing them down next day. You could also plant 'decoys', such as nasturtiums, nearby and plenty of flowers to attract ladybirds – aphids' natural predators.

The best synthetic treatments include deltamethrin and lambda-cyhalothrin – look for them in the ingredients list of pesticides in the garden centre. Thiacloprid is even more effective as it works systemically – that is, it spreads from where you spray it through the whole plant.

Always take care when applying chemical treatments and follow the instructions to the letter. Treat the undersides of leaves, where aphids cluster most densely.

correctly use an
Apostrophe

In written English, the apostrophe does two different, but equally important, jobs.

Missing letters An apostrophe can indicate that a word is a contracted form of a longer word or phrase: *don't* is short for *do not.*

Possession An apostrophe with an *s* indicates ownership: *the cat's whiskers.* The word *its* doesn't have an apostrophe in this case (*the cat twitched its whiskers*), though it does when *it's* is short for *it is.*

Plurals An apostrophe *s* is never used to denote plural nouns. If a noun is both plural and possessive then the apostrophe comes after the *s: both boys' bedroom.*

---

recognise the signs of
Appendicitis

If someone complains of severe abdominal pain, generally starting in the centre and moving to the lower-right side, often accompanied by nausea or a raised temperature, it could be a sign that the appendix – a small pouch attached to the large intestine – is inflamed.

Quick action

■ Make the person as comfortable as you can and offer a hot-water bottle to hold over the stomach. Give them a bowl if they are feeling sick.

■ Give no food, drink or medication, in case they need an anaesthetic.

■ If the pain persists or gets worse, or the person develops a high temperature, vomits or appears obviously ill, call an ambulance.

create Appliqué embellishments

Appliqué adds a personal touch to clothes and home furnishings. Devise your own patterns, trace simple shapes or use stencils.

YOU WILL NEED Fabric scraps (iron flat before you begin), template paper, tailor's chalk, medium-sized dressmaking scissors, embroidery scissors, needle, tacking cotton, thread, fusible web (for no-sew method), iron

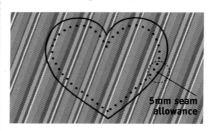

5mm seam allowance

1 Pin template to the correct side of appliqué fabric and mark a dotted line around it with chalk. Remove the template and mark a 5mm seam allowance outside dotted line. Use dressmaking scissors to cut out shape.

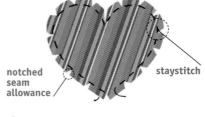

notched seam allowance

staystitch

2 Staystitch (*see* SEWING) just outside the inner seamline (dotted line) using 2mm stitches. Use embroidery scissors to snip V-shaped cuts into the seam allowance around curves and corners to make it easier to fold the fabric over.

REVERSE SIDE

Use tacking stitches to hold seam allowance.

3 Fold seam allowance back onto the wrong side along the seamline. Tack the folded edges as you go (*see* TACK).

No-sew method

1 Cut out a template without seam allowance. Place wrong side of fabric onto melting side of fusible web and iron together. Cut out the shape, iron gently paper-side up and peel off the paper.

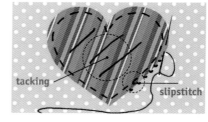

tacking

slipstitch

4 Pin shape to background fabric and secure with large tacking stitches. Secure round the edges with slipstitch (*see* SEWING) then remove the tacking.

2 Iron the appliqué (preferably over a damp cloth or from the wrong side) to fix in place. Stitch a zigzag or embroidery stitch around the edges for decoration and to prevent fraying.

win an Argument

In personal disagreements, as in total war, an all-out assault is rarely the winning strategy. Keep calm: if you lose your cool, you've lost the argument.

■ Avoid statements that are mere retrenchment (*That's rubbish!* or *How dare you say that to me?*). Instead, use words that invite the other party to let you have your say (*I think you've misunderstood what I said* or *Can I just explain why I did that?*).
■ However tempting it may be, don't resurrect old conflicts, and never make things personal (*You've never liked me, and you're just saying that because you're jealous.*). Stick to the matter in hand and the relevant facts.

cook globe Artichokes

YOU WILL NEED Large sharp knife, scissors, spoon, large stainless steel pan of boiling salted water, heatproof plate

1 Break the stalk and pull out any tough fibres. Then trim the base to allow the artichoke to sit flat.

2 Trim the spiny ends of the leaves with scissors, then use the knife to cut off the pointed top.

3 Plunge the artichokes into the boiling water, then use the heatproof plate to keep them submerged.

4 Simmer for 20-30 minutes, or until a central leaf can be pulled out easily.

5 Drain upside down so that the water runs out and allow the artichoke to cool a little.

6 Grasp the central cone and twist quickly to pull it out. Set the cone to one side.

7 Scoop out the fibrous 'choke' with the spoon, making sure it's all removed.

8 Replace the central leaf cone upside down in the centre, if you wish.

To serve
Globe artichokes make a simple, but impressive starter. They are tastiest served hot, with plain or herb butter, or cold with a vinaigrette or mayonnaise. The dressings can be spooned into the centre or set on the side for dipping the leaves in one by one.

set up a fresh water Aquarium

YOU WILL NEED Tank, gravel and rocks, water, dechlorinator, filter, lighting, water-testing kit

Clean the tank Use warm water and no detergent. Wash gravel and rocks under the tap until the water runs clear. Position the tank where it will not be in direct sunlight.

Set it up Put in 5-7cm of gravel for plants to root in. Three-quarters fill it with water and arrange plants and rocks in groups to make hideaway nooks. Install a filter where no plants will obstruct it. Top up with water that has been treated with a dechlorinator (water conditioner) or left for 24 hours to dechlorinate. Set up lighting and adjust the filter for a steady flow of bubbles.

Chemical balance Put your tank through a fishless cycle, when it will grow bacteria that remove the toxins created by fish metabolism, turning harmful ammonia into less toxic nitrites, then to much less toxic nitrates. Keep testing the water for ammonia and nitrites. Ammonia levels will rise then fall, as nitrites increase. When you get a zero reading for both, replace 50-75 per cent of the water to reduce excess nitrates.

Time for the fish Introduce just a couple of fish at first: float the bag they came in for 15 minutes, then gently release them into the tank.

recognise
Architectural styles
see pages 12-13

recognise Architectural styles

Buildings have changed greatly in appearance over the centuries, thanks to engineering progress, social demands and altering fashion. Here's a guide to recognising some of the most significant styles.

New and used A building's look isn't always a reliable guide to its age – architectural styles, like fashions in clothing, are subject to revival. Part of the interest lies in identifying the styles that have influenced a later building; the White House in Washington D.C., for example, borrows heavily from the classical era, while London's Houses of Parliament are a Gothic flight of fancy.

CLASSICAL AND RENAISSANCE
The architecture of ancient Greece and Rome was characterised by distinct 'orders', most recognisable by their style of column (below left). In the Renaissance age, architecture – like all the arts – strove to revive Greek and Roman principles. There was a new interest in classical proportions, and the five orders were re-introduced. These classical ideas were also applied to new, technically innovative features such as the tall dome (unknown to the Greeks), and architects such as Andrea Palladio (1508-80) took the idea of a columned classical temple and turned it into a façade – both ideas were copied by Christopher Wren (1632-1723) at St Paul's Cathedral in London.

TUSCAN (1) columns, introduced by the Romans, resemble the Greek Doric but are even simpler in style, with an unfluted shaft.

DORIC (2) columns generally have a simple head or 'capital'. On the long frieze above the columns are oblong blocks with vertical grooves (triglyphs).

IONIC (3) can be recognised by the scrolling on the capital, like a blanket rolled up from both ends

CORINTHIAN (4) columns have capitals that are carved to represent the bushy appearance of the acanthus plant.

1   2   3   4   5

COMPOSITE (5) The Romans combined Ionic scrolling with Corinthian acanthus leaves to create a new ornate style.

ROMANESQUE AND GOTHIC Architecture in the Middle Ages (the period between the end of the Roman Empire and the Renaissance) is best assessed by looking at windows. If a cathedral, for example, has small windows with a rounded top, set in thick walls – a continuation from Roman architecture – it's built in the Romanesque style. Such windows were the first experiments in getting light into heavy buildings without compromising their structural integrity.

Romanesque leads seamlessly into Gothic. The earliest true Gothic windows are pointed at the top like the prow of a ship. This simple shape was later elaborated upon to create large windows that incorporate tracery of great complexity and beauty – like delicate lace wrought in stone and glass. This same airy delicacy is found in other aspects of High Gothic buildings: high roofs, and elegant buttresses, like external ribs – as if the building had been pared back to its skeleton.

Gothic forms were revived in the 18th-19th centuries, particularly in public buildings such as museums and churches. This Neo-Gothic style began in Britain and spread across the world.

ROMANESQUE: Old Cathedral, Salamanca, Spain

NEO-GOTHIC: Pitt Rivers Museum, Oxford

HIGH GOTHIC: Amiens Cathedral, France

BAROQUE AND ROCOCO The simple classical lines of Renaissance architecture gradually gave way to a style that was more theatrical, sumptuous and decorative. This style is known as baroque and culminated in the frivolous and light-hearted rococo style. The first buildings in the baroque style were commissioned by the Catholic Church in late 16th-century Italy, but the style gradually travelled throughout Europe and was used in secular as well as religious buildings, including the great Palace of Versailles outside Paris. The Frauenkirche in Dresden, Germany (left), is a fine example of the late baroque period. It was built in 1726, destroyed by Allied bombing in 1945, and then rebuilt and reopened in 2005.

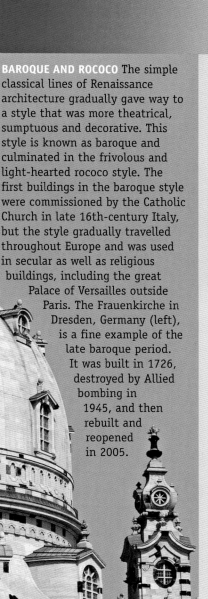

ART NOUVEAU: Elaborate doorway, Spain

ART NOUVEAU Architecture in the art nouveau style came to the fore around the turn of the 20th century. Its most noticeable feature is a playful obsession with stylised plant forms, both inside and outside a building. It might take the form of a wrought iron balcony made to look like tangled ivy, or a sinuous staircase and balustrade, lettering that's curled like roots or fronds, or walls with organic curves, as if they had grown out of the earth rather than been built to a plan. The Spanish architect Antoni Gaudi (1852-1926) filled Barcelona with such buildings, including his unfinished cathedral, the Sagrada Familia.

ART DECO The art deco style, which originated in the 1920s directly after art nouveau, is a kind of opposite: its defining characteristics are streamlined, mechanical shapes and strictly geometric patterns (think of New York's Empire State Building). Art deco buildings also feature unashamedly industrial materials such as gleaming chrome, polished enamel and expanses of glass.

ART DECO: Miami Beach, USA

prepare and cook
Asparagus

Preparation Cut or break off any woody ends – they'll snap when you bend the spears – and trim. For white or thick-stemmed green asparagus, scrape off the skin with a small sharp knife, working downwards from the tip.

Cooking Stand spears upright in an asparagus steamer and cook for 10-15 minutes in enough salted water to come halfway up their length; the stems will boil while the tips steam. Asparagus can be boiled, but take care not to overcook it.

■ If you don't have a purpose-made asparagus steamer, tie spears into a bundle and stand in a deep saucepan; wedge them upright with new potatoes. Make a dome of foil over the top of the pan to seal it.

prevent
Athlete's foot

Wash feet daily and dry well, particularly between the toes – this is a fungal infection that thrives in damp. Use talcum powder to reduce perspiration, and put cotton wool between toes at night.

Put on clean socks (cotton is best), tights or stockings twice a day and only when your feet are dry.

In changing rooms or showers, wear plastic shoes or flip-flops.

If you get athlete's foot treat it with an over-the-counter remedy from your pharmacist. Apply to the rash and 5cm of healthy skin around it. Continue for a week or two after symptoms have disappeared. In severe cases, consult a doctor.

deal with an Asthma attack

Asthma can be alarming to witness, but if you keep your cool you can help a sufferer get through it – and you might even save a life.

Quick action
If a person you're with becomes breathless, wheezy and distressed, keep calm and follow this procedure.

■ In calm tones, ask if they are having a panic attack, or have been diagnosed with asthma.
■ If they are asthmatic, encourage them to sit up, leaning slightly forward with a straight back and to take slow, steady breaths.
■ Ask if they have a reliever inhaler (normally blue). Help them to take two to four puffs, talking them through what you're doing, and preparing them to take the medication down into their lungs. Wait a few minutes before giving any more puffs of the inhaler.

■ It could be 10 minutes before the medication takes effect. If, after that time, there's no improvement or if the patient is turning blue, call the emergency services. Stay with the person, remaining calm and continuing to offer support.
■ Even if the inhaler has so far not appeared to work, continue to give puffs at 2 to 5 minute intervals. This should prevent a worsening of symptoms, speed the process of control, and give a comforting sense that something is being done.
■ If the sufferer has no inhaler, ask if anybody present has one. If not, or if this is a first attack, call an ambulance straight away. A cup of strong coffee has been shown to help as an emergency measure.

survive a snow Avalanche

If you're going to an avalanche zone, consider hiring or buying an avalanche transceiver (available online). Worn inside your clothing, it transmits a signal that can be tracked.

As soon as you stop moving, tuck your head into the crook of your arm, to create an air pocket in the snow.

Try 'swimming' to stay near the surface as you're carried along.

■ In the first moments of being involved in an avalanche, shout as loud as you can to let others know you're in trouble. Try anything, like running or rolling to get off the moving snow. If this doesn't work, brace for impact.
■ When the avalanche hits, fight to stay at the surface: 'swimming' motions sometimes help. As the

drift slows, before the snow hardens, put your face in the crook of your arm to make an air pocket.
■ Stay calm and control your breathing to conserve oxygen while you wait for help. Shout only if you hear someone close by.

keep a safe Back-up on your PC

The Windows operating system comes with an automatic back-up facility. You can specify variables such as which files you want to back up, where you want to store the files, and how often you want to run the program.

■ To set up, click on **Start**, type 'back-up' in the **Search** box, and click on **Backup and Restore.** Then follow the steps outlined on-screen.
■ You can keep your back-ups in a partition of your computer's hard drive, but it's safer to back up to a separate device, such as an external hard drive. That way, you don't lose your files if your computer gets lost or broken beyond repair.
■ For a small monthly fee you can back up your files to a secure online server (type 'online back-up' into a search engine).
■ A crude way to make back-ups is simply to drag and copy all vital files to a new folder on an external hard disk (include the date of the back-up in the folder's name). Just remember: any back-up is better than none at all.

pack a Backpack

When you pack a backpack you should have two aims in mind: to allow easy access to the stuff you need frequently or urgently, and to make sure the load isn't hard to carry.

Nothing should protrude from your rucksack into your back: the corner of a badly packed book can soon become excruciating on a long trek. Keep the weight evenly balanced: don't carry two litres of water in a side pocket. If you'll be on flat terrain, stash the weight near the top, so you can easily shift it over your centre of gravity by leaning slightly forward.

Make sure that things that belong together – such as hat and gloves – stay together in your backpack. Clothes should be wrapped tightly inside a heavy-duty rubbish bag, like the ones used for rubble on building sites.

Remove any excess packaging from your food supplies before you pack them.

If you're going on an overnight trek, put the things that you need at the end of the day – your tent and your sleeping bag – at the bottom of your backpack.

Waterproofs, snacks and first-aid kit should be near the top or in one of the side pockets.

Keep the heaviest items in your pack close to your spine.

■ Light
■ Heavy
■ Medium

master the rules of Backgammon

This game for two people is played on a board divided into 24 points, with a six point 'home' section for each player and a middle bar. Each player has 15 stones (see below), which are moved from point to point on the roll of two dice.

black moves clockwise
white moves anti-clockwise

white point 12
black point 13

white point 1
black point 24

BLACK HOME

WHITE HOME

white point 13
black point 12

white point 24
black point 1

The object is to move all 15 stones to your home, then 'bear them off' by rolling the number of the point on which a stone resides.
■ The dice scores can be used to move two separate stones, or combined to move one.
■ Two identical scores are doubled to allow four moves, separately or in any combination.
■ A point occupied by two or more stones of the same colour is blocked to the other player.
■ If your opponent lands on a point occupied by only one of your stones, your stone is moved to the bar. To re-enter it, use a later die roll to move the stone to whichever point in your opponent's home is indicated.

B

banish
Bad breath

■ As a quick fix, swill water around the mouth, spit it out, then drink a glassful.

■ Fresh parsley, cardamom and anise seeds also sweeten breath, but oral hygiene is the key.

■ Brush your teeth for a minimum of 2 minutes, at least twice a day, with a small, soft toothbrush and use a separate toothbrush or scraper for your tongue. Floss daily and see your dentist every six months.

deliver
Bad news

It's never easy to deal a verbal body blow, but sensitivity helps. Choose somewhere quiet and private.

Sit eye-to-eye with a person and give them a gentle warning to brace them: 'I'm sorry to have to tell you', 'I've just heard from the hospital', 'You know that John hasn't been well' …

Empathise with their reaction: 'I know this is hurtful', 'I realise this is a terrible shock' …

Let them cry if they want, let them say what they want, and listen to them.

Offer any help you're willing to give – and deliver on your promise, if it's accepted.

look after a
Baby
see pages 18-19

learn the basics of Badminton

This indoor court game is played by two or four people with rackets and a light feathered projectile called a shuttlecock. The speed of the shuttlecock and its swift deceleration give the game its character.

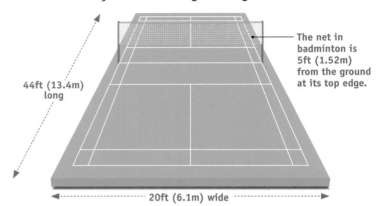

44ft (13.4m) long

The net in badminton is 5ft (1.52m) from the ground at its top edge.

20ft (6.1m) wide

Play begins with the server hitting the shuttlecock diagonally over the net towards the receiver. The players or pairs then take it in turns to hit the shuttlecock over the net.

A point is won by grounding the shuttlecock within the court on your opponent's side of the net, or by forcing your opponent to hit the shuttlecock into the net or out of the court entirely. The winner of the rally becomes the server for the next point.

To win a game a player or pair must reach 21 points. If the score reaches 20-all the game continues until either a two point lead is established or one side reaches 30 points. Matches are generally the best of three games.

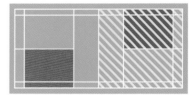

doubles

singles

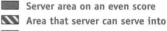

Server area on an even score
Area that server can serve into
Area of play after service

cook the perfect Baked potato

To enjoy that delicious combination of snowy white flesh encased in a crispy jacket, choose good-sized potatoes of a variety such as Desiree, King Edward or Maris Piper with a fluffy but firm texture. Scrub, wash, dry and prick all over with a fork then rub with a little olive oil, followed by some sea salt if you wish. Heat the oven to 200°C/gas 6, place the potatoes directly onto the shelf and cook for 1¼-1½ hours or until the outside is crisp and brown and the whole gives a little when squeezed. Split open and serve with anything from butter to prawn mayonnaise or chilli.

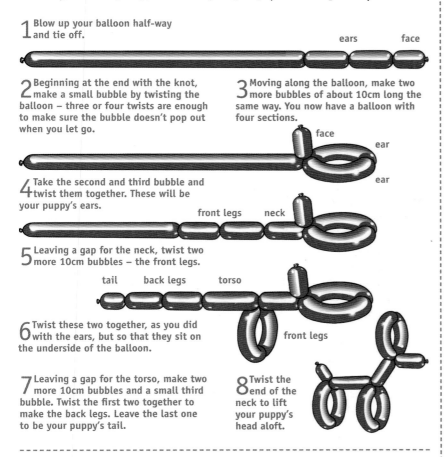

make a Balloon animal

In the world of balloon twisting, the puppy dog is the lowest form of life (with the possible exception of the balloon worm), and so the easiest for a beginner to make.

YOU WILL NEED Modelling balloons (regular length and thickness, known as 260s), balloon pump, or else bicycle pump (either is optional)

1 Blow up your balloon half-way and tie off.

ears   face

2 Beginning at the end with the knot, make a small bubble by twisting the balloon – three or four twists are enough to make sure the bubble doesn't pop out when you let go.

3 Moving along the balloon, make two more bubbles of about 10cm long the same way. You now have a balloon with four sections.

face
ear
ear

4 Take the second and third bubble and twist them together. These will be your puppy's ears.

front legs   neck

5 Leaving a gap for the neck, twist two more 10cm bubbles – the front legs.

tail   back legs   torso

front legs

6 Twist these two together, as you did with the ears, but so that they sit on the underside of the balloon.

7 Leaving a gap for the torso, make two more 10cm bubbles and a small third bubble. Twist the first two together to make the back legs. Leave the last one to be your puppy's tail.

8 Twist the end of the neck to lift your puppy's head aloft.

---

throw and catch a Ball

To throw a ball hard, take a run of six or seven paces, and turn your upper body away from the target as your throwing arm swings back. As your arm comes forwards, twist your body with it so that all your weight and momentum is behind the throw.

To maximise your chance of catching a ball that's heading your way, you should cup the hands, with fingers splayed and pointing slightly towards the ground. Watch the ball approach; keep the hands relaxed or else the ball will bounce out of your palms. Give with the ball as it enters your grasp, and close your fingers firmly around it.

B

appreciate Ballet

Ballet is pure poetry in motion, a means of using dance as narrative and to express powerful emotions. It helps to have a little background understanding to get the most out of it.

Know the plot For your first ballet choose one that tells a popular tale – *The Sleeping Beauty*, say, or *Cinderella* – so you can follow the story. Buy a CD and listen to the music, to enjoy the thrill of anticipation beforehand – and recognition on the night.

Learn about the dancers Read up about the people who'll be dancing for you – especially the principals – to understand the hard work and devotion that lies behind each of their performances.

Recognise the moves Learn about the complex and beautiful moves from which classical ballet is wrought. Look out first for the slow, enfolding movements of *adagio*, which might include a graceful *arabesque* (one leg supports the body while the other extends behind) or a *fondu* (a slow melting movement in which the supporting leg bends at the knee).

Then there's the speed and spirit of *allegro* – featuring dramatic steps of elevation such as *entrechat* (a jump into the air accompanied by a rapid crossing of the feet in front and behind) and *grand jeté* (a full leg splits in mid-air).

Enjoy the story Most importantly, allow yourself to appreciate the narrative flow of the ballet as the story is played out with such extraordinary skill and athleticism by the dancers.

B

look after a Baby

Whether you're a new parent, or a grandparent with a small baby for the first time since you had your own children, here are some hints to help you to enjoy your time together.

Keep it simple **Concentrate on meeting a baby's basic needs: feeding, comforting, sleeping and staying clean and dry. Anything beyond that is a bonus for you both. Be alert to dangers you wouldn't normally consider – even young babies can reach things that are small enough to swallow, or touch switches or sockets.**

WHY IS THE BABY CRYING?

Is the baby hungry, wet, soiled or tired? Do they have wind? If none of these is the matter, try a change of scene – go out for a stroll, put the baby in a sling and carry them as you go about the house – or take some time to play.

A routine can help to make sense of your baby's needs, even if you are feeding on demand. At around 6 months old, many babies follow a schedule similar to this:

6-7.00	Wake up, morning milk and breakfast.
9.00	Nap for up to 1 hour.
10-11.00	Mid-morning milk or snack.
12.00	Lunch followed by long nap.
2.30	Wake from nap, afternoon milk or snack.
4.00	Short afternoon nap.
5.00	Tea time.
6.00	Bath followed by bedtime milk.
7.00	Bed.
10.00	Some babies may still wake for a late-night milk feed.

SLEEP TIME FOR BABY Whether it's baby's bedtime, or they just need a nap, it's important that the conditions are right for a safe and peaceful slumber. A cot is the securest place for a small baby, so long as you follow the guidelines below. Avoid the temptation to doze off with a baby on a bed, sofa or armchair, as they may overheat or even be smothered.

1 Make sure a baby doesn't get too hot or too cold – a room temperature of around 18°C is best.

2 Dress a baby in light sleep clothing, place them on a firm, clean mattress covered in a single, fitted sheet and lay them down on their back, not on their front or side. Keep toys and teddies out of the sleep area.

3 If you need to cover a baby, use a lightweight blanket, not a duvet or quilt. Never use pillows, and keep the head uncovered. Place the baby's feet close to the foot of the cot so they can't wriggle under the cover, which should reach no higher than their chest and be tucked in securely under the sides and end of the mattress.

FEEDING Choose a calm place, without too many distractions for the baby.

Sterilising a bottle

Wash, rinse and then sterilise bottle and teat before use. Use one of the following sterilising methods.

- Use a steam steriliser: in the microwave or the plug-in variety.
- Boil in water for 10 minutes. Bottles must be fully submerged with no air bubbles inside. Cover the pan and leave the bottles in the water until you need one.
- Dissolve a sterilising tablet or mix concentrate in a tub of cold water. Submerge the bottles and leave for at least 30 minutes. Rinse with cool, boiled water before use.

Making up a bottle of formula

Allow time for boiled water to cool or make up bottles of water in advance, ready to add the powder.

1 Wash your hands. Boil a kettle of fresh water (filled from the cold tap), not water that has already been boiled, as minerals within it will be more concentrated. Let the water cool before measuring into the bottle.

2 Add scoops of formula to the water. Follow instructions on the packet, filling and levelling the scoop for accurate measurements. Shake well to combine. Use within 1 hour and discard any left over.

To warm a bottle, stand it in a jug of hot water. Never use a microwave, as this can leave dangerous 'hot spots' in the milk, even after a shake. Keep shaking and checking the milk until it's at a comfortable temperature. Never give milk to a baby without checking that it isn't too hot.

NAPPY CHANGING Always change a soiled nappy promptly. Get into the habit of changing wet nappies before or after each feed, to ensure that they are changed frequently enough to avoid nappy rash.

YOU WILL NEED Changing mat, nappy sack for soiled nappy, cotton wool and warm water or baby wipes, possibly a towel, clean nappy, nappy rash cream (if necessary)

BATHTIME Bath a baby at a time when you're both relaxed.

1 Run about 10cm water to a comfortable temperature. Soap or lotion isn't needed but can be used if a baby is more than six weeks old.

2 Undress a baby except for the nappy and wrap them in a towel while you wash the face, ears and neck with warm water and a flannel or cotton wool.

3 Remove the nappy and clean the baby's bottom.

4 Put your arm around the baby's back, holding the arm that's farther from you. Use your other hand to support the legs and buttocks as you sit the baby in the bath.

Choose a warm, safe and comfortable place: a table, the bed or on the floor. Use a changing mat to cushion the surface and to keep it clean.

1 Wash hands and gather everything you will need. Never leave a baby unattended on a table while you turn to reach for something.

2 Remove the soiled nappy and place it in a nappy sack. Clean the baby's bottom with cotton wool dipped in a bowl of warm water or with a baby wipe. Use a fresh cotton wool ball for each wipe. Always wipe a girl from front to back and clean thoroughly around a boy's testicles. Don't try to pull back a boy's foreskin, as you could damage it or make it sore.

3 Pat dry with a towel if necessary and apply cream to any areas that look red or sore. Then put on the fresh nappy, wash your hands to clean away germs and dress the baby.

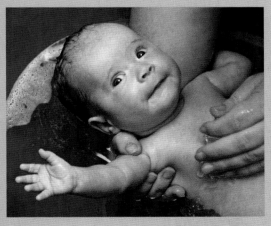

5 Keep your arm around the head and shoulders as you wash the body, rolling the baby onto their chest as you wash the back.

6 Lift the baby out, using both hands to support the body and buttocks then wrap in a soft towel and dry carefully, with attention to the skin folds.

light a
Barbecue

Don't spoil a good afternoon in the garden by fighting a pitched battle with the barbecue.

- Set up in a sheltered corner, and instead of using smelly lighter fuels, try laying scraps of lightweight cardboard (torn-up cereal boxes, for example) under and poking through the charcoal, where you can light them.
- An empty plastic squeezy bottle will do the job of bellows to fan the flames until they take hold.
- A charcoal chimney – a metal cylinder with holes around the base, which you place on the grill – is a smart buy for easy lighting. Crumple some newspaper and push it loosely in, top up with charcoal then light the paper. In 20 minutes you can decant glowing coals onto the grill.

- Start cooking when the coals are covered with fine, pale ash.

apply a Bandage

Bandage selection is vital. You need to be aware of the different uses of different types of wrap, and make your choice accordingly.

The key points When applying a bandage:
- Make sure the person is comfortable and tell them what you're doing.
- Work from the side of the affected part, not reaching across the patient.
- If you're bandaging an arm or leg, leave fingers and toes exposed so you can tell if it's interfering with circulation. If fingers or toes are really cold, with a bluish tinge to the nail beds, or the patient complains of tingling, you need to loosen the wrap.
- A bandage should be applied firmly, not tightly. Remember that the affected part may swell after being bandaged, so the wrap may need to be loosened or retied.
- Elbows and knees should be bound in a slightly bent position, which is best to remain in once the bandage is on.
- Always keep bandages clean and dry.

Roller bandages These are long strips of cotton, gauze, elasticated fabric or linen, and are used to secure dressings and support injured limbs. There are three types of roller bandage:
- Bandages made of open-weave material, which allow air to get through but don't put pressure on wounds and don't support joints.
- Elasticated bandages, which mould to the contours of the body and are used to secure dressings and support soft tissue injuries such as sprains.
- Bandages made of crepe, which are used to support injured joints.

The two most common bandaging techniques for roller bandages are the spiral and the figure-of-eight.

Spiral technique The spiral is used to wrap cylindrical parts of the body such as the lower leg and forearm.

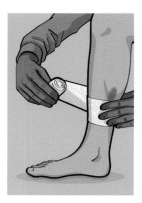 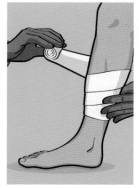 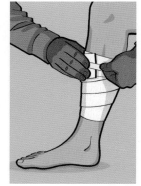

1 Start below the wound and apply one or two firm turns directly around the limb.

2 Wind the bandage around and around in a spiral, with each turn overlapping the last by a half to three-quarters.

3 Make a straight turn and fix the end with a safety pin or sticky tape.

Figure-of-eight technique This method is used to apply bandages to large joints such as elbows and knees (to hold a dressing in place on a wound or to support a sprain or strain).

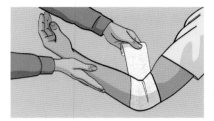

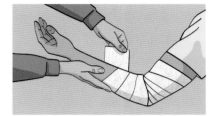

1 Flex the joint slightly. Place the end on the inside of the joint and, working away from the body, make two straight turns to hold it in place.

2 Make alternate figure-of-eight turns above and below the joint, each turn to overlap the previous one by about two-thirds.

3 Extend the bandage quite far on each side of the joint. Make a last straight full turn over the preceding one, fold in the end and fix with a safety pin or sticky tape.

Tubular bandages These are seamless tubes of fabric, which come in different sizes and types for different parts of the body. Elasticated ones can be used to support joints such as the ankle. Ones made of gauze are used to hold dressings on fingers or toes. Smaller tubular bandages are best put on using a specially designed applicator.

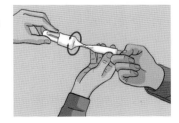

Triangular bandages These are normal bandages that come folded into a triangle shape. They can be used as large dressings, as slings to support a limb (see SLING) or to secure a dressing in place. You can also use a household item such as a scarf to make a triangular bandage.

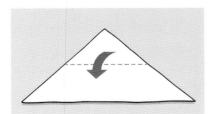

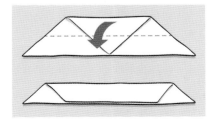

1 Before using a triangular bandage as a dressing – or to secure a dressing – fold it so that the point of the triangle touches the middle of the long edge.

2 Then fold it in half again in the same direction to make a broad strip. You can now use the spiral technique to secure the strip in place.

---

get to grips with
Baseball

The national sport of the USA is an absorbing spectacle with simple origins. Baseball evolved from the old English bat and ball game of rounders (*see* ROUNDERS) – and in all essentials it remains true to the original's 'hit and run' formula.

Baseball is played on a field, within which there's a large square or 'diamond' marked out with a 'home plate' on one corner – and a 'base' on each of the others known as 'first', 'second' and 'third'. Two teams of nine players take turns to bat and to field.

■ A pitcher in the centre of the diamond throws the ball to the hitter, standing on the home plate.
■ The hitter aims to strike the ball and run as far around the diamond as they can before the ball is fielded.
■ The hitter is 'out' if the ball is caught or if it's thrown to a fielder on the base to which the hitter is running before they can get there.
■ Hitters can choose to wait at first, second or third base if they cannot make it to the next base before the ball is fielded.
■ A second hitter then comes up to face the pitcher. Previous hitters waiting on any base can continue their run if the new player 'at the plate' hits the ball.
■ A hitter who makes it all the way around the diamond back to the home plate scores a point, and the team with the most points after nine innings wins.

It's a game of skill and strategy: fielders must be well positioned, the pitcher must induce the hitter to miss and the hitter must strike the ball in a way that maximises their opportunity to run.

reseal a Bath

There are various ways to seal a bath or shower. The one that looks best and works for most bathrooms involves squirting sealant from a 'gun'. For this 'gun' method, you need a cartridge of silicone sealant and the gun applicator.

1 First make sure that all surfaces are clean and dry, and that you've removed all the old sealant: this is best done with a flexible razor blade and, if necessary, silicone sealant remover, also sold in cartridges. Run a strip of masking tape along the wall and the rim of the bath or shower to make a gap that corresponds to the space where you want the sealant to go.

2 Apply the sealant carefully, according to the instructions on the tube. The key thing is to lay a straight, consistent bead along the middle of the gap.

3 Wet a finger and run it along the line of sealant, so as to smooth it into the gap and create a neat, concave join between the wall and the rim of the bath or shower.

4 Remove the masking tape right away, while the sealant is still wet, to make a straight edge. Any sealant that has ended up in an unwanted area can be removed with a razor blade – but wait until it's completely dry.

follow a game of Basketball

A professional basketball match is an all-action ding-dong affair in which two teams of five giant physical specimens hurl themselves – and a ball – from one basket to another at breakneck speed.

The aim of basketball is to score points by throwing the ball into the opposing team's basket. Two or three points are awarded for a basket, depending on the distance from which the shot was taken. Matches are played on a court that's just 28m long – traversable in a few seconds. So points can be scored moments apart at opposing ends, and often are. The swift and constant ratcheting-up of the score is part of the game's appeal.

Rules If the design of the court tends to make the game fast-moving, then so do the rules. The game is based on five enduring principles: a light ball that's easy to bounce and throw; a 'goal' (originally a half-bushel peach basket) fixed above head height (one reason why taller players are at an advantage); no running while holding the ball; no blocking opposing players' access to the ball; no personal contact. In addition to these rules, the modern game has regulations stating that a team gaining possession must take it into the opposing half within 10 seconds, and shoot within 30. It all adds up to an end-to-end battle of the behemoths.

stay safe in the Bathroom

With water and hard surfaces, the bathroom can be a danger zone. Follow these simple tips to avoid accidents and injury.

Water safety Slipping is the most likely hazard when your feet or the floor are wet, so always take care when getting into or out of the bath.
■ Use a bathmat if your floor is a hard surface that could be slippery.
■ Consider using a rubber suction mat or individual rubber patches inside the bath if yours doesn't have an in-built non-slip area.
■ Use the bath's grab rails, if it has them, to help you when getting out.

Children in the bathroom Never allow young children to play in the bathroom – it's neither safe nor hygienic.
■ Always run the cold water into the bath before the hot, in case a child gets in or falls in before the bath is ready. This ensures that they will not get scalded by too-hot water.
■ A thermostatic mixer tap allows you to set your desired temperature and you must then use a button if you want to override this with hotter water.
■ Always store medicines and cleaning fluids out of reach, preferably in a locked cupboard.
■ Remove the door lock or reposition it out of your child's reach.

Electrical safety Only use electrical equipment designed for use in a bathroom, and plug only into special shaver sockets. You must never attempt any wiring yourself in a bathroom.

make Batteries last

It's frustrating when a battery dies while you're using something or when you try to turn it on. And if your torch's batteries are dead just when you need it, it can even compromise your safety. There are things you can do to maximise battery life and avoid disappointment or inconvenience.

- Always buy your batteries from outlets that have a high turnover, to assure the best chance that they have been recently manufactured.
- Don't be tempted to buy a large consignment of batteries to keep in storage – they can degrade over time. Just keep a few of each type and replace your spares as you use them.
- If you have a battery-operated device (a camera, for example) that you don't plan to use for some time, take the batteries out and store them in a zip-up plastic bag, in a dry place at room temperature, until you need to reinsert them.
- If you have a device that runs both on batteries and mains power, take the batteries out and store them, as above, while you're using the mains electricity.
- Don't let batteries touch anything metal while they are in storage, as this can drain their power.
- Don't keep any battery-operated device in too warm a place, as this will reduce performance.
- Never mix new and used batteries.
- If you use rechargeable batteries, don't mix different mAh (milliampere-hour) ratings. This indicates how long the battery will last on one charge.

- -

create a simple Bead necklace

Mastering beadwork is a great way of restringing old – even heirloom – beads into attractive modern pieces. Specialist bead shops or websites will sell all the items you need.

YOU WILL NEED **Beads, piece of folded card, thread (the thickest that will fit, folded twice, through the beads), beeswax, clasp or fastening, glue (optional), beading needle, tweezers or small pliers**

Preparing beads and thread Decide how long the necklace will be, allowing at least 38cm for a choker. If you're using large or oddly shaped beads leave 13cm free at the back of the neck for comfort. Cut a piece of thread six times the intended length of the necklace, rub it in beeswax and then double it over.

Assemble your chosen beads in order in the groove of a piece of folded card.

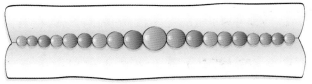

continued overleaf ➜

sink those Battleships

In this pencil-and-paper game of guesswork and deduction for two players, you're admiral of a fleet comprising a battleship, two cruisers, three destroyers and four submarines. Your opponent commands an identical fleet.

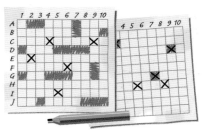

NUMBER OF SQUARES: battleship = 4, cruiser = 3, destroyer = 2, submarine = 1

How to play Each player draws up two 'ocean grids', marked with figures 1 to 10 along the top and letters A to J down the side. Screen one of your grids from your enemy and position your ships by shading the correct number of adjacent squares in straight lines horizontally or vertically, wherever you choose.

Take turns to shout out coordinates – for example, G9. If this square is occupied by part of a ship, you score a 'hit'; if it isn't, you have missed. Use your other grid to record your results and 'map' the formation of your opponent's fleet. When all of a vessel's squares are hit, it has sunk, and its admiral must reveal what sort of vessel it was. The winner is the first player to sink their opponent's entire fleet.

Strategy Space your ships well apart, as randomly as possible; avoid predictable patterns of play; if you score a hit, target the surrounding squares.

B

trim Beards and moustaches

The easiest way to neaten your beard is to use an electric trimmer. The adjustable attachment on the head of the trimmer allows you to cut your beard to a uniform length. If using a razor, make sure it's sharp. For moustaches in particular, it's also worth investing in a pair of professional barber's scissors.

For beards, pay close attention to the edges of your chosen beard style. Make sure they are sharp and that the end result is symmetrical. Shave daily to maintain definition.

For moustaches, dampen the hair slightly and comb it downwards with a fine-toothed comb. Use scissors to clip carefully and conservatively from the middle to the edge on each side in turn.

Beard styles A beard is a separate entity from a moustache or sideburns, but can be combined with either or both to create a range of styles. A goatee, for example, is a beard formed only with hair grown on the chin, while a circle beard (pictured) is a goatee joined to a moustache. When choosing a style, consider the shape and contours of your face, and the natural growth pattern of your facial hair.

Threading the necklace

1 Thread on one bead (A). Pass one end of the doubled thread through the ring of the clasp then back through the bead.

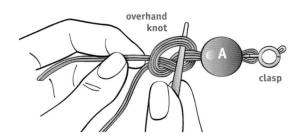

2 Make an overhand knot close to the bead and insert the threading needle into its main loop. Use the needle to guide the knot towards the bead, tightening as you remove it. Use the tweezers to hold the knot and pull the thread to compress the knot further. Leave just enough thread to pass through another bead and make another overhand knot.

3 Feed this shorter length of thread through the second bead (B) and tie a second overhand knot (as above). Cut the remainder of the short length of thread at this point, leaving only the doubled thread for further beads and knotting. Add a dab of glue, if you wish, to the knots to make them more secure.

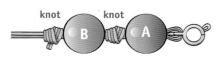

4 Keep threading beads, with an overhand knot between each and using the needle to tighten knots and beads.

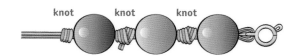

5 Continue until all the beads are in place except for the final two. Repeat steps 1, 2 and 3 with these beads and the other half of the clasp. Leave enough doubled thread at this end to pass back through the final beads and make the two knots. Cut off any spare thread, as before, at the final knot. **To leave some bare thread** at the back of the neck, you need to tie a knot an appropriate distance away from the clasp on both sides before threading the first bead.

- -

choose Beef cuts

There are dozens of cuts of beef for the cook to choose from. The key to success is selecting the right cut for the right dish.

■ The best cuts of beef tend to come from the parts of the animal that move the least – the hindquarters, ribs and forequarter. The toughest, which need long slow cooking, are the lower legs, shoulders, flank, neck and tail.
■ To be at its best, beef needs to be hung on the bone for three to four weeks. Inadequately hung beef will be bright red and shiny.
■ Some fat – which melts during cooking – is essential for a tender result.
■ Aberdeen Angus is the breed to select for superior quality. Hereford, Welsh Black, Scottish Highland, Shorthorn, Longhorn and Devon are also good.
■ Organic beef comes from steers free from treatment with antibiotics or hormones and fed only on organically certified grains and grasses.

Beef cuts

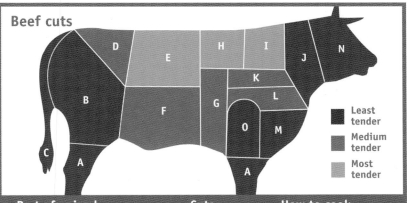

		Least tender
		Medium tender
		Most tender

Part of animal	Cuts	How to cook
LEG (A, O)	Shin Marrow bone	Stew or casserole Use for stock
HINDQUARTERS (B)	Top rump Braising steak Silverside Topside	Roast or braise Braise or stew Poach or braise Oven or pot roast
TAIL (C)	Oxtail	Stew
RUMP (D)	Rump roast Rump steak	Roast Grill or fry
SIRLOIN/WING RIB/FILLET (E)	Sirloin T-bone steak Wing rib Entrecôte steak Fillet Fillet mignon	Roast, grill or fry Grill or fry Roast, grill or fry Roast, grill or fry Roast, grill or fry Grill or fry
HINDQUARTER FLANK (F)	Flank Skirt	Poach or braise Poach or braise
FOREQUARTER FLANK (G)	Short ribs Flank steak	Roast Stew or braise
FORE RIB (H)	Fore rib	Roast, grill or fry
BACK OR TOP RIB (I)	Top rib	Roast, grill or fry
NECK (J)	Clod Neck	Stew, mince Stew, mince
CHUCK (K)	Chuck steak	Braise
TOP FORE LEG (L)	Braising steak	Braise, stew or mince
BRISKET (M)	Brisket	Poach
HEAD (N)	Cheek Tongue	Braise or stew Poach then press

make up a
Bed with sheets

Using high-quality sheets rather than a duvet adds a touch of luxury to your bedtime.

First, cover your mattress, ideally with a purpose-made cover (*see* MATTRESS).

Place the bottom sheet right side up with equal amounts of fabric hanging over the sides and with at least 30cm hanging over at the foot.
■ Tuck the bottom end firmly and neatly under the mattress from corner to corner. Do the same at the other end of the bed.
■ Standing at the foot of the bed, take hold of the sheet overhanging one side of the bed at a point 40cm along its edge away from the foot.
■ Use a finger on your other hand to press on the top corner of the mattress while pulling the edge of the sheet directly upwards. Then tuck in the small section of sheet still hanging beneath the level of the mattress nearest to the corner.
■ Place your finger back on the top corner of the mattress and lower the sheet back over the side of the bed. The sheet should now appear to drop at an angle of 45 degrees from the top corner of the mattress.
■ Tuck in the remaining fabric at the side of the bed and repeat for the remaining corners.

Add the top sheet so that when folded back its decorative edge is displayed, followed by blankets. Add pillows (see PILLOWS), with double covers, one utilitarian, the other chosen to match your bed linen. Allow two per sleeper. Cover with a bedspread, tucked under the pillow.

make Beef stock

MAKES 2 LITRES

1 tbsp sunflower oil
125g shin or clod of beef
1 onion, quartered
1 carrot, chopped
1 stick celery, chopped
2 litres water
2 bay leaves
2 sprigs each parsley and thyme
10 black peppercorns
½ tsp salt

Put oil in a large heavy-based pan and brown the beef over a high heat. Remove meat and set aside. Lower the heat, then brown the vegetables; add water and bring to the boil. Reintroduce the beef, skim off any scum, add the remaining ingredients then simmer for two hours. Strain, cool and skim off fat.

---

cope with a
Bee-sting

Bees can turn on us if we frighten them or get too close to their colony. The barbed lance of the bee's sting is torn off in the act of stinging. It remains stuck in the victim with a venom-filled sac and muscles that work the sting deeper into the flesh and increase the venom injected. A bee sting is fatal to the bee, and occasionally to the victim (*see* ALLERGIC EMERGENCY), though usually it's merely painful.

If stung, scrape the lance out using a sideways movement with your fingernail or other hard edge, such as a credit card. Never pull the sting out with tweezers, as this squeezes more poison into the skin. Minimise swelling with an antihistamine and rub with ice to quell the itch.

pour the perfect Beer

Beer is best enjoyed when poured into a glass. The foamy head releases the beer's hop aroma and retains its bitter taste.

Tilt a clean glass to an angle of 45 degrees, and begin to pour so that the beer strikes the glass in the middle of the slope. Keep the flow steady and even.

When the glass is half full, bring it upright and continue to pour into the centre of the glass. This will produce the foamy head, which should end up being about a finger's width for most beers.

---

deal with a swarm of Bees

It's an unnerving sight but a swarm of bees isn't usually a risk. Left alone, a swarm is harmless, but if you see one in your garden, keep well away, warn others to do so, and if the bees remain contact a beekeeper to move them to a new home. Beware of using noisy garden machinery close to a swarm, which will antagonise them. In the unlikely event of the swarm chasing you, stay calm and move out of the way slowly, best into the shade of a shed or tree. Don't swat at the bees, they will soon lose interest and leave you alone.

---

play Bingo at home

Bingo is a game of chance in which players hope to match a series of randomly selected numbers with those printed on their game card.

Getting started You need a set of 75 or 90 numbered bingo balls and some disposable bingo cards, each of which is made up of a grid of randomly selected numbers. One person is the caller, picking one ball at a time blindly out of a bag and calling out its number. To make it more fun, the caller should know – or learn – the traditional calls: 'Candy store – 74!' 'Was she worth it – 56!' When a number is called out, each player looks to find and mark off a match for it on their card. Depending on your preference, a player wins if they mark off all the numbers on one row of their grid (celebrating with a shout of 'line'), or on their entire card (a shout of 'house'). To raise the stakes a little, players can pay an agreed sum of money into a pot at the beginning of each round, which the winner can claim as their prize.

If no one wants to be caller there are websites that can do the job for you – though with less panache. Most of these sites also allow you to download and print bingo cards for free. Type 'online bingo caller' into a search engine.

build a Bird nesting box

YOU WILL NEED Plank of rough-sawn wood or untreated outdoor ply (15mm deep and sawn as shown below), drill, some nails, hammer, brass hinge or strip of rubber such as an old inner tube, catch

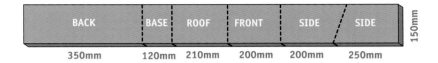

BACK	BASE	ROOF	FRONT	SIDE	SIDE	150mm
350mm	120mm	210mm	200mm	200mm	250mm	

1 Drill a few 10mm drainage holes in the base piece for the box.

2 Nail the sides to the base and then the back section to the sides.

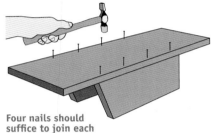

Four nails should suffice to join each side to the back.

3 Before you attach the front section, use a wide drill bit to create an entrance hole (see table below). The bottom of the hole must be positioned at least 125mm from the floor of the box so that young birds cannot fall out.

Line the nails up centrally with the section beneath.

A hinged lid allows you to open the box to clean it in autumn.

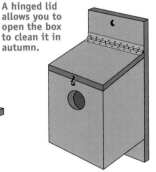

4 Nail on the front section, then attach the lid with a brass hinge, or a strip of inner tubing. Fix a catch to the front of the lid. The inside wall below the entrance hole should be rough, to help young birds clamber up and out.

5 Fix your box using a nylon bolt or wire. A piece of hose around the wire will prevent damage to the tree. The box should face between north and east and tilt down to protect it from direct sun and rain. Place the box high enough to escape the attention of cats.

The diameter of the entrance hole that you make depends on the kind of birds you want to attract.

Bluetits and coaltits	**25mm**
Great tits and tree sparrows	**28mm**
House sparrows and nuthatches	**32mm**
Starlings	**45mm**

An open front entrance is more suitable than a round hole for some birds. Here what matters is the distance of the opening from the bottom of the bird box.

Spotted flycatchers	**60mm**
Robins or pied wagtails	**100mm**
Wrens	**140mm**

---

get the knack of Blackjack

Fortunes are won and lost at this card game – but you can play at home just for fun.

Casino rules for blackjack vary. This is a simple version to be played with friends and family. However many players are at the table, blackjack is fundamentally a two-person game – you against the dealer, with the aim of gaining a hand totalling closer to 21, without going over ('busting').

Scoring Number cards are of face value. Aces can be one or 11. 'Face cards' (jack, queen, king) score 10.

Rules Each player is dealt two cards, face down; the dealer has one card turned up, the other down.
- If you're dealt an ace and a 10 or face card, you have a 'natural blackjack', an instant win – unless the dealer also has a natural, in which case there is a tie or 'push' between you and the dealer while all the other players lose.
- If nobody has a natural, each player in turn has the option to be dealt another card (a 'hit'), to stay with the cards they have (to 'stand') or to surrender if they bust.
- When all players have chosen to stand or surrender, the dealer reveals their face-down card. If they have a total of 16 or less, they must hit and as soon as they have 17 or more, they must stand. If the dealer busts, all players still in the game win. Otherwise, players with higher point totals than the dealer win.

---

maintain your
Bicycle
see pages 28-29

B

maintain your Bicycle

Your bicycle is a piece of machinery that needs to be looked after. Even if you don't ride often, there are some basic maintenance tasks that you should carry out regularly; and you'll inevitably have to do repairs and replace worn parts from time to time.

Stay safe It's crucial that all the working parts of your bike are kept in good order to minimise the chances of your brakes failing, tyres slipping or steering letting you down. Fortunately, most maintenance is simple enough that you can teach children to look after their own bikes.

TIGHTEN THE HEADSET (A)

If your handlebars are loose, you need to tighten the top bearing in the headset. On most modern bikes, with an A-head system, this is done by adjusting the top cap (sometimes under a dust cover) with an Allen key.

- Slacken the stem bolts and tighten the top cap until the looseness has gone, then retighten the stem bolts. On older bicycles and some children's cycles, you'll need spanners to make the adjustment.
- Slacken the headset locknut a little, then tighten the upper bearing cup until no 'play' is felt in the handlebars.
- Retighten the locknut and hold it securely with a spanner, then, using a second spanner, unscrew the bearing cup until it tightens against the locknut.

tightening an A-head system

ADJUST THE BRAKES (B)

The brake blocks should be positioned so that they are close to the wheel rims – but they shouldn't touch until the lever is applied, or the blocks will wear down and you'll find it harder to cycle. Minor adjustments can usually be made using the barrel adjuster at the end of the cable, either at the lever or brake mechanism.

- To tighten the cable further, use an Allen key to loosen the pinch bolt; pull the cable until you're happy with the adjustment and hold it while you retighten the bolt.

barrel adjuster

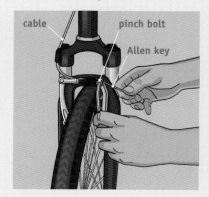

cable   pinch bolt

Allen key

BIKE MAINTENANCE CHECKLIST

A rickety bike is hard work to pedal and not safe to ride. Brakes and tyres are the main safety points to check, but every bit of your bike must be working well for you to really enjoy your ride.

Before each ride Check your tyre pressures, make sure that brakes and cables are working well and that any quick-release levers on wheels or saddle are tight.

After each ride Check tyres for any sharp stones or glass. Make sure you haven't buckled a wheel and clean off any mud.

Once a month Inspect the chain, looking for wear, any tight links or looseness. Lubricate the chain (see below). Check and lubricate brake levers, all cables and the derailleur gear mechanism. Look for wear on tyres. Check and tighten all bolts, particularly on the stem post, headset and cable mounts.

Every six months Inspect the bike thoroughly. Look for any damage on the frame or signs of rust. Check the seat post, handlebar stem, handlebars, chainrings, brake calipers and levers and make sure that all bearings (in the headset, hubs and pedals) are running smoothly.

MAINTAIN THE CHAIN (D)

Oil your chain once a month with bicycle oil. This is best done when the chain is clean: remove it using a chain tool, and then soak in white spirit, or use a cleaner that fits directly onto the chain. Chain cleaners are expensive, and not as effective as a long soak, but are quick and easy to use.

ADJUST THE GEARS (C)

Most road bikes have indexed derailleur gears that shift the chain to the next sprocket as you click the gear lever to the next number. Sometimes the mechanism gets out of synch, and the gears fail to engage correctly. The most common cause of this is a maladjusted cable, which just takes a roadside adjustment to fix.

barrel adjuster

■ The cable can be tightened or slackened using the barrel adjuster located at the point where the cable enters the rear derailleur.
■ If the derailleur isn't moving the chain far enough to engage the sprocket, turn anticlockwise.
■ If it's overshooting, turn the adjuster clockwise.
■ Test the gears after each adjustment and keep tweaking until they change smoothly.
■ If adjustments don't help, you could have bent the derailleur and may need a professional repair.

B

deal with Bleeding

Profuse bleeding can be fatal, so you need to act swiftly.

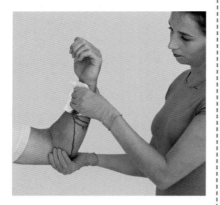

Call for an ambulance as soon as possible and be prepared to treat the patient for shock (*see* SHOCK).

Check the wound to see if there's an object embedded in it. Wear dispsosable gloves, if available.

If there isn't an object:
■ Press a dressing pad firmly against the wound.
■ If the wound is on an arm or leg, raise the limb above the head if possible – or above the level of the heart, if not – to slow blood flow to it. Take care if you think there might be a broken bone.
■ To minimise shock, lie the casualty on their back.
■ Secure the dressing with a bandage (*see* BANDAGE).
■ If blood seeps through, apply a second dressing and bandage.

If there's an object:
■ Apply pressure either side of it.
■ Raise an affected limb.
■ Lie the casualty down.
■ Cover the wound and object with a dressing, without applying pressure. Build up padding around the object until the padding is higher than the object, then bandage over the object without pressing on it.

measure a window for a Blind

A well-fitted blind – venetian or roller – blocks out light without taking up wall space on either side of the window, like curtains do.

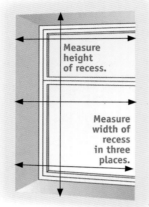

Measure height of recess.

Measure width of recess in three places.

Recessed blinds If your window has a deep recess, the blind can be fitted inside. Measure the width of the recess in three places, so that you know its narrowest point. Measure the height in the same way. When you buy your blind or have it made, the fixing should be the exact width of the narrowest point, so that it can be closed without obstruction, but cuts out light with maximum efficiency.

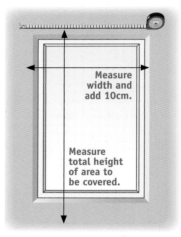

Measure width and add 10cm.

Measure total height of area to be covered.

Face-fixing blinds If there's no recess on your windows, measure the width in the same way, and add 10cm, so that the blind is 5cm wider than the window on both sides. Remember also that the blind will need to be positioned 5cm above the window too. If the window has wide mouldings, it will look better if you can tailor the blind to the exact dimensions of the mouldings.

- -

install a roller Blind

Before you begin, measure the window to determine what width your blind needs to be in order to fit properly (see above).

YOU WILL NEED **Measuring tape, junior hacksaw, long metal ruler, light pencil, scissors or trimming knife, spirit level, drill, wall plugs, screws, screwdriver**

Cutting a blind to fit Once you have established the required width of the blind, subtract the thickness of the brackets at either end to calculate how wide the roller needs to be.
■ Fully unwind the fabric and peel it away from the roller at one end. Remember that if the blind has a symmetrical pattern or shaped bottom edge, you may need to cut an equal amount off each side. Use a junior hacksaw to cut through the metal tube.
■ Use a long metal ruler and a light pencil to mark a cutting line the full

length of the fabric, 1.5mm in from the cut edge of the tube and trim off the unwanted material with a pair of scissors.

■ Use the hacksaw to cut the stiffening bar at the bottom edge of the blind, replacing the end cap when you have done it. Then re-roll the blind, tightly and evenly back onto the roller – you may need a helper to do this.

1 Using a spirit level as a guide, pencil a straight line across the wall or moulding surfaces on which you want the blind to sit.

2 Hold the blind precisely in place while you mark the screwhole positions for the brackets, either in the top of a recess, on the face of a wall or window frame or from the ceiling if it's low. You may need a helper to do this.

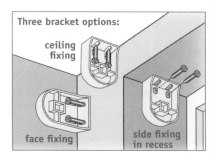
Three bracket options:
ceiling fixing
face fixing
side fixing in recess

3 Drill the screwholes and insert wall plugs into them if necessary (there's no need for plugs if you're drilling into wood).

4 Install the brackets, making sure that you place the bracket that will take the scrolling cord on the side where you want it.

5 Slide the blind into the brackets as per the manufacturer's instructions (this may mean removing the plastic covers on the brackets, and replacing them once everything is functioning smoothly).

----

play Blind man's buff

Versions of this game, which dates back 2,000 years to ancient Greece, are played around the world, from Europe to Nigeria to Papua New Guinea. One player is blindfolded then spun around until dizzy and disorientated. The other players dodge, dance and duck around him as he gropes and blunders in an attempt to catch them. When he seizes one of them, he has to guess who he has hold of. If he guesses right, the captive must assume the blindfold. If he guesses wrong, the captive is released. A favourite of children's parties, the game was once popular among adults.

----

treat Blisters

Blisters are raised areas of skin or mucous membranes under which fluids have accumulated. Never burst them. A blister caused by an infection will be teeming with bacteria or viruses, which could then spread. A blister with some non-infectious cause such as a burn or sunburn serves to protect underlying tissue, and reduces discomfort and the risk of infection.

If a blister bursts, expose it to the air in hygienic surroundings. Dress it if there's a risk of dirt getting in. See a doctor if it becomes inflamed, or if you suddenly develop widespread blisters, which suggest an underlying disease.

make Blinis

Authentic Russian blinis are best served with caviar, soured cream, onions and lemon. They are also excellent with smoked salmon and cream cheese.

MAKES ABOUT 30
350g plain flour
2 tsp easy-blend dried yeast
pinch of salt
1 tbsp caster sugar
2 large eggs, separated
300ml milk
370ml hand-hot water
25g unsalted butter
sunflower oil for frying

1 Sift the flour into a bowl, then mix in the yeast, salt and sugar. Make a well in the centre.

2 Beat the egg yolks with the milk and water. Melt and add the butter, then pour half the liquid into the well. Gradually beat in the flour to make a smooth batter, adding the remaining liquid in stages. Cover with a clean cloth and leave in a warm place until doubled in volume.

3 Whisk the egg whites to soft peaks and fold into the batter.

4 Heat the oven to 120°C/gas ½. Then heat a little oil in a heavy-based frying pan over a high heat.

5 Spoon in the batter to make blinis about 10cm wide. Cook for about 1 minute each side until golden brown. Keep hot on a wire rack in the oven until all batter is used. During cooking, stir the remaining batter occasionally.

B

start your own Blog

A blog – short for 'weblog' – is a kind of online diary that anyone can read. It's one of the many ways that you can use the internet to air your views and initiate a conversation with like-minded people.

Plan the content A blog can be personal, newsy, rambling or tightly focused on a hobby or preoccupation of your own such as the environment, local politics or parenting. Decide on a theme, come up with an engaging title that reflects the theme and will intrigue possible readers, then gather some ideas and write some material before you 'go live'. That way you'll already have a direction and a tone of voice when you make your debut.

Create your blog There are many free websites devoted to hosting blogs and giving you the support you require to set one up. One way to start if you have a PC is to use Windows Live. Once you have registered, you can follow the easy steps to design your blog, adding pictures, links and, above all, a facility for readers to leave comments so that the conversation can continue.

transfer files via
Bluetooth

Transferring data between electronic devices is easy using Bluetooth technology. You can use it to send pictures or documents over short distances from your phone to another phone or computer without having to connect the devices with a cable or use email.

For the system to work, both devices need to have Bluetooth turned on. Do this, and both devices will 'discover' each other, that is, notice the presence of another Bluetooth-enabled device. Then it's a question of following the prompts and instructions of your own phone, laptop or PC – the exact procedure varies from one device to the next.

use a home Blood pressure monitor

Most large pharmacies sell blood pressure monitors. Ask for one with a cuff that fits your arm.

Wear a loose-fitting or short-sleeved top. Sit quietly for 5 minutes, with your arm resting on the table, feet flat on the floor. Then, with your arm (always use the same one) bared, relaxed and supported, wrap the cuff around the upper arm, level with your heart.

Stay still and silent as you take your reading. Repeat once or twice, at 2 minute intervals, and take an average.
■ Ideally the average reading should be between 90/60 and 130/85.
■ If it's between 130/85 and 140/90 ('high normal'), or, more urgently, above 140/90 ('high'), you should make diet and lifestyle changes to reduce your risk of stroke.

Keep a record of your readings and see your doctor if your blood pressure is consistently raised.

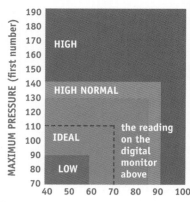

A reading of 110/70 is ideal.

BLOOD PRESSURE TABLE

MAXIMUM PRESSURE (first number)

190	HIGH
180	
170	
160	
150	
140	HIGH NORMAL
130	
120	
110	the reading
100	IDEAL on the
90	digital
80	LOW monitor
70	above

40 50 60 70 80 90 100

MINIMUM PRESSURE (second number)

read Body language

However hard we try to disguise our moods and motives, the way in which we hold and move our bodies speaks volumes about us.

We constantly telegraph unspoken messages about ourselves to one another, and learning to read those messages helps us to navigate the minefield of human relationships.

One of the most treacherous examples of body language is the blush or flush – betraying arousal, attraction, embarrassment or anger. Oh, and a yawn (sorry, are we boring you?).

A nod of the head is a gesture of approval – but persistent bobbing of the head is a giveaway of nervousness or anxiety.

Open hands speak of sincerity and a willingness to help. Clenched fists are a sign of tension or anger.

When we like or agree with someone, we lean towards them. Leaning away, with folded arms, signals dislike or disagreement.

A sudden folding of the arms signals discomfort, defensiveness or a determination to resist.

Arms behind the back signals 'stay back!' – it's an indication of anger, frustration or apprehension.

An inadvertently displayed thumbs-up or the turning up of a toe signals a positive thought or response.

Touching at the throat betrays doubt or insecurity.

calculate your Body mass index (BMI)

Adults can measure their BMI to check whether their weight is healthy for their height. Doctors consider it a useful indicator of overall health: being underweight is linked with other health problems, such as anaemia and osteoporosis, while being overweight can increase your risk of suffering problems such as heart disease, stroke and type 2 diabetes.

To calculate your BMI, all you do is divide your weight by your height squared (that is, your height multiplied by itself).

If you are, say, 1.6m tall and weigh 65kg, this is how the calculation goes:

1.6 x 1.6 = 2.56

65 ÷ 2.56 = a BMI of 25.39

Analysis A BMI between 18.5 and 24.9 is considered to be ideal. Lower than 18.5 is considered underweight, and 25 or higher is deemed overweight. If your BMI is too low or too high, you should consider talking to your doctor about ways to bring yourself within the ideal range.

Accuracy BMI can also be deceptive. Muscle weighs more than fat, so exceptionally muscular people such as weight trainers and athletes may have a high BMI but still be a healthy weight. If you're in any doubt, ask your doctor.

build a safe
Bonfire

Whether you're celebrating a special occasion or want to make a bonfire just to dispose of garden waste, it's important to construct your fire safely and sensibly. Light your bonfire when it is least likely to affect neighbours – not on a warm, sunny day.

Safety first
■ Let your neighbours know before you light your fire.
■ Make sure that someone is supervising the fire at all times, and that children and animals are kept at a safe distance.
■ Place the fire away from buildings, sheds, fences and overhanging trees.
■ Use only dry wood. Damp material, green leaves and branches from live trees will produce clouds of unpleasant smoke.
■ Don't burn household waste, especially rubber, plastics or painted materials.
■ Keep a bucket of water nearby.

To build a fire
■ Start with a heap of kindling (newspapers, small twigs, pine cones) that will burn quickly.
■ Place a log or some woody prunings at either side, and then two more logs crossways on top to make a platform.
■ Build up the pyre with more branches, brambles, logs and other woody material in this criss-cross manner, tapering towards the top.
■ Fill any big gaps with more kindling or smaller twigs and branches. Light with a newspaper torch – and never use paraffin or petrol to get the fire going.

Boil an egg perfectly

Perfection in a soft boiled egg is a firm but tender white and runny yolk, with no cracks in the shell to allow the white to seep out.

Use fresh eggs and make sure they are at room temperature to reduce the chances of them cracking during cooking.

Take a pin and make a prick in the shell at the round end (where the air pocket is). Then use a tablespoon to submerge the eggs in simmering water so that they are about 1cm below the surface. Use a small pan to stop the eggs banging together too hard during cooking.

Simmer for 3 minutes for very soft-boiled, 4 minutes for a set white and 6 minutes for *oeufs mollet* (with a soft but not runny yolk).

If the shell cracks in the pan, add a dash of vinegar or lemon juice to the water. This makes any egg white that escapes set quickly, so helping to seal any cracks.

make the best Bolognese sauce

SERVES 4-6

1 tbsp olive oil
1 onion, finely chopped
1 carrot, finely chopped
1 garlic clove, finely chopped
100g chicken livers, trimmed and chopped
450g lean minced beef (choose the best quality available)
100g mushrooms, thinly sliced
2 tbsp plain flour
400g can chopped tomatoes
salt and freshly ground black pepper
1 bay leaf
½ tsp dried marjoram or oregano
2 tbsp tomato purée
150ml red wine
300ml beef stock (stock from a cube or concentrate is acceptable if you don't have homemade)

■ Heat the oil in a heavy-based saucepan and add the onion and carrot. Cover and cook gently for about 5 minutes until the onion is tender.
■ Add the garlic, chicken livers and beef, stirring until thoroughly browned. Then add the mushrooms and fry for a few minutes.
■ Stir in the flour followed by the tomatoes, seasonings and tomato purée. Pour over the red wine and stock and bring to the boil.
■ Lower the heat, cover and simmer for 45-60 minutes. If the sauce is too liquid, remove the lid and raise the heat for the last 15 minutes, stirring occasionally.
■ Check and adjust the seasoning and remove the bayleaf before serving with spaghetti or tagliatelli. Alternatively use for a lasagne.

cover a Book

A simple protective cover for a book can be made from sturdy paper such as wallpaper or a plain grocery bag.

YOU WILL NEED Paper, ruler, scissors, clear adhesive tape

1 Measure and cut a piece of paper or plastic 5cm larger all around than the open book. Centre the book on the paper, with each cover face down. Cut diagonally across the paper at each of the four corners. Leave 1mm beyond each corner to provide an overlap.

2 Make a diagonal cut in the paper at the top of the book tapering into the top left-hand corner of the spine. Then do the same towards the top right-hand corner. Repeat at the bottom to leave two flaps of paper. which you can cut off (as left) or tuck inside the spine.

Hold the pages of the book away from the cover while you tape the paper in place.

3 Fold the side flaps in, followed by the top and bottom flaps to create a seamless border. Secure each edge with sticky tape.

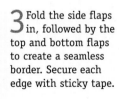

grow and care for Bonsai trees

The Chinese first grew miniature trees more than 1,000 years ago, an art later developed by Japanese monks. Almost any tree or shrub can be grown in this way.

To create an outdoor bonsai you can buy a 'from seed' kit or choose a tree seedling with a shape that you find interesting.

How to grow Pot it and leave it to establish itself for a year. The following spring, remove it, prune off any thick roots and pinch off all vigorously growing shoots. Repeat the process in the second year. In the third year, trim the roots by up to a third to fit a shop-bought bonsai tray and continually pinch out unwanted shoots. Then spiral plastic-coated wire around branches to create twisted shapes. Bear in mind that deciduous trees such as acers are most pliable in spring, whereas evergreens such as pine and juniper are best shaped in autumn.

To protect your bonsai place it in a sheltered spot outdoors. If frost is forecast, wrap it in bubble wrap.

Indoor bonsai are tropical species best bought ready-grown from a specialist and kept permanently in a place away from direct sunlight. Look for one with evenly spread roots and an elegant shape. From time to time in mild weather, they will appreciate fresh air from an open window.

B

escape Bores

It's relatively easy to get away from a bore at a drinks party, where you are upright and mobile (escape is impossible at a sit-down dinner).

If you have been pinned to the wall by someone banging on about their new conservatory, do anything to get a third person involved.

Catch the eye of an acquaintance and beckon urgently, as if you're enjoying an unmissable anecdote.

As soon as your friend arrives, drain your glass, mutter 'Excuse me while I get a refill,' and slip away without a backward glance.

You're free, and the bore will happily begin the story all over again with a new victim.

clean Bottles

For the outside of a bottle, warm water and washing-up liquid are all that's needed. Always avoid using a scouring pad on antique glass.

For the inside, where there's hardened residue, fill with warm water with washing-up liquid added and leave to soak for several hours before cleaning with a bottle brush.

For really stubborn dirt, put a tablespoon of dry rice or crushed eggshells into the bottle. Fill with water and add a denture-cleaning tablet. Let it dissolve, then cover the bottle and shake well.

For a tough white crust, try filling the bottle with white vinegar and leave it for 24 hours. Then rinse out and wash the bottle as above.

play Boules

The French term boules refers to a number of related games that involve two teams trying to place a ball or balls closest to a target.

The most popular form of boules is the Provençal version, *pétanque*. It can be a contest between two players, or teams of two or three. It's usually played on a hard gravel surface.

The game begins when a player from one side, standing inside a throwing circle, throws the small jack (or *cochonnet*) some distance away. A player from the same team then tries to throw one of their steel balls (underarm) so that it lands close to the *cochonnet*. A player from the opposing team then tries to place a ball closer still. The team that has the closest ball is said to be 'holding the point'; the team that is not 'holding' continues to throw until they are closest to the cochonnet. Then it's again the turn of the other team.

Once all balls have been thrown, the round ends. The team holding at the end wins one point for each ball closer to the *cochonnet* than the opponents' nearest. More rounds ensue, and the first team to reach 13 points wins.

tie a Bow tie

It takes practice to tie a bow tie. But once you've mastered it, it's no more difficult than tying a shoelace.

1 Drape the bow tie around your collar, so that end A is about 7cm longer than end B. Cross A over B and feed through the gap at your neck to create a base knot.

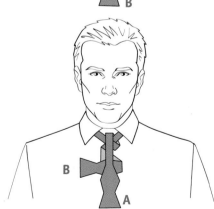

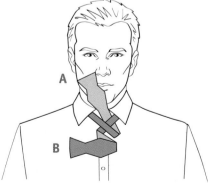

2 Hold A out of the way. With your other hand fold end B so that it forms a bow centred over the base knot – here with the folded end to your left.

3 Drop end A so it hangs over the narrow part of the bow.

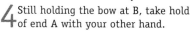

4 Still holding the bow at B, take hold of end A with your other hand.

5 Double end A on itself to form another bow and take the folded end up and behind B. Carefully feed A through the loop of the knot at your neck. You should now have a folded end and a loose end on each side of the knot at your neck.

6 Pull on the folded ends to tighten the new knot you have created, and adjust so that all ends are of an even length.

Brainstorm a new idea

Ideas generation works best when the participants can spark off each other, so get at least half a dozen lively people involved, if you can. Brainstorms are like parties: they often start slowly and may need something to break the ice. So make it fun: give people a glass of wine, or treat them to lunch. Use visual aids: if you're looking for new product ideas, have some good or bad products there on the table as conversation pieces. Scrupulously write down every idea that comes up on a whiteboard for all to see. And allow no negative criticism of any idea during the session.

clean Brass

Before cleaning brass, make sure you know whether it's protected with a lacquer coating or 'raw'.

To clean lacquered brass apply a mixture of warm water and washing-up liquid with a soft cloth or sponge. Rinse with clean water, dry thoroughly then buff with a soft cloth, chamois leather or old T-shirt.

To clean raw brass, use a soft cloth to apply a sparing amount of commercial metal polish, following the manufacturer's instructions.

To remove green corrosion, soak for several hours in washing soda, rubbing occasionally with an old cloth. Use an old toothbrush to get into crevices. Alternatively rub with a cut lemon dipped in salt. Rinse well and dry.

measure up for a Bra

Four in five women wear the wrong size of bra, affecting shape and posture. Determine the ideal size for you – and cut a better figure.

1 Wearing the best-fitting of your current bras, measure just under your breasts (A) with a dressmaker's tape measure, keeping it taut but not tugging it. If the measurement is an even number of inches, add 4in (10cm). If odd, you should add 5in (12.5cm). This gives you your band size.

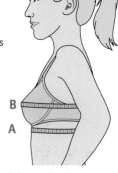

2 Now take the measure of the fullest part of your breasts (B), with the tape completely straight, flat against your back and drawn firmly, but not tightly, around your chest.

3 To find out your cup size subtract the second measure from the first:
- 'A' cup if there's no difference
- 'B' if the difference is 1in (2.5cm)
- 'C' if the difference is 2in (5cm)
- 'D' if the difference is 3in (7.5cm)
- 'DD' if the difference is 4in (10cm)

and so on through the cup sizes.

golden rules

BUYING A BRA
- Always try before you buy.
- A new bra should be a good fit on the loosest hooks. As it slackens with wear, you can use the tighter ones.
- If a bra leaves red marks on your skin, it's too tight.

B

BREAD MAKING TIPS

- Use a mixer with a dough hook (3 minutes on low speed) or mix bread ingredients in an ordinary food processor – the ball produced won't require as much kneading.
- Wholemeal flour has less gluten than white flour, so it requires less kneading.
- Speed up the rising process by using a microwave. After kneading, put the dough in an ungreased bowl and cover with lightly oiled cling film. Heat on high for 10 seconds then leave the bowl to stand for 20 minutes in the microwave or a warm place. If the dough has not doubled in size, heat on high for another 10 seconds, then leave to stand for another 10 minutes.

bake your own Bread

There's nothing quite like the smell – or taste – of home-baked bread. As well as selecting from a wide range of flours you can add seeds, nuts, raisins, sundried tomatoes, herbs or other flavourings.

TO MAKE TWO LARGE LOAVES

15g fresh yeast or 2 tsp dried
    yeast plus 1 tsp sugar or
    1 x 7g sachet easy-blend
    dried yeast
500ml lukewarm water
750g white bread flour
    (plus extra if needed)
1 tbsp salt
vegetable oil for greasing
beaten egg for glazing (optional)

VARIATIONS

Use half and half white and wholemeal flour, or choose spelt or rye flour, or granary

YOU WILL NEED Small bowl for yeast mixture, two large mixing bowls (one warmed), fork, cling film, two 450g (1lb) loaf tins, two plastic bags large enough to take a loaf tin, pastry brush for glazing

1 Dissolve fresh yeast in the water and mash well with a fork. For dried yeast, dissolve sugar in the lukewarm water, sprinkle over the yeast and stand for 10 minutes until frothy. Stir well.

2 Sift the flour with the salt into a large warmed mixing bowl; pour in the yeast mixture or add the easy-blend yeast. Mix with your hands, drawing in flour little by little to make a stiff paste. Add more flour if the dough is sticky.

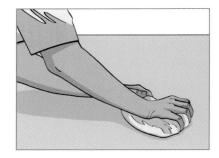

3 Turn onto a floured surface and knead for 10 minutes, flouring your hands as necessary. Work rhythmically, pushing the dough away from you, folding it back over and giving it a quarter turn each time, or knead in a mixer (see 'golden rules', left). Knead until smooth and elastic, with a slightly blistery surface.

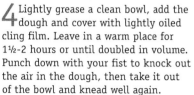

4 Lightly grease a clean bowl, add the dough and cover with lightly oiled cling film. Leave in a warm place for 1½-2 hours or until doubled in volume. Punch down with your fist to knock out the air in the dough, then take it out of the bowl and knead well again.

5 Grease two 450g (1lb) loaf tins. Divide the dough into two portions and roll each into a loaf shape to fit the tin. Pour a little oil into each bag, rub it round to cover the inside then put the tins inside, seal the opening and leave to rise (prove) for about 40 minutes at room temperature.

6 Heat the oven to 230°C/gas 8. Brush the risen dough with egg glaze if wished. Bake for 35 minutes.

7 When the bread is done, the loaves should have shrunk from the sides of the tins and sound hollow when tapped on the base. Cook for a few more minutes if necessary. Remove from tins and place on a wire rack to cool.

use up stale Bread

Stale bread has numerous uses. Try these simple suggestions to turn your leftovers into something delicious, or whizz them into breadcrumbs in a food processor and keep a bag in the freezer.

Slices without crusts Use to line a greased bowl, fill with soft fruit, top with more bread and press down with a plate and weight overnight for a summer pudding. Dip in egg and milk and fry for French toast. Layer buttered slices in a dish with sultanas and lemon zest, top with vanilla custard and bake to make a bread and butter pudding.

Cubes Fry or bake in the oven, drizzled with olive oil, to make croutons. Add to a tomato soup to create the Italian *pappa al pomodora* or to any vegetable soup to thicken it.

Breadcrumbs Mix with onions and herbs to make stuffing; fruit and nuts, such as dried apricots and almonds, can also be added. Mix with chopped herbs and use to top fish pies or other savoury dishes as an alternative to potato. Use, following flour and beaten egg, to coat food before frying. Mix with sugar and lemon zest then layer with apples, dot generously with butter and bake in the oven for an apple charlotte.

examine your Breasts

Examine your breasts monthly, just after a period. Get to know what feels normal for you, so that you'll recognise any changes. See your doctor if you notice any nipple discharge, a new lump or tenderness that lasts more than a month. Find a comfortable position: lying down or standing up.

1 Raise your arm and use your fingertips to feel the breast tissue extending into the armpit. Remember to do both sides.

2 With the flat of your fingers thoroughly examine the upper, outer quarter of the breast.

3 Examine the rest of the outer half, working towards the nipple. Then press the inner half of the breast against your ribs.

B

maximise
Broadband speed

Even if you're only browsing the internet, a poor connection speed makes pages frustratingly slow to open and to navigate around. Watching or 'streaming' video, or making online phone calls, will be stuttery or even impossible.

■ One of the most effective things you can do to increase your connection speed is upgrade your router (many providers will send you a new one for free). Older routers can handle a maximum of 54 megabits per second (Mbps) or less, while the latest ones have a maximum of more than 200 Mbps.
■ Wireless broadband works best when the computer is in the same room as the router: solid walls and furniture muffle the signal.
■ Keep your browser software up to date, and empty caches (blocks of memory) regularly.
■ Consider changing your broadband provider: another may deliver much better speeds.

✳ golden rules

BRIDGE TACTICS
■ **You should have at least four cards in a suit to call trumps.**
■ **Assess your hand: aces count as 4 points, kings 3, queens 2, jacks 1. Twelve points is good enough for an opening bid.**
■ **Don't criticise your partner or offer advice during play.**
■ **Keep a poker face if you have a bad hand: your opponents might slip up.**

master the basics of Bridge

Bridge is perhaps the most complex and sophisticated member of the whist family. But the aim is simple: to score points by winning tricks.

'Contract' bridge is played by two teams of two. The partners face each other across the table, and are known as north-south pairings and east-west pairings. A standard pack of 52 cards is dealt out to the four players.

How it begins Players conduct an auction, bidding in turn for the 'contract'. If a player bids *one diamond*, they undertake to win seven of the thirteen tricks (*one more than half the available tricks*) with *diamonds* as trumps. The next player can then bid higher in terms of the number of tricks or the trump suit: ranked in descending order, they are spades, hearts, diamonds then clubs. If you have a strong hand spread over several suits, you can bid to play without a trump suit: a *notrump* bid. *Notrump* beats all suits. A player wins the contract, say *four clubs*, when nobody outbids them. This 'declarer' is committed to winning ten tricks (four more than half), with clubs as trumps.

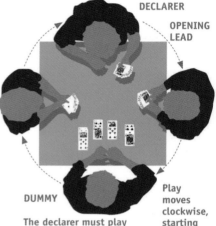

The winning bidder becomes the 'declarer' for the hand.

DECLARER

OPENING LEAD

DUMMY

Play moves clockwise, starting with the 'opening lead'.

The declarer must play the hand of the 'dummy' (see below) as well as their own.

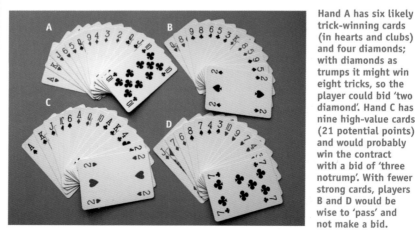

Hand A has six likely trick-winning cards (in hearts and clubs) and four diamonds; with diamonds as trumps it might win eight tricks, so the player could bid 'two diamond'. Hand C has nine high-value cards (21 potential points) and would probably win the contract with a bid of 'three notrump'. With fewer strong cards, players B and D would be wise to 'pass' and not make a bid.

The game continues The player to the left of the declarer, the 'opening lead', lays a card. The declarer's partner (the 'dummy') then lays all their cards face up on the table, sorted into suits, and takes no further part in the round; the declarer plays for them. Each trick is played in the manner of whist (*see* WHIST): every player must follow suit if they can, and the highest card wins the trick. Once all 13 tricks have been played, points are awarded for every one over six – to the declarer's team if their contract has been met, or to the opposing pair, if not.

Those are the mechanics of the game. But, as with chess, the skill in bridge lies in the ability to compute all the options, during the auction, then in trick play, and to exploit the weaknesses of the opposing pair. In bridge, as in life, it's not so much the hand that you're dealt, but how you play it.

---

help someone with a Broken bone

When a person has had a fall, your first question should always be, 'Is anything broken?' Pause to consider this before rushing to help them up to make sure that you don't inadvertently make any injury worse.

What to look for

■ Look for outward signs of a fracture, including visible swelling, bruising or discolouration of the skin around a joint; or an arm or leg or other body part that's at an unnatural angle – for instance, a leg turned outwards.
■ There may be an obvious injury: perhaps the casualty can't put weight on one leg, bend an arm or move their fingers.
■ The casualty may feel faint or dizzy and nauseous with pain, or complain of a grinding sensation in the bone. If there's any suspicion of a broken leg, on no account encourage the person to try to walk.

What, and what not, to do

■ Avoid all unnecessary movement, as broken bone ends can do damage to surrounding blood vessels and nerves. Be alert to the dangers of shock (*see* SHOCK). Put a coat or a blanket about the casualty to keep them warm, but don't offer a hot drink in case they need an anaesthetic later.
■ If there's a wound, cover it with a dressing and bandage (*see* BANDAGE) to keep it clean.
■ If a bone is poking out, lightly cover it with gauze.
■ Don't try to contrive any splint or support. Call an ambulance if the casualty cannot move.

---

mend a Broken heart

When the one who you lived for rejects you, it's tempting to wallow in pity or stew in a fury, but, in fact, it's time to live for yourself. Beware of falling for someone new on the rebound – learn to love yourself again first.

Draw support from friends and loved ones and make an effort to make yourself feel good. Eat well, get dressed up – even for a trip to the shops – and hold your head high (literally – it works).

Take exercise Walking or dancing will boost mood-enhancing endorphins and your self-image. Fill your weekends with activities you enjoy.

Make a list of all that's good about you and all that's bad about your ex. Remind yourself of your own worth and try to avoid romanticising the past.

bake Brownies

The ideal brownies are crisp on the outside and soft inside.

YOU WILL NEED Two mixing bowls, pan of water, whisk, 20cm square cake tin greased and lined with parchment

TO MAKE 20-24 BROWNIES

125g unsalted butter
200g dark chocolate, 70 per cent cocoa solids
2 eggs
250g caster sugar
1 tsp vanilla essence
60g plain flour
2 tbsp cocoa powder
100g walnuts, roughly chopped

1 Heat the oven to 180°C/gas 4. Melt the butter and 115g of the chocolate in a bowl set over simmering water, stirring occasionally. Leave to cool.

2 Whisk the eggs, gradually add the sugar and continue until the mixture is thick, foamy and leaves a ribbon-like trail when you lift out the whisk. Add the vanilla and the chocolate mixture and blend thoroughly. Sift over the flour and cocoa powder and add the nuts and remaining chocolate, chopped into small chunks. Fold it all in.

3 Pour into the prepared tin, spread evenly and bake for 30 minutes; the brownies should still have some 'give'. Cool in the tin for 10 minutes then remove paper and cut into squares.

B

treat Bruises

Bruising is caused when damaged blood vessels, especially tiny capillaries, bleed within the tissues.

■ To treat a bruise or black eye, apply a cold compress for 10-20 minutes at a time, every 2-3 hours.
■ Don't put ice directly on your skin. Make an ice pack using a bag of frozen peas or put ice cubes in a freezer bag, then wrap in a tea towel before applying.
■ Minor bruising is painful and unsightly, but nothing to worry about. Severe bruising can suggest more serious underlying damage, be accompanied by shock (see SHOCK) and require medical attention.
■ If you find you bruise easily or inexplicably, see your doctor.

disguise Bruises

You've fallen flat or walked into a door and bruised your face. There's no way round it – you look a fright.

What to do? If ordinary make-up is not up to the job, take a tip from plastic surgeons and use camouflage cosmetics. Try a concealer, which is thicker and more opaque than regular foundation, or a colour-corrector – choose a lavender tint to hide bruising and green for redness. Both of these are applied under foundation and can be just as effective on men.

In case of a black eye, apply concealer or corrector to both eyes, so they won't look too different. Concentrate on darkening the lashes with mascara (see EYES) and lightening the eyelids to draw attention away from the bruised area.

draw up a Budget

Successful budgeting depends on having complete and precise details of all your income and outgoings, while making allowance for the unexpected, such as a burst pipe, TV repair or vet's bill.

■ Get together bank statements, investment accounts, utility bills, receipts and pay slips for the last 12 months, or as long as possible.
■ Make lists on paper or, better still, in a computer spreadsheet program like Excel (see SPREADSHEET), to record all expenses under 'fixed' (such as rent, mortgage and insurance) and 'variable' (weekly shop, fuel, gifts, entertainment, holidays, emergencies). Include one-twelfth of any fixed sums that are paid annually.
■ Categorise expenses as much as possible to help you to highlight areas where you could cut back.
■ Total everything coming in and going out.

If your expenses are higher than your income, go through your lists of variable expenses to see which can be eliminated or reduced. Cut down on takeaways, use the car less or shop more economically, for example. Next, examine your fixed expenses and make sure that you have the best possible deal for your utilities and mortgage.

Set yourself limits on expenditure. Deduct the fixed expenses from your income then allocate a monthly proportion of the remainder to each of your expense categories. Be sure to keep a fund for emergencies and unexpected expenses and always prioritise the essentials, such as food and payments on any outstanding debts. Try to put some money each month into savings too.

Keep records of what you spend throughout the month so that you always know that you're within your budget.

plant Bulbs for colour

Carefully chosen, bulbs will provide colour in the garden in every season. Many spring bulbs will spread naturally in a lawn, but they are also ideal for borders and containers.

Planting bulbs in a border

1 Dig a planting hole large enough for a clump of bulbs, or use a slim trowel to make individual holes for each bulb. When planting a cluster of bulbs together – and this will give the best show – make sure that they are spaced at least their own width apart. Give more space to species that will multiply, such as grape hyacinth and crocus. For a natural effect, plant in informal groups rather than symmetrical patterns or regimented rows.

2 Scatter bone meal in the base of the hole to give bulbs a good start; fork it in and water the soil. Incorporate a little grit if your soil is heavy.

3 Gently cover the bulbs with soil, taking care not to knock them over. Firm the surface with the back of a rake and mark the area, so that you don't dig up the bulbs by accident.

In lawns Drop handfuls of bulbs from waist height, then plant them where they land using a slim trowel or a cylindrical bulb planter. Or cut the outline of a large *H* with a spade and peel away the turf. Fork in bonemeal if you wish, then plant bulbs firmly before replacing the turf.

In pots Pack a large pot with bulbs for a stunning display – a single variety is most striking. Use potting compost plus a few handfuls of grit to improve drainage. For a dense, long show of blooms, stagger bulbs in two or three layers, 5cm apart in a pot at least 30cm deep.

Planting depths for bulbs

As a rough guide, estimate the height of the bulb from tip to base, then cover it with twice that depth of soil, or three times the depth on light soils. The exceptions to this rule are lilies, which need a depth of three or four times their bulb height.

1 Chionodoxa
2 Spring crocus
3 Cyclamen coum
4 Hyacinth
5 Grape hyacinth (Muscari)
6 Daffodil
7 Siberian squill
8 Tulip
9 Allium (large)
10 Lily

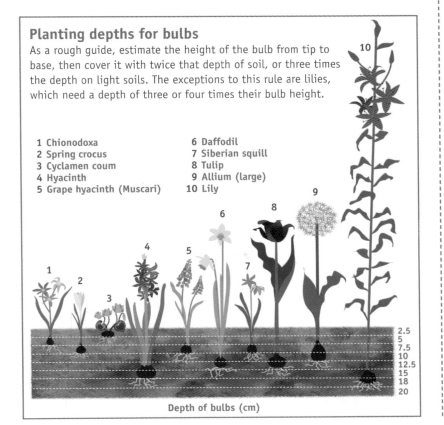

Depth of bulbs (cm)

get the better
of Bullies

Bullying can happen anywhere, in school, work or cyber space, and range from name-calling to intimidation and violence. Bullies are generally weak, jealous characters and, in most cases, will stop if you don't give them the satisfaction of a reaction. But persistent bullying can be a matter for the police.

Physical bullying If you're subjected to physical assault, or fear you're in real danger, report this to the police, or someone in authority: your human resources (HR) team or union representative if it happens at work, or a teacher if it's happening to a child at school.

Psychological bullying Your best weapon against people who try to undermine you is mental strength. Refuse to be riled by insults and negative comments. In the workplace, poor management can become bullying. Try to stay objective, keep notes of specific incidents and present a clear case to HR or a more senior manager. Most employers have a bullying policy.

Online bullying Try to avoid opening abusive emails or block the sender from your account, and stay away from social networking sites if this is where the bully contacts you. Never allow others access to your Facebook or other networking site account, where they could post embarrassing or upsetting messages in your name, and always set privacy settings as high as possible, particularly for a child's or young person's account. If you're being routinely bullied, save or print out any evidence – even anonymous posters can be traced by the police.

relieve the pain of Bunions

A bunion is a harmless swelling of the joint at the base of the big toe resulting from bone overgrowth. It's a common problem in middle-aged women, who have, perhaps for too long, squeezed their feet into too-tight, high-heeled shoes. Heredity is also a factor.

Choose broad, flat or low-heeled footwear that doesn't cram the toes. Bunion pads from the pharmacist help to stop shoes rubbing.

An ice pack (see BRUISES) can help to relieve pain and reduce swelling. Or try soaking your feet in a hot foot bath laced with Epsom salts.

Complications of bunions include stiffness in the toe joints, pain under the ball of the foot, swelling or deformity, such as 'hammer' toes, discomfort when wearing shoes, difficulty walking and corns or calluses developing over the lump.

Bunions also increase the risk of osteoarthritis to the affected joint. Your doctor may refer you to be fitted with orthoses – devices such as bunion splints to realign the bones, and specially shaped insoles to relieve pressure.

If you are in severe pain, surgery may be a consideration. It won't be offered for cosmetic reasons to improve the appearance of the foot.

Well-fitting shoes are absolutely vital for children and young people. Fashionable or not, sensible shoes will prevent the early onset of foot pain that could last a lifetime.

secure your home against Burglars

Burglars like easy targets, so make sure that your home is a difficult proposition for an opportunistic criminal. You want them to take one look and decide that it's not worth the risk or the effort.

If you do nothing else, secure all points of entry to your home. Fit visible locks to all your windows. Most burglars will think better of it straight away if they will have to break a window to get inside: they want access that's swift and silent.

A BURGLAR ALARM (1) is an effective deterrent. Some can be linked directly to the police or to your mobile phone. Don't choose an easy-to-guess deactivation code, like '0000'.

USE TIMERS (2) that turn some lights on for a few hours each evening, or even automated curtain closers. Consider fitting outside security lights that come on as anyone approaches your house.

SIDE ENTRANCE (3) If there's a side entrance or a pathway to the back of the house, make sure it has a lockable gate so that nobody can get into your garden.

VISIBLITY (4) Make sure your front door and windows are visible from the street: trim high hedges, and remove bushes that grow close to your windows and provide cover.

DEADLOCK (5) Have a five-lever (or more) mortise deadlock fitted to your front door.

SPARE KEY (6) Never hide a spare door key under a mat or pot plant: any burglar will know where to look.

GARAGE DOORS (7) are often easier to force than house doors. Fit additional locks or a barrier to prevent a garage door opening. Always lock any connecting door with the house and bolt it from the inside. If a burglar gets into the garage, they can work unseen at the inside door.

OCCUPIED Create the impression that your home is occupied even when it isn't. Cancel milk and newspaper deliveries when you're away and get a trusted neighbour to gather up your post.

make clarified Butter

Brown butter (*beurre noisette*) is served with fish and vegetables. Heat 125g butter until golden brown. Remove the pan from the heat and add 1-3 teaspoons of lemon juice. Use immediately.

Black butter (*beurre noir*), a classic accompaniment to poached skate, is heated until dark brown. Timing is crucial: it must be removed from the heat before it burns. When cooked, add 2 tablespoons drained capers. Use at once.

Clarified butter, or ghee, is used for sautéing and in Indian cookery. Melt a pat of butter in a small saucepan over very low heat and skim the froth from the surface. Pour slowly into a bowl, leaving behind the milky sediment. Or refrigerate until solid, then separate, discarding the sediment.

---

sew on a Button

Most buttons are sew-through, with two or four holes. On a shirt or blouse you can sew a button on flat; on thicker fabrics you may need the button to sit away a little by creating a thread shank (see below).

Four-hole shirt button

1 Anchor the thread on the reverse of the material with a knot and a few small stitches. Push the needle through to the front and thread on the button.

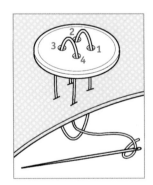

2 Take the needle down through a second hole, up through the third and down through the fourth, and continue to make about six stitches in each. You can also attach the button using the cross method: up through 1, down through 3, up through 2 and down through 4, starting again with 1. At the back of the fabric, make a few stitches through the thread to finish off, tie a small knot and snip off the excess thread.

Four-hole coat button with shank

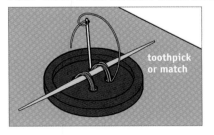

toothpick or match

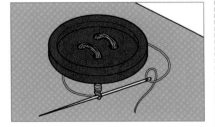

1 Secure the thread and thread on the button (above, left). As you sew, loop the stiches over a toothpick or matchstick to create some slack to make the shank.

2 Before you finish off at the back, remove the stick, pull the button away from the fabric and wind the thread firmly around the stitches between the button and the coat to make a shank. Make one stitch into the shank to secure it then push the needle through the fabric and fasten the thread at the back (above, right).

treat Burns and scalds

A burn requires immediate action to limit skin damage.

Quick action

Stop the burning process – immediately douse the burn with cold water, if possible by holding the burnt part under cold running water for at least 10 minutes, even if the pain stops. If a tap is not available, any cold fluid, such as milk, will do.

Seek medical advice or call an ambulance if any of the following applies, or if you're in any doubt about the severity of the burn:
■ burns are severe, deep or larger than the size of the victim's hand
■ burns were caused by chemicals or electricity
■ the casualty is in shock (*see* SHOCK), already in poor health or pregnant, shows signs of exhaustion, or is under 5 or over 60.

Remove clothing and jewellery around the burned area but don't pull any material stuck to the skin. After 10 to 20 minutes cooling with water, allow the area to dry then cover with a clean, non-fluffy material, such as cling film or a plastic bag.

Wrap a blanket around the person – avoiding the affected area – to guard against a dangerous drop in body temperature.

Superficial burns and scalds affecting only the surface of the skin may not need medical attention and should heal naturally.
■ Keep the burn clean, don't apply creams, and don't be tempted to burst blisters (*see* BLISTERS).

C

grow and care for Cacti

Success with growing cacti depends on imitating as far as possible the conditions from which they originate.

Desert cacti Good varieties include *Cereus, Opuntia* and *Mammillaria*; for flowers, *Parodia* and *Rebutia*.

■ A cold greenhouse is ideal, though the cacti will thrive indoors on sunny windowsills in winter.

■ Use a mixture of one part grit to three parts John Innes No.1 compost and water well between May and September, allowing the top 15mm to dry out between waterings.

■ Allow compost to dry out completely from December to February and increase watering gradually during March.

Jungle cacti These include the Easter cactus (*Rhipsalidopsis gaertneri*) and Christmas cactus (*Schlumbergera x buckleyi*).

■ Keep them out of direct sunlight at all times, provide a humid atmosphere and a temperature no lower than 10°C.

■ Pot as for desert cacti, including 30 per cent leaf mould.

■ Keep moist in winter but allow cacti to dry out completely after flowering.

golden rules

BOOSTING TIPS FOR CACTI

■ Water cacti with rainwater or cold boiled water to maximise their nutrient uptake. Never overwater or they will rot.

■ If light is one-sided turn cacti regularly to prevent distorted growth.

turn your hand to Calligraphy

Expressive, flowing handwriting in coloured ink will lend style and distinction to greetings cards and invitations.

The word calligraphy means 'beautiful handwriting', but think of it more as drawing – one perfect character at a time.

Finding a template Select and download one of the calligraphy alphabets available free online. Choose a forward-slanting alphabet or straight up and down. Don't mix styles or you'll lose the essential harmony that distinguishes calligraphy from individualised handwriting. Uniformity of size and style is more important than fancy flourishes, so practise copying letters over and over until you're confident to start writing freehand and creating your own work.

Pens A dip pen with a complete set of nibs is the choice of professionals, but cartridge calligraphy pens or calligraphy markers are less messy options for beginners. Doodle with your pens to get familiar with the nibs before you start work.

Paper and ink For the best results, use calligraphy paper of at least 90gsm and water-based, coloured calligraphy inks. You'll need a variety of each – sepia ink on cream paper will give a historic look; black or blue on white are classic and formal.

Your workspace Work on a slanted surface, such as a board propped up with a length of wood or a thick book. Use a piece of paper under your free hand to secure the sheet you're working on.

A broad, flat nib creates the distinctive thick and thin lines of calligraphy: thick when moving down and thin when writing across the page.

Always keep the angle of the nib the same, usually pointing diagonally away from you to the left. Use a light pressure and lead the nib over the paper – don't push it or lean too hard.

■ Some templates break down all the strokes that make up each letter. Draw faint guidelines to help you to keep letters regular.

■ Arrows indicate how to move your nib, in this case down from the mid point and up to the top. Lift the nib at the end of the stroke.

■ Complete the ascender, or top of the *f*, with a second curving stroke, then add the crossbar at the mid point, or x-height.

Perfect the individual strokes that build up into complete letters. Practise writing perfectly regular, parallel lines in all directions, then build on these to add curves.

cut down on Calories

By making simple, smart food choices you can reduce your energy intake, eat satisfying portions and maintain a healthy weight – for life.

- First and foremost, eat plenty of fibre in the form of whole grains, pulses, nuts and seeds, as well as the fruit and vegetables that should form the bulk of your meals. Obesity is clearly linked to low fibre intake, and just a few extra grams a day can make a difference.
- Stop eating sweetened breakfast cereals, croissants and pastries, and white bread, pasta and rice. Switch to fibre-rich bran flakes, wholemeal bread and pasta, and brown rice, which will keep you feeling full for longer.
- Choose poultry or fish over fatty, additive-laden sausages and burgers. Use super-lean mince and the leanest cuts of meat.
- Bake, grill, poach or steam your food rather than frying it. Instead of chips try a baked sweet potato.
- Go for low-fat cheese and skimmed milk. Stop buying sugary, full-fat, non-bio yoghurt. Switch to low-fat bio and eat it with plenty of fruit.
- Instead of eating a whole chocolate bar, try a couple of squares of dark chocolate that's high in cocoa solids to get your chocolate fix.
- Swap fatty, salty, packaged snack foods for an apple, a small bunch of grapes, some dried apricots or a handful of unsalted nuts.
- Switch from sugary soft drinks to mineral water or fresh fruit juice.

conjure up party Canapés

These one or two-bite savoury appetisers, served with cocktails or pre-dinner drinks, look good and are easy to eat – perfect for a party.

The best way to think of canapés is as bases with toppings. Allow ten canapés per person for pre-dinner and at least 20 for a cocktail party.

tomatoes and basil on bruschetta

salami and cheese inside a shortcrust pastry case

prawn salad on a savoury biscuit

The bases
- Bread (rye, wholemeal or sourdough triangles, pitta pieces or thin slices of baguette), with crusts removed as necessary. It can be toasted or heated in the oven.
- Savoury biscuits or pancakes (*see* BLINIS *and* PANCAKES).
- Pastry cases (shortcrust or puff).
- For low-carbohydrate alternatives use hollowed-out cherry tomatoes, sticks of celery or red pepper, crisp lettuce or chicory leaves, or fruit, such as dried apricots.

continued overleaf →

build a Camp fire

YOU WILL NEED Tinder (dry twigs, paper, pine needles), kindling (small, short sticks), firewood (dead branches or dry logs)

1 Clear a space of all combustible material. If the ground is wet, use dry wood as a platform. Have a bucket of water to hand in case the fire spreads.

2 Place a handful of tinder at the centre of your fireplace. Make a 'box' around it with kindling: build up a teepee or cone shape for cooking, and a pyramid (constructed like a log cabin) if your fire is for warmth.

3 Place firewood around the outside of the box, so that the flames spread from the tinder to the kindling to the firewood. Light from the side that's sheltered from the wind.

find the right Campsite

Don't wait until it's dark to find a place to pitch your tent (*see* TENT). Look for a spot in daylight, so you can see the lie of the land. Choose a place that's out of the wind but not directly under trees. Long grass indicates that the ground is damp, and stagnant water will attract biting insects. The best kind of campsite is a place that's flat (and so, comfortable to sleep on), level, reasonably free of undergrowth and stones, and well drained. When you put up your tent, put the back or the narrowest side facing into the wind – never the entrance.

decorate a
Cake
see pages 50-51

C

prime and stretch a
Canvas

YOU WILL NEED Wooden frame, canvas 5cm larger all round than the frame, pinking shears, staple gun, canvas-straining pliers (optional), gesso primer, brush

1 Lay your frame bevelled edge down on the canvas, aligned with the weave. Cut to fit with pinking shears, allowing 5cm overlap on each side.

2 Fold canvas along one long side and fire in a staple at the midpoint. Rotate the frame 180º, draw the canvas firmly towards you (you can use canvas-straining pliers), hold it taut with one hand and fire a staple opposite the first.

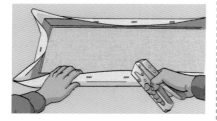

3 Repeat with the two shorter sides. Then staple 8cm to the right and left of the centre staple on all sides – grab, pull, staple each time. Repeat as necessary, rotating frame and canvas until it's taut all over.

4 At the corners, tightly fold, tuck and staple to hold the canvas firm.

5 Apply gesso primer, suitable for acrylic or oils, to the canvas and allow to dry before starting to paint. For a smooth surface, dilute the gesso with a little water and apply two or more coats.

Toppings and fillings
- Smoked salmon or gravadlax with dill and a squeeze of lemon.
- Prawn or egg mayonnaise.
- Cream cheese: plain or with herbs and/or garlic, or with smoked salmon or lumpfish roe.
- Olive tapenade (best toasted).
- Cold roast beef and horseradish.
- Pâté (liver, aubergine, or smoked mackerel, salmon or trout).

Choose from the lists of bases and toppings above or mix and match your own combinations. Alternatively spread thin slices of bread (crusts removed) with fillings such as cream cheese or smoked salmon pâté, add stuffed olives and roll up tightly. Cut into mini savoury rolls or wheels.

Don't prepare cold canapés more than an hour or so before serving.

Hot canapés
- 'Devils on horseback' (left) are a classic: wrap ready-to-eat prunes in a half a rasher of streaky bacon. Secure with a cocktail stick. Brush with olive oil and oven cook at 200ºC/gas 6 for 10 minutes until crisp.
- Or serve sausages cooked in the oven with mustard and rosemary, hot mini meatballs or mini quiches.

understand the basics of Canasta

This classic card game is usually played by four players in two pairs, with two decks, including jokers, shuffled together.

There are many intricate variations on the detailed rules of canasta, so find one version in a book or online that you and your colleagues agree on – and stick to it. Variations aside, the aim of the game is to score the highest number of 'melds' (three or more cards of the same rank, regardless of suit), including 'canastas' (melds of seven or more cards).

- Start with a deal of 11 cards to each player. The remaining pile is the 'stock', placed face down on the table. The top stock card is flipped face up and begins the 'discard' pile. The essence of the game is to pick up a card from 'stock' and discard one card from your hand at each turn to acquire melds to lay down on the table.
- Points scored for the various cards range from 100 for a red 3 (a 'bonus' card), through 50 for a joker, to 5 for a black 3. Jokers and 2s are 'wild' cards that can be added to any meld. The cards in your hands count against you, if you're left holding them when your opponents go out.
- When using wild cards, lay down jokers before 2s.
- Try to memorise the cards in the discard pile – they could come back into play, and it's worth being prepared for that moment.

make homemade Candles

All the materials for candle making can be bought from craft shops. At home it's easiest to create candles by rolling or dipping.

To make rolled candles
YOU WILL NEED Sheets of honeycomb beeswax, hairdryer, length of wick at least 2cm longer than the finished candle will be, trimming knife, metal ruler, scissors, butter knife

1 Warm the beeswax until it's pliable. Use a hairdryer on a low setting or heat the wax on a radiator.

2 Lay the wick along one edge of the wax sheet and roll it tightly and evenly, as thick as you like.

3 Use the ruler and trimming knife to cut away any excess wax, and use scissors to trim the wick. Wrap a piece of wax round wick to prime it.

4 Smooth the seam with a butter knife warmed in hot water. Slide it back and forth to seal the join and leave a smooth finish.

For the dipping method
YOU WILL NEED Stearin powder, paraffin wax granules, wax dye disc, saucepans, sugar thermometer, wick, scissors

1 Pour 40g stearin powder into a saucepan deep enough to accommodate the length of wick you want. Place the pan inside a larger pan of water and bring to the boil until the stearin melts.

2 Add a quarter of a disc of wax dye and 400g paraffin wax granules and heat to 80°C, stirring continuously.

3 Dip the wick in the wax, lift out, then pull taut and hold until the wax has set. Repeat until you have the required diameter, then trim wick.

act after a Car accident

If you have an accident in your car there are certain things you must do to make the scene safe and to ensure that the circumstances are accurately recorded.

Securing safety
■ The first thing you should do is check to see if anyone is hurt. If anyone is bleeding profusely, unconscious or in serious pain, call for an ambulance straight away.
■ Make the scene safe, if possible, without endangering yourself. Place a warning triangle at least 50m behind the scene of the accident – more if it's on a bend or the brow of a hill – but not on a motorway.
■ Move the damaged car or cars off the carriageway if it's safe to do so, but don't attempt to move anyone who is badly hurt.
■ Call the police.

Getting information
■ Gather any details that you may later need for legal or insurance purposes.
■ Take the names, addresses and registration numbers of any other drivers involved in the accident, and also of any witnesses. In some countries it's a legal requirement for drivers to swap insurance details.
■ Make a sketch or take a photo of the scene and any details of the location that may have contributed to the accident: if there were, say, roadworks or a rubbish skip, were they adequately lit? Was there a pothole, or a car parked on a blind corner, that caused one of the drivers to swerve?
■ Never admit liability at the scene of the accident even if you feel it was your fault: let the insurance companies deal with that.

C

decorate a Cake

Adding decoration to a cake need not be difficult and can give a professional look to everything from a simple sponge to cupcakes or a cake for a special family celebration.

Types of icing Icing is always effective – and tasty. Glacé, buttercream and chocolate are best for soft cakes such as sponges. Royal and ready-made fondant are best for firmer fruit cakes. As well as the decorations suggested here you can use fresh flowers, ribbons and candles.

GLACÉ ICING To cover the top and sides of an 18cm round cake or about 15 cupcakes.

175g icing sugar
2-3 tbsp hot water

Sieve the sugar into a bowl, add the water a little at a time, then add any flavourings (as for buttercream). To cover the top and sides of a cake, icing should coat the back of a spoon but flow easily. For cupcakes, icing should be a little stiffer. Leave the iced cake to set for at least an hour.

HOW TO GET A SMOOTH FINISH

Pour the icing so that it drips down the sides of the cake and use a palette knife to smooth the top and sides.

CHOCOLATE GLAZE To cover the top and sides of a 23cm round cake or about 15 cupcakes.

350g plain chocolate, broken into pieces
150g unsalted butter
120g apricot jam, sieved and warmed

Melt the chocolate in a bowl over nearly simmering water. Add the butter and stir until melted. Brush the cake with the apricot glaze. Apply the chocolate glaze to the cake and leave to set for at least 4 hours.

ROYAL ICING To cover the top and sides of a 23cm round or 20cm square cake with two thin layers.

900g icing sugar
4 egg whites
2 tsp lemon juice
2 tsp glycerine (omit for a tiered cake – it makes icing too soft)

Sieve the sugar and beat the egg whites until frothy, then add half the sugar a tablespoon at a time. Beat well for 5-10 minutes, until fluffy and increased in bulk. Gradually add the lemon juice, glycerine and remaining icing sugar, beating until it stands in peaks and loses its shine. Cover with a damp cloth and leave to stand for 2 hours. After icing the cake leave it to set for at least 4 hours before applying another layer. Allow 24 hours before adding any further decorations.

BUTTERCREAM To fill centre and cover the top of a 20cm round cake or about 15 cupcakes.

120g unsalted butter, softened
275g icing sugar, sieved
1-2 tbsp milk and/or flavouring

For flavourings, in place of some or all of the milk use:

1½ tsp coffee essence or strong black coffee
1 tbsp lemon juice and grated zest of half a lemon
2 tbsp orange juice and grated zest of half an orange
40g melted chocolate

Use a wooden spoon or food processor to cream the butter until soft. Gradually beat in the icing sugar with the flavourings (as for glacé icing), adding milk if necessary to make a smooth but stiff mixture.

buttercream

stencilled

fondant icing

chocolate leaves

Simple decorations

As well as bought decorations such as silver balls and chocolate vermicelli there are easy ways to create a great finish.

Stencil Use a stencil to create patterns when dusting with icing sugar or cocoa powder.

Sugared leaves, petals and flowers Brush leaves of sage, rose petals or whole violets with beaten egg white then dip in caster sugar. Put on a rack and leave in a warm place to set.

Crunchy lemon top Mix the juice of a lemon with 100g caster sugar. Pour onto a sponge cake as soon as it's out of the oven. When cold, add strips of lemon zest.

Feathered icing Use a pointed knife to drag the icing across the cake. Or pipe a spiral onto the cake, starting in the centre, then make lines from the centre outwards to create a marbled effect.

Fondant icing Buy it ready-made and simply roll it out for use as a cake topping. Alternatively, shape it to make all kinds of novelty cake decoration, such as flowers or faces.

Peaks Use a knife to dab blobs of royal icing onto a Christmas cake, then lift the knife sharply to shape it into peaks.

Chocolate curls Using chocolate at room temperature, scrape a swivel-style vegetable peeler over the flat side of the bar.

Chocolate shapes Spread melted chocolate onto baking parchment and cut into shapes with a knife or cutter. Or brush melted chocolate onto leaves (bay, for example), allow to set, then peel leaves away.

sugared flowers

feathered

HOW TO PIPE ICING

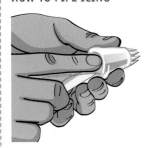

1 Fit a small round nozzle into the end of a piping bag. Twist and tuck the bag into the nozzle to stop any icing leaking out.

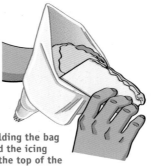

2 Make a collar by folding the bag over your hand. Add the icing with a spatula. Twist the top of the bag when full, expelling any air.

3 Ice the cake by twisting the end of the bag with one hand and pressing gently with the other.

C

unfreeze a Car lock

■ If your car is at home, soak a sponge or cloth in warm water and apply it to the lock.

■ Away from home or in extreme cold, heat the door key gently with a cigarette lighter and insert into the lock to defrost it from within.

■ If no other options are available, place your hand over the lock for a minute or two: the heat of your palm may do the trick. Don't do this with bare hands, though, as you could risk freezing your hand to the door. Try with a woollen glove on or with a piece of material between you and the cold metal.

■ Bear in mind that if the lock is frozen, then the doors may be too. So don't yank the door open or force the passenger door from the inside: you may damage the seals.

play

Car games *on*

long journeys
see pages 58-59

polish off Car cleaning inside and out

A regular wash-and-brush-up routine will make your car look good, and help to protect it from corrosion and other damage. It can even help to maintain a car's resale value.

Cleaning the interior

■ Remove the mats: vacuum them if they are made of carpet; wash with an all-purpose cleaner if they are rubber and leave to dry.

■ Carefully vacuum the upholstery and the carpets, using the crevice attachment to clean deep into the gaps.

■ Use soap and water to wash the door-jambs, and use a cotton bud to unplug the drainage holes on the bottom of the door, if necessary.

■ Clean the inside of the windscreen with a 1:8 solution of white wine vinegar and water. Spray it on then wipe dry with a soft cloth.

■ Wipe the dashboard and interior panels with a duster and a dilute household cleaning fluid.

Cleaning the exterior

■ First rinse the car gently from the roof down using a garden hose or pouring clean water from a bucket.

■ In a bucket, mix non-detergent car cleaner (never washing-up liquid) with warm water.

■ Wash one section at a time, using an old 100 per cent cotton towel: soap, rinse, dry – and move on.

■ Use a different bucket and rag to wash the wheels. Grit and stones collect here and you could transfer some to the paintwork on your cloth and scratch the car as you wash.

■ Clean the outside of the windows the same way as you did the inside: with a solution of water and white vinegar.

■ Wax your car twice a year to protect the finish.

touch up Car paint scratches

Scratches should be repaired straight away to prevent rust and corrosion attacking any metal that's left bare.

A light scratch that hasn't exposed the metalwork can be repaired using a renovating compound or restorer. First, wash the car and let it dry. Apply the compound using a clean, damp muslin cloth. Rub it onto the bodywork using a light circular motion over an area wider than the immediate damage.

Deeper scratches may need touching up with paint, which can be applied with a small paintbrush or a spray can. If you use a spray can, apply several light coats, 15 minutes apart, rather than one heavy application that's likely to run. Allow the new paint to harden for a week, then blend it into the surrounding paintwork using renovating compound, as above.

back up a Caravan

Driving forwards with a caravan or trailer is a breeze, but reversing to turn round or to manoeuvre into a space requires a little know-how and some practice. In time, though, it will be second nature to you.

1 Go very slowly. Begin by turning the steering wheel slightly in the 'wrong' direction: opposite to the way you actually want to turn.

2 As soon as the caravan starts to turn, begin to straighten up while continuing to reverse: you should feel that your car is 'following' the caravan.

3 Carry on past the neutral point of the steering wheel and begin to steer left, following the caravan.

4 Increase the lock to bring the car round the corner, just as you would without a caravan.

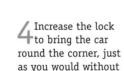

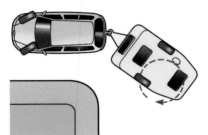

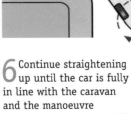

5 Start straightening up. Use your side mirrors: if more of the caravan begins to appear in the mirror, steer towards that mirror.

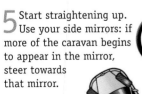

6 Continue straightening up until the car is fully in line with the caravan and the manoeuvre is complete.

---

reduce your Carbon footprint

The chances are that your carbon footprint is too large. But there are easy ways to make it smaller.

The term 'carbon footprint' is a measure of the total greenhouse gases that a person or organisation produces, usually given in terms of tons of carbon dioxide equivalent. A carbon footprint is complicated to calculate, but there are websites that estimate your footprint through an online questionnaire.

Easy ways to cut back Most simply, this means using less fuel and energy in your daily life.
- Insulate your house well, especially your roof, to cut down on energy used for heating.
- Turn your heating down a notch or two – you'll hardly notice.
- Boil only as much water as you need in your kettle – don't over-fill.
- Wash clothes at 30°C rather than 40°C or more – they will still get clean.
- Recycle as much as you can – this requires far less energy than creating every product from scratch.
- Cycle as much as you can, too: ride a bike (or walk) rather than taking the car whenever possible.
- Holiday close to home rather than fly: trains are ten times more carbon-efficient than aeroplanes.

Food impact Small changes to eating habits can make a big difference.
- Avoid buying fruit and vegetables that have been imported: 'food miles' are one of the hidden factors in your overall carbon footprint.
- Eat less meat and dairy foods, because flatulent methane emissions from livestock are one of the main contributors to greenhouse gases.

C

get stains out of a Carpet

The table below shows the best way to remove a selection of common spills and stains, but there are some general principles in carpet-cleaning that can also help.

Move fast The longer a stain is there, the harder it is to get it out without leaving a trace behind.

Don't scrub You risk rubbing the stain in deeper and spreading it over a wider area. Instead, blot liquid spills with a cloth or kitchen paper to remove as much of the stain as possible. Work inwards, so that the stain remains contained. Don't add more liquid: you'll make the job harder for yourself.

Soak it up To lift a wet stain from a carpet, the best strategy is sometimes to place a layer of clean white rags or paper towels, 1cm thick, over the spill, weigh them down with a heavy object, and leave overnight so that the liquid is absorbed up and out.

Dry-clean grease Dry-cleaning solvent is the best way to lift greasy stains: you can buy it at most hardware shops.

Finish with a wash A wash with carpet shampoo is a good final step in any carpet cleaning job. Apply it with a cloth, using just enough to moisten the area. Use a clean section of cloth as it soaks up the stain.

Stain	Treatment
BLOOD	Sponge with cold water, blotting with a towel as you go.
CANDLEWAX	Let the wax harden, then scrape off as much as you can. Cover the residue with blotting paper, brown paper or kitchen paper, and press with the tip of a barely warm iron. The wax will melt and be drawn into the absorbent paper. Don't let the iron scorch the carpet.
CHEWING GUM	Place a bag of ice cubes on the chewing gum to freeze it. You can then break the gum with a small hammer and lift off the pieces. Rub any residue with white or methylated spirits on a soft cloth.
INK	Ink marks from a ballpoint pen should be dabbed with a cottonbud that has been dipped in methylated spirits. Ink from a fountain pen should be thoroughly blotted and sponged with cold water, before using a suitable stain remover for ink. Some felt-tip pens are water-based, and ink marks from these should be treated with carpet shampoo; if the felt-tip is spirit-based, treat the marks with methylated spirits.
MUD	Allow the mud to dry completely, then brush it out. Then vacuum, and use carpet shampoo on any residual stain.
TEA AND COFFEE	Blot thoroughly, and treat with a carpet shampoo. Use a dry-cleaning solvent on any stubborn stains.
URINE	Blot with paper tissues, and treat with carpet shampoo to which white vinegar has been added (50ml of vinegar for half a litre of shampoo). Use a pet stain remover to eradicate any smell.
VOMIT	Scrape up any deposits, taking care not to spread them over a wider area. Blot thoroughly with kitchen paper. Treat with a carpet shampoo and a little disinfectant to remove any unpleasant odour.
WINE	Blot fresh spills dry, then use carpet shampoo. Don't put white wine on red wine spills or cover with salt.

Carve meat perfectly

All joints served hot will be more tender and easier to carve if the meat is covered in foil and left in warm place to 'relax' for at least 15 minutes and up to half an hour before carving.

Boneless cuts are the easiest to carve, such as a rolled beef rump or sirloin, or a boned and rolled leg of lamb. As a rule, meat is best cut across the grain. Before you start, make sure that your knife is sharp and your board isn't going to slip (lay it over a tea towel if necessary).

YOU WILL NEED Sharpened carving knife, two-pronged carving fork, carving board, small sharp knife, large warmed side plate

Rib of beef For a large joint, turn onto one side and make 5cm cuts across ribs. Lay the joint rib side down and carve several slices. Place them on a warm side dish then turn the rib back on its side and repeat. For a smaller joint, cut the meat away from the ribs in one go and then carve it into slices.

Sirloin of beef on the bone Use a small knife to loosen the meat from the bone. Carve down to the bone in thin slices, turn the meat over, remove bone and continue carving.

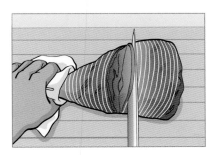

Leg of lamb or pork Place the leg meaty side up on the board. For pork, remove the crackling and put to one side. Cut a shallow V from the middle then carve slices downwards from both sides, widening the V. Turn the leg over and cut slices across the underside.

Shoulder of lamb Place joint with fat side uppermost. Cut a long slice about 15mm thick from the centre of the joint on the side opposite the bone, right down to the bone. Keep carving slices to widen the first cut then take horizontal slices from the top, over the central bone. Carve horizontal slices from the underside.

continued overleaf →

lay a foam-backed Carpet

Foam-backed carpets are much easier to lay yourself than hessian-backed ones, which need underlay and gripper strips around the edge.

Don't put carpet down on uneven boards: it will look bad and wear out quickly. If necessary, cover the floor with hardboard first to give an entirely smooth surface.

YOU WILL NEED Sheets of newspaper or roll of carpet paper, double-sided carpet tape, carpet, bolster chisel, trimming knife

1 Lay newspaper or carpet paper over the floor to prevent the foam backing sticking to the wood beneath.

2 Fix double-sided carpet tape all round the perimeter of the room, but don't peel off the backing yet. Place the carpet loosely in position so that the pile runs away from the main window (it should feel smooth when you run your hand across it, starting at the light source). Trim off the excess but leave at least 25mm on all sides.

3 Position the carpet in its correct position and make sure it's smooth and flat. Lift the edges and remove the backing from the carpet tape. Work around the room, pressing the carpet firmly into place. Use a clean bolster chisel to tamp the carpet well into the join between the floor and the skirting.

4 Cut carefully around obstacles, such as radiator pipes, and awkward shapes, such as the door frame. Trim off the excess around the edges with a trimming knife, taking great care not to cut off too much. Hold the point of the blade to the skirting, with the handle angled away from the wall. Go round the perimeter checking that all the edges are firmly stuck down.

C

digitise your old
Cassettes

It's possible to digitise cassettes using a working cassette deck, a cable that connects the deck to the line-in jack of your PC (ask at your electronics store), and a piece of software to govern the process. There are many freely downloadable programs you can use: Audacity is one of the best.

Alternatively, you can buy cassette players and record turntables that are designed specifically for the purpose of digitising these obsolescent media, and that come with the necessary software. Clean the heads of your cassette recorder before you begin so that the digital version of your tapes is as good as possible.

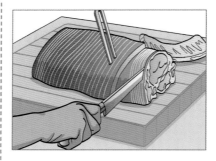

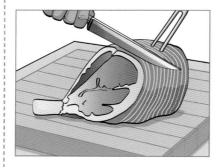

Loin of pork or lamb Use a small knife to cut between the chine bone (that runs along the joint) and the meat. Then use the carving knife to remove the bone, cutting between the meat and ribs. Remove any pork crackling. Slice the meat, finding the natural divisions between the bones and cut up the crackling.

Saddle of lamb on the bone The saddle is essentially a double loin roast including the tenderloin. Make a vertical cut across the joint away from the chump (thicker) end. Make a long cut down the length of the joint directly over the backbone then cut long thin slices parallel to the backbone. Repeat for the other side. Once you have removed all the meat this way, turn the joint over, remove the tenderloin from both sides and cut into small slices. Alternatively, remove the loins from the backbone for carving.

Ham on the bone Make a cut down to the bone just above the knuckle. Cut slices at an angle towards the knuckle.

golden rules
SUCCESS WITH CARVING
- **Always sharpen your knife before you start.**
- **A chopping board with spikes will help to hold the bird or joint steady while you work.**
- **Keep a warmed plate on the side to hold the meat as you carve it. This will help to keep it warm.**
- **With a small bird, remove the whole breast and slice it once it's off the carcass.**

Carve poultry perfectly

Small birds can simply be cut into halves or quarters for serving, but larger ones need more expert treatment to separate drumsticks, thighs and wings and to carve neat slices of meat. Aim to give each person some white breast meat and some dark meat.

YOU WILL NEED **Sharpened carving knife, two-pronged carving fork, carving board, large warmed side plate**

Removing the wishbone All poultry will be easier to carve if the wishbone is removed before cooking. Put the bird breast side up on a chopping board; pull back the skin from the neck and breast until you find the V-shaped wishbone. Expose the bone fully and cut around it with a small sharp knife until you can prise it away. If the wishbone wasn't taken out before cooking, you can use a similar procedure on a cooked bird before carving.

Carving poultry Follow these steps whether you're carving a chicken, duck, goose or a small turkey. Place the bird on its side, lift the leg up with the fork and cut under the thigh. Cut through the joint to separate the drumstick from the thigh. Slice through the breast halfway across the shoulder (below right) and cut away the shoulder, wing and a strip of breast. Carve the rest of the breast into slices, starting at the wing end, or, if it's small, cut it away in one piece and serve whole or carve on the board.

Carving turkey A large turkey (bigger than 4.5kg, for instance) is unwieldy for moving and turning on the board, as you do when carving a chicken (above), so stand it firmly on the board and carve it in one position.

1 Undo any string that's trussing the bird together. Cut between the body and the thigh on each side, cutting all around the leg and through the sinews that are holding it in place.

2 Separate the legs from the body and carve on another board or the side of your main board. Cut at an angle parallel with the bone (right) to make small slices of dark leg meat

3 Cut through the breast and down into and through the shoulder joints to remove the wings.

4 Carve thin slices of breast meat, using the back of your fork to support the slices. Try not to make holes in the meat with the fork prongs.

deal with
Caterpillars

A sudden infestation of caterpillars will chew plants to ribbons in a matter of days. Worst offenders are the yellow and black caterpillars of the large white butterfly, often known as the cabbage white. For the unsqueamish, the best solution is to remove them by hand and kill them in a strong solution of salt water. As you do so, rub off clusters of eggs on leaf undersides before they can hatch into a second generation.

Insecticide You can use a general insecticide to kill caterpillars (follow the instructions carefully) but the best organic treatment is a spray containing the microorganism *Bacillus thuringiensis berliner*, which attacks caterpillars but won't harm other insects. It can be obtained from garden centres.

Prevention You can keep caterpillars off your plants by spotting and destroying eggs before they hatch, covering plants with fine netting to prevent adult butterflies from reaching the plant to lay their eggs, and encouraging plenty of birds into your garden to prey on the insect pests.

C

play Car games on long journeys

Keeping the kids happy on a long trip is tough, very tough. 'I spy', counting colours or types of car, spelling or number challenges: these are all reliable distractions – for a while. When you have exhausted your usual games, try some of these suggestions to pass the time.

Be prepared There are things you can do before your trip to smooth the ride: buy puzzle books, make a CD of favourite music (songs that the adults can live with, too), pack a selection of snacks and treats, and plan a few games for the journey.

THREE FOR A PIG

A game for two children sitting in the back of a car, travelling through the countryside.

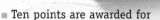

■ Each player looks out of the window on their own side of the road.
■ The aim is to spot various animals in fields on your own side, and so amass points.
■ Pigs and cows score three points, sheep one each (make a fair guess if you spot a flock of them), other animals one each.
■ There are no points awarded for birds or humans.
■ Horses earn a player minus ten points, but you cannot go below zero.

■ Ten points are awarded for a cat or dog looking out of a house or car window.
■ The first player to reach 50 points wins. Players and their parents may invent their own house rules – awarding points for men with beards, for example, or haystacks – but appoint a judge to avoid arguments.

YES OR NO

An endlessly enjoyable old favourite for all the family to play.

■ One designated person is forbidden to use the words 'yes' and 'no'. Everyone else asks them questions to trick them into saying the banned words.
■ The trick is to get the player talking about something they are interested in – football, say – then sneak in a leading question such as, 'But Brazil won the 2010 World Cup, didn't they?'

KEEP THE BEAT

A singing game that anyone can play. Put a familiar song on the car's music player.

■ One player sings along to the song. Without warning the driver or front passenger turns off the sound for a few seconds, but the person singing has to carry on.
■ If the singer is still in time with the record when the sound is turned back up, they pass.
■ Take turns until only one person is left in the game.

ROADWAY BINGO

This is a game that can be played in more than one way for all the family to enjoy during a car journey.

In its simplest version, each player picks a colour, and the first person to see ten cars of that colour shouts 'Bingo!' and wins the game.

Here is the more complex version, which involves a little preparation.
■ Before your journey, the bingomaster makes a list of ten objects for each young passenger. The lists consist of ten sights you might see along the way. Each person's list is different (though some overlap is allowed) and, if the bingo master is clever, will be tailored to the age and ability of the players. It might even take account of specific things or landmarks that are known to be on the route.
■ The first person to tick off all the objects on their list is the winner.

■ Here are some suggestions for things that might be on the lists: a cat, a castle, a street named after a person, an ambulance, a police car, a cow, a person wearing a hat, a car with foreign number plates, an aeroplane, a letterbox, a car with two children in the back (not your own), a caravan, a windmill, a sign showing the town you are headed for (or other likely destination), a burger van, a house with a green roof, a neon sign on a building, a bridge, a motorbike with two people on it, a gate with a silly name on it.

FIZZ BUZZ

This number-based game for children of about six and up can be a challenge for adults too.

■ You take turns to count upwards, remembering to say 'fizz' before any multiple of three, and 'buzz' before any multiple of five: 'one, two, fizz, three, four, buzz, five, fizz, six, seven eight, fizz, nine …' and so on. Or you can count one number each, moving around the car in turn.
■ Before multiples of both, such as 15, you say 'fizz buzz'.
■ The winner is the player who counts highest; or just see how far you can get as a family.

ALPHABETICAL SHOPPING LIST

Take turns to compile a shopping list using words starting with consecutive letters of the alphabet.

■ The first person says: 'I went to the shops and I bought apples.' The next says: 'I went to the shop and I bought apples and bananas.'
■ Each subsequent player has to recite the whole list from the beginning without making a mistake. It gets harder as the game goes on, but that is the challenge. The shopping list can be as surreal as you like: aardvark, bicycle, crab, dice …

CIRCLE OF LIFE

Quick thinking is part of the challenge of this tricky word game. Ponder too long, and you're out!

The driver thinks of an animal – a wombat, say. The next person has to think of an animal that starts with the same letter as the last letter of the previous animal – so 'wombat' might be followed by 'tortoise'. The next person has to think of an animal that begins with the last letter of that animal: 'emu'; and so on.
■ If you get stuck for more than ten seconds you're out.
■ The winner is the last person left in the game.
■ You can also play this game with any number of other categories: boys' and girls' names, towns, household objects, countries …

C

housetrain Cats

Cats are naturally clean creatures, so housetraining a kitten isn't normally a difficult job.

■ Put a layer of litter in a tray, or use sand if your cat will eventually use outdoor facilities. For two cats, provide at least two trays.
■ Place the tray in a quiet corner, away from food and water bowls.
■ If the kitten messes on the floor, transfer the puddle or solid matter to the tray. Don't be cross, but do it with a firm *This is where we do it*.
■ Clean the tray twice a day, using only hot water and detergent.
■ If your cat has an accident, wash the area with a 10 per cent solution of biological washing powder, spray with surgical spirit and scrub again.

groom Cats

Long-haired cats must be brushed and combed every day, to avoid matted, tangled fur and the skin problems that can result from a neglected coat. Start grooming a little and often from a young age. In all cats, fur balls can build up in the stomach, so even a short-haired cat will benefit from grooming.

■ Set aside a grooming area, with hygiene in mind – not the kitchen counter – and lay down a towel.
■ Talking gently all the time, fluff the cat's coat with your hand then lightly brush from roots to tip in the direction of growth. Work in sections to get rid of mats or tangles, before moving on to a wide-tooth comb, then a fine-tooth comb.
■ If the teeth of a comb snag in the fur, go back to the previous tool.
■ When you have finished, praise your cat and maybe offer a treat.

have fun with Cat's cradle

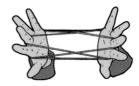

1 Slip your hands through a loop of string about 80cm long and pull them apart. Wind the string once around each of your palms.

2 Slip one middle finger through the loop on the opposite palm and pull your hands apart. Repeat with the other hand to form a 'cat's cradle'.

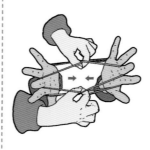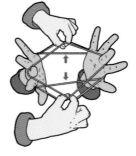

3 You need another player to join you at this point. Your playmate pinches the crisscrosses in the string.

4 They should then pull the strings outwards, then down and back under the straight sides of your cat's cradle, coming up through the centre.

5 The second player lifts the string off your hands and pulls their own fingers and hands apart to create a new shape: this is 'the soldier's bed'.

give tablets to Cats

Some cats happily take medication. Others think you're out to poison them and so giving them tablets requires patience and determination.

■ Wrap your cat in a towel and sit on the floor with them between your legs. Calmly wrap your dominant hand around the head so your fingers are under the cheekbone. Tip the head right back; the lower jaw should slacken.

■ Hold the tablet between thumb and forefinger of the other hand; use the middle finger to ease the jaw down, and place the tablet towards the back of the tongue.
■ Release the head and stroke the cat's throat to encourage it to swallow. Use a knob of butter to help the medicine go down. Watch in case it spits the pill out.

look after your CDs and DVDs

For high-quality sound and pictures, CDs and DVDs are a vast improvement on their tape-based predecessors, but they are easily damaged if you don't look after them well.

Stop skipping Dust and dirt will make CDs and DVDs prone to skipping or freezing. The simplest way to clean a grubby disk is to place it for a minute or two in a bowl of warm water with a few drops of washing-up liquid. Rinse the disk, then allow it to dry upright, like a plate in a rack. Never scrub with a wet cloth or apply any kind of pressure to the playing surface (the shiny side, without the label), and steer clear of unusual cleaning agents such as toothpaste or banana: these are often recommended, but are (at best) experimental.

Getting scratches out The surface of a disk consists of several layers. The outermost layer is a protective plastic film; a scratch that penetrates to the data layer beneath is irreparable, but shallow scratches can be 'polished out' using a soft cloth and disk-cleaning fluid. Rub gently, and always from the centre of the disk outwards: polishing round the disk in a circle is likely to cause more damage. A lateral scratch – one that follows the groove – is likely to be more damaging than a radial scratch.

paint a Ceiling

Ceilings are best painted with a roller on a long handle to avoid using trestle platforms or moving a stepladder around the room.

'Solid' ceiling paint sold in shallow rectangular boxes won't drip, but you can use any emulsion paint, poured into a roller tray. Cover the floor and furniture and wear overalls and goggles to protect against splatters. Rollers cannot paint right up to the edges, so 'cut in' by hand first. Always paint the ceiling before you decorate the walls.

Cutting in With a 38mm brush, paint the corners, a strip around the edges and just down onto the top of the wall. This will leave a neat finish when you paint or paper.

Order of work Paint the ceiling in strips, starting at the window: the reflecting light will make it easier to see where you've already been.

serve Caviar

Whether it's the real thing – the eggs of the sturgeon, lightly salted – or salmon caviar, known as red caviar or keta, caviar is best served very cold.

Because the eggs are extremely fragile they need careful handling. The traditional way of serving is to set the can in a bowl of ice and to open it at the last minute. The aim is to minimise contact with the air, which will spoil the flavour.

Caviar needs no fancy treatment: it's special enough already. Serve it with triangles of hot toast and unsalted butter or on blinis (*see* BLINIS) with soured cream as an optional extra.

To drink, champagne or vodka shots on ice are the traditional accompaniments.

copy to a CD

The most common reason for copying to a CD is to create a personalised compilation of music for the car or suchlike. On a PC this is easily done using Windows Media Player. This program allows you to select and arrange your music before 'burning' it to the CD (iTunes performs the same function on Macs and can also be used on a PC).

Archiving digital files CDs are a good medium for storing sets of files that you won't later want to modify – for example, scans of old family photos. The program that allows you to do this will launch automatically when you insert a blank CD in your computer's CD drive. Drag and drop the files you want into the appropriate window or folder then follow the instructions to save them to the disk.

C

operate a
Chainsaw safely

A chainsaw is a highly effective and time-saving tool, but it's also one of the most potentially dangerous pieces of equipment you could use. You must take precautions to ensure your safety. If in doubt, ask for advice and instructions when you hire the saw.

■ Wear a helmet, eye protection such as a pair of goggles, steel-cap boots and upper body and lower limb protection.
■ The greatest hazard that you'll encounter when using a chainsaw is 'kickback'. If the top side of the saw tip encounters an obstacle that suddenly stops the the blade, the chainsaw will jerk back dangerously towards you, the operator.

kickback danger zone

■ To minimise the possibility of a kickback injury, you should grip the front handle with your thumb curled around it.
■ Concentrate, so that you always keep the kickback danger zone free of impediments.
■ Never cut anything with one hand, or use the saw above shoulder height.
■ Don't put the saw into tight spaces, where it might catch on small branches.
■ Keep children well away.

dance the Cha-cha-cha

This dance of Cuban origin is sassy, fun and easy to learn – a great party favourite suited to many music genres.

'Smooth Operator', 'Light My Fire', 'What a Difference a Day Makes' … If you're already humming along, you're in the mood to cha-cha-cha. Its flirtatious nature is expressed in the footwork and the 'Cuban motion' swivel of your hips.

Five steps are taken to four beats: for instance, step, step, cha-cha-cha, with the first two 'cha-cha's danced quickly on the third beat. Think slow, slow, quick, quick, slow. The example below shows the man's steps – the woman's steps are the mirror image of these.

Step, step, cha-cha-cha

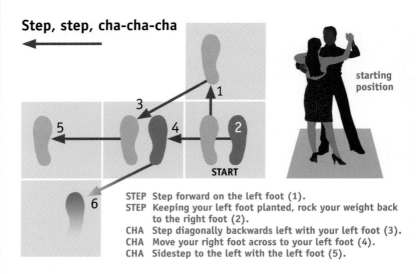

starting position

START

STEP Step forward on the left foot (1).
STEP Keeping your left foot planted, rock your weight back to the right foot (2).
CHA Step diagonally backwards left with your left foot (3).
CHA Move your right foot across to your left foot (4).
CHA Sidestep to the left with the left foot (5).

Step, step, cha-cha-cha

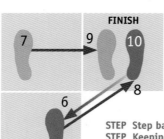

FINISH

Posture and movement
■ Hold your head high and don't look down at your feet.
■ Take short, smooth, decisive steps and transfer your weight completely with each one.
■ Don't force the swivel of your hips; master the footwork, enjoy the music and let the hip movement follow.

STEP Step backwards on the right foot (6).
STEP Keeping your right foot planted, rock your weight back to the left foot (7).
CHA Step diagonally forwards right with your right foot (8).
CHA Move your left foot to your right foot (9).
CHA Shift your weight to the right foot (10).

fix an old Chair

The spindles or rails of old wooden chairs can easily come loose or get detached. Here's how to fit them back snugly and glue them tight, and how to cure a chair that wobbles.

YOU WILL NEED Wood adhesive, cord, thick cardboard, length of wood, wooden wedge, hammer, wooden block, sandpaper, slivers of hardboard or plywood, trimming knife, varnish (optional)

Repair a loose rail

1 Sometimes all you need to do is glue the rail back, using a wood adhesive as directed on the packet. Then you must clamp the chair in position for at least 12 hours.

2 To do this, wrap a double length of cord around the chair, having placed protective pieces of thick cardboard between the cord and the chairlegs. Insert a length of wood through the cords at the front, and twist to tighten like a tourniquet. This holds everything in position. Jam the wood against a rail to keep the cord from untwisting.

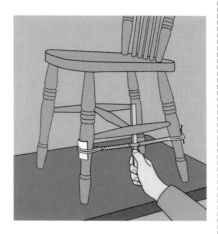

Fix a shrunken rail

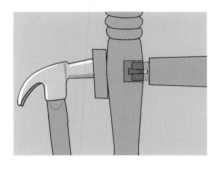

1 Sometimes the rail has shrunk in diameter, and so is too loose to glue. If so, saw a slot in the rail's end, no deeper than the hole it goes in. Insert a wooden wedge cut to the length of the slot, but don't push it all the way in.

2 Apply wood adhesive, then insert the rail into its hole. Hammer the leg onto the rail, using a wooden block to prevent damage to the chairleg. The wedge will force the rail-end open and make it fit tight.

Fix a wobbly chair

If one of the legs is too long, it's probably only by a small amount. Take some sandpaper and carefully rub away some of the leg end. Keep testing it on a smooth, hard, level surface until it stops wobbling.

If one of the chairlegs is too short, try experimenting with a series of thin slivers of hardboard or plywood.
■ Build them up one by one until the chair stops wobbling. Test it on a hard, smooth, level surface.
■ Glue the appropriate number of slivers to the leg end and to each other and allow them to dry. Trim off excess wood with a trimming knife and smooth the end with sandpaper. Stain or varnish as necessary.

---

keep the fizz in Champagne

Champagne is all about its sparkle. You can drink flat champagne, it hasn't gone 'bad' and it won't make you tipsy so quickly, but it will lack its very essence. Serve champagne in tall flutes to enhance the bubbles; they dissipate rapidly in a shallow coupe. It's a myth that a teaspoon dropped into the neck of the bottle preserves the fizz. There are two tried and tested ways to stop champagne going flat. Use a champagne saver – like a cork, but with a clamping mechanism to seal the bottle – or drink it! Alternatively, buy a half-bottle.

---

uncork Champagne

Ensure that the bottle is thoroughly chilled or it will foam too much and spill when the cork is released. Place the champagne in a bucket filled half with ice, half water, for 20-30 minutes, or refrigerate for 3-4 hours maximum.

■ Have the flutes ready to receive the first gush.
■ Strip off the foil and loosen the wire cage while covering the cork with your thumb in case it blows.
■ Drape a linen napkin or tea towel over the top of the bottle and tilt it so that it points away from you and out of harm's way (you don't want any black eyes or breakages).
■ Grip the cork and gently twist the bottle to ease the cork out.
■ As the foam subsides pour about two fingers into each glass, then top up to two-thirds.

C

dance the Charleston

This can be danced solo, side by side or opposite a partner, or together in a ballroom position. Put on some larky 1920s music ('Ain't She Sweet', 'Yes, Sir, That's my Baby', 'Don't Bring Lulu' …), and feel the beat!

Practise the elementary footwork
- You can either start right foot forward or left foot back.
- Tap your right toe forward then step back on the right foot.
- Tap your left foot behind then step forward. Repeat the cycle.
- As you step and tap, turn your toes and knees in and then out to exaggerate the swing.

Get the arms moving
- Keep your arms straight down with the palms of your hands facing the floor. Alternatively bend your arms at right angles and point your fingers to the ceiling.
- Swing your left arm back and right arm forwards as you step back with your right foot, then reverse as you tap back with the left, like swinging your arms as you walk.
- Describe circles with your arms or hands as you gain in confidence.

clean a Chandelier

The two-glove method is the best way to clean a chandelier without taking it down. Before you start, be sure to turn off the lights and remove the bulbs.

- Put on two white cotton gloves (available from DIY stores) and dampen one with glass-cleaning fluid. Massage each individual crystal with the damp glove, then wipe it with the dry glove.
- If your chandelier is really dirty you'll have to take down the crystals and wash them in a bowl half-filled with warm water to which has been added a drop of washing-up liquid and 30ml of white wine vinegar. Rinse each crystal under running water, and dry with a soft cloth.

play Charades

Two teams take turns to pick an opposition player to act out a phrase, book title, song or TV programme (*Gone with the Wind* or *Desperate Housewives*, for example), supplied by a referee. The actor may not speak or point, but may use gestures and movements to mime either the whole phrase or title, or break it down into words and syllables. By holding up fingers the actor is allowed to reveal the number of words and which word is being acted out. The first team to guess the correct answer wins. Extra points can be awarded for how quickly the answer is given, with the referee acting as timekeeper.

make a baked Cheesecake

SERVES 6-8

FOR THE BASE

100g unsalted butter, plus a little for greasing
200g plain digestive biscuits
50g caster sugar

FOR THE FILLING

3 eggs, separated
200g caster sugar
500g full fat cream cheese
2 tbsp cornflour
2 tsp finely grated lemon zest
1 tsp vanilla extract
150g fromage frais

1 Heat the oven to 180°C/gas 4. Lightly grease a 20cm loose-bottomed or springform cake tin, line with baking parchment and stand on a baking sheet.

2 Crush the biscuits in a food processor or by putting them in a polythene bag and pressing them with a rolling pin until they resemble fine crumbs. Mix with the sugar and melted butter and process for another 30 seconds or mix thoroughly to combine. Press into the base of the prepared tin. Refrigerate for 30 minutes minimum.

3 Beat the egg yolks until smooth. Add the sugar and beat until light and fluffy. Gradually add the cream cheese, followed by the remaining ingredients.

4 Beat the egg whites until stiff then fold into the mixture. Pour into the tin and bake for 10 minutes. Lower the heat to 150°C/gas 2 and cook for another hour, or until almost set. If it appears to be over-browning, cover with foil. Cool thoroughly in the tin before de-moulding. Top with raspberries or blueberries before serving.

master **Chess** basics

The game of chess is a tactical skirmish waged on a 64-square battlefield, in which the object is to capture the opposition's king.

King

Queen

Bishop   Bishop

Rook   Knight   Knight   Rook

8 pawns

Set the board up with a white square in each player's right-hand corner. Centre the king and queen on the back row – black queen on a black square, white on white. On either side place a bishop, then a knight, with the rooks (castles) in the corner. Line up the pawns in front.

How the pieces move

PAWNS can move only forward (one or two squares with the first move, one thereafter), except to capture, when they move one square diagonally.

KNIGHTS move one or two squares vertically or horizontally; two or one at right angles (that is, one straight hop, one diagonal).

ROOKS can move back or forth in straight lines over any number of unoccupied squares vertically or horizontally.

BISHOPS can move back or forth in straight lines over any number of unoccupied squares diagonally.

QUEENS can move back or forth in straight lines in any direction and over any number of unoccupied squares.

KINGS can move one square in any direction – but not to a square menaced by an opposing piece. A king can therefore not attack a king.

White starts by moving either a pawn or a knight (the only ranking piece that can pass over occupied squares, to land on an empty one or to capture a square). The players then take it in turns to move, picking off each other's pieces by landing on squares they occupy and trying not to put their own pieces in jeopardy.

The aim is to put the square occupied by your opponent's king under direct threat of being captured by your next move (putting the king 'in check'). If you can target the king in such a way that your opponent can neither move him away from the threatened square, block the line of attack or capture the attacking piece, you have achieved 'checkmate' and win the game. A draw, when a win for either player is deemed by both to be either impossible or unlikely, is called a 'stalemate'.

remove stubborn
Chewing gum

The trick for getting rid of chewing gum is to act promptly.

Try cold For a carpet, scrape off as much of the gum as possible, then apply ice cubes in a plastic bag. Scrape some more, repeating as necessary. For clothes, seal in a plastic bag and deep freeze until stiff; scrape carefully.

Try heat Blast with a hair dryer for 2 minutes, then put a clear plastic bag over your hand and remove the gum.

Try blotting Put one teaspoon of mild detergent in 200ml of water and blot. Alternatively, apply a dry-cleaning solvent.

Try oil For chewing gum in the hair, work in olive oil to soften the gum before pulling it out with a piece of kitchen towel. Shampoo and rinse.

☆ golden rules

CHESS TACTICS

■ **Gain control of the centre of the board to optimise your access to other squares.**

■ **Don't underestimate pawns. They can form powerful blockades and take more 'valuable' pieces – and if one makes it to the back line it's 'promoted' to a ranking piece.**

■ **When there are no pieces between a king and one of his rooks (and neither piece has yet moved), a king can 'castle' – that is, move two squares towards the rook, which then moves to the space directly to the other side of the king.**

C

make comforting
Chicken soup

As with any great soup, the best results begin with a good stock.

TO MAKE 2 LITRES OF STOCK

1kg chicken bones, drumsticks, wings and giblets (except liver), washed
1.5 litres water
120g onions, peeled and quartered
120g carrots, peeled and chopped
2 cloves garlic
1 large stick celery, chopped
bouquet garni
6 black peppercorns

1 Put the chicken ingredients into a large saucepan and bring slowly to the boil. Skim off any scum.

2 Add the remaining ingredients, cover and simmer for 3 hours, removing any further scum. Strain, cool and chill. Remove any fat from the surface.

SOUP FOR 4

2 tbsp olive oil
225g uncooked chicken breast or thigh meat without skin or bone, cut into small cubes
1 litre chicken stock (see above)
2 carrots, peeled and diced
2 sticks celery, diced
1 medium onion, peeled and chopped
3 tbsp parsley, chopped
85g long grain rice
salt and freshly ground black pepper

1 Heat the oil in a large saucepan. Add the chicken and brown lightly.

2 Add the stock, carrots, celery, onion, 2 tbsp parsley and the rice. Season with salt and pepper. Bring to the boil then simmer, covered, for about 20 minutes or until the rice is tender. Check and adjust the seasoning.

3 Serve in warmed soup bowls with the remaining parsley sprinkled on top.

joint a Chicken

YOU WILL NEED Chopping board, sharp knife, poultry shears or strong scissors (optional)

The trick when jointing is to be aware of the bird's anatomy and work with it. Dark meat cooks more slowly than light, so legs and thighs are best cut into smaller pieces than the breast meat. For an uncooked bird weighing 1.5kg or less, six pieces (steps 1-4) should be sufficient. For larger birds, make eight pieces by dividing the breasts (step 5) or carry on to make ten pieces by dividing the legs into thighs and drumsticks (step 6). Poultry shears or scissors aren't essential but make the job a lot easier.

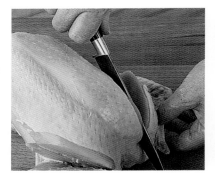

1 Place the chicken breast side up on a chopping board. Gently pull one leg out from the body, then cut through the skin between the body and leg. Bend the leg until it pops out of the socket. Cut through the flesh under the joint. Repeat with the other leg.

2 Use shears or a knife to cut off the wing pinions (ends) and discard. To separate the wings from the body, begin by making a deep cut in the breast, near the inside of each wing, angling the knife diagonally. Cut down into the meat to expose the bones.

3 To free the wings from the carcass, cut through the flesh and bone between the ball-and-socket joints with poultry shears or strong kitchen scissors. Carefully check for and remove any remaining bone splinters.

4 To remove the breast meat, use shears or scissors to cut through the thin rib cage on either side of the backbone. Discard the backbone or keep and use for stock for soup (see left).

5 Divide the breast into two, carefully cutting crossways or lengthways through the flesh using a knife, and then through the bones and cartilage with shears or scissors.

6 Cut the legs in half through the joint between thigh and drumstick.

7 Remove the skin if you wish and trim excess fat or bone from all pieces.

keep Chickens for their eggs

Fresh eggs taste far better than anything the supermarket can offer. Chickens are fun and easy to keep, and take up little space.

YOU WILL NEED Chickens (good layers include Rhode Island Reds, Leghorns or hybrid crosses, like Bovans Goldline), chicken house, wood shavings or hemcore for bedding, straw, food, grit and water containers, nest box, fencing

Housing Provide a weatherproof, roomy house with easy-to-clean surfaces, a secure door, roosting bars and at least one nest box for every three birds. Temperatures shouldn't be too extreme: egg production decreases in very cold or very warm weather. A run outside the house is essential – allow at least 1m² per bird. Chickens that roam outside could have a wing clipped to stop them straying and must be fenced in for safety against foxes. Sink the fence at least 20cm below the surface to prevent foxes digging their way in.

Cleaning Once a week clean the house, renew the straw and scrub the nest boxes and perches. Always wash your hands before and after handling birds.

Food Buy dry pellets or a mash to mix with water; 30-100g a day per bird is usually enough, but this depends on the weather, time of year, whether the hen is laying and how much free range she has. Hang grass or leafy vegetables in a string bag in the run, and provide flint grit to aid digestion and soluble grit, usually oystershell, to supply calcium for eggshells. Daily fresh water is essential.

Rhode Island Red

Laying Provide dark nest boxes with a deep bed of wood shavings, comfortable enough to accommodate a bird for up to 2 hours while she lays. Grit to peck at nearby will also help. Most hens lay in the morning after feeding.

Issues Egg production drops in autumn and winter. In late spring and early summer, remove eggs as soon as possible to stop broody chickens trying to hatch them. Consult your vet for health problems, and for more information search online for 'poultry forums'.

help with an emergency
Childbirth

When a woman goes into early labour, call for medical help and then offer calm, practical assistance.

Get prepared
■ Help the mother into a position she finds comfortable. Put clean towels under her and supply pillows.
■ Scrub your hands and nails well.

During the birth
■ When you glimpse the baby's head, urge the mother to stop pushing and instead to pant.
■ Gently support the head as it emerges, but do not pull. Remove any membrane from the face.
■ If the cord is looped around the neck, slip it over the head.
■ With the next contraction the shoulders will appear one at a time. Expect the baby's head to rotate slightly as its shoulders turn. Support the baby's body but don't pull or manipulate it.

After the birth
■ The baby will be slippery. Lay it carefully on the mother's abdomen, face down, so that mucus can drain from mouth and nose.
■ Check the baby is breathing then cover with a towel or blanket.
■ If the baby doesn't breathe within 30 seconds, gently rub its back or soles of feet. Wipe any fluids from mouth and nose. If this doesn't work, perform mouth-to-mouth: seal your mouth over the baby's mouth and nose and give two to five very gentle puffs.
■ Wait for the placenta to be expelled, and leave it attached.
■ Don't cut the cord. The midwife or paramedic will do this.
■ There will probably be some blood, so provide warm water and towels, and a sanitary towel if available.

C

clean and repair
China

Keep small or delicate china ornaments in a cabinet so that they don't collect dust.

Cleaning For ornaments, use a long-haired soft-bristled make-up brush dipped in warm water containing a drop or two of washing-up liquid.
- Rinse ornaments using a brush dipped in clean water, and leave to dry on an absorbent paper towel.
- Always wash fine crockery by hand. To prevent chipping, line the sink with a rubber mat or towel, and wash cutlery separately.

Repair Mend breaks with a two-part epoxy adhesive, which allows time to reposition the pieces, if necessary, and is waterproof.

- To position an awkwardly shaped item for gluing, place it in a box of sand, with its broken surface protruding. Apply adhesive to both pieces and carefully press together.
- A newly glued cup handle can be taped in place with gummed paper, which shrinks as it dries out, so putting pressure on the join. Repairs to handles, however, are unlikely to be strong enough to withstand normal use.

make an authentic Chilli con carne

Chilli, one of the best warming comfort foods, is believed to have been 'invented' in the 18th century by immigrants to Texas from the Spanish Canary Islands.

SERVES 6-8

175g dried red kidney beans or 2 x 400g cans, drained	750g lean minced beef
2 tbsp olive oil	2 tsp chilli powder
1 large onion, chopped	150ml red wine
2 cloves garlic, chopped	400g can chopped tomatoes
1 large red chilli, deseeded and chopped	450ml beef stock
1 small red pepper, deseeded and diced	4 tbsp tomato purée
	salt and freshly ground black pepper

1 If using dried kidney beans, soak for 12 hours or overnight in cold water. Drain, cover with fresh cold water and bring to the boil. Boil hard for 10 minutes to remove any toxins, then reduce the heat and cook for 30 minutes. Drain.

2 Heat the oil in a large flameproof casserole dish. Add the onion, garlic, chilli and pepper and cook over a low heat for 5 minutes.

3 Add the minced beef and cook, stirring, until browned. Stir in the chilli powder and red wine and cook for 3 minutes, then add the tomatoes, stock and tomato purée. Mix well.

4 Add the partially cooked beans. Bring to the boil, then reduce the heat and simmer for 1½ hours, stirring occasionally until the beans are completely tender. If using canned beans, add them for the last 30 minutes of cooking time.

5 Add salt and pepper to taste (don't salt the beans until they are cooked or the skins will become tough). Serve with rice and sour cream or guacamole if liked. A green salad also makes a good accompaniment.

play Chinese whispers

Pssst. Here's the lowdown on a wonderfully silly game, also called Grapevine or Broken Telephone. Pass it on. A group of, say, 12 of you sit in a circle. One person starts the game by whispering a brief message – once and only once – in the ear of the person on their left, who whispers it to the next person, who whispers it to the next.

Once the eleventh person has passed the message on, the last person in the circle has to say what they think they heard. If the original has done the round intact, congratulate yourselves. More probably it will have become garbled along the way – with potentially hilarious results.

If you have sufficient numbers, you can also play as two teams. A phrase is chosen at random from a book or magazine and shown to the first player on each team. The message must then be passed around each team as quickly as possible, with points awarded for speed, accuracy or a particularly funny example of miscommunication.

serve up perfect Chips

Double frying and cutting the potatoes into even-sized pieces are the secrets of deliciously tender crispy-coated chips.

YOU WILL NEED **Potatoes, potato peeler, sharp knife, tea towel or kitchen paper, chip basket and pan, vegetable oil (sunflower or corn), kitchen thermometer or cubes of stale bread**

1 For four people peel 500g potatoes and trim off the ends and sides. Cut into sticks about 75mm long and 6mm wide. Dry well in a tea towel or on kitchen paper. Put into the chip basket.

2 Heat the oil in the pan to 160°C or until a bread cube takes from 60-90 seconds to brown. Add the chips and cook for 5-6 minutes until tender and starting to brown. Drain and cool.

3 Heat the oil to 190°C (or until a bread cube browns in just under 1 minute), then fry the chips again for 1-2 minutes until crisp and brown. Drain and serve.

bake a great Chocolate cake

MAKES 8-12 SLICES

275g light muscovado sugar
25g cocoa powder
25ml water
100g butter, softened
2 large eggs, separated
225g self-raising flour
½ tsp bicarbonate of soda
½ tsp salt
150ml soured cream

FOR THE FILLING AND TOPPING

50g plain chocolate
1 tbsp coffee essence
40g butter, softened
75g icing sugar, plus extra for dusting

For the cake

1 Grease and line a 17.5cm round cake tin (springform is ideal). Heat the oven to 180°C/gas 4.

2 Put 75g sugar into a pan with the cocoa powder and water. Bring to the boil and simmer, stirring, until smooth. Leave to cool.

3 Cream the butter with the remaining sugar until fluffy. Beat in the egg yolks. Stir in the cocoa mixture followed by large spoonfuls of the remaining dry ingredients interspersed with helpings of soured cream. Beat the egg whites until stiff and fold in.

4 Pour into the prepared tin and cook for 1-1¼ hours or until a skewer inserted in the middle comes out clean. Leave to cool in the tin for 5 minutes, then remove lining paper and cool on a rack.

For the filling and topping

1 Melt the chocolate over hot water (see right) and mix in the coffee essence until smooth. Leave to cool.

2 Beat the butter until soft and creamy. Sift in the icing sugar and add the chocolate mixture. Mix well.

3 Cut the cake in half horizontally, insert the filling then replace the top half. Dust with sieved icing sugar then use the tip of a sharp knife to draw a lattice pattern.

melt Chocolate

Chocolate needs to be melted carefully or it will go grainy or 'seize'.

1 Break chocolate into small squares or chop into fine pieces. Put into a heatproof bowl.

2 Fill a saucepan one-third full of water and bring to the boil. Remove from the heat.

3 Place the bowl over the pan making sure that the base doesn't touch the water. Leave to stand, stirring the chocolate occasionally, until smooth.

You can also melt chocolate in the microwave. Break it into small pieces and heat for 30 seconds, stir, then continue in 5-10 second bursts, checking and stirring, until melted. Use a high setting for small amounts of dark chocolate, medium for more than 250g and low or medium for milk or white chocolate.

help a
Choking person

If someone is gasping, turning blue and can't speak, there's probably a blockage. If there's another person present, ask them to call the emergency services while you help the patient.

Quick action

For an adult or child

■ Remove any food or false teeth from the mouth, but don't explore the mouth with your finger.

■ Encourage the person to cough to clear the blockage. Next, bend them over forwards and slap between the shoulder blades three or four times with the heel of your hand, hard enough to induce a cough.

■ As a last resort, and only if you're sure someone is choking, perform abdominal thrusts (*see* HEIMLICH MANOEUVRE).

For a baby

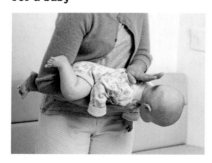

■ Lay the baby face-down along your forearm, supporting their head. Using the heel of your other hand, give five sharp blows gently but firmly between the shoulder blades. Sit down and support a larger baby across your thigh.

■ If this doesn't work, roll the baby over. Place two fingers a finger's breadth below the nipple line and press sharply inward and upward up to five times.

eat with
Chopsticks

Chopsticks work like levers, and as an extension of the fingers. Don't worry about table manners, and lift the bowl close to your mouth to avoid spills.

The upper stick is pinched between thumb and forefinger, and rests against the middle finger.

For effective use, the two ends must meet evenly, with the sticks operating in the same plane.

The lower stick rests against the third finger, with the thicker end in the crook between thumb and forefinger.

The lower is held rigid while the upper moves against it to pick up food.

mix up a
Chutney

Chutney is named from the Hindi word chatni *meaning 'hot spiced relish'. It needs to be cooked until it has the consistency of a jam.*

Chutney is essentially a sweet and sour mixture of fruit and vegetables cooked with vinegar, sugar and spices. You'll need about 3kg fruit and/or vegetables and 250g sugar to every 500ml of vinegar for a 'keeping' chutney.

Good chutneys involve mixtures such as marrow and tomato; beetroot and apple; pear, apple and sultana; dried apricots and sultanas; and blackberry and apple. Onions and garlic provide flavour, with spices such as cinnamon, cloves, cardamom, nutmeg and mace adding something more subtle. For a hotter chutney, use paprika, chilli, ginger or try garam masala or curry paste. Brown sugar (demerara or muscovado) is best for chutney. Vinegar can be malt, spirit, cider or wine, but should contain at least 5 per cent acetic acid.

Apple and tomato chutney

MAKES ABOUT 2kg

2kg tart apples, peeled, cored and sliced
2kg ripe tomatoes, peeled, seeded and coarsely chopped
4 onions, sliced
1 litre cider vinegar
400g dark brown sugar
30g salt
1 tbsp ground ginger
2 tsp whole peppercorns

YOU WILL NEED Preserving pan or large heavy-bottomed saucepan, wooden spoon, glass jars with vinegar-proof lids (plastic, coated metal or glass)

1 Combine all ingredients in a large preserving pan. Heat gently until the sugar has dissolved, then bring to the boil.

2 Simmer, stirring often, for about 1½-2 hours until the mixture is thick and pulpy, with no excess liquid.

3 Pour into sterilised jars and seal. Store in a cool, dark place, ideally for at least six months before eating.

■ Don't undercook chutney.
■ Use jars sterilised in boiling water with corrosion-proof lids.
■ Fill jars generously to within 12mm of the rim and put lids on while the chutney is still hot.

prune Climbing plants

Most climbers are easy to prune and need cutting back only to repair winter damage, though some, such as clematis, need special attention.

As well as being pruned to keep them in shape, climbers often need cutting back to prevent them from obscuring doors and windows. Those that cling can do structural damage if left unpruned (*see also* ROSES).

Wisteria Prune shoots back to about six flower buds in midsummer, then prune again, back to about three buds, in midwinter.

Self-clinging climbers Remove unwanted growth as necessary from climbers such as ivy and Virginia creeper, ideally in spring.

Twining forms Cut back climbers such as honeysuckle, passion flower and akebia between late autumn and early spring, or after flowering if really vigorous or straggly.

Herbaceous climbers Cut climbers such as hops and perennial sweet peas to ground level in late autumn.

Winter jasmine Thin out unwanted growth in late spring after flowering. Cut out dense tangled growth or unwanted long shoots at any time of year.

Clematis Pruning depends on variety and flowering time. If in doubt, treat as mid-season type.
■ Cut back early flowering varieties immediately after flowering to remove old growth and encourage new flowering stems – but only once plants are well established. Don't cut back to more than about 1m in height or plants won't flower the following year.
■ Once mid-season flowering varieties are well established, prune gently in early spring, removing only dead or damaged growth for flowers high up on stems. Prune a mature plant lower down in the same season (to about 1.5m) for flowers at head height. Cut to just above a pair of buds.

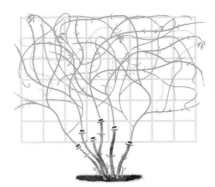

■ For varieties that flower late in the season (from midsummer onwards), prune right back in early spring to about 30cm from the ground, also to a pair of buds, before leaves are fully opened (see above).

support Climbing plants

Climbers look their best when properly trained and supported. As well as conventional solutions, a tree can make a perfect support for a vigorous climber.

However they are supported, climbers need to be tied on securely but loosely, using soft garden string or raffia (wire will damage stems rocked by the wind). Ideally, tie in shoots while they are young, flexible and easiest to manipulate. Twining climbers such as honeysuckle will need tying in only to keep them tidy.

Wires Horizontal wires placed about 45cm apart (with the bottom one 45cm from the ground) and anchored to a wall or other structure at 2m intervals with 'vine eyes' are ideal. Or, position one wire vertically up from ground level with a diagonal wire on each side to make a large V shape about 2m wide at the top. Make sure anchor points are strong and the wire is thick enough to support the weight of a large plant.

Trellis Attach trellis panels to a wall leaving at least 1cm space between them for air to circulate and to allow for tying in. Trellis panels can be mounted on wooden battens before being attached to a wall with long screws.

find and use
Clip art

Clip art graphics are a good way of livening up the documents you make on your PC. They are small images, often in a cartoon style, and thousands are available online for free. You can easily add a picture of a party hat to a birthday invitation, say, or a drawing of praying hands to a church newsletter.

If you're working in Word, you can use images that have been pre-installed on your computer as part of the Microsoft software.
■ Go to the **Insert** tab. In the 'Illustrations' group, click on **Clip Art**. From here you can browse images, or search by keyword.
■ In the Clip Art window there's a facility to access Microsoft's online library of images. Make sure that the **Include Office.com content** option is ticked. This will take you to a website containing thousands of free images. There are many other websites with similar free images.

Once you have chosen your image, you use the **Insert** command to drop it into your document. You can now manipulate the image as you wish: add borders, wrap text around it, change its colour, make it fainter so that you can run text over the top of it. You can explore these and many other possibilities using the **Picture tools** options on the **Format** tab.

Climb a tree safely

First, take a good look at your tree to be sure that there are plenty of branches you can use for suppport. Never climb wet trees – they are slippery.

■ Wear shoes with a good grip.
■ Stick to the three-point rule: keep both feet and one hand, or both hands and one foot, on the tree to support you at all times.
■ Stand only on upwardly slanting branches, as close to the trunk as you can.
■ If a branch looks dead, or too thin to hold your weight, avoid it.
■ Retrace your steps slowly and carefully as you come back down, making sure that your foot is secure before putting your whole weight on it.

iron Clothes correctly

Before ironing to remove wrinkles, check labels for symbols indicating iron temperatures. If in doubt, begin with a cool iron and increase the heat gradually. Some fabrics need to be covered with a cloth and gently pressed with an iron to avoid scorching or to prevent fabric becoming shiny. Pressing sharpens pleats, creases and lapels and neatens the shape of the garment.

> **Ironing** Use a steady back and forth motion and work methodically to avoid wrinkling sections that have already been ironed. If you don't have a steam iron, dampen badly creased areas using a spray bottle of clean water. Make sure you have a well-padded ironing board to get the best results. *See also* SHIRT.
>
> | Symbol | Fabric | Steam use |
> | --- | --- | --- |
> | COOL IRON | Acrylic, nylon, polyester | Minimal or no steam |
> | WARM IRON | Polyester mixtures, wool, silk | Moderate steam |
> | HOT IRON | Cotton, linen, viscose | Maximum steam |
> | DON'T IRON | Some synthetics | |

Pressing To press a garment or iron delicate fabrics, use a pressing cloth, such as a tea towel. Apply light pressure, especially on pockets and seams, lifting the iron quickly as you go. Most items are best pressed inside-out.

Tailored and lined jackets and trousers Press over a just-damp cloth.

Silk Use a dry pressing cloth. Place silk ties front-down on a towel.

Wool and embroidered garments Place on a folded towel and press using a damp pressing cloth.

get **Clothes** clean

Following the care labels and interpreting symbols correctly are the surest ways of getting a good result with both washing and dry cleaning. It also helps to know how to solve common problems.

The numbers in the chart below refer to the water temperature, and the bars beneath the bowl to the strength of the washing cycle and the extent to which the machine should be filled. One bar means a 'mild' wash with the machine drum no more than two-thirds full, two bars means a 'very mild' one with the drum no more than a third full. Reducing or omitting spinning is good for fabrics that crease easily. If the washing is too wet to take out, a second slow spin is better than one fast spin.

Washing symbols and fabric		Tips and variations
[95]	■ WHITE COTTON ■ LINEN WITHOUT SPECIAL FINISH	For white sheets and towels. Normal rinse, can be fully spun. Use to kill germs, such as in washable nappies.
[60]	■ COLOURFAST COTTON AND SOME POLYESTERS	Lower temperature prevents colour run. Spin fully.
[60]	■ NON-COLOURFAST COTTONS AND POLYESTERS	Use 'mild' program for easy-care fabrics and reduce or omit spinning.
[40]	■ COTTONS AND VISCOSE AND OTHER SYNTHETICS ■ WOOL	Can be fully spun.
[40]	■ NON-COLOURFAST COTTONS	Use 'mild' program for viscose and synthetics such as polyamide and reduce spinning.
[40]	■ DELICATE SYNTHETICS SUCH AS MODAL AND POLYAMIDE ■ WOOL	Use 'very mild' programme for machine washable wool. Reduce or omit spin on 'very mild' program.
[hand]	■ WOOL ■ SILK ■ CASHMERE ■ DELICATE FABRICS ■ ITEMS WITH BEADING OR OTHER DELICATE DECORATION	Wash in barely hand-hot water (maximum 40°C). Rinse well, don't rub or wring. Can be spun if crease-resistant.
[X]	■ WOOLS ■ CASHMERE ■ ANGORAS ■ LEATHER ■ SUEDE ■ MOST TAILORED GARMENTS	Don't wash.

Common problems solved

Grey whites
■ Insufficient detergent. Add more detergent, lemon juice or shop-bought whitener.
■ Water too cool. Rewash in hottest water safe for fabric.

Whites turn coloured
■ Incorrect sorting. Soak in a colour-remover and rewash. Soak new garments in vinegar to fix colour before washing.

Creasing and wrinkling
■ Incorrect cycle. Reduce temperature and/or spin cycle.
■ Overloaded machine or clothes left in for too long.

Fluff on garments
■ Lint producers (such as towels) washed with lint receivers (corduroy). Sort washing better. Remove fluff with sticky tape.
■ Tissues left in pockets. Shake and brush off when dry.
■ Clogged filter. Unblock, then run machine empty for one cycle.

Drying and dry cleaning

Check carefully before you tumble dry; even some cottons can shrink in a hot dryer.

Symbol and instruction	
	MAY BE TUMBLE DRIED
	TUMBLE DRY WITH CAUTION, REDUCE HEAT AND LENGTH OF CYCLE
	DON'T TUMBLE DRY
	DON'T DRY CLEAN OR USE STAIN REMOVERS
	DRY CLEAN PROFESSIONALLY

C

get rid of
Cockroaches

Act straight away if you see a cockroach in your house. They are are unsanitary, produce an unpleasant smell and breed incredibly fast.

■ You're most likely to find cockroaches in the kitchen by turning on a light at night. They will scurry back to their hiding places.
■ You may also see empty egg cases or skins, a dust of droppings less than 2mm in diameter or brown smears where walls and floor meet, where the cockroaches tend to run.
■ Keep your food areas scrupulously clean, empty the rubbish and don't leave pet dishes on the floor once the food has been eaten.
■ Seal any cracks that might provide hiding places – and put bleach down the drain if you suspect that's where the cockroaches are coming from.
■ Use a specific cockroach insecticide (available online, but not normally in DIY stores) to eradicate the infestation or, if all else fails, call a professional pest-control company.

☆ golden rules
CLOTHES STORAGE
■ **Store the clothes you wear most frequently in the easiest-to-reach places.**
■ **Sort garments by colour or type and store together.**
■ **Keep delicate items and those worn infrequently inside garment bags.**

select Clothes sizes around the world

Numbers used for clothes sizing follow definite patterns but are far from universal and can be unreliable because of variations between manufacturers, labelling and types of clothing. These handy charts are a good guide, but can never substitute for trying garments on in person.

WOMEN'S DRESSES										
USA	2	4	6	8	10	12	14	16	18	20	22
UK, Australia	4	6	8	10	12	14	16	18	20	22	24
Germany, Scandinavia	30	32	34	36	38	40	42	44	46	48	50
France, Spain, Portugal	32	34	36	38	40	42	44	46	48	50	52
Italy	36	38	40	42	44	46	48	50	52	54	56

MEN'S SUITS AND JACKETS									
Australia, Europe	46	48	51	52	54	56	59	60	62
USA, UK	36	38	40	41	42	44	46	47	49

MEN'S SHIRTS (BY COLLAR SIZE)									
USA, UK	14½	15	15½	16	16½	17	17½	18	18½
Australia, Europe	37	38	39	41	42	43	44	45	46

store your Clothes

Taking care about how you store your clothes will help them to last longer and look better, as well as making it easier for you to find what you want.

■ Use strong wooden or padded hangers. Store skirts on hangers with slots for loops (sew loops inside, if necessary) or clips attached, which also work for trousers. If space is at a premium, sew loops inside the waists of long dresses and hitch them up to prevent trailing. Avoid wire hangers – they can pull clothes out of shape and may even leave rust marks.
■ Hang ties over coat hangers or on purpose-made racks.
■ Fix rows of hooks inside a cupboard door for hanging belts.
■ In drawers, fold garments neatly. Store socks in matching pairs.
■ Store delicate fabrics, such as very fine wool or silk, folded between sheets of tissue paper. Roll linen to prevent it creasing.
■ Keep leather or suede in a cool, well-ventilated cupboard, and in garment bags if worn infrequently.
■ Avoid damage from clothes moths by keeping clothes clean, especially woollens, and storing them in sealed plastic bags (see MOTHS).
■ Vacuum-seal bags will save space, but clothes will need pressing before use.
■ Clean clothes before storing between seasons, but don't use fabric conditioner, which can encourage mould.

make a Cold frame

A cold frame can be improvised from a large polystyrene box covered with a sheet of thick polythene held on with masking tape, but a purpose-made frame isn't hard to construct. You can use old window frames or new wood, or even pile up bricks to make the sides. A sheet of perspex is a much safer alternative to glass for the top.

YOU WILL NEED 18mm exterior-grade plywood for front, back and side panels, preservative-treated sawn softwood battens for frame and top, saw, chisel, wood glue, 40mm and 20mm screws, screwdriver, 4 x metal angle plates for top frame, clear perspex (cut to size), glazing battens, silicone sealant, wooden beading to finish glazing, nails, hinges

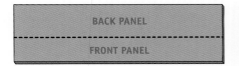

BACK PANEL

FRONT PANEL

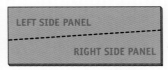

LEFT SIDE PANEL

RIGHT SIDE PANEL

1 Calculate, buy and cut the materials you need. A generous frame will be about 1.2m wide and 90cm from front to back with a front wall 25cm high and a back wall 35cm high. All the plywood can be cut from two 120cm x 60cm sheets.

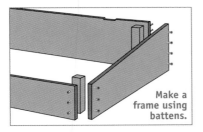

Make a frame using battens.

2 Glue and screw battens to the front and back panels, then attach the sides. Cut recesses for at least two strong hinges at the back.

3 Glue and join the top pieces using metal angle plates to make a frame for the perspex. Then fix glazing battens, glued and nailed into place, to hold the perspex. Bed the plastic on silicone sealant then finish with lengths of beading, glued and nailed in place. Attach the top to the base with hinges (using smaller screws) so that it opens easily for ventilation. It can be propped open with a strip of wood. Site the frame facing south, protected from wind.

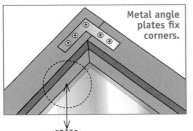

Metal angle plates fix corners.

beading
perspex
silcone
frame
glazing batten

Coconut

As well as providing flesh to be used for cooking, coconut halves can be hung in the garden as bird food.

YOU WILL NEED Small screwdriver, sieve, piece of muslin, bowl, tea towel, hammer, sharp knife

1 Use the screwdriver to pierce each of the three dark, circular 'eyes' – the weak spots at one end of the nut.

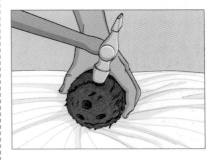

2 Drain off the liquid through a muslin-lined sieve, then lay the coconut on the tea towel and tap it with the hammer, about a third of the way down from the eyes, while turning it slowly with the other hand.

3 Continue until it breaks into two, then cut out the white coconut 'meat' with a sharp knife.

make classic
Cocktails
see pages 76-77

make classic Cocktails

Wow your guests by mixing them up some classic cocktails. These sophisticated, colourful drinks, blending alcoholic and non-alcoholic ingredients, date back to the early 19th century. Stock your drinks cabinet with a few essentials and become a mixologist.

Know your spirits Most classic cocktails are based on one of six spirits: gin, vodka, brandy, rum, tequila and whisky. You'll also need a range of liqueurs and mixers – and plenty of ice.

YOU WILL NEED

- **Measuring jug**
- **Bar strainer**
- **Lemon-squeezer**
- **Long-handled bar spoon**
- **Blender (for crushing ice)**
- **Muddler (for crushing sugar and herbs)**
- **Jigger (or shot measure)**
- **Set of measuring spoons**
- **Three-piece cocktail shaker with built-in strainer**

Choose the right glass

A martini will always look best in a martini glass. The shot glass is ideal for short, purely alcoholic cocktails, or 'shots', usually consumed in one gulp. A margarita glass is used for the drink of the same name. A fruit-juice-based cocktail, such as a Bloody Mary, fits the highball, while the lowball, also called an 'old fashioned', is good for simple, often whisky-based mixtures that can be stirred, not shaken. The goblet, or poco, is the perfect shape and size to take big, fruity cocktails like the piña colada.

shot glass

margarita glass

martini glass

highball glass

lowball glass

goblet or poco

Practice makes perfect

Cocktail-mixing is a genuine craft, and it takes practice measuring, balancing and mixing to concoct the perfect Bloody Mary or piña colada. The good news is that even your experiments, mistakes and disasters are likely to be deliciously drinkable.

NON-ALCOHOLIC COCKTAILS Some classic cocktails can be made alcohol-free, such as the Virgin Mary variation on a Bloody Mary. Experiment with your own combinations of fruit juices, bitters, grenadine, cream, milk or coconut and nobody will miss the alcohol.

MARTINI One of the earliest recorded cocktails, the martini is known the world over as James Bond's drink of choice – though he preferred it shaken, of course, not stirred, and with a little vodka added. Vary the ingredients to your taste, using dry or sweet vermouth. A dirty martini is a modern twist, made cloudy by adding two tablespoons of brine from the olive jar.

2 measures (50ml) gin
½ measure (12ml) dry vermouth
olives
orange or Angostura bitters (optional)

Pour the ingredients into a mixing glass filled with ice cubes. Stir for 30 seconds. Strain into a chilled cocktail glass. Add a dash of orange or Angostura bitters if desired. Garnish with the olives.

MOJITO A Cuban cocktail that was a favourite tipple of Ernest Hemingway's.

2 measures (50ml) rum
1 tsp caster sugar
2 tbsp (30ml) lime juice
8-10 mint leaves
1 lime
dash of sparkling water

Put the sugar and lime juice into a lowball glass. Add the mint leaves. Muddle or crush the leaves and sugar with a muddler or with the back of a spoon. Pour in the rum. Add four or five ice cubes and some lime slices. Top with sparkling water, and stir.

MARGARITA This most famous tequila-based cocktail makes for a perfect summer aperitif.

1½ measures (40ml) tequila
1 measure (25ml) Cointreau
1 tbsp (15ml) lime juice
1 lime
fine sea salt

Rub the wedge of lime around the rim of a margarita glass or a martini glass. Dip the glass into a saucer of salt, coating the whole rim. Fill a shaker with ice. Pour in the tequila, Cointreau and lime juice and shake well. Strain and add a twist of lime.

PIÑA COLADA To make this punchy, fruity cocktail extra fun to drink, serve it in the hollowed-out shell of a pineapple.

generous bowl of crushed ice
3 measures (75ml) white rum
2 measures (50ml) coconut cream
3 measures (75ml) pineapple juice
1 pineapple

Put the crushed ice into a blender. Pour in the rum, coconut cream and pineapple juice. Add the pineapple chunks. Blend until smooth. Pour straight into a tall goblet (poco) or into a pineapple shell. Top with pieces of fruit, if you wish.

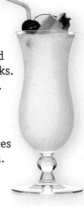

SIDECAR A delicious combination of sweetness, sourness and alcoholic strength.

2 measures (50ml) brandy
1 measure (25ml) Cointreau
1 measure (25ml) lemon juice
twist of lemon peel (optional)

Fill a shaker with ice. Add the brandy, Cointreau and lemon juice. Shake well, then strain into a lowball, old-fashioned, glass, part-filled with cracked ice. Decorate with the twist of lemon, if you wish.

BLOODY MARY The archetypal hangover cocktail.

1 measure (25ml) vodka
4 measures (100ml) tomato juice
1 tbsp (15ml) lemon juice
2 dashes Worcestershire sauce
2-3 drops Tabasco sauce
black pepper
celery stick
twist of lemon
**   or lime**

Fill a shaker with ice cubes. Add the vodka, juices, Worcestershire sauce and Tabasco. Shake, then strain into a highball filled with more ice cubes. Garnish with a little black pepper, the stick of celery and twist of lemon or lime.

MANHATTAN Some people like dry vermouth in their Manhattan, others prefer sweet. Either way, the cherry is essential.

2 measures (50ml) whisky
1 measure (25ml) vermouth
2 or 3 drops of Angostura bitters
maraschino cherry, on its stalk

Half-fill a tall glass with ice cubes. Pour in the whisky and vermouth, add the bitters and stir well to chill. Strain into a well-chilled martini glass, and drop in the cherry.

C

get rid of
Cold sores

A tingling sensation near your lips or even nostrils may mean a cold sore is coming. Act fast with over-the-counter remedies to stop it.

- Anti-viral cream applied as soon as the tingling starts will speed the healing process of the blister that develops.
- Patches that contain hydrocolloid gel aid healing and hide the sore.
- Cold sores are infectious, so avoid kissing and oral sex, and don't share crockery, lipstick, towels or flannels until a complete scab forms.
- They are caused by the herpes simplex virus HSV-1, last for eight to ten days and will often recur, especially when you're run down.

alleviate symptoms of
Colds

Pharmacy shelves groan with treatments for soothing sore throats and unblocking noses, but there's little evidence to suggest than any work better than these simple tips.

- Gargle with salt water to relieve a sore throat.
- Drink plenty of fluids.
- Try inhaling steam from hot water laced with menthol, eucalyptus or pine oil to clear blocked airways.
- Use vapour rubs to soothe symptoms in babies and children.

There have been promising studies of black elderberry (*Sambucus nigra*) to suggest it may lessen the symptoms and shorten the duration of a cold. Zinc supplement taken at the onset of symptoms may also help. Look for both in health shops.

relieve your baby's Colic

Colic is most common in babies between two weeks and four months old, after which it usually passes. Telltale signs include persistent and fractious crying for several hours at a particular time of day, passing wind and a flushed face.

Soothing solutions

There's no guaranteed cure, but there are things you can do for your baby that may help to lessen or avoid any pain and soothe the crying.
- Ask your health visitor to check your breastfeeding technique, as too much watery 'foremilk' can be a cause.
- When breastfeeding, try not to change sides too quickly or cut feeds short.
- If you're bottle feeding, ensure the hole in the teat is the right size: the milk should flow out at a drop a second without being shaken.
- Avoid caffeine and spicy food if you're breastfeeding.
- Rocking, carrying, heat, massage or 'white noise' can also calm the crying.

Try different approaches Your health visitor or pharmacist may recommend adding drops to milk to release trapped air in the digestive system or lactase drops that help to break down the protein lactose, which may cause digestive problems. Try one thing for one week. Persist if it seems effective or try something else. A cows' milk intolerance could be the cause. If breastfeeding, try avoiding dairy products in your diet, or try a hypoallergenic milk formula. See your doctor for more advice if this seems effective.

make a Collage

You don't need to be Picasso to create a successful collage. You just need the eye of a magpie, a wealth of snippets and imagination.

YOU WILL NEED **Hardboard, paper or canvas background, scissors, scraps to stick, PVA glue or wallpaper paste for sticking the paper or canvas, glue for the items you want to fix, acrylic primer and varnish (from craft shops)**

Build a collection of images cut from magazines, snapshots, greetings cards or postcards, as well as bright foil wrappers, scrunched tissue paper, labels – anything that pleases or intrigues you or has special significance. For a simple collage, you can work just with paper, but a more ambitious artwork might include buttons, shells, beads, scraps of fabric, miniature toys, trinkets, ribbons, springs, screws or anything with meaning to you.

1 Prepare the board by painting the smooth side with acrylic primer. Let it dry for about 30 minutes, cover it with glue and stick the paper or canvas to it. Don't worry about wrinkles and creases; they will add to the effect.

2 When the background is dry, lay your paper cuttings out and arrange the objects on top of them. Move things around and experiment. When you're satisfied with the effect, glue everything in place.

3 Once all the glue is dry, apply a coat of acrylic varnish to give the finished work a sheen and protective coating.

test for Colour blindness

Complete colour blindness, where someone sees only in shades of grey, is rare. The most common colour vision deficiency is red-green, which can cause sufferers to confuse shades of red, brown, green, purple and other colours with elements of red or green in them. More rare is a blue-yellow deficiency. Pseudoisochromatic plates – like these below – are often used as tests. There may be numbers within the dots or lines to trace.

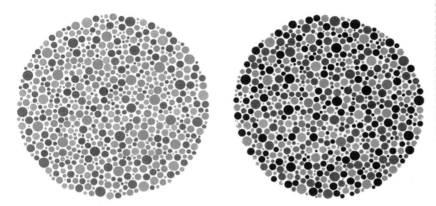

For instance, if you cannot see the figures 74 and 42 in the circles above, you may have a deficiency. There are many more online tests you can take and other types of test, too. If these lead you to suspect that you or a child has a colour deficiency it's best to consult an optician.

There's no way to correct colour blindness but it's rarely an impediment, although it may rule out some career choices, such as being an electrician or pilot, where any mistakes interpreting coloured dials, cables or warning lights could be dangerous.

Complain effectively

If you want to complain about a purchase or a service, be prompt. Delaying weakens your argument, and may affect your rights.

■ In the first instance, go back to the shop or provider and politely explain to the manager why you're dissatisfied.
■ If you're returning a purchase, remember to take your proof of purchase.
■ Know what you want: is it a replacement, a repair or a refund?
■ Stay calm and try not to get angry or emotional. Stick to the facts and be reasonable with your complaints and requests.
■ If you don't get what you require, complain in writing to the head office. Address your letter to the chief executive – you can usually find the name and the address you need online.
■ Be civil, but demand a response within a fixed time – a week or two. Explain that you've already tried and failed to get satisfaction at a local level and give the names of the employees you have spoken to.

find your way with a Compass

To use a compass, stand in an open space and hold the compass level in your hand.

The coloured end of the needle will always point to north once it settles.

Align the dial with the needle, as shown, and you can read off any other direction you need.

■ Make sure that there are no large metal objects nearby that may interfere with the reading.
■ Once the needle has settled, turn the body of the compass until the coloured end of the needle (usually red) lines up with 'north'.
■ Once you know which way is north, you can read off any other direction from the dial.
■ Bear in mind that a compass gives magnetic north; true north, the axis of the earth's rotation, is slightly to the east of magnetic north. The degree of difference varies with time and place: for most country rambles it isn't significant enough to matter, but if you're setting a bearing for a long journey, such as an ocean crossing, you should be aware of it, and compensate accordingly.

C

clean your
Computer

Screens and keyboards become dusty and grimy with daily use. It's worth spending a few minutes cleaning them up from time to time.

■ First, turn off your machine and unplug it: you shouldn't clean your computer when it's on.

■ A flat-screen monitor or laptop display needs delicate treatment. Lightly dampen a soft, lint-free cloth (don't use paper towels), and wipe from side to side, never in a circle. Never clean your screen with products containing acetone, ethyl alcohol, toluene, ethyl acid, ammonia or methyl chloride.

■ Keyboards tend to fill up with dust, fluff, crumbs and other detritus that can damage the inner workings. Unplug it (if yours is free-standing), turn it upside-down and shake, then vacuum it with the brush attachment. Cans of compressed air, available at camera shops, can be used to blow dust from between the keys. Don't use household cleaners or a wet cloth on a keyboard.

make Compost to feed your garden

Compost can be made in a heap, piled on ground that has been well forked over, but a bin is more convenient and gives better results. This can be made of plastic or from slats of wood as a 1m cube. It takes up to a year for garden waste to rot down to usable compost, so ideally you will need three bins: one filling, one rotting and one with well-rotted compost, ready for use (see below). Many plastic bins have a flap at the base for access to the ready-to-use compost, while you continue to add fresh waste at the top.

What can you compost? The best compost is made from quick-rotting green waste – vegetable peelings, grass cuttings and soft-stemmed annual weeds – plus an equal quantity of more fibrous material, such as trimmings of garden plants. If you can, add them in alternate layers, chopping or discarding any thick woody stems that will be slow to rot. Don't add a lot of grass cuttings all at once: try layering them with shredded newspaper.

As it rots, turn the heap a few times, ideally into a second bin, or simply into a pile and then back into the original bin. If it's slimy or smelly add some straw or newspaper. If it doesn't seem to be rotting, add more green matter, or a compost accelerator or sulphate of ammonia from the garden centre.

Vary what you add to your heap: don't make any one layer too thick.

Leave a full cube to rot for up to a year, turning every few months.

Use compost in the garden to improve soil texture and add nutrients.

1 Bin being filled   **2** Decomposition   **3** Compost being used

What not to compost Perennial weeds, such as couch grass and convolvulus, will grow from the smallest pieces of root left in compost. Put them in a strong plastic bag with grass mowings or soft annual weeds, tie the bag and leave for at least six months. They can then be added safely to your compost heap. Burn diseased plants or take them to your recycling centre.

Leaf mould Decomposed leaves make an excellent soil improver, but they can take two years to rot in a compost heap. Try these methods instead.
■ Put leaves into heavy-duty plastic bags, punch holes in the sides, tie them and leave for a year. If necessary, allow another six months before using.
■ To speed rotting, spread leaves out on the lawn and mow them with a rotary mower to chop them up before packing them into bags.

unfreeze a Computer

■ If one program only has locked up, go to **Windows Task Manager** and click on the **Applications** tab. You should see the status 'Not Responding' against the frozen application: click on **End Task** to quit.
■ If no programs are responding and the cursor is frozen too, reboot your computer. Press the **CTRL**, **ALT** and **DEL** keys simultaneously, and shut down when prompted. If this doesn't work, press and hold the power switch for five seconds to turn it off. Wait a minute or two before restarting.

free up Computer memory

To keep your computer working smoothly you need at least 700 megabytes (Mb) of free memory. You can check how much space you have on your hard disk (usually drive C) by clicking on the **Start** button then **Computer**. On an Apple Mac computer, double-click the icon to open your hard disk (Macintosh HD) and note the available space quoted at the bottom of the window. If you need to make more space, try some of the following tips.

■ Regularly go through old files and delete any you don't need.
■ Uninstall any software that you don't use. To do this on a PC, go to **Start**, then **Control Panel**, then **Uninstall a program.** Follow the instructions from there. On a Mac, go to the hard disk, then **Applications** and drag and drop unwanted programs into **Trash.** Empty Trash when you have finished, otherwise you will have only moved the files to a different place.
■ Move big files to an external hard disk. This is a good idea for movies, photos or music files that you want to keep but don't need to access all the time. Move or copy the files, delete the originals from your computer – and simply plug in the external drive when you need it.

guard against Computer viruses

Viruses can get onto your computer via email messages, downloads from the internet and from sharing portable storage devices, such as memory sticks.

Symptoms and cures If your PC has a virus it may run slowly or crash frequently; dialogue boxes and other elements on screen may look different; you may hear the hard disk whirring when it should be inactive. Run your anti-virus software immediately or seek help from a computer professional.

Beating off viruses Install anti-virus software and keep it up to date. Be careful about what you allow onto your computer: only download from reputable websites, and be wary of unsolicited or odd-looking emails, even if they appear to have come from a friend. Delete any that seem suspect without opening them (viruses are often hidden in an attachment).

deal with Concussion

If a blow to the head has rendered someone briefly unconscious, or they are staggering or looking dazed and confused, suspect concussion.

Quick action

■ If the person is unconscious, don't move them: call for an ambulance. If the person is conscious, help them to sit up and place a cold pack of ice wrapped in a clean cloth on any injury to reduce swelling.
■ Call an ambulance if the patient's condition deteriorates.
■ Get the patient assessed by a doctor even if they were only unconscious for a few moments.
■ Continue to monitor the patient's condition: they should rest under supervision for 24 hours. Call the doctor or an ambulance if they suffer nausea or vomiting, visual disturbance, breathing difficulties or disorientation.

deal with
Condensation

Condensation occurs when warm, moist air comes into contact with a cold surface such as an external wall or a single pane of glass. It's most common in bathrooms and kitchens. To reduce condensation, you must tackle both the humid air and the cold surfaces.

■ Open a window while you shower or immediately after.
■ Cover saucepans with a lid when you cook.
■ Install an extractor fan in your kitchen and your bathroom and use them. Leave bathroom fans running for a while after you finish to clear the moisture.
■ Keep your bathroom warm for the first hour or two of the day, when it's most in use.
■ Use anti-condensation paint (which contains a fungicide) on bathroom walls.
■ Ensure adequate ventilation in rooms fitted with draughtproofed windows. Have trickle vents fitted in the frames if necessary.

write a letter of Condolence

Getting started is often the hardest part of writing a letter of condolence, but it's best to be straightforward, with a simple *I am writing to say how sorry I am to hear about David's death*. Explain what the deceased meant to you and why you loved or admired them: *He was the centre of any gathering*, *She taught me so much about …* or just *He always had a friendly smile*. If you can, include a story about the deceased that the bereaved person might not know; a fond anecdote that sums up the personality that's now gone. If that story happens to be funny, then so much the better: in times of grief, it's wonderful to be reminded that there were moments of joy and laughter.

treat Conjunctivitis

Allergy, irritation or infection in the eye can cause a gritty sensation, itching, sharp pain or just a persistent feeling of 'something in my eye'. There may also be a discharge, causing blurred vision or leaving eyelids stuck together when you wake. Soothe the irritation as follows.

■ Soak a clean flannel or cotton wool pad in cool, boiled water and hold it to the eye to relieve itchiness and clean away any discharge. Wash the flannel after use and between eyes, and don't share facecloths or towels until the infection clears up: conjunctivitis is very contagious.
■ Consult a doctor or pharmacist, who may prescribe an oral medication, cream or eye drops. If you wear contact lenses, stop until you're better.

conquer at Conkers

Arm yourself with a fine specimen of a horse chestnut. Choose a conker that's firm, of even shape and free of cracks. Drop it in a bowl of water: if it floats, it's damaged. Find a better one. Drive a hole through your conker with a skewer or hand drill, and thread and knot a length of string.

■ One opponent dangles their conker while the other takes a swing at it.
■ If a player spins their opponent's conker full circle, they get an extra crack at it. The winner is the one with a conker left on their string when the other has been smashed.

plant out flower Containers

Flowering plants in containers will thrive for longer than many border displays and need minimal maintenance. You can pack the plants in more tightly, too, for a really striking splash of colour.

First choose a pot. Too small, and it will quickly become rootbound, too large and it will be prone to waterlogging. Plastic retains water better than terracotta, which must also be treated to be frostproof. Next, choose your compost. A multipurpose mix is fine for short-term displays, but for permanent plantings, mix this 50:50 with John Innes No.3. Container compost includes added feed and water-retaining compounds, which can reduce maintenance when you're away (see over page).

1 Fill the pot with drainage material to a tenth of its height. Use coarse gravel, bits of broken terracotta pot or polystyrene plant trays. Add compost until the pot is about two-thirds full and push it down with your fingers. If using a large pot, water it now.

2 Position plants in their individual pots until you're happy with the display, then start planting, beginning with the largest. Set the plants in the container, planting them to the same depth as they were in their previous pots.

3 Fill in with compost as you go, leaving at least 2.5cm between the finished surface and pot rim. Pack compost around the roots.

4 Gently firm, water well and put the container in position, ideally on 'feet' to keep drainage holes clear and to help to prevent waterlogging.

avoid and treat
Constipation

A diet that provides insufficient fluid and fibre is a prime cause of this condition. It's normally easy to treat, but also to prevent.

■ The best way to avoid constipation is to drink six to eight glasses of fluid a day, preferably water, and eat plenty of fruit and vegetables, wholemeal bread and brown rice. Take regular brisk exercise, too. This same advice can also help to treat the problem.
■ Your doctor may prescribe laxatives, but if you don't respond you may require a suppository.
■ Some experts recommend taking a psyllium supplement with plenty of water in the early evening. Ask your doctor if this is appropriate for you.
■ Never ignore or rush calls of nature, and don't strain.

✳ golden rules

DAZZLING DISPLAYS IN CONTAINERS
■ **Don't over-compress the compost as you plant.**
■ **Reduce maintenance by adding water-retaining gel and slow-release fertiliser.**
■ **Use special ericaceous compost for acid-loving plants, such as camellias.**
■ **Prevent pots from blowing over by adding heavy stones in the base.**

C

be confident holding a
Conversation

Maintaining a conversation is a skill, like driving a car, that anyone can master.

A conversation is more about engaged listening than talking. Often the hardest thing is getting started, but a reliable technique is to ask a few questions about the person in front of you.

■ If you're a guest at a wedding, for example, enquire how the person knows the couple.

■ In a social situation, paying a mild compliment is a good way to get a chat started: *I like that brooch, where did you get it?* or *Your children are behaving beautifully – how old are they?*

■ If it's a professional situation, ask a question that might establish some common ground: *Are you in X's team?* or *Do you work on the Y account?*

Keep the conversation going

■ If the conversation moves on to personal matters, listen, but resist the temptation to offer advice.

■ When talk turns to big questions – religion or politics – state your view honestly, modestly and with good humour: an argument is the worst form of conversation.

■ Never talk for more than a minute at a time without letting someone else have a say: a monologue isn't a conversation.

Time to move on It's perfectly polite to bring a conversation to a close when you need to. You should say something like: *I'm sorry, but I really have to go now – but thank you so much: I really enjoyed talking with you.*

keep Containers blooming without you

If you don't have a neighbour to water your pots while you're away, cut off any surplus growth to reduce water loss, then try the following methods.

■ Sink small pots into larger ones filled with wet sand or compost.

■ Group them in a shady spot or bury them in a damp compost heap or empty flowerbed.

■ Incorporate water-retaining gel into the compost when you plant.

■ Sit pots in troughs covered with dampened capillary matting dipped into a bucket of water at one end.

■ False-bottomed pots and troughs have a water reservoir in the base, that will last longer than if you water compost from above.

■ Cut off the base of a plastic bottle, remove the cap and stuff the neck with plenty of cotton wool. Push the bottle, neck downwards into the soil and tie it to a stake to keep it upright. Fill with water just before you leave and it will drain through slowly. Make one for each container.

■ If you're away for long periods, install an automatic watering system that delivers a fine spray of water to each container. Some have a timer to control the watering.

bake Cookies for all occasions

Cookies can be made in endless variety. Plain ones can be made in fancy shapes or iced, or the dough flavoured with fruit, nuts, spices or chocolate. Whatever you choose, they should be crumbly and moreish.

Raisin oat cookies

MAKES ABOUT 30

125g butter, plus extra for greasing
125g light brown muscovado sugar
175g wholemeal self-raising flour
50g rolled (porridge) oats
pinch of salt

50g seedless raisins
1½ tbsp golden syrup
1 medium egg, beaten

VARIATION Substitute chopped mixed peel or nuts for the raisins.

1 Preheat the oven to 180°C/gas 4. Grease three baking sheets with a little of the butter and melt the remainder in a large pan over gentle heat. Take off the heat, add the remaining ingredients and stir until well mixed.

2 Use a teaspoon to form the mixture into small balls and place well apart on the baking sheets: they will spread. Bake for 12-15 minutes until golden and set. Leave to sit for 1-2 minutes, then transfer to a wire rack to cool completely.

Chocolate chip cookies

MAKES ABOUT 24

175g soft margarine or softened
    butter, plus extra for greasing
225g golden caster sugar
2 eggs
350g self-raising flour
100g chocolate chips or roughly
    chopped plain or milk chocolate
½ tsp vanilla essence

1 Preheat the oven to 180ºC/gas 4.
Grease three large baking trays with
a little butter.

2 Put all the ingredients into a bowl
and mix to a smooth dough. A food
processor will do this quickly.

**VARIATIONS Substitute half the
chocolate chips with chopped
toasted hazelnuts or pecans.
Use 1 tsp coffee essence in place
of the vanilla. Use light muscovado
sugar for a deeper flavour.**

3 Place the dough on the trays in large
spoonfuls, pressing them down with
the back of the spoon or a palette knife.

4 Bake for 15-20 minutes until golden
brown and just firm to the touch.
Cool on a wire rack.

Cut-and-come-again cookies

MAKES ABOUT 50

250g softened butter
125g icing sugar, sifted
375g plain flour
90g dried apricots, finely chopped
70g roasted hazelnuts, finely
    chopped

1 Preheat the oven to
180ºC/gas 4. Line two
baking trays with baking
parchment.

2 Put the butter and
icing sugar in a bowl
and beat until light and
creamy. Transfer to a
larger bowl, sift in the
flour and combine.

3 Add the flavourings to
this basic dough and
mix together gently. Turn
the dough onto a lightly
floured surface and knead
until smooth. Divide in
two and roll each portion
into a log.

4 Wrap each log in greaseproof paper
or cling film and refrigerate for an
hour. The dough will keep for seven to
ten days, or freeze for three months.

**VARIATION Substitute other fruit
and nut combinations for the
apricots and hazelnuts, such
as raisins and pistachios. For
children, add a handful of small
sweets to the basic dough mixture.**

5 Slice the dough into discs 1cm thick
and place on trays, 3cm apart. Bake
for 10 minutes, until just firm, and cool
on the trays, then a wire rack.

clean tarnished
Copper

Decorative copper items are usually
lacquered. Cookware is unlacquered.

For lacquered copper Wipe with a
damp cloth. Use warm soapy water
to remove grease and a medium
bristled brush to get into crevices.

For unlacquered copper Never use
a scourer (it will scratch) and avoid
bleach, which causes discolouration.
Instead, sprinkle with salt and a
little white vinegar, or use the cut
side of half a lemon dipped in salt.

■ For heatproof items, boil in a
large pan of water with 100ml white
vinegar and 50g salt. Rinse well and
dry with a tea towel.

■ For grimy crevices use an old soft
toothbrush and methylated spirits.

■ Remove green corrosion by
soaking in washing soda.

■ Swab small items with ketchup,
using a make-up sponge.

golden rules

IRRESISTIBLE COOKIES

■ **Space cookies well apart to
allow them to spread.**

■ **Time cooking carefully:
cookies burn easily. If in
doubt, lower the temperature.**

■ **Cookies will crisp up as they
cool, so don't overcook.**

■ **Don't add too much egg or
other liquid – the mixture
should be stiff.**

■ **Most cookies will keep for a
week in an airtight container.
Finished cookies and uncooked
dough both freeze well.**

C

treat Corns on feet

A corn is an area of thick, dry skin that develops due to excessive pressure or friction.

- First identify and avoid the cause, such as shoes that rub or pinch.
- Use a pumice stone to rub down skin that's getting thick, but never cut away a corn yourself. That's a job for your doctor or chiropodist.
- If you talk to a doctor, chiropodist or pharmacist, ask about creams to rehydrate thick skin, and plasters, padding and insoles to ease or redistribute pressure on your foot.
- To prevent a recurrence, change socks or tights daily, choose comfortable footwear, thoroughly wash and dry your feet every night and apply foot-moisturising cream.

tackle a Cough

A cough is the body's way of clearing mucus or irritants from the throat and lungs. It's usually caused by a respiratory tract infection resulting from a virus, such as a cold, flu or bronchitis.

- For a dry throaty cough (one that produces no phlegm) make a warm drink of honey and lemon. The honey coats the throat, relieving the irritation that causes coughing.
- For a chesty cough that produces phlegm, ask your pharmacist to recommend an expectorant cough medicine. This helps to loosen up mucus, so making it easier to cough up out of your system.
- Avoid spreading germs; cough into your elbow. If you cough into your hands, wash them (see HANDS).
- If you have had a cough for more than two weeks, if it's getting progressively worse or if you cough blood, see your doctor.

produce a classic Coq au vin

SERVES 4
1 chicken weighing 1.5-2kg
550ml red wine, ideally Burgundy
salt and freshly ground black pepper
1 tbsp olive oil
100g streaky bacon, diced
2 tbsp brandy
100g button onions, peeled
100g mushrooms, sliced
2 cloves of garlic, crushed

about 300ml chicken stock
25g butter, softened
about 4 tbsp plain flour

TO GARNISH
4 small white onions
25g unsalted butter
1 tsp sugar
50g button mushrooms
1 tbsp chopped parsley

1 Tenderise an older bird by marinating in the red wine for 24 hours, then clean, truss and season the bird (saving the wine for use during cooking). Heat the oil in a flameproof casserole and fry the bacon until the fat runs. Remove and set aside. Add the bird and brown. Pour off all but 3 tbsp fat.

2 Warm the brandy in a small pan, set it alight and pour it over the bird. When the flames subside, pour in the wine and add the bacon, onions, mushrooms and garlic plus enough stock to come halfway up the bird.

3 Cover with a lid and cook on the top of the stove or in an oven preheated to 150°C/gas 2 for 1½-2 hours or until the thigh juices run clear when pierced with a skewer.

4 Meanwhile, mix the butter and flour with a fork. Boil the white onions for 5 minutes, then toss them in butter in a frying pan for 3 minutes. Add the sugar and cook for 3-4 minutes until caramelised. Fry the mushrooms ready for the garnish.

5 Remove the chicken, divide into joints and place on a serving dish. Lift the mushrooms, onions and bacon from the casserole with a slotted spoon and arrange over the meat. Keep warm.

6 Place the casserole over a high heat and boil hard to reduce by a third. Lower the heat and add the butter and flour mix in small pieces, stirring, until the sauce thickens. Check the seasoning and pour over the bird. Garnish with the onions, button mushrooms and parsley.

perform CPR

Cardiopulmonary resuscitation (CPR) is used to treat someone who has stopped breathing, but the method varies depending on the cause.

CPR always involves chest compressions, but in some cases mouth-to-mouth resuscitation via 'rescue breaths' should also be given. Your first step must be to assess the patient's condition.

Assess the scene
- Tap or gently shake the patient. Shout *Can you hear me? Open your eyes. Squeeze my hand.* If there's no response, shout for help. Get someone to summon an ambulance and to confirm they have done so. Make sure they tell the ambulance controller that a cardiac arrest is suspected.
- Kneel by the patient and roll them onto their back, pulling from the hip. Tilt the head back, lifting the chin with your fingers to open the airway.

■ Put your ear close to their mouth and listen for breathing. If the patient is breathing normally, place them in the recovery position (*see* RECOVERY POSITION) and don't start CPR.

■ If the patient isn't breathing normally, or is coughing, breathless or motionless, apply CPR. If drowning or asphyxiation is suspected, alternate 100 chest compressions with two rescue breaths. Otherwise start by applying 600 chest compressions and then alternate as above.

Chest compressions

1 Kneeling over the patient place the heel of your hand at the centre of their chest. Cover that hand with the other and lace your fingers, keeping the fingers of the lower hand raised, away from the patient's ribcage.

2 Lean forward with your arms straight till your shoulders are over the chest and press straight down 5-6cm. Keep your hands in place but ease the pressure to let the chest rise. Repeat 30 times at a rate of 100-120 per minute.

3 If the patient starts breathing normally again, place them in the recovery position. If the patient isn't responsive after 6 minutes of compressions, continue by alternating two rescue breaths (see below) with 30 compressions until help arrives. If you cannot or do not want to give rescue breaths, give chest compressions on their own. Carry on until help arrives or the patient regains consciousness or starts breathing again – or until you are too tired to continue.

Rescue breaths

1 Place a hand on the person's forehead and tilt the head back, supporting the chin with your fingers. Pinch their nose to close it, draw a normal breath, seal your lips around the mouth and blow until the chest rises.

2 Watch the chest fall – the complete cycle should take about one second – and repeat once more before resuming chest compressions. If you have enlisted a fellow first-aider, take it in turns; stop pumping the chest while your partner gives rescue breaths, and vice versa.

make a Corsage

A corsage is essentially three buttonholes tied with a bow, pinned to a dress or worn on the wrist. When choosing flowers keep in mind the fabric to which your corsage will attach: don't make it too heavy.

YOU WILL NEED Three perfect rosebuds, secateurs, corsage wire, wire cutters, florist's tape, baby's breath as a filler flower, fronds of foliage, safety pin and ribbon

1 De-thorn and trim each rose stem to around 5cm in length. Poke a wire about 12cm long halfway through the fleshy base of each rose, bend downward in a U-shape and tape to the stem.

2 Add a spray of filler flower and a frond of foliage to each rose. Bind to the stem with florist's tape.

3 Tape all three rose bundles together into a triangle and twist the wires together at the base. Wrap florist's tape around the wires.

4 Wrap the safety pin in wire and tape. Secure the pin by twisting its wire to the back of the corsage just beneath the top rose. This ensures that, when pinned, the corsage remains upright.

5 Finish with a ribbon tied in a bow around the stem tops.

C

go Crabbing

There are various ways to go about crabbing, some more hi-tech and equipment-heavy than others. If you're crabbing just for the fun of it, the easiest and simplest way to catch crabs is to attach some bait – rancid bacon works well – to a length of string or twine, and lower it into a rock pool or into the water below a quay.

- When you get a bite, gently lift the line and the crab will come with it, clinging on to the bait.
- Keep your catch in a bucket of seawater, away from the sun. Don't put too many crabs in together: they will fight.
- Return them to the water when you're finished.

treat Cradle cap

In their first three months or so, babies may develop yellow, greasy, scaly patches on the scalp. The condition is harmless, rarely causes discomfort, and usually lasts for no more than a few weeks or months.

- Massage a little petroleum jelly, olive oil or baby oil into the scalp at night to soften the patches. Use a soft baby brush or a cloth in the morning to remove particles, then wash the hair and scalp with baby shampoo.
- If the cradle cap doesn't clear up on its own, or becomes inflamed or infected, consult a doctor, who may prescribe medication.

prepare and dress a Crab

The meat of a crab is well guarded within its tough armoured shell, but cooking, extracting and presenting it is a satisfying culinary challenge.

YOU WILL NEED Large saucepan, claw cracker or small hammer, skewer or lobster pick, two bowls, teaspoon

1 Cook a fresh crab in boiling water with 1 tbsp lemon juice, a bay leaf, some parsley stalks and a few black peppercorns. Allow 15-20 minutes for a 1-1.5kg crab. Let it cool. Lay the crab on its back and twist off the legs and claws. Open the claws with the cracker or hammer and remove the meat into a bowl using the skewer or lobster pick. Do the same with any other reasonably sized legs.

2 Twist off the tail flap and discard. Then push out the flesh of the central body chamber from the upper shell with your hands.

3 Remove and discard the gills ('dead men's fingers') from around the body. Pick up the back shell and remove the stomach sac from just below the head.

4 Break the body into halves or quarters and prise out the white meat, discarding any small pieces of membrane.

5 Spoon the brown meat and any coral in the shell into a separate bowl.

6 Trim the washed empty shell, cutting around the edge to neaten. Season the meat and replace in the shell, white to the sides and brown in the middle. Serve with mayonnaise, with lemon and buttered brown bread or with a salad.

create the perfect Crème brûlée

Perfection in a crème brûlée lies in the crispness of its sugar coat and the richness of its custard filling. Fruit such as raspberries, blueberries or nectarines can also be added below the custard mixture.

SERVES 4

600ml double cream
8 egg yolks
1 tbsp caster sugar
½ tsp vanilla essence
about 75g caster sugar, to finish

1 Put the cream in a heatproof bowl over a pan of simmering water. Beat the egg yolks with the caster sugar and vanilla essence, then stir into the warm cream. Cook, stirring continuously, until the custard thickens enough to coat the back of a spoon.

2 Strain through a fine sieve into four heatproof ramekins. Refrigerate for at least 4 hours, or overnight.

3 Cover each custard with a thick, even layer of sugar then use a cook's blowtorch or a high grill to melt and caramelise the sugar. Cool and chill for 2-3 hours before serving.

make classic Crêpes suzette

Best finished on a table-side burner amid a flourish of flame, these sumptuous pancakes are a dinner party classic.

SERVES 4

8 pancakes made with sugar added
(*see* PANCAKES)
25g unsalted butter
50g caster sugar

juice of 2 large oranges, strained
juice of ½ lemon, strained
2-3 tbsp orange liqueur

1 Heat the oven to 120°C/gas ½. Cook the pancakes and place between layers of greaseproof paper. Put on a large plate, cover with foil and keep warm in the oven.

2 Melt the butter in a large frying pan, stir in the sugar and cook until it becomes golden brown and caramelised. Add the orange and lemon juice and stir until the caramel has dissolved and the sauce is thick.

3 Put a pancake into the pan and fold it in half, then in half again. Push to the side of the pan, then add the next pancake and fold in the same way. Continue until all the pancakes are in the pan. If you have a table-side burner, switch the pan to it now and lower the lights for a touch more drama.

4 Add the liqueur, allow it to warm for a few seconds, then set it alight, shaking the pan so that the sauce becomes well mixed. Serve the pancakes with the still-burning sauce spooned over.

treat Cramp

Most cramps are brief episodes of intensely absorbing pain, when muscles go into involuntary spasm. You need to stretch the affected muscles to reverse the effect. Drink plenty of fluids if you're prone to cramp, as this can help to prevent it.

Quick action

■ For a cramped foot stand on it and lean forward to stretch the muscles on the sole. Rub firmly.
■ For cramp of the front of the thigh, lie down and bend the knee. Rub the front of the leg.
■ For cramp of the back of the thigh, straighten the leg and massage the back of it.
■ Relieve cramp in a calf by flexing the ankle, pointing the toes up.

C

understand
Cricket terms

Part of the charm of cricket lies in the lexicon of terms employed to describe every facet of play. Here are some of the most common ones.

Run out A dismissal in which the ball hits the wicket while the batsman is still running between the stumps.

Stumped The batsman steps outside the crease (see right) while attempting to play the ball, but the ball comes through to the wicketkeeper who breaks the wicket using the ball in their hand.

LBW 'Leg before wicket', meaning broadly that the batsman blocks with his body (not necessarily his leg) a delivery that would otherwise have hit the wicket.

Maiden An over of six balls during which a batsman fails to score.

Spin A form of bowling in which the bowler gives the ball a flick as it's bowled in the hope of causing it to arc and bounce off the pitch in an unexpected way.

Duck A score of zero made by a batsman, described as 'golden' if the dismissal is on the first delivery.

All-rounder A player skilled at both bowling and batting.

Bouncer A delivery that hits the pitch and rears up near to or over the batsman's head.

Swing The lateral movement of the ball in the air as it's delivered.

No ball A delivery deemed illegal, usually because the bowler stepped beyond the crease before releasing the ball.

follow Cricket

The game has a reputation for arcane rules and impenetrable jargon – but the basic principles are actually quite simple.

Cricket is a game of bat and ball between two teams of 11 players. Two batsmen take to the field at any one time. Each has a 'wicket' to guard made up of three upright pieces of wood ('stumps') with two smaller pieces ('bails') laid across the top. The two wickets are positioned at either end of a thin rectangular pitch 22 yards (20.12m) long in the centre of the playing field.

The bowler delivers the ball overarm from one wicket to the other. The batsman aims to hit it before or after it bounces and then both batsmen run as many times as possible between the two sets of stumps before the ball can be returned to the wicket. Each must reach the safety of the opposite 'crease' (a line drawn 4ft – 1.2m – forward of the stumps) for a run to be scored. After every six deliveries (an 'over'), a new bowler takes aim from the other end.

Cricket fielding positions (right-handed batsman)

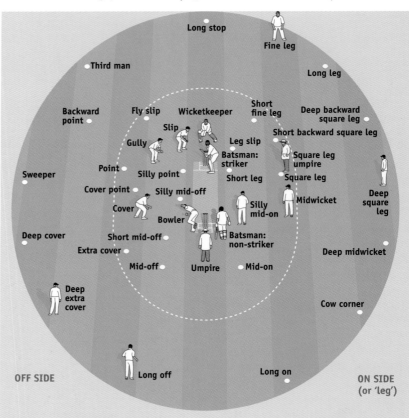

The captain and bowler 'set a field', placing fielders where they are most likely to catch or inhibit the batsman, according to the bowler's style. The figures above show a 'defensive field', intended to limit the runs a batsman might score. An 'attacking field' would include more 'slips' close to the batsman, ready for a catch.

Understanding the ins and outs

The bowler's primary aim is to 'bowl' the batsman out by hitting his wicket with the ball, but he may also try to trick the batsman into hitting the ball high so that he can be caught out by a fielder. The batsman must choose whether to try to score runs or just to guard his wicket until an easier ball comes along. If he manages to hit the ball to the boundary of the playing area (usually no less than 69m from the wicket) he scores four runs, or six if the ball doesn't bounce until it has cleared the boundary.

An innings ends when ten batsmen are out. The opposing team then tries to beat the first team's score. Games consist of one innings each (a one day game), or two innings (played over three, four or five day games).

learn basic Crochet

Crochet is a way of making fabric by linking together loops of yarn. One loop is held in position by a hook (*crochet* in French) while another loop is fed through it. These instructions show how to make a foundation chain of loops, the base for all stitches, and how to work a basic stitch into it. Reverse the hand positions if you are left-handed.

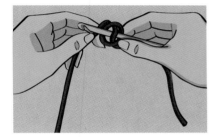

1 Make a slip knot about 15cm from the yarn end and insert the hook through it from right to left.

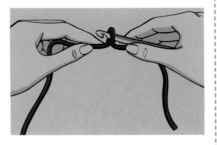

2 Pulling both yarn ends, draw in the loop until it's close but not tight to the hook.

3 Holding the slip knot with your left thumb and middle finger, and pulling the yarn tight over your index finger, push the hook forward and twist it so that the yarn passes over the hook and is caught in its slot.

4 Draw the yarn through the loop, so forming a new loop (chain) on the hook. This should be loose enough for the next chain to be drawn through it in the same way. Repeat until you have the desired number of chains.

continued overleaf ➜

win at Croquet

Croquet looks like a genteel game, but its rules reward players who show no mercy.

Croquet is a game for two players or pairs of players. Each has two balls (black and blue, or red and yellow), which they must hit through six hoops twice in a set order and direction, and finally against a central peg (as shown).

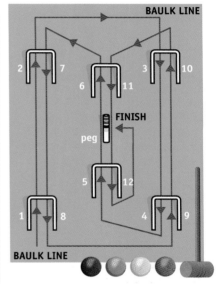

■ Begin by striking the balls into play from one of two 'baulk' (start) lines, diagonally opposite one another on the lawn.

■ In turn, players strike a ball to go through ('run') its next hoop or hit ('roquet') another ball.

■ For running a hoop, take an extra stroke. A roquet wins two; place your ball next to the 'roqueted' ball and propel both at once.

■ If both balls are yours, direct them to your advantage. If one is your opponent's, despatch it to the most inconvenient spot you can find.

■ A turn ends when you have made all the strokes you are entitled to or if you send a ball off court.

C

master the
Cross-stitch

Cross-stitch is a form of counted thread embroidery, which, as the name suggests, involves counting fabric threads. It's usually stitched on Aida or evenweave fabric that has easy-to-count threads. Often the stitcher follows a chart where the cross-stitches are displayed as clearly marked symbols.

Both the simplicity of the cross-stitch technique itself – each stitch is worked over the same number of threads to form a neat X-shape – and the easy-to-follow charts mean you can stitch designs that are perfect in every detail, even if you're a beginner.

1 To start working from right to left, push the needle through a hole from the back of the fabric to the front. Insert it one hole up and to the left, and bring it out to the front again one hole down. Continue like this to form a row of diagonal stitches.

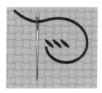

2 Now work from left to right to turn each diagonal stitch into a cross. Bring the needle out one hole below the top of the last stitch. Insert it one hole up and to the right. Bring it out one hole down. Continue to form a row of completed cross-stitches.

 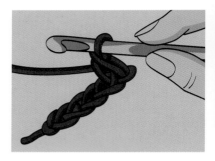

5 To begin a second row, keep the last chain on the hook and feed the hook through the second knot down on the chain. Then catch the yarn as before.

6 Pull the yarn through both loops on the hook to complete a turning stitch and then continue as before to add stitches to your new row.

7 When you've finished, trim the remaining yarn to 10cm, then pull through the loop. Work back along your final row, using the hook to pull the yarn through each stitch in turn, weaving it into the crochet. Part way along, make a knot to secure the yarn. Trim the loose end and repeat with the tail left from the start of the crochet.

tackle a cryptic Crossword puzzle

Cryptic crosswords are an immensely satisfying form of mental exercise, a battle of wits between you and the setter.

The key to cryptic crosswords is that no element of a clue is superfluous. A crossword setter will call on a number of conventions when devising a clue, so the first step to becoming an aficionado is to learn the main ones. The ones listed here account for perhaps half the answers in any given crossword.

Synonyms The answer is often a synonym for the first or last word or phrase in the clue. Think: 'What is the answer going to mean?' In 'Roughly put down cheap wine (5)', the answer is a synonym for both parts of the clue: PLONK.

Anagrams Many clues are disguised anagrams, and these are often the easiest to spot. Look out for words that might point to an anagram, such as 'confused', 'about' or 'mixed', then see if there are words in the clue that add up to the right number of letters. The solution to 'Claimed USA plotted conflict (10)' is POSTULATED – an anagram of 'usa plotted' signalled by the word 'conflict' (and a synonym for 'claimed').

Abbreviations Cryptic clues make great use of common abbreviations or colloquialisms. 'Politician' can imply the letters MP; 'fashionable' or 'home' suggest IN; 'about' implies CA or RE; C can be derived from 'hundred' (Roman numeral) or 'cold'; father can be 'PA'; mother, 'MA'; 'soldier', GI or RE (Royal Engineer); 'doctor', MO, MD or DOC. If interpreted correctly, these letters, combined with other elements of the clue, will then feature in the solution.

Hidden words Sometimes the solution is actually spelled out in the clue, but split across one or more word breaks. The solution to 'Find a seat in stalls of arena (4)', for example, is SOFA, its letters hidden in 'stall**s of a**rena'.

get about on Crutches

Crutches are invaluable for keeping mobile when you have injured a leg, but using them takes some practice to perfect.

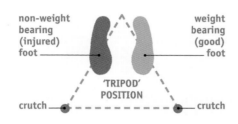

non-weight bearing (injured) foot

weight bearing (good) foot

'TRIPOD' POSITION

crutch ———— crutch

To get out of a chair hold both crutches upright with the hand on your injured side and push against the chair with your free hand to stand on the uninjured leg. Move a crutch around to that side and get a comfortable grip. The crutches should be angled outward slightly, about 10-15cm to the side and in front of your feet – the 'tripod' position.

Share the load between crutches and injured leg.

Step forward with the sound leg.

To get moving, shift the crutches and injured leg forward together to share the load, then step forward with the sound leg. If you cannot put any weight on your injured leg, your arms and shoulders will have to work hard. Move both crutches forward, put your weight on them, swing your bad leg level then step forward with the other leg.

To go upstairs, if there's no handrail to hold, push down through your hands and mount the first step with your good leg. Stand firm on that leg, push down through your hands, bring your weight over the step, bring your bad leg up beside the good one, followed by the crutches – and so on. Coming down, crutches advance a step, followed by the bad leg. Balance your weight down through the crutches and lift yourself down with your good leg. Alternatively, you can negotiate stairs by sitting.

Step down by placing crutches first, then bad leg, then good.

Step up by moving good leg first, then bad, then crutches.

organise your Cupboards

Use your cupboards only for everyday items, don't pack them with things that can go into storage.

■ Make the most of your kitchen corner unit storage by fitting carousel shelving to the doors to hold pots and pans. Nesting pots and pans together also saves space.

■ To optimise cupboard space for storing tins, dried goods and so on, install cheap, freestanding shelving or display steps.

■ Where you have similar perishable items, put those with the longest shelf life to the back.

■ When storing toxic cleaning products under the sink, secure the doors if you have young children.

■ Get to grips with an overflowing wardrobe. Remove all the clothes and divide into piles 'yes', 'maybe' and 'discard' – the clothes that fit and are regularly worn, those that you might wear occasionally, and the has-beens for the charity shop or recycle bin. The exercise can throw up some forgotten garments, to be promoted from 'maybe' to 'yes'.

■ Keep linen cupboards tidy, with bed linen in sets or with sheets of similar size all together. Sort towels into colours and sizes and lay them with the folded side to the fore. Always rotate clean sheets and towels: put the newly laundered ones to the bottom of the pile and take clean ones from the top.

C

Curriculum vitae

Your CV needs to catch the eye of a prospective employer. Pay attention to presentation, choose a clear, easy-to-read font, and keep it succinct. Always tailor your CV to each individual application. Study the job advert to see what strengths are required and concentrate on displaying your relevant abilities.

Start by giving your personal details – name and contact information – and relating briefly and positively (not boastfully) what skills you possess that fit you for the job. Focus on your achievements. Bring your top selling points to the fore. And, throughout your CV, recount your successes rather than labour the responsibilities.

Follow up with your qualifications, training, education and employment history, starting with the most recent. Keep it relevant. Don't mention every night class or Boy Scout badge, but do include anything that might set you apart from other candidates – fluency in languages, IT skills, field trips …

golden rules

IMPROVE YOUR CV
- **Run a spell and grammar check, then read and re-read to iron out any errors.**
- **Avoid jargon and cliché such as 'team player' and 'think outside the box', in favour of clear, lucid language.**
- **Don't start every sentence with 'I', 'me' or 'my'; that kind of repetition is wearing.**

---

bake delicious Cupcakes

Cupcakes have never been more popular. Ice them simply or dress them up with fancy piping or toppings for a special occasion.

MAKES 12
- **100g softened butter or soft margarine**
- **100g caster sugar**
- **2 eggs**
- **100g self-raising flour**
- **1 tsp baking powder**
- **1 tbsp milk (optional)**

FOR THE ICING
- **75g butter, softened**
- **150g icing sugar**
- **1-2 tbsp milk**
- **1 tsp vanilla essence**
- **food colouring, if wished**

1 Preheat the oven to 180°C/gas 4. Put 12 paper cases into a bun tin. Place all the ingredients into a food processor or mixing bowl and beat until smooth. If the mixture seems too thick, add the milk. Spoon into the paper cases, filling to about two-thirds. Bake for 15-20 minutes until risen, golden brown and springy to the touch. Cool on a wire rack before decorating.

2 Cream the butter and icing sugar, adding enough milk to give a creamy texture, and the vanilla essence, plus any colouring or alternative flavouring you like. Smooth or pipe over the cakes. Or decorate in any other way (*see* CAKE).

Variations
- Replace 25g of flour with cocoa powder for chocolate cupcakes.
- Add the grated zest of two lemons or a large orange for citrus flavours.
- Fold in 1 tbsp coffee essence or strong espresso and/or 50g chopped pecans or other nuts.

---

cook an authentic Indian Curry

The hallmark of Indian curry lies in its spices, which are mixed with a thickening agent, such as onions, yoghurt, coconut milk, tomatoes or split peas (*dahl*). The heat will depend on the amount of chilli or cayenne you use. An authentic recipe such as the one below takes some time and effort.

Lamb rogan josh

SERVES 4
- **75g natural yoghurt**
- **½-1 tsp cayenne**
- **2 tsp ground coriander**
- **1½ tsp ground cumin**
- **2 large cloves of garlic, crushed**
- **2 tsp grated fresh ginger**

- **1 tsp paprika**
- **½ tsp ground turmeric**
- **2 tbsp vegetable oil**
- **550g lamb leg steak, cut into 5cm cubes**
- **300g onions, finely chopped**
- **1½ tbsp tomato purée**
- **salt**

- **25g unsalted butter**
- **2 bay leaves, crumbled**
- **2 green cardamom pods, split open**
- **5cm cinnamon stick, broken in half**
- **4 whole cloves**
- **½ tsp freshly grated nutmeg**

TO SERVE Rice and accompaniments such as poppadoms, naan bread, fruit chutney, and a raita made with yoghurt, cucumber and mint.

1 Mix the yoghurt, cayenne, coriander, cumin, garlic, ginger, paprika and turmeric. Heat the oil in a heavy-based casserole, add the lamb and onions and stir until lightly browned. Add the yoghurt mixture and fry for a few minutes. Then lower the heat, cover and cook for 30 minutes or until the lamb has released its juices.

2 Remove the lid and cook on a high heat, stirring for about 5 minutes until the sauce has a paste-like consistency. Add the tomato purée, salt and 15g butter, reduce the heat and simmer for 3-4 minutes. Pour in 350ml boiling water, cover and simmer for a further 15 minutes.

3 Melt the remaining butter over a low heat, add the bay leaves, cardamom, cinnamon and cloves and sizzle for 40 seconds. Add the nutmeg, stir and then pour over the meat. Mix well, cover and cook for another 10-12 minutes.

---

measure up and hang Curtains

Use these general guidelines for length and width.

Length Measure from the bottom of the track to 2.5cm above floor covering (A), to 10cm below a window sill (B) or 5cm above a radiator (C). If making curtains, add 15cm for a hem and 7.5cm for a top turning, plus enough fabric for a 'heading' to conceal any track. If using a pole, alter the heading to conceal all or part of it, as preferred.

Width Multiply the width of the track or pole (D) by the factor required for your heading style:
- 1.5 to 2 for gathers
- 2.25-2.5 for pencil pleats
- 2 for pinch pleats.
For made-to-measure curtains add 30cm for side turnings and overlaps where curtains meet.

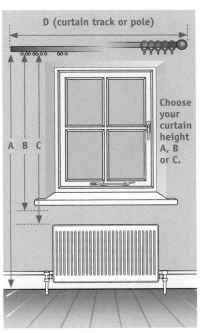

D (curtain track or pole)

Choose your curtain height A, B or C.

A B C

Curtain track Any track must be strong enough for your chosen fabric and be securely fastened to the wall or ceiling.
- Most tracks are fixed with brackets spaced about 20cm apart, but poles are held with one bracket at each end and, for heavy curtains, may need an extra central bracket.
- Buy track to extend at least 15cm beyond the window at each end. In bay windows, fit track to run beyond the bay and onto the wall at each side.

To keep heavy curtains hanging straight, sew small lead weights to the hem on the wrong (reverse) side – these can be bought ready covered with fabric. Weighted beads threaded through the hems of sheer curtains will prevent them from billowing.

serve up a Thai
Curry

Thai curries are typified by their mixture of dried spices and fresh ingredients, spiked with the acidity of lime and the heat of chilli.

Thai prawn curry

SERVES 4

5cm piece root ginger, peeled and chopped
2 stems lemongrass, bruised and chopped
3 cloves garlic, chopped
1 tsp ground coriander
1 tsp ground cumin
2 kaffir lime leaves
3 tbsp vegetable oil
1 bunch spring onions, chopped
3 large green chillis, deseeded and shredded
160ml coconut milk
juice of 2 limes
500g cooked shelled prawns
2 tbsp chopped fresh coriander
freshly ground black pepper

TO SERVE Plain boiled basmati rice

1 Put the ginger, lemongrass, garlic, coriander, cumin, kaffir lime leaves and half the oil into a food processor with 3 tbsp of cold water and blend to a paste.

2 Heat the remaining oil in a large pan. Add the spring onions, chillis and spice paste and stir fry for 2-3 minutes until aromatic. Stir in the coconut milk and lime juice and simmer, stirring regularly, for 10-15 minutes until reduced and thickened. Add the prawns and cook until just heated through. Adjust the seasoning and serve.

C

lengthen and shorten Curtains

YOU WILL NEED Tape measure, scissors, tailor's chalk, pins, thread, needle, decorative tape (optional), seam unpicker, curtain and lining fabrics, iron

- Match new and old fabrics depending on their weight and laundering requirements.
- Let down old hems and clean curtains, following manufacturer's instructions, before making alterations.
- Double check that both curtains are exactly the same length.

To shorten Measure the new length, adding at least 5cm for the hem. Cut off unwanted fabric from the bottom. Fold up the seam allowances then pin, tack (*see* TACK) and stitch the new hems into position by hand or machine.

To lengthen If there's enough fabric, make a smaller hem. If the previous hem mark is very obvious, disguise it with decorative tape. Replace or re-gather the heading tape.

- Alternatively, insert extra contrasting fabric. Measure the new length, adding 2.5cm for each additional seam, then unpick any lining. Cut a strip of the new fabric to the width of the curtain, allowing 2.5cm seam allowances at each side. Mark cutting lines on the reverse of the curtains with tailor's chalk, then cut. Pin, tack and stitch in the new fabric bands, right sides together, then press the seams. Lengthen the linings by the same amount, working from the bottom. Turn up and stitch lining hems. Restitch the linings into place.

create a simple Cushion cover

This project shows you how to cover a square cushion. Making the cover slightly smaller than the cushion allows it to plump up when filled.

YOU WILL NEED Cushion, fabric, tape measure, scissors, pins, thread, needle, sewing machine, iron

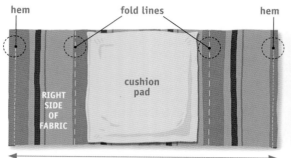
hem | fold lines | hem
RIGHT SIDE OF FABRIC
cushion pad
twice the length of cushion + 10cm

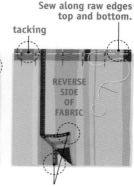
Sew along raw edges top and bottom.
tacking
REVERSE SIDE OF FABRIC
doubled-over hems

1 Measure the cushion. Cut a piece of fabric the right height and twice the length plus 10cm. Mark two fold lines the same distance in from the sides – 25cm for a 40cm cushion, 27.5cm for a 45cm cushion or 35cm for a 60cm cushion. Turn under 5mm then 5mm again at each end to form hems. Pin, tack and sew. Remove tacking and press.

2 Fold fabric, right sides in, at fold lines. Allow 8cm overlap at the join. Pin and tack the two raw edges then sew a 1.25cm seam along each. Trim the hem diagonally at the corners to make them neater once the fabric is right side out. Remove tacking. Turn right side out and press. Insert the cushion in the slit at the back of the cover.

make real Custard

Custard can be served with any hot dessert or cold with fruit. It's an essential ingredient of trifle and the basis for many ice creams.

MAKES 500ml

500ml whole milk
1 vanilla pod, split,
or ½ tsp vanilla essence
5 egg yolks
40g caster sugar

Bring the milk slowly to the boil in a heavy-based saucepan. Add the vanilla pod, leave to infuse for 10 minutes then remove. Whisk egg yolks and sugar until thick, add vanilla essence, if using, and stir in the hot milk. Clean the pan, strain the mixture back into it, then heat gently, stirring with a wooden spoon until it thickens.

- Never allow custard to boil or it will curdle. If it starts to 'turn' remove it from the heat at once and put it into a blender or processor. Or strain it into a bowl sitting in an outer bowl of ice cubes and beat vigorously.
- If you don't have a heavy-based saucepan, cook custard over a pan of barely simmering water.

take plant Cuttings

Use cuttings to save money and propagate your garden favourites, selecting your method according to the type of plant.

YOU WILL NEED Sharp knife, secateurs, plastic bags, rooting hormone, pots filled with a mixture of loam-based compost and sharp sand, trowel

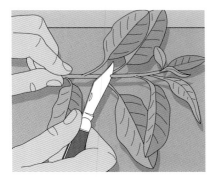

Softwood cuttings Before midsummer, cut off the soft, sappy tips of non-flowering shoots, with four or five pairs of leaves on each. Remove the lowest pair and the top pair just below the leaf joint. Pot up and cover with a plastic bag. Keep warm until rooted. Use for plants such as pelargoniums and busy lizzies.

Basal cuttings In early spring dig away soil from plant bases and cut off young growth. Pot up as for softwood cuttings, making sure that cuttings don't touch in the pot when planted. Use this method for species such as lupins, chrysanthemums and delphiniums.

Semi-ripe cuttings Take cuttings in late summer from shoots that have begun to harden at the base. Prepare and root as for softwood cuttings, but dip into rooting hormone before planting. Use for hebes and other shrubs. For clematis trim between, not just below, leaf joints.

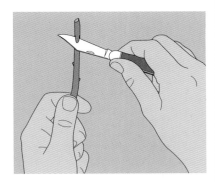

Hardwood cuttings Take cuttings in winter from the youngest shoots. Cut to about 25-30cm and remove a thin sliver of wood from the base of each. Dip into rooting hormone and insert into large pots or a shallow trench lined with coarse sand or grit. Ideal for roses.

deal with Cuts

A small surface cut or abrasion can be dealt with at home. Before you dress the wound, wash and dry your hands thoroughly (*see* HANDS).

Clean the wound under warm running water using a cotton-wool swab, and pat dry with a fresh towel. If you need several swabs, discard each one after one use. Don't use antiseptic as this can damage the tissue and slow the healing process, but do apply a sterile plaster.

Change the dressing frequently and remove it at night if the wound is unlikely to rub on bedclothes. To keep the wound dry choose a waterproof dressing that can withstand light wetting such as a shower. When the wound is no longer moist and in need of protection, don't dress it but watch for signs of infection.

See a doctor if you notice any swelling, redness spreading around the wound, the formation of pus or an increase in pain, or if you feel unwell, develop a fever or have swollen glands.

If a cut is deep, though it may not appear large, there may be underlying damage to blood vessels, nerves, muscles, tendons and ligaments. Act quickly to stem the bleeding (*see* BLEEDING) and seek medical attention, because of the risk of complications such as tetanus.

tackle Dandruff

Although harmless, dandruff can be itchy, and the appearance of white flakes of dead skin in the hair and on clothing is unsightly and can be embarrassing. Its exact cause is unknown but it isn't linked to poor hygiene.

- Treat with medicated shampoo or tea tree oil shampoo. Wash at least three times a week and rinse thoroughly.
- Massage rather than scratch your scalp when using shampoo, to avoid causing unnecessary irritation.
- Brush hair daily to help remove flakes of dead skin, but avoid scraping the scalp too roughly.
- Change or stop using hair products, such as gels and sprays, to see if your dandruff improves.
- See a doctor if the dandruff does not respond to home treatment, or if your scalp is irritated, or is infected by scratching.
- Continue using medicated shampoo at least once a week after your dandruff clears up.

weave a pretty Daisy chain

Children love to wear necklaces and garlands of daisy or dandelion chains, and will enjoy the process of making them.

- Gather flowers with thick, strong, long stems.

1 Use a thumbnail to make a split in a stem just big enough to allow you to poke another stem through and continue until you have your chain.

2 Try to make each split the same distance from the flower head. The closer to the head, the more dense and colourful the chain.

3 To close the circle, poke the last stem through a small split in the top of the first flower and pull.

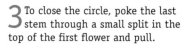

spot signs of Damp

There are two main causes of damp in the home: condensation inside the house, and a leak coming in from outside.

If you have crumbling plaster or peeling wallpaper in cold, dry weather, the chances are that the damp is caused by condensation (*see* CONDENSATION). If the damp problem manifests itself in warm, rainy weather, then it's more likely that the damp is coming in from outside, and is due to a structural problem in your house.

Damp patches at skirting-board level, or a tide-mark on wallpaper anywhere up to 1m from the floor, may indicate a problem with your damp-proof course. Check outside to see if there's visible damage to the damp course. Repairing it is a job for a professional.

Rising damp can also occur if, say, a path or a flower bed is bridging (or overlapping) the damp course, and so letting rainwater in. In such instances, the flowerbed or path must be lowered, or a channel cut so that it doesn't touch the walls of the house.

Damp higher up the walls can be caused by cracked or missing tiles on the roof, or by leaking or blocked guttering. Get a professional to assess the cause, and get it repaired straight away.

throw good Darts

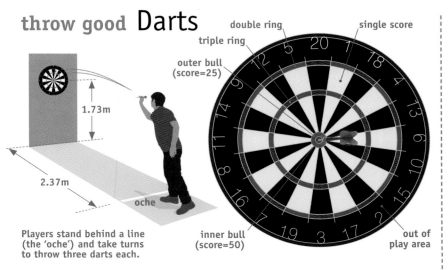

double ring

triple ring

single score

outer bull (score=25)

1.73m

2.37m

oche

inner bull (score=50)

out of play area

Players stand behind a line (the 'oche') and take turns to throw three darts each.

There are many games that can be played on a standard dartboard; the most common is 501.

■ Two players take turns ('legs') to throw three darts each. The score from each set of three darts is subtracted from 501, and the winner is the player who first reduces their tally to exactly zero.

■ Players must end on a 'double', a dart landed in the double ring, for which the score is twice the number shown in that segment.

■ The triple ring scores three times the number shown. It follows that the highest, most valuable score that can be made with three darts is 180 (a triple 20 scored with each of your three throws).

■ If you score more points in a leg than you require, you're adjudged to have 'bust' and the total at the end of your previous leg is reinstated.

impress on a Date

Dates, especially first dates, are fraught with potential for disaster. Most can be avoided if you're polite, and also honest about yourself.

■ If you're a man, show some old-fashioned chivalry: compliment your date's appearance, hold open doors. If you're a woman, allow the man to do this: it's not compromising your independence, just a display of courtesy.

■ Don't bail out if the date isn't going well, or if there's no chemistry. It's rude for one thing, but more importantly a bad start isn't always fatal.

■ Dress up a little. It's polite to make some effort, however casual the date.

■ Avoid any remark that sounds like a chat-up line. The only worthwhile chat-up line in all the world is: *Tell me about yourself*, so be a good listener.

■ Don't boast about yourself. And don't tell self-aggrandising fibs that you might later have to retract (*I'm in the special forces*).

■ Don't talk about exes, divorces, failed relationships. Be positive and happy: present cheerfulness is always more attractive than past sadnesses.

■ Pay attention. Maintain eye contact, and don't look around to see who else might be available.

Darn a sock

The basic darning technique is essentially reweaving, and can be used on woollens and woven fabrics of all kinds.

An old-fashioned 'darning mushroom' gives you a firm base for the job, but the smooth underside of a small jar is a good substitute. Don't stretch the fabric over the mushroom or jar, otherwise the darned section won't fit the hole properly.

YOU WILL NEED Darning needle, matching wool or thread, darning mushroom (or equivalent), scissors

1 With the sock right side out, insert the darning mushroom or jar. Then thread the needle and run a neat frame of small stitches round the hole, working in a strong, undamaged area of the fabric.

2 Lay a warp of threads across the hole in one direction, leaving a small loop at the end of each row to allow for any shrinkage. Then weave a series of weft threads at right angles to the first set, taking a small anchoring stitch at each side. Fasten off securely on the wrong side, out of sight.

⚡ **golden rules**

DEADHEAD GARDEN PLANTS
■ Use sharp secateurs for deadheading, working neatly, and clean them well afterwards to remove any sap or disease-carrying organisms.

---

clean a Decanter

Wash dust and grime from a decorative decanter from time to time and clean thoroughly inside after each use.

Outside Wash by hand in warm soapy water using a sponge and a soft-bristled brush. If antique, or made of crystal or cut glass, lay a folded tea towel in the bottom of the sink to protect against chipping.

Inside Half fill with warm soapy water and shake gently with your hand over the top. If still stained, try swirling around a mixture of vinegar and coarse rock (sea) salt. Or buy special abrasive-coated cleaning balls to swirl around instead. For stubborn wine stains use warm water, rock salt and bicarbonate of soda. Alternatively, fill with water, add a denture cleaning tablet and soak overnight.

To dry Effective drying is essential to prevent 'fogging' and contamination by microorganisms lingering in any water. Drain thoroughly then insert a long-handled wooden spoon wrapped in paper towel. Leave overnight. Or blow in warm air with a hair dryer – but beware of the glass overheating and cracking.

Deadhead your garden plants

As well as making the garden look tidier, deadheading is the best way of lengthening the flowering season of many plants. Because plants put a lot of energy into seed formation, stopping them from doing this can also strengthen them and encourage strong foliage. Resist deadheading any plants whose seedheads make good winter shapes or food for birds if left uncut.

Bulbs and corms Deadhead flowers to ground level as soon as they fade to divert resources into the underground storage organs. Keep well watered until the foliage dies down.

Perennials Remove dead flower spikes. In plants such as lupins and delphiniums this will encourage the growth of flowering side shoots. Cut spring and early summer flowering perennials such as hardy geraniums and oriental poppies down to ground level after flowering. Some will even flower a second time.

Annuals Because they will stop flowering once they have set seed, deadhead pansies, antirrhinums (snapdragons) and petunias to ensure continued blooms. Tidy up other annuals such as carnations and marigolds as flowers fade.

Roses Remove flowers down to the first pair of leaves.

---

prepare surfaces for Decorating

Whatever the surface, the time and effort that you put into preparing for decoration make a world of difference to the finished look.

Painted wood need be stripped only if more coats would affect the functions – as with sash windows, for example. Wood need not be stripped if it's in good condition, but it should be cleaned with sugar soap and water. Gloss surfaces should be keyed – roughened with sandpaper – so that the new paint adheres.

Exposed brick should be brushed to remove dust. Interior brick surfaces can be painted with emulsion.

Old wallpaper should be removed before new paper is hung. Soften the paper with warm water containing washing-up liquid, then scrape off with a scraper. Painted wallpaper may need to be scored with the corner of your scraper – especially if there are several layers. A steam stripper makes the whole job much easier, but take care not to over-steam and soften the plaster underneath. *See also* WALLPAPER.

Old bare plaster might need some repair before it's papered over. Cracks and small holes left by picture hooks should be filled with a DIY wall filler. Crumbly patches should be removed back to sound plaster and replastered with a repair plaster (*see* PLASTER).

Newly plastered ceilings can be painted directly with emulsion: there's no need to paper. *See also* CEILING.

build a simple Deck in your garden

Decking remains a popular choice for a garden seating area. After some initial setting out and levelling, it's quick and easy to construct a basic structure.

YOU WILL NEED 100mm x 100mm support posts, cement, weed-suppressing membrane to cover the area, 150mm x 50mm tanalised timber joists for the frame, 100mm x 50mm tanalised timber lengths for cross-members, wall plate (if you want to fix to the house wall), joist hangers, bolts, 100mm nails, decking planks, screws, spirit level, string line, hammer, screwdriver, saw

Start by drawing a plan so that you can calculate how much timber you need. Follow the minimum spacings between joists and support posts indicated on the plan below. Don't be tempted to stretch these distances to suit your final measurement, but put in additional supports instead. Lay down a weed-suppressing membrane to cover the area that will be directly beneath the decking.

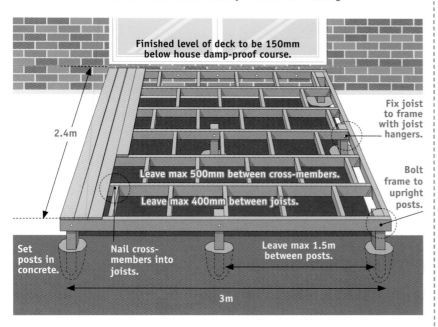

Finished level of deck to be 150mm below house damp-proof course.

Fix joist to frame with joist hangers.

Bolt frame to upright posts.

2.4m

Leave max 500mm between cross-members.

Leave max 400mm between joists.

Set posts in concrete.

Nail cross-members into joists.

Leave max 1.5m between posts.

3m

1 Set support posts in cement, no more than 1.5m apart in each direction. Use a spirit level to make sure that they are perpendicular.

2 When the concrete has set, bolt the outer frame to the supports, checking carefully with the longest spirit level you have that it's level, with just a slight fall away from the house for drainage. Make sure that the finished level of the deck will be 150mm below the level of the house's damp-proof course. Saw off the support posts flush with the frame.

3 Use joist hangers to fix joists within the main frame, no more than 400mm apart, and nails to fix cross-members, no more than 500mm apart. Decking planks must be laid at right angles to the joists, so decide which way to lay them now.

continued overleaf ➜

---

avoid Deep vein thrombosis
when flying

During air travel, prolonged immobility can cause blood to clot in a deep vein, usually in the leg or pelvis. Part of the clot may detach and travel to the lung, causing a life-threatening blockage.

■ Avoid alcohol and drink plenty of water to avoid dehydration.
■ To improve circulation, take short walks and follow the exercises below. Wear elastic compression socks or stockings.
■ Consult a member of the crew if you have any swelling in your limbs.

Exercise your legs for 3-4 minutes every hour. Lift your feet off the floor and flex them by pointing your toes up and down.

Raise each knee in turn, so that the back of your thigh is lifted off the seat.

With your knee raised, rotate your ankle by describing a circle with your outstretched toes. Switch legs and repeat.

Descale a kettle or shower head

Special descaling solutions are available to buy, but white vinegar is ideal for attacking limescale.

For a kettle dilute white vinegar 50:50 with water. Fill the kettle and leave it overnight. Empty, rinse, refill with water, reboil and empty. It's now ready to use. No taste of vinegar will remain.

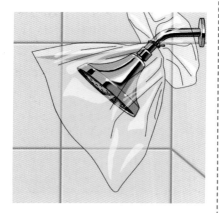

For a shower head unscrew the head and soak overnight in a bowl of white vinegar (if it has several parts, unscrew these if possible and soak them separately). Remove any remaining deposits with an old toothbrush. If the shower head can't be unscrewed, pour the vinegar into a plastic bag and pull it up around the head to immerse it. Secure firmly in place with twist ties or string and leave overnight before finishing off with the toothbrush.

4 Cut the decking and 'dry lay' it in place. Make sure that you're happy with the overall look, either arranging the joins in the planks to be staggered randomly or regularly, or neatly aligned. Adjust the boards to minimise waste.

5 Use a power drill to screw two 63mm screws through the board and into the joist below at each fixing point; use a string line to help you to keep the screws in a neat line. Use nails or a piece of card as spacers to leave a 5mm drainage gap between the boards.

6 Finish the edges of the decking with a cover strip of matching wood, nailed in place, if wished.

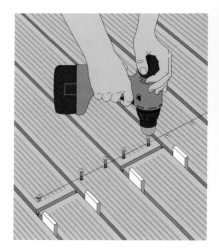

Defrost food safely

When food is defrosting, as soon as it rises above 4°C any bacteria it contained before freezing begin to multiply. Poultry, especially large birds, must always be completely thawed before cooking to remove the risk of salmonella being activated during cooking.

Defrosting in the refrigerator is the safest method. If using the microwave, cook food immediately after defrosting because some parts may become warm and stimulate bacterial growth during the process.

Timing is crucial
- For meat and poultry allow 6 hours per 500g in the fridge and half this time at room temperature.
- For fish and shellfish allow 4 hours per 500g in the fridge or 2 hours per 500g at room temperature.

deal with Diarrhoea

Although the symptoms of diarrhoea can be extremely uncomfortable, the main danger of the condition is the dehydration it can cause.

- Take small, frequent sips of water or diluted juice.
- Talk to the pharmacist about medication and rehydration preparations, such as Dioralyte, which contain the correct balance of water, salt and sugar.
- Eat some carbohydrate food such as bread, rice or potatoes as soon as possible, adding in other foods when you can face them.
- New research suggests that taking a probiotic will reduce the length of a bout of diarrhoea and the risk of it lasting more than four days.
- If symptoms persist for a fortnight (five days in children, 48 hours in babies) or if you pass blood or pus with the diarrhoea, see a doctor.

eat a healthy, balanced Diet

Build your food intake around the eat-well plate and you can increase your prospects for a long and healthy life.

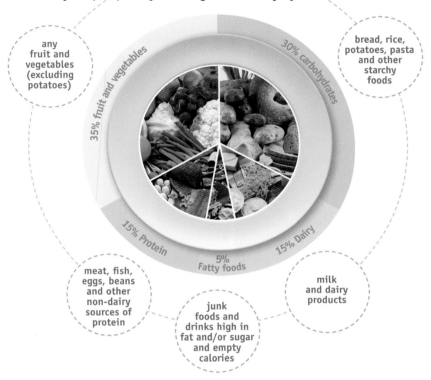

any fruit and vegetables (excluding potatoes)

35% fruit and vegetables

30% carbohydrates

bread, rice, potatoes, pasta and other starchy foods

15% Protein

5% Fatty foods

15% Dairy

meat, fish, eggs, beans and other non-dairy sources of protein

junk foods and drinks high in fat and/or sugar and empty calories

milk and dairy products

A healthy meal should be based on starchy foods, such as wholegrain bread, cereals, potatoes and pasta. They are the fuel on which our bodies run and are a prime source of nutrients and dietary fibre, which makes for good bowel and colon health and helps to control cholesterol. Try to choose wholemeal or wholegrain varieties. They contain more fibre, vitamins and minerals.

Fruit and vegetables should make up more than a third of your diet. Fresh plants contain phytochemicals, powerful antidotes to the rogue oxygen molecules called 'free radicals' that damage cells and cause disease. A little less meat, a little more veg on your plate, will make a real difference.

Cut right down on fatty, sugary snacks and soft drinks – they are a fattening source of 'empty calories'. Try dried fruit for a snack rather than a chocolate bar, and drink diluted fruit juice rather than a fizzy drink.

Meat, fish, eggs and beans are good sources of protein, needed for the growth and repair of our bodies. Try to choose lean cuts of meat and skinless poultry to cut down on fat, and aim for at least two portions of fish a week.

Dairy products are also a good source of protein and contain the calcium we need to keep our bones healthy. Choose lower-fat options to avoid raising your blood cholesterol levels and so increasing your risk of heart disease.

throw a faultless Dinner party

There are two vital ground rules for a smooth-running dinner party: plan ahead and don't over-reach yourself.

■ Invite no more people than your table can accommodate. Six is a good number (including yourself) that facilitates round-the-table conversation. Eight is a sensible maximum number.

■ Ask in advance if your guests are vegetarian, or have special dietary requirements. (A polite guest will volunteer this information, rather than turn up and say they can't eat your food.)

■ Plan your menu so that it's full of contrasts: meat starter, fish main; rich main, light dessert; no more than one spicy course. Avoid repetition: a creamy chicken casserole followed by a cream pudding, say, or a steak pie followed by an apple pie.

■ Choose tried-and-tested recipes that you know you can get right on the night. Don't treat your guests as guinea pigs for culinary experimentation.

■ Serve one course that you can prepare entirely in advance – a chilled pudding, say. You don't want to neglect your guests while you slave away at the stove. Avoid dishes such as individual steaks that require last-minute attention.

■ Make sure there are enough drinks; don't rely on guests to bring a bottle. As a rule, keep white wine chilled, allow red wine to breathe and be sure to provide a soft drink alternative as well as water.

■ Above all, be attentive to your guests. Making them feel at home and at ease is at least as important as the food you put on the table.

D

stack a
Dishwasher

For maximum efficiency it pays to run a dishwasher fully and properly loaded. Make sure items won't prevent the spinning arms moving freely or obstruct tubes, sprayers or the opening of the soap dispenser, and that breakables don't risk touching if they vibrate during the cycle. Check that all items are dishwasher safe.

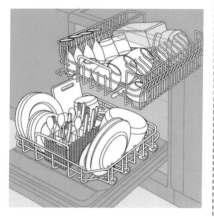

Plates Insert in slots in lower section, facing towards the centre.

Cups, glasses and bowls Place in the top section. Stack bowls on an incline. Put glasses upside down between, not over, prongs.

Plastic items Place on top rack away from the heating element in the lower section that can cause melting.

Pots and pans Place upside down in the lower section.

Cutlery Place forks and spoons handles downwards into utensil baskets, and knives handles upwards. Mix them so that they don't 'nest' into one another. Lay larger utensils horizontally across the top section.

Cutting boards and baking trays Place on the outermost edges of the bottom section.

clear a blockage in your Dishwasher

Your dishwasher has filters where the water goes in, and where it flows out. This is where blockages can occur.

The outlet filters, set inside each other like cups, are to be found in the bottom of the dishwasher cabinet. They collect grease and food particles, so are prone to blockages.

Unclip the filters as advised in the manual, rinse them clean under warm running water, soak and wash in warm soapy water, using washing-up liquid to disperse the grease, and replace.

To clear the inlet filter, turn off the water at the stopcock, then disconnect the inlet hose. Remove any rubber seal and pull out the filter with long-nosed pliers. Clean it with a nail brush. Inlet filters rarely get blocked.

Dive into a swimming pool

A well-executed dive is by far the most graceful way to launch yourself into a pool and can generate momentum for your swimming stroke.

Hook your thumbs, and wrap the fingers of the upper hand around the other.

Push your chin into your chest.

Fix your eyes on a point about 1m into the pool: this is what you're aiming for.

Bend slightly at the waist.

Always check that the water is deep enough for diving. Never dive into water less than 1.5m in depth.

1 Stand with the toes of one leg (the one you kick with) at the pool's edge. Set your other foot slightly back from the edge.

2 Bend both knees slightly and allow yourself to tip forwards.

3 As you strike the water, straighten your legs, keep your hands linked, your arms aloft, and your body in a straight line.

4 As your downward momentum slows, steer your body up towards the surface, kicking your legs for added speed.

take care of your Dog

Keeping your dog clean and well-groomed is one of the key things you can do to keep it happy and healthy. Regular grooming can become a special and affectionate ritual that strengthens your emotional bond, but it also allows you to spot new lumps or tumours, skin complaints and parasites, such as fleas or ticks, and tackle them before the problem becomes severe.

Grooming the coat

When grooming a long coat, hold the hair down at the roots so you don't tug the skin. Don't yank at knots but work patiently.
■ Use a flat, wide-tooth steel comb when the slicker brush fails.
■ A dematting comb, which has blades, can be used to cut through stubborn mat. Alternatively cut vertically with scissors and brush out.

Short coats are easier to groom than long ones, but can be prone to matting.
■ Use a slicker brush to remove tangles. Apply firm, long strokes down the body and tail.

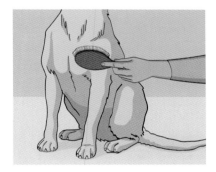

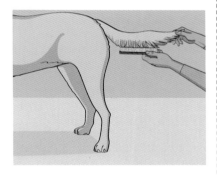

■ Next brush the entire coat, not forgetting tail and legs, with a bristle brush to remove dirt and dead hair.

■ Run a fine comb through feathery hair on the legs and tail.

Bath time Always brush and comb your dog before you put them in the bath, and check the feet for grass seeds. Bathe them only when they are dirty or need a flea bath. Too much bathing can leave the skin dry and flaky. Use a gentle dog shampoo, or one designed for a specific problem such as fleas or a skin condition.

■ Put a rubber mat in the tub so your dog doesn't slip. Use lukewarm water to wet them from neck to tail. Shampoo the hind legs, tail and rear end, then the body, chest and front legs.
■ Carefully wet the head, then shampoo, covering your dog's ears and eyes so that no lather gets in. Check ears for wax, which can indicate mites.
■ Rinse until the water runs clear: head, face and ears, then body, hind quarters and tail and finally the underside.
■ Wrap the dog in a towel to soak up excess, then dry from top to tail. Finish with a hairdryer on low temperature, taking care not to hold it too close.

seek out water with a
Divining rod

To perform this esoteric art you'll need a Y-shaped stick (ideally willow), called a 'water witch', or L-shaped 'dowsing rods', from specialist suppliers (search online).

■ If using a stick, hold it pointed-end down, with your palms face up and thumbs pointing outwards. Walk over the chosen area. If the stick is drawn convulsively down, it's telling you there's water beneath the surface.

■ If using rods, hold them loosely in each hand with the top wire pointing slightly down. If they swing apart or cross, start digging.

This ancient skill requires practice and sensitivity. Scientists dismiss it but Einstein believed it worked – although nobody knew how.

continued overleaf ➔

treat a Dog bite

All dog bites pose an infection risk, and the most savage may cause severe lacerations, tendon and nerve damage – even broken bones. Treat bleeding (*see* BLEEDING) and watch for shock (*see* SHOCK).

Quick action

For a small bite, thoroughly wash under warm, running water, gently squeeze to encourage bleeding, pat dry and cover with a sterile dressing. Unless you are certain that the victim had a full course of five tetanus injections as a child, consult a doctor. If the bite is to the face, hands or feet, if a tooth has punctured deeply into the flesh or if any signs of infection develop, such as high temperature or chills, seek medical advice promptly.

For a serious bite, wash as above and call an ambulance. If a finger or other body part has been bitten off, wash it with tap water, and put it in a plastic bag or sealed container in a tub of iced water; a surgeon may be able to reattach it.

Trimming claws A dog's nails are softer after a bath, so now is the time to trim them if necessary. Most dogs' nails wear down naturally.
- Use canine nail clippers to cut the nails diagonally, taking off no more than a few millimetres. Ask your vet to show you how much to cut if you are unsure. Gently smooth rough edges with a nail file or sandpaper.
- Take great care not to cut the nails to the 'quick', the pink area inside the nail; it's living tissue with blood supply and nerves.

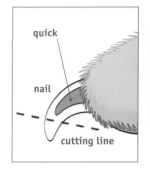

House training Use reward, not punishment, to teach your dog good toilet habits. Go for frequent walks – first thing in the morning, last thing at night, after meals, even every hour – to give them opportunities to learn where to go to the toilet. Watch for signs that they need to go out, such as fidgeting, sniffing, going round in circles or squatting. Once outside and in a suitable place, wait with and encourage the dog. When they have finished, collect the waste (if need be), praise them, then continue the walk for a while so they learn that walkies don't end when they have been to the toilet. It's important to ignore mistakes; if you give a dog attention (even if it isn't 'nice' attention) when they get it wrong, you'll only confuse them and the training will take longer.

---

train your Dog

A well-trained dog is a happy dog, so it's worth taking the time to build a confident relationship between you and your pet.

Sit, stay and come

The sit command is one of the easiest to teach a dog.
- Face the dog with a treat in your hand and, as they trot towards you, hold it over their head. Keeping their eyes on the treat, the dog will back up and sit down. As they do so, say 'Sit!' Reward them with the treat. Don't say 'sit down': this will confuse the dog when you try to teach them 'down'.
- Don't push the dog's bottom down to make them sit, just keep repeating the command and give lots of praise.

Teaching to stay then come is trickier, since 'stay' is an abstract concept for a dog, whereas sitting is a physical act.
- Have a reward in each hand.
- Tell the dog to sit and give them a treat.
- Hold up your empty hand as if you were stopping traffic and back slowly away, issuing a firm, clear command of 'Stay!'

Back slowly away, saying a firm, clear 'Stay!'

Call out an enthusiastic 'Come!'

When the dog comes, give them a reward.

■ Keep facing and looking at the dog. When you've put a small distance between you, call out an enthusiastic 'Come!' When the dog comes to you, reward them with the other treat.

■ If they try to get up and approach you before you call, say a definite 'No!', ask them to sit again, and start the exercise over again.

Bring a dog to heel In the excitement of a walk a dog may naturally tug and scrabble. If your dog starts to pull the instant you clip the lead on, stand still and wait. Don't go anywhere until they have calmed down.

■ Choose which side you want your dog to walk on and stick to it. Hold the lead in the opposite hand and put a treat in the other hand. Show the dog the treat to get their attention and walk forwards. As the dog follows your hand, say 'heel' and give a little of the treat. Keep going, repeat 'heel' and give a little more of the treat. Don't stop walking.

■ If the dog doesn't keep up with you or pulls in a different direction, suddenly change direction and encourage the dog to come with you.

■ Whenever your dog falls in step with you, praise them.

Start your training in your garden, if you have one. Work up to going to the park at quiet times when there are few distractions. Get someone to drive you to the park, and walk home; your dog is less likely to pull on the way back. Gradually the dog will get the message.

If your dog has lots of energy, let them burn off a bit of it in the garden before walking outside.

If the dog pulls, change direction and say 'Heel'.

Stop jumping up In natural exuberance, your dog may bound up to greet you or others. To discourage this undesirable behaviour, you and all the family must take the same line. When the dog jumps up, don't make eye contact with them, don't touch them or talk to them. Instead, walk away or gently push them away. If a dog is ignored they will learn that this isn't the way to get attention, and that it's calm behaviour that wins rewards.

play Dominoes

Twenty-eight solid domino pieces are 'shuffled' face down on a table. Each domino's face is split into two halves, bearing a set of between zero and six pips. Opponents draw a piece and the one who scores closest to the highest pip count of 12 gets to start.

■ Each of the two, three or four players draws seven pieces. Any remaining pieces are left in 'stock'.
■ The leader lays a piece – usually of the highest count.
■ The next player has to match one of the two pip counts on the piece by laying a domino bearing the same pip count end to end with it. Doubles are placed crossways.
■ A player who cannot make a match calls 'Go' and play passes on to the next player.
■ The first player to lay down all their pieces wins. If nobody can make a match, the winner is the one with the lowest pip count in their 'hand'.

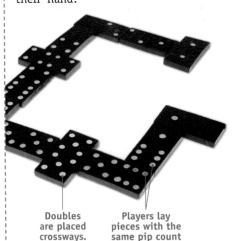

Doubles are placed crossways.

Players lay pieces with the same pip count end to end.

paint a panelled
Door

Always open a door before you paint, and slide plenty of newspaper underneath to catch the drips.
■ Remove handles and other door furniture such as escutcheons.

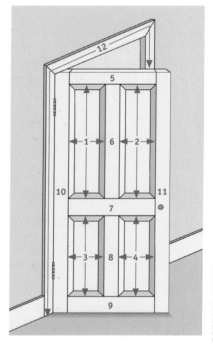

Solid doors Paint the panels first, in the order shown above. Use a thin brush for the mouldings, one that's no wider than the mouldings themselves. Don't overload the brush: this leads to drips and runs. Once you've done the panels, do the horizontal sections between them (eliminating any runs as you go), then the vertical sections.

Glass doors If there are glass panels in the door, use masking tape or a paint shield to help to keep paint off the glass. If any paint does dry on the glass, it should be carefully scraped off with a glass scraping tool or a razorblade.

change your Door locks

If, for security reasons, you want to change a cylinder lock (of which the night latch is the most common type) you need only replace the working parts. The same applies to mortise locks.

YOU WILL NEED Screwdrivers, self-grip wrench, pliers, new cylinder and keys (for a night latch), junior hacksaw (if necessary), hammer, new set of levers and keys (for a mortise)

Changing a cylinder Be aware that you cannot change the cylinder on a night latch with a locking interior handle; this method works only for the simple night latch design like the one illustrated below.

1 Unscrew the lock cover on the inside of the door so that you can get at the screws that hold the cylinder in place.

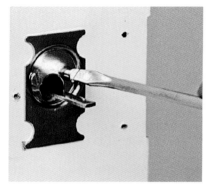

2 Unscrew the cylinder and pull it out. The connecting bar will come with it.

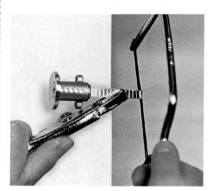

3 Take your new cylinder: this too has a bar attached. The bar is divided into segments along its length. Hold the new connecting bar tightly in a self-grip wrench, and use the junior hacksaw to cut it to the same length as the old one.

4 Make sure that the new connecting screws are the right length. If they aren't, you'll have to trim them with a junior hacksaw. Insert the new cylinder into the hole. Tighten the screws, and then screw the cover back in place, making sure that the handle of the lock has slotted onto the bar.

Changing a mortise lock Mortise locks come in various shapes and sizes. Take the old one with you when you go to buy a new one to avoid having to chisel out a larger slot in the door.

1 Unscrew the two screws that fix the cover plate and lock-face to the edge of the door. Turn the key so that the bolt shoots out, then remove the key.

2 Use a pair of pliers to grip the projecting bolt and slide the lock out of the door.

3 Put the new lock back in the slot, making sure it is the right way round. Screw it and the cover plate in place, and make sure that the key turns smoothly.

fix a Door that squeaks or sticks

When a door squeaks, the problem is with the hinges. Squirt a tiny amount of aerosol lubricant onto the hinge pins, and then work the door back and forth a few times. With rising butt hinges (*see* HINGE), lift the door off the hinge pins, lightly smear them with grease or petroleum jelly, then replace the door (this is a job much more easily done by two people).

A sticking door is usually caused by a build-up of paint on one edge. The problem usually arises in damp wet weather, when the wood of an exterior door is liable to swell. Rubbing the edge of the door with a candle may suffice to cure slight sticking. Otherwise, wait for a dry spell, then strip the paint from the door edge and frame. Repaint only when the door is completely dry. If the door sticks on the bottom edge, which is often the case, there's nothing for it but to take the door off (in a dry spell) and plane or file with a rasp to shave a whisker off the bottom.

Download music and video online

If you have plenty of free disk space on your PC (*see* COMPUTER MEMORY) and a good internet connection (*see* BROADBAND SPEED), downloading music and video is a convenient, quick and simple process.

Open an account with a website that offers a download service, such as 7digital, Amazon or iTunes, the best-known music download site. Some sites ask you to pay a monthly subscription, in return for which you can download unlimited amounts of music; others ask you to pay individually for each track, album or movie that you buy.

Your payment details will be stored securely by the website so that no unauthorised transactions can take place. You'll be asked to provide security details such as a password before any transaction is completed. This also gives you an opportunity to check that you have selected the intended song or film before going ahead.

Before playing a purchased file, you may need to download a piece of software such as Microsoft Media Player – which is itself freely available from Microsoft's own site (*see* DOWNLOAD SOFTWARE). You may be provided with this software automatically when you open an account with a download site. If not, check the site for details of which software you require.

Files can be stored on your PC, iPod or MP3 player, or, depending on the download site you're using, can be transferred to disc (*see* CD).

Download software
from the internet

Many software manufacturers now sell their products in the form of internet downloads, rather than on discs retailed through shops.

■ Browse the manufacturer's website to locate the desired software.
■ Look for and click on a button marked 'download' or similar.
■ Enter your payment details (they will be stored securely on the site).
■ Confirm where on your computer you want to store the software and then click to begin downloading.
■ Click on the downloaded file to complete the installation process.

Look out for free trials, at the end of which you can often pay to be given a code that you can enter to 'unlock' the program permanently.

find free Downloads

Many programs are available as 'freeware'. For example, you can freely download word-processing software that has almost as much functionality and flexibility as the commercially available packages that you have to pay for. Most freeware consists of small programs such as games and anti-virus scanners.

■ Free software can be browsed and downloaded through websites such as Tucows, Jumbo! and CNET.
■ Compare reviews on several sites before you download.
■ Make certain that the item you want is compatible with your computer's operating system.

unblock an outside Drain

Blockages often occur at the gully, which is the square drain, usually outside the back door. If the gully is blocked, you may hear a bubbling sound when you drain the kitchen sink.

■ The grille covering the gully can become clogged with leaves and debris. Lift it with a garden fork and hose it clean or scrub it well with a stiff brush in hot, soapy water.
■ If the trapped water doesn't flow away immediately, then the blockage is deeper. Put on long rubber gloves, plunge your arm in, and scoop any debris out by hand. Finish by flushing the drain through with water from a hose.

play Draughts

Draughts is a cut-throat game, in which two players attempt to be the first to remove all of the other's pieces from the board.

To play Set up the board with the dark corners to the left. Toss for who plays which colour. Place your 12 'men' on the dark squares in three rows. Dark starts. Moves are made one square forward and diagonally. The aim is to block your opponent or to eliminate their pieces by jumping over them, diagonally, from an adjacent square, into an empty one beyond. With a satisfying click, click, click, you might make a series of such jumps.

Three optional 'nasty rules'
■ If you fail to spot and make a possible jump you can be 'huffed' (that is, your opponent can remove the defaulting man).
■ If you have a choice of two jumps in one turn, you can make only one, while the other is huffed.
■ If you touch a piece you must move it.

A man who reaches the opposing 'crown row' becomes a 'king'. He's crowned with a previously captured piece, may move back as well as forth, and cannot be huffed.

The game is up when one player's men have been captured, all moves are blocked or there are too few men to offer hope of a win. A draw is declared when neither player can win.

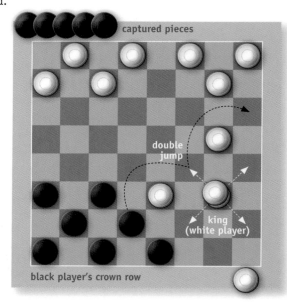

captured pieces

double jump

king (white player)

black player's crown row

Draw a face

Learn the basics of symmetry and proportion and you have the beginnings of a portrait that you can flesh out into a true likeness.

YOU WILL NEED **Sketch pad, hard and soft pencils, ruler, eraser**

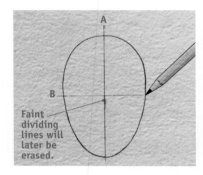

Faint dividing lines will later be erased.

1 Draw an oval, tapered at the chin. Add faint lines to divide it in half vertically (A) and horizontally (B).

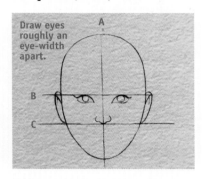

Draw eyes roughly an eye-width apart.

2 Bisect the bottom half with another line (C) and sketch the ears roughly between lines B and C. Add the eyes just under line B.

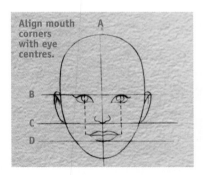

Align mouth corners with eye centres.

3 Add a further line (D), halfway between C and the point of the chin. Sketch the nose and mouth – the nose so its tip rests on the intersection of A and C, and the mouth so the bottom lip sits on D.

4 Add eyebrows and hair. Erase your guide lines, taking care not to lose any of the facial detail you've drawn.

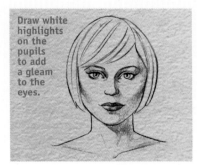

Draw white highlights on the pupils to add a gleam to the eyes.

5 Take a softer pencil and add shadow and detail, such as the irises and pupils of the eye, to bring your portrait to life. Imagine the light to be coming from top left, so add soft shadows on the right side of the nose and face, and under mouth, chin, eyebrows and cheekbones.

prevent Draughts

Draughtproofing doors and windows makes your home a more comfortable place to be – and cheaper to run.

Casement windows can be sealed using a foam strip or a self-adhesive rubber strip. Foam strips tend to wear out more quickly than rubber ones. Apply the adhesive strip to the window frame. For large or uneven gaps, use silicone sealant, following the manufacturer's instructions on the tube.

Sash windows are notoriously draughty. Fit a foam strip along the top and bottom of the frame. Use a brush strip or a V-shaped plastic strip to create a seal along the moving parts of the window.

Front doors are a prime source of draughts in winter. A traditional sprung strip of copper tacked to the frame is the most durable excluder. The metal strip is tacked along one side, then bent slightly outwards, so that it presses against the door's edge when it's shut and thus forms a seal. Rubber, foam or brush excluders are more commonly available today.

■ Fix a threshold draught excluder at the bottom of your front door. This comes in two interlocking parts, one for the door and the other for the threshold, and it keeps out rain as well as wind.
■ A surprisingly strong current of cold air can come through the letterbox. A brush excluder fitted on the inside will solve the problem.
■ For an effective additional barrier, you can also mount a thick curtain behind the door. Be sure to leave enough room on the rail or pole to allow the curtain to be drawn aside when opening the door.

D

Drive in bad weather

When taking to the road in adverse weather conditions, always put safety before punctuality. Better to arrive late, and in one piece, than take unnecessary risks.

Before you go ... **Know your vehicle. Familiarise yourself with the position and operation of its controls. Plan your route to avoid back roads, and memorise it, so that you're not distracted by looking at directions or a map. Tune the radio to pick up travel bulletins.**

WHATEVER THE WEATHER

The cardinal rules in any kind of bad weather are to limit your speed and keep your distance. In wet weather you need to allow more room, and when roads are frozen stopping distances can increase tenfold. Where visibility is reduced by mist, fog, driving rain or blizzards, hold well back from the vehicle ahead. When you cannot see for more than 100m, use headlights.

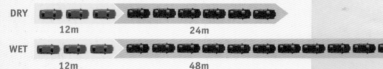

DRY — 12m — 24m

WET — 12m — 48m

| Thinking distance |
| Braking distance |

STOPPING DISTANCES AT 40MPH On wet roads, the braking distance is at least twice as long as in the dry. At 40mph (above), allow at least 60m total stopping distance in the wet (six car lengths greater than in the dry) – and preferably as much as three times the braking distance.

IN HIGH WINDS

Buffeting winds can rock a car and make steering difficult, as well as blowing tree branches and other debris into your path. Keep your eyes peeled for hazards and grasp the wheel firmly with both hands, especially when overtaking another vehicle. Be particularly careful around caravans and bikes, which may be blown off course.

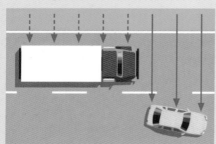

A high-sided vehicle may act as a windbreak while you're overtaking it. You should expect to encounter a sudden gust of wind as you complete the manoeuvre.

PREPARE YOUR VEHICLE FOR BAD WEATHER

Ask yourself if your journey is really necessary. Never drive in extreme weather if you don't have to. Prepare your vehicle by making the following checks.

Clean the windscreen and mirrors, scrape ice off all windows.

In winter top up antifreeze and windscreen de-icer.

Check the battery, since heaters, lights and wipers will drain it.

Check the pressure and tread of the tyres, including the spare.

Make sure that all the bulbs are working, including fog lights.

Ensure you have all you might need in an emergency: de-icer, scraper, mobile phone, torch, tow ropes, jump leads, jack and spare wheel, shovel, warning triangle, sacking to lay under stuck wheels, extra clothing, blanket, hot drink in a flask. In heavy snow, you might need snow chains.

IN SNOW AND ICE

Make patient preparations to ready yourself for your journey and drive cautiously to avoid having to deal with hazards such as skidding (*see* SKID)**.**

Wear comfortable, dry shoes that won't slip on the pedals, and take a pair of boots. Don't drive in heavy boots that might make you clumsy when using the pedals. Give a frosted windscreen time to clear completely: don't drive off peering through a small 'porthole' (*see* WINDSCREEN). Brush snow off the roof so it can't slide down the windscreen.

Gentle manoeuvres and a steady pace are the way forward. Move off in second gear to avoid wheelspin. If you drive an automatic, check that you know how to downshift into a lower gear, to reduce dependence on the brakes. If you have a 'winter' gear mode, select it: it locks out first gear to reduce wheelspin.

Drive at low speed in as high a gear as possible and don't brake or accelerate sharply. Before braking, drop into low gear sooner than normal to slow the car, then, if you don't have anti-lock braking, apply gentle, pumping pressure.

If the steering feels light or the tyres on the road surface are eerily silent, suspect black ice and use your gears to reduce speed. If the car skids when you brake, and you have a manual gearbox, release the brake and press the clutch.

To climb a hill, drop a gear to build momentum on the approach, then take it at a steady pace. Coming down, use a low gear to avoid having to brake.

Brake well before a bend, where it's all too easy to lose control. Don't wrench the wheel; steer smoothly.

If the car gets bogged down in snow, straighten the steering, clear snow from under the wheels, use sacking or an old rug in front of the driving wheels to give them something to bite on, and accelerate gently. Once you get going, try to continue until you find better road conditions.

In a blizzard, when the wipers can't work hard enough to clear the screen, abandon your journey and seek shelter. A heavy fall of snow can make roads impassable in minutes.

If you're trapped in your car, wrap up in rugs, coats, blankets – even newspaper. Use fuel sparingly, running the engine and heater for 15 minutes in any hour, with the window open a crack. Try to stay awake as you await rescue. If other motorists are trapped too, 'car share' to increase warmth, save fuel and keep your spirits up.

Always clear your windscreen and car roof as thoroughly as possible before you set off.

IN HEAVY RAIN

Don't underestimate the twin risks of poor visibility and slippery road surfaces. Allow twice the normal stopping distance and test your brakes. Lightly press the brake pedal from time to time as the friction will help to keep them dry. Drive with dipped headlights to decrease glare, and put your wipers on fast mode.

If the tyres can't get a grip and you find yourself aquaplaning, don't brake but ease off the accelerator to slow down gradually. Grip the wheel and get ready: when the tyres regain their hold it can cause the car to swerve and you should prepare to steer through it.

Never drive into standing water too deep for your car. Drive through shallow water at a steady crawl, keeping the revs high by using a low gear, then test your brakes as soon afterwards as it's safe to do so. If you can't tell how deep the water is, don't venture in.

D

use a Drill properly

Always disconnect a drill from the power source when you're changing bits, or when you're leaving the drill unattended (this applies to all power tools).

■ When working with a drill, grip it firmly with both hands: this is safer, and it will make your drill hole neater and more accurate.
■ When drilling holes in walls or floors, check first for cables and pipes below the surface using a battery-operated detector.
■ When using the hammer-drilling function, wear safety spectacles to protect against the increased risk of flying debris, and ear defenders to shield you from the additional noise.
■ When sanding with a drill, wear a dust mask.
■ Always use the right kind of bit for the material that you're drilling, whether it be wood, masonry, metal or glass.

interpret your Dreams

Dreams are rich with metaphor and symbols. Two of the most common recurring themes are dreams of being naked or flying.

A dream that you are naked may express a fear of exposure, of being left defenceless – perhaps you dread disgrace or ridicule, or have been pretending to be something you're not.

If you dream you're flying and looking down, you may have gained a new perspective. If you can control your flight perhaps you enjoy an exalted sense of power – while falling could suggest insecurity, instability or loss of control.

Dream dictionaries can help you to understand common symbolism, but you're uniquely placed to interpret your own dreams, so try to hold onto them. On waking, lie still, gather in dream remnants and then jot them down at once. Within a few minutes they can have faded. Look out for puns and wordplay, rather like deciphering a cryptic crossword clue.

Keep a dream journal in which you write down not just what you dreamt, but the location, your emotional responses and physical sensations. You may find enlightening patterns or cycles that emerge.

save someone from Drowning

Don't try to leap into the water and rescue someone unless you're a trained lifesaver. You could easily become a casualty yourself.

Rescue from water

■ Shout for help.
■ Call the emergency services, or ideally get someone else to do it so you don't take your eyes off the victim.
■ If there's a buoyancy aid – a lifebelt or any other object that floats, such as a ball – throw it. Look around for a lifebuoy on a line as your first choice or tie a lifevest to a rope.
■ If there's no lifesaving equipment nearby, throw something as a lifeline, such as a tow rope, or reach out with a pole, oar, fishing rod or tree branch.
■ Don't go into the water unless you're trained in rescue. If you have to wade out, stay within your depth and ask someone onshore to hold a rope tied round your waist. Take a buoyancy aid for the person to hold on to.

Treat the casualty

Pull the person to safety and out of the water. Remove any mud or weed from the nose and throat and perform CPR if needed (*see* CPR).
■ If vomiting or regurgitation occurs after you begin CPR, roll the victim on to their side to clear their airways.
■ Treat for hypothermia (*see* HYPOTHERMIA).
■ Keep trying to revive the casualty until professional help arrives.

build a Drystone wall

A drystone wall is one constructed from stones without any mortar to bind them. If care is taken over the selection and positioning of each stone, a drystone wall can stand for hundreds of years.

YOU WILL NEED Wooden A-frames shaped like the finished wall, string, stones sorted into piles of various sizes

1 First dig out a trench 20cm deep, corresponding to the dimensions of the wall you intend to build. Line the bottom of the trench with big, flat heavy stones.

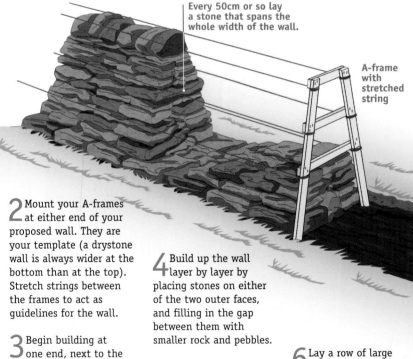

Every 50cm or so lay a stone that spans the whole width of the wall.

A-frame with stretched string

2 Mount your A-frames at either end of your proposed wall. They are your template (a drystone wall is always wider at the bottom than at the top). Stretch strings between the frames to act as guidelines for the wall.

3 Begin building at one end, next to the A-frame. The butt-end (known as the quoin) must be perfectly square and solid, so take extra care when choosing and laying your stones.

4 Build up the wall layer by layer by placing stones on either of the two outer faces, and filling in the gap between them with smaller rock and pebbles.

5 When you position the next layer, be sure that each stone bridges the joint between the two beneath it, as in an ordinary brick wall.

6 Lay a row of large heavy stones on top of the wall. Their weight serves to press together the stones beneath, so making the whole structure more stable.

recognise and tackle a
Drug overdose

Any drug – legal, illegal, prescribed or bought over-the-counter – can cause adverse reactions, even at the stated dose. Reactions are even more severe when the drug is taken in excess, in combination with other drugs or alcohol or by susceptible individuals.

Acute symptoms can range from drowsiness, shallow breathing, racing pulse, abdominal pain, vomiting, profuse sweating, distended pupils, hallucinations, paranoia, irrational behaviour, disorientation, tremors, tinnitus and seizures, to loss of consciousness and heart failure. Over hours or days paracetamol poisoning can cause jaundice and liver damage.

If you suspect an overdose, make the patient comfortable, lying on their side to guard against choking on vomit, and ask what they have taken, when and how much. Ask others who may know, or look for bottles, packaging or other evidence. If you find a hypodermic needle don't touch it. Call an ambulance, telling the operator all you can.

Note down changes in the casualty while you wait, checking breathing, pulse and level of consciousness. If the patient falls unconscious, check their breathing and be ready to give CPR (*see* CPR). If they are breathing, place them in the recovery position (*see* RECOVERY POSITION). If they vomit, keep a sample for analysis, but don't try to make them sick.

Drive in bad weather
see pages 112-113

shift Dust

The aim of good dusting is to remove dust, not disperse it.

- Vacuum as many surfaces as possible before you dust.
- Use a just-damp microfibre cloth for most surfaces. For a highly polished surface, on which water may leave a permanent mark, use a dry cloth and furniture polish.
- Dust from the top of a room down so settling dust can be removed.
- A feather duster is good for blinds, but must be shaken outside frequently as you work. Or wipe slats with a cloth dampened with vinegar (which also disinfects).
- For tricky crevices, use a small, medium-bristled paintbrush.
- To remove stubborn dust from upholstery or clothing, wind masking or packing tape around your hand, sticky side out, then rub.

Dye clothes

Take care when dyeing. Wear rubber gloves and an apron, and cover work surfaces and floors with newspaper.

Hot water dyes Wash item and leave it damp. Submerge in dye mixture, bring slowly to the boil and simmer. Cool in the water. Rinse in warm water.

Cold water dyes Dissolve powder in hot water, add fixative and salt. Soak for an hour before rinsing. (For wool, substitute vinegar for salt and fixative.) *See also* TIE-DYE.

Machine dyes Ideal for bulky items. After dyeing, run through wash cycle with detergent at hottest temperature, then again with the machine empty to clear dye residue that could stain other washing.

avoid a fight with a Duvet cover

With the right technique, inserting a duvet into its cover is a simple process, involving a second or two of preparation, a straightforward flick of the wrists and a few moments more to complete the job.

1 Put the duvet flat on the bed. Turn the cover inside out then reach inside to grasp the two corners farthest from the opening.

2 With your hands inside the cover, take hold of the top corners of the duvet and lift both of them together.

3 Flick your wrists and shake the two corners you're holding so that the duvet cover unfurls over the duvet the right way out.

4 Hold the corners in the air, and carry on shaking. If you're not very tall, you may need to stand on the bed. Then smooth out the cover and close the end.

calculate the date of Easter

Easter, unlike Christmas, is a 'moveable feast'. It occurs on a different calendar date each year, determined by a complex compromise between astronomy and ecclesiastical necessity.

In its simplest terms, Easter falls on the first Sunday after the first full moon after March 21 (the vernal equinox). In practice, the calculation is not so straightforward, because the full moon appears at different times depending on where you are in the world. If the first full moon after March 21 were to appear late on Saturday in some places, and early on Sunday elsewhere, Easter would end up being celebrated a week apart in those locations.

To get round this problem, the Church publishes tables of 'paschal full moons', in which the calendar is superimposed on a cycle of 19 years consisting of lunar months that are 29 or 30 days long. This scheme yields a rough model of the astronomical facts: the actual first full moon after the spring equinox is never more than a day or two removed from the notional paschal full moon.

Once you know the date of the paschal full moon, the rest is easy: the following Sunday is Easter Day.

---

buy and sell on eBay

eBay is the biggest and best-known internet auction house. It's easy to sell unwanted possessions and to bid for items that other people have put up for sale – all through your home computer.

To use eBay you must first register with the site. Go to the website and fill in the online form. If you're planning to sell, or if you're using an anonymous email address, you'll be asked to provide credit card details. This is purely for identification purposes.

Looking to buy
You're now ready to look for items that might interest you. Browse categories, or use eBay's search facility. If you find something you want to buy, read the description carefully, and check that you're happy with the delivery arrangements and the payment options.
- You can email the seller to ask questions before you place a bid.
- Note when the auction is due to end. It's often worth waiting before bidding, so that you don't push the price up early in the auction.
- Check the seller's feedback from other transactions for clues to their reliability and service. As with a 'bricks-and-mortar' auction house, once you bid, you're obliged to buy if your bid wins.

Looking to sell
If you're planning to sell on eBay, click on **Sell** and follow the instructions for creating 'listings' of items. Take great care over the descriptions that you write and the starting price that you set. Also, check mailing costs if you plan to send items to buyers by post.

treat Earache

Pain in the ear is commonly caused by infection, or by a build-up of mucous after a cold. It will usually clear within two to three days but there are steps you can take to help to alleviate the discomfort.

Quick action
- Try holding a warmed, soft cloth over the ear, but avoid getting water in it.
- Drink plenty of fluids and avoid cigarette smoke, which can irritate the membranes in the ear.
- See a doctor if the pain is intense, you have blood or fluid draining from the ear, are generally unwell or have a high temperature, or if a foreign body is lodged in your ear.
- Never poke a cotton bud or anything else into your ear to attempt to clear a blockage; you can cause serious damage.

Doctors try not to use antibiotic ear drops, especially in young children, as they can lead to a build-up of drug-resistant bacteria and fungi. However, sometimes you or your child may be prescribed antibiotic, steroid or other drops to help to speed recovery.

---

golden rules

eBAY BUYING AND SELLING
- **When selling, include good clear photographs of your goods and write an honest, detailed description.**
- **Don't get carried away. You can sometimes buy a brand new item from another online retailer or a shop for only a little more, but with more consumer protection.**

organise an
Egg hunt

A treasure hunt with chocolate eggs for prizes is a fun Easter activity for young children.

■ Choose places around the house or garden to hide clutches of tiny confectionery eggs, one for every child in each location. They might be behind a clock, in the fruit bowl, under a bush ...

■ Make sure all hiding places are accessible to the smallest child.

■ Devise a series of clues to the hiding places, give each child something to put their treasure in, and send them on a bunny trail, with one clue leading to another.

■ Give them the run-around: back and forth, up and down. The first to come back to 'base' with their full complement of eggs wins a prize.

golden rules

EGG SAFETY

■ **Decorated eggs should not be eaten unless you're sure they have been safely cooked and stored and that decoration is non toxic.**

observe an Eclipse safely

The only time it's safe to train the naked eye on the sun is during the brief darkness of a total eclipse, when the moon completely covers the sun. To observe a partial eclipse you need a filter to prevent damage to your eyes. Some people use inexpensive shade 14 welder's goggles (sunglasses aren't adequate), but the cheapest method is to use a pinhole projector.

viewing opening

Line up pinhole with hole in box.

1 Cut a 1cm square opening at the end of a cardboard box, such as a shoebox, and another, large enough to look through, in the side.

2 Tape down the lid of the box. Use a pin to make a hole in a piece of tin foil and tape it over the end opening.

image of the sun

3 Place the box on your shoulder and aim the pinhole at the sun, while peering through the side opening. You'll see the spectacle projected on the inside of the box. Never look through the pinhole at the sun.

get creative with Egg decorating

White-shelled eggs are best for decorating, as they take up the colour best. Place eggs in a single layer in a pan with dye and 2 tbsp vinegar for every litre of water.

Adding colour Use spinach water for green, beetroot water for crimson, cranberry juice for pink, paprika for orange-red, turmeric for yellow, blueberries or red grape juice for lavender, strong coffee for brown, red wine for deep purple. Or add a few drops of food colouring. For a mottled brown effect, wrap onion skins tied with cotton thread around eggs. Simmer eggs for 15-20 minutes. For more intense colour, leave to cool in the pan.

Adding a pattern before boiling For a marbled effect, add 1 tbsp olive oil to the dye water, draw on a pattern with a white wax crayon or wrap the egg in rubber bands before boiling. You can repeat the wax crayon method in several stages, dipping the eggs into dyes of increasing intensity for about 5 minutes each time. To wipe away any unwanted wax, put in a warm oven with the door open until the wax melts, then dab off with a paper towel.

rubber band patterns

marbled effect with
olive oil in water

wax crayon patterns

masking tape patterns

hand-painted

metallic spray paint

Creating designs For geometric patterns stick on masking tape before dyeing; when peeled off it will leave white areas. Use the same method for fancy shapes such as leaves and flowers. Use crayons, pens, quick-drying acrylic or watercolours to create designs by hand, or spray with paint from a can.

treat Electric shock

If you find someone unconscious, look for clues as to what has happened, particularly any electrical equipment that could have given them a shock. Take care not to endanger yourself. Always make the situation safe first.

Quick action

■ If someone has been electrocuted in the home, don't touch them before you break the current. Unplug the appliance at the socket or cut off the mains supply entirely at the household consumer unit or fuse box. Don't touch the switch on the device itself: it may be faulty.

■ If this isn't possible, stand on some insulating material such as a pile of newspapers or a rubber mat, and use something nonconductive, such as a wooden broom (never a damp mop), to separate the casualty from the electrical source.

continued overleaf ➔

test Eggs for freshness

A fresh egg feels heavy in the hand, but without another egg to compare, the easiest testing method is to put it into a bowl of cold water. A fresh egg will sink to the bottom and lie flat on its side. As it starts to lose its freshness more air accumulates inside and the egg will stand upright with the broader end uppermost. If it floats to the surface it should be discarded.

As a double check, break an egg into a bowl or saucer before you use it. A stale egg has a flat (not firm and rounded) yolk and a runny white. If it's bad, it will smell.

separate Eggs

An egg separator (above) allows the white to drain through holes, while retaining the yolk, but you don't need any special equipment to perform this simple task. Wash your eggs and hands before cooking to minimise any risk of infection.

■ Working over a bowl, crack the egg at its broadest point. Use your thumbs to break the shell apart, letting the white fall into the bowl, but retaining the yolk. Tip the egg from shell to shell until only the yolk is left. Nip off any threads of white with your fingertips.

E

Exfoliate skin on your face

Sloughing off dead skin cells from the face boosts circulation and lends a radiance to the complexion. There's no need for salon visits or expensive products. Always cleanse your face first to avoid rubbing dirt into the skin.

- Make a paste of 2 tsp of fine raw porridge oats, 1 tsp of bicarbonate of soda, and water.
- Gently massage the paste into the skin with circular motions, avoiding the eye area. Rinse and pat dry.
- For a luxury treatment use equal parts sugar and vegetable oil, scented with almond oil or vanilla extract. Step into the shower and apply when you're thoroughly wet; massage in and rinse off.
- Always moisturise after exfoliating and don't exfoliate the face more than once a week.

✳ golden rules

EXPERT EMBROIDERY
- Insert the needle with a stabbing motion for the most even stitch tension.
- Let the needle dangle freely occasionally to let thread unwind.
- Use an embroidery hoop to keep fabric taut but remove it each time you finish working to prevent marking.
- Keep stitches a consistent size and even tension.

- Assess the casualty's condition. They may have suffered superficial or more serious burns (*see* BURNS AND SCALDS), internal injuries, fractures from having been thrown, shock (*see* SHOCK), unconsciousness or cardiac arrest. Unless the electric shock was mild, call the emergency services.
- Check their pulse and breathing and give CPR if needed (*see* CPR).

Shock from a power line Even domestic electricity can kill, but high-voltage electric shock, from power lines for example, is usually fatal. Don't go within 18m of someone who has been felled by such a shock and keep others away, too. The current can travel a considerable distance.
- Call the emergency services and the local electricity supply authority (you should find the number on a nearby cable support or pylon).
- If the victim is conscious, call out reassurance. Don't attempt first aid until the scene is declared safe.

create Embroidery stitches

Embroidery can be used to decorate everything from table linen to clothes and cushions. As you grow in confidence, you could embroider pictures or simple samplers to frame and display.

Materials Choose tightly woven plain fabrics, evenweaves such as linen, which have the same number of threads in both warp and weft, or regularly patterned fabrics, such as gingham.

Threads and needles Stranded cottons or silks, which can be separated to give a finer thread, are most versatile. Or choose 2, 3 or 4 ply wool. For fine work use a sharp-pointed, medium length crewel needle. For heavier threads choose chenille needles. For thicker wool, select a tapestry needle.

Securing the thread To start a new thread, hold the end against the reverse side of the fabric and work stitches over it for about 4cm. To finish off at a thread end, slide it through about 4cm of worked stitches on the reverse side.

Stitches

Chain stitch is a commonly used stitch for outlines, but also for filling.

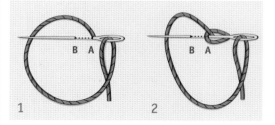

- Bring the needle out at A. Insert very close to the same hole and out at B, carrying the thread under the needle point. Pull the thread through to make the first chain link. Insert needle very close to B and repeat the stitch to sew a chain.

- Finish off by making a small stitch over the end of the last loop in the chain.

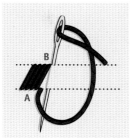

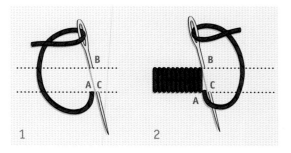

Satin stitch is a filling stitch. Working from left to right, bring the needle up at A and insert it directly above at B. Bring it up at C, just to the right of A and continue in a neat row.

You can also work on a slant, offsetting the position of A and B.

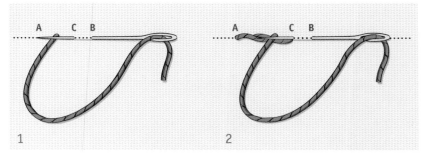

Stem stitch is an invaluable outline stitch for floral designs. Working left to right, bring the needle out at A, insert it at B and bring it out at C, half a stitch length back. Repeat, keeping thread below the needle and to the left.
■ Outlines sewn in stem stitch are often filled in with satin stitch, above. For a leaf, for example, fill in half at a time, each slanted a different way to emulate the pattern of veins in an actual leaf.

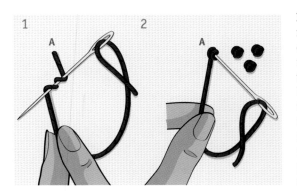

French knots create raised and textured effects. Bring the needle up at A. Holding the thread in one hand, wrap it around the needle twice, then tighten. Insert the needle near A, hold the thread taut and pull through to make a knot.

Other useful stitches Cross-stitch can be used for decorative borders and as a filling stitch (*see* CROSS-STITCH) and to sew entire patterns. Backstitch creates a neat line for outlining shapes and herringbone stitch is used for decorative borders (*see* SEWING *for both*).

shape your Eyebrows

A beautifully arched brow lightens and opens up your eyes, but work carefully. If you pluck too much you'll look permanently startled.

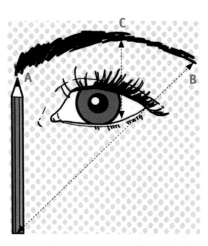

■ Hold a pencil straight up against one nostril. This will show you where your eyebrow should begin (A).
■ Hold it diagonally from the nostril so it crosses the outer corner of the eye: this is where it will end (B). Your aim is to achieve an arch directly above the outside of the iris when you are looking straight on (C). The brow should then taper.
■ Comb out your eyebrows and use an eyebrow pencil to draw the shape you want.
■ Tweeze unwanted eyebrow hairs one at a time, pulling in the direction of growth.
■ Soothe the area with toner when you've finished.

apply false
Eyelashes

YOU WILL NEED **Tweezers, eyelash strips and glue, small scissors, eyebrow pencil, mascara, eyeliner**

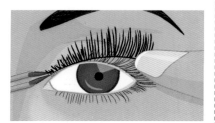

1 Use tweezers to hold the eyelash strip. Measure it against your own eye and trim the ends to fit. Draw a fine line with dark eyebrow pencil along your upper lid and smudge it a little.

2 Squeeze eyelash glue onto the back of your hand and draw the base of the strip through it. Using tweezers, apply the lashes as close to the natural eyelash line as you can.

3 Press from end to end and wait for the glue to dry.

4 Apply mascara to blend the false eyelashes with the natural ones and use eyeliner to fill any gap between the false and the natural lashes.

make Eyes up beautifully

You can enhance the natural beauty of your eyes with subtle highlighting and shadow, or create a more dramatic, smoky effect.

Sit in front of a magnifying mirror in a good light and set out your palette: eyeliner, three complementary tones of shadow, highlighter, brushes and mascara. Be prepared to take your time and experiment to get the right look.

Eyeliner

1 Use your eyeliner of choice – pencil or brush – to frame your eyes. Start from the outside corners of the upper eyelids and work inwards, as close as you can to the lashes.

2 Line under the eye, as close as possible to the lashes, starting only from the middle and working outwards. Gently smudge this bottom line with a cotton bud so that it isn't too stark.

Eyeshadow

1 Apply a base colour of shadow that almost matches your eyelids, sweeping it across the lid from the inside out, and up to the brow bones.

2 Add a slightly darker shade to the lid only, not up to the brow bone. Finally, add the darkest shade in the crease at the top of your eyelid.

3 Blend the three shades into one another, to create a subtle grading effect, using a cotton bud or blending sponge. Apply a dab of highlighter to your brow bone and blend from the mid brow outwards. Now try a professional tip from make-up artists: brighten the eye by adding a dab of highlighter to the inner corner of each eye where upper and lower lids meet.

Mascara

1 With your chin pulled downwards and your eyes looking up, brush the lower lashes of each eye with mascara. Remove excess mascara from the brush first.

2 Look down and stroke mascara onto the upper lashes, separating them as you work. Move the brush side to side at the roots, then outwards, so the lashes fan out.

3 Mascara looks best when applied in thin layers. Let each layer dry before building on it. If the lashes clump, brush them out with a mascara comb once they are dry.

keep your personal information safe on Facebook

The whole point of Facebook is to let people know that you're out there, and tell them what you're doing. But you might not want to reveal everything to everybody.

Facebook is equipped with privacy settings that allow you to decide exactly who sees which bits of your 'profile': the sum total of all that you write on the site, the pictures you post, and the information you give about your life.

■ At the top right of your home or profile page there's a tab called **Account**. Click on it, then choose **Privacy Settings**. Go through each element of your profile and choose how wide a circle of people can see it: just you, just your Facebook friends, your Facebook friends and all their Facebook friends, or anyone who happens on your profile while browsing the internet. If you're concerned about your privacy, choose **Friends Only** as your default setting.
■ If, as most people do, you accepted some distant acquaintances as friends when you first joined Facebook, you might want to bar them from seeing personal details such as your home. You can do this through the 'Customize' setting. No one will know that they have been excluded from your inner circle.

treat a child to a Face-paint

Face-painting is always a hit with children. Use your imagination or follow one of our simple designs for a tiger or a butterfly.

YOU WILL NEED **Soft paint brushes or make-up brushes, water, sponges, non-toxic face-paints**

A tiger face

1 Add yellow from the eyebrows down to the chin. Use a sponge to paint a white muzzle.

2 Use bright orange to frame the middle of the face. Then, from the brow line, paint in a pair of white eyebrows.

3 Add white stripes to the cheeks and paint in whiskers. Paint a black tip to the nose, a black mouth and stripes.

continued overleaf ➔

cleanse your Face

You should cleanse your face gently, no more than twice a day, to remove dirt, make-up and other debris without robbing the skin of its natural moisturisers.

■ Avoid normal hand soap, which contains detergents that dry out the skin.
■ Choose a cleanser formulated for your skin type. Moisten your face with tepid water, and apply cleanser with your fingertips, lightly massaging it in with tight circular motions. Thoroughly rinse off with tepid water (hot water is dehydrating), leaving no residue, and use a soft towel to pat – not to rub – dry.
■ If you're using moisturiser, apply it while the skin is still slightly damp. *See also* EXFOLIATE SKIN.

✱ golden rules

FACE-PAINT LOOKOUTS
■ **Test the paint before use on anyone with an allergy.**
■ **Don't apply paint if the child has any cuts or sores or an infectious skin condition.**
■ **Use a sponge to shade in a large area, and brushes for more detailed work.**
■ **Apply each colour with a different brush or sponge, or wash brushes between uses.**

read Facial expressions

There are certain facial expressions that are the same in all cultures. Among them are happiness, sadness, surprise, fear and disgust. These universal expressions are easy to read, but it's often the case that a person is saying one thing while their face is sending a different message. When a person smiles at you, look at the eyes: unless you see crow's feet wrinkles, and movement in the muscle that orbits the eye, the smile isn't genuine. You should also watch out for 'micro-expressions', moments when a person's real feelings flit across the face. They are only fleetingly visible, but extremely revealing if you can spot them.

deal with Fainting

Someone is feeling sick and dizzy – they could be about to pass out.

Quick action

■ Help them to lie on the floor, on their back. Kneel by them, raise their legs and rest them on one of your shoulders.
■ If you cannot get the person to lie down, have them sit, head between their knees, and tell them to push their head up against your hand, while you apply firm, gentle downward pressure. This encourages blood flow to the brain.
■ If the person faints and doesn't come around in 1-2 minutes, put them in the recovery position (*see* RECOVERY POSITION) and call for medical help. The reason behind the fainting episode may need to be investigated.

4 Add an outline of black to define the whiskers and eyebrows. Finally, stipple the muzzle with dots.

Or paint on a butterfly face
Paint the outline of a butterfly wing on either side of the face. Fill in the wings, blending two pretty colours, then outline the wings in another colour. Paint the butterfly's body on the nose, and add a round head and elegant feelers on the forehead. Finish by embellishing the wings.

draw up your Family tree

A family tree is an instantly readable representation of your personal heritage, linking you back to your ancestors.

Start with notes of all the names and dates of birth, marriage and death for all the relatives you can identify. Ask everyone in the family what they remember. Take a large sheet of paper and make a rough draft. To begin with you might find it helps to write the names on pieces of card, and move them around till you have everyone in place.

Making a simple tree In its most basic form, a family tree is called a 'pedigree chart' or 'birth brief', which begins with one individual (yourself), and goes backwards, to include only direct ancestors – two parents, four grandparents, eight great-grandparents and so on, but no aunts, uncles, cousins or siblings. It might be arranged horizontally, from left to right (as below), or vertically, from top to bottom.

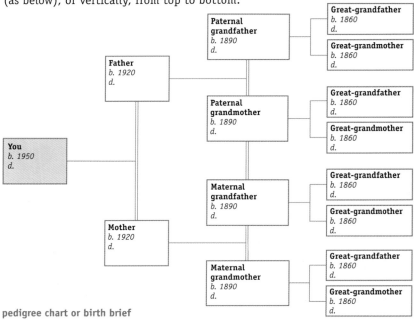

pedigree chart or birth brief

Embrace the wider family When you start to research your family history, you may want to move both forwards and back in time, to include your own children and grandchildren, and even aunts, uncles and cousins, back into the distant past. For this, you want the 'drop-line' format (see below), in which the most distant relatives are listed at the top and the lines of descent drop down the chart from one generation to the next.

drop-line chart

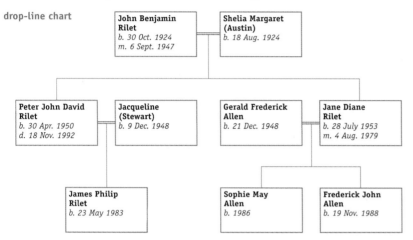

Family tree conventions

■ List women by their maiden names and use double lines to join spouses. List second spouses to the partner's other side, and number them 1 and 2.

■ Use a vertical line to link parents to children, and a horizontal line to link siblings, listing them chronologically from left to right.

■ Save space by using the common abbreviations shown right.

COMMON ABBREVIATIONS	
b.	born
bap.	baptised
m.	married
d.	died
bur.	buried
d.s.p.	died childless (*decessit sine prole*)
ob. inf.	died in infancy (*obiit*)
(c.)	approximately (*circa*)
?	uncertain or unknown
2	second marriage
════	married
= = = =	unmarried

great-grandparent

great uncle/ aunt — grandparent

first cousin once removed — uncle/aunt — parent — one parent remarried — step parent

second cousin — first cousin — you — brother/ sister — half brother/ half sister — stepbrother/ stepsister

second cousin once removed — first cousin once removed — nephew/ niece

second cousin twice removed — first cousin twice removed — great nephew/ great niece

A drop-line chart can help you to understand family relationships such as first and second cousins, and first cousin once removed.

---

create a children's
Fancy dress kit

Children love to get in costume and act out their fantasies. Delight them by creating a dressing-up box or wardrobe, and see how they play.

There's no need to splurge on specialist costumes; it's more fun to mix and match. Start by bringing together old family hand-me-downs or charity shop finds, cleaned or laundered. Hats, a velvet muff, a silk kimono, a bridal veil, a poncho … anything to fuel a child's imagination. Add accessories such as handbags, wigs, parasol, sunglasses, feather boa, baubles, bangles and beads.

Get the kids to help you to improvise more costumes for their burgeoning wardrobe.

■ For a wicked witch, you might adapt a dark dress with a ragged net skirt underneath – and add a toy black cat for her 'familiar'.

■ For a swashbuckling pirate, bring together cut-off jeans, a striped top, a bandana and an eye-patch.

■ For a fairy princess, adorn a pink leotard with silk or tissue flowers, then add a net skirt, white tights and a tiara.

■ To make gossamer wings, use fine-gauge aluminium wire for the frame, and cover with the cut-off legs from a large pair of fine tights. Tie with ribbons, so that the wings can be worn backpack fashion.

■ A pointy hat for a wizard? Roll a newspaper into a cone, hold it together with sticky tape and roll up the bottom edge until it's a snug fit for a small head.

■ A silk nightdress, a tiara and strings of fake pearls is all that a princess needs.

F

respond to a Fever

A fever – when the sustained body temperature is above 38°C (100°F) or 37.5°C (99.5°F) in children under five – is an immune response to illness or infection, and can usually be managed at home with pain relief and bed rest.

Quick action

■ Contact your doctor if a child with a fever is showing any additional symptoms of serious illness, such as severe pain, persistent and unusual crying, drowsiness, failure to drink, a non-blanching rash (*see* SPOTS AND RASHES), stiff neck or difficulty breathing.

■ For a baby under three months old, contact your doctor if their temperature is 38°C (100°F) or higher. Do the same for a baby aged three to six months, if their temperature is 39°C (102°F) or higher.

■ Don't overheat the patient's room, and make sure fresh air circulates.

■ Cover the patient with no more than a thin sheet, and keep nightclothes to a minimum.

■ If the fever is making the person uncomfortable, offer medication, such as paracetamol or ibuprofen, to bring the temperature down. Make sure to check the label for the appropriate dose.

■ Provide plenty of cool, clear drinks to replace lost fluids.

■ Check the patient's temperature (*see* TEMPERATURE) every few hours. Consult a doctor if it remains high or if other symptoms (see above) give cause for concern.

■ Be especially vigilant with young children. Fever in the under-fives can cause convulsions (*see* FITS).

replace an old Fence panel

Panel fences will rot if they haven't been properly treated, and they are subject to damage in storms and high winds. But it's not difficult to replace individual panels that are beyond repair.

1 Before you insert the new panel, paint it with a wood preservative, taking care to treat any joints or end grain that will be inaccessible once the panel is in place. You should apply preservative even if the panel has been pre-treated by the manufacturer. Use an old paint brush then throw it away.

2 It's simple to replace a fence panel that's supported by slotted concrete posts. The panels come in a standard length of 6ft (1.8m), so you need only buy a new one and slide it into the slots from above. For this you'll need a ladder, and the help of another person.

3 If you're fitting a panel to wooden posts, the new section has to fit exactly in the gap. If it's too big, you may have to plane a small amount off the frame on both sides. If it's a little too small, then you'll have to fill the gap with a narrow fillet of wood inserted between the post and the panel. Treat the fillet with preservative. Drive in the new nails at a slight angle through frame, fillet and post. This is easier if you drill pilot holes for the nails before you fit the panel. Three on each side should be sufficient.

change computer File formats

'File format' simply means the program in which any given document was created, and also the version of that program.

You'll sometimes need to change the file format of a document to make it readable on computers that use different programs from yours, or older versions of the same program. Someone using Word 97, say, won't be able to open a document that you've created in Word 2008 – unless you first change the file format.

To do this, go to **File** and select **Save As.** Click on the **Format** drop-down menu and select **Word 97-2004.** Check that the **Append File Extension** box is ticked. Click **Save.** You'll now have created a copy of your Word 2008 document that's readable by the older Word 97 program. It will have the file extension '.doc'. It's important to include the file extension, because sometimes another computer won't be able to recognise the file type unless the extension is present, and so won't be able to open it.

This example using Word is just one instance. Most programs have a **Save As** option that allows you to 'save back' to older versions, or to change the file format in other ways.

take Film worth watching

Technology has made it easy for anyone to try their hand at being a cameraman or film director. But it's not so easy to make a film that's really worth sharing with others.

Keep still The first and worst mistake that most people make is allowing the camera to shake and jiggle. It distracts viewers, and affects the quality of the shot. Brace your camera in both hands and, if you can, lean on a fence or other immovable object. Alternatively, for fixed-position shots, use a tripod.

Take your time Don't pan quickly from side to side. This error is known as 'firehosing', and it makes your film impossible to watch. The same applies to zooming in and out: do it in a measured way and not too often. Let the camera roll: a 3 second videobite of someone blowing out the candles on their cake isn't interesting. Capture the build-up, and then the aftermath.

Get plenty of material Shoot lots of footage, then edit it on your computer. Invest in some good video-editing software and use it to rearrange your film into a narrative. Pick out only the very best bits, and ruthlessly discard everything else. When you edit, mix things up so as to vary the pace and the mood of your film. This is the time to add effects such as wipes (where one scene changes to another as if 'wiped' from the screen) and fades (where the action dissolves gradually from the screen).

Be scared of the dark Camcorders work best in bright light. Films made in the evening or in the dim light of a party can easily end up looking like they were shot down a coalmine.

Change the angle
Don't shoot everything from shoulder height: this soon gets boring. Get up on a balcony from time to time or crouch down. If someone is talking to the camera, position yourself so that their head is not in the dead centre of the frame.

Crouch down so that you film children at their level (not always with their faces turned upwards to the camera). Or change the point of view even further by filming from a position below the children's eyeline.

transfer Files
to and from your PC

Sometimes you'll want to move documents and other files onto your PC, or to move files from your PC to another storage device. The simplest way to copy files is to 'drag and drop' them onto a different drive.

■ Plug a storage device – a memory stick or an external hard disk – into one of the USB ports on your computer. Click on the **Start** button, then on **Computer** from the Start menu. Your storage device will be displayed in the left pane, below Computer. Navigate on the 'C:' drive to the files that you want to move. Highlight the folders or individual files, drag them over to the **Removable Disk (E:)** icon, and drop them. They will all be copied over.
■ If your aim is to free up space on your computer, you should now delete those same files from 'Local Disk (C:)'.

When you buy a new computer, you'll want to transfer all your files to the new machine. You can do this 'manually', but it's easier and safer to use the Files and Settings Transfer Wizard, an inbuilt program designed specifically for this purpose. The Wizard works on older versions of Windows, so is ideal if you're upgrading to a better, newer machine.

choose the right
Fire extinguisher

For small fires involving paper, wood or soft furnishings you can use water extinguishers, though they are unwieldy. Never use for chip-pan or electrical fires.

For flammable liquids such as petrol, and synthetic fibres in soft furnishings and carpets, use aqueous, film-forming extinguishers.

On burning liquids, and for fires involving computer and other electrical equipment, carbon dioxide extinguishers can be used, without causing any damage. Don't use for chip-pan fires: the jet of gas will blast the fat out of the fryer.

Powder extinguishers are a powerful all-rounder, though not to be used in confined spaces, where powder might be inhaled. They also cause great mess and damage.

For kitchen fires involving burning oil, or small, localised fires, use wet chemical extinguishers. They deliver a cooling layer of foam via a lance.

The label on a fire extinguisher explains the type of fire on which it can be used, and gives operating instructions. Commit this information to memory before you have reason to use the extinguisher.

tackle a Fire in the home

A house fire is potentially devastating. Take every precaution to avoid one, and be ready to act if the worst should happen.

No home is completely fireproof, but faulty wiring and appliances, overloaded sockets, inattention to the stove, negligent smoking and badly placed candles are all fire hazards that are easily avoided. A working smoke alarm, a fire blanket and extinguisher (see left) can prove vital in saving your life and possessions. Learn how to use them by heart; you won't have time to revise in the event of a blaze. Plan escape routes and ensure they are kept clear.

Press the test button once a month to check that your smoke alarm is working.

When there's a fire in the home

If you smell smoke, or the smoke alarm sounds, or there are flames, call everyone together, and lead them out by the safest route without pausing to investigate. Close doors behind you to help to contain the fire. The instant you're clear of the building call the fire brigade. Follow the simple rules below to stay safe while you're in the building.

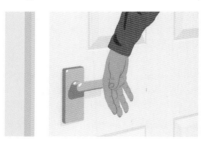

■ In a choking cloud of smoke, stoop low where the air is clearer.
■ Don't waste time trying to salvage your possessions.

■ Before you open a door, check the top and handle with the back of your hand. If it's warm, there's fire on the other side. If cool, stand behind it and open it a crack. If it opens towards you, brace your foot against it so hot gases don't blow it wide.

■ If smoke and fire block your progress, and there's no other way out, marshal everyone into a refuge room. Use bedding, rugs or rolled-up carpet to block the gap under the door, to keep out smoke and fumes. If you can get to a phone, dial the fire service. Open a window and shout for help. Wave a 'flag' of some fabric to attract attention.

Kitchen fires

■ More than half of domestic fires arise from cooking accidents, and most commonly start as a 'chip-pan fire'. If your deep-fat frying pan catches light on the hob, don't try to move it, but turn off the heat supply at the hob or at the main power source – the main electrical supply or the gas tap, for

example, if you cannot safely reach the hob controls. Get out of the room and close the door. Evacuate the house and call the fire service.
■ Never use water on an oil fire as it can cause a fireball, while a fire extinguisher can spread the flames. Fire services caution against the old technique of covering the pan with a damp tea towel and rolling it over the flames, away from you; it's simply too risky. Even the use of a fire blanket isn't advised. Summon the professionals.

Electrical fires
■ Faulty wiring carries the risks of both shock (*see* ELECTRIC SHOCK) and fire. Maintain wiring and appliances to a high standard with regular checks, and watch for warning signs of faults, such as fuses that frequently blow, lights that flicker and scorches around sockets. The best advice for avoiding electrical fires is to unplug appliances whenever they are not in use.
■ In the case of an electrical fire, if you can get to the mains supply without endangering yourself, cut it off. Don't touch or try to pull out a plug or remove an appliance until you've done this. A fire blanket, or a dry powder or carbon dioxide fire extinguisher (see left), can be used on a small, localised electrical fire. Otherwise evacuate the house as quickly as possible and call the emergency services.

lay and light a fire in your Fireplace

■ Make sure that the flue is open before you begin, otherwise you'll fill your house with smoke.
■ Place one or two firelighters or some twists of newspaper in the bottom of the grate.
■ On top, lay some twigs or thin scraps of wood in a criss-cross pattern, so that plenty of air can circulate. The more of this kindling you have, the better.

■ Lean two smallish logs against each other in a tent-shaped arrangement on top of the kindling, disturbing it as little as possible.
■ Hardwoods such as oak and apple will burn hotter and longer than softwoods such as pine and cedar.
■ Light a match or long taper and hold it to your newspapers or firelighters. Once the fire is well established, add some bigger logs.

clean your Fireplace

If you have a working fireplace in your home, you should have your chimney professionally swept once a year – during the warmer months when it's not in use. This is also the time to do a thorough clean of the firebox (the area where you build the fire). Remove the firescreen and the grate, then sweep up all the ashes; it's a good idea to sprinkle damp tea leaves on first to reduce dust. Clean any build-up of creosote with a wire brush. If that doesn't get the firebox clean enough, dissolve 50ml of soda crystals in 4 litres of water, and apply with a sponge – then go at it with the wire brush, and rinse with clean water.

chop Firewood

Frozen logs are easiest to split – but warm an axe that has been left in the cold before use to prevent the blade from chipping.

■ Stand your log upright on a platform such as a tree stump.

■ Set your feet so that you wield the axe with force and accuracy. Tee up to the log, then bring your axe over the shoulder of your dominant hand, swinging down hard. Your dominant hand should slide down the shaft of the axe as you swing.
■ If the log doesn't split at the first blow, repeat your swing. Try to strike in the same spot, or in any crack that appears in the log.
■ Always wear safety shoes with steel toecaps when using an axe. They will not only protect your toes if you miss with the axe, but also protect them from falling pieces of wood.

put together a
First-aid kit

Keep your first-aid kit in a cool, dry place, locked away from children, and replenished as necessary. Include a first-aid manual and useful information, such as family blood groups and contact details for your GP or local minor injury unit.

A household first-aid kit for routine emergencies should contain:
- assorted sticking plasters and tape
- sterile gauze dressings
- sterile eye dressings
- triangular, elasticated and crepe bandages; clips and safety pins
- disposable sterile gloves
- sharp scissors
- tweezers
- alcohol-free wipes to clean cuts and grazes
- digital thermometer
- skin-rash cream
- antiseptic cream and liquid
- insect bite or sting relief
- ibuprofen or paracetamol (both available as a syrup for children)
- antihistamine tablets
- calamine lotion for burns or rashes
- distilled water
- eyebath.

For a first-aid kit in a car add an emergency thermal blanket, hand sanitiser gel, disposable hot/cold pack and a clinical waste bag.

When travelling abroad, add laxatives; diarrhoea medicine and rehydration salts; antacids; sun block and soothers; travel sickness pills and antihistamines. For certain destinations, health professionals recommend carrying a supply of sterile syringes and scalpels; water purification tablets and a single 500mg tablet of the antibiotic ciprofloxacin, which must be obtained on prescription.

cook Fish

Always test that fish is properly cooked by prodding it gently with the prongs of a fork. The meat should be just opaque and flake easily. The exception is tuna, which can be served rare.

Method	Suitable for	Cooking tips	Timing
SAUTÉING AND PAN FRYING	Any firm fish	Use hot oil and butter mixture. Put in skin side down. Can be dusted with seasoned flour then rolled into egg and breadcrumbs.	2-3 minutes each side
DEEP FRYING	Any firm fish	Can be covered in batter or egg and breadcrumbs. Use a frying basket and vegetable oil heated to 180°C (or so that a bread cube browns in 1 minute).	6-7 minutes for a fillet, 3-4 for whitebait
STEAMING	Any fish fillet, steak or small to medium whole fish	Use fish stock (*see* FISH STOCK) or a court bouillon (water with onions, herbs and seasoning added).	8-12 minutes for fillets or steaks
POACHING	Any fish or cut, including whole fish	Cook in a court bouillon on the stovetop or in the oven at 180°C/gas 4. Use a fish kettle for large fish. Leave to cool in the poaching liquid.	10 minutes for fillets, 10 minutes per 450g for a whole fish
GRILLING AND BARBECUING	Whole oily fish; firm textured steaks or fillets	Brush with oil and add fresh herbs. Ensure grill or barbecue is very hot.	4-5 minutes per side
BAKING	Any fish, whole or cut, especially delicate fish	Bake in a shallow buttered dish. Or wrap loosely in foil or greaseproof paper. Score (make deep cuts) into whole fish.	15-20 minutes for fillets or medium whole fish

Batter for fried fish To make a basic coating batter, whisk together or mix in a food processor 100g plain flour, a pinch of salt, 1 egg and 150ml milk or beer. Stand for 30 minutes before using.

create a classic Fish soup

Both white fish and shellfish make excellent soups. Choose from a hearty, rustic version or a smooth and sophisticated bisque.

Fish soup Provençal

SERVES 4-6

3 tbsp olive oil
1 large onion, chopped
2 cloves garlic, chopped
1 celery stick, chopped
1 small head fennel, chopped
400g can chopped tomatoes
2 tbsp tomato purée
150g each whiting, plaice and
    ling fillets or other white fish,
    skinned and trimmed, cut into
    5cm pieces

juice of 1 orange
1 strip orange zest
500ml fish stock (*see* FISH STOCK)
bouquet garni of 2 sprigs each
    parsley, thyme and rosemary and
    2 bayleaves, tied with string
salt and freshly ground black
    pepper

TO GARNISH

1 stick French bread, sliced
olive oil
4 tbsp double cream

1 Heat the oil in a heavy-based pan and cook the onion until soft, but not browned. Add the garlic and cook for another 1-2 minutes before adding the celery, fennel, tomatoes, tomato purée, orange juice and zest. Simmer for about 15 minutes stirring occasionally.

2 Add the fish, stock and bouquet garni and bring to the boil. Cover and simmer for 20 minutes. Remove the bouquet garni and orange zest, leave to cool for a few minutes, then liquidise until smooth. Return to the pan, bring back nearly to the boil and adjust the seasoning.

3 Brush slices of French bread with olive oil and grill until golden brown, turning once. Ladle soup into bowls. Swirl 1 tbsp cream into each bowl and top with the slices of French bread.

Prawn bisque

SERVES 4-6

15g butter
1 carrot, diced
1 small onion, diced
500g uncooked prawns
100ml white wine
1½ tbsp brandy
1 litre fish or shellfish stock
    (*see* FISH STOCK)

bouquet garni (as above)
20g rice
salt and pepper

TO SERVE

4 tbsp double cream
4 tsp sherry or Madeira
pinches of cayenne pepper
few extra cooked prawns, unpeeled
croutons

1 Melt the butter in a large saucepan. Add the vegetables and cook until soft. Add the shellfish and cook, stirring for 2-3 minutes. Pour in the wine and brandy and boil for 1-2 minutes to reduce. Add about 100ml stock and simmer until the prawns are tender. Remove and peel them, discarding any intestinal veins (*see* PRAWNS).

2 Return the prawns to the pan with the remaining stock, rice, salt and pepper. Cover and simmer for 15-20 minutes. Discard the bouquet garni, purée the mixture then pass it through a sieve. Return to the pan, bring almost to the boil and check the seasoning. Pour into bowls, then stir in the cream and sherry or Madeira and a pinch of cayenne. Decorate with the additional prawns and croutons.

---

make a versatile Fish stock

Bones and trimmings such as heads and skin are ideal for fish stock, but remove any gills from fish heads before using.

White fish are the best choice for making stock – darker ones can impart a bitter taste. For a shellfish stock, substitute shells of prawn, crab, mussels or lobster. Fish stock freezes well but should be used within three months of being made.

MAKES ABOUT 1.5 LITRES

1kg white fish trimmings (can
    include inexpensive white fish
    such as pollack) or shells
1 onion, thinly sliced
4 sprigs parsley
2 bay leaves
2 carrots, chopped
2 sticks celery, chopped
4 black peppercorns
1.5 litres boiling water or 1 litre
    water and 500ml dry white wine

1 Rinse the fish trimmings well and place in a large saucepan with the onion, parsley, bay leaves, carrots, celery and peppercorns. Pour on the boiling water and wine (if using). Return to the boil and simmer gently for about 30 minutes, skimming off any scum from the surface.

2 Remove from the heat, cool for 10 minutes, then strain through a fine sieve (plus muslin if using shellfish, to catch any fine particles of grit). Use at once or chill.

---

master
Fish preparation
see pages 132-133

F

master Fish preparation

Good fishmongers will usually prepare fish, but it's useful to know how to do it yourself, particularly if you have the chance to buy it fresh from market or harbourside stalls.

smells of the sea
rather than fish

tight scales

bright red gills

clear eyes

bright slippery skin

YOU WILL NEED Scissors, small sharp knife, polythene bag, chopping board, large cook's knife, teaspoon, filleting or medium-sized cook's knife, tweezers

A fresh fish has bright, slippery skin, tight scales and bright eyes and gills. It should feel firm to the touch and should smell of the sea rather than 'fishy'. Before cooking, fish may need to be trimmed and scaled, cleaned (gutted), boned and skinned. The methods used for most of these tasks differ depending on whether you're preparing round fish or flatfish.

Prepare a round fish

Before handling any fish, wash your hands thoroughly and improve your grip by dipping your fingers into salt. Wash your hands again when you're finished.

Trimming Use scissors or a small sharp knife to cut fins from both sides and along the back.

Scaling Put the fish into a polythene bag and onto a chopping board. Hold the tail in one hand and work the knife from tail to head, using the bag to catch the scales.

Skinning You need only skin fish if your recipe requires it. With a sharp knife, loosen the skin around the head then gently insert and draw the knife beneath the skin towards the tail. Repeat for the other side.

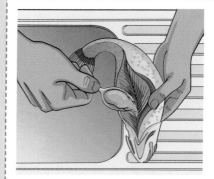

CLEANING A WHOLE ROUND FISH

1 Hold the fish on its side and slit it along the belly with a small sharp knife until you reach the head.

2 Pull the opening apart to widen it then scrape out the intestines with a knife or teaspoon.

3 Rinse the fish well under cold running water, running a teaspoon along the backbone to remove any blood clots.

BONING A WHOLE ROUND FISH
A filleting knife with a flexible blade makes this job easier. If you don't have one, use a medium-sized cook's knife. If you leave the head on it will help the fish to keep its shape during cooking.

1 Hold the fish with its cleaned cavity toward you. Slide the knife between the ribs and the flesh on both sides, freeing all the ribs down the backbone and taking care not to cut through to the skin.

2 Use scissors to cut through and release each end of the backbone. Then gently peel it away from the flesh, beginning at the head, using a small knife to ease it if necessary.

3 Check that no small bones remain, especially around the edges. Use tweezers to remove any left behind. Bones can be kept and used to make fish stock (see FISH STOCK).

CUTTING FISH STEAKS Use a large cook's knife to cut steaks 2-3cm thick, starting from the widest part of the body. Only remove the central bone after cooking.

Prepare a flatfish

After being scaled, cleaned and trimmed, a flatfish can be cooked whole, with or without the head. Wash your hands before and after preparation.

Scaling Use the same method as for round fish.

Cleaning Make a semicircular slit just behind the head, on the dark side to open up the body cavity. Scrape the entrails out with a small sharp knife and/or a teaspoon. Wash well under cold running water. Cut off the fins with scissors, close to the body.

Skinning Put the fish on a board, dark side uppermost. Make a slit across the skin just above the tail. Holding the tail tightly, pull the skin towards the head. Remove the white skin in the same way.

Boning Only large flatfish such as Dover sole, shown right, are suitable for boning. Smaller ones like plaice are too delicate. Once a fish has been boned, it can be stuffed.

FILLETING A WHOLE ROUND FISH
A round fish provides two fillets, one on each side of the backbone. Remove the head before you start, but leave the skin in place. The head can be used when making stock (*see* FISH STOCK).

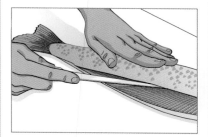

1 Put the fish on its side with the tail towards you. Working from head to tail, cut along the length of its back right through to the backbone with the knife, parallel to the work surface.

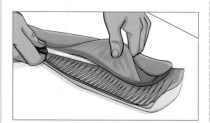

2 Starting at the head end, free the flesh from the rib bones on one side. Work the knife along the underside until the top fillet comes away.

3 Then, pulling on it gently, cut away the second lower fillet. Remove any bones with tweezers.

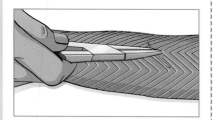

FILLETING A FLATFISH A flatfish will make four fillets, two from each side. Keep the knife as close to the bones as possible and make bold strokes – tentative ones are more likely to damage delicate flesh. There will already be a small incision in the fish where the guts were removed at sea.

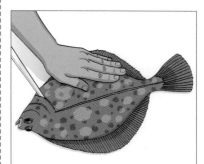

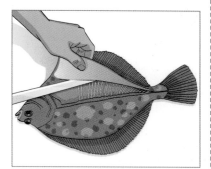

1 Put the fish dark side up on a board and cut off the fins. Working from head to tail, cut along the backbone. Make a semicircular cut just below the head, through half the thickness of the fish.

2 Slant the knife against the backbone and use short strokes to separate the left-hand fillet from the bone.

3 Make a thick cut just above the tail and remove the fillet. Repeat for the right-hand fillet and for the two fillets on the other side.

make Fishcakes

You can use white fish, salmon or smoked fish to make fishcakes.

SERVES 4

400g potatoes, cooked and mashed with 25g butter
375g white fish, poached in milk
3 spring onions finely chopped
3 tbsp chopped parsley
salt and freshly ground pepper
30g plain flour
1 large egg, beaten
85g fine fresh wholemeal breadcrumbs combined with 30g freshly grated Parmesan cheese

1 Heat the oven to 190°C/gas 5.

2 Mix the potatoes with 2 tbsp poaching milk, fish, onions and parsley to make a soft mixture. Season with salt and pepper.

3 Form into eight cakes. Dust cakes with the flour, dip into the beaten egg then into the breadcrumb mixture.

4 Cook on a non-stick baking sheet for 20 minutes until golden. Alternatively, fry in vegetable oil.

cast a Fishing line

In coarse fishing, the goal is to land your bait at a point in the water where you believe the fish are feeding. The technique used for casting your fishing line is the same whether you are using a ledger weight or a float.

1 Hold the rod in front of you at an angle that's a little below the vertical, with a short play of line dangling from the end. Grip the rod near the reel seat using the hand you write with. Place the other hand at the butt of the rod.

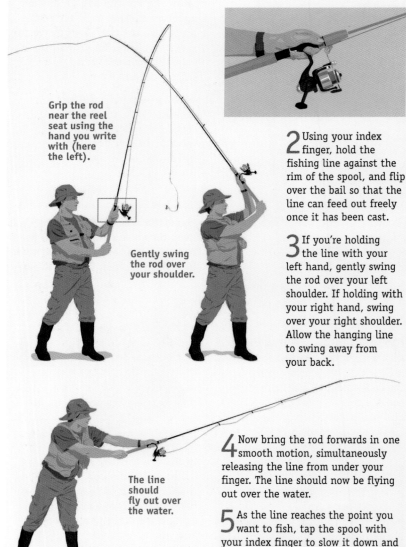

Grip the rod near the reel seat using the hand you write with (here the left).

Gently swing the rod over your shoulder.

The line should fly out over the water.

2 Using your index finger, hold the fishing line against the rim of the spool, and flip over the bail so that the line can feed out freely once it has been cast.

3 If you're holding the line with your left hand, gently swing the rod over your left shoulder. If holding with your right hand, swing over your right shoulder. Allow the hanging line to swing away from your back.

4 Now bring the rod forwards in one smooth motion, simultaneously releasing the line from under your finger. The line should now be flying out over the water.

5 As the line reaches the point you want to fish, tap the spool with your index finger to slow it down and drop it in the water without too big a splash. Close the bail arm.

deal with Fits

Witnessing a fit is frightening, but they are seldom as alarming as they first appear. Stay calm and follow these tips to keep the patient safe from injury.

Quick action

Seizures may be recurrent, as in epilepsy (often triggered by flashing or flickering lights), or isolated. A sufferer may stagger, utter meaningless sounds, or fall to the floor and convulse. Never restrain their movements or put anything in their mouth.

■ If the person suffering the fit is on the floor, provide padding with clothing, rugs and blankets to prevent injury, particularly to the head (left). If possible, move any nearby furniture if they are indoors.

■ When the jerking stops, roll the person onto their side and check that the airway is clear (*see* RECOVERY POSITION). Let them lie quietly to recover.
■ Call an ambulance if the fit is someone's first, lasts for more than 5 minutes or recurs. Call also if the person has been injured or is unconscious for 10 minutes or more.

When a child has a febrile convulsion

Before the age of 5 a child may suffer convulsions caused by a fever (*see* FEVER). Though these are usually harmless and last no more than 2 minutes, you should take the following measures.

■ Call an ambulance if a child shows other symptoms of serious illness, such as a rash or stiff neck, if the fit lasts more than 5 minutes, or if they have not fully recovered within an hour. Seek medical advice if this is a first fit.
■ During the fit, to help prevent any injury lie the child on a soft surface if you can move them safely. If possible, lie them on their side to keep the airway open and avoid choking if they vomit.
■ As soon as you can, remove warm clothing or bedclothes and loosen tight clothing. Don't allow the child to get too cold and don't sponge the skin with cold water. Let them cool down naturally.
■ When the child is fully conscious, give paracetamol or ibuprofen if you wish, to help to bring the temperature down.
■ Monitor the child's pulse, breathing and temperature every 10-15 minutes until the temperature starts to fall.

raise a Flag

The act of running a flag up a pole is a technical task, but there are also matters of etiquette.

The technical aspect is straightforward. On the rope there are two snaphooks.

1 Attach the higher snaphook to the grommet (brass ring) at the upper right of the flag.

2 Raise the flag a little, then attach the lower snaphook to the grommet at the bottom corner of the flag.

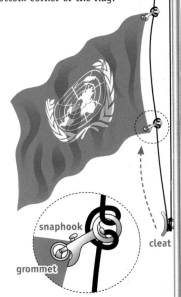

snaphook

cleat

grommet

3 Hoist the flag to the top of the pole, then secure the rope at the base using the cleat.

Etiquette

■ Take care to fly a British flag the right way up. The broader white diagonal stripe should be uppermost on the side of the flag nearest to the flagpole.
■ An American flag must not touch the ground at any point during lowering or raising.

F

deal with Fleas

If you have fleas in your home, start by treating your dog or cat to remove the initial cause.

■ Consult your vet for the safest and most suitable treatment. Never use on a cat a treatment intended for a dog or vice versa.
■ Wash your pet's bedding, then wash or thoroughly vacuum any furniture where your pet is allowed to sit. Remove the vacuum bag as soon as you've finished, seal in a plastic bag and throw away.
■ For serious flea infestations in the home, you may need to call in a professional pest-control company.

get a Flight upgrade

Free upgrades are rare, but to stand any chance of getting one you need to look the part.

■ If you're dressed scruffily, your chances of wangling your way into Business Class are slim.
■ An appearance that says SFU ('suitable for upgrade') is more likely to pay dividends if you check in late, once the cheap seats are full. But this is a risky strategy: you might just end up with the worst seat in Economy.
■ You're more likely to be upgraded if you're travelling alone.
■ The best tactic is to join an airline's loyalty scheme and try to use that carrier whenever you fly. Frequent flyers tend to go to the front of the upgrade queue.

get ready for a Flooding

When a flood threatens your home there are measures you can take to minimise the risk of damage and to keep you safe.

■ Have drinking water to hand. Fill jugs and saucepans from the kitchen tap before the floods hit: the tap supply may become contaminated.
■ If water gets inside the house, turn off the electricity at the mains before you begin to clear up, and open windows if you smell gas.
■ Never leave your house during the flood, unless you feel your life is in danger there. Move upstairs and wait for help.
■ In high-risk flood areas, choose easy-to-clean ceramic tiles and loose rugs for flooring, rather than fitted carpets downstairs, which will need to be replaced after a flood.
■ If your house regularly floods, raise electrical sockets and switches to at least 1.5m above the floor and run ground floor cabling through the ceiling void and down the wall to keep the wiring above water level.

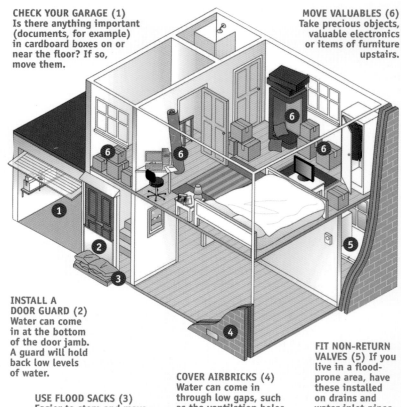

CHECK YOUR GARAGE (1)
Is there anything important (documents, for example) in cardboard boxes on or near the floor? If so, move them.

MOVE VALUABLES (6)
Take precious objects, valuable electronics or items of furniture upstairs.

INSTALL A DOOR GUARD (2)
Water can come in at the bottom of the door jamb. A guard will hold back low levels of water.

USE FLOOD SACKS (3)
Easier to store and move than traditional sandbags, flood sacks inflate in water to create a water-tight barrier.

COVER AIRBRICKS (4)
Water can come in through low gaps, such as the ventilation holes in airbricks. You can buy effective covers that still allow the airbrick to do its job.

FIT NON-RETURN VALVES (5) If you live in a flood-prone area, have these installed on drains and water inlet pipes to prevent foul flood water from getting back into the water system.

prepare and sand Floorboards

YOU WILL NEED Dust mask and ear defenders, claw hammer, nail punch, floor sander, sanding belts (coarse, medium and fine), edging sander

1 Sanding floors is a noisy business that creates lots of dust, so wear a dust mask and ear defenders. Before you begin, make sure that the room is entirely empty of furnishings, which includes taking down the curtains.

2 Carefully check over the floor, and use your claw hammer to remove any tacks that may remain from previous floor coverings. Look at all the floorboard nails: if any are protruding, firmly nail them down with the punch and hammer.

3 Now you can begin to sand. Fit a coarse-grade sanding belt first. Beginning at one edge of the room, work along the length of the boards. You'll feel the sander drag you forwards: hold it slightly in check so that it moves at a controlled rate.

4 If any of your boards are curled (a common problem in old houses), then do your first pass diagonally (as left) to smooth the edges.

5 When you have finished one strip, move on to the adjacent section of floor. Take care to lift the belt from the floor as you turn the machine around, and never try to pull it backwards. Once you have covered the whole floor, repeat the process with the medium belt, and then the fine-grade belt (don't sand diagonally with these finer belts).

6 The edges of the room have to be tackled separately with an edging sander. The corners must be done with a scraper, or with a hand-held sander designed specifically for the task. When you have finished, vacuum the floor thoroughly, then wipe over with a clean, dry, lint-free cloth to remove the last of the dust. Finish with several coats of oil, varnish, stain or paint.

replace damaged Floorboards

YOU WILL NEED Claw hammer, steel bolster, scrap wood battens, new floorboard, nails, stain or varnish

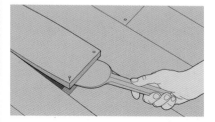

1 Lift the damaged board. Take a hammer and a steel bolster (a chisel with a wide blade). Tap the bolster into the gap at the end of the board and lever up the board a little, so that the nearest nails are partly pulled out. Then ease them out with the claw hammer.

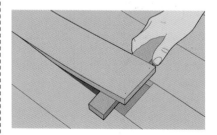

2 Lift the board again and slip battens of scrap wood under to hold it up while you free the subsequent sets of nails until the board itself comes free.

3 If the damage is superficial (a burn, say, or a bad dent) it may be enough just to turn the floorboard over and nail it back down. If your board needs replacing, take it to a wood merchant and get a new board made up to the same width and thickness – this varies greatly with the age and style of a house, so don't attempt to guess.

4 Slot the new board into place and nail it down, using the old nails if they are good enough. Stain or varnish the new board so that it looks the same as the rest of the floor if you aren't going to carpet over it.

press Flowers

YOU WILL NEED Blotting paper, tray, newspaper or paper towels, heavy books or heavy microwave-proof dish and microwave

Pressing with books

■ Put three or four sheets of newspaper on a tray and cover with a sheet of blotting paper. Place the flowers on top, well spaced out.

■ Cover with another sheet of blotting paper and three or four sheets of newspaper. Place heavy books on top and leave for two weeks in a cool, dry place.

■ Remove blotting paper carefully to avoid damaging flowers. Leave for another week if not completely dry.

In the microwave

■ Prepare as above, but using paper towels, rather than newspaper, and a microwave-proof plate or the turntable, rather than a tray. Place a heavy dish on top, then microwave on medium power in 1 minute bursts, checking for dryness each time. Flowers should be stiff and the paper still slightly damp – it should take 3-4 minutes.

make cut Flowers
last longer

■ Pick flowers early in the morning or in the evening.

■ Remove all lower leaves that will be under water.

■ Cut off the bottom 1.5-2.5cm of each stem at a sharp angle, then soak stems in lukewarm water for at least 2 hours (use cold for flowers from bulbs, such as tulips and lilies).

■ Make sure vases are scrupulously clean before use.

■ Change the water every two days.

create a beautiful
Flower arrangement

The key to making a flower arrangement is to think of it as a three-dimensional triangle built up in a series of layers. Using odd numbers of each stem helps to achieve this.

YOU WILL NEED Flowers, vase, flower food, scissors, florists' tape. Optional: florist's foam, bucket, knife

1 Fill the vase with water and add flower food. Arrange three long stems (usually foliage) to make the basic shape of your arrangement.

2 Add more foliage to fill out the shape. Some florists make a grid of clear tape over the neck of the vase to help to support the stems.

3 Start adding tapered flowers to enhance the arrangement's shape. Choose slender flowers, such as delphiniums, or unopened buds.

4 Fill in gaps with rounder flowers, which will form the bulk of the arrangement and add volume and colour.

5 Next, position one or three eye-catching focal flowers, such as large lilies or bright sunflowers.

6 Finish with 'fillers' for additional texture or an airy contrast to bold flowers. Try gypsophilia or even grasses.

Using florist's foam For shallow and flat arrangements a block of foam allows stems to be inserted at any angle. Soak the foam in a bucket of cold water and submerge for about 5 minutes or until wet through. Use a sharp knife to cut to shape, 2.5cm higher than the container, and remove a V from one corner for adding water. Secure with florist's tape.

dry Flowers

YOU WILL NEED Cut flowers, elastic bands, string and coat hangers, or silica gel crystals, shallow airtight glass or plastic container and microwave oven (optional)

Air drying
- Strip off untidy lower leaves.
- Secure bunches of up to ten stems with an elastic band (the stems will shrink as they dry and fall out if tied with string), tie to hangers with string of different lengths and hang in a dark, warm, well-ventilated place for up to two weeks.

Using silica gel
- Line the base of an airtight container with 2.5cm of silica gel then push in trimmed flower heads, face upwards and spaced well apart.
- Cover with another 2.5cm layer of gel, seal and leave for three to five days. Alternatively, microwave on high for 2 minutes for delicate blooms and 4 minutes for fleshier ones.
- Cool for 20 minutes. Check that flowers are totally dry before removing.

be safe with Food storage

To store food safely you need to control the multiplication of bacteria, which contaminate food and produce harmful toxins. Similar toxins are also produced by the moulds (fungi) that flourish on poorly stored food.

In the fridge
- Keep the temperature no higher than 5°C to help to prevent bacteria and moulds reproducing.
- Store dairy foods at the top of the fridge or in the door space.
- Cover cooked foods with cling film or store in sealed containers at the top of the fridge.
- Cool cooked foods before storing.
- Store raw meats on the bottom shelf, below cooked foods.
- Don't mix different meats in the same container, or meat with fish.
- Keep fruit, vegetables, dairy and any food that won't be cooked away from raw meat and fish.
- Keep fruit and vegetables in salad drawers.
- Put fresher items behind older ones to use them in order.

In a cupboard or larder
- Keep dry ingredients in airtight containers to prevent deterioration and deter insects. Clothes pegs or purpose-made clips are ideal for sealing opened packets.

Basic food hygiene
- Reheat cooked food thoroughly. Most bacteria are killed at 70°C, so heat until steaming hot and keep

continued overleaf →

distinguish Flu from a cold

You have a sore throat and a cough. Your head is pounding. You can't eat, ache all over and feel wiped out. Is it a cold or flu? The two share many of the same symptoms, but are caused by different viruses – and influenza is far more serious.

- Flu tends to come on suddenly, with a high fever (*see* FEVER).
- There may be aching muscles, a dry cough and exhaustion.
- With a cold, you should start feeling better within a few days. Flu symptoms persist for up to a week and leave you still feeling tired.
- If you have flu, you know it! With a cold it's still possible to move around and function, with flu you won't want to get out of bed.

If you have flu or a bad cold, always cough or sneeze into a tissue and wash your hands after disposing of it. Avoid close contact with others, if possible. Seek medical advice for the over 65s, under 5s, pregnant women and otherwise vulnerable patients, such as those with asthma, heart or other chest complaints, diabetes or a weakened immune system.

golden rules
FRESH FOOD, SAFE FOOD
- **The sell-by and use-by dates on foods are just a guideline. Use your eyes and nose as well to tell whether food is safe.**
- **In hot weather, take a coolbox to the supermarket to keep fresh food as chilled as possible while you get it home.**
- **Clean the fridge once a week.**

head a Football

With the ball in front of you, jump and strike the ball downwards, just above its 'equator' to send it low into the goal.

If you're heading to score, you need timing, accuracy and power. Time your jump so as to get above the ball, but also above the heads of the defenders. Arch back and spring forwards as you make contact with the ball, so that all the power of your back and neck goes into the impact. Aim low, because a ball near ground level is much harder for a goalkeeper to deal with.

Strike the ball from below as you jump to send it up and away from the attacking play.

If you're heading defensively, make contact just below the ball's equator, so that it flies out of the danger zone over the heads of the attacking players.

food at that temperature for at least 2 minutes, even if you then let it cool again slightly before serving.
■ Once opened, transfer perishable foods, such as canned goods, to the fridge. Always follow the storage instructions on a product's label.
■ Wash your hands thoroughly before and after handling food,
even when shopping and unpacking your groceries (*see* HANDS).
■ To avoid contaminating food or spreading bacteria, never use the same knife for different kinds of food unless you wash it thoroughly in between. Keep a separate chopping board just for use with raw meat and poultry.

calculate and cut Food miles

The purpose of cutting your food miles is to reduce the fuel consumption involved in transporting food from its place of production to your plate. In doing this, you help to reduce the emission of the greenhouse gas carbon dioxide into the atmosphere. Food labels stating place and country of origin can reveal much about the eco-friendliness of your purchases.

Calculate food miles on the basis that, on average, transporting 1kg of food 1,000km by air generates 1.1kg of carbon dioxide compared with 23g if transported by boat, 290g if carried by road and less than 30g if moved by rail. As a rule, highly perishable foods such as strawberries and green beans are air freighted, less perishable ones such as onions and potatoes, plus canned goods, are carried by boat, road or rail. To check, look for the air-freighted symbols used by some supermarkets.

Cut food miles by buying local produce whenever possible and eating seasonally. Out-of-season foods are invariably transported long distances, grown in heated greenhouses or both. When you can, grow your own food and preserve any surplus for use throughout the year.

treat Food poisoning

The body can react violently to contaminated food, with diarrhoea, vomiting, stomach cramps, abdominal and muscle pains, fever and chills. The symptoms, though unpleasant, can generally be soothed and usually abate within a week.

Seek medical help if symptoms persist or are extreme, if being unable to keep liquids down lasts for longer than a day, if the patient is very young or old, pregnant or has other medical conditions that make them vulnerable, such as a weakened immune system.

■ Sip slowly at least 2 litres of water a day, plus 200ml for every loose stool.
■ For elderly or vulnerable people, include rehydration salts, available from a pharmacist.

■ When appetite starts to return, introduce small portions of plain food such as rice, bread or pasta in the first 24 hours.

kick a Football

There are many ways to kick a ball. It all depends on what you're trying to achieve: a straightforward pass or nifty ball manoeuvre.

A short pass is best made with the instep of the foot, which should be at right angles to the direction of the pass.

To drive the ball fast and low, use the laces, or top of the foot: keep the toes pointing down, and the non-kicking foot close to the ball.

To swerve the ball, you must make it spin, and that means striking it off-centre with the inside or (more challenging) the outside of the foot.

To chip the ball, stab down, under the ball, creating uplift and backspin, so the ball rises and drops steeply.

---

take a Football penalty

When taking a penalty, you face a series of choices. The key is to make a quick decision and stick to it.

■ Power or placement? Power means using the instep to blast the ball as hard as possible. The goalkeeper has little chance to react, but you can all too easily hit high or wide or straight at the keeper. Placement means using the instep to put the ball in the corner, beyond the keeper's reach, but gives him time to assess your shot and get to the slower-moving ball.
■ Left or right? You have four permutations to work with: power left, power right, placement left, placement right. Or you might, as a fifth option, shoot straight down the middle in the hope that the keeper will be diving away from the centre.
■ Stick to your guns. The worst thing you can do is change your mind on the run-up. Most missed penalties are the result of the striker's indecision.

use correct Forms of address

Pete or *Mr Brown*? Will you be court-martialled if you muddle your Majors and Generals? Even in these less formal times, it helps to know how to address people of certain ranks and professions. Here are some hints for modern manners.

Ms or Miss? *Miss* is used mainly to address girls of under 18. Use *Ms* if you aren't certain of a woman's marital status. If a woman retains her maiden name after marriage, she usually uses the prefix *Ms*, rather than *Miss* or *Mrs*.

First-name terms How do you feel when a stranger addresses you by your first name? Or when an email arrives with a strangely formal *Dear Mr Smith*? Let common sense be your guide, reserving formality for more senior colleagues, people you don't know or people you know would appreciate the gesture.

Doctors and physicians are Doctor (*Dr*, in writing) unless they are surgeons, when they revert to being addressed as *Mr* or *Ms/Miss/Mrs*. Dentists are dental surgeons, so do not use the *Dr* prefix.

A military officer is addressed by full rank in writing, with letters after their name to denote orders and decorations. In speech, address all Generals (Generals, Lieutenant Generals and Major Generals) as *General* and likewise with other groups of ranks.

Mixing with Majesty Even the Royal family is moving with the times. While senior royals should still be addressed as *Your Majesty*, *Ma'am*, *Your Royal Highness* or similar, many of the younger royals prefer a less stuffy approach.

apply
Foundation

As its name suggests, foundation provides the background to your make-up look and shouldn't stand out. Aim for a subtle, dewy finish, not an unnatural glow.

■ Choose the ideal shade by testing on your jaw line; check it in daylight, not just artificial light.
■ Apply a thin veil of moisturiser and wait for it to dry.

■ Use a brush or your middle finger to spread foundation. Work outwards from the centre of your face, covering a small area at a time.
■ Blend around the hair and jaw lines to avoid an obvious 'seam' between foundation and your natural skin tone. Use a clean sponge instead of your fingers, if you prefer.
■ If you have dry skin, 'set' the foundation by blotting with a tissue. For medium or oily skin, use a light dusting of powder.

discourage Foxes from your garden

Foxes can cause a nuisance in gardens by digging and fouling. And they can keep you up at night by barking and screaming in the main breeding seasons of autumn and winter.

■ Think twice about paying a pest controller to remove or destroy the trespasser; a successor is likely to move in within weeks.
■ A fox uses scent-marking to identify territory, so fool it by using an artificial scent-mark product, available from garden centres. Some people claim that collecting your own urine and distributing it around the perimeter of your property will make a fox hesitate about crossing your territory.
■ Close sheds to avoid providing shelter for the animal and keep food waste inside bins with secure lids to limit scavenging.
■ Avoid fertilisers that contain fish bone or blood products. These can attract hungry foxes, who will dig up lawns and borders in search of the food they think is nearby.
■ Use netting over fruit and vegetable crops, pick up windfalls and keep pet rabbits and chickens secure to deny foxes an easy meal (*see* CHICKENS).

dance a Foxtrot like Fred Astaire

Put on some evocative swing music – 'You Make Me Feel so Young', 'Night and Day', 'Cheek to Cheek'. Ladies, place your right hand in his left, and left hand resting on his right arm. Gentlemen, place your right hand on her left shoulder blade.

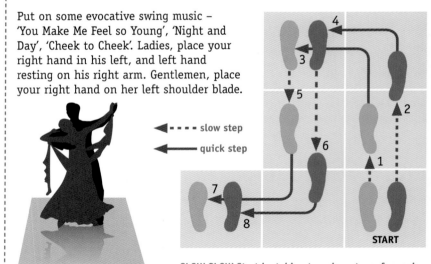

SMOOTH AND SOPHISTICATED
The slow foxtrot is danced with grace and flair: think Fred Astaire and Ginger Rogers. It should flow, with a natural rise and fall created by the changing pace of the steps. Go low with the slow steps and rise up with the quicks. A 'social foxtrot' (right) is easier, with no rise and fall.

SLOW SLOW Start by taking two slow steps, forwards for the gentleman (1) and (2), left then right.

QUICK QUICK Take one quick sidestep, gentleman to the left (3), and another to bring feet together (4).

SLOW SLOW The gentleman takes two slow steps backwards, left then right, (5) and (6). Ladies moving forward, right then left.

QUICK QUICK Another quick sidestep – gentleman to the left (7) and (8), lady to the right. And a quick step to bring feet together before starting again. Repeat the sequence as you move round the floor.

Freeze food safely for storage

A well-stocked freezer can save you money and time, but is wasteful if you aren't selective or don't use foods in time. Many ready-prepared dishes can be cooked from frozen, as can small pieces of raw fish; otherwise defrost food slowly and thoroughly first.

The more water a food contains the less likely it is to freeze well. Many fruits and vegetables, including tomatoes, are better puréed or made into sauces, soups or cooked dishes. Vegetables need blanching in boiling water, then cooling quickly in cold water to inhibit the enzymes that detract from their colour, flavour and nutritional value. Freeze food in watertight bags or rigid containers that will make the best use of your freezer space. Items can also be wrapped in foil or film.

Tips for a safe and efficient freezer
- A full freezer runs most efficiently.
- Freeze foods when they are as fresh as possible.
- Allow room for liquids to expand as they freeze.
- Never refreeze any food already defrosted.
- Label items you freeze with the name and date.

Food and maximum keeping time		Comments
MEAT AND POULTRY		
Beef, lamb, poultry (uncooked)	12 months	Buy in bulk from a butcher, farmer or market.
Pork	9 months	Buy in bulk.
Minced meat (uncooked)	2 months	Shape into burgers before freezing.
Sausages, bacon, ham	3 months	Ideally, freeze uncooked.
Cooked meat	4 months	Same timing for casseroles and other cooked meat dishes.
SOUPS AND STOCKS	3-6 months	Use shorter time for soups.
FISH AND SHELLFISH		
Fish (uncooked)	4 months	Keep up to 6 months for white fish.
Shellfish (uncooked)	3 months	Same timing for bought, cooked, frozen prawns.
VEGETABLES, FRUIT, HERBS		
Asparagus, peas, sweetcorn, and broad, french and runner beans	12 months	Blanch for 2-3 minutes before freezing.
Spinach	12 months	Blanch for 2 minutes first, then squeeze out excess water.
Herbs	12 months	Chop and freeze in ice cube trays then bag up for easy use.
Fruit	12 months	*See* FRUIT for best methods of freezing.
DAIRY AND EGGS		
Double cream, unsalted butter	8 months	Reduce by 2 months for salted butter.
Cheese	4 months	Best frozen grated. Becomes more flaky after freezing.
Eggs	10 months	Must be out of their shells.
Ice cream	3 months	Similar time for frozen yoghurt.
BREAD, PASTA, PASTRY AND CAKES		
Bread	6 months	Freeze ready-sliced and as breadcrumbs for easy use.
Pizza	2 months	Freeze according to the topping ingredients.
Pasta, uncooked	4 months	Same timing for lasagne and similar cooked dishes.
Cakes	6 months	Freeze before icing if possible.
Pastry, uncooked	3 months	Pre-roll for easy use.
Cooked pastry dishes	3 months	Freeze according to the filling ingredients.

F

defrost your Freezer

An iced-up freezer won't run efficiently, so it's worth defrosting regularly. Run down your supplies first, so you have less food to keep cold while you work.

1 Choose a cold day. Switch off and unplug the freezer. Remove ice trays, racks and containers. Pack food into bin bags and put them outside. Or wrap in newspaper and blankets and leave in the coolest place indoors. Use coolboxes for ice cream or soup, which melt quickly, and pack them tightly – this way, food should stay frozen for several hours.

2 Put old towels covered with newspaper on the floor and your largest roasting pan on the bottom shelf inside the freezer to catch excess moisture. Leave the door open. Mop up as the ice melts. Don't chip away ice with a knife – use a plastic scraper.

3 To remove lingering smells, clean the freezer with 2 tsp bicarbonate of soda in 1 litre of warm water, then dry thoroughly. Wash racks and drawers in warm soapy water and dry. Rub the inside with glycerine before you put them back – ice will come away much more easily next time you defrost.

4 Check food before you replace it and discard anything that's out of date or has deteriorated. Repack with the oldest food most readily accessible.

To speed defrosting
■ Put saucepans of hot water inside the freezer and refill as necessary.
■ Spray the inside with a shop-bought defroster.
■ Use a steam cleaner sold as safe for the purpose – never a hair dryer, which could electrocute you if it gets wet.

throw a Frisbee

1 First you need to get the grip right. Your thumb rests on top of the frisbee, your index finger lies along the curved rim, and the other three fingers support the disk underneath.

2 With this grip, curl your arm in towards your body, holding the frisbee level with the ground. Point your shoulder towards your target.

3 With a smooth and swift action, uncurl your arm and hand. Release the frisbee at the last moment, as your arm becomes completely straight.

4 The frisbee should fly true and level to the catcher, who should pluck it out of the air by grabbing the rim.

preserve Fruit

Fruit seasons are short, but harvests plentiful, so try preserving your crops for use when the fresh fruit has passed its best.

Make jams or chutneys (*see* JAM *and* CHUTNEY) or use one of these methods. Wash and dry fruit first.

Freezing is the easiest method. Although it may sacrifice some of its texture, frozen fruit retains all the flavour of fresh.

Dry freezing Use this method for berries and soft fruit. Spread on trays lined with wax paper, freeze for 1 hour then pack into boxes and return to the freezer.

In sugar Pack fruit between layers of caster sugar. Allow 100-175g sugar per 500g of fruit.

In syrup Put fruits, mixed in with the syrup, into rigid containers before freezing. Make a simple syrup using 250g sugar to every 250ml water.

Poached or puréed This method is ideal for less-than-perfect specimens. Poach fruit for a few minutes in a sugar syrup then cool before freezing. Or purée in a blender and freeze in batches.

Bottling Most fruits can be bottled, either in a sugar syrup or in alcohol, but only use unblemished fruits. Use ovenproof bottles with an airtight seal – those with a rubber ring and metal spring clip are best. Peel, core and slice apples and pears; skin, halve and stone apricots and peaches; and bottle plums, damsons and soft fruits whole. Pack them into sterilised bottles and top up with boiling syrup (left). Put lids on loosely and sterilise the bottles again in the oven. Stand them on cardboard in the centre of the oven at 150°C/gas 2 for 40-60 minutes, then seal. To bottle in alcohol, layer fruit with sugar then top up with any spirit more than 40 per cent proof, shaking every few days for a month to dissolve the sugar.

make a traditional Fruit cake

Covered with marzipan and iced, this is a perfect special-occasion cake for Christmas or a celebration. Or eat it plain for afternoon tea.

If you don't plan to ice the cake, press some almonds or glacé cherries (or both) into the top before baking. This cake is best left to mature for six weeks after cooking, tightly wrapped in a double layer of greaseproof paper, then in foil. You can add more brandy over this period if you wish.

MAKES A 20cm ROUND CAKE

100g glacé cherries, washed and dried
100g mixed peel, finely chopped
225g currants
225g large raisins
225g sultanas
50g ground almonds
50g whole almonds, roughly chopped
225g plain flour

½ tsp salt
1 tsp mixed spice
225g salted butter
225g soft dark muscovado sugar
4 eggs, lightly beaten
1 tbsp black treacle
½ tsp vanilla essence
finely grated zest of 1 orange or lemon
2 tbsp milk
2 tbsp brandy

1 Heat the oven to 150°C/gas 2. Grease a 20cm round cake tin and line it with a double layer of baking parchment. Tie a double layer of brown paper around the outside of the tin. Mix the cherries with the peel, dried fruit and almonds. Sift the flour, salt and mixed spice into a bowl, add 4 tbsp of the fruit mixture and toss together.

2 Cream the butter and sugar together until the mixture is light and fluffy. Add the eggs a little at a time, plus a spoonful of flour mixture at each addition to stop the mix from curdling. Once all the egg has been incorporated, fold in the remaining flour. Then add the rest of the fruit mixture, the treacle, vanilla, zest and milk and mix well.

3 Carefully spoon the mixture into the prepared tin and smooth it level. Arrange some almonds or cherries in the top if you wish (see above). Bake for 2 hours then lower the temperature to 140°C/gas 1 and cook for another 1½-2 hours, or until a skewer pushed into the centre of the cake comes out clean. If the top of the cake is browning too quickly, cover it loosely with foil.

4 Cool in the tin for 1 hour, then turn out the cake and continue cooling on a wire rack. When completely cool, pierce the top several times with a skewer and spoon over the brandy, allowing it to soak in.

thaw Frozen pipes

Find the pipe that's blocked with ice, which will naturally be in a cold part of the house. Be prepared to turn off the water supply in case the thawing process reveals a burst joint or a pipe has split in the freeze.

If no taps are working, the problem is with the cold-supply pipe from the cold-water cistern – most likely in the loft. If a single tap runs dry, then the blockage is in the pipe leading to that tap.

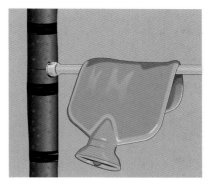

Remove any insulation from the affected pipe and open the tap, so that you will know when the water is flowing again. If the pipe is copper, use a hair dryer to heat it until the water starts to flow, or hang a part-filled hot water bottle on it. If the pipe is plastic, wrap it in towels soaked in hot water.

✳ golden rules

STOP FRUIT FROM SINKING
■ **Always wash and dry the glacé cherries thoroughly before adding them to the cake mixture. This will prevent them from sinking to the bottom of the cake.**

F

KEEPING BIRDS AND FRUIT SAFE

■ **Prevent birds from getting entangled by using small mesh netting with holes no bigger than 18mm x 18mm.**
■ **Check netting regularly for bigger holes.**
■ **Check for gaps at ground level** – some birds will stroll in on foot and then get trapped.
■ **Put out dishes of water near your crops** – thirsty birds do most damage.

make Fudge

MAKES 64 SQUARES

450g light brown muscovado sugar
225ml milk
115g unsalted butter, plus extra for brushing tin
1 tsp vanilla essence
115g chopped nuts (optional)

1 Line a 20cm x 20cm x 5cm square tin with foil and brush with melted butter. Put the sugar, milk and butter into a large saucepan and stir over low heat until the sugar dissolves.

2 Bring to the boil and boil for about 20 minutes, stirring constantly, until the mixture reaches 114°C on a sugar thermometer or when a teaspoon of mixture dropped into cold water forms a soft ball. Remove from the heat and stir in the vanilla and nuts (if using).

3 Leave until lukewarm, beat until creamy, then pour into the tin. When nearly set, mark squares with a knife. Break into squares when set.

protect Fruit trees and bushes from hungry birds

Birds have voracious appetites for soft fruit of all kinds, which makes protecting crops essential. Protection is easiest for bush fruit, such as raspberries and blackcurrants, and for low-growing strawberries.

Trees such as cherries and plums are hard to protect but you can throw netting over a small tree for short periods. Or hang old CDs, strands of cassette tape or pieces of scrunched-up foil secured with string onto the branches. These may work for a while but birds quickly become immune to them.

For individual bushes set three or four canes around each bush, top with glass jars and drape netting over the top. Pull it taut, then secure at the base with wire pegs.

For strawberries make a cane framework for netting around the whole bed or push sturdy hoops into the ground and stretch netting over.

For a large area construct a fruit cage high enough to walk inside. Buy a kit with metal uprights or make a frame using 75mm x 50mm pressure-treated timber for the corner posts and 50mm x 50mm timber for intermediate posts placed 2m apart. Link all posts with heavy-duty wire stretched taut and allow for a door of some kind, which can be well-overlapped pieces of netting or a wooden construction. Attach the netting with staples and secure at ground level with wire pegs or with bricks or stones.

prune and train Fruit trees and bushes for a good crop

Well-pruned fruit bushes will stay healthy and produce maximum yields. Training fruit trees against walls and fences saves space and is ideal for warmth-loving types, such as peaches and apricots.

Soft fruit bushes
Prune soft fruits according to their time of fruiting and the type of wood on which the fruits grow.

Raspberries For summer-fruiting types, remove dead canes after fruiting. For autumn-fruiting varieties, cut back to ground level in autumn or early spring.

Currants Blackcurrants fruit on new wood, so prune the bushes as you harvest, leaving eight to ten branches less than three years old to grow and fruit next year. Red and white currants fruit on old wood. Prune them in winter, shortening tall new growth by half. Cut side branches (laterals) back to one bud.

Fruit trees

Winter pruning Prune to create a strong framework. Remove crossing branches, those blocking light or air, and any dead wood. To promote new growth, prune back main growing shoots (leaders) to just above a healthy growth bud, slanting the cut upwards. Prune back side shoots (laterals) to form a fruiting spur or leave them to grow into new branches. Growth buds are easily distinguished from fruit ones because they lie flat to the stem; fruit buds are plumper and stand prouder by comparison.

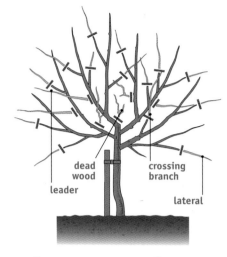

dead wood
leader
crossing branch
lateral

fruit bud

growth bud

pruning cuts just above a bud

fruiting spur

Summer pruning Apple trees can be pruned to promote fruiting. Prune new sideshoots to about six or seven buds, cutting just above a plump fruit bud.

Training Blackberries, loganberries and other bushes that grow untidily are best trained onto wires spaced 20cm apart, cutting out dead wood each autumn after fruiting. For other fruit use one of the following two methods.

Espaliers Plant 20cm from a wall or fence. In early summer, select three shoots, one at the top (to be trained vertically) and one on either side of the main stem, 30cm above ground level. Remove all other shoots and buds. As sideshoots grow, attach them to wires on the wall. In early spring select more sideshoots for training and remove unwanted growth. Allow shoots to grow every 10-15cm on the sideshoots, removing the rest. On new growth, cut back shoots with flower buds at their base to one or two leaves.

Cordons This method is ideal for apples and pears that bear fruit on short sideshoots (spurs). Cordons are best established with trees planted 60-90cm apart at a 45 degree angle against a fence or wall onto which you've secured horizontal wires 60cm apart. After planting, leave the leader and any short laterals intact. Cut back all laterals longer than 10cm to three buds. Between July and September cut back all laterals to one good leaf from the base and sub-laterals to one or two buds.

cut down your Fuel consumption

There are lots of small things you can do to make your car more fuel-efficient, but the most significant is to drive smoothly. Going fast then braking hard wastefully burns fuel.

Check your tyre pressures at least once a month. Tyres only have to be a little bit under-inflated for fuel consumption to rise considerably.

Don't use your boot as a cupboard Take out the toys, the toolbox and anything else that doesn't have to be there. Extra weight costs fuel.

Keep short trips to a mimimum Cars use more fuel when they are running cold, so if you're taking the car out, run as many errands as possible with each trip.

Plan your route There's no more pointless waste of petrol than driving round looking for your destination because you didn't look at a map before you set out.

Use the gears to slow down gradually, and the brakes only to bring your car to a stop. Try to change gear up at 2,000-2,500 revs to make the best use of your fuel.

Negotiate traffic-calming obstacles at a constant speed rather than braking suddenly and then accelerating.

Use air-conditioning sparingly as it burns a lot of fuel. At low speeds an open window is better. Don't open windows at high speeds, though, as this increases drag on the car and increases fuel consumption.

illuminate
Garden features

With the right type of lighting, features such as ornaments and statues, as well as individual plants, can become the stars of your night-time garden.

The simplest option is to use lighting that doesn't need cabling, such as garden candles or solar-powered lamps.

Mains-powered lighting should be installed by a professional. To protect cables from damage, they should be buried under walls, lawns and paths, which is easiest when creating a new garden.

Low-voltage lights are easier to install, as the cable need not be buried. DIY kits are available with a transformer that just plugs into an existing electrical socket in the house or garage.

Uplighting works particularly well for picking out individual garden features. Simply place a light right at the base of the item.

Spike-mounted lights are good for illuminating pathways or providing light for a garden bench.

Water features take on a new lease of life if lit at night. Submersible lights, to which coloured lenses can be fitted, are especially effective.

⭐ golden rules
GARDEN LIGHTING SAFETY
- Have mains cabling checked by a professional every few years.
- Know where mains cables run to avoid accidental damage when digging in the garden.

create Garnishes

A well-chosen garnish will contrast with a dish in colour and texture. It should enhance both its look and its taste.

Savoury garnishes These can be as simple as slices of lemon cut into butterfly shapes, parsley sprigs or a sprinkling of fried breadcrumbs. Alternatively use croutons or fried sage leaves.

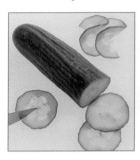  

Cucumber twists Use a small sharp knife to cut the cucumber into thin slices. Make a single radial cut from the edge to the centre of each slice, then twist either side of the cut in opposite directions.

Fluted mushrooms Score each cap from the centre to the edge with a small sharp knife, tracing a curved shape and removing a narrow strip of flesh each time. Remove the stem.

Radish roses Remove the stalk and slice across the base so that the radish stands upright. Make partial scalloped incisions in the radish. Place in iced water for an hour. Dry before use.

Sweet garnishes **Frosted fruit** Brush fruit such as grapes, cherries (with stalks), sprigs of redcurrants or mint leaves with lightly beaten egg white, dredge with caster sugar then dry on wire racks. **Citrus strips** Remove the rind from lemons or oranges without pith and cut into thin strips. Boil in a sugar syrup, drain and dry. **Dipped fruit** Half dip fruit such as strawberries into melted chocolate and place on baking parchment to dry. **Chocolate curls** *see* CAKE.

deal with a Gas leak

If you smell gas indoors it's time for fast action
- **Don't turn on a light** or use any electrical switch.
- **Don't strike a match** or use any naked flame.
- **Open doors** and windows straight away.
- **Turn off any gas appliance** that has been left on – a ring on the stove, say.
- **Shut off the gas supply** at the meter or mains if the source of the gas is not immediately apparent, but don't attempt this if the meter is located in the cellar, where levels of gas may be higher.
- **Call the National Gas Emergency Service** on 0800 111 999 as soon as you have taken these measures.

cut a pane of Glass

YOU WILL NEED **Pane of glass, newspaper, chinagraph pencil, glasscutter's wheel, white spirit, straightedge**

1 Lay your pane of glass on an open newspaper. Using the rules and lines of print on the page, align your glass. With a chinagraph pencil, mark the line along which you plan to cut.

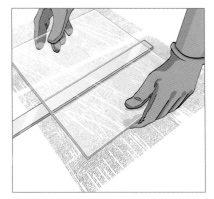

2 Lubricate a glasscutter's wheel with white spirit. Position a straightedge on the cutting line. Hold the cutter so that your index finger applies pressure to the wheel. Starting at the furthest point from you, run the cutter the full length of the glass without stopping.

3 Lift the glass and tap lightly underneath with the ball-end of the cutter. Then place the glass so that the scored line is immediately above the edge of the straightedge. Press firmly on both sides, and the glass will snap cleanly along the scored line.

clean and care for Glass ornaments

Glass can be hard to wash because it's so easily broken. Caution and patience are the key to cleaning ornaments with the minimum of risk.

Always wash fine glassware by hand, and with the utmost care. Remove any jewellery that may scratch the glass – diamonds are particularly hazardous. Wash your ornaments in soapy water, having first placed a rubber mat in the bottom of the sink (remember to swing the tap head out of the way, too). Always wash one item at a time. Rinse items in a bowl of clean water. Don't attempt to wipe glass objets d'art, particularly if they have delicate parts. Allow them to dry naturally in the air.

Dealing with really delicate glass Some ornaments may be too precious or fragile to put through the process of washing-up, but they can still be cleaned. Put on rubber or surgical gloves. Make up a solution consisting of equal parts methylated spirits and water, then add a few drops of ammonia. Apply the solution with cotton wool. Don't use this technique on glass that has decorative gilt, as it may make the gold come away.

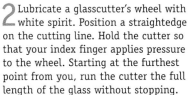

bake
Gingerbread men

Children love helping to make these traditional treats, which taste just as good whatever size and shape of cutter you use.

MAKES ABOUT 16
175g soft brown sugar
4 tbsp golden syrup
1½ tsp ground ginger
½ tsp cinnamon
1½ tbsp water
100g butter, diced
½ tsp bicarbonate of soda
350g plain flour
currants, to decorate

1 Put the sugar, syrup, spices and water into a large saucepan and bring to the boil, stirring constantly. Remove from the heat and add the butter and bicarbonate of soda. Stir in the flour (add some extra if necessary) to make a smooth dough. Cover and refrigerate for 20 minutes.

2 Heat the oven to 180°C/gas 4. Roll out the dough on a floured surface to 4-5mm thick, then cut into shapes using a gingerbread man cutter. Place on greased baking sheets and add currants for eyes and buttons. Bake for 12-15 minutes until brown. Cool slightly before transferring to a wire rack.

G

take care of
Goldfish

These colourful creatures can be rewarding pets, especially for children, and are relatively easy to keep. Look after a goldfish and it could live for 20 years or more.

Provide enough space You should allow 20 litres of water for each goldfish you keep, so use a tank rather than a traditional bowl.

Keep the water clean Goldfish have to swim in their own waste, and polluted water will make them sick. Even traces of the ammonia in their urine can be deadly to them.
■ Use a small net to skim off any fish waste or leftover food flakes.
■ Every two weeks, replace a third of the water with treated water (*see* AQUARIUM), of the same temperature as that in the tank.
■ Buy a siphon to vacuum dirt from the gravel. Make sure any equipment that you use with the fish is kept clean.
■ Add plants to the tank. Living plants oxygenate the water, while plastic ones attract algae, an additional feeding source for the fish. They also make for a more interesting environment.

Feed them well Buy food specifically prepared for goldfish from a pet shop or supermarket.
■ Don't overfeed; leftover food will go off in the water.
■ If you have to go away for more than a couple of days, ask someone to feed your fish.

get your Gold to gleam

Gold needs regular cleaning to keep it shiny. Avoid immersing delicate gold jewellery in chlorinated water (as in swimming pools), which can make it deteriorate. For a really professional clean take gold to a jeweller or invest in an ultrasonic cleaning machine, available from electrical stores. These two methods, though, will have your gold looking great.

Mild method Make a bowl of suds with warm water and a little washing-up liquid. Soak the gold item briefly then scrub gently with a soft toothbrush or eyebrow brush. Rinse in a wire sieve under warm running water. Dry with a soft, clean cloth or chamois.

Stronger method Mix equal parts of cold water and ammonia and soak the gold piece for 30 minutes. Then scrub, rinse and dry as above.

choose the right Glue for the job

To bind two materials together effectively you must first select the right adhesive for the task, a choice which depends on the materials you want to bind. You must then follow the manufacturer's instructions for preparing the surfaces and applying the adhesive correctly.

Type	Uses
CLEAR RESIN	Good for flexible materials such as card, leather and fabric-backed plastic.
CONTACT ADHESIVE	Use with non-porous sheet materials – for example, laminate trims for kitchen worktops.
EPOXY RESIN	Use for metal, china or glass. Good for mixed materials – for example, a glass pendant in a metal setting.
PVA	Suitable for paper and wood, also for fixing ceramic to other materials such as felt.
PVC	Use to glue plastic to plastic. Good for repairing plastic macs, blow-up children's toys and so on.
LATEX (white)	Best used for fabrics and leather – for example, fashion embellishments or carpet edges.
SUPER GLUE	Good for small objects, such as china ornaments and rigid plastic toys, and for binding metal parts to other materials.

make an authentic Goulash

SERVES 4

2 tbsp olive oil
1kg boneless veal shoulder or
   braising steak, cut into
   3cm cubes
1½ tbsp butter
2 large onions, thinly sliced
2 cloves garlic, chopped
2 large red peppers, in chunks
2 tbsp paprika (plain or smoked)
1 tbsp caraway seeds
1 tbsp plain flour
500ml tomato passata
250ml beef stock – for best results,
   use homemade (*see* BEEF STOCK)
1 tsp dried marjoram or oregano,
   plus a few fresh leaves

1 Heat the oil in a large frying pan over a medium heat, brown the meat in batches and set aside. Melt the butter over a medium-low heat in a large deep saucepan. Add the onions, garlic and peppers and cook for 2 minutes, or until the onion is soft, stirring occasionally. Add the paprika and caraway seeds. Stir for 30 seconds, then add the flour and stir constantly for 1 minute.

2 Stir in the passata, stock and dried marjoram or oregano. Bring to the boil, then reduce the heat to low. Add the meat and simmer, uncovered, for 1½ hours, or until the veal is tender. Stir occasionally and add a little more stock or water if needed to keep the meat covered. Garnish with fresh oregano or marjoram and serve with mashed potato or noodles. A dollop of sour cream, while not traditional, adds a little richness.

treat an attack of Gout

Gout is a form of arthritis caused by a build-up of uric acid in the blood. Too much uric acid, a waste product usually excreted by the kidneys, can cause crystals to form in the joints, which then become inflamed and painful.

When pain strikes
■ Rest, with the affected limb elevated.
■ Keep the joint cool. Don't cover it. Remove clothing from around it and apply ice packs wrapped in a tea towel for 20 minutes at a time.
■ Drink plenty of water and a couple of glasses of black cherry juice a day.

Managing your gout
■ Maintain your ideal weight (*see* BODY MASS INDEX) and avoid alcohol.
■ Eat plenty of fresh fruit and vegetables.
■ Be very sparing with: meat (especially liver, kidneys, veal and turkey); seafood (especially anchovies, herrings, mackerel, sardines, mussels, scallops or roe); asparagus, kidney beans, lentils and spinach; yeast extract.

speak the language of Golf scores

Golf, like cricket, is a game of eccentric charm, with jargon to match. This is especially true when it comes to describing the score.

Par The number of shots you're expected to take to complete an individual hole or an entire round.

Birdie One shot fewer than the par amount ('under par') for a hole.

Eagle Two shots under par for a hole.

Albatross Three shots under par.

Bogey One shot over par.

Double bogey Two shots over par.

say Grace

When offering this prayer of thanks before a meal, make an effort to be gracious. Thank the Almighty for the food on the table, the company of family and friends, and perhaps for one other thing specifically related to the occasion, such as the presence of a much-missed relative or the safe conclusion of another year. Those at table should listen in silence – so don't tempt them by making jokes. Everyone should have their hands folded in front of them. As with any other kind of speech, keep it pithy and brief: dinner is getting cold, after all.

get to grips with
Golf
see pages 152-153

G

get to grips with Golf

The game of golf involves hitting a tiny ball into a tiny hole several hundred metres away while playing as few shots as possible. Power, precision – and stoicism – are key.

Swing is king The best golfers are simply the ones who hit the ball the right distance in the right direction more often than most. A good set of clubs helps but, whether you need to hit the ball 20m or 200m, it's consistency of grip and swing that really matters. Master those basics and you'll get better with every round you play.

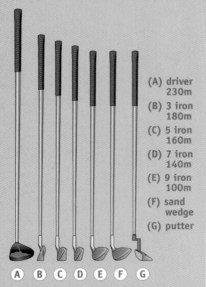

(A) driver 230m
(B) 3 iron 180m
(C) 5 iron 160m
(D) 7 iron 140m
(E) 9 iron 100m
(F) sand wedge
(G) putter

Ⓐ Ⓑ Ⓒ Ⓓ Ⓔ Ⓕ Ⓖ

BEGINNER'S SET OF CLUBS showing men's average distance achieved.

CLUBS FOR THE OCCASION
To play golf you will need a set of clubs. Seven is enough for most beginners: a putter, a driver, a sand wedge and four irons – numbers 3, 5, 7 and 9 make for a good initial selection. It makes sense to buy secondhand if you're an absolute beginner, but be sure that your clubs are all of the same type or make, so that they all 'feel' the same when you play: don't just buy a ragbag set of oddments. Take advice on equipment from a more experienced player, or from the golf pro at your golf club.

HOW TO GRIP
You should also get some initial advice on your grip: it's impossible to play accurate shots if your grip is bad – so invest in a few lessons at the start of your golfing life. This will pay dividends later on, when you begin to improve through regular practice sessions. By far the most popular method of holding a club is the 'Vardon grip' (see below), and like every aspect of the game it takes time to perfect. The grip locks the two hands together on the shaft of the club, so that they act as a single dynamic unit when you swing.

THE VARDON GRIP These instructions are for a right-handed golfer but can be reversed for a left-hander.

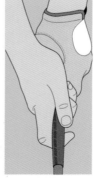

BACK VIEW Put the little finger of your right hand between the middle and index fingers of the left.

FRONT VIEW Use your right hand to grip both the club shaft and the thumb of your left hand.

DRIVING: POWER AND ACCURACY
Your aim when you drive a golf ball off the tee is to strike that ball with maximum force and precise direction.

It's important to stay relaxed. Don't allow tension to build up in your hands and forearms. This is why some professionals waggle the club before they drive to loosen up. To achieve power, you have to twist your body

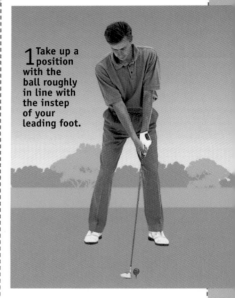

1 Take up a position with the ball roughly in line with the instep of your leading foot.

and lift your club so that, when you unwind, all the energy in your body and in the moving head of the club is delivered sweetly to the ball at the moment of impact. In order to have accuracy at the same time, your club must make the same smooth arc through the air on the way down as it did when you (slowly) lifted it up and back. All parts of your body, as well as the club (which should be seen as a kind of extension of your body), must be aligned in the instant when you make contact. The ball should be slightly forward of your centre, level with your left instep (if you're right-handed), so that it's hoisted into the air by the strike.

PUTTING: THE GAME WITHIN A GAME

A round of golf is won or lost on the green. That's to say, missed putts are what make the difference in a competitive situation – so it makes sense to concentrate a good deal of your practice time on putting. But there are other things you can do to improve your putting game. One is to make a habit of 'walking the green', as it's called. When you have a putt to make, pace out the distance between the ball and the hole, so that you get a feel for how far the ball needs to go, and weight your shot accordingly. It also helps to visualise a point beyond the hole as your target. Aim for an imaginary flag half a metre beyond a line connecting your ball and the hole: this will help you keep the ball on track when you putt.

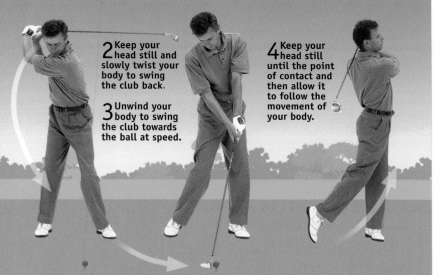

2 Keep your head still and slowly twist your body to swing the club back.

3 Unwind your body to swing the club towards the ball at speed.

4 Keep your head still until the point of contact and then allow it to follow the movement of your body.

THE SECOND SHOT:
THINKING STRATEGICALLY

Don't just slam the ball down the middle of the fairway: consider what you're going to do next. Think about how you're going to approach the hole. Sometimes you have to tack or zigzag towards it. Consider hazards such as water and bunkers, and whether you dare risk placing your ball close to them. This is a question of measuring your own confidence and ability, as well as gauging the lie of the course.

TO COMPLETE THIS PAR 5 HOLE, you're expected to make three approach shots and two putts.

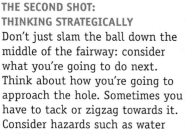

GETTING OUT OF A BUNKER:
DAMAGE LIMITATION

If it all goes wrong, and you find yourself in a sandtrap, take a moment to assess the situation. Your main objective is to get out of the bunker so you can continue towards the hole. If you're in a fairway bunker, you may have to escape by lofting the ball high over the lip of the bunker. You'll need the correct club to clear the lip, but this means you might not be able to get enough distance to reach the green. The same is true if the ball is lying deep in the sand: to get it out at all, you'll have to sacrifice distance.

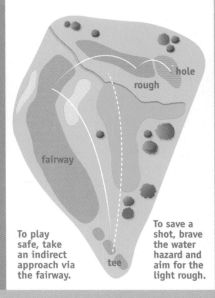

hole

rough

fairway

To play safe, take an indirect approach via the fairway.

tee

To save a shot, brave the water hazard and aim for the light rough.

G

protect
Greenhouse
plants from scorching

Although greenhouses are designed to provide a higher temperature for raising delicate plants and seedlings, at the height of summer they can reach oven temperatures that will bake the plants inside. Keep a watch on heat levels with a maximum-minimum thermometer.

Provide shade In midsummer heat, greenhouse plants need protection from the sun and even on a bright spring day seedlings may benefit from some shade. The cheapest solution is to brush greenhouse shade paint onto the outside of the glass. Choose one of the new paints that turns opaque in bright sunlight but becomes more transparent on dull days and is impervious to rain.

Allow air to circulate On warm days open greenhouse vents and doors, then shut them before the evening temperature drops. Automatic vent openers are inexpensive and easy to fit and will open and close the windows according to the temperature inside the greenhouse.

Water regularly Watering is essential for plants to survive hot weather inside a greenhouse. Water at the beginning or end of the day, when the temperatures are at their lowest to minimise the amount of water lost through evaporation before it can get to the plant. Use a plant mister to spray water on leaves as well as watering at the roots, and water the greenhouse floor, too, if it's stone – this water will evaporate in the sun and help to raise the humidity inside.

make perfect Gravy

Using a good stock makes all the difference when making gravy, and won't mask the true flavours of your roast meat (*see* BEEF STOCK *or* VEGETABLE STOCK). Failing this, save the water in which vegetables have been cooked, or use a can of beef or poultry consommé.

1 Pour excess fat from the roasting tin, leaving the sediment and enough fat to cover the base thinly. Gradually stir in 500ml hot stock or vegetable water, and blend thoroughly over medium heat, scraping up all the sediment.

2 Pour the pan juices into a saucepan. Blend some flour or cornflour with a little water to a smooth paste and add to the pan juices. Cook, stirring over medium heat, until the gravy has reduced and thickened.

For extra flavour add red or white wine or sherry to match the meat you're serving. For lamb or game, stir in a few spoonfuls of redcurrant jelly. Mustard and spices such as nutmeg can also be used. If you add herbs such as rosemary or thyme the gravy will need straining.

clean a Greenhouse

A thorough annual clean will help to keep your greenhouse free of pests and diseases and allow maximum light penetration. Early autumn, once crops such as tomatoes have finished, is the best time to do this.

1 Before you begin, remove all plants, except those growing in fixed borders, and take out all pots, boxes and trays, and any staging that can be dismantled. Turn off the electricity and protect any sockets with masking tape.

2 Using a brush and a hosepipe, or buckets of water, clean the outside of the glass, then the inside. Use the end of a plant label or an old knife to prise dirt from between overlapping panes and wash away with a jet of water.

3 Disinfect all the internal surfaces. You can use a strong chemical cleaner, but even better are biodegradable products that combine cleaning with disinfecting and attack algae, mosses and fungi as well as bacteria and viruses. Follow the manufacturer's instructions to the letter.

4 Wash and scrub all pots, boxes and trays, pieces of staging and disinfect in a similar way. Replace all these, plus the plants, and close all the vents.

create Greetings cards

Save interesting images of all kinds, pressed flowers and even pieces of fabric to stick on cards, either alone or as collages. Or be more ambitious with these effective but easy ideas.

YOU WILL NEED Card, cutting board, metal ruler, scalpel (optional), leaves or petals, low-tack adhesive spray, PVA adhesive, spray paint, thick coloured paper, pencil, scissors, eraser, crayons, pens or paints (optional)

Stencilled card As well as leaves or petals you can use any cut-out shapes as stencils in this method.

1 Place the base card on a cutting board and cut it to size using scissors or a metal ruler and scalpel. Then fix one or more leaves or petals to it with low-tack spray adhesive.

2 Spray paint over the plant material, following the manufacturer's instructions, and leave to dry. Peel off the leaves or petals and carefully rub off any traces of glue. Finish by folding the card ready for use.

Pop-up Valentine card

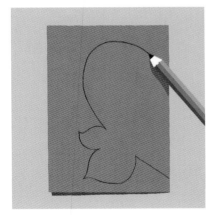

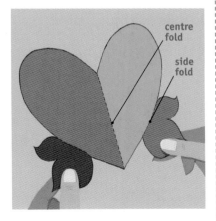

centre fold

side fold

1 Choose a piece of thick coloured paper to contrast with your base card (see over) and fold it in half, pressing it down flat. Draw one half the 'winged heart' design with the centre of the design against the fold. Cut it out, just inside your drawing line to make a symmetrical piece that will be used to create the pop-up element of your card.

2 Fold and unfold along the centre fold line several times to make it flexible. Fold in the 'wings' at the sides of the heart to crease them, then open them out to the sides. Hold with the main centre fold pointing forwards as shown. Add any further decorations to the heart using crayons, pens or paints and allow them to dry thoroughly.

continued overleaf →

tune a Guitar

It doesn't matter how good a guitar player you are: if the strings on your guitar are out of tune, it will sound awful. The action of playing a guitar can easily cause the strings to fall out of the correct tension, so every time you pick your instrument up, and at regular intervals as you play, you should spend a couple of minutes making the appropriate adjustments. The best way to tune your guitar to itself is to use the 4th/5th fret method.

Start by tuning the bottom E string as precisely as you can, using a piano or tuning fork.

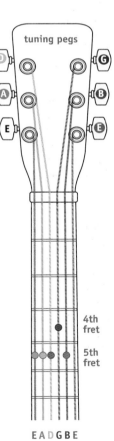

● **A STRING** Fret bottom E at 5. Play the open A string. If it sounds lower or higher than the fretted E string, gently adjust the A tuning peg until the two strings sound the same.

● **D STRING** Fret the A string at 5. Tune the open D string until you have the same note.

● **G STRING** Fret the D string at 5. Tune the open G string to it.

● **B STRING** Fret the G string at 4 and tune the open B string to it.

● **TOP E STRING** Fret the B string at 5 and tune the open top E string.

tuning pegs

4th fret

5th fret

E A D G B E

clear Gutters

Clearing gutters is a maintenance job best done late in autumn, after all the leaves, the most likely cause of a blockage, have fallen. But you may find that your gutters suddenly start overflowing at any time of year.

Before you climb a ladder to inspect your gutters, place a piece of hardboard at the bottom of the downpipe to prevent any debris getting into the gully or the drain. If the downpipe goes straight into the ground, your first job on climbing the ladder should be to stuff a piece of rag into the top of the downpipe.

Check the contents of your gutter
Scoop out any silt, leaves, moss, old tennis balls or other debris – and put it in a bucket. Don't allow any of the debris to go down the downpipe, or indeed down the wall of your house, where it will make an unsightly stain.

Once you have removed all the debris, position your ladder at the far end, away from the downpipe, and pour three or four buckets of water into the gutter to sluice it through (remember first to remove your rag, if you used one). You might find it easier to use a hose for this part of the job.

3 Measure the rectangular base card to at least 5cm larger all around than the pop-up shape and cut it out. Using a ruler and pencil for accuracy, fold it exactly in half widthwise. Rub off any pencil marks. Place the pop-up piece inside of the card, standing proud as it will be in the finished item, and use a pencil to mark where the 'wings' will be stuck to the card (right). The pop-up piece needs to fold neatly into the finished card, or can protrude a little if desired. Apply PVA adhesive to these areas, then immediately fix the pop-up design in place.

4 Allow to dry, then carefully rub off any excess adhesive with your fingertips and erase any pencil marks. Carefully close the card, folding the pop-up along its centre line. The outside of the base card can be decorated further if you wish.

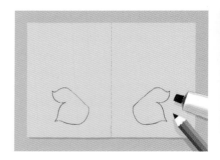

replace a Guitar string

If you're changing a string on a steel-string acoustic, turn the appropriate capstan to loosen the old string so that it isn't under tension, and have a cloth ready to clean the guitar beneath where the string usually sits.

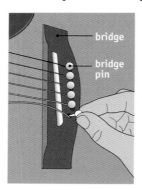

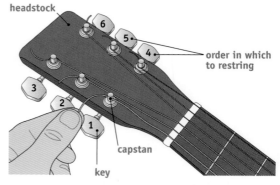

1 First pull up the little peg (bridge pin) that holds the string in place. You may need a pair of pliers or wirecutters to do this. Insert the ball-end of the new string into the hole, and replace the pin.

2 Thread the other end of the string tip into the capstan on the headstock, and pull through so that there's 3-5cm of slack. Bend the string to one side, then tighten by winding the key attached to the capstan. Trim the excess with wirecutters, or wind it into a neat loop. If you're changing all the strings at once, begin with the one nearest the neck on the near side and follow the order shown above.

write a Haiku

A haiku is a minimal Japanese verse form consisting of three lines and 17 syllables. Beyond that, everything is entirely up to you.

In Japan, strict rules govern the elements of the haiku. It has to consist of three untitled, unrhyming lines of five, seven and five syllables respectively. There should be 'cutting' – a division of the poem into two ideas that contrast and illuminate each other. The haiku should allusively describe a concrete scene or image or event, and it should contain a word called a kigo, that hints at the season in which it's set (the 'green' that suggests spring in the example below). Metaphors and personal emotions aren't allowed, though the odd one may creep in. Here's a translation of a classical haiku (about a frog):

> At the ancient pond
> A sudden flash of green legs;
> The ghost of a splash.

Some will say you must stick to the classical form, or it's not a haiku. But in poetry you're at liberty to meddle with the form if you feel that the result will be a better poem. So, if you wish, you can give your haiku a title, make it rhyme, use imagery … . Above all, you should feel free to express any feelings or make any point that inspires you.

---

remove unwanted Hair

If you don't want an expensive salon habit, there are a number of ways to remove unwanted facial and body hair in the privacy of your own home.

Shaving is quick and inexpensive, but it's a temporary solution as it cuts the hair off only at the surface of the skin. When the hair grows back it can be more noticeable, because it has blunt tips rather than a natural taper. Always moisturise first to minimise snagging and razor rash.

Epilators are electrical devices that roll over the skin plucking out hairs, so results are longer lasting than with a razor. They are only moderately expensive, quick and effective. Most are for use on clean dry skin. Before you start, stroke the hairs against the direction of growth so they stand on end.

Waxing kits for use at home also work by pulling out hairs at the root. Practise on your legs before you try this on more sensitive areas, where waxing may irritate the skin.

Sugaring works on a similar principle to waxing, but is a less messy and more natural method, first used in ancient Egypt. Products are available over the counter. Like waxing, sugaring can irritate the skin.

Depilatory creams dissolve hairs at the skin's surface. They contain harsh chemicals, so always test a new product on a small patch before wider use.

Tweezers are ideal for plucking out stubborn facial hairs and tidying eyebrows (*see* EYEBROWS).

understand British Hallmarks

Reading hallmarks is simply a matter of learning the symbols, or knowing where to look them up.

SPONSOR'S MARK (A) There will always be a sponsor's mark, identifying the craftsman who made the object.

STANDARD MARK (B) A standard mark (below) indicates the purity of the metal and the background shape identifies the metal. A lion (on pendant, right) indicates sterling silver, 92.5 per cent.

Sterling silver | Gold 18 carat | Platinum 90 per cent

ASSAY OFFICE MARK (C) This records where the silver was assayed, or checked.

Birmingham | London

Edinburgh | Sheffield

DATE MARK (D) A letter of the alphabet indicates the year of manufacture. The same letters recur every 25 years (J isn't used), but often in minutely altered styles that take years of experience to decipher. Date marks are no longer compulsory.

 2000
 1900
 1800

Together with a reference guide for each Assay Office, these marks allow you to establish some of the history of any piece of silver, gold, platinum or palladium.

wash your Hands

Thorough washing is vital to prevent the spread of infection. Use liquid soap, not a shared bar, and a clean towel.

- Wet hands and apply soap. Rub hands together for 15-30 seconds under warm running water, paying attention to fingertips, nails, thumbs and right up to the wrist.
- Work the hands together, palm to palm, palm to back and fingers interlacing, for as long as it takes to sing 'Happy Birthday' through twice.
- Dry thoroughly: moist hands spread germs. Choose clean paper towels over a hand dryer – it may recycle dirty air and take a long time to dry hands thoroughly, encouraging you to walk away without completing the job.

choose and use a Hammer correctly

Make sure you have the right hammer for the job.

CLUB HAMMER Good for light demolition work.

CROSS-PEIN HAMMER For nailing in tacks and pins.

CLAW HAMMER For driving nails into wood and removing old nails.

- Hold the hammer near the end of the handle, and keep your eye on the nail.
- Tap gently at first to fix the nail in position. For the heavier blows, pivot your arm from the elbow, so that the handle is at right angles to the nail at the moment of impact.

make a great Hamburger

The secret of a good hamburger is to use best-quality lean beef and mince it yourself, in a mincer using a coarse blade or in a food processor. Alternatively chop it by hand with a large knife, occasionally turning and lifting the meat until it resembles fine mince. Always cook shop-bought mince until no pink remains.

SERVES 4

750g lean minced beef
salt and freshly ground
    black pepper
1 small onion, grated (optional)
½ tbsp oil (optional)
1 tsp mixed herbs
1 tbsp Worcestershire sauce

1 Season the beef. Sweat the onion lightly in heated oil (if using) and add with the herbs and Worcestershire sauce. Mix very well.

2 Using wet hands, form into even sized patties 2.5cm thick. Cook under a preheated grill for 4-6 minutes per side or to taste.

plant a Hanging basket

Choose drought-tolerant plants for a hanging basket and add water-retaining gel and slow-release plant food granules to the compost to reduce watering. Do this and you can enjoy months of colour with minimal maintenance.

YOU WILL NEED Hanging basket, bucket, moss (optional), liner, trimming knife, trailing plants and some bushy varieties for the top, newspaper, soil-less potting compost, filled watering can, hairpins (optional)

1 Remove the detachable hanging chains if possible and stand the basket on top of the bucket. Line the basket with moss, if you have it, then the liner. You can buy rigid cardboard or cellulose liners, flexible ones made of felt, jute or other fibres, or use a piece of hessian.

2 Starting from the bottom, use the knife to make holes in the lining. If plants are delicate, wrap them in newspaper to protect the stems. Push the plants in roots-first from the outside, filling in with compost as you go. Space plants evenly, staggering them in rows.

3 Put the tallest plants in the centre at the top, making a depression in the soil around them to help retain the moisture. Plant more trailing plants around the rim, using hairpins, if necessary, to attach stems to the frame, encouraging them to hang down.

4 Drench the basket with water and allow excess water to drain through. Attach the chains, then hang the basket, taking care not to squash any stems with the chains.

play Hangman

This simple word game is ideal for two to four players and easy for children to learn. You can play it anywhere with only a pencil and paper. Players take turns to be the hangman, who must have a word in mind. His opponents, condemned to hang, hope to earn a reprieve by guessing the word.

■ The hangman marks out the appropriate number of dashes – for instance, _ _ _ _ _ _ _ _ .
■ The condemned players guess, one at a time, letters that might be in the word. Say the word is GERANIUM and the first suggested letter a vowel, A, the hangman enters it thus: _ _ _ A _ _ _ _ .
■ Say the next suggested letter is a C. With this first wrong guess begins the hanging. The gallows are drawn in bit by bit: base, upright, crossbar, diagonal bar, noose. Then, with each subsequent wrong guess, the hangman adds head, body, one arm, one leg, a second arm – and with the second leg the execution is complete.
■ To help younger players, keep a note of wrong guesses and maybe decide on a theme for the game or a minimum or maximum number of letters.

Winning tip Obscure words and little-used letters can be winners for either hangman or guesser (XEROX would be make or break), but a three-letter word that has two letters in common with lots of others can be a real killer.

cure a Hangover

Nausea, a pounding head, dry mouth, light-sensitivity, shame, self-reproach … It's the morning after the night before!

Rehydrate Alcohol is a diuretic, promoting the production of urine, so drink lots of water to get rid of that furry tongue and headache. Avoid caffeinated drinks, which are also diuretic.

Honey on toast The concentrated sugar in honey converts the toxins left in the body from alcohol to acetic acid, which is burned as part of the normal metabolic cycle. Toast adds potassium and sodium, which also help the body to cope.

Eggs for breakfast You might crave a fry-up, but it's the eggs you really need. They contain cysteine, an amino acid that can help to mop up the toxins.

Never again! Of course, the best 'cure' is prevention. Try alternating alcoholic drinks with soft drinks or water, and avoid red wine, brandy or whisky in excess – these contain chemicals known as 'congeners' that contribute to the agony the next morning. After drinking, rehydrate with two glasses of water before going to bed.

dazzle with
Hair up-dos
see pages 160-161

dazzle with Hair up-dos

'Up-do' hairstyles have a timeless appeal. Think of Audrey Hepburn's chignon in Breakfast at Tiffany's, *as desirable today as it was in 1961. Not that you need to be up for an Oscar to create a film-star look. If you can manage a ponytail, you can create any of the styles here.*

YOU WILL NEED Natural bristle brush, hairspray, stretchy hair band, hairpins and possibly straightening irons. Optional: hair gel or wax, flowers, hair jewels or ornamental combs for embellishment

GET TO KNOW YOUR HAIR

It's easiest to put your hair up the day after it has been washed. Silky, newly shampooed hair can be difficult to work with. If you have just washed your hair, apply gel when it's still damp, blow dry and then mist it with hairspray, in sections, to make it more malleable.

Plan the look Dragging your hair into a tight top knot can create too severe an effect, so start by experimenting with what best suits you. Study yourself in the mirror as you sweep your hair backwards, upwards, downwards and choose a flattering line. How will you frame your face? A fringe, half-fringe or none? Stray fronds, curls or ringlets? Will you go for a side or centre parting, or sweep your hair straight back? How much height do you want?

Dressy or messy? Practice makes perfect – but imperfections can be part of the charm. Artful dishevelment (below), an off-centre 'do' and stray ends can lend a more modern look to a traditional style. You can also embellish your hair with flowers, jewelled pins, ornamental combs, or skewer with lacquered chopsticks.

CLASSIC BUN

The style favoured by ballet dancers, a formal bun (below left) should be centred on the back of the head, lying flat to it and firmly secured. Trace the line of your cheekbones: the bun will sit on the point where these lines meet.

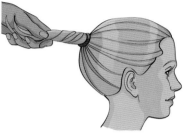

1 Dampen, then smooth the hair and form a ponytail, secured with a stretchy hair band. Give a couple of twists to the top of the ponytail to form a short section of 'rope'.

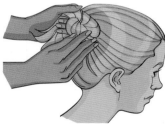

2 Working in the same direction as your twist, start to coil the 'rope' around the base of the ponytail. Twist and wrap, twist and wrap, until the hair is all neatly coiled.

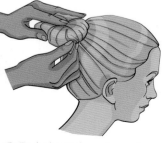

3 Tuck the ends under and secure the bun with hairpins close to the scalp.

SOPHISTICATED FRENCH TWIST

For a formal occasion, a French twist can be dressed with flowers or jewels along the line of pins. If you prefer, curl the ends of the ponytail and leave them loose, or pin them in loose curls or loops around the crown of the head.

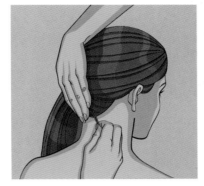

1 Brush the hair completely smooth across to one side at the back, applying a veil of hairspray in the direction that you brush. Use hair grips to pin the hair at the nape of the neck to hold it in place. The twist will come back across these pins.

ELEGANT CHIGNON

The word 'chignon' derives from *chignon du cou*, meaning nape of the neck. This soft style is worn low, showing off the neck and shoulders and accentuating cheekbones.

Don't brush the hair too smooth or pull it too tight – a chignon looks best when it's a little loose.

1 Brush your hair and apply a mist of hairspray. Brush it back into a ponytail and secure it with a band towards the nape of the neck.

2 Divide the ponytail into two and push the hair in each section back up towards the head, as if gently backcombing it to add volume. Twist the two sections around each other in a two-strand 'plait'.

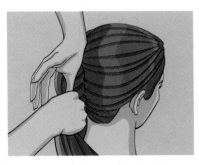

2 Grasp the hair gently, then lay your left thumb against the head and pull the hair over and around it to create a twist. For a twist that lies the other way, use your right thumb.

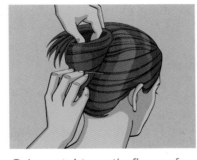

3 As you twist, use the fingers of the left hand to coil the hair upwards. Fix with pins, picking up a little of the twisted hair and pushing pins into the hair under the twist.

3 Coil the twisted hair around the base of the ponytail in a loose bun at the nape of the neck.

4 Coil the ends of the hair and tuck into the twist then pin to close the loose top of the coil.

5 Lightly brush the surface to smooth any loose hairs. Add more pins to secure and a final fix of spray.

4 Secure the hair with pins as you coil it, then tuck the end back into and under the chignon and pin it all in place.

treat and avoid
Hay fever

This common allergic disorder can be a minor irritation or more severe. Pollen stimulates the production of histamines – one of the body's defences against infection – leading to streaming noses and puffy eyes.

As the hay fever season nears, start taking a daily spoonful of raw (unpasteurised) local honey. Traces of pollen in it can help to desensitise the body.

Reduce exposure to pollen. Keep away from grassy areas and stay indoors when the pollen count is high, with windows closed. Damp-dust and vacuum regularly. When you go out, wear sunglasses and keep car windows closed. If you suffer badly, consider fitting a pollen filter to the car's ventilation system. Change clothes and take a shower as soon as you get in.

Spread petroleum jelly inside your nostrils to intercept the pollen.

Eat onions They are rich in quercitin, which is said to help to ward off hay fever.

Try butterbur, a traditional herbal remedy that has been used for centuries and has shown promise in a Swiss clinical trial.

Talk to your doctor about which prescription and over-the-counter treatments might help you. Make sure you tell them about any natural remedies you already take.

If you find no relief, ask your doctor about immunotherapy, a highly specialised procedure in which minute amounts of allergens are introduced to accustom the body to them and lessen the allergic reaction they normally trigger.

make a paper Hat

YOU WILL NEED **Double page of a broadsheet newspaper, sticky tape**

1 Fold the newspaper pages back on themselves to form a double layer. Fold in half, top to bottom.

2 Fold the corners in to the middle to form a pointed top and a triangular body for the hat.

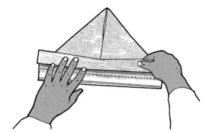

3 Now for the brim. Fold one side of the bottom of the paper up to meet the bottom of the triangle. Fold again so that it overlaps. Turn it over and do the same with the other side. Secure with sticky tape, then pull the bottom of the brim apart. Wear side to side, front to back, or at a rakish angle.

relieve a painful Headache

In a common tension headache, pressure is felt on both sides of the head, sometimes with sensitivity to light and noise. Here's what to do to bring relief, without necessarily having to take a tablet.

- Drink water. A lot of headaches are caused by dehydration.
- Take a hot shower, letting the water play on your neck and lower back to help to relax tense muscles that may be causing the headache. If this isn't possible, apply a warm face cloth to the forehead or neck.
- Put a few drops of lavender oil on a handkerchief and sniff it to relax you or try rubbing peppermint oil into your neck – it will energise you and help to relieve any congestion that may be causing a sinus headache.
- Try a drink of coffee, tea or cola. Caffeine will constrict your blood vessels and can relieve an aching head as well as providing a helpful pick-you-up.
- As a last resort, take a painkiller, such as paracetamol or ibuprofen, but beware overuse of medications and always stick to the stated dose.

recognise and deal with a Heart attack

With a heart attack, every second counts, so learn to spot the signs and act at once. A casualty is three times more likely to survive if specialist medical help is given within the hour.

Should you call an ambulance? If someone appears unwell and any of the following symptoms are present, dial the emergency services without hesitation, saying clearly that you suspect a heart attack, or enlist someone else to do so while you stay with the patient. Comfort the patient and monitor their condition while you wait for the emergency services.

Symptoms

■ Vice-like chest pains that may spread to the jaw and down one or both arms, although not all heart attacks are accompanied by chest pain.
■ The patient feels dizzy and faint, and is stricken with panic or a sense of impending doom.
■ Their skin is ashen and clammy; their lips are turning blue and they are gasping for air.
■ Their pulse is weak, racing or erratic.
■ They experience discomfort high in the abdomen, or suffer nausea, vomiting or loss of consciousness.

If the casualty remains conscious

Help them into a half-seated position with head and shoulders supported, legs raised and knees bent to ease strain on the heart. If possible, support the knees on pillows, cushions or rolled up coats for comfort.

Loosen clothing at the collar, chest and waist.

Offer reassurance that help will soon arrive. If you're in a public place, call out to see whether there's a doctor nearby who could help, but try to keep intrusive bystanders away from the patient.

Give medication if the casualty suffers from angina and has their tablets or spray to hand. They may need you to help to find their medication and to administer it.

Continuously monitor the casualty, checking their breathing, pulse and state of consciousness. Don't leave them alone.

continued overleaf ➜

deal with
Head injuries

Severe head injuries or a patient who has been knocked unconscious need immediate medical attention. A minor bump, though it may cause mild swelling, bruising, nausea, headache and dizziness, is unlikely to do long-term damage.

Quick action

■ Sit the casualty down and give reassurance.
■ If there's a swelling at the site, apply an ice pack (*see* CONCUSSION).
■ Bleeding from a scalp wound can be heavy. Place a sterile pad over it and apply gentle pressure for a couple of minutes to staunch the flow. Secure with a bandage wrapped around the head.
■ Avoid excitement and offer paracetamol as a painkiller (not aspirin or ibuprofen, which can increase the risk of bleeding within the skull). Keep meals light.

Delayed symptoms

■ Keep an eye on the patient for 48 hours for signs of more serious injury: slurred speech, drowsiness, difficulty in writing or understanding, loss of consciousness, seizure, double vision, unequal pupils, loss of balance, weakness, clear or bloody fluid leaking from nose or ear, severe headache or stiff neck, or unusual behaviour.

Be safe, rather than sorry

■ If you're in any doubt following a head injury, seek medical advice.
■ If a child vomits or seems drowsy after a bang on the head, take them to hospital to be checked.
■ Stay off work and rest until you have completely recovered. Don't drive or operate machinery.

H

relieve the pain of
Heartburn

This common condition occurs when stomach acids pass backwards into the oesophagus, or gullet. Try these natural remedies to douse the burning pain.
- Sip sparkling water, lemonade or a little bicarbonate of soda dissolved in water.
- Try ginger or camomile tea.
- Suck a peppermint.
- Chew a dozen or so unsalted almonds.

Over-the-counter antacids
will usually relieve a bout of heartburn quickly, but overuse of them has been linked to increased risk of infection, nutritional deficiencies and the very symptoms they are designed to assuage.

To minimise the risk of heartburn
avoid eating too much fatty food or chocolate and drinking excessive amounts of alcohol or coffee. Smoking can also be a trigger. Raise the head of your bed, and try to avoid large meals, being overweight, tight waistbands and bending over or lying down after a meal.

See also INDIGESTION.

If the casualty is unconscious
Open their airways, check for breathing and prepare to begin CPR (*see* CPR).

Call for a defibrillator Public buildings may be equipped with an automated external defibrillator (AED), which comes with clear instructions, and can deliver a shock to correct an abnormal heart rhythm (ventricular fibrillation or cardiac arrest). Don't be tentative, but trust this smart machine: it will deliver a shock only if necessary. Leave the pads in place until the ambulance arrives, even if the casualty seems to be recovering. If an AED is provided there should also be trained staff available.

treat Heat stroke

Heat stroke, and its precursor, heat exhaustion, can be fatal. Act immediately to lower body temperature and stop the overheating.

Heat exhaustion occurs when the body's core temperature rises above 37°C/98.6°F. Water and salt levels in the body drop, causing nausea, heavy sweating and faintness. There may also be fatigue, confusion, vomiting and a racing heartbeat. Ultimately, it can lead to organ failure from heat stroke.

- Get the sufferer to rest in a cool place and give fluids – water or rehydrating sports drinks, but never coffee or alcohol.
- Loosen their clothing and make sure they have air.
- Cool them with cold water – a shower or bath, or wet flannels applied to the skin.
- Call an ambulance if the person is no better within half an hour. Heat exhaustion can lead to heat stroke.

Heat stroke occurs when the body temperature exceeds 40°C/104°F. Symptoms include rapid heartbeat and breathing, cramp, mental confusion, loss of coordination, anxiety, hallucinations, seizures and unconsciousness. Untreated, it can cause brain damage, organ failure and death.

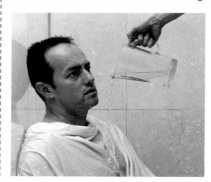

- Call an ambulance.
- Move the patient to a cool place. Fan them and give fluids, as above.
- Shower or immerse the patient in cool (not cold) water, or cover the skin with cool, damp towels.
- Massage gently to encourage circulation.
- Be prepared for their condition to deteriorate. *See also* CPR and RECOVERY POSITION.

plant a Hedge for privacy and shelter

A hedge, if chosen well, will be an attractive boundary all year round. Always avoid Leylandii cypress, which is too vigorous in any domestic setting.

1 Prepare the soil in late summer. Dig deeply and thoroughly, then allow the soil a few weeks to settle. In autumn, buy plants. Water container-grown plants well and soak bare-rooted plants for 2 hours. Tease out the roots and trim off any that are damaged or overlong.

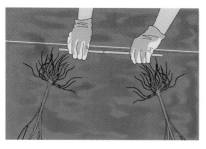

2 Mark the line of the hedge with string. Lay out the plants, spacing them an even distance apart. Use a piece of pre-cut cane to ensure that the spacings are even.

3 Make planting holes and position plants at the same depth as they were growing previously. Firm the soil around each plant and water them. Add a layer of mulch if you wish, to lock in the moisture.

perform the Heimlich manoeuvre

Otherwise known as an abdominal thrust, the Heimlich manoeuvre can be a life-saver for a choking patient if applied correctly.

Use this procedure to expel a blockage in a person's airway that cannot be shifted by pressure applied to the back (*see* CHOKING). If not carried out properly, it can cause injury, so this should be seen only as a last resort and should not be used on babies under one year old or pregnant women.

■ Stand behind the casualty, wrap your arms around them.
■ Place a clenched fist just above the navel. Grasp the fist with your other hand and pull sharply upwards and inwards. Don't squeeze the ribs; let your hands do the work. Repeat as necessary.
■ If you yourself are choking, lean over a table or chair back and press your abdomen against it to create the thrust.

trim a Hedge

Trimming a hedge in mid to late summer allows new growth to ripen before winter sets in.

■ Quick-growing conifers need trimming at about eight week intervals through the growing season.
■ When possible, trim small conifer hedges with secateurs to avoid cutting across leaf sprays.

Preparation Tie strong string along the hedge on one side to mark the desired height, making sure it's taut and horizontal. Fix the string to long bamboo canes, if you have some tall enough, or to strong stems within the hedge.

Trimming Cut the sides of the hedge with shears or a hedge trimmer using an upward motion. Taper the hedge slightly towards the top. Cut the top to the string level.

golden rules

TIPS FOR A TIDY HEDGE
■ **Sharpen shears before you begin.**
■ **Trim a wide hedge in two stages, working to the centre from each side.**
■ **Wear goggles and gloves when using an electric hedge trimmer and make long, sweeping strokes.**

turn up a skirt Hem

Take down and iron flat an existing hem then mark the new length with pins and turn the skirt inside out.

YOU WILL NEED Skirt, tape measure, pins, needle, tacking cotton, chalk, scissors, sewing thread

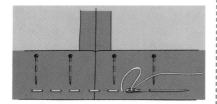

1 Lay the skirt flat, fold up and pin hem at right angles to the edge. Check skirt for length then tack close to the fold (*see* TACK). Remove pins and press.

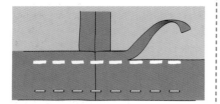

2 Measure and mark with chalk the hem allowance (how deep the hem is): 7cm for a straight skirt, less for a flared one. Trim excess fabric at the chalk mark.

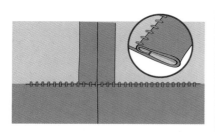

3 Turn the hem edge under 6mm, iron flat, then hemstitch in place (*see* SEWING). Remove the tacking.

plan and plant a Herbaceous border

Carefully planned and planted, a herbaceous border will give colour from spring right through to autumn. And if you choose the right plants for your conditions, a border will last for many years.

Plan first, plant later To make an impact, a border should be at least 1.5m deep. Draw a plan before you buy any plants.

■ Even if you want a mixed colour scheme, choose a dominant shade or two: pastel lilacs and pinks (good in light shade); hot reds and golds; cool blues and whites; or purples, limes and oranges. Work out how these will link with the seasons and your garden conditions.

■ Start with plants that work well together, using them in groups of odd numbers and repeat patterns along the border.

■ Spring and autumn bulbs set between perennials will add extra colour.

1 Bear's breeches
  Acanthus mollis
2 *Miscanthus sinensis*
  'Morning Light'
3 *Delphinium* 'Magic
  Fountains Dark Blue'
4 Globe thistle
  Echinops ritro
5 *Eryngium giganteum*
6 Horned violet
  Viola cornuta
7 *Thymus vulgaris*
  'Silver Posie'
8 Lily turf *Ophiopogon
  planiscapus* 'Nigrescens'
9 *Festuca glauca*
  'Elijah Blue'

Don't forget foliage Choose a variety of foliage types, colours and textures from deep to pale green – including variegated leaves – and from smooth and shiny to almost furry. Make use of grasses with textural foliage and consider including a few edible plants, such as cut-and-come-again lettuces or strawberries, plus chives, fennel and other herbs.

Height and impact Put the tallest plants at the back of the border and lower, ground-covering ones towards the front. For an island bed, position the tallest plants in the centre. To lead your eye along a long border, use architectural plants and splashes of bright colour at intervals.

Planting Enrich the soil with a balanced fertiliser, such as bonemeal, before planting and dig in some well-rotted manure. Insert plants to the same depth as they were growing when they were purchased.

choose Herbs to match food

The distinctive tastes of herbs work brilliantly with many foods. Choose the right ones and they will boost flavour, and liven up relatively bland ingredients such as pasta, fish and chicken.

Herb	Goes best with	Tips
BASIL	Tomatoes, peppers, aubergines, cheese dishes, pasta, poultry, eggs	Tear immediately before using. Blend with oil, garlic, pine nuts and parmesan for a pesto sauce.
BAY	Fish, red meat, game, goose, pâtés, beans, lentils	A pronounced flavour, especially when dried. Best used sparingly.
CHIVES	Leafy salads, potatoes, mayonnaise	Mild onion flavour. Also available in a garlic version.
DILL	Fish, seafood, lamb, cucumber	Mild aniseed flavour. Best used fresh. Use seeds for a stronger flavour and in breads.
CORIANDER	Curries and all other spiced dishes, salsas	Use stalks as well as leaves for extra flavour. Cook minimally.
MARJORAM	Tomatoes, lamb, pork, poultry, beans and pulses, pasta	Very useful dried. Similar in flavour to oregano.
MINT	Lamb, peas, carrots, potatoes, cucumber	Best fresh. Pour boiling water on fresh leaves for mint tea.
PARSLEY	Fish, poultry, stuffings, vegetables of all kinds, béchamel sauce	Flat-leaved parsley has more flavour. Perfect as a garnish for almost every dish.
ROSEMARY	Fish, lamb, pork, poultry, game, potatoes and root vegetables	Coarse leaves may need to be finely chopped.
SAGE	Oily fish, pork, duck, cheese, pasta	Dries well, intense flavour. Leaves are delicious fried.
TARRAGON	Fish, seafood, poultry, eggs, mushrooms, mayonnaise	Choose the French variety for best flavour. Buy freeze-dried.
THYME	All meats and fish, tomatoes	Dries well, very versatile.

maintain a Herbaceous border

Keep a herbaceous border neat with regular deadheading (*see* DEADHEAD). In addition, cut back to their bases the stalks of plants that bloom before midsummer to stimulate a second flush of flowers. Later-flowering plants can be neatened after flowering or left to provide winter interest then cut down in spring. Weed regularly. Mulching in spring will suppress weed growth.

Moving plants Autumn and early spring, when plants are dormant, are the best times for moving them, and for lifting and dividing those that have become too large. After being dug up, smaller plants can be pulled apart with your hands. Trim off any damaged or rotten roots and replant. For large matted perennials, use two forks set back to back to separate them once they have been dug up. Cut away any woody shoots and dead roots before replanting.

golden rules
COOKING WITH HERBS
- **Add delicately flavoured fresh herbs such as basil and tarragon at the end of cooking.**
- **Use strongly flavoured herbs such as sage to cut through the oiliness of foods like pork.**
- **Use finely chopped stalks of fresh tender-stemmed herbs for an even better flavour.**
- **Buy herbs in small quantities and use quickly to prevent them from going stale.**

stop Hiccups

A sliver of unpeeled lemon dredged with Worcestershire sauce and sugar, chewed and swallowed, is strangely effective. Alternatively, stir a teaspoon of sugar or honey in warm water, hold the mixture on the back of the tongue and then swallow it. If you have no such ingredients, take a deep breath and hold it for as long as you can. Take quick sips of cold water, or try bending over, head down, and drinking from the 'wrong' side of a glass. Breathe in and out of a paper (never plastic) bag. See your doctor if hiccups persist for more than 48 hours.

walk in
High heels

High heels aren't worn for comfort or practicality, they are designed to make an impression. Learning how to walk in them with style is essential if you want to be noticed for the right reasons.

■ Buy shoes that are a perfect fit – ideally ones that can be firmly strapped to your feet.
■ Begin with lower heels with a thicker base and work up. Keep torturous high heels for 'best'. If you're going out, wear flat shoes there and back and change when you arrive.
■ Avoid tights that cause your feet to slip inside the shoes.
■ Practise at home before braving the outside world. Stand tall; the heels will stop you falling backwards.
■ Keep your legs close together. Take short steps, coming down with a heel-toe motion and placing most of the weight on the ball of the foot. Swing your hips to help you to move.

dry Herbs

YOU WILL NEED String, cake rack, kitchen paper, airtight storage jars, labels, microwave (optional)

Air drying Tie in bunches and hang upside down in a dark, dry airy place until leaves snap easily. Or spread sprigs over a cake rack and put in a warm dry place, turning several times for the first two days. Remove leaves by rubbing stems between your hands over kitchen paper. Store herbs immediately in jars and keep in the dark to prevent flavours

deteriorating. Add a label to each jar identifying the herb for future use.

Microwave drying Place herbs on kitchen paper and heat on low for about 3 minutes, watching all the time, as some herbs can catch fire. Check dryness after the first minute and then every 30 seconds. Cool before removing leaves.

Strip ripe seeds from herbs such as fennel and dill and air dry on trays following the same method for storing as used after air drying.

fit a simple Hinge to a door

Fitting hinges is the trickiest part of hanging a replacement door. It requires accurate measuring, and some basic carpentry skills.

YOU WILL NEED Hinges, trimming knife, marking gauge, chisel, screws, screwdriver, wedges

1 If your door is new, you must first cut recesses in which the hinges will sit, matching them with the hinge positions on the door frame. Hold the door against the frame, supporting it on wedges, and mark the positions of the hinges. Then hold the hinges in place, and mark around the flap of each with a knife.

2 Set the marking gauge to the thickness of the hinge flap, and use it to mark the depth of the recess required on the edge of the door.

3 Cut around the perimeter of your recess with a sharp chisel, then make a series of cuts about 5mm apart across the grain of the wood. Carefully pare away the waste with the chisel, bevel side downwards. Try to leave as level a surface as possible on which to mount the hinge, but take care not to make so many adjustments that the recess becomes too deep.

4 Screw the hinge flaps into the door recesses with just one or two screws.

5 Put the door up to the frame, using wedges to support it, open. Screw the free hinge flaps to the recesses in the frame with two screws. Check that the door swings freely. If it does, insert the remaining hinge screws. If it doesn't open or close properly, the hinge positions may have to be adjusted.

make and rescue Hollandaise sauce

A double saucepan is ideal for making this variation on mayonnaise, served hot with fish, eggs or vegetables such as asparagus. Béarnaise sauce is similar but flavoured with tarragon and served cold with grilled meat or fish.

MAKES 300ml

3 tbsp lemon juice or white wine vinegar
15ml water
6 black peppercorns

1 bay leaf
3 egg yolks
175g butter, softened
salt and freshly ground black pepper

1 Before you start, part fill a large basin with cold water (see 'Rescue the sauce' below).

2 Boil the lemon juice or white wine vinegar, water, peppercorns and bay leaf together until the liquid is reduced to about 1 tbsp. Cool.

3 Cream the egg yolks with 15g butter and a pinch of salt in a heatproof bowl. Strain in the lemon juice and set over a pan of barely simmering water and turn off the heat. Whisk in the remaining butter about 5g at a time until the sauce is glossy and has the consistency of thick cream. Season.

Make in a food processor Lightly blend the egg yolks and lemon or vinegar reduction, then pour in warm melted butter in a thin stream, keeping the motor of the processor running.

Rescue the sauce If the sauce becomes granular or starts to curdle, immediately put the bowl into the basin of cold water and stir vigorously to cool. Or remove from the heat and beat in 1 tbsp of cold water.

Béarnaise Reduce 2 tbsp white wine vinegar and 2 tbsp tarragon vinegar with half a small onion, finely chopped. Cool, then follow step 3 above.

play
Hopscotch

This simple playground game can be played by two to four people and requires only some hard ground, a piece of chalk and some stones.

Start by chalking out ten numbered squares in seven rows, alternately made up of a single and then two squares.

As you get better, you can vary the layout of the grid as you like.

Begin to play
■ Give each player a stone to mark their progress.
■ Throw your stone into square 1 and hop over it into square 2. Then proceed to 10 and back, hopping in rows with only one square, putting two feet down in rows with two.
■ Once back at square 2, balance on one foot and retrieve your stone. Then, hop back into square 1.
■ Turn and throw your stone into square 2, then hop directly from 1 to 3, and proceed as before. Next time throw the stone into square 3, then 4 and so on, always hopping over the square with the stone in it.
■ Continue until you put a foot wrong, or your stone misses a square. Then place it on that square and stand down while the next player has a turn.
■ The game gets progressively more challenging, as no player may enter any square with a stone on it. First to claim square 10 is the winner.

repair a garden
Hose

You can temporarily repair a pinhole leak in a rubber hose by jamming a wooden toothpick into the hole, breaking it off flush, and taping over with insulating tape. For a long-term repair, the only effective way is to use a hose repair connector.

■ Disconnect your hose from the tap, and cut through it on either side of the damage with a sharp knife, so that you leave a clean edge on both parts.
■ Fit the connector according to the manufacturer's instructions. Since your connector is going to be permanent, screw the sections together as tightly as possible.

groom a Horse

Grooming is not just for show. It ensures a horse's well-being and allows you to check it over for minor injuries. Follow these techniques for horses that live outside or horses that are not clipped.

YOU WILL NEED Rubber curry comb or grooming mitt, dandy brush, body brush, face brush, clean sponges or soft cloth, plastic mane comb, hoof pick, hoof oil

1 Start on one side, working down from the neck, using the rubber curry comb (above) or grooming mitt in circular sweeps to loosen dirt, following the direction of the hair. Go gently over bony parts, and sensitive spots such as the belly and between the hind legs. Do the same on the other side. Then use a dandy brush to sweep out the loosened dirt, and a body brush to remove any residues and to smooth the coat.

2 Gently whisk clean the broader parts of the face, ears and throat with the face brush and use it to remove any remaining dust that you missed with the body brush. Clean carefully around the eyes, ears and muzzle with a damp sponge or soft cloth (above).

3 Hold the tail out and up then clean the dock with a damp sponge. Then gently comb out the mane and the tail. If necessary, use the body brush (above) to remove loosened dirt from the mane or tail.

4 Use the hoof pick to scrape out mud and stones, which can cause lameness. Work from heel to toe, as you're less likely to dig into the horny pad in the sole – the 'frog'. If your farrier recommends it, oil the hooves to prevent cracking.

get started with riding a Horse

Before you get on a horse, you should get into the right clothes: a riding safety helmet that conforms to current safety standards is essential, and it's advisable to wear strong boots and a body protector.

Mounting a horse

As with all riding skills, mounting is best learnt at a riding school. If available, a mounting block makes it easier to get on, especially for children and beginners, and puts less strain on the horse. The guidelines below apply whether or not you use a block.

1 Mount from the left. Ensure the girth is tight enough to stop the saddle slipping then take the reins in your left hand just behind the mane. Turn the stirrup (so that it isn't twisted once you're seated) and put the toes of your left foot in.

2 Grasp the pommel at the front of the saddle with your right hand. You'll now be facing the horse's flank, with your left foot up.

3 Spring up off the right foot and swing your right leg over the horse's back (taking care not to kick it by mistake). Land as gently as you can on the saddle and take up the reins.

Sitting on a horse

- Double-check the stirrup length. Take your feet out and let them hang straight, the bottom of the stirrup iron should be level with your ankles.
- Once checked, place your feet securely in the stirrups.
- Make sure you're seated in the deepest part of the saddle.
- Keep your upper body straight, but not stiff.

- Hold reins in both hands above the withers, thumbs on top facing forwards.
- Keep a firm, not tight, pressure.

Walking and halting a horse

TO WALK, squeeze gently with your lower legs. Relax once the horse responds. Be flexible from the elbows, so your arms and hands move back and forth with the nod of the horse's head.

TO HALT, sit up tall, squeeze with your legs, brace the hands and clench your fingers on the reins as if squeezing water out of a sponge. Relax your legs and reins once you've stopped.

---

deal with
Hot flushes

Hot flushes and night sweats are an uncomfortable, at times embarrassing, symptom of the menopause. But you can develop practical coping strategies to get you through.

- Wear lightweight fabrics made from cotton or linen. Avoid silk and synthetics and high-necked tops. Dress in layers so you can shed clothing if necessary.
- In the morning, try a tepid bath for 20 minutes. Throughout the day, turn the central heating down, carry a small battery-operated fan and have iced water to hand to sip if you feel a flush coming on.
- Every day, do at least 20 minutes of aerobic exercise (*see* AEROBIC EXERCISE). Its impact on hot flushes is just one of the many benefits. A low-fat diet, over time, and loss of excess weight can also help, but losing too much weight makes symptoms worse.
- Keep a record of the things that trigger your hot flushes and avoid them, where possible. For instance, caffeine, alcohol and spicy foods are all prime suspects.
- Stress is another major factor. Anxiety can increase the frequency and severity of hot flushes, so try to relax. Yoga (*see* YOGA), meditation (*see* MEDITATE) and breathing exercises can help to put you back in control.
- Try drinking soothing sage tea. Many women report that it helps, particularly with night sweats.
- Before bed take a cool shower, then sleep on cotton sheets in cotton nightwear.

make a
Hot toddy

A roaring fire and a hot punch are just the thing on a bitter winter's night. Pour 50ml of whisky, rum or brandy (that's two alcohol units) into a heatproof glass or pottery mug. Add a teaspoon of soft, dark-brown sugar, a teaspoon of runny honey, a cinnamon stick, the juice of half an orange or lemon and a strip of pared rind. A toddy may not be a cure for a cold or flu, but it can certainly make you feel better. Sip slowly and let the vapours do their stuff.

----

treat
Hypothermia

When core temperature drops below 35°C (95°F), the body diverts blood supply from the surface of the skin to the vital organs, leading to hypothermia. In severe cases, a casualty may seem confused, lethargic and disorientated, drawing slow and shallow breaths. Their skin will look and feel cold.

Quick action
■ Call the emergency services, and while you wait, try to warm the person gradually, but don't apply heat directly.
■ Move them quickly to the warmest place available.
■ Remove any wet clothing, dry them and swaddle them in layers of blankets, in particular wrapping head and torso. Hug the person gently to share your own warmth.
■ Provide warm (not hot) drinks and a high-energy food such as a chocolate bar.

impress with a Hula hoop

Hooping is fun and challenging. It's also a great form of exercise, providing a low-intensity work-out, increasing strength and flexibility.

Choose a size and weight of hoop that feels comfortable. It should be between stomach and chest height when you stand it on the floor in front of you. A child's hoop from a toy shop is no good for an adult. A large hoop is great for a beginner, as it will spin more slowly, giving you more time to get the feel of the technique.

Getting the hoop habit The aim is to use the momentum of your body to keep the hoop revolving around it. For a great toning exercise, as you become proficient, alternate the direction of spin.

Raise your forearms.

Thrust your hips forward (don't circle them).

Slightly bend and straighten the forward leg to shift your weight.

Keep one foot forward.

■ Stand with one foot a little forward and hold the hoop with both hands, horizontally against the small of your back.
■ Give it a whirl in your preferred direction to set it in motion and raise your forearms. As the hoop crosses your belly, thrust your hips forward (don't circle them). Round and round goes the hoop as you thrust your hips and belly forward then pull back, slightly bending and straightening the forward leg to shift your weight.

----

keep Houseplants alive

Houseplants need careful attention, but if you look after them they could reward your investment with years of attractive, healthy growth.

Water Don't overwater (the commonest cause of houseplant death). It kills the roots, making plants collapse. Always let the surface of the compost dry out before watering and allow excess to drain away. Or water from below by standing plants in a bowl of water. Reduce watering to a minimum during winter. Mist regularly in dry conditions such as in centrally heated rooms.

Temperature Provide stable conditions away from draughts. If necessary, move plants away from open fires, or from cold windows at night.

Light and air Bright filtered light, not scorching direct sunlight, is ideal. Foliage plants are best suited to low light levels.

Food Use a shop-bought liquid feed from spring through to autumn, while plants are growing actively.

make delicious Ice cream

Homemade ice cream, using the best-quality ingredients, is superior in taste and quality to any you can buy in the shops and is easily made by hand – you don't need a special machine.

The classic base for most ice cream is a simple custard (below), with fruit or other flavours added according to taste or what you have to hand. But you can also make quick and easy frozen desserts based on just cream or yoghurt (bottom). Try traditional favourite flavours or invent your own combinations.

Vanilla ice cream

SERVES 4-6

500ml double cream
1 vanilla pod, split
125g caster sugar
150ml water
4 egg yolks

Variations Instead of the vanilla pod use 1½ tsp vanilla extract, adding it direct to the cream. Before freezing, add nuts, coffee essence, chocolate buttons or chopped chocolate.

1 Bring the cream almost to boiling point, remove from the heat and drop in the vanilla pod. Leave to cool. Scrape the seeds from the pod and leave them in the mixture, discarding the pod itself.

2 Dissolve the sugar in the water and boil until syrupy (it should form threads between finger and thumb when cooled). Whisk the egg yolks in a large bowl, gradually pouring in the syrup, followed by the cream. Pour into a plastic container and freeze for 1-2 hours or until the edges are frozen.

3 Tip the mixture into a bowl and whisk well: this breaks down any ice crystals in the mix. Return to the container and freeze again. Repeat the freezing and whisking twice more until the ice cream is smooth and completely frozen.

Summer fruit ice cream

SERVES 4

500g mixed soft fruit: blackberries, raspberries or strawberries
1 tbsp lemon juice
175g icing sugar
300ml double cream

Variation Substitute full-fat yoghurt for half the cream.

1 Blend the fruit, lemon juice and icing sugar in a food processor until smooth. Press through a nylon sieve into a large bowl. Discard the seeds. Whip the cream to form soft peaks. Fold gently into fruit mixture.

2 Pour into a container and freeze as for vanilla ice cream (above), freezing and whisking in turn.

---

deal with
Ice on paths

In winter, icy paths and drives can become potentially dangerous skating rinks. You can prevent the ice forming in the first place or take simple measures to clear it.

Start early As soon as snow has settled, or first thing in the morning after an overnight fall, clear your paths. Snow is easier to shift when fresh rather than compacted. If the sun comes out it will help to melt any ice uncovered underneath.

Clear the ice
■ If you use water to melt any ice, remember it could refreeze and turn to black ice, which is even more hazardous.
■ Chip away at the ice with a spade and spread salt on any area you have cleared. Ordinary table or dishwasher salt will do, but take care not to spread any on grass or plants or they will be damaged. If you don't have enough salt, you can use sand or ash, though they aren't as effective.
■ Cover cleared paths with more salt, sand or ash before nightfall to give a grip in case of overnight freezing temperatures.

⚡golden rules

ICE CREAM TIPS
■ **Chill all equipment and ingredients before you start.**
■ **Use the fast freeze setting on your freezer.**
■ **Measure accurately – too little sugar or cream will make the mixture granular.**

I

protect your Identity

Identity theft is increasingly common. But you can make it harder for the criminals.

- The misuse of credit card details is one of the most common forms of identity theft, so check credit card statements as soon as you receive them. If there are any unauthorised or inexplicable purchases, inform the card provider immediately and check any other accounts you have.
- Be suspicious if you're refused a loan despite a good credit history, or if important letters from your bank fail to arrive.
- Tell the police if you lose any documents that contain your name, address and date of birth – such as your driving licence or passport.
- Shred anything containing personal information: official letters, credit card receipts, bank statements and even junk mail.
- Never give personal information to cold callers, and never, ever give out your PIN over the phone: no one should be asking for it.
- If you move house, redirect your mail for at least six months and promptly inform your bank and any other financial organisations you deal with, so that all letters go to the right address.

stand and move on Ice skates

When you first put on skates it feels impossible to stand, let alone move. But the knack for it comes quickly, with just a little practice.

How to stay upright Spend a minute or two getting used to your boots before you venture out onto the rink. Stand in them, and walk around in them (if you have covers for the blades). Find your balance. When you're ready, remove the covers and go out onto the ice. Keep a hold of the barrier and pull yourself away from the entrance, sliding on your skates as you go. Don't attempt to take normal steps, and don't worry that your grip on the bar is the only thing keeping you upright at this point.

 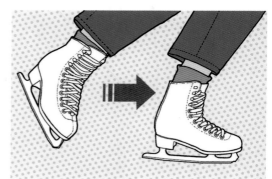

How to make your first move Hold your head up and your body straight, but bend your knees slightly. Position your feet so that they form an inverted T, with your left heel touching your right instep. Shift your weight slightly to the left foot, while digging into the ice with the inside of your right skate. Push off by straightening your right leg – and you'll sail off, slowly and, with luck, gracefully, across the ice.

treat painful Indigestion

You could take a tablet, but there are also some simple, natural remedies that can swiftly ease your discomfort.

Drink a cup of herbal tea The warmth itself will be soothing, but the herbs you choose will also have an effect. Try ginger, which has long been used to relieve the bloating and flatulence that can make indigestion so uncomfortable. Peppermint and camomile teas are also good choices.

A tablespoon of apple cider vinegar in a glass of water, sipped slowly, can also bring relief – especially when taken with a meal.

For better digestion, naturally, take a regular probiotic supplement of beneficial bacteria, including *Lactobacillus* and *Bifidobacterium* to inhibit the growth of harmful bacteria in the gut. Avoid big, rich, spicy meals, don't bolt your food and try to avoid eating too late at night. If you smoke, give up, and keep your alcohol consumption at a moderate level (*see* ALCOHOL UNITS).

put Insomnia to bed

Sleeping pills may knock you out, but they provide poor-quality sleep, may stay in your system in the daytime, encourage dependency and don't get to the root cause of your wakefulness. Try these drug-free solutions, instead.

Stress and worry can come between you and your sleep, so address these first, with simple relaxation techniques or a course of cognitive behavioural therapy (*see* STRESS *and* RELAXATION).

Take daily exercise – but not within 4 hours of bedtime. This helps to combat stress and encourages restful sleep.

Adopt a bedtime routine and don't take daytime naps. A warm bath and a milky drink or camomile tea before going to bed can help to make you drowsy.

Avoid watching the clock and fretting as the minutes – and hours – tick by. If it takes you more than 30 minutes to drift off, get up and go to another room. Read or watch television for a while. Write down your worries and possible resolutions then put them from your mind until morning.

Address the fundamentals: peace, quiet and comfort. Choose a mattress and pillows that allow you the best sleeping posture (*see* MATTRESS *and* PILLOWS), have freshly laundered bedclothes, put up heavy curtains to exclude the light and use earplugs if noise is a problem. *See also* SLEEP.

Insulate water pipes

There are two types of protection – tubing and wrap – that provide good insulation for pipes. Never leave a joint or corner exposed: these are the points most likely to freeze – and burst – in a cold snap.

Snap-on foam tubing is the quickest and simplest choice for lagging straight runs of pipe. The insulation is made to fit standard diameters of pipe and is slit along its length so that you just need to cut it to length and snap it onto the pipes. Make neat, notched joints with a knife at corners and T-junctions (right), and wrap the joints in PVC insulation tape to keep them closed.

Self-adhesive foam wrap is good for pipes that have lots of bends or are otherwise difficult to clad in tubing. Wrap the foam round the pipe like a bandage with a generous overlap of about a third of the width of the wrap. Be sure to wrap stoptaps and valves as you go, leaving only the handle or turn screw exposed so that they can still be operated.

protect against
Infections

Frequent hand-washing is the single most important factor in combating the spread of infectious diseases (*see* HANDS). Throughout the day, as you open a door, exchange money, pet a dog, handle raw food, flush the toilet, tap the keyboard, answer the phone, you pick up and spread germs, which can infect you if you then touch your eyes, nose or mouth. Much of this is unavoidable, but good hygiene can help to protect you from infection.

Try not to sneeze into your hands, and if you do so, wash them immediately. Be cautious about shaking hands with someone who obviously has a cold; be sure not to touch your face until you have washed.

At home, respect the rules of basic food hygiene (*see* FOOD), and avoid catering outlets that you suspect of poor hygiene practices.

Hospitals are breeding grounds for viruses and bacteria. Always use the alcohol-based hand rubs provided, on arrival and leaving. Don't visit a patient if you have sickness or diarrhoea. Unwell people are particularly vulnerable to infection.

Your immune system is your first line of defence against disease, so give it the best fighting chance by adopting a good diet (*see* DIET) and taking regular exercise (*see* AEROBIC EXERCISE).

protect children on the Internet

Take these simple steps to make the web a safe place for your children to explore.

■ Have your computer somewhere in the house where you can keep an eye on it, and on anyone using it. There's no substitute for real-life parental supervision.

■ Monitor your children's internet use by checking the 'History' function in your web browser. This is a complete list of all the sites that have been accessed recently. Bear in mind that a reasonably adept user (that is, any teenager) will know how to disable or edit the History list.

■ Make use of the 'Content Advisor' that comes with Windows. From the **Start** menu, open the **Control Panel**. Select **Network and Internet** then **Internet Options**. In the Internet Properties dialogue box click on the **Content** tab, then the **Enable** button under Content Advisor. Click the **Ratings** tab and use the slider to set a level of access that excludes categories such as nudity, depiction of weapon use and so forth. You'll be asked to create a supervisor password so that only you can amend the settings.

■ Many internet browsers have a built-in content filter, but you can also buy software such as Net Nanny and Cyber Patrol that filters inappropriate content, blocks access to chat sites, and creates an activity log that only the nominated supervisor can access. Some such programs can be installed on internet-enabled mobile phones.

Insulate your loft

Good loft insulation is essential to keeping valuable heat inside your house in winter – and keeping it out at the height of summer, too. Your insulation should be at least 270mm thick.

Choosing insulation The quickest and easiest type of loft insulation to use is blanket roll. Sold in widths that match the standard gaps between joists, the insulation is rolled out in the loft and cut to length. It comes in different thicknesses, to fit within the joists or lay at right angles over them.
■ 'Sleeved blanket' is easier to handle than the cheaper 'plain blanket' If you're using the plain variety, you should lay a vapour barrier first, to prevent condensation forming as heat rises from the room below.
■ Rigid glass fibre boards, or batts, can be fixed to the underside of the roof, between the rafters. This helps to maintain a constant temperature within the roof space if you're storing anything that must stay warm and dry.

YOU WILL NEED Scissors or trimming knife, face mask, protective gloves, rolls of insulating blanket

The fibres in plain (unsleeved) insulation can irritate the skin, so wear a mask and tuck your sleeves into gloves, and trousers into socks. Only open the packaging in the loft, and do all the cutting there, to minimise the spread of fibres.

1 Start at one end of the loft, leaving a gap of about 50mm in the eaves for ventilation. Unroll the blanket between two joists, pressing lightly so that it lies flat. Don't squash it down, as this will reduce the insulating properties.

2 Cut the roll as necessary, butting the ends up tight against each other when making a join.

3 Keep cables above the insulation so that they don't overheat, but water pipes below it, to keep them warm. Never insulate under the cold-water tank, or it will be more likely to freeze in winter, but do stick a square of blanket on the loft hatch.

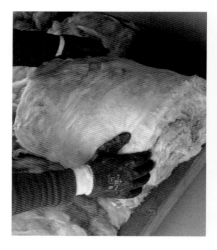

pay safely on the Internet

Buying products over the internet can be quick, easy and convenient, and perfectly safe, so long as you follow a few golden rules.

Check out the website that you're planning to buy from. Look for a link entitled 'Contact us' or something similar, and make a note of any physical address or phone number. Ring the number and see if anyone answers. If the page only gives an email address, send a short message: if it's a genuine and reputable site, someone should respond to your query promptly.

The payment process should take place on a secure webpage. Look at the address: it should begin with the letters https rather than just http. In Windows 7 you should also be able to see a padlock symbol at the top of the page; double-click on it to see the site's security certificate. Avoid any sites without a certificate or where the certificate has expired.

Check the delivery times and costs before you commit. The postage and packing costs might negate any saving you're hoping to make by buying on the internet or you may have a long wait for delivery.

Pay for big items by credit card for the consumer protection that your card issuer provides. For small transactions, use 'electronic cash' with an e-cash account. PayPal is the best known and most universally accepted.

------

make a success of Internet dating

The internet is a marvellous way to meet people when you're looking for love or simply companionship. Be sure that you make the most of its potential and avoid the possible pitfalls.

Post a photo Most people will be keenly interested in what you look like and you'll have a much better response rate if you make a picture available. Choose one in which you look your best, and make it a recent and honest headshot (not a snap of you sitting in your friend's Ferrari ten years ago).

Make a good statement All sites allow you to write something about yourself. Be reasonably open and frank, and make it meaningful. *I love cooking for my friends – especially Thai food ...* tells others about your interests and the kind of person you are. Avoid clichés like *I enjoy candlelit dinners* or *I'm a glass-half-full person*, as they are unlikely to set you apart from others. Similarly, steer clear of bald statements, like *My friends say I have a good sense of humour*. It's much more telling if you prove your humour through the information you give and the way you give it.

Stay close to home There's little point in striking up an online friendship with someone who lives at the other end of the country: remember, the aim is to find someone you can have a real relationship with.

Get together If the signs look good, meet up for a drink (rather than a meal: save that for the second date). Even if romance doesn't spark, you might end up enlarging your circle of friends, which itself increases the odds that you'll meet someone you want to be with.

Be careful Meet your new date in a public place, and don't accept an offer of a lift, especially to or from your home. Always tell a family member or friend where you're going to be and what time you expect to be home, and make sure your mobile phone is fully charged so that you can make contact if you need to. Avoid the temptation to drink too much – you need to like the person sober. If you're at all uncomfortable, make your excuses and leave.

carry out an effective
Internet search

When looking for information on the internet, your aim should be to define your search as narrowly as possible to generate the best and most appropriate results.

Use four or five key words If you're looking to find a shop in your area that sells Fender guitars, for instance, it's not enough to key in the words 'guitar' and 'shop', as you'll get suggestions of shops all over the world. Try something that better defines your wishes, such as: 'Fender guitar retailer Boston Lincolnshire'.

Use quotes If you put double quotes around a phrase, the search engine will prioritise hits where those words occur together. This is useful if you want something with a specific name – a 1973 Fender Jazz bass, for example. Put exactly that in double quotes: "1973 Fender Jazz bass". Quotes are helpful if your search naturally takes the form of a phrase – a line of a poem that you want to identify, or the title of an out-of-print book you want to find.

Exclude words Sometimes a search can be overwhelmed by sites that contain the right word in the wrong context. If you're searching for a guitar shop in the English town of Boston, you'll get lots of hits, or results, for Boston, Massachusetts. You can exclude these by adding words you don't want and putting a minus sign in front of them, for example, '-Massachusetts', and any other variations of the word, such as '-Mass' and '-MA'.

I

Introduce people to each other

Provide names to both the people being introduced, and explain who they are – just enough information to kick off a conversation. Your primary aim is to put people at ease, but there are some etiquette conventions to follow.

■ Always introduce a man to a woman: *Jane Brown, I would like to introduce Jack Black.*

■ The older or more senior person should 'receive' the younger, *Dad, this is my old French teacher, John Stewart; John, this is my father, Harry Smith.*

send and reply to Invitations

■ Make sure that any invitation, however informal, contains all the vital information: the name of the host; the nature of the occasion; the time, date and venue (including directions or a full address and postcode); a time that the event finishes; an address, phone number or email for RSVPs; and any special information such as a dress code or requests to bring something.

■ Include the names of all invitees, and make it clear whether children are invited too. If you're inviting friends by email or through Facebook, take extra care not to invite the wrong people by mistake.

■ For big events, send invitations 10-12 weeks in advance. Include an RSVP date to give you time to invite more people if some decline.

■ If you're replying to an RSVP, be prompt, especially if the occasion is something formal, like a wedding, which requires a lot of planning.

conduct a job Interview

Your job as an interviewer is to allow interviewees to make a case for themselves, and to get them to reveal something of their personality.

Set the tone and take control Explain the purpose of the interview and give an indication of how long it will last. Introduce yourself and anyone else who is taking part by name. But don't speak for too long at the start: get the interviewee involved as soon as possible.

Ask open-ended questions A good question is *What would you say has been your finest achievement?* This allows candidates to showcase their strong points, while their manner when answering will give you a good idea of what they are like, what qualities they value and how articulate they are.

Keep your responses neutral Encourage the candidate with occasional nods of the head. Be interested and try not to look surprised by any of the interviewee's responses.

Record the interview It's hard to take notes and stay engaged with the interviewee. If a sound recording isn't possible or appropriate, have someone on hand to take detailed notes for you.

Make notes afterwards As soon as the interviewee leaves, jot down a few thoughts while the impression of that person is still fresh in your mind.

perform well in a job Interview

Preparation is the secret of making a good impression at interview. Be sure of your facts and confident in your ability.

Prepare yourself Think about why you're qualified for the job, and write down your strong points. Identify triumphs and successes from previous jobs, and be ready to talk about them succinctly and convincingly.

Practise your interview technique If possible, get a friend to conduct a trial interview with you, and give you honest feedback.

Know the firm Read up on the company that you're applying to work with and, if possible, talk to people who already work there. Then you can tailor your responses to the way the company works and ask relevant questions.

Sell yourself on the day Smile, maintain eye contact and a relaxed pose, be courteous and speak clearly. Remember the interviewer's name and use it.

Remember some critical 'Don'ts' These all-too-common pitfalls could cost you the job, but are easy to avoid.

■ Don't be late. No excuse is good enough to counteract the bad impression this makes.

■ Don't dress casually. If anything, dress more smartly and formally than you would in a normal work situation.

■ Don't be overfamiliar. You won't get the job by trying to make friends.

save battery life on your iPhone

Your iPhone may be carrying out lots of little tasks that you don't require. Turn off these functions, and your battery will last longer between charges.

■ Disable 'push notifications' on applications. These alert you to things going on within your applications ('apps') that might be of interest to you. If you turn them off you'll still get the information when you open the app.
■ Check for mail less frequently. Set the default to check hourly.
■ Lock your phone. Put your iPhone to sleep whenever it's not in use, and set the Auto-Lock function to the shortest possible time.
■ Turn down the brightness. Keep the screen as dim as you can manage.

remove scratches from your iPod

The iPod is a desirable object that gets a battering with day-to-day use. There are steps you can take to restore some of its original gloss.

■ Always use a soft, dry, lint-free cloth to avoid making more scratches as you clean. Polish regularly to remove the lightest scratches.
■ Some people recommend banana or toothpaste to remove scratches, but you'll get the best results with shop-bought cleaning products.
■ Scratch removers work by rubbing down the surrounding area to the depth of the scratch, so deep scratches can only be removed with very abrasive products, that could damage the rest of the device.

Protect your Touch The iPod Touch relies on the sensitivity of its screen, so fit an adhesive screen protector as soon as you take it out of the box. They are sold in packs of 12, so that you can replace them as they get scratched.

Earlier iPods, with the clickwheel interface, are fast becoming design classics – and so are worth looking after. Buff the back gently with Brasso but use a shop-bought cleaning fluid for the front.

unfreeze an iPod

If your iPod Touch freezes or crashes, the problem is likely to be with an application rather than the iPod itself. For a classic iPod, try turning it off and on again to reboot the software.

■ Try to force-quit the current application by pressing and holding the sleep-wake button for a few seconds, then pressing and holding the home button when the red slider appears.
■ If that doesn't work, the time-honoured method of turning the device off and on again should do the trick. If not, then you can 'reset' an iPod Touch (and an iPad, too) by holding down both the sleep-wake and the home button for at least 10 seconds, until the Apple logo appears.

compile an iTunes playlist

In iTunes, it's easy to make manual playlists for different moods and occasions by selecting albums or individual songs and dragging them into folders. But you can also use iTunes to generate other kinds of playlists for you.

Smart Playlist In iTunes, go to File then select New Smart Playlist. Here you can set search parameters, such as artist, year or genre, and iTunes will compile the songs in your library that fit the bill.

Smart Playlist can be set to exclude all sound files that aren't actually music (such as podcasts or audio books). You can set the 'Last Played' option to exclude any songs that you've listened to in the last week or month, or tag songs according to categories of your own (party favourites, music for jogging) so that you always get the right sounds for the occasion.

Genius The iTunes 'Genius' function automatically generates playlists from the songs in your library. Choose one track, and Genius finds other similar songs, and also makes recommendations of songs that you might like to purchase.

J

remove lids from Jars

If a jar lid seems to have been welded on, wear rubber gloves or try placing a rubber band around the lid rim to give yourself a better grip.

Still no luck? Run hot (not boiling) water over the lid for 20 seconds, directing the stream onto the centre rather than the rim so that it expands a lot more than the glass. Dry it off and try again.

■ Three good whacks to the base of the jar with the heel of the hand can break the vacuum seal.
■ Alternatively, try inverting the jar and banging it (not too hard) on the counter top, or tapping around the side of the lid with the handle of a knife to loosen the seal.

---

make great Jam

Jam is often made using equal weights of fruit and sugar, but the secret of a good set is pectin, a natural fruit sugar.

Fruit such as apples, redcurrants and plums are pectin-rich and can be added in small quantities to low-pectin fruits such as strawberries and raspberries. Alternatively, you can add lemon juice or jam sugar (it has pectin added), or use ready-bought pectin powder or liquid, following the instructions on the label. A preserving pan, sugar thermometer and a wide-necked funnel for filling jars are good investments if you make jam regularly.

YOU WILL NEED **Jam ingredients, preserving pan or large heavy-based saucepan, sugar thermometer, saucer, skimming spoon, ladle, sterilised jars and lids, labels. Optional: wide-necked funnel, waxed discs, cellophane covers, elastic bands**

Raspberry jam

MAKES ABOUT 4 X 450g JARS

1kg raspberries
1kg granulated sugar or jam sugar, warmed in a low oven
50ml lemon juice (if not using jam sugar)

1 Put the fruit into a preserving pan. Add the lemon juice (if using) and heat gently until the juices run. Simmer until the liquid is reduced by about a third. Add the sugar and boil rapidly for about 20 minutes until the setting point is reached (104°C on a sugar thermometer – see right).

2 To test for set, put a teaspoon of jam onto a cooled saucer. If the skin crinkles when pushed with a finger, it's ready.

3 Quickly skim off any scum with a skimming tool or spoon then pot into warmed jars. The jam can be covered with waxed disks (wax side down) if you wish. Wetted cellophane covers held in place with elastic bands can be used in place of lids.

make Jelly

Jelly is both a preserve and a dish made with gelatine or agar-agar. Preserves are an excellent way of using summer and autumn soft fruits, including blackberries and apples, and well worth the effort of straining the juice. As a dish, dessert jelly is a traditional and easy-to-make favourite.

Preserve jellies Jelly is best made in small quantities, no more than can be accommodated in one jelly bag. A purpose-made bag (right) is ideal for straining, but you can make one yourself from a piece of muslin.

Redcurrant jelly

MAKES ABOUT 4 X 250g JARS

1kg redcurrants, including stalks, rinsed
250ml water
granulated sugar (see recipe for amount required)

YOU WILL NEED **Jelly ingredients, preserving pan or large heavy-based saucepan, bowl, jelly bag and stand (or equivalent), measuring jug, saucer, skimming spoon, ladle, sterilised jars and lids, labels. Optional: wide-necked funnel, sugar thermometer, waxed discs, cellophane covers, elastic bands**

1 Put the fruit into a preserving pan with the water. Simmer for about 30 minutes. Strain into a bowl overnight through a jelly bag suspended on a purpose-made stand or an improvised alternative such as an upended stool. Measure the juice into a jug and allow 250g sugar for every 250ml.

2 Reheat the juice until nearly boiling, stir in the sugar and boil rapidly until setting point is reached (*see* JAM). Pour into jars, label and store.

Dessert jellies Strained fruit juices make an ideal base for jelly. They can be used alone, with wine or spirits added, or with cream to give a slightly denser texture. Dessert jellies are made with the animal extract gelatine or with agar-agar, a vegetarian alternative derived from seaweed.

Gelatine comes in powdered or leaf form. If using powder, allow 1 tbsp per 600ml of liquid for a firm set. Sprinkle over a little cold water in a heatproof basin and leave, without stirring, until spongy. Set over a basin of simmering water and stir until dissolved. Add to warm liquid. If using leaf gelatine, bear in mind that six sheets equal 1 tbsp of powder. Soak in cold water for 15-20 minutes until soft. Squeeze lightly to extract surplus water, and add to the amount of liquid recommended by the recipe you're using. Stand in a bowl over hot water and heat, without boiling, until the gelatine has dissolved.

Agar-agar tends to set more firmly and at a higher temperature than gelatine. Always check the packet for advice on quantities and method.

beat Jet-lag

■ Eat carbohydrates before bed when you arrive. Food such as pasta helps you to sleep.

■ Don't drink alcohol on the flight and avoid caffeine too. But drink lots of water while you're airborne.

■ If you're flying while it's night time at your destination, do all you can to sleep. Use an eyeshade and earplugs, and turn the cold air to high: a cooler temperature tells your body it's night.

■ When it's daylight where you're going, try to stay awake – in sunlight if you can.

■ Eat eggs for breakfast. The protein will help you through that first day in a new time zone.

■ Switch to local time as soon as you can if you're staying more than a day or two. Stay up till local bedtime, and don't take an afternoon nap.

■ Get some exercise: a swim, or jog in the hotel gym, will encourage natural sleep.

clean Jewellery

For diamonds and hard stones such as rubies and emeralds, if settings are secure, use washing-up liquid and soak for 10 minutes in hot, sudsy water in a small bowl. Use an old toothbrush to remove ingrained dirt around settings. Rinse, then dry with a soft cloth.

For soft stones such as opals and coral, wipe with a silk cloth but never wash.

For pearls and strung beads, wipe after each wearing with a barely damp, really soft cloth. Very occasionally, wash quickly in mild soap suds in lukewarm water. Rinse, then dry with a soft cloth.

J

tell a funny Joke

Telling a joke is like singing a song: it requires rhythm and a confident delivery – and you have to know the whole thing from start to finish.

Don't spoil the joke before you start If you've just said: *You know that joke where it turns out he's the old lady's butler?*, then don't bother telling it. And don't begin by saying: *I know this really hilarious joke* – a phrase guaranteed to make everyone's heart sink.

Have your joke off pat If you find yourself saying things like *Oh, I should've said earlier that the second man had an ostrich on a leash* … then your joke is already dead and buried.

Don't laugh at the joke yourself – at least until you've got the punchline out. Laughing at all is poor form, but giggling just as you get to the best bit wrecks the timing, and may mean that nobody hears the payoff line.

Don't recycle half-remembered incidents from *The Simpsons*, *Seinfeld* or any other TV show. They are not jokes and, however funny they were to watch, it will be torture to listen to your retelling.

Know your audience A joke that was hilarious in the pub with your friends may clang like a cracked bell at lunch with the in-laws.

If all else fails, and all your jokes seem old and tired, make that the point of your joke: *A wrestler, a bald priest and a piece of string walk into a bar. The bartender takes one look and says, 'Sorry, but is this some sort of joke?'*

do the Jive

This dance developed from the Jitterbug and Boogie Woogie. It should be performed with great verve, with legs pumping and the mood of the music and the dance sassy and loud.

The basic count of six beats begins with a 'rock step' (beats 1 and 2), followed by two triple steps that are counted 3-a-4, 5-a-6. Put on a CD of jive music (such as Elvis Presley's 'Hound Dog' or Dion's 'Runaround Sue') and feel the beat. Study the steps described below and count them in time to the music. When you have them fixed in your mind, start the music again, get up and rock around the clock till it's broad daylight.

Starting position Stand facing each other. The man takes his partner's right hand loosely in his left, holds it aloft, and leads her through the steps shown below. As she follows, her every step mirrors his: if the man steps back with his left foot, the woman also steps back, but with her right and so on.

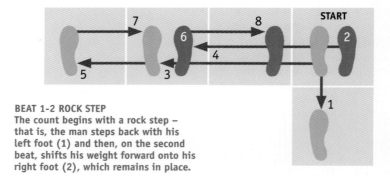

BEAT 1-2 ROCK STEP
The count begins with a rock step – that is, the man steps back with his left foot (1) and then, on the second beat, shifts his weight forward onto his right foot (2), which remains in place.

BEAT 3-a-4, 5-a-6 THREE SIDE CHASSÉS
There's now a gliding three-step sequence. The man chassés to the left – that is, sidesteps with his left foot (3). He then brings his right foot across next to his left (4).

He takes another sidestep to the left with his left foot (5). Then he shifts his weight back onto his right foot (6).

Finally he sidesteps to the right with his left foot (7) and then sidesteps to the right with his right foot (8).

Advanced When you have perfected these steps, try adding the spins so characteristic of this dance. Start with one or both partners performing a spin instead of a second chassé. If only one partner spins, the other should complete the second chassé as usual but keep their sideways movement to a minimum.

master some essential Judo moves

Judo is a combat sport, a form of wrestling derived from the Japanese martial art of ju-jitsu. Your aim is to win by throwing or immobilising your opponent, while defending yourself from attack.

Safe landings Before you learn to win at judo, you should learn how to lose at judo – that is, you need to know how to fall when you're thrown. This is the first thing that you'll be taught if you join a judo club. The essence of the 'breakfall', as it's known, is to roll rather than hit the mat flat.

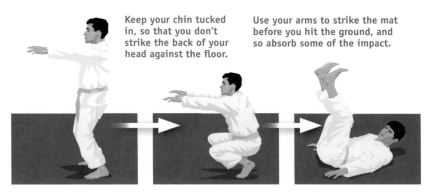

Keep your chin tucked in, so that you don't strike the back of your head against the floor.

Use your arms to strike the mat before you hit the ground, and so absorb some of the impact.

Learning to throw There are many effective ways of throwing an opponent. But in competitive judo you're aiming not merely to land your opponent on the mat, but to do so with good technique, since this is what wins points. *Osoto-gari* is one of the basic judo throws.

1 Pull downwards on your opponent's right sleeve with your left hand, while using your right hand to push on their left shoulder.

2 Swing your right leg behind your opponent's. Use your forward motion to push with your arms and unbalance your opponent.

3 As your opponent's left leg lifts, rotate your body so that your opponent falls swiftly and unstoppably on their back.

Winning the bout A controlled throw that lifts an opponent off their feet and onto their back scores an *ippon* – a full point – and the match is won. There are other ways of scoring an *ippon*: pinning an opponent on their back for 25 seconds, and applying an arm-lock or a stranglehold that forces the opponent to submit. **Arm-locks and strangleholds can be dangerous:** they should only be performed by experienced *judoka* (judo fighters).

learn to Juggle

Stand with your back against a wall to discourage a tendency to move forward. The pattern should be an arc, not a circle, with balls crossing paths in the air.

1 Hold your hands at waist level, and start by tossing a single ball from one hand to the other, cresting at eye level, and allowing it to plop down into your palm. As you toss it back and forth the ball should always describe the same arc.

2 When this exercise is second nature, bring another ball into play. Toss the first ball from one hand, and as it loops at the top of its arc, toss the other one from the other hand. Pause. Do the same thing in reverse. Practise to make perfect.

3 Add a third ball. Hold balls 1 and 3 in the hand you favour (usually the right) and ball 2 in the other (left). Launch ball 1, cross it with ball 2 and catch ball 1. As ball 2 reaches its high point, launch ball 3. As ball 3 reaches its high point send ball 1 left to right. Catch 3 in your left hand, and so on.

prepare Kebabs

Any meat, fish or vegetables suitable for grilling will make good kebabs, which can also be barbecued. Or try fruit brushed with melted butter and sprinkled with sugar for an unusual dessert. Marinating ingredients before cooking adds greatly to their flavour and tenderness.

Choose ingredients that will complement each other in terms of their taste (sweet pepper with salty pork) and texture (crunchy onion with succulent beef). Three or four ingredients is usually plenty.

Prepare a marinade based on an acidic ingredient such as tomato, vinegar or lemon juice, which helps to tenderise the meat or fish. Add other ingredients for their flavour, such as garlic, fresh ginger, olive oil, sherry, brown sugar and soy sauce. Place cubes of meat or fish in the marinade, cover and leave to stand in a refrigerator for at least 30 minutes – or even overnight.

Before cooking remove the meat or fish from the marinade and thread on to skewers, interspersing the fruit or vegetable ingredients as you do so. While cooking, brush the remaining marinade on the kebabs to keep them moist. Make sure the meat is cooked through and then serve immediately.

golden rules
PREPARE KEBABS
■ **Soak wooden skewers for 20-30 minutes before using so that they don't burn.**
■ **Cut ingredients into chunky equal-sized pieces to ensure even cooking.**

understand the principles of Karate

Students of karate learn to channel their own or an opponent's energy to maximum effect – in order to deliver a powerful blow to or unbalance that opponent.

Karate is a form of self-defence that has an almost balletic grace. If you take up karate, you'll spend a great deal of time performing *katas*, set sequences of fight-moves that, to an outside observer, look like a rather war-like dance routine. The purpose of the *katas* is to teach you to concentrate all the energy you can muster into fight-winning blows. The idea at the core of karate is that a strong strike, delivered with precision to the weakest points on an opponent's body, can make a decisive difference. By applying this approach a smaller, physically less powerful protagonist can overcome a much larger, stronger enemy. However, in modern karate, the focus is more on discipline, self-control, fitness and confidence than in actual self-defence.

Making an impact One way to make a strike as strong as it can be is to reduce the area of impact, so that the force of the blow is concentrated in a small spot. To this end, karate practitioners (*karatekas*) recognise certain 'points of contact', which are the weapons in the practitioner's armoury: the knifehand, often termed the 'karate chop', is perhaps the best known. *Karatekas* also stress the importance of following through the blow beyond the moment of contact, and they practise resisting the temptation to pull punches (hence the spectacular feats of smashing tiles or planks with the hand or forehead).

Positive energy When you practise karate, you should think about your opponent's power as well as your own. You must learn to block intelligently and effectively, so as to deflect blows aimed at you. You can also use an opponent's energetic movement against them, to tip their balance and topple them over. When karate is practised as a sport (as it usually is) all these skills are honed through *kumite*, or freestyle sparring, in which two *karatekas* fight – but deliberately avoid making contact with their blows.

retrieve a broken Key

This method can be used for the locks found on car doors and for the cylinder locks on front doors.

■ Spray the lock with aerosol lubricant (not generally recommended for cylinder locks – but this is an emergency).
■ Insert a thin piece of fretsaw blade into the keyway. Position the blade so that its serrated teeth are pointing back towards you.
■ Manoeuvre the blade so that its teeth catch on the notches in the key, then gently pull back to draw the key out slightly.
■ As soon as a small part of the shaft is protruding, use needle-nose pliers to get hold of it and extract it from the lock.

make a simple paper Kite

This simple paper kite costs next to nothing and is quick to make. You could have lift-off within 15-20 minutes.

YOU WILL NEED Sheet of A3 paper (decorated if desired), sticky tape, wooden skewer (about 25cm long), ribbon, hole punch, ball of fine string

1 Lay the sheet of paper on a work surface in front of you with the long sides to top and bottom, fold it in half from right to left, and make a firm crease down the middle.

2 Rotate the paper so that the folded edge is facing you. Make a diagonal fold so that two triangles of paper protrude from beneath the folded section, one about four times larger than the other. Make a firm crease.

3 Turn the paper over and unfurl one leaf of the uppermost folded section. Apply tape along the join revealed to create the spine of your kite.

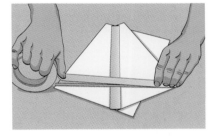

4 To hold the wings in place on either side of the spine, tape the wooden skewer across the widest section of the paper at right angles to the spine.

5 Tape the ribbon to the bottom of the spine, then turn the kite over. The fold of paper beneath the wings is the kite's keel. Fold it back and forth so that it stands at right angles to the wings.

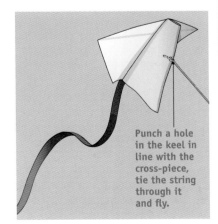

Punch a hole in the keel in line with the cross-piece, tie the string through it and fly.

fly a Kite

Find a wide open space, a safe distance from roads or power lines and well away from hills, trees and buildings that cause turbulence.

How much wind a kite needs depends on its design. Heavy kites require more wind to get off the ground. Some are made especially to fly in light wind, but most are designed for average wind speeds. If you can feel wind in your face, or see fluttering leaves, there should be enough puff to launch your kite.

■ Stand with your back to the wind and hold your kite as high as you can, its nose pointing straight up.
■ Gently give it over to the wind. If the breeze is strong enough it will start to ascend. Pay out a little line and the kite will drop. Before it lands, tighten your grip and it will rise again. Repeat this until it's high enough to find steady winds.
■ If the line slackens, bring it in a little. If the kite tugs hard, pay more line out. Don't feed your kite too much line: 30-60m is ample, allowing you to keep it within sight.
■ Watch the kite like a hawk to avert a crash. A dive-bombing kite can cause injury.

choose the right
Knife

Using the correct knife for the job will make food preparation easier. A basic set of kitchen knives will meet most of your needs.

■ Hold a knife before you buy to check its comfort and balance.

■ Choose knives with handles riveted to the blade or made all in one piece.

■ A few good knives are better than many of poor quality. High-carbon stainless steel is easy to sharpen and stays sharp longest (see opposite).

LARGE COOK'S KNIFE (A) An especially versatile knife used for chopping, slicing, jointing and paring.

SMALL VEGETABLE KNIFE (B) A knife for more intricate jobs such as boning meat or fish or making garnishes – as well as for preparing vegetables.

SMALL FRUIT KNIFE (C) For cutting through skins without tearing delicate flesh.

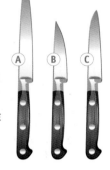

PALETTE KNIFE (D) For smoothing and lifting. It's particularly useful when applying icing, and for lifting biscuits from baking trays.

BREAD KNIFE (E) The best bread knives come with deep serrations and a long, straight 30cm blade.

CARVING KNIFE (F) Best with a broad, tapering blade at least 20cm long.

learn the basics of Knitting

Knitting is creative, absorbing – and easy to master. And it enables you to make things that are totally individual in colour and style.

The basic process of knitting starts with 'casting on' a first row of stitches (see steps below) using your chosen yarn and a pair of needles. You then build up the work, row by row, using a combination of stitches: knit (plain) and purl (hence the phrase 'knit one, purl one'). When you have reached the desired length, you 'cast off' the finished rows to prevent your knitting unravelling.

The basic tools Knitting can be done in almost any yarn, including wool, wool mixtures, cotton, linen and silk – or you can mix them as you wish. You can choose needles in metal, plastic and also in bamboo and wood, which are the most expensive but the easiest to use. For best results you need to match yarn and needles. As a rule the thicker the yarn the larger the needles should be. You'll need to practise to achieve the correct tension – the number of stitches and rows to a given measurement – stated in the knitting pattern.

Knowing the stitches Knit and purl stitches are used in combination to create three basic styles of knitted work:

Garter stitch Knit stitches on every row – creates horizontal ridges.

Stocking stitch Alternate rows of knit and purl – resulting in a basic smooth knitting stitch.

Ribbing Alternate knits and purls with the pattern reversed on alternate rows – producing firm but stretchy ridges useful for edges such as cuffs.

Casting on

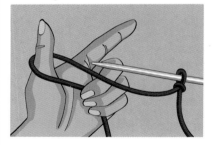

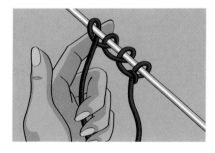

1 Tie a slip knot round a needle and hold that needle in your right hand. Wrap the yarn from the ball end around your left thumb, then grasp the yarn firmly between the palm of your hand and the tips of your fingers.

2 Turn your hand so that the back of your thumb is facing you, forming a loose loop. Insert the needle from front to back through the loop.

3 Slip your thumb out of the loop and at the same time pull the yarn downward to close the loop around the needle. Repeat to make first row.

Stitches

Knit (plain) stitch

1 Insert the right needle into the first cast-on stitch and behind the left needle. Loop the ball-end yarn anti-clockwise around the right needle.

2 Use the right needle to draw the loop forwards through the stitch. At the same time push the stitch on the left needle up towards the tip.

3 As you pull the loop away with the right needle, allow the stitch on the left needle to slip off. Pull it tight to the right needle to make the stitch.

Purl stitch

1 Insert the right needle in front of the left needle (not behind) and behind the ball-end yarn rather than in front.

2 Wrap the yarn around the right needle as before, pull it through and push the stitch on the left needle towards the tip.

3 Allow the stitch to slip off the left needle and tighten it against the loop on the right needle on to make a purl stitch.

Casting off

  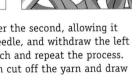

1 Knit the first two stitches in the row. Insert the tip of the left needle into the front of the first stitch knitted.

2 Lift the first stitch over the second, allowing it to slip off the right needle, and withdraw the left needle. Knit the next stitch and repeat the process. Continue to the end, then cut off the yarn and draw the cut end through the last stitch.

sharpen
Knives

The extra chromium in a stainless steel knife keeps it sharp for longer than ordinary steel, but all knives become blunt with use and should be sharpened regularly.

Purpose-made wheel sharpener
Simply draw the blade through the V formed by the two sets of hardened blades.

On a steel Hold the steel at a slight angle, point down. Place the widest part of the knife blade at the top of the steel, at an angle of about 20 degrees.

■ Draw the knife down the steel, keeping it at the same angle but gradually pulling the blade towards you so that, when you complete the stroke, only the tip of the knife is touching the end of the steel.

■ To sharpen the other side of the knife blade, place it at the same angle against the underside of the steel and then draw it down in the same way. Alternate these diagonal strokes until both sides of the knife blade are sharp.

create a
Knot garden

The fragrant knot garden, a favourite in Elizabethan times, will work well in both large and smaller spaces. Within its low hedges you can grow aromatic herbs such as thyme, sage, rosemary and camomile.

Design Draw a design, to scale, on squared paper, marking key measurements and plant choices. The garden should be at least 2m square, or 3m in diameter for a circular plan.

Plants Select boxes of different varieties, including variegated types, and hardy English lavenders. Other good choices are germander, rosemary, hyssop and the grey-leaved cotton lavender. You can also add purple sage or a purple-leaved berberis.

Preparation and planting Dig over the area, adding plenty of compost. Mark out your design using stakes and string. Set plants in place, allowing growing room, with 'crossing' plants placed appropriately within each line. Box plants need to be 30-35cm apart, lavenders and rosemary 30-45cm apart. Keep well watered. Fill in open areas with gravel.

Training and care Cut back 'underneath' plants at crossing points and allow the 'over' ones to grow continuously. Enhance the knot effect by allowing the plants in the upper lines to grow taller than those below.

tie Knots

There are scores of different knots but five basic types will cover most of your needs. Practise tying them with pieces of string and try to remember the tasks for which each type of knot is suitable.

Uses for knots

Reef or square knot This simple knot lies flat when finished, so is useful for tying bandages. It's also used for joining two ropes of equal thickness, but should be used only with natural rope, not rope made out of synthetic fibres.

Sheet bend An essential knot for securely joining ropes. If they are of different thicknesses, the thinner rope should be the active partner in tying the knot.

Bowline If you need to make a loop that won't slip at the end of a length of rope – for instance, as a rescue knot when throwing a line to someone in trouble in the water – this one is quick to tie.

Round turn, two half hitches A knot that's useful for tethering a horse or mooring a boat to a post or ring.

Constrictor This is used to tie a rope around a fixed object such as a bollard, rail or jetty post.

How to tie knots

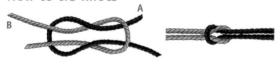

Reef knot Wind the 'working' rope end (A) in your right hand over and then under the 'standing' rope end (B) in your left. Swap hands, so that the working rope is in your left hand, then loop it back over and under the end of the standing rope and pull tight.

Sheet bend Make a loop in the thicker rope (A). Feed the end of the thinner rope (B) through the loop; wrap it round the two lengths of thicker rope and under its own standing part. Pull the lengths of thicker rope to tighten.

Round turn Loop the rope twice around the post or ring, with the second loop overlapping the first. Make a half hitch by taking the end around the main rope and passing it through between the post and the rope. Repeat, then slide the two half hitches up and pull tight.

Bow line Form a small loop (A) near the rope end. Pass the end (B) through the loop, hook it around the standing rope and then back through the loop. Pull the standing rope and rope end to tighten the knot and form a fixed loop.

Constrictor knot Wind the rope around the post or rail in a figure of eight. Feed the end of the rope under the second loop, then over and under the first loop and pull to tighten.

choose cuts of Lamb

Lamb is a tender meat, sweetest of all when 'new season', from the youngest animals with a pale pink flesh and creamy white fat. Meat from older animals is darker in colour. Nearly all lamb cuts are tender enough to be roasted or grilled apart from neck joints and shanks.

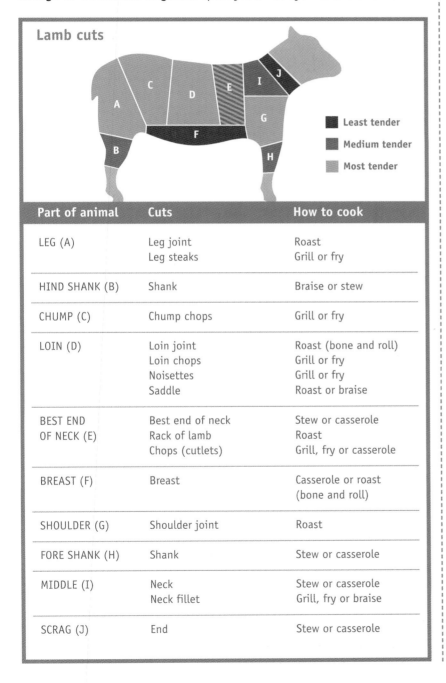

Lamb cuts

Least tender
Medium tender
Most tender

Part of animal	Cuts	How to cook
LEG (A)	Leg joint Leg steaks	Roast Grill or fry
HIND SHANK (B)	Shank	Braise or stew
CHUMP (C)	Chump chops	Grill or fry
LOIN (D)	Loin joint Loin chops Noisettes Saddle	Roast (bone and roll) Grill or fry Grill or fry Roast or braise
BEST END OF NECK (E)	Best end of neck Rack of lamb Chops (cutlets)	Stew or casserole Roast Grill, fry or casserole
BREAST (F)	Breast	Casserole or roast (bone and roll)
SHOULDER (G)	Shoulder joint	Roast
FORE SHANK (H)	Shank	Stew or casserole
MIDDLE (I)	Neck Neck fillet	Stew or casserole Grill, fry or braise
SCRAG (J)	End	Stew or casserole

use a Ladder safely

■ Set straight ladders at an angle of about 75 degrees, or one out, four up – for example, if you're putting a ladder 4m up a wall, stand it 1m out from the wall.
■ For time-consuming jobs, tie the ladder to sturdy pegs driven into the ground on either side.
■ On hard surfaces, get someone to stand on the bottom rung to prevent slippage.
■ Use cordless tools: cables are a hazard when working up a ladder.
■ Hold the rungs when climbing up or down the ladder.
■ Don't go up a ladder with your hands full: raise and lower items in a bucket on a rope, and hang the bucket on an S-hook.
■ The top four rungs are for handholds only.
■ Don't set up a ladder in front of an unlocked door.
■ Never leave a raised ladder unattended.

treat Laryngitis

An inflamed larynx or voice box is usually caused by a virus, and will usually get better with simple home treatments. Persistent cases may be due to bacteria and require antibiotics.

■ Drink plenty of fluids, especially water, and try not to swallow or cough excessively.
■ If you have a hoarse voice, rest your vocal cords. Don't shout, talk, sing or whisper for long periods.
■ Gargling with a mouthwash or salty water can help to ease a sore throat (*see* SORE THROAT). Menthol inhalation and an air humidifier help to clear the airways.
■ If you smoke, it's time to stop.

fix a central heating
Leaking pipe

A leaky pipe should be fixed promptly – not just to prevent water damage, but because leaks allow oxygen into the system, which can cause boiler and radiators to rust.

It's most likely that your leaking joint is a 'compression fitting'. This consists of a nut attached to a fitting that has a screw thread around its outside. A small ring of soft metal – called an 'olive' – forms a seal between these two parts. To stop a leak, it may be enough just to tighten the nut a quarter of a turn (no more than that, or you'll damage the olive).

Still got a leak? Fit a new olive or try wrapping the old olive with plumber's tape.
■ Drain the system, or isolate the leak by closing valves on either side.
■ Undo the leaking joint, and drain any residual water into a bucket.
■ Pull the pipe slightly away from the nut. Wrap two or three turns of PTFE tape (also known as 'plumber's tape') around the olive.
■ Reinsert the pipe, tighten up the nut, and then refill the system.

---

golden rules
LAYING A LAWN
■ **Choose a seed treated with a bird repellent.**
■ **Check turf samples for firmness, colour and absence of weeds.**
■ **Keep a new lawn well watered in dry spells.**
■ **Don't mow until the grass is 5cm high.**

lay a Lawn

Spring and autumn are the best times to create a new lawn. You'll need to prepare the ground at least a month in advance and decide whether to grow a lawn from seed or lay ready-prepared turf.

Prepare the ground
■ A firm, level surface is essential. Trample the earth and break up clods with a rake, removing weeds and large stones.
■ Compact the soil to make it firm by taking small overlapping steps with your weight on your heels.
■ Rake over the ground several times in different directions to create a crumbly, even surface.
■ Select seed or turf to meet your requirements – lawns that will get repeated use by a family need hard-wearing grass mixtures. Fine grasses with a 'bowling green' effect will be less resilient.

Laying turf Putting down turf has the advantage of giving you an immediate and more predictable result, and can be done in summer if necessary, but is much more costly than sowing seed.

1 Buy turves and set in a shaded area. If they can't be laid within 24 hours of purchase water them lightly.

2 Set a plank on your prepared area and lay the first turves against the straight edge. Lay alternate courses of turves in staggered rows, working from the plank.

3 Bang the surface with the back of a rake to firm in. Brush fine topsoil into the cracks and water in. Repeat if any cracks open up later.

4 Don't worry at this stage about shaping turves to fit your lawn area. Wait until they have taken, then trim any excess with a knife or lawn edger.

Sowing This method is quick and inexpensive, and there is a wider range of grass types to choose from, but a new lawn of this type can take six months to mature and is susceptible to bird and cat damage. Whichever type of seed you choose, allow 30-60g per m².

Peg out strings 1m apart then place bamboo canes across them to form an area of 1m². Sprinkle the seed evenly across the square. Repeat for the remaining area, repositioning the bamboo canes as you go. Rake seed in lightly and evenly. Deter birds with bird scarers or crisscross black cotton thread 5-8cm above the surface, between pegs.

patch a Lawn

A lawn can be repaired with seed or turf, ideally in spring or autumn. If a replacement patch is needed, try to use the same grass type.

Broken edges Make three neat cuts in the turf around the broken edge. Lift the cut section and turn it round so that the ragged edge is on the inside.

Seeding bare patches
- Use a half-moon edging tool to cut out the damaged area in a neat square or rectangle. Lightly fork over the soil and add some replacement topsoil or compost. Scatter grass seed at 30-60g per m². Sprinkle lightly with topsoil and protect from birds as for a new lawn (see above). Water if necessary.
- Alternatively, pre-germinate the seed. Mix seed with moist compost in a bucket, cover with cling film and put in a warm place for three days or until you see roots beginning to develop. Then sow as above.

Turfing bare patches
- Cut away the damaged area and prepare the patch as above. Cut a bought piece of turf to size, place in position and brush in some top dressing. Press it in neatly with the back of a rake. Water well. Alternatively, for an ideal match, use an identically sized piece of turf from a less conspicuous area of your lawn.

make Lemonade

Nothing is more refreshing on a fine summer's afternoon than a glass of homemade lemonade – so much better than the fizzy stuff. This syrup will keep in the fridge for up to a week.

350g caster sugar (or to taste)
750ml boiling water
juice of 8 large lemons
2 tbsp finely grated lemon zest

TO SERVE

ice cubes
sprigs of lemon balm, lemon verbena or mint

Put the sugar into a pan with the water and stir until the sugar has dissolved. Leave to cool. Stir in the lemon juice and zest until well blended. Strain if you wish. Chill before serving, then dilute with water to taste, pour over ice cubes and top with herbs.

clean Leather

Leather comes in its natural form or, as in shoes, leather garments and upholstery, dyed and coated with polyurethane. The two need different treatment, as does suede, a leather with a napped finish used for shoes (*see* SHOES) and handbags.

Natural leather Dust frequently with a soft cloth. Try removing any dirt or marks with an art rubber, available from specialist stores, but be aware that it may still leave a smudge.

Coated leather Dust regularly with a cloth and occasionally with one dampened with cold water. Wash every six months or so with saddle soap. First remove any loose dirt with a stiff brush or damp cloth. Then rub a damp cloth on saddle soap and work up a lather on the leather, rubbing with a circular motion. Allow to air dry then buff with a clean, soft cloth. Finish with a protective leather cream.

Suede Brush regularly with a suede brush or clean dry kitchen sponge to restore the nap. Use a slow, circular brushing motion.

golden rules

CLEANING LEATHER
- **Test any cleaning method on a small inconspicuous area.**
- **Have valuable items professionally cleaned.**
- **Never dry wet leather near a heat source – it may shrink.**
- **Treat greasy spots with talcum powder, leave overnight and brush off.**
- **Never use a solvent-based spot remover.**

Lift items safely

Before lifting anything heavy, assess it carefully. Notice anything that might snag or scratch you or slip through your fingers. Never try to lift more than your capacity, and if possible use mechanical help such as a hand truck or trolley.

- If you fear that the load might be too heavy, and you have no mechanical help, take no chances, and recruit a helper.
- If you have a helper, take control. Issue clear, concise instructions for lifting, moving and setting down, such as *up*, *left*, *right*, *down*.
- Stand close to the load, with feet apart, and one slightly in front of the other for stability.

Bend at the knees, not the waist, and tuck your chin in. Keep your back as vertical as possible and take a firm grasp of the object.

Don't lift with straight legs and bent back as this risks injury to the back and abdomen.

Make your legs do the work: begin to straighten them as you slowly lift, taking care not to twist your torso.

Once you're standing, hold the object close to your body to minimise stress to your lower back.

find a perfect Level

Establishing a correct horizontal line is vital for many DIY jobs, such as putting up shelving, laying decking and building fences.

A spirit level is the essential tool for any job requiring a horizontal line. You will need a full-size one, at least 60cm long, for building work such as fencing and concreting. A short 'torpedo level' – 15-20cm long – will do for indoor shelving jobs. A line level, one that hooks onto a taut string, is useful for bricklaying. All levels have a clear vial filled with liquid. When the level is horizontal, a bubble in the liquid floats between two lines marked on the vial.

A water level, or length of transparent hose, can be used to fix a level between two distant points – on two walls of a room, say, or around an outside corner of a house. Fill the hose with water, making sure that there are no air bubbles. Tip a little out, so that there's a small amount of space in the hose. Hold your thumb over one end of the hose and ask a helper to do the same at the other end, then each take up position at the points between which you want to fix a level. Hold each end upwards and remove your thumbs from the hose. Ask your helper to align the water level inside the hose with the first reference point. The surface of the water at your end will always be at the same height as your helper's, allowing you to fix a level.

compose a witty Limerick

A limerick is a comic five line poem. It has a characteristic galloping rhythm (loosely a string of anapaests). The fourth and fifth line are short, and rhyme with each other; the three longer lines also share a rhyme. Here's an early classic of the genre, by Edward Lear:

> There was an Old Man of Calcutta,
> Who perpetually ate bread and butter,
> Till a great bit of muffin,
> On which he was stuffing,
> Choked that horrid Old Man of Calcutta.

To modern tastes this is not hilarious, and the repeat of the rhyme-word Calcutta is a little disappointing. When you attempt to write your own limerick, make sure that the first line ends in a word that has plenty of rhyming possibilities. You'll do well to retain the central character introduced in the first line: *There once was a ...* person of some sort from somewhere. Then just use the five lines to tell a little short story.

Modern limericks also tend to be somewhat bawdy. They don't have to be ribald at all, but they should be amusing:

> There was a young man from Argyll,
> Who sharpened his teeth with a file.
> It meant he could eat
> The most leathery meat,
> But it made for an unnerving smile.

cook, prepare and eat Lobster

YOU WILL NEED Plastic bag, large pan, salt, chopping board, cook's knife, large napkin, finger bowl of warm water and lemon slices, fork, small hammer or lobster (or nut) crackers, lobster fork or skewer

Cooking The most humane way to treat a live lobster is to rinse it, put it in a plastic bag and freeze it for 2 hours before plunging it into boiling water to which you've added 100g salt per litre. Cook for 12 minutes for the first 500g weight, 10 minutes for the next 500g and then 5 minutes for each additional 500g. Drain off the water and leave to cool.

Preparation

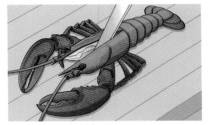

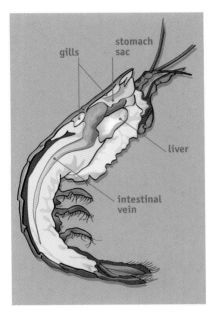

- Lie the lobster on its back on a chopping board and slice in half from head to tail.
- Spread out the two halves and remove the gills, stomach sac (in the head) and the dark intestinal veins running down the tail.
- Remove the liver (also in the head) and, from female lobsters, the coral-red roe in the tail. Set aside for garnish.

Eating Tuck in a large napkin and prepare a finger bowl. Serve with mayonnaise and lemon wedges or with a hollandaise sauce (*see* HOLLANDAISE SAUCE).

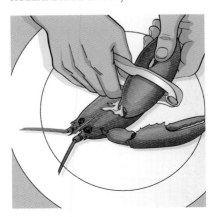

- Use a fork to remove as much meat as possible from head, body and tail. Then crack the claws in several places using a small hammer or lobster or nutcrackers and use the lobster fork or skewer to extract as much meat as possible from either side of the thin membrane running down the centre of each claw.
- Break off the smaller side feelers, crack open and suck out the meat.

apply Lipstick

YOU WILL NEED Lip liner pencil in a nude or natural shade, lip brushes, lipstick, gloss

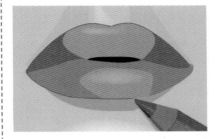

1 Carefully outline the shape of your mouth with the lip liner pencil using gentle strokes.

2 Next fill in with your lipstick. You can do so directly from the tube, but a lip brush gives you more control. Start from the middle of your bottom lip and work out, applying an even layer, then do the same with your top lip. Use the brush to blend lipstick and lip liner.

3 Blot with a tissue and apply a second light coating of lipstick. Work your lips together to ensure an even coverage.

4 Finish by adding a layer of lip gloss, starting at the centre of the lips and moving outwards.

create a company
Logo

A well-designed logo helps you to stand out from the crowd and tells your customers something about the type of business you are. To devise a logo you need a professional designer.

Find a designer Ask around or look online for designers who do work for businesses. Contact up to three and arrange an initial meeting.

Create a brief Think about what the designer needs to know.
■ What is your business, and what are its values? Are you modern and innovative? Caring and customer-focused? Reassuringly traditional? This will affect the images and typography that the designer uses.
■ Where will your logo appear? On your letterhead and business cards, but what about websites, billboards, packaging or as the livery on vans?
■ What is your budget? Have a figure in mind, then agree a price with the designer before they start work.

Protect your logo All logos are protected under copyright law as 'artistic works'. For better protection, register your logo as a trademark with the Intellectual Property Office.

The FedEx logo is modern, efficient and clever (spot the hidden arrow): qualities the company would like customers to associate with its courier service.

free up a stiff Lock

Various things can make a lock mechanism go wrong, but most problems are easily fixed. If your problem is with a latch bolt that won't close properly, it could be that the door has sagged slightly, so that the bolt is out of alignment with the slot in the striking plate. A small misalignment can be fixed by filing down the bottom edge of the slot with a metal file. If the misalignment is larger, you'll have to remove the striking plate from the door frame and reposition it.

Mortise locks on exterior doors may dry out or corrode if the wind and rain gets at the mechanism. In the first instance, spray an aerosol lubricator into the keyhole and operate the lock a few times to allow the lubricant to disperse. If that doesn't work, you'll have to take the lock mechanism out.
■ Remove the door handles, and the two screws holding the lock in the doorframe, then prise the mechanism out (*see* DOOR LOCKS). Carefully open the casing by removing the screws.
■ Apply car grease or petroleum jelly to all working parts, and put them back in the order that you took them out. Close the case and replace the lock.

Cylinder locks Don't use aerosol lubricant on cylinder locks (of the Yale type). They should be treated with a dry lubricant such as graphite or PTFE powder, available from DIY stores.

make emergency repairs to Luggage

A suitcase can come in for a battering by baggage handlers or succumb to wear and tear. But you can make running repairs.

A breaking handle can be temporarily fixed by binding it with self-adhesive fabric tape or strapping tape. If a handle breaks completely, and is attached by D rings, prise them open with pliers, remove the handle and replace it with an old tie or other suitable makeshift. Keep the handle. You can later take it to a leatherwork shop and buy a similar one. If the handle is retractable, and screwed in on the inside, you'll need to open up the case to locate and remove the fixings, which may mean detaching the lining.

If the case itself tears, undo any lining around the tear, and patch it with leather or fabric. For a vinyl case, you can buy vinyl cement and vinyl patches. Apply the appropriate adhesive to the case interior and the patch. Wait until it's touch-dry, then position the patch and press to the surface. Hammer lightly at the edges to affix it. Use fabric glue to reattach the lining.

A broken zipper can be a nightmare, but a luggage strap bound round your case gives belt-and-braces security – and makes it easier to spot on a baggage carousel.

A dent in a metal suitcase can be knocked out by gentle tapping on the inside with a piece of wood.

dance the Macarena

The Spanish song 'Macarena', by Los del Rio, became an instant hit on its release in 1995, inspiring a craze for this exuberant dance.

Don't worry if you have two left feet or no willing dance partner. This dance requires only that you move your hands, arms and body – with a Latin swing and sway. Every movement is sensuous. Put on the 'Macarena' and feel the beat. *Oh, when I dance, they call me Macarena / And the boys, they say that I am buena …*

BEAT 1 Stretch the right arm out in front of you at shoulder height, palm down.
BEAT 2 Follow with the left arm.

BEAT 3 Turn up your right palm.
BEAT 4 Turn your left arm palm up.

BEAT 5 Put your right hand on your left shoulder.
BEAT 6 Put your left hand on your right shoulder.

BEAT 7 Clasp your right hand to the back of your head.
BEAT 8 Clasp your left hand to the back of your head.

BEAT 9 Right hand to front of left hip.
BEAT 10 Left hand to right front hip.

BEAT 11 Right hand to right buttock.
BEAT 12 Left hand to left buttock.

BEATS 13, 14, 15 Swing your hips to the right, left, then right again.

BEAT 16 Clap hands and jump-turn 90 degrees to the right – then start again.

remove Make-up

Remove make-up with as much care as you took to apply it. Use cotton-wool pads and separate products specially formulated for eyes and face, or try using milk or yoghurt, or olive oil, for removing eye make-up.
■ Start with your eyes, working gently around each one. Close your eyes and work from root to tip to remove mascara. Then use a cleanser (not soap) – or milk – to remove foundation, powder, lipstick and blusher. Rinse with warm (not hot) water and pat dry with a soft towel. Finish with toner.

peel and cut a Mango

A mango is easiest to prepare when it's fully ripe. The skin should yield slightly when pressed gently and it should smell sweet and fruity.

1 Hold the mango horizontally and cut into two lengthwise, just missing the stone. Repeat on the other side, leaving a thin layer of flesh around the stone.

2 Slash the flesh in a lattice, cutting down to, but not through, the peel. Holding the flesh upwards, push the centre of the peel with your thumb, turning it inside out and opening out the cubes of flesh. These can then be easily cut off.

Alternatively, remove the peel with a potato peeler or sharp knife and cut off the flesh in slices until you reach the stone. Cut away any remaining flesh in chunks.

conjure up
Magic tricks
see pages 198-199

read Map contours

A short walk isn't necessarily an easy stroll if it's all uphill. Learn how to interpret map contours to get a measure of the gradient before you set off.

The most commonly used walker's map in Britain is the Ordnance Survey's Explorer series. It shows variations in the height of the ground with brown contour lines, which join together places of the same height above sea level.

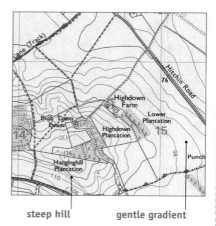

steep hill   gentle gradient

■ Each line indicates a rise or fall of 5m or 10m, depending on the scale of the map.
■ Numbered lines indicate the actual height of the ground. Use these to work out whether the ground is rising or falling with the direction of your route.
■ Tightly packed contour lines indicate a steep hill. If the contour lines are widely spaced, then the climb (or descent) is less steep.
■ The highest number is always at the top of the hill, but the bottom of the hill is rarely at 0m (sea level). To calculate your climb, subtract the starting height from the height at the top.

treat yourself to a French Manicure

A French manicure achieves a natural look by the use of pearly tinted varnish and white-painted tips on carefully tended nails.

YOU WILL NEED **Warm water, towel, cotton wool, nail-polish remover, emery boards, cuticle conditioner, rubber-tipped hoof stick, nail buffer, hand cream, pink or peachy nail polish, white polish, self-adhesive tip guides (optional), clear top-coat polish**

1 If your nails are already painted, remove all polish, paying particular attention to cuticles. Wash and dry your hands.

2 Shape nails with the emery board, using the fine side at a 45 degree angle, working from the outer corners to the centre. Aim for smooth, rounded tips or a slightly square finish, if you prefer. Smooth rough edges with light downward strokes on the top layer of each nail and upward strokes on the bottom layer.

3 Gently work cuticle cream into the base of each nail. Using the rubber-tipped stick, loosen the skin around each nail bed, then immerse hands in warm water for a few minutes before drying them. Use your stick to ease the cuticles back, working from the centre out.

4 Use a buffer to buff your nails, working in one direction only.

5 Apply a light hand cream that will soak in quickly to smooth hands.

6 Apply a base coat of the coloured polish to each nail, let it dry and apply a top coat. *See also* NAILS.

7 Use tip guides or work freehand to apply white polish. The length of the tips will depend on the length of your nails, but keep them uniform.

8 Once the tips are dry, finish off with a top coat of hard-wearing, clear varnish to protect the tips from chipping.

get started on Marathon training

To run a marathon, you must first be able to tackle a half-marathon. The key to success is to run regularly: training with friends or a running club can make it more enjoyable and give you commitments to stick to. Build your stamina with one long run a week, and shorter or less strenuous sessions in between, plus some gym-based strength and conditioning sessions and one full rest day. *See also* AEROBIC EXCERCISE *and* RUNNING ROUTINE.

Training programme for beginners The programme below will take you from a standing start to your first half-marathon in 21 weeks.

Week	TUESDAY	THURSDAY	FRIDAY	SUNDAY
1	5 mile walk		20 min jog	5 mile walk
2	10 min jog		20 min jog	10 min jog
3	20 min jog		20 min jog	20 min jog
4	10 min jog		25 min jog	30 min jog
5	25 min jog		25 min jog	30 min jog
6	30 min jog		30 min jog	40 min jog
7	35 min jog		35 min jog	45 min jog
8	50 min jog		50 min jog	60 min jog
9	50 min jog		50 min jog	60 min jog
10	60 min jog		60 min jog	70 min jog
11	60 min jog	5 mile jog	70 min jog	70 min jog
12	60 min jog	5 mile jog	70 min jog	70 min jog
13	5 mile run	6 mile jog	70 min jog	60 min run on grass
14	5 mile run	6 mile jog	70 min jog	60 min run on grass
15	60 min run	6 mile run	5 mile run	60 min run
16	60 min run	6 mile run	5 mile run	70 min run
17	60 min run	7 mile run	60 min run	85 min run
18	60 min run	7 mile run	60 min run	85 min run
19	60 min run, 10 min hard	60 min run, 10 min hard	6 mile easy	95 min run
20	60 min run, 10 min hard	60 min run, 10 min hard	6 mile easy	6 miles with friends
21	6 mile jog	3 mile jog	3 mile jog	**HALF-MARATHON DAY**

What next? Allow a few weeks to recover but don't stop running or you'll lose your hard-won fitness. Go out three or four times a week and run for at least an hour, increasing your distance week by week. Use a cross-trainer or go swimming once a week to minimise wear on your joints. It's important to build in 'fartlek' ('speed play' in Swedish) sessions, where you run hard for short bursts as part of a longer run. Your local running club will offer advice and support if you want to work towards the full marathon.

clean Marble

Because marble is porous, it needs care and gentle treatment. Always wipe away any spills immediately, then rinse and dry thoroughly. Never apply abrasive cleaners, ammonia or any acid, such as vinegar. It also marks easily, so seal the surface annually with stone sealer, available online.

General cleaning Mix about 2 tbsp of mild liquid soap in 2 litres of water and apply with a soft sponge or sponge mop. Rinse, then dry with a soft cloth.

Surface stains Use a marble polishing powder such as tin oxide, available from DIY stores. If the item isn't valuable, try applying a thick paste of baking soda and water, leave for 10-15 minutes then rinse off with warm water and dry.

play Marbles

There are countless marble-based games. This one is known as 'ringer'.

■ First, draw a ring on the ground, about 3m across. Arrange 13 equally sized marbles in a cross at the centre of the ring, leaving about 10cm between each marble.
■ Two to six players, positioned at the edge of the ring, take turns to try to knock marbles out the circle using a 'shooter' marble. A point is awarded for each marble knocked out of the ring and players can keep point-scoring marbles. A player's turn ends when they fail to knock a marble out of the ring or if their own shooter is knocked out of the ring.
■ The player with the highest score when the last marble is knocked out wins.

M

conjure up Magic tricks

It's amazing how impressive a simple magic trick can be. With a little knowledge and a few hours of practice, you can astonish and impress your family and friends.

Tricks of the trade **You must rehearse until your routine is smooth and fault-free. And you need to develop a good patter: many tricks depend on distracting the audience – so you must be able to chat and joke as you perform. Here are some magic tricks that are easy to learn, and require no specialised props.**

PICK A CARD

Here's a classic find-the-card trick. You'll need an elastic band.

1 Shuffle a deck of cards and ask a volunteer to take one and show it to the audience. Turn your back to assure them you can't see it.

2 While your back is to the audience, turn the pack of cards face up, and turn the top card over and place it face down on the pack.

3 Turn back to the audience, and showily wrap the elastic band round the pack widthways. With the pack in your left hand, ask the volunteer to push their card face down into the pack.

4 Now the sleight of hand: pass the pack from your left hand to your right, left palm down. Now pass it back to your left hand. Ask the volunteer to twang the elastic 'to release the magic'.

5 Remove the band and fan the cards out (but don't let the audience look too closely). The volunteer's card will be face up in the middle of the pack – allowing you to name it with a triumphant flourish.

MIND READING

Ask a volunteer to do the following calculation in their head, so that you zero in on their brainwaves.

'Pick a number between one and ten ... multiply it by nine ... if it's a two-digit number add them together ... subtract five.'

Now say, 'Pick the letter of the alphabet that corresponds to that letter, whatever it may be: A for 1, B for 2, and so on ...'

'Now think of a country that begins with that letter. Think of an animal that begins with the second letter of that country. Think of the colour of that animal.'

Now say, 'That's odd: I'm getting a vision of a grey elephant in Denmark!' Nine times out of ten you'll be right, because the answer to the calculation is always four, Denmark is the obvious country beginning with D, and an elephant the obvious animal beginning with E – but they don't know that.

THE OBEDIENT WAND

A great trick to do early in your set, this will establish your magical credentials.

The audience sees that your wand wondrously sticks to the palm of your hand though you aren't holding onto it. They don't see that the wand is held in place by a pencil that you're holding in your other hand. You could try tucking the pencil into the band of your wristwatch, but you'll have to practise hiding it at the end of the trick.

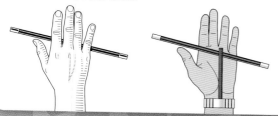

THE MYSTIC BANANA

This trick is simply a matter of advance preparation.

Take a banana and insert a needle through the skin near the top. Twist the needle from side to side, keeping it level, so as to neatly slice the banana. Repeat down the length of the banana. The pinholes will be barely visible. During your performance take a knife, and mime chopping the banana – without the knife ever touching the fruit. Now unpeel the banana. The pieces of fruit will fall out, as if chopped by magic inside the skin.

THE DISAPPEARING COIN

The ability to palm a coin is crucial to the magician's art, and the only trick to it is lots of practice.

1 Hold a small coin between the thumb, index and middle fingers of your right hand.

2 Pretend to take it into your left hand, but instead push it into the palm of your right hand, wedging it into the folds of skin, and slightly cupping your palm if necessary (it's hard to make this look natural: use a mirror to see how it looks from the audience's point of view).

3 Keep it there until you're ready to make it 'reappear' in an unexpected place – behind someone's ear, for example. Look surprised when you find it there.

THE INDESTRUCTIBLE SHOELACE

In this trick you clearly cut a shoelace in half, but somehow it remains in one piece.

1 You need one whole shoelace, and a 5cm length of an identical shoelace.

2 Make a loop of the short piece, and conceal it behind the fingers of your left hand. Pick up the long lace in such a way that the two ends dangle down. The loop of the long lace should remain concealed behind your fingers, but unnoticed you move the short loop into view, so that it appears to be part of the long lace.

3 Cut the little loop repeatedly, tossing the pieces aside, until all you have left in your hand is the long lace. Take one end and triumphantly pull it through your fingers to show that it's whole.

create a flavour-packed
Marinade

The aim of marinating is to tenderise and add flavour to meat and fish. It's particularly useful for some of the otherwise tough, cheaper cuts of meat.

Marinades must include acid ingredients (wine, lemon juice or vinegar), herbs or spices and oil, plus vegetables, such as onions and garlic. Yoghurt or crème fraîche can also be used, particularly in Indian tikka dishes (*see* CURRY). A marinade will help to keep chunks of kebab meat tender (*see* KEBABS).

When marinating red meat, use red wine and red wine vinegar with a bouquet garni of parsely, rosemary, thyme and a bay leaf. Leave in the fridge for up to three days, turning from time to time.

Drain and pat the food dry before cooking or it won't brown. Save the marinade, though, for basting or for adding to a sauce.

White wine marinade for chicken or fish

MAKES ABOUT 250ml

1 small onion, sliced
1 small carrot, diced
½ stalk celery, sliced
1 clove of garlic, crushed (optional)
50ml olive oil
50ml dry white wine
125ml white wine vinegar
juice of 2 lemons or 4 limes
bouquet garni of parsley, rosemary and thyme
6 whole peppercorns

Mix all the ingredients well and pour over the chicken or fish. Cover and leave in the fridge for at least 30 minutes before cooking but no longer than 24 hours.

serve up classic breakfast Marmalade

Marmalade can be made from most citrus fruits, alone or mixed, but bitter Seville oranges give the best flavour to this classic orange preserve. They have only a short season: look for them in late winter.

YOU WILL NEED **Oranges (or other citrus fruit), stiff brush for scrubbing fruit, tea towel, small sharp knife, citrus squeezer, bowl, muslin, string, preserving pan or large saucepan, sieve, skimming spoon, sterilised jars and lids, labels. Optional: potato peeler, sugar thermometer**

Chunky Seville orange marmalade

MAKES ABOUT 10 X 500g JARS

1.5kg Seville or bitter oranges
juice of 2 lemons
3.5 litres water
3kg preserving (jam) sugar

1 Remove any stalk ends from the oranges, scrub and dry in the tea towel. Peel off the rind using a sharp knife or potato peeler, avoiding the pith. Cut into strips, as chunky as you like your marmalade, and set aside. Halve and squeeze the oranges, saving the pips, then remove any pith and bundle it, with the pips, in a square of muslin tied with string.

2 Cut the squeezed orange flesh into small chunks and put into the preserving pan with the peel and the muslin bundle. Strain the orange juice into the pan and add the strained lemon juice and water. Bring to the boil and simmer, uncovered, for about 2 hours or until the peel is soft and the pan contents reduced by about half. Remove the muslin bag and let it cool a little while you add the sugar, stirring constantly over a low heat until it has dissolved.

3 Squeeze the jelly-like juices from the muslin bag into the pan – these are high in pectin and will help the marmalade to set. Turn up the heat and boil hard until the mixture reaches setting point and wrinkles when tested on a cool saucer (*see* JAM) or registers 103°C on the sugar thermometer. Skim, leave to stand for 30 minutes then pot in prepared jars (*see* JAM). The rind will float if you pot it too hot. When cool, seal the lids, label the jars and store them in a cool, dry place.

guarantee lump-free Mashed potato

For smooth and fluffy mash, select floury main crop potatoes such as Desiree or Maris Piper. Boil in lightly salted water for 15-20 minutes until just tender and drain. Then:

By hand Add a little milk (warm is best, but cold will do) and a knob of butter. Mash thoroughly until all lumps have gone, moving the mixture from the sides to the centre of the pan as you work.

Potato ricer or food mill Press the cooked potatoes through the sieve or mill and return to the pan with a little milk and a knob of butter.

After mashing, adjust seasoning, and warm through for just long enough to remove any excess moisture if necessary. Add further seasonings or other ingredients to taste, such as mustard, grated cheese or even pesto.

---

give a neck and shoulder Massage

You don't need special training or equipment to give someone this wonderfully relaxing treatment in your own home. Choose a warm, quiet room with soft lighting, and even add some soothing music.

1 Ask the person you want to massage to lie face down, on a firm, comfortable surface with a pillow under their chest. Pour a little massage oil such as sweet almond (check for any nut allergies first) into your palm and rub your hands together to warm it. Spread the oil smoothly and evenly over the shoulders and neck.

 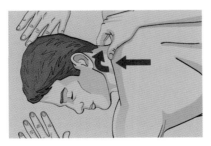

2 Squeeze and knead the shoulders, moving from the outside towards the neck. Do this for 5-10 minutes, working harder as you feel the muscles relax. Ask how it feels from time to time to see how much pressure the person wants.

3 Move to the base of the neck, making small circular motions with your right thumb on the left side, for 3-4 minutes, gradually increasing the pressure. Repeat with the left thumb on the right side of the neck.

4 With your hands on the shoulders, use both thumbs and the same small circular motions across the base of the neck. Work your thumbs up the sides of the neck. Perform this sequence a few times, easing up on the pressure towards the end.

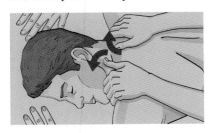

make and use Marzipan

Marzipan, usually covered with icing, is a traditional topping to a rich fruit cake such as a Christmas or wedding cake. It can also be moulded into spheres or fruit shapes, which can be tinted with food colouring, dipped in chocolate or both. *See also* CAKE.

FOR TOP AND SIDES OF 18cm CAKE

**100g icing sugar, sifted, plus extra for rolling
100g caster sugar
225g ground almonds
1 tsp lemon juice
few drops almond essence
1 egg, beaten**

1 Put the sugars and ground almonds into a bowl and mix. Add lemon juice and almond essence and gradually stir in the beaten egg until the mixture is firm but manageable. Knead gently. Store for up to one week in an airtight tin.

2 To make the marzipan stick to the cake, it's best to apply it over an apricot glaze (see below).

FOR THE GLAZE

**225g apricot jam
½ tbsp lemon juice
2 tbsp water**

1 Bring all the ingredients to the boil, stirring. Rub through a sieve, return to the pan and boil for 2 minutes. Cool. Place your cake on a rack and brush glaze over the top and sides of the cake.

2 Dust the work surface with icing sugar and roll out the marzipan until large enough to cover the top and sides of the cake. Wrap around the rolling pin and unroll it over the cake. Press gently all over, and trim off any excess. If not being covered with icing, the marzipan can be grilled to brown it, though take care as it scorches easily.

give a face Massage

This is a great way to relieve stress, improve facial tone and bring a radiant glow to the complexion. Spend no more than 20 minutes overall and cleanse the face first. Ask the person to lie on their back and stand behind them as you work.

1 Apply a massage oil formulated for the face, with a gliding movement and a deft, light touch. Stroke the face with your fingertips, upwards and outwards towards the temples.

2 Massage along the jaw line with your fingertips.

3 Work on the nose, mouth, forehead and around the eyes. Use a circular motion to massage the temples.

4 Use thumbs and forefingers to give little pinches along the eyebrows. Finish by massaging the neck muscles with firm upward strokes.

send Mattress bed bugs packing

If you wake with an itchy rash or find bloodstains or dark spots of insect fecal waste on the sheet, it could be that a bug has moved into your mattress. A smell of almonds or overripe raspberries is another clue.

■ Once the bugs are in, they mean to stay. There are a number of old wives' remedies and modern gadgets, such as UV hand wands, that claim to shift them, but the best way to do it yourself is to steam-clean the bed and the surrounding room, including skirting boards, where the bugs hide in the day.
■ If steam-cleaning fails, call a professional pest controller.

choose the best Mattress for you

Sit on the edge of your mattress. If it sags, it's time for a new one. No more waking up feeling ragged, and racked with aches and pains.

You get what you pay for Even a good mattress needs replacing after seven to ten years. Cheap ones may be good for just a couple of years.

If you have back trouble, you may be tempted by an 'orthopaedic' mattress, but this simply means a firm one and you need both support and comfort. Too hard a mattress will not be comfortable and a too-soft mattress will not offer enough support. The right mattress will conform to the shape of your body, allowing for the curves of your hips, spine and shoulders.

Little and large Body weight is a major factor in getting the right firmness. If you're an 8 stone woman married to a bodybuilder, choose a combination mattress with a softer side for you, and firmer side for him. Zip-together single mattresses are another option. Always go together to choose.

If your bed mate is a fidget, avoid 'continuous coil' mattresses, in which a single looped wire moves as one, with a trampoline effect. Choose an open-coil mattress, made from single springs wired together, or, better yet, a pocket-sprung mattress, with individual springs, each supporting a small part of the sleeper.

If you have painful joints, a memory-foam mattress may help. The foam is affected by room temperature, body heat and pressure, so the mattress can feel cold and hard when you first get into bed. As it warms, it softens and moulds to your body shape, which feels cosy but may inhibit movement.

If you suffer allergies, a hypoallergenic pure foam or latex mattress is a wise choice.

Try before you buy Take off your coat and shoes and lie down in your normal sleeping position for at least ten minutes. On your back, you should be able to slide your hand under the small of your back. If there's a large gap, the mattress is too hard. If there's no gap it's too soft. When trying a memory mattress, lie still for a few minutes then see if you can move freely.

See also SLEEP.

convert Measurements

Thanks to the pocket calculator, you don't have to be a latter-day Einstein to convert metric and imperial or other measures – you just need to employ these basic formulas. Enter the original value and multiply by the appropriate conversion factor.

LENGTH AND AREA		
FROM	TO	MULTIPLY
inches	mm	25.4
mm	inches	0.0394
inches	cm	2.54
cm	inches	0.3937
feet	metres	0.3048
metres	feet	3.2808
yards	metres	0.9144
metres	yards	1.0936
miles	km	1.6093
km	miles	0.6214
sq inches	cm²	6.4516
cm²	sq inches	0.155
sq feet	m²	0.0929
m²	sq feet	10.7639
sq yards	m²	0.8361
m²	sq yards	1.196
sq miles	km²	2.5899
km²	sq miles	0.3861
acres	hectares	0.4047
hectares	acres	2.471

VOLUMES		
FROM	TO	MULTIPLY
pints	litres	0.5682
US pints	litres	0.4731
litres	pints	1.7598
litres	US pints	2.114
gallons	litres	4.546
US gallons	litres	3.785
litres	gallons	0.22
litres	US gallons	0.2642
fl oz	litres	0.0284
litres	fl oz	35.195

WEIGHTS		
FROM	TO	MULTIPLY
ounces	grammes	28.3495
grammes	ounces	0.0352
pounds	grammes	453.6
grammes	pounds	0.0022
pounds	kg	0.4536
kg	pounds	2.2046

Temperature conversion
- Fahrenheit to Celsius: subtract 32, then divide by 1.8.
- Celsius to Fahrenheit: multiply by 1.8, then add 32.

In the kitchen Most recipes use round measurements, rendering 1oz as 25g and 4oz as 110g, for example, rather than the exact mathematical conversion. This approximation is close enough for recipes to work, but always choose to use either the metric or imperial quantities, and not a mixture of the two in one dish.
- Be aware of transatlantic differences: 'pint-sized' might mean an imperial pint (a little more than half a litre) or a US pint (a little less than half a litre). US recipes may call for a 'stick' of butter: this is 110g. Or they may measure ingredients by volume (cups) rather than weight. One cup of flour is 150g; white sugar is 225g and brown sugar 175g; one cup of uncooked rice weighs 200g; and butter, 225g.

mix your own Mayonnaise

Homemade mayonnaise is far nicer than anything out of a jar. It's easy to make and you can add your own flavours. A light olive oil is the best base, or you can use a mixture of vegetable oils. Extra virgin oil gives a really strong flavour.

MAKES 300ml
2 egg yolks or 1 whole egg
½ tsp Dijon mustard
½ tsp salt
300ml olive oil
1-2 tbsp white wine vinegar
or lemon juice

By hand Beat egg yolks, mustard and salt in a bowl using a whisk or electric beater. Add half the oil, drop by drop, beating continuously until the mixture begins to thicken. Add the vinegar or lemon juice, then drizzle in the remaining oil, still beating all the time.

In a blender Blend yolks or whole egg with mustard, salt and vinegar or lemon juice for a few seconds. With the motor running, add the oil, first drop by drop then in a steady stream.

Rescuing curdled mayonnaise
If the mixture begins to separate add a tablespoon of warm water. Or start again with one egg yolk and gradually add the curdled mixture.

Adding flavours Spice up a basic mayonnaise by adding finely chopped garlic or herbs – basil, chives, dill, parsley, tarragon and thyme are all good on their own or as a mixture. Try using a tablespoon of Dijon mustard and the same of honey, or make a paste of sundried tomatoes and garlic in a blender and stir into the finished mayonnaise.

learn to Meditate

Regular meditation is deeply relaxing and restorative, with a multitude of health benefits for both body and mind.

Don't try to meditate too soon after eating or drinking. Set aside a quiet space for your meditation practice.

1 Sit comfortably, upright on a supportive chair, and rest your hands, palms down, on your lap. Some people choose to lie down with their eyes closed, but this can induce sleep.

2 Clear your mind of 'chatter'. To do so you might fix on one calmly pleasing thought, or repeat to yourself over and over, in your head, some meaningless syllable (what some would call a mantra). Alternatively, focus on your breathing: count the breaths in and out, taking as long to exhale as to inhale, expelling all the air.

3 Thoughts and worries will steal in. Acknowledge that they have come and just bat them away like balloons, airy notions.

4 Try imagining that you're in a place of great beauty and peace. Hear the splashing of a stream and the breeze in the trees; smell the roses; transport yourself mentally away from your actual domestic surroundings.

5 After about 20 minutes, come back into yourself. Shuffle in your chair. Flex your muscles. Get up slowly. Don't spring to your feet. Meditation can lower blood pressure, so you may feel dizzy if you stand too quickly.

chair a Meeting effectively

Keep it small Only invite people who are directly involved with the subject to be discussed.

Circulate an agenda beforehand Summarise at the beginning of the meeting what is to be discussed and what you aim to achieve. Then work through the agenda point by point.

Stay on track Your task as chair is to channel the flow of ideas. Don't allow the discussion to deviate. If there are six points on the agenda, and you have scheduled an hour, insist that the discussion moves on to a new point every 10 minutes.

Minute the discussion Appoint someone else to take notes – you cannot both chair and take minutes

effectively. Make sure all action points are minuted, and assign someone to take on each task.

Make it brief The longer the meeting, the less productive it becomes. Don't aim to tackle too much at once. Better to have a follow-up meeting at a later date.

Timing is everything Try to avoid organising meetings for first thing in the morning, when people are most busy, or late afternoon, when energy levels have flagged.

Outlaw monologues No one person should be allowed to dominate proceedings – especially not you. Make sure everyone has their say.

See also MINUTES.

improve your Memory

There are tricks – known as mnemonics – that use verse, phrases and acronyms to assist mental recall. These are useful props, but there are much simpler things you can do to really boost the power of your memory.

Stretch your brain Tackle a new skill. Take a course in a subject about which you know little but that fascinates you. Perhaps learn a new language.

Stretch your legs Research among older adults has shown that walking 6-9 miles a week reduces the risk of memory loss.

Practise neurobics New routines activate new brain circuitry. If you're right-handed, try doing things with your left. Eat with your eyes closed. Take a new route to work. Go to new shops.

Cut down or cut out alcohol The old saying 'I drink to forget' is all too true.

Feed the grey matter A diet rich in nutrients will boost brain function. Eat plenty of fresh fruit, vegetables and whole grains. Increase your intake of omega-3 fatty acids, found in oily fish, such as herrings and mackerel, walnut and flaxseed oils.

Sleep on it Many studies have shown that taking a daytime nap after studying speeds up long-term memory consolidation. In one experiment, two groups of participants were asked to learn a task. One group then stayed awake, while the other took a 90 minute nap. The group that were allowed to sleep showed a significant improvement in their task performance by the evening.

make wafer-thin Melba toast

This makes a sophisticated accompaniment to pâtés of all kinds, or soup. It's also a good way of using thick or medium slices of stale white bread that you might otherwise throw away.

Toast slices lightly in a toaster or under the grill, cut off the crusts and use a sharp thin knife to cut each in half horizontally into two very thin slices. Toast uncooked sides under the grill until crisp and curly. Alternatively, cut crusts from wafer-thin slices of bread and bake in the oven at 180°C/gas 4 until evenly brown. Once cool, you can store the slices in an airtight container.

whip up the perfect Meringue

Absolute cleanliness of equipment and scrupulous care when you separate your eggs are the keys to making perfect meringues.

MAKES 20 MERINGUE SHELLS

3 egg whites
150g caster sugar, plus extra
**   for sprinkling**

1 Heat the oven to 110°C/gas ¼. Whisk the egg whites until stiff in a large, grease-free copper, stainless steel, glass or china bowl. You can do this with a hand whisk, but it will be quicker with an electric model. Gradually blend in half the sugar, whisking well after each addition then fold in the remaining sugar, using a clean, metal spoon.

2 Spoon or pipe the glossy mixture onto a baking tray lined with baking parchment, sprinkle lightly with caster sugar and bake for 2½-3 hours or until crisp. When cooled, store the shells in an airtight tin, ideally in a warm place such as an airing cupboard. For serving, they can be sandwiched together with whipped cream, which can be flavoured with vanilla and sugar if you wish.

Bake immediately after mixing or meringues may 'weep' a watery syrup. Don't be tempted to raise the oven temperature to speed up baking – this is another common cause of 'weeping'. To make more room for filling, press the base of each shell lightly with your finger halfway through cooking.

spot the signs of Meningitis

The onset of meningitis is usually sudden. If in any doubt or if any of the symptoms below are accompanied by a fever, call for an ambulance.

Symptoms

Meningitis is most common in children, but can strike an any age. Early symptoms can be similar to those for flu, and include:
- cold hands and feet
- limb pains or neck stiffness
- pallor
- blotchy skin
- vomiting.

More alarming symptoms may follow, such as:
- severe headache
- stomach cramps
- a blank stare and delirium
- sensitivity to light.

The glass test The most serious form of meningitis may be accompanied by a tell-tale rash of red or brown pinpricks on the limbs, which may develop into red or purple blotches or blood blisters.

If you press the side of a glass to the rash and it doesn't fade, call for emergency help. If someone is feeling seriously unwell, don't wait to see whether a rash develops before calling for an ambulance.

find treasure with a
Metal detector

Be legal Make sure you know the law regarding metal-detecting wherever you happen to be. The Treasure Act means that you cannot necessarily keep what you find, and in some places you need a permit even to search. Be careful, too, not to trespass on private property. The National Council for Metal Detecting is a good source of advice.

Develop a technique Long slow sweeps close to the ground yield the best results. Practise covering the ground methodically.

Pick your spot Focus on areas where there's known to have been human activity in the past: a beach or the site of a forgotten village is more likely to yield treasure – or at least something of interest – than a bare mountain-top.

Stay safe If you discover anything that looks like live ammunition or an unexploded bomb, stop digging or searching, mark the site carefully, and inform the police.

get rid of Mice

Mice breed rapidly. If you see any sign of infestation – such as rod-shaped droppings about 4mm long – you must act as soon as possible.

- Clean scrupulously in your kitchen. Leave no food out, and seal waste bins.
- Seal cracks or holes in walls and skirting with steel wool, which mice cannot chew through.
- Set traps around the perimeter of the room, baited side facing the wall. For bait, use small pieces of bacon or offal (not the traditional cheese).

treat and prevent a Migraine

Every migraine sufferer has their own particular symptoms and tried-and-tested relief remedies, often retreating to a quiet, darkened room as a first resort. These tips, though, may also help.

- At the first signs of an aura (flashing lights or zigzags), try sucking barley sugar or eat a spoonful of honey.
- Eat regular, light meals to keep blood sugar levels constant. Keep a food diary to identify potential triggers in your diet.
- Stay active. Although strenuous exercise can bring on migraine, moderate aerobic exercise promotes general well-being and can reduce the frequency and severity of attacks.
- Painkillers can help to nip an attack in the bud, but avoid those containing codeine, which can cause rebound headaches. Painkillers containing caffeine, or even just a strong coffee, may help some sufferers.
- The herb feverfew – available as a supplement from pharmacists – is a much-used headache remedy and some people find that it can help to prevent migraines, though medical studies are inconclusive.
- If you're taking the contraceptive pill, consider trying another brand, as hormone cycles can be linked to migraine. If you experience migraines with an aura, avoid the pill altogether, as this can increase the risk of stroke.

See also HEADACHE.

take the Minutes of a meeting

- Talk to the person chairing the meeting (*see* MEETING) beforehand. Find out the purpose of the meeting, get a copy of the agenda and a list of invitees.
- During the meeting, don't try to take down every remark. Concentrate on actions to be taken (noting who they are assigned to), and write down any decisions that are made. These two categories – actions and decisions – should form the bulk of your minutes.
- Show a draft of your finished document to the chair of the meeting before circulating it to the invitees and any other relevant people.

clean a Mirror for a clear view

Don't just treat your mirror like a pane of glass. A shop-bought glass cleaner, squirted liberally onto the mirror, can seep around the edges and affect the backing, oxidising the silver and making it black, brittle and flaky. It can also damage the frame. Spray cleaning fluids onto a lint-free cloth and use this to clean and polish the surface, or try these household tips.

- Use a chamois leather, dipped in a solution of 1 tbsp white vinegar in 2.5 litres of warm water and squeezed out.
- If hairspray has become caked onto the mirror, wipe it off with a little surgical spirit on a soft cloth.
- Avoid scratchy abrasive cleaners and acidic ones that can damage the reflective backing.

hang a Mirror

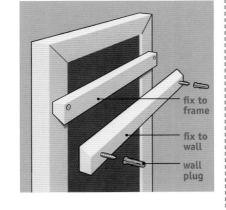

Large framed mirrors are heavy and should be hung on battens. Make an interlocking batten from a length of wood approximately 5cm x 2cm and slightly shorter than the width of the mirror. Cut along its length at an angle, as shown (right). Fix one part of the batten to the wall and the other to the back of the mirror so that they slot together when the mirror is hung.

fix to frame
fix to wall
wall plug

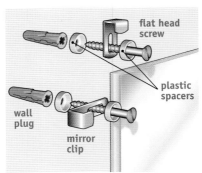

flat head screw
plastic spacers
wall plug
mirror clip

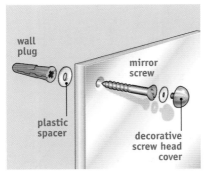

wall plug
mirror screw
plastic spacer
decorative screw head cover

Sliding mirror clips are used for frameless mirrors. Use fixed clips at the bottom and then two sliding clips at the top, and at the side, too, for large mirrors. Position clips so the screws are hidden and they can slide in and out for fitting or removing the mirror.

Use mirror screws to hang a mirror with screw holes. Use plastic spacers between the back of the mirror and the wall to allow air to circulate and avoid cracking the mirror as you tighten the screws. Don't attempt to drill holes in a mirror yourself: this is a job for a glazier.

back up your Mobile phone contacts

If you're afraid of losing your phone, and all your contacts with it, consider uploading them to the internet for safekeeping. Various companies provide this service. If you have an iPhone, you can easily transfer all your contacts to your own computer when you 'sync', and you can install similar software to do the same with other phones. To transfer contacts to another phone, copy them to your SIM card: your phone's removable memory. Check your phone's manual or online help file to find out how. When you put your SIM in your new phone, your contacts will be stored there. If your SIM memory is not big enough, upload your contacts to the internet as described above, then download to your new phone.

dry out a soaked Mobile phone

- If you drop your mobile in water, fish it out as quickly as possible. Remove the battery and the SIM card straight away.
- Shake the phone to get as much off the water out of its workings as possible, and dab it with paper towels to absorb even more.
- Place your phone in a bowl of uncooked rice. Leave it for three days: the rice will draw out the moisture from inside the phone.

If the phone still doesn't work then it's probably damaged beyond repair. But your phone dealer should still be able to retrieve the data on your SIM card if you don't have your contacts backed up (see above).

keep Money safe when you travel

Don't have all your money, cards and ID in one place.

Do take out only as much cash as you need for the day, and spread it around your person: in a money belt, a neck pouch inside your clothes, in hard-to-access pockets.

Don't flash your wallet around, especially in busy places.

Do carry your wallet or purse in the front pocket of your trousers: it's almost impossible for a pickpocket to steal it from there.

Do leave the rest of your cash at your hotel in a safebox. If there's no safe, lock your cash in a suitcase.

win at Monopoly

It's partly a game of chance. But there are winning strategies.

■ Buy as much property as you can early on. You're then in a strong position to trade for a complete set of three properties.

■ Aim to get the orange properties: they're cheap to build on (just £100 per house), and so provide a high return. Moreover, their position on the board, on the run after 'Jail', means that they have a high probability of being visited. The red properties are also good, but avoid green, yellow or blue: the odds are against your getting rich with them.

■ When you build, stop at four houses: converting to hotels doesn't bring that much additional revenue. More importantly, it's good tactics to create a housing shortage so that your opponents cannot build on their properties little by little. If you're pulling in the rent while preventing your opponents from doing the same, then sooner or later you'll win.

read and send Morse code

Morse code is a method of transmitting messages using sound or a flashing light. It's a useful way of communicating over long distances, or when face-to-face communication is impossible.

Letters of the alphabet

Morse provides a means of representing each letter of the alphabet using combinations of dots (short bursts of light or sound) or dashes (longer bursts, equivalent to three dots). The sender spells out the message letter by letter, leaving an interval the length of one dash between letters, two dashes between words. To write or read Morse fluently takes time and practice, and there's no shortcut to mastering it. In the days when Morse was widely used in wireless telegraphy and by ships at sea there were many skilled operators. Knowledge of Morse code is now rare – but it's still worth everyone's while to know the Morse distress signal, which is the three letters SOS – or dot-dot-dot, dash-dash-dash, dot-dot-dot.

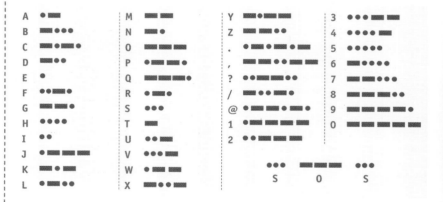

make a beautiful Mosaic

Specialist craft shops or internet sites sell all the basic materials needed for making mosaics, but you can also use your own collections of stones, shells or even pieces of broken pottery.

YOU WILL NEED **Pencil, squared paper, safety goggles, tiles (or other material suchh as broken-up plates), tile cutter, PVA glue or tile adhesive, tweezers, plywood backing cut to size, cement-based grouting, rubber scraper or palette knife, strips of wood, masking tape, brown parcel paper, water soluble paste or wallpaper paste, brush, heavy books, stiff-bristled brush**

Direct method – for simple geometric designs

Draw your design on squared paper. Put on safety goggles and cut tiles to shape and size, coat with adhesive and use tweezers to place pieces in position on the plywood. Leave to dry. Apply grouting with the scraper or palette knife. Allow to dry overnight. Scrape off any excess. Trim backing.

Indirect method – for building a picture

1 Draw your design, and tape wood strips around the edge. Arrange unglued pieces in place, cutting them as you go, beginning with the shape outline. Apply paste to the parcel paper and lay it over the mosaic, taking care not to move the pieces. Leave to dry, loosen the tape, then turn the mosaic over.

Stick parcel paper over finished design.

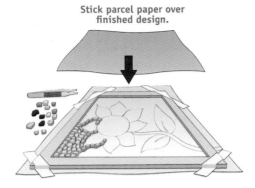

Apply plywood to back of mosaic.

Peel back paper to reveal design.

2 Apply PVA glue to the plywood backing and place over back of mosaic. Weight with books and leave to dry.

3 Moisten the parcel paper and peel off. Grout as for direct method and grout a second time if necessary.

keep Mosquitoes at bay

■ Mosquitoes are attracted by the carbon dioxide in human breath, but also by floral fragrances in perfumes and toiletry products. Avoid fragrant lotions to reduce your chance of being bitten.

■ If mosquitoes trouble you in your home, eliminate all pools of stagnant or dirty water. Be sure to change the water in fountains or birdbaths. Empty buckets, plant pots and wheelbarrows of accumulated rainwater. Drain any puddles that form on patios or lawns. Remember that even a pet's drinking bowl can become a breeding ground for mosquitoes.

■ Citronella oil, the active ingredient in most 'natural' mosquito repellents, can work for a hour or two when applied to the skin. However, citronella candles, often used outdoors in the evening, are no more effective against mosquitoes than ordinary candles: it seems the flame acts as a decoy source of warmth and light.

■ By far the most effective 'topical' repellents are those containing the chemical DEET. A repellent with a DEET concentration of 35 per cent is adequate for most situations, but travellers in countries where malaria is endemic should use a more concentrated formula.

deal with
Mosquito bites

In parts of Africa, Asia and South America a 'bite' from one of these parasitic blood-suckers can cause malaria. In temperate regions, itchy lumps, and possibly blisters and inflammation, are usually as bad as it gets.

■ Don't scratch! It can make the bite more itchy and swollen and cause secondary infection.
■ Wash the bitten area with soap and water.
■ Apply a cold compress, such as a bag of ice or even frozen peas wrapped in a cloth, to reduce swelling. Don't apply ice directly to the skin.
■ Soothe the itch. Calamine lotion, ibuprofen gel or antihistamine cream can bring relief and reduce the likelihood of infection and swelling – but don't use them on broken skin. Alternatively a paste of baking soda and witch hazel is a trusted natural remedy.
■ Watch for an allergic reaction (*see* ALLERGIC EMERGENCY).
■ Mosquitoes are at their busiest from 2 hours before dusk and again at dawn – so go indoors before the sun goes down and don't venture out too early without protection.

avoid Moths

Regular cleaning of clothes is the best way of avoiding moths but far from foolproof. Sweat, hair oil and food attract moths and make attack more likely. Wool and cashmere are most vulnerable, but moth larvae will munch on cotton and even heavily stained synthetics.

Clothes
■ Never put clothes away dirty.
■ Store valuable items such as cashmere sweaters in plastic storage bags all year. Do the same for clothes you're storing for a season.
■ Shop-bought moth-killer strips work better as a deterrent than mothballs and are odour-free. Cedar balls can work well, too. Sprays are also available for treating the inside of wardrobes and drawers.

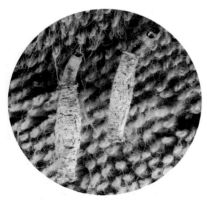

clothes moth larvae magnified

Carpets and furniture
■ Shampoo or clean items regularly.
■ Purpose-made chemical sprays are available but must be applied following the manufacturer's specific instructions.
■ Carpet areas that get least traffic need most attention.
■ If buying secondhand carpets, look for the tell-tale white threads left by moth larvae.

drive safely on a Motorway

Smart driving on the motorway
■ Leave 2 seconds' worth of space between you and the driver in front. Use a marker such as a bridge (see right) or a tree to help you to measure the space – count the time between the car in front passing it and you passing it.
■ Keep to the inside lane unless you're overtaking.
■ Observe the speed limit.
■ Indicate whenever you want to change lanes.
■ Take particular care when passing large vehicles (see also DRIVE).

If you break down
■ Get your car as far over onto the hard shoulder as you can, switch on your hazard lights, then exit the car by the door nearest the verge.
■ Use a motorway emergency phone, not your mobile, to call for help. This makes it easy to locate you. Regular marker posts indicate the nearest one.

Leave 2 seconds' worth of space between you and the driver in front.

make an authentic Moussaka

Beef can be used in place of lamb in this recipe, to cut down on salt and fat. Modern aubergine varieties aren't bitter, as they once were, so it isn't necessary to salt them before cooking. If you have time, cook and refrigerate the meat in advance, then skim any fat from the surface. Serve with a salad.

SERVES 4-6

3-4 tbsp olive oil
1 large onion, finely chopped
450g lean minced lamb
2 tsp tomato paste
150ml meat or vegetable stock

salt and freshly ground black pepper
4 medium aubergines, thinly sliced
25g butter
25g plain flour
275ml milk
1 egg

1 Heat 1 tbsp oil in a heavy-based pan and gently fry the onion for about 5 minutes. Gradually add the lamb and fry, stirring, until thoroughly sealed. Stir in the tomato paste and stock, season then bring to the boil and simmer for 30 minutes or until the meat is tender and the liquid almost absorbed. Cool and remove any fat if you wish.

2 Lightly brush the aubergines with the remaining oil and grill on both sides until soft and golden brown. Beginning and ending with aubergines, layer them with the meat in a large, lightly greased ovenproof dish.

3 Heat the oven to 180°C/gas 4. Melt the butter over low heat and stir in the flour. Cook for 1 minute then mix in the milk. Season then simmer for 1-2 minutes. Take the pan off the heat and beat in the egg. Spoon over the moussaka and bake in the oven for 35-40 minutes until brown and bubbling.

minimise the stress of Moving home

Moving from one house or flat to another is a notoriously stressful thing to do. To minimise the worry, you should plan well in advance.

Three weeks, or more, before you move
- If you're moving yourself, get boxes and begin packing non-essentials such as books, pictures and ornaments.
- Get at least three quotes for van hire.
- If you're using a removal firm (a far less stressful option), have some firms come round to your house to quote for the job. Be sure to discuss matters such as parking problems and items that will need special handling, such as a piano or aquarium.
- Arrange to have your post redirected to your new address.

A week before you move
- Whether you're using a removal firm or not, pack a box with precious items – jewellery, heirlooms, ornaments – ready to take them with you in your car.
- If you're moving yourself, consider taking out goods-in-transit insurance.

On the day
- Get an early start: it takes longer than you think.
- Make sure all boxes are labelled.
- Speak to the removal man in charge when he arrives and give instructions only to him. Keep the workers supplied with tea and biscuits.
- Pack a small box of essentials, such as a kettle, cups, tea bags and toilet paper, which you can get to immediately once you've moved.
- Phone through all utility meter readings to the relevant companies.

Before you go
- Lock all doors and windows before you hand over the keys.
- Check you have done everything you agreed with the new owners.
- Leave your new address, so that they can forward stray post.

mix up your own Muesli

You can vary muesli ingredients to suit your taste, but a generous base of cereal is always required.

MAKES 8-10 BREAKFAST PORTIONS
50g wheat bran
50g sunflower seeds
125g nuts (such as brazils, toasted hazelnuts, almonds), chopped
225g mixed dried fruit (such as sultanas, apricots, figs), chopped
125g dried banana chips
225g jumbo oats
125g barley flakes
2 tsp ground cinnamon (optional)

Dry fry the bran and sunflower seeds in a large non-stick frying pan for 3-4 minutes until golden and aromatic. Cool, then mix with the remaining ingredients. Store in an airtight container. Serve with milk or yoghurt and, if you wish, fresh fruit such as grated apple, raspberries or banana.

choose and use a Mulch

Mulches are soil coverings that come in two types – biodegradable and non-biodegradable. All help to retain moisture, suppress weeds, protect plant roots from extreme heat and cold, and encourage earthworms and other beneficial soil organisms.

Biodegradable mulches such as leaf mould, mushroom compost or wood chippings also release additional nutrients into the soil as they rot.

Non-biodegradable options include shingle, gravel or pebbles, and plastic or fabric sheets. The latter are good at suppressing weeds and retaining moisture but can be unattractive and, unless you choose a permeable fabric, cut slits or leave gaps, won't let water penetrate.

- Apply mulch from late spring to autumn when the soil is moist and warm. Lay it over an entire bed or border, or around individual plants.
- Lay biodegradable mulches to a thickness of at least 5cm.
- Weed thoroughly before mulching.
- Don't smother small plants.
- Don't pile mulch up the stems of shrubs and other woody plants.

golden rules

MUSHROOM REMINDERS

■ **Never cook a wild mushroom unless you're totally sure you have identified it correctly.**
■ **Remember that mushrooms can produce large amounts of liquid, especially when cooked slowly.**

warm up with
Mulled wine

Sweet and spicy mulled wine is wonderfully reviving on a cold winter's night. The Germans call it Glühwein – *glow wine – a name that couldn't be more apt.*

SERVES 12

4 bottles fruity, dry red wine
6oz granulated sugar
**thinly pared rind of 2 lemons
   and 2 oranges**
juice of 2 oranges
12 cloves
generous grating of nutmeg
2 cinnamon sticks
115ml brandy
thinly sliced lemon

1 Pour the wine into a large pan and add the sugar, citrus peel and juices, and spices. Set over a low heat and stir occasionally until the sugar is dissolved.

2 Remove the pan from the heat and leave it to stand for half an hour to allow the flavours to mingle.

3 Return the pan to a low heat, warm until the liquid is just beginning to steam, thenwwwhe brandy.

4 Strain into a punchbowl, garnish with the slices of lemon and ladle into heatproof glasses.

prepare and cook Mushrooms

Mushrooms are versatile ingredients that can be cooked and served on their own or added to everything from soups to casseroles. As well as cultivated mushrooms, wild varieties such as shiitake and chanterelles are widely available, especially in autumn. Their delicate flavour makes them ideal for serving on toast or as accompaniments to chicken and fish. Dried porcini mushrooms, with their robust flavour, are excellent for risottos (*see* RISOTTO) and meat dishes, and make a useful store cupboard ingredient.

Wipe with a damp cloth to clean If covered with excessive dirt, plunge into cold water then shake. Morels and other mushrooms with deep indentations should be left in water for 5 minutes before cleaning. But don't let other kinds of mushroom soak or they will absorb too much liquid.

Trim the stalks Peel the skins from large field mushrooms. Then quarter, slice or dice as required. Pour boiling water over dried mushrooms, soak for 20 minutes, then strain and dry on kitchen paper. (The flavour-rich soaking liquid can be re-strained through muslin and used in stock or soup.)

Fry in a mixture of oil and butter Add mushrooms to a hot pan and cook over medium heat. As juices appear, turn the heat to high to boil them off quickly. Season well with salt and freshly ground black pepper. Tarragon is also an excellent flavouring, or add lemon juice or a dash of chilli. Or brush with butter and grill for 6-8 minutes, turning once. Stuff large field mushrooms with a breadcrumb-based stuffing or a cheese mixture and grill or bake.

compose a perfect Music compilation

Creating a music mix is fun and absorbing. It allows you to include only favourite tracks and makes a very personal gift.

Use online music stores such as iTunes for digital singles. The choice is almost limitless.

Make a playlist Search for songs by name or title, listen to them and drag those you want into your playlist. This will be a rough 'draft'. Edit it as you go; add to it, drop things, change the running order.

Start with a couple of stunners Draw the listener in.

Vary the pace Follow a soft and dreamy track with something loud and electrifying.

Make it meaningful Choose songs that evoke memories of the day you met, a romantic holiday, that first date – or that show how you feel.

Don't get carried away Anything more than 16-20 tracks, however good the music, will become a slog.

Make the final track count Choose something that stays in the mind. Let it impart something significant to the listener.

When you're thrilled with your mix, burn a disk (*see* CD).

Add finishing touches Create artwork for your CD and give it a title. You can print off artworks on iTunes. Go to the **Advanced** menu and choose **Get Album Artwork**.

master the basics of Music notation

When reading or playing music from the page, there are two things you need to know about every note: what the pitch is (how high or low it is), and how long you should play the note for. Musical notation conveys this information, and much more, using a highly readable and economical system. The short example below is taken from the horn part of J.S. Bach's Mass in B Minor.

The length of a note is signified by the precise shape of the tadpole-like symbols on the page. A black note with a stick-like tail is played for one beat.

A note with a curly hook on its tail (or, when they occur in pairs, with a thick horizontal lid) is played for half a beat.

A note with a doubled tail or lid is played for a quarter of a beat.

The five lines of the stave, and the four gaps between them, represent the notes of the scale. The higher up the stave the note is placed, the higher the note to be played.

Each space or line on the stave is one note up the scale from the one below.

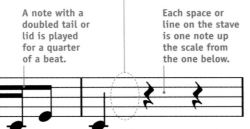

Other symbols represent rests: an instruction to the player to be silent for a set duration such as one beat (a vertical squiggle, right) or half a beat (above, shaped like a curly '7').

The symbols for standard notes and rests are shown in the table opposite. There are many other symbols signifying, for example, how to play rather than what to play – quietly, crisply, running the notes together.

NUMBER OF BEATS	STANDARD NOTATION	REST	NAME
4	o		semibreve
3			dotted minim
2			minim
1			crotchet
½			quaver
¼			semiquaver

grow Mustard and cress

These little plants are so easy to grow. They are great fun for children – and a tasty addition to a salad.

YOU WILL NEED **Plastic tray without drainage holes, kitchen paper, seeds, scissors**

■ Line the tray with kitchen paper and dampen.
■ Sprinkle in the mustard seeds and leave in a light place for three or four days, keeping the paper moist but not sodden. Then add the cress seeds (which germinate faster).
■ Leave until well grown, moistening as necessary. Harvest with scissors.

tackle and cook
Mussels

Hidden within the hinged darkness of a mussel's shell lies a succulent morsel of orange flesh.

To store As soon as you get them home, put mussels into the fridge or a large bucket of cold salted water.

To prepare Scrub with a stiff brush to remove grit, and scrape off any barnacles with a sharp knife. Rinse well. Finally scrape away the strands of the 'beard' emerging from the shell (pictured), plus any seaweed.

To cook Put in a large pan with 1cm water or white wine, plus some chopped parsley and chopped shallots or onions. Cover and cook on high heat, shaking occasionally, for about 5 minutes or until the mussels open. Remove mussels with a slotted spoon. Strain the cooking liquid through a muslin-lined sieve to remove any grit and serve.

golden rules

SPOTTING BAD MUSSELS
■ Discard any mussels with broken shells, or which float when soaked in water.
■ Before cooking, discard any mussel that doesn't close after being prised open a little, or that opens easily.
■ Never eat a mussel that doesn't open once cooked.

paint your Nails

YOU WILL NEED Nail polish remover, cotton wool pads, cotton buds, protective base polish, coloured polish

■ Remove any remnants of polish from the nails. Dip a cotton bud into the polish remover and work around the cuticles.

■ Rest your hands by turn on a firm surface. Work from the little finger in. Apply the base coat in three rotating strokes – centre and to right and left – right to the edges. Wait for it to dry.

■ Roll the enamel bottle between your palms to mix. Paint on a thin layer in three strokes. Be sure the first coat is dry. Apply a second, covering any gaps in the first.

Start your first stroke at the point shown.

Brush back towards the cuticle.

Then brush forward to your nail tip.

Make a parallel stroke to one side, brushing from cuticle to tip.

Apply a third stroke on the other side, again from cuticle to tip.

Once the whole nail is covered, dry, then repeat to apply a second coat.

use the right Nails

You should select the correct nails for the job in hand – and then take care hammering them in.

Use	Nail type
ROUGH CARPENTRY 	**Round wire nails** are best for fixing large pieces of wood together in situations where appearance isn't key. They come in various sizes. Always nail the thinner piece of wood to the thicker one.
JOINERY 	Use **oval wire nails** where you want the nail to be invisible. Align the long axis of the head with the grain of the wood then sink it with a nail punch, and fill the hole. These are good for wood that you might want to paint, such as a piece of furniture.
PLYWOOD OR MDF 	Use **panel pins** for fixing sheet materials to timber frameworks. Panel pins, being small and unobtrusive, are also good for fixing wooden mouldings. You can sink the head with a nail punch and fill the hole.
ROOFING FELT/ WIRE FENCING 	**Clout nails** have large heads that hold pliable materials firmly in place. Use galvanised ones for outdoor jobs.
PLASTERBOARD 	There are special **plasterboard nails** that have jagged shanks and large heads to increase their holding power. Use the ringed (annular) type for plasterboarding ceilings.
BRICKWORK 	**Masonry nails** are specially hardened so that they can penetrate brick. Drive them into the body of the brick, not into the mortar courses between them. The nails may shatter if not struck straight, so wear goggles when using them.

stop Nail-biting

Nibbling your nails is a largely unconscious act. Keep a record of when you do it. This will increase your awareness and interrupt the process. If you find, for instance, that you bite your nails when you're alone, reading, wear gloves before you pick up a book.

Give yourself a weekly manicure Pride in your hands can discourage biting (*see left and* MANICURE).

Keep your fingers busy, with fidget toys, sewing, doodling or worry beads – any handcraft or activity that provides an alternative.

Try a bitter-tasting anti-biting preparation This can be painted onto nails and is available from pharmacists.

change your Name

Under English law, you need not undergo any legal process to change your name. At any time, you can simply choose to be known by a different name (so long as you don't intend to defraud or deceive).

You may sometimes, though, need proof of your name change for administrative reasons – in order to obtain a passport in your new name, for example. The document that attests to your name change is known informally as a 'deed poll'. A deed poll can be obtained via various agencies: search on the internet and you'll find many companies that issue deed polls. Pick one that looks reputable and reliable.

To receive your deed poll, you apply by post or online and pay a small fee. You'll be sent a prepared document that states your old name and your new one. By signing the document in the presence of a witness, you're making a formal commitment to be known only by your new name from then on. You don't have to return the document: it's yours to keep, and is your legal proof of name change.

Inform all relevant organisations of your name change: banks, tax authorities, the DVLA and so on. You should receive a checklist of such organisations with your deed poll document.

remember Names

If you say you have a head like a sieve when it comes to names, consider this: it might be more like a brick wall. Demolish those mental barriers.

Take an interest When you're introduced to someone, study them and want to know more about them.

If you don't quite catch a name, ask to hear it again. If necessary you should ask for the spelling.

Repetition, repetition Say their name back to them, repeat it mentally to yourself and drop it subtly into the conversation.

If you've forgotten a name, apologise and ask to be reminded.

Make associations Think of someone else with the same name. Picture that person. If someone is called Basil, or Rose or Ruby, visualise those things.

On leaving, say goodbye to your new friend by name. Write their name down afterwards.

fold a simple
Napkin

A crisp linen napkin, sharply folded, adds an elegant finishing touch to a dinner table setting.

Pyramid napkin

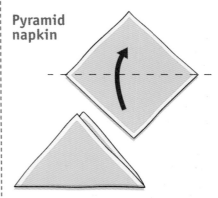

1 Use a spotless starched napkin that will take a shape and stand, not flop. Lay it out in front of you on the diagonal and fold the bottom corner to the top to form a triangle. Smooth the crease.

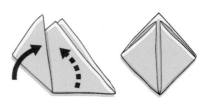

2 Bring the bottom corners up to meet at the top point.

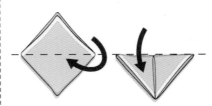

3 Turn the napkin over and fold it in half by bringing the top point of the diamond towards you.

4 Turn the napkin over again, fold along the centre line and stand it on the base of the triangle with the crease facing the diner.

repair a Necklace

It's advisable to have valuable jewellery professionally repaired, but there are some renovations you can do yourself. A broken necklace is best totally restrung (*see* BEAD NECKLACE). Replacement clasps can be obtained from jewellers, bead shops or specialist suppliers.

Untangling Sprinkle a knot with talcum powder, cornflour or vegetable oil to lubricate the links. Then place on a firm surface and use the points of two pins to prise knots apart. Wash in a mild detergent, rinse and dry with a soft cloth.

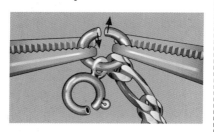

Repairing or replacing a clasp or loop Use a single pair of pliers to close up a gap in a clasp or loop. To replace a clasp, use two pairs of small pliers to twist open the loop attached to the clasp. Remove the old clasp and replace with a new one, then use the pliers to close the loop.

Tightening a V-spring Insert a knife blade between the two parts or 'leaves' of the V-spring and turn it a little to push the leaves apart. Test for fit into the clasp sheath and repeat as necessary.

thread a Needle easily

■ Choose a needle with an eye of appropriate size for the thickness of thread you're planning to use.
■ Hold the thread against a background of contrasting colour.
■ Lick or dampen the end of the thread or apply some hairspray.
■ For thick thread such as wool, tie on a length of thin cotton and thread that through the needle first, pulling the wool through behind it.
■ Use an old-fashioned wire needle-threader. Pass the thin loop of wire through the needle, feed the thread through the loop and pull back through.
■ Buy an automatic threader, which you can usually find online.

start basic Needlepoint

Needlepoint, or tapestry, is stitching worked on canvas. It's versatile and easy to master and can be done almost anywhere.

The mesh of the canvas provides a grid onto which you can stitch differently coloured threads to create a pattern or design. You begin with simple stitches, then add more as you progress. The completed canvas can be incorporated into a cushion or chair cover, or framed as a wall hanging or picture.

YOU WILL NEED Canvas, yarns, round-ended tapestry needle

Patterns, yarns and stitches Canvases can be bought from craft shops or online with pre-printed patterns on them, or you can work from printed charts. Tapestry wool, viscose, cotton and silk are all suitable yarns for needlepoint, and should match the size of the canvas holes (its gauge). Yarn should be thick enough to cover the canvas when stitches are formed, but slip easily through the holes without distorting the canvas or scuffing the yarn. Cross-stitch (*see* CROSS-STITCH) and tent stitch are the most common needlepoint stitches.

Continental tent stitch

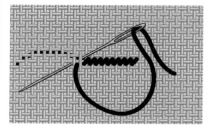

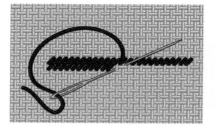

1 Pull the needle through the canvas to the right side, leaving 5-6cm of yarn at the back. Work the first row from right to left as shown, catching in the tail of yarn with the first few stitches.

2 Add the next row of stitches below the first one, working from left to right as shown. Continue working alternately from right to left and then from left to right.

Basketweave tent stitch

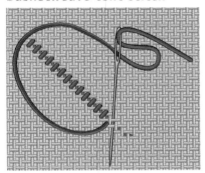

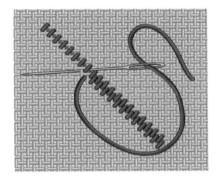

1 Beginning at the upper left of the area to be worked, bring the needle out to the front and insert it one square up to the right. Bring it back out again two squares down, then repeat until you've made the required number of stitches diagonally down the mesh.

2 To begin the 'up' row, complete your last down stitch by bringing the needle out two squares down but one to the left. Put the needle in one square up to the right, then out again two to the left. Repeat until you have the required number of diagonal rows up and down.

Finishing Bring needle and yarn to the back of the canvas. Weave yarn through the underside of the last few stitches you've made. Trim off excess.

---

use Newsgroups to keep in touch

Newsgroups allow you to conduct discussions and share information with like-minded people all over the world.

The term 'newsgroups' is a little misleading, because they aren't really about news. A newsgroup is a forum dedicated to talking about a particular subject – films, human rights, DIY, model trains, computer programming, parenting, cars ... You post a message that all subscribers to that group can see and reply to. It's a great way to find answers to problems and make online friends.

To find a newsgroup, search online for a key word describing your interest and you may find that a newsgroup comes up in the search results. Alternatively, browse the list of categories online at **Google groups**.

To use a newsgroup, you must register with a valid email address, which will be kept private. You then set up a username and password. Some forums require payment, but many are free to use. You'll then be ready to read all the discussions that have taken place, receive new posts as they are written, and make contributions of your own. Take care to follow the golden rule of newsgroups: only post the type of messages that you'd like to see posted by others. Posts are monitored by moderators, who will remove unsuitable content, but always remember that these are open forums and be cautious about the information you share and the advice you follow.

Negotiate
a better price

It's amazing how many stores will offer you a discount if you ask for it. You just have to know the right things to say.

Most stores will negotiate on large items such as fridges and TVs. When it comes to secondhand items, such as cars and antiques, the seller positively expects to haggle, and will have set the price accordingly.

Build a rapport with the seller. Be warm, but don't make friends. Conversely, don't try to bully the retailer into selling (*I'm not paying that price!*); you're trying to reach an agreement about the price, not win an argument.

Make it clear that you're not a time-waster, and imply that the price is just a small obstacle standing in the way of a sale. Say something like: *I'm really interested, but I'd need you to do me a deal on that.*

Don't accept the first offer In fact, don't say anything about it at all. Just look doubtful or wince, and wait to see what the seller says next: they may name a lower price.

Look for ways to add value that don't affect the price: ask for free delivery if you're buying electrical goods, a year's tax or a better music system if it's a car.

detect and deal with
Nits

There's no disgrace in having head lice. They are spread by head-to-head contact and feel just as at home in clean as in unwashed hair.

Your child can't stop scratching an itchy scalp. It could be a sign of a head lice infestation, which may have been present for weeks, even months. These parasites are most common among school children under 11, especially girls. Lice eggs stick to the hair, close to the scalp, until they hatch. 'Nits' refers to their eggshells after hatching. A rash on the back of the neck may occur as an allergic reaction to louse faeces.

Search and destroy

If your child displays telltale signs, inspect their scalp minutely. Live lice are the only sure sign of a current infestation, and they are hard to see. Look also for the tear-shaped eggs or shells, which can be mistaken for dandruff. Inspect collars and pillows for black specks of droppings.

Wet combing the hair with a fine-toothed lice comb is an effective and non-toxic, if time-consuming, way to eradicate lice. Apply plenty of conditioner, then comb thoroughly.

■ Comb through first with an ordinary comb.
■ Divide the hair into sections and work through each in turn with the lice comb.
■ Start each stroke from as close to the scalp as possible and wipe the comb with a tissue after each stroke. If you find lice on the tissue, repeat every three to four days for a fortnight to eliminate any new hatchlings.

create a Newsletter on your PC

A family newsletter is a great way to keep distant family friends in touch with your life, and it's an easy thing to produce.

First gather together your material. You'll need articles or snippets of news about your life – written by you or family members – and a selection of eye-catching photographs. Decide how long your newsletter will be: four pages is probably enough.

Edit your text carefully and thoughtfully. When you mention triumphs and successes, try not to sound smug (*Alice was chosen to dance the lead in her ballet show – again!!!*). Modesty, ideally laced with some humour, is the best policy. And concentrate on events of common interest – a detailed chronology of your holiday, for instance, however thrilling it was at the time, is unlikely to make interesting reading for others. Save paper and postage by emailing your newsletter to computer-owning recipients.

1 Microsoft Word has a selection of newsletter templates that you can use. They come with spaces for the words and pictures, and with decorative details such as borders and panels. Access all the templates by opening a new document, then selecting **Newsletters** from the dialogue box.

2 In your template, replace the default text with your own, by clicking in the text box and typing. You can resize the box by clicking on it and dragging the tiny square and circular 'handles' on its borders.

3 To add your own pictures, click in a picture box and use the dialogue box to locate your digital image. You can resize the picture boxes in the same way you did the text boxes.

cure Noisy pipes

There's no need to put up with bumps, bangs and hisses from your household plumbing. Most noises can be diagnosed and cured.

Creaking and clicking This kind of noise is caused by the pipes rubbing against wood, or against each other, as they expand and contract. One likely source of the noise is the point where the pipes come up through the floorboards. If you can get the floorboards up, use a rasp to enlarge the hole slightly, and cover the pipes with felt or lagging. If the noise is coming from under the floor, lift a board above it. It may be that the pipes are running through a notch that's too tight. Use a tenon saw to make the notch wider, and pack the space with lagging.

Rushing water There's air in the system. Turn the heating off and vent the radiators (*see* RADIATOR). With a rag ready to catch drips, use a radiator key to loosen the vent. The air will hiss as it emerges. As soon as the hissing stops and water comes out, tighten the vent. Check for leaks then vent the next radiator.

Banging If you hear loud banging noises from your plumbing system, the most likely cause is 'water hammer' – a shock wave caused by water being shut off too quickly. It can usually be cured by replacing worn tap washers, closing the mains cold water stop valve a little or by replacing a piston-type ball valve on the cold water cistern with an equilibrium-type ball valve instead.

remember Numbers

We live in a world of numbers, and it's near impossible to remember them all. There are some simple tricks, though, to keep random series of numbers such as security codes in your head.

■ Break them down. Just as phone numbers would be harder to recall if they didn't divide into area codes and unique numbers, any long numbers can be divided into manageable 'chunks'. Instead of a 16-digit bank card number, memorise four four-digit numbers.
■ Use rhythm and repetition. Reciting numbers in threes is really effective as it resembles normal speech patterns. If the long number doesn't divide into threes, add 'and' or 'and a', for example 146 289 722 and a 9.
■ Use rhyme. Substitute bun (one), shoe (two), tree (three), paw (four), hive (five), bricks (six), heaven (seven), gate (eight), line (nine), hen (ten) – pictures you can visualise – for digits.

stop a
Nosebleed

Unless they are frequent and persistent, or caused by a serious blow to the face, nosebleeds are more an inconvenience than a medical emergency. They can usually be halted in a matter of minutes.

Do lean forward – ideally over a basin – so the blood can drain down and out of your nose.
Don't tilt your head back; it will cause the blood to drain down the back of your throat. If any blood does reach your throat, spit it out, don't swallow it.
Do breathe through your mouth and pinch the soft part of the nose to stem the flow.
Don't sniff, swallow or cough while clots are forming.
Do continue to pinch for 10 minutes, then release and see if bleeding has stopped. If not, pinch again. A covered ice pack held against your cheek can also help reduce bleeding.
Don't blow your nose after the bleeding has stopped. Use a damp cloth to clean around the nose.
Don't put a coin in your mouth, a key down your back or tie string around the little finger of your left hand. These methods don't work.

follow the Offside rule in football

The offside rule isn't as complex as people think. But in some cases its enforcement relies on the judgment of the referee.

An offside player is one who is nearer to the opponents' goal line than both the ball and the second last opponent. The last defending player will usuallly, but not necessarily, be the goalkeeper. The ball must be played forwards to the offside player for the foul to be called.

An attacking player (A) isn't offside if there's an opposition player (B), other than the goalkeeper, in line with or in front of them at the moment the passing player (C) kicks the ball.

offside

There is, though, a troublesome grey area. A player in an offside position (D) isn't deemed to be offside if not interfering with play. If they were, as here, far from the action of an attack that resulted in a goal, that goal would most likely stand.

The problem is: even if a player is utterly uninvolved in an attack, their mere presence might be enough to attract the attention of a defender, who then plays differently. It's for the referee to judge if an attacker's position or actions amount to 'interfering with play'. Herein lies the source of much of the confusion around the offside rule.

get started with Oil painting

The rich pigments of oil paints make them a joy to work with. Learn the basics and you could be producing your own small masterpiece.

YOU WILL NEED Bristle brushes and soft brush (see below), canvas, easel, charcoal, palette, 'student-grade' oil paints, turpentine

Select your brushes The strong, springy bristles of hogs'-hair brushes are ideal for the heavy texture of oil paint. Bristle brushes come in different shapes, such as Flat, Round and Bright, and in numbered sizes: 12 the largest and 00 the smallest. For a beginner, the three shown below will cover most tasks. One soft synthetic brush is also useful for small-scale or detailed work.

NO. 5 FLAT Ideal for applying broad, rectangular strokes and areas of thick, bold colour as well as short dabs of colour. Use the side of the brush for thin lines and sharp details.

NO. 8 ROUND Suitable for early composition, making long, bold marks and laying in large areas of colour.

NO. 2 BRIGHT Good for detailed work thanks to its shorter, stiffer bristles. A round-ended No. 4 synthetic brush is also useful for fine detail or for laying in an area of thin colour.

Set the scene Decide on your subject – for instance, a landscape. Place the canvas level and perpendicular. When painting outdoors, position the canvas so that the sun doesn't shine on it.

Do the groundwork Use charcoal or thinned paint to 'sketch' the composition. Include one dominant element, such as a castle, and some subordinate items, such as trees or livestock. Give the dominant element due prominence in size or position. The horizon should be on one-third or two-thirds of the canvas. Keep it low if you want to paint tall trees or close-up buildings.

Prepare your palette The colours you plan to use should go to the sides. Mix them in the middle to make an infinity of new shades.

Start painting If you have a dark sky, keep the landscape light, or vice versa. Paint the foreground in detail; keep the background vague – as the eye sees it. Make most use of contrast in the foreground. Oil paints can be applied 'as is', straight from the tube, but are easier to use when mixed ('thinned') with turpentine. Simply stir in turpentine until you have the required consistency.

Wet-on-wet painting requires a single layer of paint, and is usually executed in one sitting ('direct'). Think of the fluid energy of such Impressionists as Monet and Cézanne. Blending wet colours can produce subtle tonal changes.

Fat over lean is slower and more controlled ('indirect') painting, often starting with a tonal under-painting in grey or brown. Think of such Old Masters as Rembrandt. 'Fat' describes the buttery paint straight from the tube. Start with thin paint then gradually build in thickness, waiting for each layer to dry.

So which are you – a Monet or a Rembrandt?

---

appreciate Opera

Opera is all about intense emotion – that of the composer, the characters and of the spectator, who is swept away on a flood tide of music and spectacle. Evening wear isn't required.

An opera is a drama in music, with dance, lavish costumes and sets. Like any stage play it has different acts and scene changes. Unlike a musical, most opera has no spoken lines and is entirely composed of song with musical overture and interludes.

Understanding the language of opera

The written lyric is called the *libretto*, delivered as melodic arias (solos), duets and dialogue between the various players. The greatest operas combine several memorable arias, a tragic tale and intriguing characters. A female star of great rank or pretension (often in life as in art) is called a diva – a goddess. 'Tenor' describes the highest natural male voice, 'basso profundo' the lowest. 'Soprano' is the highest female voice followed by 'mezzo soprano' and 'contralto'. The varied singing styles and techniques give opera its rich texture and complexity.

What's it all about? Driven humanity, passion and towering emotion.

But isn't it elitist? Don't think of opera as 'not for you'. You'll have found yourself singing along to 'Song of the Toreador' from Georges Bizet's *Carmen* (1875) or 'La donna è mobile' from Guiseppe Verdi's *Rigoletto* (1851). You may even have been persuaded to buy trainers, aftershave, breakfast cereals or fizzy drinks by opera. Advertisers use it because it evokes an emotional response.

But it's in a foreign language There are English operas, too, but the language of opera is the universal language of the heart.

Where do I start? The most accessible operas are from the 'Romantic' period in the second half of the 19th century, usually sung in Italian. Try anything by Giacomo Puccini (*Tosca, La Bohème, Madame Butterfly*), or Verdi's *Aida, Rigoletto, La Traviata* or *Falstaff*. For an English-language opera, try *Peter Grimes* by Benjamin Britten. Before seeing your chosen opera live, get to know it on DVD first. This will increase your appreciation of it on the night and add to your sense of anticipation, which is a powerful part of the experience.

make a perfect Omelette

You can add herbs to this omelette mixture if you wish and, before folding, add ingredients such as grated cheese, sliced cooked mushrooms or diced ham, to taste. Cook in a small frying pan or a purpose-made omelette pan.

SERVES 1

**2 eggs
1 tbsp milk or water
¼ tsp salt
freshly ground black pepper
15g butter**

Beat all the ingredients together with a fork. Melt the butter until hot but not brown. Pour in the mixture, lifting it up around the edges and pulling the cooked parts to the centre with a fork or spatula to let any uncooked mixture run into the gap created, tipping the pan as necessary.

When the entire mixture is almost set, and the underside is golden, fold in half or into three with the spatula or a fish slice. Remove from the pan and serve immediately.

grow and care for
Orchids

The rare exoticism and beauty of orchids can make them expensive to buy, but with proper care they should flower again and again. They can be grown as houseplants or in the greenhouse with equal success.

Orchids are extremely difficult to grow from seed so are best bought ready grown. For the best repeat flowering choose the white-flowered moth orchid *Phalaenopsis*.

■ Position orchids in good light but not full sun, and in a humid environment, ideally provided by standing pots in trays filled with moist gravel.

■ Mist them regularly with rainwater. Keep plants moist between spring and autumn by plunging pots into a bucket of rainwater once a week, but water only sparingly (about once every 14 days) in the winter months.

■ The aerial (above ground) roots of orchids are good indicators of health. If yellow or brown at their ends, plants need attention. Try repotting them in a specifically formulated compost from a garden centre. But, because orchid needs vary widely from species to species, feed them only according to the guidelines provided by the grower.

fold an Origami frog

In origami, a wide variety of finished pieces are based on set initial folds. There is, for example, a bird base and a frog base. Here we use the frog base to make … a frog.

Make the preliminary fold

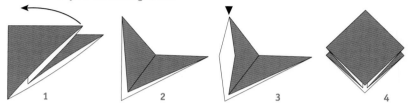

Fold a square piece of paper in half diagonally to make a triangle and then fold that in half again to make two smaller triangles (1). Lie the paper on a flat surface and lift the top triangle so that it stands perpendicular to the bottom one (2). Press the upper point of this triangle directly down (3) until it meets the fold line dividing the two triangles. Flatten the paper out to either side to make a diamond shape. Turn the model over, lift the other triangle and repeat to complete the preliminary fold (4).

Turn preliminary fold into a frog

1 Raise one flap so that it's perpendicular and squash it flat as shown to make an inverted kite shape.

2 Fold in the left and right points of the kite so that they make two small flaps that meet at the centre line.

3 Fold the whole base in half and unfold again. Open up the flaps that you have just made, and take hold of the horizontal edge beneath. Lift this edge – making the two flaps 'yawn'. Continue lifting the edge until the two flaps meet at the centre again to make another, smaller kite shape. Repeat steps 1-3 on back and both sides.

4 You'll now have a neat lozenge shape. Turn the left flap of your lozenge (as shown), as if you were turning a page, to reveal a flat surface. Turn the lozenge over and repeat on the back. You'll now have a flat surface front and back and four flaps on each side.

5 Fold in the right and left tips of the top layer to meet in the middle. Repeat on the back and sides.

6 Turn the top right flap to the left – again like a page. Turn the model over and repeat on the back. The four long thin flaps at the bottom of the model will be the frog's limbs.

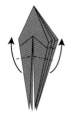

7 Fold and unfold the front limbs to make a crease in both. Open slightly and push out the inner fold line to switch the direction of the fold (a 'reverse fold') so that the two limbs point up diagonally. Crease the back limbs along the different lines indicated above and make a reverse fold in each to bring them up into a horizontal line.

8 Make further creases in each of the four limbs as shown. Then make two more reverse folds in each limb along those lines. You'll now have four fully jointed limbs.

9 To complete the frog, blow into the opening at the base of the model to inflate its head and torso, then draw on a froggy face if you wish.

prepare and eat Oysters

Oysters are a delicacy usually eaten live. If eaten uncooked they must be opened just before serving and always on the day they are bought.

YOU WILL NEED Stiff brush, thick tea towel, strong short-bladed or purpose-made oyster knife, bowl, plates, crushed ice, serving accompaniments and cooking ingredients, small fork, finger bowl with lemon

Preparation

1 Scrub and scrape shells to remove any sand and dirt. Wrap your hand in the tea towel then grip the oyster in the protected hand, rounded side down. Insert the tip of the knife into the hinge and twist it to prise the shell apart.

2 Run the knife between the shells to cut through the muscles holding them together. Lift off the top shell, then cut out the oyster with the knife. If the oyster is to be served raw, carefully retain all the juices. If not, drain into the bowl.

Serving and eating Present on a plate, on a bed of crushed ice, with lemon wedges, salt and pepper, Tabasco, finely chopped shallots and brown bread and butter. Supply a small fork and a finger bowl for each diner.

Cooking Trickle over a little melted butter and grill for 3-4 minutes or until just opaque. Serve at once or cool and add to a seafood salad. Good toppings to add before grilling include breadcrumbs, herbs (dill, chervil or fennel), or grated parmesan or pecorino cheese.

banish grease from your Oven

Regular, thorough cleaning improves an oven's efficiency, extends its life and prevents a smoke-filled kitchen or even the risk of fire.

Prevention To avoid grease build-up:

- Wipe spills with a moist sponge immediately, while the surface of the oven is still warm.
- Regularly wipe the inside of the oven with a vinegar-soaked cloth.
- When possible, cover food with a lid or foil while it cooks.
- Don't overfill dishes; put any that may overspill onto baking trays.

Cleaning routine

1 Remove oven racks and grill pan. Wash with washing-up liquid, using a non-abrasive scrubber. Or you can leave your racks to soak inside a specially designed cleaning bag filled with oven-cleaning solution.

2 Fill a glass bowl with about 100ml of full-strength ammonia. Put into a cold oven, close the door and leave overnight. Remove the bowl, then clean off the loosened deposits with a cloth or sponge.

3 Prise off stubborn grease with a silicone spatula and/or scour with a non-abrasive scrubber dipped in kitchen surface cleaner.

Caustic commercial cleaners Use only as a last-ditch solution and always on a cold oven. Wear long sleeves and rubber gloves, keep the kitchen well ventilated, and follow the maker's instructions.

make Paella

Traditionally, this Spanish rice dish is cooked and served in a two-handled iron pan. A big frying pan or wok will also work well.

SERVES 6

about 1 litre chicken stock
350g mussels
50ml olive oil
750g boneless chicken portions
100g chorizo, cut into chunks
1 large onion, chopped
2 cloves garlic, chopped
350g paella or risotto rice
225g tomatoes, skinned and chopped
1 red pepper, deseeded and chopped
175g large peeled cooked prawns
225g frozen peas, defrosted
pinch of saffron strands
salt and freshly ground black pepper

TO GARNISH

6 large unshelled cooked prawns
6 lemon wedges

1 Heat 300ml stock in a large pan. Add the mussels, cover and simmer for 5-7 minutes until opened. Strain the stock through a muslin-lined sieve and set it aside. Remove top shells from mussels, discarding any that haven't opened.

2 Heat the oil in the pan over moderate heat and fry the chicken until golden. Remove and cut into smaller chunks. Fry the chorizo and remove when browned. Then fry the onion and garlic, add the rice and stir until pale brown.

3 Return the chicken and chorizo to the pan with the tomatoes and pepper. Add the mussel stock plus enough chicken stock to cover. Bring to the boil, reduce the heat, cover and simmer for 30-40 minutes, or until the rice is tender and the stock absorbed (add a little more if necessary). About 5 minutes before serving, stir in the mussels, prawns, peas and saffron. Season to taste, then serve garnished with the prawns and lemon.

match Paint to surfaces

Both for aesthetic and for practical reasons, it's important to use the correct paint for the job. Most paints now come in versions that are low in VOCs (volatile organic compounds), and are less polluting than traditional paints. You can also buy quick-drying, water-based undercoat and topcoat paints, which are generally solvent-based.

Surface	Application and paint type
BARE WOOD/METAL	The surface should first be clean and dry, and then painted with **primer**. An **undercoat** should be applied as soon as possible.
BARE PLASTER	Newly plastered interior walls can be painted with **emulsion** so long as the surface is good. If the surface is old or slightly damaged, paper with thick lining paper, then paint with emulsion.
BATHROOM WALLS	Use **anti-condensation** paint in bathrooms, and also in steamy kitchens. It doesn't 'cure' condensation but inhibits the build-up of water droplets on the painted surface and doesn't peel away when exposed to lots of moisture.
PRIMED WOOD/METAL	One or two coats of **undercoat** should be applied when painting primed wood or metal.
BRICKS/ PEBBLEDASH	Specially formulated **masonry paint** should be used on the outsides of houses. Two main types are available – textured and smooth. Textured is good for concealing minor blemishes like hairline cracks. Smooth paint goes a lot further.
FLOORS	Ordinary paint isn't hard-wearing enough for wooden floorboards. Use a dedicated **floor paint**, or **varnish** and thin down the first coat.
WINDOWS/DOORS	Interior wooden surfaces, including window frames, doors and door jambs, skirting and banisters, should be finished with a single **topcoat** in the desired colour. **Gloss** is shiny; **semi-gloss** (also known as **satin**, **silk** or **eggshell**) slightly more understated. The same topcoat can be used on undercoated metal.
CHILDREN'S TOYS AND FURNITURE	Use non-toxic **enamel** paint on metallic or wooden toys or furniture. No primer or undercoat required.

strip away old Paint

Most paint stripping jobs require the old paint to be softened up, by applying heat or chemicals. Then it's all about laborious scraping.

- You'll need a variety of scrapers if you're removing paint from mouldings on, say, a sash window: flat-blade scrapers, large and small; a shave hook; a long-handled scraper with a replaceable blade.
- A hot-air gun is good on wooden doors. Apply heat until the paint begins to bubble. Wear gloves, and take care that the hot paint doesn't fall on your hand as you scrape. Never put newspaper on the floor when using any type of heat stripper.
- If you're using a chemical stripper, begin scraping when the paint is wrinkled and broken. Start too soon, and the paint won't come away; leave it too long, and the paint will dry out and go hard again.
- Chemical strippers are best for objects with awkward nooks and crannies – old cast-iron fireplaces, for example. But consider having such objects professionally sand-blasted: it may be worth the expense because it will save you many long hours of work.
- When scraping wood, work along the grain as much as possible. If you're going to repaint, you need not get off every scrap of the old paint.

select Paintbrushes and rollers

Buy the best brushes you can afford. Cheaper ones cover less well, and the bristles tend to fall out and get stuck on the surface you're painting. You're likely to need a number of brushes in varying widths – you should have a set of four at least. Natural bristle brushes are not suitable for painting fences and synthetic brushes are also better for applying emulsion to walls.

100mm for large expanses of wall or fencing

50mm for smaller areas such as door panels, and also for some corners and edges

25mm and 12mm for windows and other tricky areas

cutting-in brush with angled tip for painting windows without getting paint on the glass

Paint rollers take much of the effort out of painting emulsion on walls. The synthetic pile type is good for most jobs. Invest in an extension pole to paint ceilings or the high parts of walls, and a little roller for painting behind radiators without removing them. You can also hire 'power rollers' that use a pump to feed paint to the head so you don't have to stop to reload.

calculate how much Paint you need

Most paint tins indicate the area that the contents can be expected to cover. Bear in mind that you'll have to double the amount for a second coat, and bare plaster soaks up paint like a sponge, so the first coat on a fresh wall will require more paint than the tin suggests.

1 Calculate wall area (m²) = height (m) x width (m)

2 Add ceiling area (m²) = length (m) x width (m)

3 Subtract area of doors (m²)

4 Subtract area of windows (m²) = total area to paint (m²)

Always add a little to the total figure – better to have some paint left over than run out mid-job.

properly clean your Paintbrushes

Remove as much excess paint as possible before cleaning. Lay the brush on newspaper, and use an old knife to scrape along the bristles from the base to the tip. Wash out emulsion paint under a running tap. Rub a little washing-up liquid into the bristles as you work the brush with your fingers.

Solvent-based paints have to be cleaned with white spirit or paintbrush cleaner. Half-fill a jam jar with the cleaner and soak small brushes for a few minutes, then wash the brushes in running water and washing-up liquid, and rinse. Shake off water outdoors, allow the brushes to air-dry, then put away.

cook the best
Pancakes

For an extra-smooth result, leave the batter to stand before using. This allows the air to disperse and the starch grains in the flour to swell.

MAKES 8-10 PANCAKES

100g plain flour
pinch of salt
2 eggs
300ml semi-skimmed milk
oil or melted butter for frying

1 Sift flour and salt into a large bowl, make a well in the centre and add the lightly beaten eggs. Slowly work in half the milk, then beat with a hand whisk or electric whisk until smooth. Then add the rest of the milk, beating until bubbly. Or put all the ingredients into a blender and mix for 1-2 minutes until smooth, scraping down any mixture from the sides with a spatula. Leave batter to stand for 30-60 minutes, stir well and add a little more milk if the mixture is too thick.

2 Brush enough oil or butter into a frying pan to coat lightly. Heat until really hot then ladle in just enough batter to form a thin layer. Cook for about 1 minute or until the underside is golden, then turn over and cook the other side. Serve with sugar and lemon juice.

build a Paper plane that flies

Paper planes have become ever more sophisticated. The fascination may begin in childhood, but grown men compete to set new records. All you need is a crisp sheet of paper (A4 is ideal). Success depends on making precise, sharp creases to ensure the integrity of the structure.

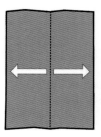 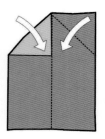 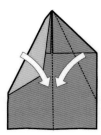 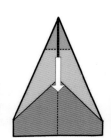

1 Lay the paper on the table portrait fashion and make a fold in it lengthways, matching corner to corner and smoothing the crease. Open it out and lay it with the creased edge forming a valley.

2 Fold the top corners in so that they meet at the centre line and form two triangles and a point. Smooth down the creases.

3 Fold in again from the outer point of each triangle, so the two points meet on the centre line to make a more streamlined shape.

4 The next step is unexpected if you were picturing a dart. Fold the point of the plane down to meet the points on the centre line.

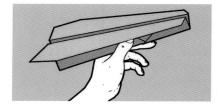

5 Fold the whole paper back on itself along the centre line so all the folded parts are on the outside. Fold down a wing to either side of the plane.

When you fly your plane, angle the wings upwards ever so slightly before you launch it. If the plane climbs, stalls and plummets to earth, angle the wings downward a little. If the plane then nosedives, angle the wing-tips up slightly.

mould a Papier mâché piggy bank

YOU WILL NEED Old newspaper, cold water, water-based glue, plastic bowl, balloon, scissors, egg box, sticky tape, paints, brushes

Preparation Protect your work area. Lay down an old tablecloth, some newspaper or other covering – you'll be making a mess.
- Tear the newpaper into small uneven strips.
- Pour a cup of cold water and 1 tablespoon of glue into your plastic bowl and mix to make a weak gluey solution.
- To make your papier mâché mix, immerse a handful of paper strips in the glue. Be ready to add more strips to the mix as you go along.

Make your piggy bank

1 Blow up your balloon to the size of piggy bank you want. Then spread the gluey strips of paper one at a time over the balloon.

2 Apply five or six layers of papier mâché, leaving the knot to stick out at one end to grip. Leave overnight to dry the paper out completely.

3 Pop the balloon and remove it through the hole. Cut out feet, snout and ears from an egg box and fix them to the pig's body with sticky tape.

4 Cover ears, feet and snout with more papier mâché and leave to dry. Then paint the pig, leave to dry again and finish by cutting a slot in the top big enough to take a coin. Getting money out will be more of a challenge …

Park a car in a tight space

1 Position yourself parallel to the kerb and slightly forward of the car that's in front of the space you want to occupy: you're going to back in. Check that it's safe to begin the manoeuvre.

2 Reverse slowly, and when the rear of your car is level with the rear of the other car, turn your steering wheel one full turn towards the kerb, until the front of your car is pointing to about 2 o'clock.

3 Straighten the steering wheel and reverse until the offside front corner of your car passes the back of the car in front. Turn the wheel two full turns in the other direction and continue reversing.

4 Reverse slowly into the space, taking care not to clip the car in front. Straighten the wheel as your front end nears the kerb. Make adjustments so the car is parallet to, and no more than around 30cm from, the kerb.

wrap a Parcel efficiently

When you wrap a parcel, your twin aims are to protect the contents and keep the weight to an absolute minimum.

■ Use a padded envelope for any items that are irregularly shaped or have hard edges.

■ Non-breakable, rectangular items are best wrapped in brown paper, which weighs little and so keeps the cost of postage down. Seal joins with wide parcel tape: ordinary adhesive tape may not be strong enough.

■ The binding and corners of books can easily get knocked or damaged in the post. Don't wrap books in brown paper; instead, use a corrugated fibreboard book pack with at least 2.5cm clearance at each end. Small books can be sent in padded envelopes.

■ Perishable items must be clearly marked as such.

■ Attach a 'FRAGILE' sticker prominently on any breakable item.

■ Always write a return address on the back of a parcel or important package in case it cannot be delivered for any reason.

■ The safest way to send maps, drawings and plans is in a rigid cardboard tube.

■ Liquids and creams should be wrapped in polythene and sealed with tape, then sent in a leakproof container. Powders and grains (including items such as leaf tea) should be sealed in a strong polythene bag and shipped in a rigid corrugated box.

calculate quantities for Parties

Just the right amount – without a lot of leftovers and wasted food and expense – is the aim of any party planner. Work out your quantities by person and by time.

Canapés Allow four pieces per person to accompany drinks before dinner, 12-15 per head for a 2 hour cocktail party (*see* CANAPÉS).

Food Allow around 700g food per person in total for a three course main meal. For a dinner or lunch, serve a main course consisting of around 200g of protein such as meat or fish, 125-150g of carbohydrate such as potatoes, rice or pasta and a remaining 125-150g of accompanying vegetables. If serving pasta as a main course or a substantial starter, work on the basis of 100-125g per person.

Drinks A 75cl bottle of wine will yield six glasses. Calculate on the basis of three to four glasses per person for a 2 hour cocktail party, evening meal or a celebration lunch. A 75cl bottle of spirits will make about 30 shots of 25ml each. On average, allow four shots per person for a drinks party lasting 2 hours – plus 100ml of mixer for each shot. For soft drinks such as orange juice, allow about 400ml per person.

golden rules

PARTIES ON A BUDGET
- **For economy serve a sit-down meal, for which quantities are easier to calculate than they are for a buffet.**
- **Buy wine in bulk on a sale or return basis and ask for free glass hire.**

choose a secure Password

You need to think of a password that you can easily remember, but nobody else can easily guess. That means that you should avoid your mother's maiden name, and the names of your children or pets. The worst password in the world is PASSWORD. To be effective, passwords should be at least six characters long and include a combination of letters, numbers and punctuation. So if you choose the city you most love, add the year you first went there, and replace one of the letters with a punctuation mark: NEWY*RK98. If you must use the name of a loved one, add the year of their birth in some unguessable way, such as mid-word: M!CH11AEL.

---

produce your own egg Pasta

Pasta is hugely versatile and simple to make at home. It can be frozen after making or dried completely and kept in an airtight jar. It's even quicker and easier to make if you invest in a pasta machine.

SERVES 4

300g plain or strong white flour, plus extra for working and rolling
3 medium eggs, lightly beaten
pinch of salt
1 tsp olive oil

1 Put the flour onto a clean work surface and make a well in the centre. Add the eggs, salt and oil then use a fork to draw in flour from the rim. Use your fingers to form a moist but not sticky dough.

2 Lightly flour the work surface then knead the dough for about 10 minutes, alternately folding it using your fingers and pressing it with the heel of your hand. Form into a ball, wrap in cling film and rest in a cool place for 20 minutes.

3 Divide dough into four portions (roll each separately). Flour both work surface and rolling pin well. Pat the dough down, then roll, lifting and turning the dough occasionally to form a neat oblong or square. Leave to dry for about 10 minutes. For flat pasta such as lasagne, use a large knife to cut it as required. Leave to dry for least 15 minutes before cooking.

4 For ribbon noodles, flour the dough and fold it several times to make a loose roll. Cut into 4-6mm strips before unravelling them and leaving them to dry on a clean, floured tea towel for at least 15 minutes before using.

Using a pasta machine

Make the dough using durum wheat (Italian '00') flour if possible. Divide into batches and pass through the machine's rollers six to eight times, starting with the thickest setting then adjusting the machine with each rolling until you have the required thinness. Dry for 10 minutes then, if you wish, attach a cutting head to make ribbon noodles. Dry as above.

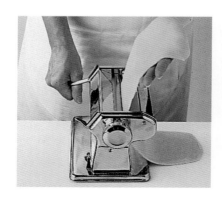

match Pasta with the right sauce

Choose sauce for pasta according to the texture, shape and size of the pasta and the thickness or chunkiness of the sauce: as a rule, the thinner the pasta the lighter the sauce. Never drown the pasta in sauce – stir it in to give the pasta a light coating.

Pasta	Sauce
THIN PASTAS spaghetti, linguine, vermicelli and fine bucatini 	Thinner sauces or those containing oil, cream, cheese or tomatoes. Examples include carbonara (eggs, garlic, pancetta and cheese), puttanesca (tomatoes, olives, capers and garlic), bolognese and pesto (*see* BOLOGNESE SAUCE *and* PESTO).
RIBBON PASTAS tagliatelle, linguine, fettucine and other ribbon pastas 	The most versatile. Match with seafood-based sauces and almost any others except the thickest.
TUBULAR SHAPES penne, rigatoni, macaroni and lumache (snails) 	Chunky meat and vegetable sauces that fit into the 'crevices' of the pasta, including sauces with small meatballs. Also good for thick cheese sauce or aubergine and tomato melanzane for baking in the oven.
SHAPED PASTAS farfalle (bows), fusilli (spirals) and radiatore (ruffled) 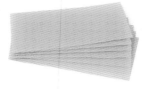	Versatile, but best with thicker sauces such as mushroom, sausage and tomato or meat ragus.
LASAGNE 	Thick sauces such as bolognese or sauces made with duck or rabbit. Usually baked in the oven.

make shortcrust
Pastry

Homemade pastry has a texture and taste superior to ready-bought, and is well worth the extra effort. It also freezes well.

This all-purpose pastry is best made with equal parts butter and fat, but can be made just with butter or block margarine if you want. For a rich, sweet pastry, add 2 tbsp caster sugar to the mixture after rubbing in, and one egg yolk in place of 1 tbsp of water. It's usually cooked at 180°C/gas 4 or 200°C/gas 6.

MAKES 440g (ENOUGH TO LINE A 25cm TART TIN TO SERVE 4-6)

250g plain flour
1 tsp salt
75g unsalted butter, chilled, cubed
75g vegetable shortening or lard, cubed
about 4 tbsp cold water

1 Sift flour and salt into a bowl. Add the butter and fat and rub in with your fingertips until the mixture resembles fine breadcrumbs. Make a well in the centre and add the water.

2 Use a round-bladed knife to mix, adding another 1-2 tbsp water if too dry. Press with your fingers to make a ball of soft, not sticky, dough. Wrap in cling film and refrigerate for 15-20 minutes before rolling out.

make a simple Pâté

A pâté is usually made from liver, but you can also use mushrooms or other vegetables, or smoked fish such as salmon or mackerel, as the main ingredient. A good pâté should have a smooth texture, in contrast to a terrine, which should contain definite pieces.

Chicken liver pâté

SERVES 6

450g chicken livers
50g butter
1 small onion, finely chopped
2 bay leaves
2 tsp chopped thyme
salt and freshly ground black pepper
2 tbsp brandy or balsamic vinegar

1 Trim the chicken livers, cutting away any green or gristly bits. Divide into small pieces and set aside. Melt the butter and fry the onion, bay leaves and thyme for 2-3 minutes. Add the chicken pieces and cook gently for 5 minutes or until they are just cooked through. Remove and discard the bay leaves.

2 Transfer the mixture to a food processor and process until smooth, or put twice through a mincer. Season to taste and stir in the brandy or balsamic vinegar. Transfer to a dish, cover and refrigerate for several hours, preferably overnight.

Alternatives Cook 450g mushrooms with seasonings such as mace and paprika then drain off any liquid and process with 225g cream cheese. Or blend 150g smoked salmon or mackerel with 3 tbsp low-fat crème fraîche, 1 tbsp lemon juice and 1 tbsp horseradish sauce.

play Patience

This card game for one player and an imaginary adversary is also known as solitaire, suggesting French origins. Napoleon certainly whiled away his exile on St Helena with versions of it.

The aim is to build up four full suits of cards, from ace up to king.

To start, deal out a pack of cards to form a tableau (see below). There should be seven columns of cards, with one card in the far left column and one more in each subsequent column so that there are seven in the far right one.

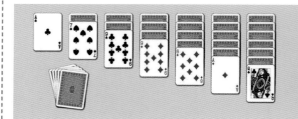

Deal out the columns from left to right with the final card in each column turned face up. Place the rest of the pack ('the stock') face down in front of you. You're ready to play.

■ Study the tableau. If there's an ace showing put it aside as a 'foundation card' and turn up the card immediately underneath it.
■ Move exposed cards onto other columns if you can – red on black, black on red, in descending rank or value. Turn up any face-down card you uncover at the foot of a column. Sequences of cards in the tableau can be moved from column to column according to the same rules.
■ If you empty a column you can start a new one by moving a king, or a sequence beginning with a king, into the space.
■ Whenever possible, move cards onto the foundations sequentially within suits, ace to king.
■ If you can't move any of the exposed cards, take three cards from 'stock' and fan them face up on the table. If the top card – and subsequently those under it – can be added to the tableau or foundation piles, do so. Then turn another three cards face up on top of these and continue in this fashion.
■ When you've worked through the stock, turn the pack over and go through as before. You win if you liberate four full suits of cards. Whether you succeed depends on key cards becoming exposed during the course of play.

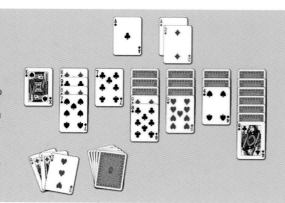

Here the ace of clubs and ace of diamonds have been moved from the tableau to start foundations. Sequences have been built on the columns using turned-up or stock cards. The three available stock cards can all be played – red three on the black four, red jack on black queen and red queen on black king. The game is afoot.

lay garden Paving

With any paving project, whatever materials you're using, the most important things are to lay a firm foundation and keep the surface level. Plan the layout before you start, to avoid awkward cuts or poor alignment with features such as a door or path. Allow for a 10mm joint between slabs. If you're laying irregular-sized slabs, draw a plan.

Prepare the foundation

1 Mark out the area to be paved with pegs and string. Drive pegs into the earth to the depth that you need to dig out (depending on the kind of surface you're laying). Mark pegs with the proposed depth of hardcore (crushed bricks and broken stone), concrete sub-base and paving slabs or bricks.

2 All paving materials need a good base of hardcore, about 100mm deep. A tonne covers an area of about 6m². Spread it in the excavated area, and ram it down using an earth rammer or, for large areas, a plate vibrator.

3 Spread a 10mm layer of ballast or sand to fill the gaps, and ram down. Use a string line to ensure that the surface is smooth and flat, with a slight fall away from any building for drainage.

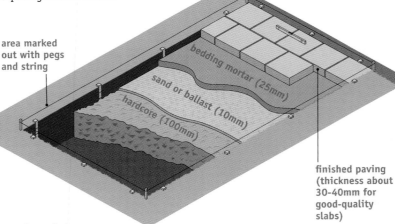

area marked out with pegs and string

bedding mortar (25mm)

sand or ballast (10mm)

hardcore (100mm)

finished paving (thickness about 30-40mm for good-quality slabs)

Lay the slabs

1 To create mortar, buy a pre-mixed packet or combine six parts sand to one part cement and add water (with a little washing-up liquid) a bit at a time until the mortar is like a stiff cake mix. Spread a 35-40mm layer over the sand.

2 Position the slabs – a small area at a time – then tamp down with a piece of timber and a club hammer until the mortar bed is just 25mm deep, and the slabs are level and firm. Make any cuts using an angle grinder with a masonry cutting disc – wear gloves and goggles.

3 Wait two days before pointing the gaps between slabs with a dry mortar mix of one part cement to two parts sharp sand, using a pointing trowel to get a neat finish.

whisk up a Pavlova

A pavlova makes a perfect dinner party or celebration dessert. The vinegar and cornflour added to the meringue help to make it crisp on the outside and soft and sticky in the centre.

Summer berry pavlova

SERVES 6-8

3 egg whites
175g caster sugar
a few drops vanilla essence
½ tsp white wine vinegar
1 tsp cornflour
300ml double cream
25g icing sugar, sifted
350g fresh soft fruit, such as raspberries, hulled strawberries, blackcurrants, blueberries

1 Heat the oven to 150°C/gas 2. Draw an 18cm circle on a piece of baking parchment and place this, marked side down, onto a baking sheet. In a large bowl, whisk the egg whites until stiff. Gradually add half the sugar, whisking well. Fold in the remaining sugar with the vanilla, vinegar and cornflour.

2 Spread or pipe the meringue over the circle on the paper, piling it up at the edges to form a rim. Bake for about 1 hour, or until crisp and dry on the outside. Transfer to a wire rack to dry. Alternatively, for a really crunchy exterior, leave the meringue to dry in the oven for several hours or overnight. Remove the paper and place the meringue on a serving plate.

3 Whip the cream until stiff and add the icing sugar. Pile or pipe it onto the pavlova then add the fruit on top and serve immediately.

whizz up a Pesto

This Italian pasta sauce, originally from Genoa, is also good mixed into salad dressing or added to mashed potato.

MAKES 450ml

45g basil leaves, roughly chopped
6 cloves garlic, chopped
40g pine nuts
125g parmesan cheese, grated
175ml extra virgin olive oil, plus extra for sealing
salt and freshly ground black pepper

Purée the basil, garlic, nuts and cheese in a food processor with 2-3 tbsp oil. Then, on low speed, add the remaining oil in a steady stream. Season to taste. Alternatively, pound the basil, garlic, nuts and cheese with a pestle and mortar, gradually add the oil, then season. Store in an airtight jar with a little oil poured on top to seal. Pesto also freezes well.

indulge yourself with a Pedicure

Looking after your feet is an essential and often neglected part of any self-care and beauty routine, especially in warmer weather when you're planning to wear sandals or peep-toe shoes.

YOU WILL NEED **Nail polish remover, exfoliating cream, bath oil, pumice, toenail clippers, emery board, cuticle remover, cotton buds, body moisturiser, cotton wool, nail varnish**

■ Remove any trace of nail polish (flecks and chips of old polish send the misleading message that you don't wash your feet).
■ Use exfoliating cream to rub away dead skin.
■ Give your feet a lovely soaking in a bowl of warm water laced with bath oil for a relaxing 5 minutes to soften skin and nails.
■ Use pumice to rub away hard skin from the heels and balls of the feet.
■ Dry your feet completely and trim your toenails. Smooth them with the coarse side of the emery board. The nails should be quite square, not shaped.
■ Apply cuticle remover to the cuticles and use a cotton bud to ease them gently back. Wash off any excess and dry thoroughly once more.
■ Massage a moisturising cream into your feet.

■ Use cotton wool or a shop-bought toe separator to hold your toes apart and – working from left to right if you're right-handed, vice versa if you're left-handed – apply a base coat of varnish in three strokes, one down the centre and one to each side. Allow to dry and apply another coat or two.
■ Put your best foot forward.

choose a Pet for children

Pets give children a valuable sense of responsibility and an outlet for affection. They need looking after, though, and you need to choose one to suit your child – and you.

■ Talk it over. Find out what your child wants from a pet. Stress that animals aren't toys.
■ Wait a few months to see if the desire was more than just a whim.
■ Set a budget. Decide what expenses you can meet.
■ Consider your home. A small flat with no access to the outside is an unhappy environment for dogs and cats, which, in turn, can be messy and destructive.
■ Consider safety. Cats scratch. Dogs bite. Young children can cause injury to fragile creatures.
■ Do extensive homework. Study animals' varying needs.

■ Start small. Cats and dogs are demanding of time and money (*see* CATS *and* DOG). Lower-maintenance animals can provide a good introduction to caring for a furry friend.

Mice, hamsters and gerbils look sweet and need only small cages, but they require gentle handling and are generally more active at night.

Guinea pigs need shelter, hiding places and an exercise area safe from predators. They are loveable and responsive: the more they are handled (gently) from the start, the tamer they become. They are extremely active, will get bored if cooped up and crave the company of other piggies; not for them solitary confinement.

Domestic rats become attached to their owners, and love to snuggle in a pocket or up a sleeve. They are intelligent and crave handling. Rarely do they bite. They should be kept in same-sex pairs – ideally siblings. Given the run of the home, they will mess indiscriminately.

Rabbits are endearing, cuddly and sociable. They need space and companionship – human and bunny. They may be kept outdoors with a hutch and an exercise run, but can live indoors and be housetrained.

Prepare for bereavement Rabbits can live five to ten years, guinea pigs five to seven years, mice, rats, hamsters and gerbils only two to three. For longevity (50-100 years) choose a tortoise.

See also AQUARIUM *and* GOLDFISH.

---

take more professional Photos

Photography is an art, so there are no absolute rules. But keeping certain principles in mind will help you to get the best possible shot out of any situation.

Be camera-ready Carry your camera with you at all times – there's nothing more frustrating than seeing something that would make a great picture, but not being able to capture it.

Be aware of the light If the light is behind your subjects, they will be underexposed or silhouetted; if the light is in front of your subjects, they may come out overexposed or washed out (and sunlight tends to make people squint). It's best to have your light source coming in from the side.

Keep off-centre Good composition makes the difference between a dull photograph and a memorable one. The most basic principle is: don't put the subject in the dead centre of the frame. The girl on the beach, the church tower, the leaping goalscorer – they will all look more interesting in the left or right-hand third of the frame.

Look past the subject The background is always important. Avoid a cluttered backdrop; be sure that no electricity pylons are sprouting from your subject's head; make use of attractive or dramatic cloud formations.

master the
Photographic portrait

Portraits are one of the hardest photographic genres, because the act of taking a picture affects the way that the sitter behaves – and this can ruin the shot.

Put the sitter at ease Talk to them as you set up and shoot. Tell them how well they are doing. Flatter them shamelessly.

Don't say, 'Say cheese' A natural expression is generally better than a pose. Get your sitter to tell a joke or to talk about something that interests them. Take lots of shots, so that you catch the moment when emotion shows on their face.

Vary the angle Don't always shoot straight on at eye-level. Shoot upwards from chest-height or climb a ladder to catch the sitter from above.

Get in close Sometimes the face is everything. Experiment with close-ups; the results can be stunning.

Frame the subject Think of ways to draw attention to the subject's face. Have them look through a letter box or peep from behind a tree. Think what suits the sitter's personality and the feeling you want to convey.

store Photos safely

Photographic prints are fragile and need to be handled and stored with care. Digital images are easier to look after.

If you have a great many digital images, it's worth investing in a detachable hard disk on which to keep them. Having your photographs on a disk of their own has several advantages: they are not taking up large amounts of space on your computer's internal hard drive; they aren't in danger of being lost or damaged if your computer breaks down; and you'll not have the bother of transfering all your pictures when you change or upgrade your PC.

Paper photos

You should store these in a bone-dry part of your house where the temperature doesn't fluctuate – a cupboard, rather than a basement or attic. Your best shots should be mounted in an album, using plastic or paper photo corners, and these pictures shouldn't be viewed in strong sunlight. Other photographs can be stored in plastic sleeves or paper envelopes – but the plastic should be non-PVC, and the paper should be acid-free. You can buy plastic boxes that are specially designed for containing sheaves of photographs. Ask at your local photographic shop.

share Photos over the internet

The simplest way to share individual digital photographs with loved ones is to send them direct as email attachments. But there are more sophisticated and more public ways to share large numbers of photographs. Websites such as Flickr (www.flickr.com) and Picasa (picasa.google.com) invite you to download some free software, which you then use to edit and manipulate your photos with a view to posting them as 'albums' on the internet. Here anyone – or anyone you designate – can see your pictures and (if you let them) comment on them. These sites operate much like social networking sites such as Facebook, but with photography as the main focus of activity.

transfer Photos to your PC

If you take pictures on a digital camera, it's easy to transfer them to your PC. This might involve connecting your camera with a lead to a USB port, or removing the camera's memory card and slotting that into your PC. Some PCs have a slot designed to take the SD memory cards found in many cameras; if your computer doesn't have that kind of slot, you might need a USB adapter to connect your memory card to your PC. Photos taken on mobile phones can be transferred using Bluetooth (*see* BLUETOOTH). Generally, your PC will automatically launch a picture transfer program when it detects the camera or memory card. This program will also ask if you want to delete the transferred pictures from the camera's memory, to make room for new shots.

Turning paper photos digital

To transfer the printed pictures in your photo album onto your computer you need a scanner, a machine that turns your pictures into digital computer files. Scanners are quite cheap, and many modern printers also function as scanners. You can only scan one photograph at a time on a home scanner, so it's a time-consuming process. But it's really worthwhile, because snapshots taken 30 or 40 years ago tend to fade away. By scanning the pictures, you're ensuring that you have the image forever. And 'heirloom' photographs, once scanned, can be digitally restored using programs such as Photoshop. You can edit out creases or tears, and (if you wish) make prints that look like new.

play a tune on the Piano

Learning the basics of playing the piano is a little like learning to touch-type. Once you have the position of the keys at your fingertips it's as easy as A, B, C, D, E, F, G.

One of the advantages of learning to play the piano is that, unlike wind and reed instruments, it's easy to produce a pleasing note right from the start; you just press a key. It takes a little longer to learn the principles of scales, chords and tunes but, as with all instruments, practice makes perfect.

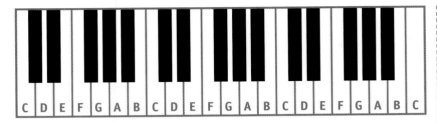

C D E F G A B C D E F G A B C D E F G A B C

Get to know the keyboard A full keyboard consists of 88 black and white keys that form a repeating pattern. The black keys – the sharps and flats, or half notes – are grouped in twos and threes. The white notes are named alphabetically A, B, C, D, E, F, G. At the centre is middle C, so the preceding keys are A and B, the following are D, E, F, G – then you start over at A again.

Play the scales The underpinning of popular and classical music, the scales are a series of eight ascending or descending notes, always ending on the starting note – otherwise known as 'tonic'. Play the C major scale: Do, re, mi, fa, so, la, ti, do – C, D, E, F, G, A, B, C. Play it up, play it down. Keep your mind focused on the notes as you strike them. This is just an introduction. There are 12 major scales to learn, but you're getting a feel for your piano.

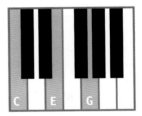

C E G

C MAJOR SCALE Use thumb, middle finger and little finger to play the scale.

Now for chords Of course, to make music on the piano requires more than picking about with the digits. Look at the C major scale (see above). Play C, E and G together. Hear how much more depth it has. That's your C major chord. Playing the first, third and fifth notes from any major scale gives you a major chord with the same name as the scale you're using. Practise the major chords at the same time as you practise scales.

Play your first tune All right, it's only 'Chopsticks', not beautiful music, but it helps to get you used to the keys.

C D E F G A B C

1 Index fingers on F and G – play it six times.

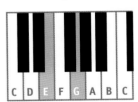

C D E F G A B C

2 Left finger on E, right on G – play six times.

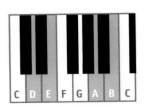

C D E F G A B C

3 Left on D, right moves up to B – play six times.

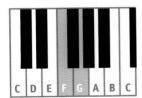

C D E F G A B C

4 Move each finger out one note to the next C – play four times.

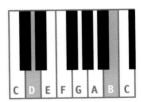

C D E F G A B C

5 Moving your fingers back towards each other, play D-B and E-A once each.

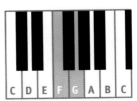

C D E F G A B C

6 Index fingers on F and G – play six times and you're off again.

make Pickled onions

Pickled onions should be kept for six months to mature before eating. They marry best with cheese, bread and cold meats such as ham.

MAKES 2 X 500ml JARS

2kg small white pickling onions or shallots
300g salt
10 black peppercorns
4 bay leaves
2 litres cider or white wine vinegar

1 Put the onions or shallots in a bowl, cover with boiling water and leave for 5 minutes. Remove the outer skins and trim neatly. Cover with cold water, add the salt, mix well and leave for 12 hours or overnight. Drain.

2 Pack with the peppercorns and bayleaves into sterilised jars (*see* STERILISE). Pour over the vinegar, seal and keep in a cool dark place.

pack Picnic food

Carefully packed, picnic food will arrive at its destination fresh, wholesome and intact. If you picnic often, invest in good-quality containers. And don't forget to include napkins, utensils and condiments too.

Choose plastic containers with replaceable lids. Each can contain a personal 'mini meal' such as a salad. Or, wrap food well in foil or cling film to keep it fresh and insect-proof.

Pack food in coolboxes or bags If you're taking both hot and cold food, have one box or bag for each. Keep food extra cool with sealed bags of ice cubes or cooled freezer packs. If you don't have a coolbox, line a picnic bag or basket with a large sheet of bubble wrap plus cold drinks cans or bags of ice cubes – they will keep food cool for an hour or so.

Thermos flasks are ideal for hot or cold drinks. Choose wide-necked flasks for soups.

On a hot day, pre-freeze sandwiches and yoghurt and put direct into the coolbox. They will defrost as you travel. Avoid foods such as egg mayonnaise, potato salad, fish and pasta and rice dishes, which are most prone to food poisoning bacteria.

hang a Picture

Pictures add life to a room. Plan their positioning carefully so that they have room to breathe and sufficient light to be enjoyed.

Use fixings strong enough to support your picture and check that the plaster is sound. Pin-type picture hooks, driven in by a hammer, usually suffice. Or drill into the wall and insert a round-head screw into a wall plug.

A heavy or wide picture should hang on two hooks positioned near each end, not one central one. The hooks must be at the same level: use a spirit level to mark a true horizontal line on the wall, and fix the hooks accurately on it.

To hang a picture on a single hook, get someone to hold it up against the wall, and with a pencil lightly mark the wall where the top of the frame is, at the central point. Lay the picture on its face, mark the top centre, and use your picture hook to pull the wire tight towards the mark. Measure the distance between the top of the frame and the top of the hook. Measure this same distance down from the mark you made on the wall and make a new mark. Hammer in the hook so that its top is level with this new mark.

Heavy pictures and large framed mirrors should be hung on battens rather than hooks (*see* MIRROR).

choose the right kind of Picture frame

A picture frame should play a full supporting role – not just structurally, but visually. It can give a more finished look to a painting and define the boundaries of an artwork.

Stealing beauty A frame that draws attention to itself will distance the viewer from a painting and render it a mere object. An eye-catching frame can work with a strong painting, but remember – it should complete, not compete.

A large frame for a small picture is possible, provided the picture has sufficient impact not to be overwhelmed. Indeed, where a small painting might be lost on a wall, a wide frame can give it presence.

Choose a frame colour to complement the hues of the painting or picture – not to blend with a room. Paintings with predominantly warm pigments such as reds can sit happily in a gilt frame. For studies in black and white go for black or silver. Complement pale hues with a light wood frame. Cool colours such as blues, lilacs and whites are beautifully set off by silver.

Gilding and mouldings send a message. Keep them for grand, formal, rich oil paintings, not delicate watercolours.

For perspective pictures choose an inward-sloping border that seems to retreat towards the horizon, drawing your eye in.

For modern paintings generally choose simple, flat contemporary frames that project the work out towards the viewer.

make a Pie crust

YOU WILL NEED Pie funnel, dish, pastry brush, pastry, flour, rolling pin, knife, fork. Optional: beaten egg, milk

Before you begin To prevent the crust becoming soggy, put a pie funnel into the dish to allow steam to escape. For a pie without a pastry lining, brush the rim of the pie dish with a little cold water. For a pie with a pastry lining, brush the edge of the pastry where it meets the rim of the dish.

Rolling out If your pie doesn't have a pastry lining, roll out and cut a strip of pastry. Place the pastry strip all around the rim and brush with water. Then roll out the pastry for the top of the pie on a floured surface and use the rolling pin to transfer it into position. Press the edges together to seal.

Finishing
■ 'Knock up' the edges by holding a knife horizontally and tapping it against the outside rim of the pastry while pressing the top of the pastry on the inside of the rim with the back of your index finger. Repeat all around the rim. Then use the tines of a floured fork to make a pattern all around.

■ Alternatively pinch the edges of the pastry between thumb and finger for a crimped edge or use a knife to make a scalloped edge.
■ Use any left-over pastry to cut diamonds or other shapes for decoration. Brush with water then place in a pattern on the crust. Finally, brush with beaten egg or milk for a glazed effect if you wish.

learn simple Pilates exercises

This subtle but powerful exercise method builds core strength, improves posture and makes for a longer, leaner, toned outline. It's suitable for all ages, and enhances agility, mobility and stamina.

These elementary exercises will give you a feel for Pilates. Wear clothing that allows freedom of movement. You'll need an exercise mat. Before starting any exercise, relax the body and focus on the muscles you'll be using.

Navel to spine breathing technique
This is fundamental to creating stability and allowing centred movement. Practise it. Breathe in, and as you exhale draw your abdominal muscles up and in; visualise your navel being drawn to your spine. Notice how the technique is incorporated into the following exercises.

continued overleaf →

choose Pillows

A good pillow provides both comfort and support. A squashy one that causes the head to flop, or one so hard it causes a crick, can result in neck ache.

The volume of filling in a pillow will determine its level of softness. Tightly packed filling makes for a firmer pillow, loose filling makes for softness. If you sleep on your back, try a flatter pillow than if you sleep on your side or your stomach.

Down and feather pillows can be moulded to a shape that suits you. They feel luxurious but aren't good for allergy sufferers unless the pillow is hypoallergenic. Choose a closely woven covering so the sharp ends won't poke through.

Latex foam pillows hold their shape and give good support so are helpful if you have neck or back pain. They are also resistant to house dust mites – good news if you have allergies.

Polyester filling in a variety of thicknesses is again recommended if you're asthmatic or allergic.

Tempur or memory foam pillows are designed to mould to the contours of the head and neck, giving strong support and relief to the neck and shoulder muscles.

golden rules
PILLOW WISDOM
■ **Plump pillows every day.**
■ **Protect with a good-quality pillowcase and wash often.**
■ **Replace pillows as they become stained and misshapen or lose their 'loft height'.**

choose a memorable
PIN

Since they all consist of four digits, there are only 10,000 possible PIN codes. To make yours as secure as possible, you need to avoid obvious combinations, such as the day and month of your own birth. It's much better to think of a memorable four-word phrase in which each word contains the same number of letters as the digits in your PIN. So if your PIN is 1455, a good phrase might be: *I LOVE FRIED BREAD.* Choose something that's true and unforgettable. Or, select a simple letter and trace its pattern on the keypad – for example, 'C': 3179.

prepare and cut a
Pineapple

For rings Slice off the leafy top and stem end. Using a sharp knife, cut off the skin and woody 'eyes' from the flesh. Cut into slices 1cm thick. Then use a small pastry cutter or apple corer to remove the woody centre of each ring.

For chunks Leave the top and stem in place and cut the pineapple in half lengthwise. Use a small sharp knife to remove the core and a serrated fruit knife to cut out the flesh. Cut into chunks. If you wish, serve in the pineapple shell.

Roll down – roll up

1 Sit tall on the mat with your knees drawn up, feet flat on the floor in front of you and arms outstretched.

2 Breathe out as you begin to roll down, curling your lower back in a C shape and drawing your navel to your spine. Keep your feet firmly planted as you roll slowly all the way down. Rest your arms by your sides.

3 Take a deep breath, filling your lungs and expanding your back. Exhale as you peel yourself off the floor, rolling up as you rolled down, arms outstretched by your sides. Keep your chin tucked in and lift your head first, drawing navel to spine.

4 Reach your arms forward to rest on your feet and use those hollowed abdominals to hold you in a C curve. Then inhale and lift up from the base of your spine to take up your original position. Do this three times.

Pelvic curl

1 Lie on your back with your knees bent, feet flat on the floor, arms rested by your sides.

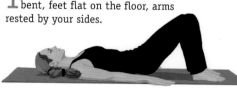

2 Exhale and draw your navel to your spine, moving your tailbone upwards. Continue to lift your spine from the floor, not like a board, but one vertebra at a time. Keep your feet firmly planted.

3 When you have raised yourself onto your shoulders, with your body forming a straight line from knees to shoulders, hold the position, inhaling. Relax your neck, shoulders and ribcage while bracing hips, thighs and ankles.

4 Exhale, drawing your navel to your spine, and uncoil slowly back down to your starting position, vertebra by vertebra, working from the top of your spine.

bend a copper Pipe

To bend a copper pipe you'll need bending springs (available from a DIY store) of the right diameter. If the pipe is longer than the spring, you'll also need a length of string, which you should tie to the end of the spring.

■ Grease the spring well and push it into the pipe, making sure it reaches the point where you're to make the bend. Pull the spring through with string if the pipe is long. The pipe can then be quite easily bent across your knee.
■ It's best to bend it slightly further than the required angle, then ease it back. This makes it easier to withdraw the spring: insert a screwdriver through the spring loop or the end of the string, and pull.

make a great Pizza

Homemade pizza is not only tastier than ready-made, but is lower in fat and salt. It's worth making large batches of dough, dividing them up and keeping them in the freezer. Pizza toppings, usually set onto a tomato base, can easily be varied according to individual tastes. Variations on this recipe could include finely sliced mushrooms, capers, peppers, anchovies or artichoke hearts.

MAKES 1 LARGE OR 2 SMALL PIZZAS TO SERVE 2-4

BASE	TOPPING
350g strong white flour	**400g can chopped plum tomatoes**
½ tsp salt	**2 garlic cloves, crushed**
½ tsp fast-action dried yeast	**2 tbsp chopped fresh basil and/or oregano**
150ml warm water	**pinch of sugar**
15ml olive oil	**3 tbsp olive oil**
	salt and freshly ground black pepper
	150g mozzarella cheese, thinly sliced
	75g chorizo, thinly sliced
	16 black olives

1 Sift the flour and salt into a large bowl. Add the yeast. Make a well in the centre and gradually work in the water and oil to form a soft dough. Knead lightly on a floured surface. Place in an oiled bowl, cover with cling film and leave to rise for about 1 hour until doubled in size.

2 Meanwhile, put the tomatoes, oil, garlic, herbs and sugar in a pan and simmer for 20 minutes until thickened. Season to taste, then cool.

3 Heat the oven to 230°C/gas 8. Knock back the dough (*see* BREAD) and roll out into one thin 30-35cm or two 15-20cm rounds on a floured surface. Place on floured baking sheets. Top with the tomato sauce, mozzarella, chorizo and olives and bake for 8-10 minutes until dough is crisp and golden and cheese melted and bubbling.

For extra crispness Pre-heat extra baking sheets in the oven and put the pizzas (on their trays) on top of these. The additional heat will cook the bases quickly and evenly.

put Plaits in hair

A basic plait or braid is a simple and attractive way to keep long hair tidy. All you need are a brush and comb, and an elasticated band.

Simple plait

1 Thoroughly brush and comb dry hair to remove tangles. Gather the hair as for a ponytail where you want the plait to be – usually the nape of the neck, or high on the back of the head. Divide the hair into three sections.

2 Holding the right (blue) and middle (green) sections in your left hand, separated by your fingers, take the left (red) section across the middle. Then take the right (blue) section and cross it over that.

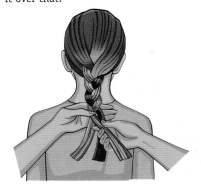

3 Continuously changing hands, take sections alternately from the left and right over the middle, pulling tightly as you please. When the plait is as you want it, secure the end with a band.

Plane wood

Your plane will have a lateral adjustment lever behind the blade; use it to make sure that the blade is square to the plane body. You can set how far the blade projects – and therefore the thickness of each cut – using the knurled nut between the blade and the handle.

■ Mark a cutting line on both sides of the piece of wood you want to plane. Clamp it firmly in a vice or workbench.

■ Position your plane so that it's ready to run the full length of your piece of wood. Your stronger hand should be on the handle at the back of the plane, while your other hand guides the front.

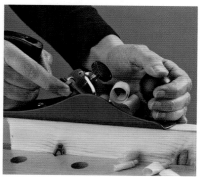

■ Plane from one end to the other, always working with the grain, and in long smooth strokes. Regularly check how close you are to your marked cutting lines.

tackle common Plant diseases

Diseases can make plants look unsightly or even kill them, marring the beauty of the flower garden and reducing the yields of crops. As well as the diseases included here, both roses (*see* ROSES) and seedlings (*see* SEEDS AND SEEDLINGS) are particularly prone to attack.

Disease	Signs and treatment
BLIGHT *summer, especially when wet* 	Leaves turn brown and rot. Tubers and fruits also rot. Affects potatoes and tomatoes. **Treatment** Spray with a copper-based fungicide or mancozeb every seven to ten days.
CANKER *any time* 	Brown, cracked and sunken patches on bark. Oozing slime from affected areas, which die back. Affects many trees and shrubs, including apple, ash and poplar. **Treatment** Spray with copper-based fungicide. Destroy a badly infected tree.
CHLOROSIS *growing season* 	Foliage turns yellow all over, on margins or veins or in lines or rings. Affects a large range of plants. **Treatment** Dig in peat and/or a lime-free fertiliser. Add a chelated iron compound (iron formulated for easy absorption). Control aphids, which spread viral disease (*see* APHIDS).
CLUB ROOT *growing season* 	Roots become swollen and distorted. Leaves of brassicas turn red, purple or yellow. Affects brassicas, wallflowers, stocks, turnips, radishes. **Treatment** Lime soil in winter to keep it neutral or slightly alkaline. Raise plants in sterilised compost. Don't re-grow on affected soil.
CORAL SPOT *any time when plants under stress* 	Rashes of pink or coral-red spots on dead twigs. Plants vulnerable when over-dry, waterlogged or recently transplanted. Affects many trees and shrubs, including acers, beeches, maples, magnolias and redcurrants. **Treatment** Prune to 15cm below affected area. Avoid injuries to bark, through which infection can enter.

Disease	Signs and treatment
HONEY FUNGUS *autumn*	Toadstools at base of trunk. Black bootlace threads on diseased roots. Plants die. Affects most trees and shrubs and some herbaceous perennials and bulbs. **Treatment** No chemical control.
LEAF CURL *before bud burst*	Leaves develop big red blisters, turn white then brown and fall prematurely. Affects flowering cherries and other ornamental *Prunus* species, also apricots and peaches. **Treatment** Treat with mancozeb or a copper-based fungicide in late winter.
LEAF SPOT *late spring onwards*	Leaves and stems develop round or oval brown spots that may have a black pinpoint. Leaves fall prematurely. Affects many ornamental plants, also celery, spinach, blackcurrants, gooseberries. **Treatment** Treat with mancozeb or a copper-based fungicide.
POWDERY MILDEW *growing season*	White powdery patches spreading on leaves, flowers and fruit. Affects many ornamental plants, fruits and vegetables. **Treatment** Treat with fungicides such as difenoconazole or myclobutanil.
ROOT ROT *warm, wet periods*	Foliage dies back and plants may die. Roots may look black and mushy. Affects trees and shrubs, including rhododendrons and azaleas. **Treatment** No cure for some pathogens but try applying an anti-pythium fungicide.
RUSTS *spring and summer*	Shoots covered with orange fungal spores; may become malformed. Affects leeks, mint and many decorative plants such as hollyhocks, fuchsias and antirrhinums. **Treatment** Spray with mancozeb or myclobutanil at first signs of attack.
SCAB *growing season*	Ragged-edged scabs on tubers or roots. Affects potatoes, beetroot, radishes, swedes and turnips. **Treatment** Compost well before planting, avoid adding lime.

P

apply a coat of
Plaster

For any large plastering job, you need a hawk (a large flat tray with a handle beneath) and a steel plastering trowel. You carry the plaster to the wall on the hawk, and apply it with the trowel. Plastering is a skilled job and it takes practice to get a smooth finish.

▪ Mix the plaster in a clean bucket to a consistency between porridge and whipped cream. If the plaster is too wet or too thick, it won't adhere to the wall. Alternatively, use a ready-mixed plaster.

▪ Load a manageable amount of plaster onto your hawk. With the hawk close to the wall, scoop a little at a time onto your trowel, and holding the trowel at roughly 45 degrees, sweep upwards to push the plaster onto the wall, flattening it slightly at the end of the stroke.
▪ Apply a finishing coat about 2 hours after the undercoat. Mix it to the consistency of melting ice cream, and spread with the same kind of motion as before. About 20 minutes after application, spray with a household water spray and use the trowel to smooth to a perfect finish.

Pluck poultry

Game birds, such as pheasants, are often sold complete with feathers by traditional butchers or, if you live in the country, may be presented to you direct from the field. Ideally they need to be hung in a cool dark place for a week to ten days before they are plucked to allow the muscle to slacken and flavour to develop.

- The way to pluck poultry is the same, whatever bird you have.
- Sit with the bird on your lap. Starting with the legs and wings, pull out two or three feathers at a time, using sharp, backward tugs against the direction of growth. Take care not to tear the skin.
- Leave the breast feathers until last. Start at the top and pull towards the head.
- Using a lighted taper or cook's blowtorch, quickly singe off any remaining down or hairs.
- Wipe the bird with a damp cloth and use tweezers to pull out any remaining long hairs or feather ends.

repair damaged Plaster

Repairing small areas of damaged plaster is relatively easy, and a good way to learn the plasterer's art.

YOU WILL NEED **Bolster chisel, hammer, paintbrush, ready-mixed repair and finishing plaster, spray water bottle, plasterer's trowel, length of batten wider than the area to be patched, fine abrasive paper or sander**

1 Use the chisel and hammer to chip away loose or crumbling plaster until you have an area that's firm all around the edges. Brush the whole area with an old paintbrush to remove any remaining dust and spray lightly with water.

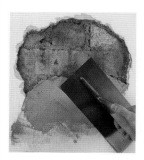  

2 Apply the repair plaster using a plasterer's trowel (above). Build up the damaged surface in thin layers, waiting for each layer to stiffen, but not dry out, before applying the next.

3 If the wall is to be papered, level over the patch. Work fast, keeping both ends of the batten in contact with the solid wall, as you move it from side to side and up across the repaired area. Sand smooth when dry.

4 If the wall is to be painted, fill to 3mm below the surface, then apply a layer of finishing plaster. Do this with a large brush, using upward strokes, then spread and smooth with a plastic spreader. Sand when dry.

Poach fish

Poaching is especially good for white fish, which can be dry when grilled, or for whole salmon or trout. A fish kettle is the best pan to use, but you can use a large saucepan or cover a shallow dish with foil and poach in the oven.

Preparation A court bouillon – a flavoured poaching liquid that's discarded after use – will give poached fish the best possible taste.

MAKES ABOUT 1.5 LITRES

2 carrots, finely chopped
1 large onion, finely chopped
2 sticks celery, finely chopped
1 bay leaf
3 parsley stalks, chopped
2 sprigs thyme
1 bay leaf

2 tbsp lemon juice
long strip of lemon rind
250ml dry white wine or dry cider
   (or the same quantity of water)
1.25 litres water
6 black peppercorns
1½ tsp salt

Put all the ingredients in a large saucepan, bring to the boil, skim off any scum and simmer on a low heat for 15 minutes. Cool a little then strain. Pour it over the fish to be poached. Tie a whole fish in muslin before poaching, securing it at each end with string. Leave long enough ends on the string to lift out the bundle when the fish is cooked.

Complete poaching If a whole fish is to be cooked and served cold, poaching is the perfect method. Simmer the fish slowly in the court bouillon, either on the stove or in an oven set to 180°C/gas 4, allowing 8-10 minutes per 450g. Allow the fish to cool in the liquid, then lift out with fish slices and drain on kitchen paper to prevent it from 'weeping' liquid on the plate.

To serve, carefully scrape off the skin with a sharp knife, stopping at the gills, so the head remains intact, and just before the tail. Or remove the head and tail, if you prefer. Thinly sliced cucumber is a traditional garnish, whether you cover the fish as if with pale green scales, or surround it on the plate. Watercress and lemon are other good accompaniments.

create your own Podcast

A podcast is rather like a homemade radio programme, published on the internet rather than broadcast over the airwaves. You can listen to it on your computer or download it to an MP3 player. A good podcast requires both a creative idea (you need something to say) and some technical expertise (you have to know how to record, edit and publish your work).

Your subject The content is up to you. It might be a dramatic monologue, a spoken-voice tour of your town or nearest museum, or an oral history project in which you interview local people, war veterans or family members.

Equipment A microphone is vital, preferably a USB microphone that plugs directly into your computer and records a digital file straight onto it. Use an omnidirectional microphone if you plan to feature more than one voice at a time or a unidirectional one if your podcast consists just of one person talking. You might also need a USB mixer, so that you can modify the sound as you record, and a pop guard to soften plosive 'P' sounds.

Software Editing software allows you to bring together the elements of your podcast into a professional-sounding finished product. This is where you add background music, cut and edit interviews, add your commentary and clean up background noise. If you have a Mac, all this can be done with the Garage Band application. Other available programs include Adobe Soundbooth and Audacity (which is free to download).

Publishing To make your podcast available, you must upload it to a web server (check your internet service provider's website). You must also create a webfeed; this is a text file that allows people to subscribe to your podcasts and alerts them when you post a new instalment. Many web servers automatically generate the webfeed for you. Finally, advertise your podcast by posting a link on your own website or on a social networking site, or by mailing the link to your friends and family.

cook the perfect
Poached egg

The perfect poached egg, with a just-firm white and a runny yolk, is as delicious eaten on toast as it is in dishes such as eggs Benedict. Add vinegar to the poaching water to help the eggs to keep their shape.

1 Fill a large, deep frying pan or large saucepan with water to a depth of about 7.5cm. Bring to the boil and add 2 tsp vinegar.

2 Break an egg into a cup, swirl a patch of water with a spoon and gently slip the egg into the 'whirlpool'.

3 Reduce the heat and simmer for 4 minutes or until the white is set and the yolk soft. To test, lift out the egg on a slotted spoon and press it gently with your fingertip – the yolk should give a little.

4 Lift out the cooked egg, then trim any ragged edges with a knife or scissors before serving.

golden rules
PERFECT EGG POACHING
■ **Never add salt to the poaching water or the egg whites will break down.**

learn a Poem

Memorising and reciting poetry by heart is a rewarding challenge and brilliant exercise for your brain.

To begin, browse an anthology and choose a poem that appeals to you, or that contains a line you like. Pick a piece that has a memorable rhyme scheme and is manageably short – two or three stanzas, or verses.

Write it out by hand, keep the text with you, and look at it whenever you have spare moment.

Learn the first two lines, testing yourself throughout the day so that you have them word-perfect by nightfall. The next day, learn two lines more. That way you can master a sonnet in a week.

Recite the whole poem out loud to yourself, and doodle it in idle moments – in newspaper margins, on scraps of paper – until it's firmly rooted in your mind.

POISONING – ACT FAST
- **If you suspect that someone has ingested a potentially dangerous chemical or dose of medication, don't hesitate to call the emergency services.**
- **Stay calm and gather together as much evidence and information as you can.**

deal with Poisoning

Cases of poisoning are rarely fatal, but most homes contain an array of toxic substances, so it's important to be familiar with the symptoms and to know what action to take. Most poisoning involves small children, but ingesting tainted food or a dosing error with medication can happen to anyone.

Quick action If you think someone has swallowed a poisonous substance, call an ambulance straight away.

- If the casualty is unconscious don't put your finger into their mouth to make them vomit, but try to wake them and encourage them to spit out what they have taken.
- Put the casualty in the recovery position (see RECOVERY POSITION).
- Look for clues to the poisoning cause: open bottles of household chemicals; nearby berries or leaves; tablet bottles or packets. Take them with you to the emergency department.
- If the person has vomited, keep a sample for examination.

At the hospital Be prepared to give as much information as you can to medical staff to help them to treat the casualty appropriately. Be ready with the following information – write it down while you wait for the ambulance. If you're flustered, it will help to calm you down as well as assist the doctors.

- The substance that you think may have been swallowed (or inhaled or splashed on the skin).
- Precisely when it was taken.
- How much of it was ingested.
- The symptoms you have noted.
- The age of the patient and any known medical conditions.

Carbon monoxide poisoning Tasteless, colourless, odourless and poisonous carbon monoxide (CO) is a major cause of brain damage and death. As well as vehicle exhaust, common sources in the home include faulty boilers, gas appliances and fires, blocked flues and chimneys.

The symptoms of mild CO poisoning are similar to those of flu or food poisoning – headache, nausea, abdominal pain and dizziness, shortness of breath and a cough (although without a temperature). More severe poisoning induces a racing and irregular heartbeat, hyperventilation (fast breathing), confusion, drowsiness, respiratory problems, seizures, chest pain, clumsiness and unconsciousness.

If you, your workmates, family or pets experience any of these, get everyone into the fresh air and call the Gas Emergency Services phone line (0800 111 999 in the UK) for them to check the premises for possible sources of a leak. Anyone who displayed any of the symptoms listed above should be checked over urgently by a doctor or hospital.

understand the basics of Poker

No card game has a greater aura of glamour, mystique and James Bond cool than poker – the ultimate game of bluff.

Players bet on having the highest-scoring hand, but only they know what cards they hold. With nerve, a cool exterior and good judgment, the player with the lowest hand might tough it out and win. It's all about reading your opponents' body language while keeping your own 'poker face' inscrutable.

ASSESSING YOUR HAND The highest-scoring hand in poker is a 'royal flush' (A): 10, jack, queen, king and ace, all of the same suit. Next comes a 'straight flush' (B), a single-suit run of any other consecutive cards. 'Four of a kind' (C) is next, with the highest-value card set winning in a tie, followed by a 'full house' (D): three of a kind and a pair. Any five cards in suit is a 'flush' (E), just beating a 'straight' (F) – any five consecutive cards, whatever the suit. Next come 'three of a kind' (G), 'two pair' (H) and a 'pair' (I). If you have no scoring groups of cards (J), your hand is valued by its highest card – here, the ace.

For straight poker you need six to eight players (ideally) and one 52-card deck. A jack may be added as a wild card or the dealer may designate any card as wild (*dealer's choice*). Aces are high except in a straight or straight flush (5-4-3-2-A).

To start Players buy into the game with a stake in the pot (the *ante*). One player takes the deck and starts to deal cards face up. The first to receive a jack is dealer. Any player may shuffle the pack but dealer takes last shuffle. The turn to deal passes one to the left with every game. Cards are dealt clockwise. Each new deal is a separate game so you're betting on your current hand.

The play Each player receives five cards. The player to the left of the dealer stakes money on his hand or discards it (*folds*). The next player must match the bet (*call*), make a higher one (*raise* it – in a show of confidence or bravado), or fold.

The showdown Every player has a chance to bid – the *betting interval*. Since a player may not raise their own bet, an interval ends when the betting has returned to the player who made the last raise. Players left in the game then show their hands and the winner takes all the stake money in the pot. In the event of a tie the pot is split. A fresh game begins with a new deal.

grow winter salads in a
Polytunnel

Polytunnels are plastic substitutes for a small greenhouse or rows of cloches. They offer warmth and light and extend the growing season of many crops to provide home-grown salad through the winter and the earliest crops of summer fruits.

What to sow Hardy oriental greens, such as mizuna and mustard greens, along with rocket, land cress, radicchio and endive (frisée) are ideal choices. Spring onions and frost-tolerant lettuces such as 'Valdor' and 'Artic King' will also do well. Salad seeds can be bought in ready-prepared mixtures or as packets of a single variety.

Prepare the polytunnel Choose a double-skinned polytunnel for best insulation and ensure that it has a free flow of air within. For extra insulation, line the inside of the tunnel with bubble wrap, held in place with duct or strong masking tape. Make sure the tunnel is firmly secured to the ground and won't be blown away by the wind.

Sow the seeds Make shallow drills 5mm deep and sow directly into the ground from autumn onwards, allowing 20-30cm between rows. Keep watered, as necessary, and apply a liquid feed every two weeks. If the weather is warm enough, further sowings can be made in early winter and early spring. If the weather is very cold, protect plants with fleece.

Harvest the crop Loose-leaved salads can be cut with scissors. Larger 'headed' ones such as lettuce and radicchio can be pulled out. If plants are closely packed, thin them out, eating the thinnings.

play Pool

There are many forms of pool, but '8-ball' is the most widespread. The aim, as in all cue games, is to pocket balls in the correct manner.

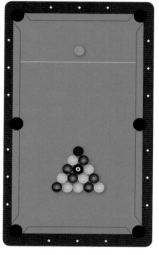

There are two sets of seven balls, one set is red, the other yellow. There's also a white cue ball and a black '8' ball.

The coloured 'object' balls are arranged in a triangle, with the base parallel with the end of the table. The black must be in the centre of the third row, and positioned over the spot on the table. The other balls are arranged as shown here.

The game One player breaks, striking the cue ball from a point behind the 'baulk' line on the table. If one or more balls are potted off the break, the player must nominate which colour they want to play. The first legal shot after this determines which colour they are on for the rest of the frame. If they pot nothing, the other player takes a shot. The first player to pot all seven of their balls and then the black wins. A player who inadvertently pots the black out of sequence loses.

create a simple garden Pond

Water adds an extra dimension to any garden, and a pond is easy to install using a ready-made flexible lining. If you're unaccustomed to heavy digging, work in short sessions to protect your back.

YOU WILL NEED **Hosepipe, sand, spade, plank, spirit level, protective underlay, butyl liner, large scissors, paving or edging stones**

1 Lay out the shape with the hosepipe, then trickle sand round the edge and remove the hose. Dig out, sloping the sides at a 20 degree angle. Remove a strip of turf all round for edging stones.

2 Make a 25cm wide ledge for marginal plants about 25cm down from the top. Use a spirit level on a plank to check that sides are level all around, building them back up as necessary.

3 Line the hole with damp sand, then underlay. This will protect the liner from sharp stones and root growth. Put the lining in place, hold down edges with stones or bricks and fill with water, easing the liner into the corners of the ledges.

4 Trim the liner to within 10cm of the water's edge. Cover with soil and lay paving stones or other decorative edging stones around the perimeter.

How much lining? Measure the width, length and depth of the pond. Then double the depth and add it to the length and width measurements. So a pool 2m wide, 4m long and 0.5m deep needs a lining sheet 3m wide by 5m long. Then add an extra 30-50cm all around for overlap.

Planting Add plants to the pond in containers to prevent muddying the water and to allow you to move them around until you're happy with their position. Line and cover the tops of pots with stones or heavy pebbles.
- **Underwater plants** Choose Canadian pondweed and water milfoil, which are excellent at aerating the water and keeping down algae.
- **Marginal plants** Colourful choices include marsh marigolds, irises and water mint. Set them on a ledge near the pond rim. Rushes are also suitable.
- **Surface plants** Water lilies are ideal and come in a wide variety of colours and shapes. If a water lily is too short to reach the water surface, cut off the leaves before immersing it. New ones will grow to the correct level. Nuphar lilies and water hawthorn are other good choices.

choose and cook cuts of Pork

Almost every bit of the pig, from snout to tail, can be eaten, although the least tender cuts require long, slow cooking. Here's how to cook each part of the animal for the best results.

Pork cuts

Least tender
Medium tender
Most tender

Part of animal	How to cook
HEAD (A)	▪ Cheeks – poach or braise ▪ Ears – braise or grill
SPARE RIB (B) AND SHOULDER	▪ Spare rib – roast, grill or barbecue ▪ Shoulder – oven or pot roast, casserole ▪ Back fat – use for larding (adding fat to very lean meat)
HAND (C)	Oven or pot roast
HOCK (D)	▪ Hock – poach or braise ▪ Knuckle – poach or braise
TROTTER (E)	Braise
LOIN (F)	▪ Loin chops – grill or fry (loin cured as back bacon) ▪ Escalope – grill or fry ▪ Tenderloin (fillet) – roast or fry ▪ Chump chops – grill or fry
BELLY (G)	▪ Rack of spare ribs – roast ▪ Belly – roast, braise or grill (also cured as streaky bacon)
LEG (H)	Roast (cure as ham), braise or casserole
TAIL (I)	Poach or braise

make crisp and crunchy Pork crackling

Perfect crackling is a treat to accompany a pork roast. Many cooks have their own secret methods, but one important rule is that the skin needs to be completely dry and scored with deep parallel cuts before cooking. Some cooks rub olive oil and sea salt liberally into the skin before putting the joint in the oven, others recommend raising the temperature for the last 20 minutes of the roasting time to 220°C/gas 7.

If your crackling fails, you can rescue it by carefully cutting the skin away from the cooked meat with a sharp knife and crisping it under a hot grill or in the microwave for a couple of minutes.

golden rules
GET THE BEST FROM PORK
▪ **Pork must be thoroughly cooked and should never be served rare or even pink.**
▪ **Tangy accompaniments, such as apple sauce or sage and onion stuffing, counter the fattiness of the pork and make the meat more digestible.**
▪ **Good-quality pork is pale pink with a fine grain. The fat should be white with a milky tinge and pink skin.**

improve your
Posture

Standing tall boosts well-being and self-confidence and staves off aches and pains. Try these exercises in front of a long mirror.

FEET Stand with your feet apart and firmly planted. Rock back and forth and side to side to get centred and put weight on the balls of your feet, not the heels.

KNEES Stand with knees relaxed, not locked, and your body weight 'dropping' through your feet.

PELVIS Circle your pelvis one way then the other to release tension in your lower back.

SHOULDERS Bring your shoulders up to your ears, hold – 1, 2, 3 – and let them drop. Repeat. Pull shoulders down from the ears and relax them. As your hands hang by your sides see if your shoulders are level. If not, there's work to do.

NECK Loll your head gently to one side, to the front and then to the other side. Do it twice. Extend your neck so your head sits easily balanced and freely on the top of your spine, with your chin neither thrust forward nor tucked in.

STAND TALL Imagine there's an invisible cord linking the top of your head to the ceiling. Picture how it draws you up so you stand tall but still relaxed, not ramrod straight. Enjoy the feeling. Practise daily.

grow Potatoes

When it comes to flavour there's no contest between home-grown and shop-bought potatoes. They are one of the easiest vegetables to cultivate, come in dozens of varieties and have the added advantage of helping to clear the ground of weeds.

Potatoes are bred to mature at different times in the year and to resist diseases such as scab and blight, and pests such as wireworms. Select for disease-resistance first and then choose earlies, which will be ready in early and midsummer, and main crop seed potatoes, which are harvested in late summer or early autumn for winter storage. That way it's easy to enjoy home-grown potatoes nearly all year round.

Chitting In late winter, set seed potatoes nose end up in cardboard boxes or slatted trays. Leave in a cool, light place for about six weeks until strong, short shoots develop.

Planting Dig trenches about 10cm deep and 45-60cm apart, using well dug and composted soil. Rub off all but the strongest two or three shoots and plant shoots uppermost along the trenches 25-30cm apart.

Earthing up Use a rake to draw the soil up over the row into a ridge. Continue to earth up when leaves appear and as foliage grows. Cover any potatoes near the surface or they will turn green and be inedible.

Harvesting Harvest after flowers appear. Use a fork and work from the edge of the row to avoid piercing. Before lifting the crop, test one or two potatoes by rubbing the skin with your thumb. If it doesn't rub off, the crop is ready.

In a barrel Grow new potatoes in a barrel with holes in the base for drainage. Put in a 15cm layer of compost, then add the potatoes and cover with 7.5cm of compost. Once the stems have grown so that they protrude about 15cm above the surface, add another 7.5cm layer of compost. Keep well watered and continue adding compost layers until the barrel is almost full, then harvest.

freshen your home with Pot-pourri

Fill bowls with pot-pourri to scent your rooms. Or use it to fill pillows or sachets to put into cupboards and drawers.

YOU WILL NEED **Fragrant flowers and herbs, newspaper, scissors, orange or lemon peel, cardboard box with a lid, whole crushed spices such as cloves, cinnamon and coriander, orris root fixative, essential oils (optional)**

1 Dry flowers and herbs by hanging them in a warm dark place (*see* HERBS *and* FLOWERS) or spread on newspaper, removing petals from large flowers and cutting up large leaves.

2 Leave the flowers or herbs for three or four weeks, turning every day to ensure even drying. Cut the citrus peel into slivers and dry separately over the same period.

3 Put the dried material into the box and add 2 tsp orris root fixative and 4 tbsp of crushed spices for every 100g of dried material. Cover and leave for four weeks, shaking occasionally.

In place of spices, you can use a few drops of an essential oil such as lavender or lemon verbena. But avoid using this pot pourri for pillows or sachets as the oil will leak out.

prepare and cook Prawns

Small prawns are best shelled after cooking, but the shells of large king or Dublin Bay varieties are best removed beforehand. Use them in everything from a prawn cocktail to a curry or a seafood pasta.

Small prawns If not bought ready-cooked, plunge into boiling water for 5 minutes and cool in their liquid. Drain. Then hold the tail of each shell tightly and pull it off. Twist off the head and finally peel off the body shell. Check for any intestinal veins and remove if necessary.

Large prawns Before cooking, remove the head and shell but leave the end of the tail in place (see below). Make a shallow cut along the back with a small sharp knife and prise out the dark intestinal vein running along it. To cook, brush with oil and grill, barbecue or fry, or add to curries or other dishes.

Power-walk
for fitness

Power-walking is faster than a stroll, slower than a run, and an all-round good way to get some fitness-building exercise.

■ Wear good running shoes, not walking shoes. Also wear synthetic sports socks that are designed to prevent blisters.

■ Start slowly, so as to warm up your muscles. A sudden start to any aerobic exercise puts you at risk of pulled muscles or other injuries.

■ Don't carry weights, and certainly don't place weights on your ankles; it will hamper your natural gait and place undue stress on your ligaments, tendons and joints.

■ Breathe normally. If you get completely out of puff, slow down or rest. You should be able to maintain a conversation as you power-walk.

■ Fix your gaze on a point about 8m ahead. Don't stare at your feet.

■ When you power-walk, think about standing tall with your head high – as though suspended from a string.

■ Don't lean forward or hunch your shoulders.

■ Swing your arms in a relaxed and natural way, keeping your elbows bent at a right angle and your hands loosely curled.

■ Don't elongate your stride to increase your speed. Instead, move your legs faster. Keep your steps small and even.

treat Prickly heat

This intensely irritating skin rash is thought to be caused by excessive sweat leaking from glands into surrounding tissue. The medical term, *miliaria rubra*, or 'red millet', describes the appearance. In some cases salt crystals form in sweat gland ducts, causing blisters.

■ To reduce sweating, avoid excessive heat and humidity. If you have to go out in really hot weather, wear loose clothing of natural fibres. Taking a cool bath or shower will provide some relief.
■ Antihistamine tablets or creams can help to reduce itching. Or try applying hydrocortisone cream (not to the face) or calamine lotion. Aloe vera gel is pleasantly soothing. Natural yoghurt spread on the rash is messy but often effective.

Publicise an event

Once you've settled on the who, what, when, where and why of your event, it's time to spread the word.

Create a 'hub' Put all the details of the event on a website (*see* WEBSITE) or a Facebook page. Mention this hub in every other form of publicity you use.

Use your contacts Email or 'tweet' details of the event to everyone you know, and ask them to pass the news on (*see* TWITTER).

Use traditional media Contact local papers and broadcasters, send a press release or a letter to the editor. Say you're available for interview. Notify the 'what's on' columns.

Be seen Print posters and ask local shopkeepers to display them. Print a flyer to be delivered door to door.

prepare an effective Presentation

Whether you use Powerpoint, an overhead projector or a flipchart, presentations are all about employing the material effectively, and with a touch of visual flair.

■ Before you begin to make slides or other visual material, work out your presentation on paper. How long will you be talking? How many slides or pictures will your presentation need to contain? What photographs, graphs or other artworks do you intend to use? Make rough sketches of your ideas.
■ Only put the headline information on your slides. If you have three points, just give the headings, then expand on them in your talk. The slide is there primarily to remind your audience of the structure of what you're saying. Don't simply stand there and read out what's on the slides.
■ Use alliteration and acronyms to bind your points together. A slide that says 'Strategy, Security, Sanity' is punchier than one that says: 'Have a plan, try to make sure it won't go wrong, and use your head when you implement it.'
■ Turn any statistics into a chart or diagram, with minimal labelling, and then explain what it means as part of your speech. Make the visual as large as you can: a graphic can never be too big.
■ If you're working in Powerpoint, use the 'theme' facility to give a unified visual look to design elements such as colours and fonts. Use the software to add video and audio – but do so sparingly. Keep clips brief, and use them to illustrate your point rather than as a substitute for speaking yourself.
■ Know what you're going to say. Write out your entire script if that helps, and rehearse it so that you know exactly how long your presentation lasts.
■ Above all, speak clearly. Don't waffle, and never mumble.

repair a bicycle Puncture

1 Remove the wheel by unscrewing the nuts or opening the quick-release lever, working a rear wheel free from any gear cogs as you go. Let the air out of the tyre.

2 Insert a tyre lever between the wheel rim and the tyre, taking care not to catch the inner tube. Prise the bead of the tyre away from the rim, and hook the lever on a spoke. Insert a second lever about 15cm further on to release the next section of the tyre. Repeat until you can pull out the inner tube.

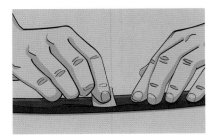

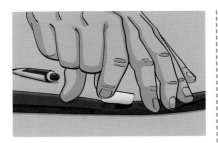

3 Pump up the inner tube, and listen for hissing air to locate the puncture, or immerse the tube in a bowl of water and look for bubbles. Mark the hole with chalk or crayon, deflate the tyre, and roughen the area around the puncture with sandpaper. Apply rubber solution, wait until touch-dry, then stick on a patch.

4 Inflate the tube slightly, insert the valve into its hole, and slide the tube little by little under the wheel rim. Push the bead over the rim with your thumbs, working your way round until it's in place. Refit the wheel on the bike, then pump up the tyre.

carve a Pumpkin for Halloween

YOU WILL NEED **Big round pumpkin, sharp serrated knife, serving spoon, marker pen, tea light**

1 Set the pumpkin stalk side up and scalp it. Use a careful, deliberate sawing motion. Set the top aside.

2 Scoop out the seeds and fibres, holding the bowl of the spoon for leverage. Scoop out most of the flesh; set aside for pumpkin pie.

3 Draw triangular eyes, nose and a grinning, toothy mouth. Cut around the features and press them out with your thumb from the inside.

4 Put a tea light into the base of the pumpkin, light with a long cook's match and pop the top back on. Dim the lights. Spooky!

take a Pulse

Your pulse is your heart rate, and is measured in beats per minute. It's lower when you're at rest and raised by exertion. To take it, you need a watch or clock with a second hand, or a minute timer.

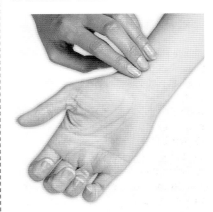

■ Lay your index, second and third fingers lightly on the inside of the wrist, close to the base of the thumb. Alternatively, place the tips of the index and second finger on the neck to the side of the windpipe. Move them around until you feel the insistent rhythm of coursing blood.

■ Count the beats for a full minute, or for 15 seconds multiplied by four. The normal adult pulse rate at rest is 60-80 beats for men, 65-85 for women. It's considerably faster in children.

escape from
Quicksand

This viscous waterlogged sand is rarely deep, so you're unlikely to drown. But you'll need to find a way to get out – quick.

Quicksand is loose wet sand that yields easily to pressure. You sink into it slowly, especially if you're standing up.

▪ If you step onto quicksand and your feet start to sink, sit down or fall backwards so that your upper body is on dry land.
▪ Pull out your feet one at a time – sacrificing your wellies if need be.

▪ If you sink in to your midriff, don't panic and don't thrash about. Lean back and paddle very slowly with your legs to inch yourself towards firmer ground. Then turn over and crawl on your elbows and stomach until you're clear.

dance the Quickstep

The quickstep evolved in the 1920s from the foxtrot and Charleston, and contains elements of both. It's fun and lively, to be danced with brio.

Put on some catchy quickstep music – 'It Don't Mean a Thing', 'Too Hot to Hold', 'Let's Face the Music and Dance'. Get to know the rhythm: slow, quick, quick, slow … slow, quick, quick, slow …

Posture and movement Because of the speed of this dance, you'll be mostly up on your toes for the quick steps and should move like a cat on hot bricks. Longer, slow steps are taken on the heel. The upper body should remain smooth and unaffected, as the feet work quickly underneath.

Get started Engage your partner in a classic ballroom hold (the lady slightly offset to the man's right). The man leads, the lady follows. The example below shows the basic man's steps, without any turns around the floor – the woman's steps are the mirror image of these.

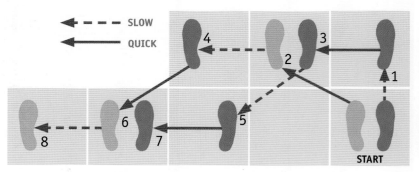

SLOW Take a good step forward with your right foot (1).
QUICK QUICK SLOW Now for a chassé (sidestep-slide-sidestep). Step forward and to the left with your left foot (2) and close your right foot to meet your left (3); then step left again with your left foot (4).
SLOW Take a long step back and to the left with your right foot (5).
QUICK QUICK SLOW Step back and to the left with your left foot (6) and close your right to meet your left (7); then take another step to the left with your left foot (8).

Change the angle As you take any of the slow steps, try rotating your foot so that it lands at an angle to where it was originally pointing. You can then use this foot as a pivot to execute a simple turn. As you grow in confidence, you can also add 'lock steps' by crossing one foot behind or in front of the other, and 'variations' by throwing in some fast little hopping movements. Have fun!

Quilt a simple cover

Warming quilted covers can easily be created using plain or patterned fabrics or sheets of patchwork.

YOU WILL NEED **Smooth light or medium-weight fabric, tape measure, scissors, polyester fibre wadding, dressmaker's pencil, ruler, masking tape, pins, ordinary sharp and quilting needles, quilting thread**

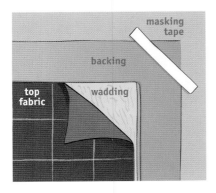

1 Cut out fabric for the quilt top and backing, adding at least 10cm to the desired width and depth to allow for the 'shrinkage' the quilting will cause. Make the backing 5cm larger all round than the front. Cut the wadding to the same size as the quilt top. Use a dressmaker's pencil and a ruler to mark a geometric pattern on the top fabric. Lay the backing fabric, wrong side up, on a hard, flat surface. Pull it taut and attach with masking tape. Spread the wadding on top. Put on the top fabric, right side up.

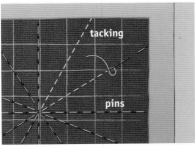

2 Pin through all three layers, starting at the centre of the quilt and working outwards to make a sunburst effect. Once all the pins are in place, remove the masking tape from the backing fabric. Then apply tacking stitches along the pin lines to hold the layers together more firmly. Remove the pins as you go.

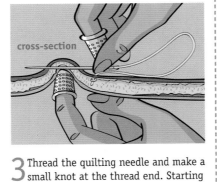

3 Thread the quilting needle and make a small knot at the thread end. Starting at the centre, insert the needle through the top layer only, bring it back up on a quilting line and pull hard so that the knot lodges in the wadding. Sew through all three layers along your pre-marked pencil lines a stitch at a time, using running stitch (*see* SEWING). Secure the thread end with a few backstitches on the underside. Remove tacking as you go.

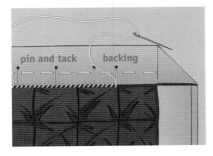

4 Fold the excess backing over the top layer, turning the raw edge under by 10mm, then pin and tack into place through all three layers. With the sharp needle, use slipstitch (*see* SEWING) to attach the backing to the front of the finished quilt. Turn corners in on the diagonal before folding in backing edges to finish with neat mitred corners.

---

run a Quiz night

To host a good quiz night you need to do more than shout out a few questions.

■ Get your questions from an impeccable source. Check all facts if you're writing them yourself, and make sure that there's only one possible correct answer. So if the question is *In what year did 'Rock Around the Clock' reach number one in the charts?* – specify whether you mean the charts in the US, the UK or some other country.

■ Don't make the quiz too long. Try eight sets of ten questions – plus perhaps a picture round or two that teams can work on at their tables.

■ Get the technical side set up well in advance. Designate a technically savvy helper to test and operate the sound system, the overhead projector, the electronic scoresheet.

■ Have at least two other helpers on hand – to do the marking and collate the scores.

■ Practise reading the questions so that you're aware of awkward turns of phrase. Check the pronunciation of any obscure words or names.

■ On the night, read each question twice, with a gap of, say, 30 seconds. Don't rush: discussing possible answers is the bit participants love.

■ Speak with authority, and don't be put off by hecklers or know-alls. Your decision is final. At the same time, don't terrorise the participants; you are a quizmaster, not a headmaster, and everyone is there to have fun.

■ If the answer to a question appears to be wrong, declare that question void so that no points are scored. Explain that this is the fairest way to proceed, and apologise graciously.

■ Make a bit of a show of announcing the winners and presenting the prize.

R

golden rules

LOOKING AFTER RABBITS

- Take rabbits to the vet for regular health checks.
- Rabbits are happiest as a compatible pair. Keep a neutered male with a neutered female.
- Provide an exercise run, where rabbits have enough room to run around.

bleed a Radiator

You should bleed a radiator if it remains cold at the top when the central heating is turned on and the rest of the radiator is hot. This means there's air trapped inside that has to be released. You'll need a radiator key and a rag.

- Turn off the central heating.
- Fit the key over the air vent that's situated on one end of the radiator, at the top.
- Turn it slightly anticlockwise. Air should start to hiss out. Stop turning as soon as you hear the hissing – if you turn the key too much the vent will screw right out.
- Hold the rag underneath to catch any drops of water that escape as the last of the air is released. As soon as water starts to appear, turn the key back to close the vent.
- Turn the heating on again.

look after pet Rabbits

Happy bunnies have a roomy purpose-made hutch with a wire-mesh door, in a sheltered spot, and access to a secure pen for exercise.

Food

- Feed rabbits two meals a day, at regular times, in a heavy earthenware dish that won't move as they eat. Use a second dish for fresh water.
- Good-quality hay and grass should make up most of your rabbits' diet. Feed them at least their own bodyweight in hay every day. The only treat you should give is a root vegetable like carrot, or fruit, in small amounts.
- Don't give rabbits rhubarb, potato shoots, mown grass (unless newly cut), buttercups, daisies or any weeds or wild flowers sprayed with pesticide.

Housing

- Line the hutch floor with newspaper or clean wood shavings, with soft hay or straw on top. Clean the hutch every day by removing any shavings or bedding that are wet and dirty, remove any uneaten fresh food and cleaning the foot and water containers before refilling them
- A hutch must have separate areas for eating, sleeping and toilet, and be large enough for a rabbit to stand on its hind legs without the ears touching the top. Ensure a hutch has safe places where rabbits can hide when afraid.

Handling

- Lift a rabbit with one hand under its abdomen then support it under the rump with the other hand. Hold it to your chest, supporting the head and ears. Keep movements slow and gentle; don't startle your pet. Never lift a rabbit by its ears as this causes unnecessary suffering. With correct and frequent handling from a young age you can build a relationship of affection and trust.

stop wild Rabbits feasting in your garden

Rabbits can eat through an entire crop in one night or destroy your prize flowers just for a snack. Your first line of defence is a chicken-wire fence, which must enclose the entire garden or vegetable patch.

- Hammer metre-long stakes into the ground about 1.5m apart. Unroll a metre-wide roll of chicken-wire and make a bend about 20cm deep along its length. Stand the wire against the stakes so that the bent portion faces outwards to stop the rabbits from digging underneath. Another tactic is to bury the bottom 20cm of the wire fence in the ground. Fix the wire to the stakes.
- In addition, use commercial repellents – which should be applied in the evenings (when rabbits come out to feed) and after rain. Serious rabbit infestations may need to be dealt with by professional pest controllers.

construct a Raised bed

Raised beds are ideal for growing vegetables and fruit such as strawberries. Once built, they don't need to be dug, help to combat perennial weeds and can be tended without treading on the soil.

YOU WILL NEED Tape measure, canes, string, spade, saw, eight 1,200mm x 150mm lengths of treated wood or gravel board, four posts each 750mm x 100mm x 100mm, 16 x 75mm galvanised nails, hammer, compost, rake. Optional: bark chippings, weed-proof fabric

1 Mark out an area 1.2m square. Measure diagonally from corner to corner – if the bed is square the diagonals will be equal. Clear all weeds and dig to a depth of 20-30cm, piling the soil into the centre.

2 Nail corner posts flush with the tops and edges of two pieces of board, then fix a second, lower board to each. Position the edging boards on opposite sides of the bed, 1.2m apart, and tap down until the lower edge of the lower board is flush with the surface level.

3 Nail the side boards into place. Mix compost into the dug soil and rake level. Surround the bed with bark chippings if you wish. Water well if necessary and add plants.

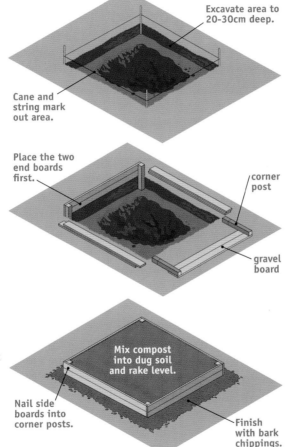

Excavate area to 20-30cm deep.

Cane and string mark out area.

Place the two end boards first.

corner post

gravel board

Mix compost into dug soil and rake level.

Nail side boards into corner posts.

Finish with bark chippings.

Tips and alternatives

■ Sleepers make excellent raised beds and don't need nailing to corner posts. But make sure you buy new sleepers: reclaimed railway stock will be steeped in toxic oil that's harmful to plants and people.

■ If your ground is weed-prone, remove all the soil as you dig and line the bed with weed-proof fabric. Fill the bed with fresh topsoil and compost.

■ Make sure beds are small enough for you to reach across without treading or leaning on the soil. For a higher bed (and less bending) use longer corner posts and more boards.

■ Make paths between beds wide enough to push a wheelbarrow through.

learn to Rap

Freestyle rap involves improvised rhythmic speaking to a beat. You need the ability to think on your feet and impeccable timing.

Learn the language Rap rejoices in the use of street slang and is woven through with terms such as *cupcakin* (acting lovey-dovey), *burbalatin* (happening), *livin large* (doing big *thangs*), *off the hook* (crazy and wild), *scallywag* (uncool) and *parlayin* (relaxing with friends). Remember that *-ing* is always said as *-in*, or you'll ruin the effect of what you say.

■ Build a stock of rhyming words, and words with similar sounds or endings. Search for 'rap dictionary' online to find a wide selection of rap, or hip hop, slang.
■ Work out a narrative. Your rap should tell a story or state a case, expressing your opinion. Decide what you want to say.
■ To begin with, forget about rhyme. Practise flowing until you get the hang of improvising, or 'freestyling', to a rhythm.
■ Now start to introduce rhyme. Don't worry if you make mistakes or talk yourself into dead ends; this is how to learn. Accomplished rappers are able to acknowledge a slip and build it into the rap. Let your mind run ahead a little: as you finish line one you should have line two in your head.
■ A neat rappers' trick is to have a store of all-purpose fill-in rhyming couplets that you can throw into the mix to buy yourself some time to think of the next few lines.

make Ratatouille

Slow simmering is the key to a good ratatouille. The dish is best in late summer, when all the main ingredients are in season.

SERVES 6-8

3 small aubergines, cut into
    5mm slices
75ml olive oil
1 large onion, chopped
2 cloves of garlic, chopped
2 large courgettes, cut into
    5mm slices
5 large tomatoes, skinned,
    deseeded and chopped
1 green pepper, deseeded
    and sliced
1 red pepper, deseeded and sliced
salt and freshly ground black pepper

1 Brush the aubergine slices with oil and grill on high until lightly browned on each side but not softened.

2 Heat the remaining oil in a large lidded frying pan or shallow casserole dish that's suitable for use on the hob. Cook the onions and garlic until the onion is softened.

3 Add the courgettes, tomatoes and peppers, season and simmer for about 35 minutes, stirring occasionally, until vegetables are just soft, but not pulpy. Stir in the grilled aubergines and heat thoroughly before serving.

get rid of Rats

Rats inside the home are a serious health risk, since they spread diseases such as salmonella, *E. coli* and leptospirosis (Weil's disease), which is potentially fatal. You can help to discourage rats by never leaving pet bowls or rubbish bags outside and not putting meat on your compost heap.

Act swiftly if you detect signs of rats in the garden, under decking (a favourite nesting spot) or in a garage. You may see rod-shaped droppings 8-12mm long or holes gnawed in skirting boards or packaging, or may notice a distinctive musky smell.

Set a large number of traps with poisoned bait, such as garlic sausage or bacon. Bait the traps unset for a week before activating them, since rats tend to avoid anything new. If the infestation doesn't clear up quickly, call in your local authority's pest control service before the rats multiply.

---

use the Recovery position

Someone is unconscious but breathing. Once you have dealt with any potentially life-threatening issues, and while you wait for the emergency services, you must make them safe, to prevent choking (*see* CHOKING). If the casualty is left lying on their back, there's a danger that vomit, saliva, blood or their own tongue could block the windpipe. Don't roll the person if there's any possibility of a spinal injury, and keep the airway open by lifting the jaw carefully and tilting the head back without moving the neck.

1 Keep the person's airway open (see above). Straighten their legs. Kneel at their side, at chest level, and place the arm nearest to you at right angles to the body.

2 Take the other arm across the chest and support the head, resting the cheek on the back of the casualty's hand. Bend the farther knee upwards and pull it to roll the person owards you.

3 Take great care to protect the head while rolling the person over. Ensure that the one knee remains bent to prevent rolling too far.

4 If you have rolled the casualty onto their left side, the bent right knee and right arm will provide support – and vice versa.

5 Continue to support the head and tilt the chin up and head back to keep the airways open and to allow fluids to drain without risk of choking.

6 Monitor the pulse (*see* PULSE) and breathing until help arrives. If help is delayed, switch the person to the other side every 30 minutes.

write an effective Reference letter

When you write a reference for someone, whether they are applying for a job, a place at college or another position of responsibility, your must be fair and truthful. Never say anything libellous. If you have doubts about the person or their suitability, it's better to decline to write them a reference altogether.

■ Your reference letter should begin by stating your connection to the applicant, and should say something positive early on. *I was Georgina's line manager at the Acme Corporation for four years, and in that time I found her to be thoroughly trustworthy/hard-working/efficient/...* Make sure you include a reference to how long your have known the candidate.

■ You should say something specific about why you feel that this person is right for the role in question – so make sure you know what the job or position is. Ask the applicant or the person who has approached you for more information if necessary.

■ End on a high note: *I recommend Georgina wholeheartedly, and know she is a fine candidate for the post.*

keep your Refrigerator clean and cool

Regular cleaning is essential to prevent the build-up of potentially dangerous bacteria and fungi and to eliminate unwanted odours. You should also keep the temperature low enough to prevent the growth of harmful bacteria.

Cleaning

■ A quick wipe once a week will keep your fridge clean, but every six months do a thorough clean-up of all the shelves, drawers and storage pockets.

■ Remove food from shelves and keep in a cool place. On a really hot day, put perishable items into a coolbox or work one shelf at a time, so that most of the food can stay in the fridge.

continued overleaf ➜

banish Red-eye from photos

The curse of red-eye is easy to avoid and, nowadays, not difficult to put right.

Red-eye in photographs occurs when you use a flash, so take your pictures in natural light if possible.

■ A camera with internal flash is more likely to lead to red-eye, because the source of the light is close to the lens – which is where the subject tends to be looking.

■ Have your subjects look away from the camera if that suits your shot; if you need them to be looking directly at the camera, use an external flash.

■ Some cameras have a red-eye reduction setting, which produces a small blink of light before the main flash. This causes the subjects' pupils to contract, and so restricts the amount of light reflecting off the retina (which is the cause of red-eye).

Easy PC fix Red-eye removal pens can touch out the telltale red stare on photo prints, but with digital photographs it's an easy thing to put right using your computer. Import your pictures onto your PC (or scan the prints if your camera isn't digital).

■ Open the images in the image-editing software that came with your camera or your PC. Many have a built-in red-eye function: it's simply a matter of highlighting the eyes in your image, and clicking on the button.

Re-point
damaged brickwork

Re-pointing is a straightforward DIY job so long as the affected area is small.

The trickiest part of re-pointing is making mortar that matches the surrounding joints. The only way to do this is to experiment by making up small batches using varying amounts of sand and lime with the cement. Re-point a small area with each different batch, having first taken note of the quantities. Wait for the mortar to dry – for a week at least – before settling on the mix that's the best match. You may have to rake out your unsuccessful experiments.

1 The first task is to remove cracked or crumbling mortar from between the bricks. This can be done with a 'plugging chisel' that has a tapered edge specially designed for this task – use it with a club hammer. If you own an angle grinder, a special diamond cutting wheel does the trick. Whichever method you use, you should cleanly remove the old mortar to a depth of around 15mm.

2 Brush the bricks to remove dust and debris, then wet them. Copy the shape of the mortar in the surrounding joints, using a pointing trowel or a special pointing tool (see above) – or you can improvise with a piece of cane or even a length of hosepipe.

■ Remove shelves and clean with a disinfecting cleaner to reduce the risk of salmonella and *E. coli* infection. These thrive on meat or poultry juices. Rinse shelves and dry with a clean tea towel or kitchen paper.
■ Clean the interior surfaces, including the door storage areas, with the same cleaner. A little white vinegar will quickly cut through any grease.
■ Remove drawers, squirt in some washing-up liquid and soak in the sink in hot water for 10 minutes. Use a brush to remove any stubborn or trapped pieces of dirt. Rinse and dry.

Maintenance
■ Check the temperature regularly. For safety it should always be between 2°C and 4°C. If your fridge doesn't have a built-in thermometer, buy a fridge thermometer and store it inside.
■ If the door doesn't close properly, your fridge won't operate efficiently and may not be cool enough. Try shutting a piece of paper in the door – the seal around it should be strong enough to make it difficult to pull the paper out. If the seal doesn't seem good enough, use a mild detergent solution to clean the rubber sealing strip, making sure to clean in all the grooves.
■ Dust and dirt on the condenser coils will also reduce the efficiency. Every six months, pull out the fridge and gently vacuum the back.

practise deep Relaxation

The pace of modern life can lead to stress and exhaustion, but just minutes of the right kind of relaxation can be enough to calm the mind and refresh the body.

Find a quiet space, take off your shoes, loosen your clothing and try the following techniques.

Take a deep breath Breathing exercises promote calm and clarity of mind, and ease tension. Lie on your back on the floor with your head cushioned and with something to rest the backs of your knees on.

From the diaphragm Rest your hands on your abdomen and use your diaphragm to draw air into and then completely out of your lungs, as your hands move up and down with the rhythm. Deep, abdominal, breathing can be done in any comfortable position, sitting or lying.

Sink into the floor Lie on your back with your spine aligned from neck to tailbone, feet up and arms a little way from your body.
■ Start to isolate, tense and relax different muscles from top to toe, concentrating in turn on each part of your body.
■ Crease your forehead for a count of five and relax. Do it again. Squeeze your eyes tight shut. Then move down your body.
■ When you have worked your way down to your ankles – one arm, one leg at a time – lie still, release all tension and imagine yourself floating.

organise a Reunion

An exchange of Christmas cards is all very well, but bringing together a group of old classmates or colleagues is a far richer experience – if you get it right. Here are some tips for a successful gathering.

Who will be there? Make your list then start to spread the word. If you have lost touch with a friend, the chances are that someone else is still in contact. Try approaching whoever organised the last reunion for their list.
■ Approach an alumni representative at your old school, college or university.
■ Don't overlook the phone book. Your friend may have moved on, but their parents might still live at the old address.
■ Use the internet and reach out across the world. Try social networking sites and chatrooms such as Facebook or Twitter. Try the dedicated reunion websites such as Friends Reunited, and people searches such as yaba.com.

When? If years have slipped by, what's another six months? Give everyone plenty of notice of your intention and gauge enthusiasm. Suggest a couple of possible dates and ask for feedback before settling on a final day.

Where? Is it to be a restaurant, bar, at your own home? You might decide to meet up informally in a bar, then to move on for a meal nearby. Consider the type of venue: you're going to want to talk above all, to catch up, show photographs, bring news, so avoid anywhere too busy or loud. Wherever you decide to meet, make it somewhere central and accessible to all.

Set a budget Remember some party-goers will have to bear the cost of travel and possibly overnight accommodation, so be practical about your plans.
■ For a large gathering, allow for food, drink, venue hire, music and flowers.
■ Don't hand over your own credit card without firm promises from attendees. Explain that acceptance is a commitment – or consider selling tickets.

When everything is booked send round a confirmation. State the time, date, venue and who else so far has 'signed up' for the do.

---

relieve Rheumatic pain

Rheumatic pain can be symptomatic of a wide range of diseases, but whatever the cause there are ways to ease the discomfort. Try following these three tips to soothe your aching joints.

Stay active to maintain muscle function and avoid stiffness. Swimming is great as it strengthens muscles and joints without placing too great a load on them. Don't overdo the exercise, though; rest is important, too.

Avoid fatty foods and sugars, which can cause inflammation, as well as weight gain, putting pressure on the joints. A healthy, balanced diet makes a real difference (*see* DIET).

Go for 'good fats' Omega-3 fatty acids – found in oily fish, walnuts, pecans and hazelnuts, flax seeds and certain other plant foods – can help to bring relief. Borage seed oil and evening primrose oil, which contain beneficial forms of omega-6 fatty acids, also have anti-inflammatory properties.

cook perfect white Rice

Perfect rice is light and fluffy, not soggy and stuck. It's easy when you know how.

Rice can be cooked in a large pan of boiling, salted water for 10-15 minutes and then drained, but this 2:1 absorption method gives even better results.

SERVES 4

1 Put 250g long-grain white rice in a heavy-based saucepan with 500ml of cold water and a pinch of salt.

2 Bring to the boil, stir once, cover, then simmer on a very low heat for 10 minutes.

3 Remove from the heat and leave, with the lid on, for another 10 minutes. Fork through to separate the grains and serve immediately.

golden rules
RICE TRICKS AND TIPS
■ **Make sure the pan lid fits tightly.**
■ **If the rice sticks, transfer it to a sieve, rinse thoroughly with boiling water, shake off any excess liquid, return to the pan, cover and leave undisturbed for 5 minutes.**

R

remove a stuck Ring

When a ring is so tight you can't get it off, the worst thing you can do is to wrench at it in panic. Stay calm.

Run it under cold water, raise your hand above your head to decrease blood flow, use any lubricant to hand – olive oil, washing-up liquid, hair conditioner – then twist the ring back and forth to ease it off.

Try dental floss

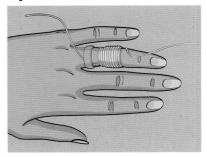

Poke the end of a length of dental floss under the ring, then wind the floss from the dispenser firmly around and up the finger from the ring towards and over the knuckle.

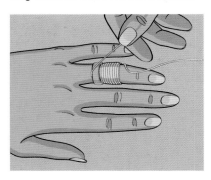

Then start to unwind the string by pulling on the loose end beneath the ring to edge it up your finger and over the knuckle.

Take care Don't tie a knot in the floss or leave it on for more than 5 minutes. Remove the floss at once if your fingertip turns blue.

make a simple Risotto

The round grains of risotto rice are essential for absorbing the stock in a risotto. You can add vegetables, chicken or seafood to this basic recipe, but if using seafood, omit the parmesan.

SERVES 4-6

50g butter
1 tbsp olive oil
1 small onion, finely chopped
1 small clove of garlic,
    finely chopped
225g risotto rice
150ml dry white wine
about 1.2 litres hot chicken or
    vegetable stock
75g parmesan cheese, freshly grated
salt and freshly ground black pepper

1 Melt half the butter with the oil in a large, shallow pan. Add the onion and garlic and fry over moderate heat until the onion is transparent. Add the rice and cook, stirring, until the grains begin to change colour. Pour in the wine and a quarter of the stock and bring to the boil.

2 Put the remaining stock into a separate pan and keep at simmering point. As stock is absorbed into the risotto, add more, a ladleful at a time, stirring constantly for about 20 minutes. The risotto is done when the rice is just tender, the liquid absorbed and the mixture creamy. Stir in the remaining butter and the cheese, check the seasoning and serve at once.

■ Use good – preferably homemade – stock (*see* CHICKEN SOUP *and* VEGETABLE STOCK).
■ Make sure the risotto doesn't dry out.

avoid a Road rage incident

If another driver becomes angry with you as a result of an accident or a near-miss, your main goal should be to keep yourself safe. If in doubt, stay in your car.

■ Try to defuse the situation. Hold up your hands as a conciliatory gesture, though avoid saying sorry as this could be seen as admitting liability.
■ Don't make the situation worse by arguing.
■ If you've stopped and got out of your car, get back in and lock the doors at any point that you feel threatened.
■ Don't hesitate to drive away if you feel that the driver is becoming violent.
■ If the driver follows you, don't head home. Instead, drive straight to the nearest police station or a public place such as a petrol filling station or drive-through restaurant, sticking to busy, well-lit roads. If the situation remains dangerous, stop, and use your mobile phone to call the police from your car.

Roast meat **without worry**

Before cooking but after they have been prepared and had any stuffing added, all joints or birds need to be weighed. Season the meat, brush with a little oil if it's very lean, then put it on a trivet to allow fat to drip and air to circulate freely. The meat can be loosely wrapped in foil to stop it from drying out, but always remove foil for the last 30 minutes of cooking to allow the surface of the meat to brown.

A meat thermometer is a handy tester. Insert it into the thickest part of the meat, making sure it doesn't touch either bone or the roasting tin.

Meat	Cooking times	Meat temperature

Cooking times below are from when the oven is pre-heated.

BEEF AND LAMB	180°C/gas 4	
▪ Rare	35 mins/kg + 15min	60°C
▪ Medium	45 mins/kg + 20 min	71°C
▪ Well done	55 mins/kg + 25 min	80°C

Cook at 220°C/gas 7 for the first 20 minutes to brown. The rarer the meat the more it will 'give' when pressed (*see* STEAK).

PORK	200°C/gas 6	75°C
	55 mins/kg	

Must be well cooked all through. For good crackling, score the skin with deep parallel cuts. Cook for last 15-20 minutes at 220°C/gas 7 (*see* PORK CRACKLING).

CHICKEN	200°C/gas 6	71°C
	35-45 mins/kg	
	+ 15-20 mins	

Baste often. When the thickest part is pricked, the juices should run clear.

TURKEY	180°C/gas 4	71°C
	45 mins/kg + 20 mins	

Baste often. When the thickest part is pricked, the juices should run clear.

- ▪ For joints off the bone add 5 minutes per 450g, plus 5 minutes overall.
- ▪ Bring meat to room temperature before roasting.
- ▪ Ensure that the surface of the meat is completely dry.
- ▪ When the cooking time is up, stand the roast on a warm serving platter in a warm place for at least 15 minutes before carving. This allows the fibres of the meat to firm up, making it easier to carve.

cook the perfect
Roast potatoes

For roast potatoes that are crisp on the outside and fluffy within, use floury maincrop potatoes such as Desiree or Maris Piper, and cook them in lard or goose fat. For a vegetarian version, use good vegetable fat. Shaking them well roughens the surface and helps to make them extra crunchy.

SERVES 6

**1.5kg potatoes, peeled
and cut into pieces**
salt
100g lard or goose fat

Heat the oven to 220°C/gas 7. Boil the potatoes in salted water for 5 minutes then drain. With the lid on the pan, shake them well. Heat the fat in a roasting pan until very hot, add the potatoes and baste well. Cook for 40-50 minutes until crisp and golden brown, turning once.

golden rules
BEST ROAST POTATOES
- ▪ **Keep potato pieces to an even size.**
- ▪ **Make sure each piece is completely covered with fat when you baste.**

build and plant a
Rock garden

A rock garden adds a bit of rugged drama to sunny, open sites and is a good way to plant on an awkward slope.

For best results, the soil shouldn't be too rich and you should avoid overhanging trees, which will drop leaves on your display.

YOU WILL NEED Spade, hardcore or builder's rubble, sharp sand, assortment of large and small rocks and stones, trowel, plants, bulbs, pea shingle (optional)

Start with the stones Get your stones from a builders' merchant, garden centre or quarry: they will deliver if you're buying a large enough quantity. Limestone resists frosts and weathers attractively but isn't good for acid-loving plants, such as summer-flowering heathers. Sandstone is lighter and cheaper but less frost-resistant, and tufa is excellent but expensive.

1 Dig the topsoil to 30cm, creating a slope downwards from a plateau. Add 15cm of hardcore or rubble to help drainage. Cover this with 5cm of sharp sand, then 10cm of topsoil. Place rocks and stones in tiers, embedding two-thirds of each below the surface and placing all grooves and fissures running in the same direction. Butt some up closely and leave planting spaces between others.

2 Allow soil to settle for three to four weeks, then plant with alpines, such as alyssums, sedums and saxifrages. Mulch with small stones or pea shingle. Plant bulbs such as miniature daffodils, alliums and tulips in early autumn, followed by heathers and dwarf shrubs and conifers in late autumn.

launch your own Rocket

This simple rocket won't go into Earth orbit, but it flies using exactly the same ballistic principles as the Apollo moonshot.

YOU WILL NEED Sheet of A4 paper, pencil, scissors, plastic pot with a lid that fits inside the tube (an old-fashioned 35mm film canister is ideal), sticky tape, water, measuring cup or spoons, antacid tablet (such as Alka Seltzer) or effervescent health salts (Epsom salts)

1 Mark up the paper as shown, and cut out the shapes. Use a lid or saucer to draw around for the nosecone (experiment to find the right size for your pot) and keep all the fins the same size. Decorate the paper components if you want them to look even more like a rocket.

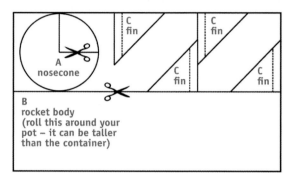

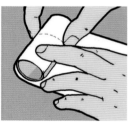

2 Take the long oblong of paper and wrap it around the canister, securing it in place with sticky tape. The canister should be positioned at the bottom of the paper cylinder you have made, with its open end pointing outwards.

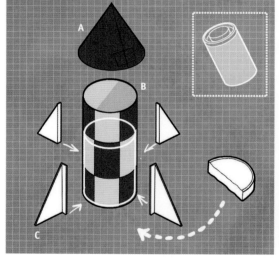

3 Cut a quarter out of the circular piece of paper, and discard. Use sticky tape to stick the two straight edges together – this is your nosecone (A). Stick the nosecone to the top of the body (B) of the rocket (the opposite end to the canister).

4 Make a fold in the long edge of each of the rocket's fins (C) and secure them to the base of the rocket with sticky tape, spacing them evenly.

5 Turn your rocket over, and carefully fill the canister one-third full with water. Then put in half an antacid tablet or ½ tsp health salts for each 10ml of water and very quickly snap on the lid. Place your rocket on a hard level surface and stand well back. In a few seconds, it will launch itself into the air.

climb a Rope ladder

Climbing a rope ladder with wooden rungs isn't the same as climbing a 'stiff' ladder (*see* LADDER). If the ladder is hanging free – that is, not resting against a tree or a wall – then you should tackle the ascent from the side, not the front: left arm and leg to one face of the ladder, right arm and leg to the other. That way, the ladder does not swing away from your body as you climb. If the ladder rests against a vertical surface, you can only climb up the front. Move your left arm and right leg together, and vice versa, to keep more or less equal pressure on both ropes as you move, and minimise the sway.

handle Ropes properly on a boat

Coil a rope All sailors need to know how to coil a rope for safe, tangle-free stowage. This method offers a secure way of stowing ropes that won't be hung up. Coil clockwise, beginning from the fixed end and working your way to the free end. Make each loop the same size – about the length of your outstretched arm – and twist the rope as you go if you need to work out any kinks. When you have 1.5m left, make three or four turns around the bundle, then push a loop of the free end through the coil (1) and pull it back over the top (2). Pull the free end to tighten (3) then tuck it through the coil to finish off (4).

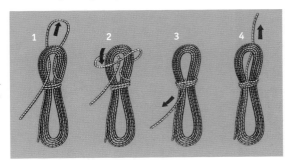

Throw a rope First uncoil and recoil the rope. Making sure that the line is attached to the boat (see left), split the coil into two with slack between. Hold the fixed end of the rope in your left hand (if you're right-handed) and throw the first half and then release the second immediately after. This will reach the greatest distance and make the rope easier to catch. Don't aim straight at the receiver, but just to one side.

Tying up To tie the free end of the line when mooring, for instance, use a round turn and two half hitches to make fast to a bollard or a mooring ring, or a bowline for dropping a loop over a post (*see* KNOTS). These are the two most essential knots for part-time sailors. To make fast to a cleat, take the rope around the cleat, add one or two more figures of eight and make another round turn to secure.

read Roman numerals

The Romans had a numerical system based on seven letters, representing seven numbers.

These letters are:

- **I** (one)
- **V** (five)
- **X** (ten)
- **L** (fifty)
- **C** (one hundred)
- **D** (five hundred)
- **M** (one thousand)

Other numbers can be generated by adding these together, with the largest figure coming first:

MCCLVI stands for **1,256.**

M (1,000) + CC (200) + L (50) + VI (6) = 1,256

If a smaller number comes before a larger one, then the lesser figure is subtracted from the higher one:

XC means 90 (100 – 10)
IV means 4 (5 – 1)

This was a cumbersome and inefficient way of counting, but Roman numerals continued to be used long after Roman times to express dates on civic monuments, such as on buildings and statues.

grow perfect
Roses
see pages 264-265

R

grow perfect Roses

A rose is not simply a rose. The plant comes in an extraordinary range of colours and forms, often combined with a heady scent, and will ramble up walls and over trellises, as well as thriving in borders alongside other shrubs and herbaceous perennials, or in pots.

Choosing and siting roses

All roses need sunshine for at least part of the day and do best in well-manured, slightly acid, water-retentive soil. Choose the right type of rose for your needs from the categories listed below, considering colour and scent, as well as growing habit.

BUYING GUIDE Roses can be bought container-grown or bare-rooted, and should do well as long as you follow these guidelines:
- Buy from a reputable grower and ask for disease-resistant varieties.
- Check plant details carefully if buying by mail order or online, to ensure it's what you want.
- Always unwrap mail-order plants promptly when they are delivered, check their condition and plant them as soon as possible.
- When choosing a variety, check that it's repeat flowering (blooms more than once each season) if you want a long-lasting display.
- Choose plants with at least three or four strong shoots and plenty of roots. Avoid old, pot-bound ones.
- Never buy roses showing signs of pests or disease.

Rosa 'Excelsa' (climber)

A ROSE FOR EVERY PLACE

Rosa 'Ballerina' (shrub)

Shrub roses This group includes many well-known types, such as China, damask and Old English roses, which mostly flower only once a year. They are good in mixed borders and can be trained up posts. Also in this group are rugosa roses, which are good for hedging and have large attractive hips, and ground cover roses, many of which are repeat flowering.

Hybrid teas These are smaller than shrub roses, with large, usually scented double blooms. Hybrid teas are easy to grow, come in many colours, and flower in two main flushes in early and late summer, and even through to the first frosts. They are the ideal roses for a dedicated rose bed but can also be mixed with other plants.

Climbers You usually get fewer but larger blooms with climbers, borne on young wood made in the same year. They make a framework of long, strong shoots, which look excellent growing through a tree or on pergolas and trellises.

Patio and miniature roses These roses are bred for small spaces and containers. They bear pretty, small blooms but tend to be prone to blackspot and mildew.

Ramblers Vigorous growers with large trusses of small flowers borne once each season on flexible wood made in the previous year. Easily trained, but best around pillars and over arches.

Floribundas Usually unscented, but flower in profusion over a long period. They are easy to grow in a dedicated bed or in a mixed border in the same way as hybrid teas.

Rosa 'Iceberg' (floribunda)

PLANTING Plant bare-rooted roses in mid to late autumn (see TREE), and container-grown ones at any time, as for other shrubs (see SHRUB).

■ Soak roots of bare-rooted plants overnight in a bucket of water before planting, or water container-grown plants thoroughly.

■ Trim back all stems to about 15cm above outward-facing buds and remove any thick, coarse roots. Take care not to damage the thin fibrous roots.

■ Most roses are grafted and the 'union' between the rootstock and the grafted stems must be below ground, but not planted too deeply. Lay a cane across the hole to help you to gauge the depth.

PRUNING The methods for pruning roses vary according to their type, but it's an essential routine to encourage strong growth and abundant flowers.

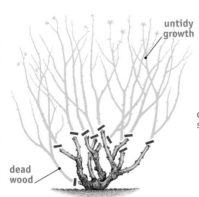

untidy growth

dead wood

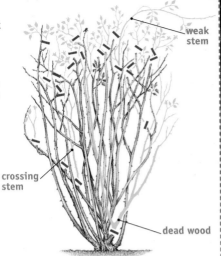

weak stem

crossing stem

dead wood

Shrub roses Prune every two years. Thin out and trim back untidy growth in early winter or spring to leave strong new shoots. Remove all dead wood and old weak stems. You can use sharp shears for this.

Hybrid tea, floribunda and patio roses Cut out dead wood and remove weak or crossing stems, then cut back to healthy buds in late winter. Prune hybrid teas and miniatures to 10cm, floribundas to about 30cm.

Climbers Immediately after blooming, trim back shoots that have flowered to new buds – don't wait until energy-sapping hips form. Then in early winter cut spindly, dead and diseased wood back to strong new shoots. Prune back old shoots that haven't produced any new growth by about half.

Ramblers In early autumn, cut some of the old flowered shoots ('canes') down to ground level, leaving new growth springing from the base. If there aren't enough new shoots to maintain the shape of the plant, leave more old stems in place, but cut back to a strong shoot (right) higher up.

PESTS AND DISEASES Good health is the best prevention, but roses are still vulnerable to attack. Aphids (see APHIDS) are a problem, as are rusts and powdery mildew (see PLANT DISEASES). The following are also major problems for roses.

black spot

Black spot A common fungal disease causing unsightly dark spots on leaves. Spray every two weeks from late winter onwards with rose fungicide, according to the manufacturer's instructions. Burn fallen leaves and all prunings to stop the fungus spreading.

Rose sickness Sometimes roses suddenly die back for no apparent reason, possibly as a result of fungal build-up in the soil. Remove a dead rose with its root ball and burn it, then dig out all the surrounding soil to a depth and diameter of 50cm. Replace the soil with fresh compost, then wait for three years before planting another rose in the same spot.

Row a boat

The aim is to combine a series of movements into a cyclical action in which the blades of the oars move in a smooth oval.

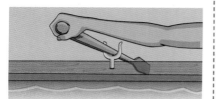

1 Grip the oars with your arms held straight out in front of you, parallel to the water. The blades should be vertical, and just out of the water. Your wrists should be straight.

2 Now lift your arms slightly so that the blades dip into the water, and, once buried, lean back with your body, keeping your arms parallel. This will get you moving. Finally, bend your arms to complete the stroke.

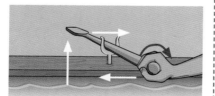

3 At the end of this first stroke, push down on the oars to raise the blades out of the water; bend your wrists, as if revving a motorbike, so the blades are horizontal, and simultaneously push your arms forwards to make ready for the next stroke.

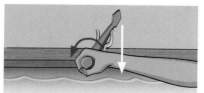

4 As your arms straighten, turn your wrists back so that the blades are vertical once more. Lift your arms slightly to drop the blades into the water, and pull again.

place bets in Roulette

You bet against the 'House' in this casino game, predicting which of 37 slots on a wheel (38 on American wheels) a ball will land in when the croupier spins it.

To bet, place chips on a table layout of red and black boxes representing each number on the wheel, and outer boxes representing various combinations of numbers.

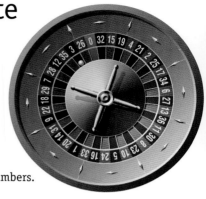

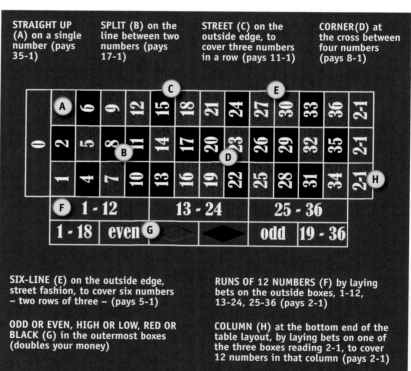

STRAIGHT UP (A) on a single number (pays 35-1)

SPLIT (B) on the line between two numbers (pays 17-1)

STREET (C) on the outside edge, to cover three numbers in a row (pays 11-1)

CORNER(D) at the cross between four numbers (pays 8-1)

SIX-LINE (E) on the outside edge, street fashion, to cover six numbers – two rows of three – (pays 5-1)

ODD OR EVEN, HIGH OR LOW, RED OR BLACK (G) in the outermost boxes (doubles your money)

RUNS OF 12 NUMBERS (F) by laying bets on the outside boxes, 1-12, 13-24, 25-36 (pays 2-1)

COLUMN (H) at the bottom end of the table layout, by laying bets on one of the three boxes reading 2-1, to cover 12 numbers in that column (pays 2-1)

play Rounders

Rounders is a hit-and-run game like cricket and baseball – its direct descendant. The game is often played informally, in parks for instance, but also as a serious sport, with an official set of rules and a governing body. A rounders bat is short, like a kind of truncheon, and is usually wielded with one hand. The ball is hard and covered in leather – a smaller version of the kind used in baseball. In formal games, each team has nine players on the pitch at a time – but the game can easily be played with as few as six a side.

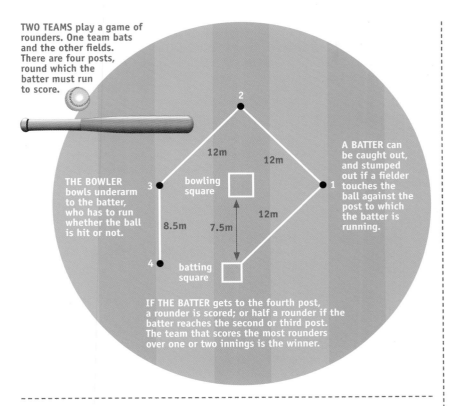

TWO TEAMS play a game of rounders. One team bats and the other fields. There are four posts, round which the batter must run to score.

THE BOWLER bowls underarm to the batter, who has to run whether the ball is hit or not.

12m

12m

12m

2

3   bowling square

1

8.5m   7.5m

4   batting square

A BATTER can be caught out, and stumped out if a fielder touches the ball against the post to which the batter is running.

IF THE BATTER gets to the fourth post, a rounder is scored; or half a rounder if the batter reaches the second or third post. The team that scores the most rounders over one or two innings is the winner.

understand the basics of Rugby

The game of rugby has two distinct versions – Union and League. The skills are similar, but there are some key differences.

In both forms of rugby football (to give it its full title), the aim of the game is to score points by taking the ball over the goal-line, which stretches over the entire width of the field, or to kick it between the uprights and over the cross-bar of the tall H-shaped posts. The ovoid ball may be kicked, but it's mostly carried and passed between players by throwing (see right).

The Union game A Rugby Union team consists of 15 players. A game begins when one side kicks the ball deep into the opposing half. The team in that half collects the ball and works it forwards by running with the ball while passing it sideways or backwards. It's against the rules to pass the ball forwards with the hands, though it can be kicked towards the goal-line. The defending team attempts to regain possession of the ball either by intercepting the ball, or by bodily tackling the player holding the ball – who's obliged to release it after falling to the ground. A scrum – called for technical infringements – is one of the distinctive features of the game. Eight players from each side lock together in a kind of tense huddle then the ball is thrown into the gap between the two front rows. The 'hooker' drags it back with their foot so as to win possession of the ball. A try – five points –

make a
Rugby pass

1 Hold the ball firmly with the thumbs and fingers of each hand positioned on the seams. The fingers should be splayed, and your palms shouldn't touch the ball. Aim to pass at chest height, so that the receiver doesn't have to take their eye off their run, and so that you're passing over the head of any opponent tackling you at waist-height.

2 Draw your arms and the ball to one side of your body, then swing them across and release the ball directly at the target. The ball must not travel forwards to the receiving player. The referee will penalise a 'forward pass' by awarding a scrum (see left) to the opposition.

continued overleaf ➜

Running routine

Running is a straightforward way to get fitter. Just pull on your shoes, and you're ready to go.

The only special equipment you need if you want to run is a good pair of running shoes. Go to a dedicated running shop, where the experts will watch your running technique and advise you on what pair to buy.

The health benefits of running will come to you if you do it regularly, and build up slowly. Three 10 minute runs over the course of the week will do you more good than one half-hour run – and are far less likely to cause injury. Rest for a day between every run (so the maximum is three or four runs in a week). Don't increase the time or distance that you run by more than 10 per cent from one week to the next. If you get breathless when you run, stop and walk for 30 seconds or so.

Make a regular time to run Early mornings can be an exhilarating time to be out – but beware: your muscles may be stiff, so do some dynamic warm-up exercises before you start (*see* AEROBIC EXERCISE). Never run on a full stomach. Motivation is important, so find yourself a 'running buddy', and choose a pleasant route for your run: along the seafront, through the park, down a towpath.

See also MARATHON.

is scored if a team places the ball on the ground beyond the opposing goal-line. Three points are scored for a 'drop-goal' or 'penalty goal' (kicking a ball over the crossbar and between the goalposts). After each try, two additional points can be scored for a 'conversion', which is a kick taken in the same way as a penalty goal.

The League game Rugby League differs from Rugby Union in several significant ways. In the League game, teams consist of 13 players, and there's a rule that the team in possession must concede the ball if tackled six times in succession. The scoring system differs too: four points for a try, two for a kicked goal.

stop Rugs from slipping

A rug on a polished surface is prone to slip, which can be dangerous. The best way to prevent this from happening is to put a rubber mat or rubberised netting underneath. The netting should be cut to a size that's a little shorter and narrower than the rug itself. Another way of achieving the same result is to apply spray-on rug adhesive to the back of a rug or mat. The rug will stick to the floor without harming the surface, but can still easily be lifted and repositioned. Don't use carpet adhesive on valuable or antique rugs.

prevent and remove Rust

This flaky corrosive coating damages tools and machinery, and is an unsightly blemish on metalwork – but you can prevent it.

Rust occurs when water and air chemically react with iron or steel. The best way to prevent rust is to stop the water and air coming into contact with the metal in the first place. Painting metal fixtures such as railings and window frames is the obvious way to keep the corrosive elements at bay, but the paint must be kept in good condition. Even small scratches in paintwork will allow rust patches to form. If this happens, you need to repair and repaint promptly.
■ Scrape away the damaged paint, making sure that all the rust is exposed.
■ Remove surface rust with emery paper, cleaning back to bare bright metal. Use an old paintbrush to remove all dust.
■ Repaint with a zinc-rich metal primer, followed by undercoat and topcoat.

Large areas of rust on outdoor items such as wheelbarrows or barbecues can also be treated in the same way.
■ Wearing safety spectacles, gloves and mask, remove the rust scales using a power drill with wire-brush attachment.
■ Rub down the surface with emery paper and dust clean, then fill the pitted area with two-part epoxy paste before repainting as above.
■ Alternatively, use a rust-killing paint (such as Hammerite) directly on the rusted metal. No primer or undercoat is needed; paint can be brushed on or sprayed from an aerosol.

take a first step in Salsa

Salsa is fun, sexy and great exercise. It's easy to pick up, with a simple eight-beat rhythm. Here's a basic step for you to practise.

Holding your partner If you're leading, face your partner (the follower) and place your right hand on the small of their back. Lift your left arm to chest height, bend the elbow at a right angle and raise your palm. Take your partner's right hand in a loose grip and place their left hand on your right shoulder. This is known as the 'closed' position. Alternatively, you can simply hold your partner's hands, with one raised to shoulder height – the 'open' position.

Basic forward and back These are the steps for the leader. Start with your feet together and your weight on your right foot. The follower starts with feet together and their weight on the left foot, using the backward step as in beat 5.

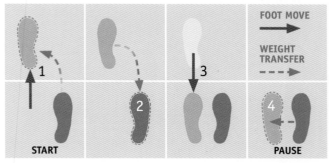

BEAT 1 Step forward with your left foot, shifting your weight on to that foot (1).

BEAT 2 Rock your weight back from your left foot to your right (2).

BEAT 3 Step back with your left foot, keeping your weight on your right (3).

BEAT 4 Pause for the fourth beat, but transfer your weight on to your left foot (4).

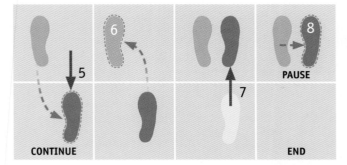

BEAT 5 Step back with your right foot and shift your weight on to it (5).

BEAT 6 Transfer weight from your right foot to your left (6).

BEAT 7 Step forward with your right foot (7).

BEAT 8 Shift your weight to your right foot (8), then begin again.

mix a classic
Salad dressing

MAKES 200ml

9 tbsp extra virgin olive oil
3 tbsp white (or red) wine vinegar
2 tsp Dijon mustard
½ tsp salt
½ tsp black pepper
½ tsp sugar (optional)

Whisk or shake all the ingredients together. You can add a twist with any of the following ingredients: one or two crushed garlic cloves; 2 tbsp chopped tarragon or chives; 1 tbsp tomato purée and a pinch of paprika; 1 tbsp honey.

spice up a party with
Salsa dip

SERVES 12

4 large tomatoes, diced
½ large onion, minced
3 cloves garlic, chopped
handful chopped fresh coriander
2 tbsp fresh lime juice
1 jalapeño chilli, seeded and minced
salt to taste

Mix the tomatoes, onion, garlic, coriander and juice. Add the chilli half a teaspoon at a time, tasting after each addition to see how hot the salsa is. Add salt to your taste.

S

Sand by hand

It may take longer, but sometimes sanding is a job best done with your own hands. Different tasks require different techniques – and the right choice of sanding material.

■ Glasspaper (the more accurate term for sandpaper) is the cheapest option for hand-sanding. Aluminium oxide paper is more expensive, but works better and lasts longer. Silicon-carbide paper – sometimes called wet-and-dry – is primarily used for smoothing metal surfaces and keying painted wood before decoration. Garnet paper is for the fine finishing of furniture that's to be varnished or polished.

■ If you're sanding a flat surface by hand, wrap the paper round a sanding block made of cork or wood (an offcut will do for many purposes). Always work along the grain of the wood. Scratches across the grain are hard to remove, and will show up if the wood is later varnished.

■ It's best to hand-sand furniture: it takes longer but gives a better finish. When you're sanding curved areas, shape the paper with your palm rather than use a block.

■ Use the right grade of paper. A coarse grade is adequate for rubbing down paintwork before painting, but use only fine grades for finishing planed timber.

■ Don't use sandpaper to remove paint: the friction will quickly melt the paint and clog up the abrasive surface, rendering it useless.

launch into
Sailing
see pages 272-273

be the king of the Sandcastle

Sandcastle building keeps the kids amused for hours and you can be the envy of all on the beach. Choose a site below the tide line away from the incoming tide.

YOU WILL NEED **Good-quality spade (preferably with a metal digging plate), two buckets with one full of sea water to keep sand damp, small funnel, old plastic or wooden spatula, or picnic knife**

1 Scoop up plenty of wet sand to form a circular flat-topped base for the castle. Build in layers, packing each one down and pouring on water to keep moist.

2 Dig down into the centre of the mound and clear the sand to reveal a circular courtyard and inner castle walls. Use a spatula to finish the inner and outer walls of the castle off to a smooth face.

3 Make the outline of an arched doorway in the outer wall. Excavate the entrance to about halfway through the wall and repeat from the other side.

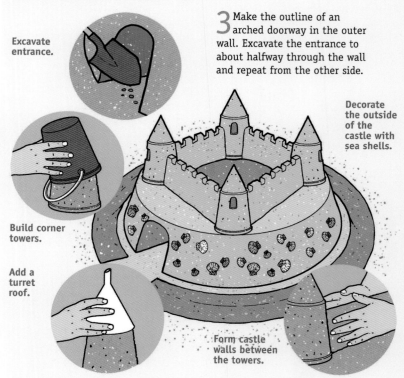

Excavate entrance.

Build corner towers.

Add a turret roof.

Decorate the outside of the castle with sea shells.

Form castle walls between the towers.

4 Use your bucket to make the first tower near the edge of the mound. Repeat to make more towers.

5 To make roofs for your towers, fill a funnel with moist sand, pack it down, and place on top of each tower. Use a picnic knife to carve details such as stairs and slits for windows.

6 Build up castle walls between the towers with your hands. With a knife carve crenellations along the top.

7 Dig a moat around the outer wall and fill with water.

play the game of Sardines

Sardines is similar to the old favourite hide-and-seek, but with a twist – it starts with only one person hiding, while everyone else seeks.

The game is great fun to play indoors or outdoors. As few as three people can take part, but the more who join in the better.

Begin by deciding who's going to hide. Then, the seekers close their eyes and count to a predetermined number – say, 20 or 50 – while the hider hides. When the time is up, the seekers spread out and the hunt begins. As each seeker finds the hiding place they join the hider, cramming together like, well, sardines in a can. The last person to discover the hider is the loser and becomes the hider in the next game. Play sardines indoors, using cupboards, under the stairs and even under beds, and the game really lives up to its tightly packed name.

rescue Sauces

Even the best cooks can have problems with sauces, so it pays to know what to do when trouble arises.

Lumpy sauce or gravy Off the heat, whisk hard in the pan with a balloon whisk or purpose-made smoothing whisk. If this doesn't work, process in a blender or rub through a sieve, then reheat.

Too thin In a bowl, use a fork to mix 2 tbsp of plain flour into 20g of butter. Add to the sauce a little at a time, stirring, until it thickens.

Too salty Add 1-2 tsp sugar or a little milk or yoghurt.

Too sweet Add a little lemon juice.

Curdled custard Blend or process or strain into a cold dish sitting in a bowl of ice cubes and beat vigorously.

Separated mayonnaise Add 1 tbsp of warm water. Or start again with one egg yolk and gradually add the curdled mixture.

Curdled hollandaise Remove from the heat, then beat in 1 tbsp of cold water a little at a time until the sauce becomes smooth. Or, off the heat, stir an ice cube into the warm sauce. Or beat in an additional egg yolk in a clean pan until thick, then, over low heat, gradually beat in the curdled sauce until smooth.

Grainy or 'seized' chocolate sauce Try adding warm water, a little at a time, while stirring vigorously.

cook perfect
Sauté potatoes

The best sauté potatoes are crisp on the outside and soft within. Really hot fat is critical.

SERVES 2-4

500g potatoes, peeled
10g butter
3-4 tbsp sunflower or olive oil
sea salt

1 Boil potatoes in salted water for about 10 minutes until barely tender. Cut into small even chunks.

2 Heat the butter and oil in a large frying pan, add the potatoes and fry quickly, shaking the pan and turning them two or three times until well browned all over.

3 Lift out with a fish slice and drain on kitchen paper. Sprinkle with sea salt and serve immediately.

⭐ golden rules

SAUTÉ SECRETS
- **Make sure the fat is really hot before adding the potatoes.**
- **Don't lower the cooking temperature or the potatoes will 'stew' and become soggy.**
- **For larger quantities, cook in two or more batches.**

S

launch into Sailing

Sailing of any kind demands a certain amount of seamanship: you need to be able to recognise the moods of the sea, and you need to learn how to catch the wind in the sails so as to propel the boat.

Know the ropes You should start on a small boat. Most have two sails – the mainsail and the jib – or try a dinghy, which has a mainsail alone. The best way to learn to sail is to spend time on the water with an experienced and responsible sailor, perhaps as part of a training course.

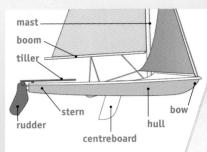

PARTS OF A BOAT Sailboats come in all shapes and sizes but most share a core set of common parts.

mast
boom
tiller
stern
rudder
centreboard
hull
bow

THE WIND The wind is your boat's engine. The skill of sailing lies in harnessing the wind to take you in your chosen direction. Sailing in the same direction as the wind ('running') is a simple matter: the wind naturally pushes you along, and you go where it leads you. Sailing 'upwind' is much trickier. You have to work hard to manipulate the sails, so as to catch the wind and drive the boat against its natural inclination.

SHEETS AND SAILS When sailing you need to constantly adjust or 'trim' the sails. You have to do this when the boat changes direction, when the wind itself changes direction, or when you want to slow down or speed up. The sails are controlled by ropes known (confusingly for non-sailors) as sheets. When you complete a tacking manoeuvre (see opposite), the jib must be moved across to the other side of the boat by slackening one of the sheets that controls it and tightening the other. This must be done swiftly, and at the right moment; judging and executing this correctly is one of the key skills of sailing.

wind direction

into wind
(in irons)

close
hauled

close
hauled

close
reach

close
reach

no go zone

beam
reach

beam
reach

broad
reach

broad
reach

dead run

mainsail

wind direction

jib
sail

jib sheet

main sheet

HOW TO SAIL By angling the mainsail and jib, you can run with the wind or 'reach' across it. The only direction you can't travel in directly is the 45 degree 'no go zone' to either side of the headwind. Instead you must use a zigzag approach called 'tacking' (see opposite).

TACKING

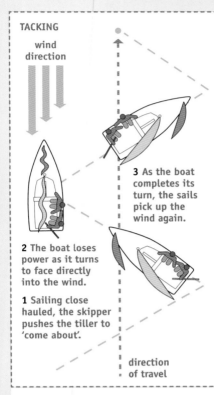

wind direction

3 As the boat completes its turn, the sails pick up the wind again.

2 The boat loses power as it turns to face directly into the wind.

1 Sailing close hauled, the skipper pushes the tiller to 'come about'.

direction of travel

TACKING You can't sail a boat directly into the wind; you have to zigzag to and fro, like a slalom skier. This means sailing close hauled on, say, a starboard tack (with the wind hitting the right-hand side of the boat first) then turning the boat through the wind to sail on a port tack. As you pass through the wind, there will be a moment when there's no force in the sails. For this reason you should build up speed before you make your move, so that the momentum will carry you through from one side of the tack to the other.

GYBING Gybing (or jibing) means taking the stern of the boat across the wind. This is trickier than tacking because it causes the boom – the heavy horizontal pole to which the mainsail is attached – to swing at speed right across the boat. Timing is everything when you gybe – not just to make sure that the boat keeps moving, but also to make sure that you don't get hit by the boom when it swings. You have to be ready to duck out of the way.

GYBING

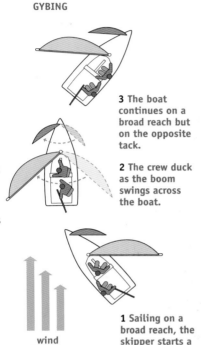

3 The boat continues on a broad reach but on the opposite tack.

2 The crew duck as the boom swings across the boat.

1 Sailing on a broad reach, the skipper starts a slow turn.

wind direction

DOCKING You should come into a dock or mooring with the wind as nearly ahead of you as possible. Come to a stop by slackening the main sheet, so that the sail flaps. If you must dock with the wind behind you, lower the sail when you're 15–20m away, so that the boat loses momentum and coasts in, guided by the tiller.
See also ROPES.

THE TILLER Some boats have steering wheels, as on a car. Others have a tiller, a long pole attached directly to the rudder. With a tiller (but not with a wheel), you steer to the right by pushing to the left, and vice versa. Do this very gently and smoothly, especially when changing tack, or you run the risk of capsizing.

SAFETY Always wear a buoyancy aid when sailing, and always hold on with one hand when moving around a boat.

■ If your boat capsizes and is lying on its side, free the sheets then climb onto the centreboard, With your feet close to the hull, take hold of the gunwale (the rim of the boat) and lean back – your weight should pull the boat upright. Move round to the stern, keeping hold of the boat, and climb back in.

RULES OF THE ROAD Where differently powered boats of differing sizes use the same body of water, it's important that everybody knows who has right of way. There are certain rules that all boat users must observe.

■ You must give way to boats that can't change course without the risk of running aground.
■ Powerboats give way to boats under sail.
■ A sailing boat with the wind on its port side (the left of the boat if you're facing the bow) gives way to a sailing boat with the wind on its starboard (right-hand) side.
■ A boat that's overtaking gives way to the boat being overtaken.
■ If in doubt, take a positive course of action, make it obvious to the other vessel and perform it in plenty of time.

choose the right
Saw for the job

hacksaw

CUTTING METAL Replaceable hacksaw blades have extra-hard teeth, designed to cut through metal. Hacksaws are ideal for cutting pipes.

tenon saw

WOOD JOINTS A tenon saw has a small blade with a solid metal strip along the top. It's designed for making woodworking joints. It can be used for any small wood-cutting task.

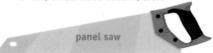
panel saw

CUTTING WOOD A panel saw is the one to choose for most DIY jobs. Its long, flexible blade, usually around 500mm in length, is ideal for cutting up panels of wood or board.

coping saw

CUTING SHAPES The blade on a coping saw can be rotated to any angle, so as to cut shapes and slots in wood, plastic and glass fibre.

ROUGH-CUT LOGS
A bow saw, designed for rough-cutting logs and greenwood branches. Two-handed saws can be used to cut through large logs.

bow saw

use a hand Saw correctly

Safety and accuracy should be your watchwords when sawing. Always use a workbench or sawhorses to support the wood as you cut.

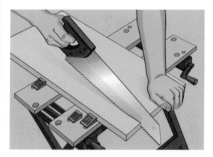

Panel saw Begin by making a few short backwards strokes to create a nick. Guide the blade with the thumb knuckle of your free hand. Once the cut is started, move your free hand, hold the saw at 45 degrees to the wood and saw in even strokes. Use the full length of the blade and keep your arm relaxed. Move the wood forward as you cut.

Coping saw Be sure that the work is gripped firmly in a vice. Use short strokes, adjusting the angle of the blade as necessary as you go.

Hacksaw Use your free hand to hold the front of the D-frame and steady your stroke. Friction might make the blade hot as you work; allow it to cool from time to time.

sharpen a blunt pair of Scissors

YOU WILL NEED Fine file, slipstone (or oilstone), light machine oil

1 Open the scissors and hold them firmly. Use the file to remove any nicks in the blades of the scissors until you have two straight edges.

2 Put a few drops of oil on the slipstone. Hold the scissors firmly, and brace the back of the blade against a solid surface such as a tabletop.

3 Run the slipstone along the cutting edge of the blade, keeping the stone at the same angle as the edge of the blade. Work in smooth strokes. Then run the stone flat along the inner face of the blade to remove any raised 'burr' that may have formed.

4 Sharpen the other blade then tighten the securing screw if necessary.

win at Scrabble

It may not be the player who knows all the long words who wins this highly competitive game, but the crafty technician with an arsenal of short ones and a mastery of letter combinations.

In this crossword game, two to four players hold a running stock of seven lettered tiles of different values, and use them to build word on word. Premium squares, such as 'double word score' and 'triple letter score', yield extra points. There is a bonus of 50 for laying down all seven tiles in one go. Here are some of the secrets of the champions.

■ Learn two-letter words (*al, ai, em, en, ax, ex* ...) and you'll rarely be stuck for something to put down.
■ Learn where 'Q' can be used without a 'U' – *faqir chews qat while typing on his qwerty keyboard.*
■ Try to use 'S' to make a plural at the same time as a new word and score two words for the price of one.
■ Focus on the board, not on your rack. Where you put a word and the options it opens up is at least as important as what you put down.
■ Keep abreast of which tiles have been used – or used up.
■ Aim to use a premium square with every move.
■ Don't hoard high-score tiles. As play progresses it gets ever harder to lay them down, and any you're left with count against you.
■ When laying down the high-scorers you'll want to place them where others can't make use of them – but then nor can you. Consider your tactics and whether to take a chance on a second crack or risk your opponent laying down a feeble spoiler.
■ Get the best score you can with every turn. Holding back because you have nearly got a seven-letter word, or because you might be able to get that triple-word bonus, is a loser's game. While you're hanging out in the hope of something, others can be notching up consistently good scores.

make perfect Scrambled egg

Gentle cooking and meticulous timing are the keys to the best scrambled egg. Use a heavy-based saucepan – a non-stick one is ideal. The freshest eggs are best cooked with a little milk.

SERVES 1-2

2-3 eggs
1 tbsp milk (optional)
salt and freshly ground black pepper
30g butter plus (optional) extra to finish
1 tbsp single cream (optional)

■ Whisk the eggs lightly. Melt the butter over medium heat, add the eggs, lower the heat and cook, stirring constantly with a wooden spoon. As the eggs begin to solidify, scrape them away from the base and sides of the pan.
■ When they are creamy and a little runny, remove from the heat. Serve at once. They will finish cooking in their own heat.
■ For extra richness, add a little more butter and the single cream at the end of cooking if you wish.

remove Scratches
from furniture

There are various ways to remove or disguise scratches, depending on the damage and the surface.

Waxed wood You can remove a light scratch in waxed wood with a retouch crayon or pen, or by sanding with fine abrasive paper or garnet paper (available from craft shops) dipped in linseed oil. Repolish the area, taking care to blend the newly waxed area with its surroundings.
■ A deep scratch can be filled with a wax filler stick, available in various wood colours. Apply by hand, following the instructions, and remove excess with a cloth, making sure that it fills the scratch. Once it has set, polish with wax polish.

Varnished wood Dilute matching varnish with white spirit and apply with a soft brush (above).
■ Work along the length of scratch, brushing in the direction of the grain. Let the varnish dry, then re-apply until surface is slightly raised.
■ Level off with fine glasspaper, dust and apply more varnish to blend with the surface.

Dents in solid wood You can restore a dent in solid wood (not veneer) using a household iron over a damp cloth. The wood will swell, then dry, then you can sand and repolish.

choose the right
Screws

It's important to select the right type and size of screw for the job.

Woodscrew For fixing to wood. Use countersunk screws (right) when joining wood to wood, round-head screws (left) for other fittings.

Coach screw A large screw for fastening bulky pieces of wood together. Has a head like a bolt, so that it can be tightly fixed.

Masonry screw Has a wide thread that can be driven straight into concrete or brick. Some masonry screws have hexagonal washer heads.

Self-tapping screw Cuts its own thread as it's screwed in. Good for fixing to sheet metal and plastic.

raise
Seeds and seedlings
see pages 282-283

Seal gaps around the home

Gaps around door and window frames, holes where pipes go through walls and warped or poorly fitted skirting boards let heat escape and moisture creep in. Seal them with these simple techniques.

Choose the right sealant for the job. For gaps between different materials (brick and wood, for example), you need a flexible acrylic or silicone-based sealant that will allow for any slight movement in future. Flexible sealants come in cylindrical cartridges that fit into a trigger-operated cartridge gun for use. For larger gaps, use expanding foam filler or decorating filler, built up in stages.

Before you start, make sure that the area you're going to work on is clean and sound, otherwise the sealant won't stick.
■ Clean off dirt and dust with a cloth and check that any paintwork is in good condition. Rub it down and repaint it, if necessary, before tackling the sealing.
■ Scrape out any old sealant with a putty knife, screwdriver or a razor blade, taking care to remove it all.

Applying sealant Snip off the end of the nozzle at a 45 degree angle so that the hole at the tip is about half as wide as the crack you have to fill. Don't make it too wide.
■ Squeeze the trigger of the cartridge gun to start the flow of sealant.
■ Start at one end of the gap and, with a steady hand, move slowly and evenly along the gap. You'll need to release and squeeze the trigger again from time to time.
■ Use your thumb to release the locking bar on the piston to stop the sealant flowing when you have finished or need to stop.
■ Use a wet finger or a special sealant-shaping tool to make sure that the sealant has a neat finish and is well bedded into the crack.

Expanding foam filler For deep, wide or awkward-shaped gaps, expanding foam is the easiest solution for a neat finish.
■ Always wear the gloves supplied, as the filler is very sticky when wet.
■ Practise with the can before you start the job. The foam comes out surprisingly fast and expands to up to 60 times its original volume.
■ Spray the gap with a little water to dampen it before filling.
■ Squirt a bead of foam into the gap and allow it to expand.
■ Leave it to dry for up to 2 hours, then cut away the excess with a hacksaw or sharp knife. Wear a face mask to protect you from the dust.
■ Sand the surface smooth if you want to paint over the repair.

make a Seam to join fabric

Seams are used to sew pieces of fabric together. The width of the seam, or 'seam allowance', is usually about 15mm. After stitching, the raw edges need to be finished in some way. Stitch seams by machine or use backstitch or, on very fine fabric, the smallest possible running stitch (*see* SEWING).

Basic plain seam Place fabric pieces right sides together and secure with pins at right angles to the seam. Tack, then remove the pins and stitch by machine or by hand close to the tacking stitches, following the line exactly (*see* TACK).

WRONG SIDE

Pressing and finishing Remove tacking. If a seam is curved – at the top of a sleeve, for example – use small, sharp scissors to make small cuts in the seam allowance to help it to lie flat. Keep well clear of the stitching. Press seam open.

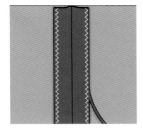
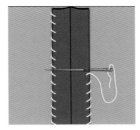

■ For non-fraying fabrics, use pinking shears to cut along the edges of the seam allowance.

■ For fabrics that will fray, use machine overlocking, or sew a zigzag stitch close to the raw edge. Cut any excess fabric close to the stitching.

■ To finish by hand, if you prefer, or if machine stitching is impractical, use overcasting. Make even stitches 3mm in depth and 6mm apart over the raw edges.

ward off Seasickness

If you don't have an over-the-counter remedy to hand, try these strategies to quell your nausea.
■ Get up on deck, preferably at the middle of the vessel, and breathe fresh air. Face toward the direction of travel and focus on something other than the pitching ship – the nearest land or the horizon.
■ Keep busy and occupy your mind, but avoid close work such as reading.

■ If it's warm and sunny lie in a deckchair and close your eyes.
■ Ginger is a trusted herbal remedy for sickness. Crystallised ginger is fine, but some ginger ales don't contain the real thing.
■ Drink plenty of water.
■ Console yourself with the fact that your brain will eventually adjust and you'll find your sea legs – if you don't reach dry land again first.

understand Semaphore

As long as two people can see one another, they can use flags and arm movements to send short, simple messages over long distances.

There are eight arm positions: straight up and down, horizontal (left and right), diagonally up (left and right) and diagonally down.

Each letter of the alphabet is a combination of two arm positions – imagine hands pointing to a clockface of 8 hours. Once you have learned the semaphore alphabet, you simply spell out your message, one letter at a time.

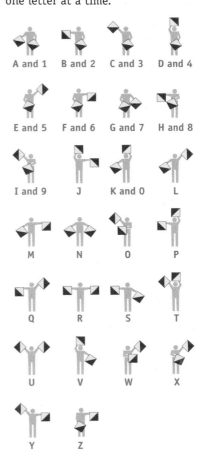

A and 1   B and 2   C and 3   D and 4

E and 5   F and 6   G and 7   H and 8

I and 9   J   K and 0   L

M   N   O   P

Q   R   S   T

U   V   W   X

Y   Z

S

put on a Shadow puppet show

Shadow puppets are silhouettes of animals made by forming a shape with the hands. To make shadow puppets you need only a reading lamp and an expanse of white or light-coloured wall. When you put on your show, position yourself and the light source so that the shadows – not your hands – are the centre of attention. Put on some music to add atmosphere. Withdraw your hands from the light as you form the puppets, so that each one enters the limelight with a flourish.

goat

rabbit

grasp the basics of Sewing by hand

Sewing is the means of joining and decorating pieces of fabric by drawing a threaded needle in and out of the fabric in a variety of ways. By practising and perfecting a few essential stitches it's possible to create clothes and furnishings and make repairs and alterations. Even if you use a sewing machine, hand stitching is essential to many sewing tasks.

Needle types Needles are sized in numbers 1-28 (the higher the number, the thinner the needle), and described according to their type of point. For most jobs 'Sharps' in sizes 7 and 8 are the best choice but have small eyes. 'Crewel' needles in these sizes have larger eyes and are easier to thread. Larger crewels have blunter points and are used for jobs such as wool work, darning and needlepoint. Tapestry needles have blunt ends. Short 'Betweens' are good for fine fabric.

Starting and finishing For all hand stitching and quilting the thread needs to be secured on the wrong (reverse) side of the fabric with a small knot at the thread end or with a few stitches worked over each other on the wrong side. Except for herringbone stitches, always work from right to left. Finish off with a few stitches worked over each other, then cut the thread close to the fabric.

Running stitch Used for tacking, quilting and making gathers. Weave the point of the needle in and out of the fabric several times, then pull the whole needle through. Weave the needle so that both the stitches and the spaces between them are small and even for quilting and gathering, longer for tacking.

Backstitch Used for seams and embroidery. Pull the thread through from the wrong to the right side. Insert the needle 1.5-3mm or half a stitch length behind the point where the thread emerges. Bring it out again at the same distance in front of that point and repeat.

Herringbone Firm and flat for hems. Working left to right, insert the needle diagonally across and above the hem edge and bring it through just to the left of that point. Take the needle back diagonally over the hem edge and insert it, bringing it up just to the left of that point. Repeat as necessary.

Hemstitch (vertical)

Used for a near-invisible finish on hems. Start by bringing the needle through the hem edge. Directly opposite this point,

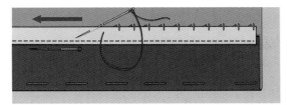

catch a single thread of the fabric. Then direct the needle diagonally to go through the hem edge 6-10mm to the left. Continue along the hem in this way for succeeding stitches.

Blind hemstitch For

an invisible finish, fold back the hem edge and secure the thread inside it. Take very small stitches 6mm apart, catching a single thread of first the garment

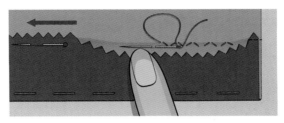

fabric, then the hem fabric. Continue to alternate stitches in this way. Be careful not to pull the stitches too tightly as you go or the material will become gathered.

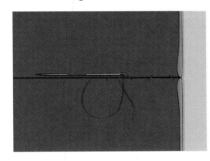

Slipstitch For joining two folded edges (left) or a folded edge to a flat surface. Fasten thread and bring the needle through the folded edge. Make a very small stitch into the flat surface, then take the needle back through the folded edge, bringing it out about 6mm away. Continue to make stitches in this way so that most of the thread is hidden.

See also APPLIQUÉ, CROSS-STITCH, CUSHION COVER, EMBROIDERY, HEM, NEEDLEPOINT, QUILT, SEAM, TACK, ZIP.

---

put up adjustable Shelving

Upright-and-bracket adjustable shelving is economical, versatile, strong and durable – a good option for most domestic purposes.

YOU WILL NEED Tape measure, uprights and brackets, pencil, spirit level or plumb line, drill, wall plugs, screws, screwdriver, bradawl

1 Measure the wall for the uprights. You'll need two uprights for shelves up to 900mm, three (or more) for longer shelves. Hold the first upright to the wall, and mark the position of the top screw with a pencil. Using a spirit level or plumb line, draw a vertical line.

continued overleaf ➜

---

build a survival
Shelter

If you're stranded outdoors for the night, you must find a way to keep warm and dry.

Don't wait until it's getting dark. Find a safe place in daylight, while there's a chance to check for hazards such as rockfalls or a hornets' nest. If you have a tarpaulin or a groundsheet and a length of rope, then you have the makings of a basic shelter.

■ Tie your line between two trees, and lay the tarp over it.

■ Peg the lower edges to the ground to make a tent: most tarps have eyelets for this purpose.

If you have no tarp, build an A-frame.

1 Find a dry spot, a branch 2-3m long and two shorter ones of 1.5m or so. Use the two shorter branches to make an A by pushing both branches into the ground, and tying their tops together. Then push one end of your longer 'ridgepole' into the ground, and tie the other end to the apex of your A. Make sure it's aligned so that the lower end faces the prevailing wind.

2 Fix more branches to the ridgepole, and weave twigs between them. Fill the gaps with evergreen branches or bracken, and cover the ground inside with ferns or conifer branches to provide additional insulation.

S

soothe Shingles

After chickenpox infection, the virus can lie dormant and be reactivated to cause shingles. It's known as *herpes zoster*, from the Greek 'to creep' and 'girdle', because it manifests as a blistering rash that spreads around one side of the body, most often on the trunk. A doctor will prescribe medication, but you can help yourself. If shingles appears on the face, though, consult a doctor urgently as the eyes may be affected.

■ Wear loose clothing that doesn't catch or rub.
■ Take two or three cool baths a day (don't apply talcum powder).
■ Apply calamine lotion.
■ Try adding three drops each of geranium, sage and thyme oil to 20ml of carrier oil and dab it on.

clean and revive a Shirt collar

The collars of shirts are prone to attracting stains from hair grease, make-up and the like. Try treating them with these methods.

■ Use a clean nailbrush to apply a little shampoo formulated for greasy hair or some liquid detergent. Leave for 15 minutes then wash in a washing machine at the hottest setting. For a quick treatment, wash the collar only, by hand, rinse well, rub as dry as possible in a thick towel then iron completely dry.
■ Spray with a stain remover, leave for 10 minutes, or as directed, then wash in the washing machine, again at the hottest safe setting.
■ For lipstick, rub in some white toothpaste as a pre-wash treatment or use a stain remover as above.

2 Draw a parallel vertical line for the second upright. Use a spirit level to pinpoint the exact point at which the top screwhole for the second upright should be drilled. It's crucial that the two top screwholes are made at precisely the same height, otherwise the shelves won't be level.

3 Drill and plug the top two screwholes. Screw the uprights temporarily in position. Use a bradawl to mark the positions of the other screwholes, then swing the uprights aside to drill and plug each one. Then screw the uprights permanently in position.

4 Fit the brackets at the required height, and place the shelves on top, making sure they are all in line. Use the bradawl to mark screwholes in the underside of the shelves, then take them off and make pilot holes. Put them back on the brackets and screw them firmly in place.

fold a Shirt

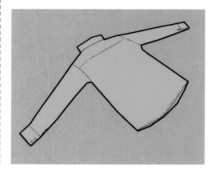

Properly folded shirts and blouses will stay wrinkle free. They are also easier to store neatly on shelves and in drawers. Always start with a well-ironed shirt or blouse (see opposite).

1 If the shirt has buttons, do them up and smooth out any wrinkles. Then place the shirt face down on a flat surface with the arms extended.

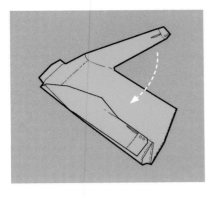

2 Fold in the left shirt side to the centre line of the shirt back, then fold back the sleeve so that its upper edge meets the shirt side seam. Repeat for the other side.

3 Fold up the bottom third of the fabric, then fold over again. Turn the shirt over.

iron a Shirt

Ironing each part of the shirt in the correct order is the key to success: first collar, then cuffs, yoke, sleeves, back and front.

1 Using a pre-heated iron, iron the outside then the inside (the side visible when worn) of the collar (1). Next, iron the inside then the outside of both cuffs (2).

2 Slide the shirt over the pointed end of the ironing board and iron one shoulder of the yoke (3) and then the other.

3 Iron the sleeves (4) on each side, followed by the back (5), again with the fabric spread over the end of the ironing board. Turn the shirt over and iron the front (6), the right side followed by the left side. Button up and then hang or fold the shirt neatly (see opposite).

recognise and deal with Shock

This clinical term doesn't describe emotional trauma, but a dangerous physical response to illness or injury, a complication that itself needs urgent intervention.

Shock occurs most usually as the result of a drop in circulation, often due to blood loss, depriving the vital organs of oxygen. Severe burns, vomiting, a heart attack, bacterial infection or allergy, near-drowning, extreme pain and blood poisoning are among other possible causes.

Suspect shock if the patient is:
- pale, cold and clammy – or sweating profusely
- breathing rapidly, yawning or sighing
- weak and dizzy
- feeling sick or vomiting
- complaining of thirst.

Quick action
- Call an ambulance.
- Be prepared to administer cardio-pulmonary resuscitation (*see* CPR).
- Treat any injuries appropriately (*see* BLEEDING, BURNS AND SCALDS, DROWNING *and* HEART ATTACK).

If the casualty is conscious and their injuries allow it:
- Lie them down with their head lower than their heart to increase blood flow to the brain.
- Unless it interferes with breathing, raise and support their legs.
- Keep them warm – cover with a coat or blanket but don't swaddle them tightly.
- Offer comfort and reassurance.

If the patient is unconscious:
- Place them in the recovery position (*see* RECOVERY POSITION).
- Keep them warm (as above).

In all cases, don't give anything to eat or drink.

See also ALLERGIC EMERGENCY, INFECTIONS.

S

raise Seeds and seedlings

Growing plants from seed is rewarding and economical, but all seeds and seedlings need careful treatment if young plants are to grow and thrive. Perennials take a long time to establish from seed, but vegetables and annual and biennial flowers offer a better chance of success.

Sowing seed Seeds can be sown into pots or trays, or direct into the ground in the warmer months. Sow in spring or summer for a summer or autumn harvest, and autumn for crops that will mature the following year.

YOU WILL NEED Seed compost, vermiculite or sharp sand, pots or trays, small block of wood, water-misting spray or watering can with fine rose, glass, horticultural fleece, masking tape, plastic bags, elastic bands, rake, hoe, garden line, labels, dibber, multipurpose compost. Optional: tamping board, folded card, propagator, cloches, pencil, kitchen fork

START IN POTS OR TRAYS

1 Mix one part sand or vermiculite with every two parts of compost to help drainage. Fill seed trays or small pots, level and tamp down.

2 Moisten compost, then sow seeds, either individually by hand, or by tapping them out of your palm or a folded piece of card using your finger. If seeds are very small, mix them with sand or coffee grounds before planting to make it easier to spread them evenly.

3 Except for very fine seeds, cover with a fine layer of sifted compost. Mist with water. Finish if you wish with a layer of finely ground vermiculite to help to keep the temperature even. Label the pots.

4 Cover each tray with a lid or a sheet of glass or fleece. Place plastic bags over individual pots and secure with elastic bands.

5 Once growth appears, remove the lid or coverings.

SOW DIRECT INTO THE GROUND

Seeds of annuals such as cornflowers, clarkias and Californian poppies that don't transplant well are best scattered direct onto garden beds and raked in lightly. Use sand to mark out areas for each plant, flowing and overlapping for a natural look, and sow in drifts across each section, not in regimented rows.

For vegetables use this method:

1 Rake well-prepared ground and use garden line to mark out rows for your crop, spaced according to the seed packet.

2 Use a hoe to scrape out seed drills to the recommended depth. Plant the seeds as for sowing in trays (left). Cover with soil, firm in with your fingers, water lightly and label. Add an additional covering of fleece or cloches if you wish. If using cloches, water regularly.

HELP THE GERMINATION PROCESS Use these tips to help seeds to germinate better and produce stronger, healthier plants.

- Soak hard-skinned seeds like lupins, beans and peas in warm water for 24 hours before planting to soften them.
- Rub sweet pea seeds with sandpaper or make a nick in each one with a clean sharp knife before planting.
- Plant flat seeds of melons, cucumbers and their relatives on their sides.
- Plant seeds that develop deep roots, such as runner beans, in root trainers – individual, reusable cells which can be folded open to remove seedlings without damage to roots or stems.

PRICKING OUT Many seedlings need more space to mature than their seed tray or first pot allows. Tender plants need the shelter of a cold frame or greenhouse, but a loose covering of fleece can also work well for outdoor seedlings.

1 Fill the bottom half of a tray or pots with a 2:1 mixture of moist multipurpose potting compost and sand or vermiculite. Top up with compost and firm down. Make planting holes at least 2.5-3.5cm apart using a dibber or pencil.

2 Lever up a clump of seedlings with the dibber or an old kitchen fork. Tease out seedlings individually, holding them by their seed leaves – the first to appear, which usually look different from the true leaves.

3 Plant in the holes and firm in with your fingers. Water lightly.

BUYING AND SAVING SEEDS
Seeds are usually sold loose in packets, but some vegetables are now also supplied on tapes that you bury in the ground, with no thinning or transplanting.

■ To save seed from garden plants, allow seed heads to ripen for as long as possible. Collect direct from the plants or cut off seed heads, dry them in a warm place then shake or pick off the seeds.

HARDENING OFF Frost-tender plants need hardening off before they are planted out. If they are being grown indoors, put them out during the day and bring them in again at night. If they are in a cold frame or greenhouse, open the ventilation for a few hours each day, and close it up at night. Gradually increase the ventilation until protection is no longer required. Watch out for late frosts.

THINNING AND TRANSPLANTING
Without thinning out and transplanting, young plants will grow weakly. These jobs are best done when the soil is damp (water them if necessary) but remember that seedlings of root vegetables such as carrots and beetroot won't transplant satisfactorily.

■ Use one hand to pull out an unwanted seedling while pressing the other down on the soil.
■ Firm in all remaining plants and water well.
■ Select the best seedlings with good, healthy leaves and strong roots for transplanting. Discard any weak or damaged plants.
■ Use a small dibber or trowel to make holes for new plants and insert them.
■ Firm in with your fingers and water well.

cure squeaky Shoes

Eliminating unwanted friction between parts of a shoe is the way to cure squeaks. Spraying the squeaky area with WD-40, or dusting it with talcum powder, are two good cure-alls. If the squeak seems to be coming from the inside of the shoe, partially lift the inner sole and dust inside with powder. If the tongue is rubbing against the laces, apply saddle soap or a similar leather conditioner to the tongue and re-apply as necessary. If a heel is loose, take it to be repaired professionally or try to secure it with bonding glue.

stretch tight Shoes

Nearly all shoes stretch in time, and if a little too tight it's worth wearing them around the house for a while to break them in. If this doesn't work, try one of these remedies before resorting to professional treatment.

- Stuff shoes as tightly as possible with crumpled wet newspaper or peeled potatoes. Leave to dry out slowly, then wear shoes for a few hours – they should have more 'give'.
- For leather shoes, put on thick socks and squeeze your feet in. Heat the troublesome area for 20 to 30 seconds with a hair dryer while bending and unbending your toes.
- Swab the insides of leather shoes with surgical spirit, concentrating on the tightest areas. Put the shoes on and walk around for a few minutes. Or soak an old pair of socks with the spirit, put them on and wear the shoes.

work out Shoe sizes around the world

ADULT'S		Sizes will vary, so use these two charts as a guide only.		
UK/AUSTRALIA/ NEW ZEALAND	EUROPE	USA/CANADA Women	Men	JAPAN
2	34	4½	-	21.5
2½	35	5	-	22
3	35.5	5½	-	22.5
3½	36	6	-	23
4	37	6½	-	23
4½	37.5	7	-	23.5
5	38	7½	5½	24
5½	38.5	8	6	24
6	39	8½	6½	24.5
6½	39.5	9	7	25
7	40	9½	7½	25.5
7½	41	10	8	26
8	42	10½	8½	26.5
8½	42.5	-	9	27
9	43	-	9½	27.5
9½	44	-	10	28
10	44.5	-	10½	28.5
10½	45	-	11	29
11	46	-	11½	29.5
11½	46.5	-	12	30
12	47	-	12½	30.5

CHILDREN'S			
UK/AUSTRALIA/ NEW ZEALAND	EUROPE	USA/CANADA	JAPAN
5½	23	6½	-
6	23.5	7	14
6½	24	7½	-
7	24.5	8	15
7½	25	8½	-
8	25.5	9	16
8½	26	9½	-
9	26.5	10	16.5
9½	27	10½	-
10	27.5	11	17.5
10½	28	11½	-
11	28.5	12	18.5
11½	29	12½	-
12	30	13	19
13	31	1	20
13	31.5	1½	20.5
1	32.5	2	21
1½	33	2½	21.5
2	33.5	3	22

lace and tie Shoes

Most of us learn to tie our shoes as infants with a rudimentary bow – and spend the rest of our lives stooping to retie them. A bit late in the day, but learn better ways to lace and tie your shoes.

Ace lace This lacing method gives you a neat ladder-like finish on top of the shoe with tight and secure criss-crossing underneath.

1 Thread the lace ends down through the eyelets at the toe-end.

2 Bring the orange end as shown up through the next but one eyelet on the opposite side; take it across, then down through the eyelet directly across.

3 Take the red end as shown diagonally over the other and bring it up through the next empty eyelet opposite, then draw it straight across and thread it down through the opposite eyelet.

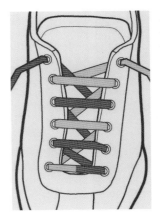

4 Repeat the actions of step 2 with each end in turn. You'll find that the orange lace will skip an eyelet one more time, while the red lace will perform the action twice.

5 Keep running lace ends in this way diagonally on the underside and straight across on the top until they reach the final eyelets at the top.

Tie the knot An easy variation of the basic knot, this is known as a 'bunny ears' knot because you create two loops at once rather than work with a loop and a single strand.

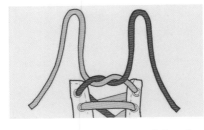

1 Start as normal, right over left and under; pull tight.

2 Make a loop in both strands and cross them over.

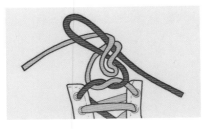

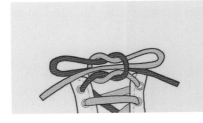

3 Wrap the lower loop around the upper and feed the end of it through the gap between the upper loop and the starter knot.

4 Take hold of both loops and draw tight. It will stay tied all day.

look after and clean Shoes

Shoes will keep their shape and last longer if well cared for and cleaned regularly. Take them to be repaired before heels wear right down into the body of the shoe and before soles become thin and uncomfortable.

Shoe care
- If possible, switch to a different pair of shoes every couple of days.
- Insert shoe trees into good leather shoes to keep them in shape.
- Dry wet shoes away from direct heat. Stuff them with newspaper or rolled-up magazines to keep them in shape and absorb moisture.
- Remove salt stains by rubbing with equal parts of water and vinegar applied on a cotton pad.
- Protect new shoes with a waterproof stain-repellent spray and repeat applications regularly before going out in bad weather.

Shoe cleaning
Leather Brush off loose dirt with a stiff brush. Apply polish with a clean cotton cloth or soft brush. Leave to dry for 10 minutes then buff with a clean cloth or brush. Remove laces before cleaning. If dirty, clean with saddle soap using given directions.

Patent leather Shine with purpose-made cream, baby oil or petroleum jelly using a clean cloth. Remove scuffs with a clean pencil eraser.

Suede Use a plastic or fine metal brush to clean and brush the nap. Dust oily stains with baby powder and brush off.

Canvas Spray with stain remover then scrub by hand with detergent. Or machine wash, adding towels to stop them from bouncing around.

S

bake the best
Shortbread

Butter is an essential ingredient of shortbread, a Scottish speciality. Add rice flour or semolina for a fine-grained but deliciously crunchy texture.

MAKES 8 WEDGES

100g plain flour
50g rice flour or semolina
50g caster sugar, plus extra for dusting
100g salted butter, chilled

1 Sift the flours into a bowl, add the sugar and grate in the butter using a coarse grater. Rub in the butter until the dough resembles breadcrumbs. Press into an 18cm straight-sided sandwich tin and level the top. Prick all over with a fork.

2 Chill in the fridge for 1 hour. Heat the oven to 150°C/gas 2 and bake for about 1 hour or until straw-coloured. Cool in the tin for 10 minutes then cool further on a wire rack. While it's still warm, mark into eight wedges. Dredge with caster sugar and separate into wedges before serving.

golden rules

PLANTING SHRUBS
- **Always choose shrubs to match your garden conditions. Check your soil type** (see SOIL) **and read labels carefully.**
- **Don't skimp on hole size.**
- **Water frequently and generously until established.**
- **Put in supports before, not after, planting.**

Shop responsibly

With a bit of thought you can use your buying choices to benefit causes that matter to you, such as the environment, local businesses, ethical trading, international development or animal welfare.

For the environment
- Buy less. If you're constantly throwing food away, edit your shopping list.
- Shop close to home. By using independent neighbourhood stores and services, you can save on car use – and support your local community.
- Choose locally sourced goods. In general these will have required less transportation, and therefore had less impact on the environment.
- Opt for organic – but be discriminating. Organic food crops, free from chemical fertilisers and pesticides, confer benefits to the workforce, the consumer and the environment where they are grown. However, organic fare flown in from overseas may have a greater overall impact on the environment than non-organic foods grown locally.
- Think before you eat. There are plenty more fish in the sea, for example, than the most endangered species. Be adventurous, try new species, look for the 'approved' certification. Buy 'dolphin-friendly' tuna.
- Choose goods that are packaged in an efficient and easy-to-recycle way.
- Take your own shopping bags with you rather than accumulating a mountain of unwanted plastic bags back at home.

For ethical trading
- Favour Fairtrade. The label guarantees a better deal for producers in the developing world, while a proportion is invested in development projects.
- Favour manufacturers with a good company profile (read their mission statements), over makers of shoddy, cut-price throwaway goods.
- Use charity shops. Pass unwanted clothing and goods on to a charity outlet and buy from there yourself (you may be amazed at what you find).
- Shop at cooperative-style stores, where a greater percentage of the profits will go to the store workers themselves.

For animal welfare
- Choose free-range meat, poultry and eggs rather than cheaper but intensively farmed alternatives.
- Avoid cosmetics or household goods that have been tested on animals. Look for the internationally recognised Leaping Bunny logo, a guarantee that no such testing has taken place during the product's development.

plant a Shrub

Shrubs are the backbone of the garden. They are best planted in autumn, while dormant, or in early spring before they sprout into growth. Except for acid lovers such as azaleas and rhododendrons, all shrubs, including roses, will benefit from the addition of granules containing mycorrhizal fungi, which encourage root growth. Follow the maker's instructions, making sure that roots and granules are in contact.

Before planting Prepare a planting mixture of 2.5 litres each of well-rotted manure and garden compost plus 100g of sterilised bone meal. Dig over the planting area to one spade's depth, removing all perennial weeds. Have some mulch ready to cover the soil around the new shrub (*see* MULCH).

Planting Most shrubs are bought container-grown, but can also be obtained bare-rooted (*see* TREE). Before buying container-grown shrubs, remove them from the pot and check that there are several white roots around the rootball.

1 Dig a hole as deep as, and slightly wider than, the plant's rootball. When you place the plant in the hole, the base of its stem should be at the same level as the surrounding soil.

2 Water the plant and remove its container, if applicable. If the roots are wound around the outside of the rootball, tease out some of the outer roots so that they will establish more quickly in the surrounding soil.

3 Holding the plant by its stem, and supporting the rootball, place it in the hole. Fill the hole to the top with the planting mixture and tread down firmly. Top up and tread down again, then water thoroughly.

master Shrub pruning

Regular light pruning is the best way to keep shrubs in good health and to ensure that they produce flowers each year. Rather than pruning them precisely, shrubs with many thin stems such as *Spiraea* and *Potentilla* are best cut back and shaped with shears.

Before pruning a shrub to shape cut out all dead and diseased wood. (This can be done at any time of year.)

Shrubs that flower after midsummer Late bloomers such as *Lavatera* (mallow) and buddleja (right) should be pruned in early spring, before new growth starts. Cut back last year's flowering stems and any weak shoots. The harder you prune the more new growth – on which flowers will develop – will be produced.

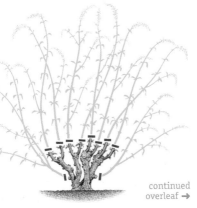

continued overleaf ➜

overcome Shyness

Don't be a shrinking violet. Work on your confidence and blossom at work and play.

■ Understand your shyness, notice where and when it strikes and ask yourself what it is that you fear. Note down the negative messages that you send yourself then list the assumptions on which they are based. Remind yourself that they are assumptions not facts.

■ Feel the fear and do it anyway. Strike up a conversation, go for that interview, make that phone call, go to that party. If you duck out of challenging situations you only reinforce your problem.

■ Set a target. Don't go to a party expecting to talk to every single guest. Challenge yourself to talk to, say, three people you don't know.

■ Break social encounters down into smaller, simpler steps. Start with everything but conversation: stand tall, look around you, make eye contact, smile. A friendly approach is usually welcome and reciprocated.

■ Keep conversation simple (see CONVERSATION). Say hello, introduce yourself, find out the other person's name, make a comment, ask a question. Above all, take an interest in what the other person has to say: don't worry what they think about you.

■ Remember that you have something in common with the other person: you are both in the same place at the same time. Think about why: do you have a shared acquaintance, interest or job? Use this to fuel your conversation.

■ Be polite. Thank people warmly for any service. Be appreciative. Make them feel good. It will help you to feel the same way.

S

golden rules

PRUNE SHRUBS

- Use sharp secateurs and make cuts as clean as possible.
- Cut back to an outward-facing pair of buds if you can.
- Remove all green shoots from variegated shrubs as soon as they appear. This prevents them from taking over the whole plant.

keep Silver clean

As well as pastes and liquid, you can buy polishing gloves and cloths to buff up silver regularly. For valuable items try a jeweller's rouge cloth (available online). Always wash silver by hand in warm water with mild washing-up liquid and dry at once to avoid leaving marks.

Cutlery Clean with paste or polish applied and buffed off with a soft cloth. Solid silver – but never silver plate – can be immersed in a silver dip according to the instructions. The dip will strip off plating, especially if it's damaged.

Ornate pieces Sprinkle on some bicarbonate of soda (baking soda) and rub off with a soft cloth. Use a soft brush to get into any crevices.

Jewellery Clean as for silver-plated cutlery. Dip an old toothbrush in bicarbonate of soda for cleaning crevices. Wash in warm water and dry well.

Shrubs that flower before midsummer Early bloomers such as *Forsythia*, *Philadelphus* and *Weigela* (right) produce flowers on wood grown by the shrub the previous season. They should be pruned as soon as flowers fade, cutting back only to the highest new shoot or bud. This gives the shrub time to grow mature wood ready to flower again the following season.

Shrubs grown for coloured stems Prune in early spring, cutting back all the previous year's growth to near ground level or to an established framework of branches.

Evergreen shrubs Prune to keep them in shape, to shorten over-long shoots and to thin out congested plants in late spring and summer.

empty a fish tank using a Siphon

Transferring liquid from one receptacle to another can be laborious and messy, especially when a container is really heavy and difficult to move – like an aquarium. The easy way is to siphon it out. All you need are flexible tubing, a bucket and a helping hand from gravity and atmospheric pressure.

1 Place your bucket on the ground, close to the tank. The bottom of the tank must be higher than the bucket – the greater the vertical distance the quicker the liquid will flow. If there are any fish in the tank, transfer them to a safe place.

2 Find a length of flexible plastic tubing long enough to reach easily from the bottom of the tank to the bottom on the bucket. If possible, use transparent tubing so that you can monitor the flow of liquid. Holding the tubing in an even U shape, carefully fill it from a tap until the water reaches nearly to the top of each end. Cover each end with a thumb. This will be easier if you have someone to help.

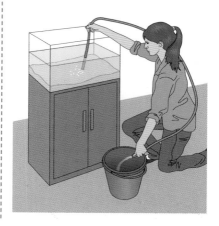

3 Move to the tank and, keeping your thumbs in place, insert one end of the tube into the bottom of the tank and the other into the bucket. Remove your thumb from the end in the tank and then do the same with the end in the bucket. The water will now flow out from the tank. The tube will also suck away mess at the bottom of the tank.

4 To stop the flow, if, for example, the bucket is full, lift the tube out of the tank water – the water left in the tube will empty out. To start again, refill the tube as in step 2. If the tank is large, you'll need several buckets to hand.

unblock a Sink or basin

If water isn't draining away from your sink or basin, then there's a blockage somewhere below the plughole.

First, try using a plunger If that works you won't have to dismantle any of the pipework. Place a sink plunger squarely over the plughole, and hold a damp cloth tightly against the overflow. Pump the plunger sharply up and down.

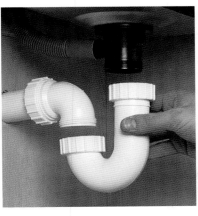

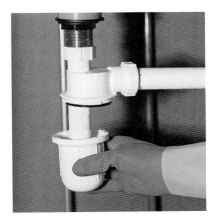

If plunging fails, look at the pipework underneath the sink or basin. Directly beneath the plughole there will be a plastic 'bottle trap' (above, right) or a P-shaped sink trap (above, left). Put the plug in the plughole of the sink, and place a bucket underneath the trap to catch any dirty water that may be blocked up in there. Unscrew the trap carefully (there's one central screw on a bottle trap, one on each end of a P-shaped trap). Wash it thoroughly if it's blocked with hair, grease or food debris, and then screw it back in place.

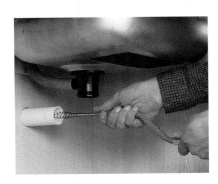

If the sink or basin still won't drain, the blockage is further down the pipe. You'll need a 'plumber's snake', a spiral device that can be bought or hired. Disconnect the trap once more, and feed the wire into the pipe. Turn the handle to rotate the spiral, which should break up any blockage it encounters. Re-assemble the trap, remove the plug from the plughole and run the tap to test.

alleviate Sinusitis

When infection causes the linings of the sinuses (small cavities behind the cheekbones and forehead, opening into the nose cavity) to become inflamed, it can cause fever, pain, tenderness and a blocked or runny nose. Sinusitis usually clears up on its own, but if symptoms persist you should see your doctor. In the meantime, there are a number of ways to ease the problem.

Try a steam inhalation of a decongestant. You can buy a ready-made mixture from a pharmacist or make one yourself at home.
■ Put two drops of tea tree, pine or eucalyptus essential oil in a bowl and pour in a litre of hot water.
■ Lean over the bowl with a towel draped over your head and breathe in the soothing vapours for 10 minutes, inhaling as far as possible through the nose.
■ If you're having trouble breathing, rub a couple of drops of tea tree oil between your palms and inhale from your cupped hands.

Eat horseradish For a strong decongestant blast try chewing and swallowing ½ tsp of freshly grated horseradish root. To avoid stomach irritation, use this remedy only after a snack or meal.

Add pepper to a meal One of the quickest ways to loosen up blocked sinuses is to sprinkle cayenne pepper on your food.

embrace life after
Sixty

Once upon a time, 60 was 'old'. Advances in medicine, healthier lifestyles and a revolution in attitudes to age have changed all that, but there are still key actions you can take to give you the best chance of staying well after 60.

Worry less about losing weight
If you do drop weight after 60, you could be losing muscle and even bone density, making you weaker, with less balance and flexibility, and so more likely to have a fall. An obese person, though, should still be looking to lose some weight.

Eat more food but fewer calories
Concentrate on eating for good nutrition and disease prevention. Pile your plate high with fruit and vegetables, add beans and wholegrains, and cut down on high-calorie culprits such as burgers and cream sauces. *See also* DIET.

Keep excercising Even day-to-day chores such as mowing the lawn or sweeping leaves a few times a week will keep you mobile and active for longer, and even stave off heart disease and diabetes. *See also* AEROBIC EXERCISE.

Do something interesting Join a choir, do charity work, take up painting and you'll have less stress, better moods and even lower blood pressure. Indulge in puzzles and other brain-stretchers and you could even lower your risk of Alzheimer's and other forms of dementia.

Have a laugh Share plenty of time with friends, watch funny films, look on the bright side, and the endorphins released will make you more relaxed, less stressed and likely to fight off infections.

Sit properly

The teacher who told you to 'sit up straight' had a point. Good sitting posture is important to your health – but holding yourself rigid can be as bad as slouching.

Change your sitting posture regularly to alter the forces on your joints and muscles. If you're reading a document or are on the phone, move in your chair, perhaps sit back and relax a little, or stand up to take a call.

Working at a computer Pay attention to the height of your chair in relation to your desk, your monitor and your own height.

Your head should be freely poised, shoulders relaxed, and your knees slightly apart.

The top of the screen should be slightly below your eye level. If it's too low use a stand for it. The screen should be positioned so it doesn't reflect glare and cause avoidable eye strain.

Choose an ergonomic chair with lower-back support for good posture.

Hold your forearms level or tilt them up slightly.

Avoid slouching, crossing your legs or twisting your body. To lean forward, keep your bottom on the chair and bend from the hip joint.

The work surface should be at about elbow level and afford clearance below for your knees.

Aim to sit with your feet flat and your thighs parallel to the floor. Adjust your chair height with these factors in mind.

Check and correct your posture periodically, and take regular breaks to stand up and walk around.

At the wheel Sitting incorrectly when you drive can not only cause back strain but affect the quality of your driving and place you in danger in an emergency. When you get into your vehicle make sure the seat is optimally positioned for you. Don't sit too far back so that you can barely grasp the bottom of the wheel – or too far forward so that you're hanging on to it.
- Your legs should be comfortable when you press a pedal to the floor.
- Hold the upper part of the steering wheel with your free hand and adjust the seat back so that your arms are not bent at the elbow when holding the wheel and your back is comfortably supported.

steer out of a Skid

You've lost control of your car; keep a grip on your nerves.
A panic reaction will make the situation more dangerous.

Front-wheel skid You're approaching a bend in the road and turn the wheel but your car continues to travel straight on.

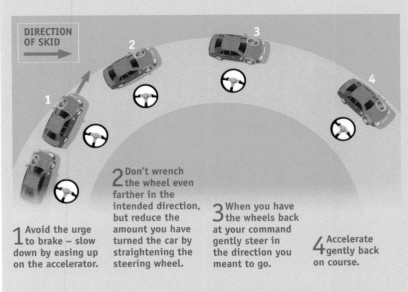

DIRECTION OF SKID

1 Avoid the urge to brake – slow down by easing up on the accelerator.

2 Don't wrench the wheel even farther in the intended direction, but reduce the amount you have turned the car by straightening the steering wheel.

3 When you have the wheels back at your command gently steer in the direction you meant to go.

4 Accelerate gently back on course.

Rear-wheel skid As you round a bend, the back of the car begins to slew as if it might break away or spin you around.

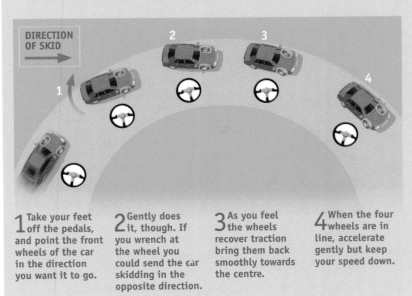

DIRECTION OF SKID

1 Take your feet off the pedals, and point the front wheels of the car in the direction you want it to go.

2 Gently does it, though. If you wrench at the wheel you could send the car skidding in the opposite direction.

3 As you feel the wheels recover traction bring them back smoothly towards the centre.

4 When the four wheels are in line, accelerate gently but keep your speed down.

---

get on board with
Skateboarding

As with skating and bicycling, everything in skateboarding is easier once you're balanced.

■ All beginners fall off their skateboards, so invest in knee and elbow pads and a helmet. Specialised skateboarding shoes, designed to grip the board, might make the early stages easier for you.

■ First, get balanced. Stand, feet apart, on the flat section of the board. Your dominant foot should be at the front, or 'nose', of the skateboard (this end is usually curved up slightly higher than the tail-end). Place your feet at right angles to the length of the board, and turn body and head towards the front.
■ To 'roll', or move forwards, angle your front foot towards the nose, and use your back foot to push, as with a child's scooter. When you pick up speed, put both feet on the board and adopt the balancing position.
■ To steer, move your centre of gravity to one side of the board or the other. Shift your weight to the right, and you'll go into a wide, right-hand turn. To slow down, lean towards the back of the board.

S

Skim stones
across the water

Choose your stone carefully. Look for an oval one about the size of your palm. It should be flat, thin and as light as possible. Bear in mind that you'll get more bounces if the surface of the water is calm.

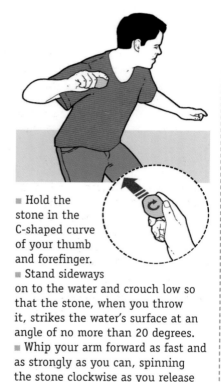

■ Hold the stone in the C-shaped curve of your thumb and forefinger.
■ Stand sideways on to the water and crouch low so that the stone, when you throw it, strikes the water's surface at an angle of no more than 20 degrees.
■ Whip your arm forward as fast and as strongly as you can, spinning the stone clockwise as you release it. Then watch it bounce, bounce, bounce towards the horizon …

master the basics of Skiing

The key to skiing well is good balance. Concentrate on that and everything else will follow.

In skiing, the quality of your gear makes a difference. Stood on end, your skis should come up to around eye level: long skis are harder to control. Buy the best boots that you can afford: good boots make skiing easier. Your poles, like your skis, should be the right length. Turn them upside down and grasp them below the basket (the hoop near the tip). With the poles resting on the ground, your elbow should be bent at a right angle.

In a starting position, ready to push off, your ankles, knees and hips should be slightly bent, and your weight should be in the centre of your feet. But your body should be upright, and you shouldn't be leaning steeply forward from the waist.

To begin skiing down a gentle slope, push off with your poles, then hold them so that they are pointing backwards, clear of the ground. Once you're gliding downhill, you shouldn't need to use the poles to propel you. Bend your ankles, knees and hips, enough to feel the pressure on the tongues of your boots. Look ahead – not at your feet – and allow your body to take care of your balance.

To slow down, angle your legs so the tips of your skis are pointing at each other – a position known as the wedge or snow-plough. Keep your knees apart and your weight forward and equal on both feet, and don't allow your ski tips to cross. The wider your wedge (the further apart the back of the skis) the slower you'll go. Keep making it wider, and, if on easy terrain, you'll come to a stop.

install Skype and make free calls

Skype is a computer program that lets you make free phone calls from one computer to another across the internet. You'll need to connect microphone and speakers if they aren't built in to your computer.

First go to www.skype.com and follow the instructions that you find there to download the software. Once the software has downloaded, run the installation 'Wizard'. You'll have to assign yourself a Skype name – your actual name is fine. This will be the equivalent of your Skype phone number.

When you launch for the first time, go to the **Contacts** menu and click on **Search for People on Skype**. Type in the name of a friend you know is on Skype already. Make sure you choose the right person from the list of people with that name (either by asking their username in advance, or by checking the name against that user's given location). Click **Add contact**, then click **OK**. That person will be added to your address book once they respond, and you'll be able to see when they are logged on to Skype.

To make a call, click on a name in your contacts list that's highlighted with a green tick. Then click on the phone icon if you want to speak to that person without a visual link – or on the camera icon if you'd like to see each other (both computers need a webcam for this to work – *see* WEBCAM).

---

get a good night's Sleep

A good bed and bedding, and a clean, tidy, well-aired and fresh-smelling bedroom, are key to unbroken, restorative sleep.

Love your bedroom You spend about a third of your life there. Dedicate it to sleep. Banish the computer and television to other rooms. Eliminate dust and mess. Hang up clothes, return books to the shelves.

Launder the sheets often They should smell fresh. Also, lightly spray with lavender water – the perfume is said to aid sleep and relaxation.

Set a routine Keep regular hours and start to wind down as you look forward to going to bed. Create a ritual to prepare for bed. Read, write down your thoughts, watch television (but not thrillers or horror), whatever relaxes you.

Not too hot, not too cold Set a comfortable temperature for your bedroom.

Sleep in complete darkness – and seek sunlight in the morning. As bedtime approaches start to dim your lights; don't sit in glare.

Try to soundproof your bedroom Exposure to noise at night can suppress the immune system – even if it doesn't wake you.

Use an old-fashioned alarm clock The tiny luminous particles from a digital clock are enough to disturb sleep, while the sheer visibility of digits as the hours tick away makes for fretfulness if you're wakeful. Electrical alarms and other devices may also transmit electrical fields or faint sounds to disturb sleep and penetrate consciousness. *See also* INSOMNIA, MATTRESS, PILLOWS.

Skip
for health or for fun

Group skipping with a long rope is a popular playground game, but skipping isn't just child's play. For adults, solo skipping is an exhilarating way to burn calories and keep fit.

Solo skipping
■ Use the right length of rope: if you stand on the middle you should be able to bring the ends of the rope up to your armpits.
■ Start with the rope hanging to the floor behind your heels, arms angled out from the hips.
■ Twirl the rope forward using small circular wrist movements.
■ Keep your feet together and bend your knees slightly as you jump.
■ For a basic workout, skip for 30 seconds, rest for 30 seconds. Repeat ten times. Gradually progress to 60 second intervals over 20 minutes.

Playground games
Skippers do stints as 'enders', to turn the rope for their playmates.

'I like ...' First skipper ducks under the turning rope and starts to skip, before calling in a friend (let's say Sam), by chanting *I like coffee, I like tea, I like Sam in with me*. Sam joins in and both jump rope. Then it's *I don't like coffee, I don't like tea, I don't like Sam in with me!* Sam has to exit and another friend is called. The aim is to keep going for as long as possible without a fault.

'Teddy bear ...' Four players skip in time to a chant: *Teddy bear, teddy bear, turn around. Teddy bear, teddy bear, touch the ground. Teddy bear, teddy bear, go upstairs. Teddy bear, teddy bear, say your prayers*. The skippers have not only to jump the rope but also mime these actions.

S

win the battle against
Slugs and snails

These slimy little creatures destroy plants virtually overnight. Their particular penchant is for the soft foliage of salad vegetables and herbaceous perennials such as hostas, and for strawberries. Although plants at soil level are most vulnerable, slugs and snails will also climb up and eat young clematis.

- Try to avoid having dark havens in the garden, such as behind pieces of wood or loose bricks.
- Sprinkle slug pellets sparingly. These are now available in organic formulations.
- Hand-pick and destroy slugs and snails, particularly when they emerge after rain and at dusk.
- Sink glass jars filled 50:50 with beer and water into the ground. The creatures will be lured into them and then drown.
- Surround plants with glass or gravel chippings, or with coffee grounds.

- Wrap copper bands around pots (above). Slugs and snails can't tolerate the metal.
- Scoop out grapefruit halves and place them upside down beside vulnerable plants where slugs and snails will accumulate overnight and can be removed and destroyed.

make a Sling for an injured person

If your first-aid kit doesn't have a sling, you can support an injured arm with a triangular bandage (*see* BANDAGE). Treat any wound before applying a sling.

1 Place the arm across the body with the hand slightly above the elbow and thumb uppermost. Handle with great care if you suspect a break. Slide a triangular bandage between the arm and chest so that the corner opposite the longest edge of the bandage is behind the elbow of the injured arm. Take the top corner around the back of the neck to the front of the shoulder on the injured side.

2 Carefully support the site of the injury with soft padding such as a towel. Then bring the bottom corner of the bandage up and over the injured arm. Tie it to the top corner using a reef knot (*see* KNOTS) just over the hollow in front of the shoulder.

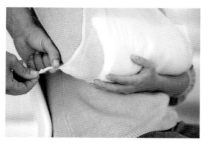

3 Twist the excess fabric at the elbow so that the sling fits snugly around the joint, then tuck the twisted end into the fabric. The weight of the arm in the sling will then hold the twisted end in place. Monitor the fingers to check they aren't turning pale or blue. Check the pulse and ask the casualty about any tingling – if there are signs of loss of circulation, loosen the sling.

Improvised jacket sling If the casualty is wearing a jacket, this will serve very well as a support for the injured arm.

For an injury to the forearm, hand or wrist
- Undo the jacket's fastenings.
- Ask the casualty to support the injured arm as you bring the hem up and over, ensuring that the elbow is supported (see left).
- Fasten the hem to the jacket with safety pins.

For an upper-arm injury
- Gently unzip or unbutton the jacket a little way down from the top.
- Slide the casualty's hand into the jacket opening and, if you're unsure of the solidity of the zip or buttons, fasten beneath it with safety pins.

build your own fish Smokery

Hot-smoking is a great way to cook fish such as mackerel and salmon. A smokery is easy to make from everyday household equipment.

YOU WILL NEED **Roasting tin, bricks, sawdust, grill rack, cooking oil, fish, brine (water saturated with salt), baking sheet, methylated spirit burners**

1 Take an ordinary roasting tin and place it on four bricks, outdoors. Sprinkle in 2 tbsp of sawdust – hickory, oak or maple. (This 'smoke dust' can be bought from fishing-tackle shops or barbecue shops.) Place a grill rack inside the roasting tin, so that it sits above the sawdust.

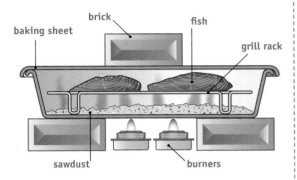

baking sheet · brick · fish · grill rack · sawdust · burners

2 Wipe some oil on the rack to keep your food from sticking. Put the fish on the rack having first soaked it in brine for 30 minutes and patted it dry. If the fish is filleted, place it skin-side down. Use a baking sheet to cover the roasting tin and weigh it down with another brick.

3 Half-fill two burners (available from camping shops) with methylated spirit. Position them underneath your homemade smokery, between the supporting bricks, and carefully light the meths with a match.

4 Don't worry if smoke seeps out of the burner: that's as it should be. Refill the burners if they run out of meths – but take great care when doing so, as they will be hot. Cook the fish for 20 minutes or so, remove it from the smoker, and allow to cool before serving.

---

prepare, cook and eat Snails

Although garden snails are edible, they need careful preparation to remove harmful toxins. It's best instead to buy snails in tins with the shells supplied alongside. They are traditionally cooked with garlic butter in *escargotières* – earthenware dishes with indents to hold the shells. They are best eaten with the help of purpose-made tongs and small, sharp forks.

SERVES 4

200g butter, softened
2 tbsp brandy or white wine
4 tbsp chopped parsley
2 large garlic cloves, crushed
4 tbsp breadcrumbs
salt and freshly ground black pepper, to taste
24 canned snails, drained and rinsed, plus shells

Heat the oven to 200°C/gas 6. Put the butter, brandy, parsley, garlic and breadcrumbs in a bowl and mix well with a fork. With a teaspoon, put a little of the mixture into each shell, add a snail, then fill each shell up to the rim with more mixture. Transfer to *escargotières* or four shallow ovenproof dishes. Bake for about 10 minutes, until the butter is bubbling.

give up Smoking

The addiction to tobacco is powerful – but so is the human will. Make up your mind to quit and you'll do so.

Set a date for giving up Tell everyone of your intention.

Write down the reasons why you want to give up They will be compelling.

Prepare for withdrawal symptoms For a while you may feel out of temper, confused, anxious or restless. You may have a headache or insomnia, but these don't last for ever. Symptoms tend to peak in two to three days, reducing over two to four weeks. Nicotine patches or nicotine chewing gum can help. You may also, perversely, have a cough. All this just signals that your body is ridding itself of toxins.

Take some exercise It will reduce those wretched symptoms, enhance your mood and improve your chances of success.

Try acupuncture It has a good track record for treating addictions and symptoms of withdrawal.

Get rid of ashtrays and lighters You have no more use for smokers' paraphernalia.

Avoid places and situations you associate with smoking And, where possible, avoid associating with continuing smokers.

Have your teeth cleaned by the dentist Enjoy the novelty of a fresh mouth.

Bank the money you would have spent on cigarettes If you have a 20-a-day habit, think what a holiday you can have after a year as a non-smoker. Just don't celebrate with a cigarette.

use a Snorkel

Safe snorkelling means having the right kit. The mask should fit snugly; the snorkel should be a J-shaped breathing tube with a mouthpiece that sits comfortably between your teeth. Only snorkel if you can swim well, and never snorkel alone.

■ Put on the mask and snorkel and check that they fit well.

■ With your head still above water, take a few practice breaths in and out of your snorkel. Get used to breathing only through your mouth rather than your nose.

■ Start swimming and duck your face just below the surface of the water. Continue breathing steadily through the mouthpiece and watch in wonder as a new world opens up to you beneath the waves.

It's possible to dive underwater with a snorkel, but you'll need to clear the tube of water afterwards. Tilt your head well back as you rise to the surface. Exhale as you break the surface and keep on breathing out as you tilt your head forwards.

If your mask fills with water, look up, press the top of the mask, and breathe out through your nose until the mask is clear.

learn the basics of Snooker

Snooker is a game of great skill in which you use a cue and a white cue ball to steer balls around a table. Points are scored by knocking ('potting') the balls into six 'pockets' on the table edge.

■ There are 15 red balls, each worth one point, and six coloured balls: yellow (two points), green (three), brown (four), blue (five), pink (six) and black (seven). The game begins with the balls arranged as shown.

■ A player must first pot a red, then a colour, then another red, and so on.

■ If a colour is potted after a red, it's placed back on its starting spot.

■ If a player fails to make a pot, the other player takes over and begins by attempting to pot any available red.

■ Once the reds are gone, the colours are potted in value order. The player with the most points by the time the black is potted wins the 'frame'.

Game within a game

Snooker is more than marksmanship, though. A good snooker player – like a chess player – must think ahead and map out all the many possibilities on the table. That way each shot can be played to set up the next one. And where there isn't a clear scoring opportunity, a good player will position the cue ball so that their opponent doesn't have a direct shot and has to use the angles of the table to hit a red or the next colour ball. This situation is called a 'snooker' and, if not successfully escaped from, incurs a penalty of at least four points.

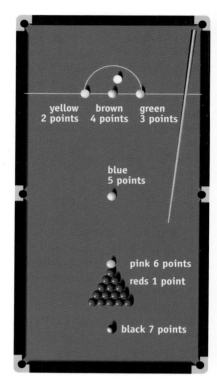

yellow 2 points   brown 4 points   green 3 points

blue 5 points

pink 6 points
reds 1 point

black 7 points

stop Snoring

See a doctor if snoring is extreme, and especially if breathing stops for a period and then re-starts noisily. Otherwise, try the following to ease snoring.

■ Slightly raise the head-end of the bed on blocks.

■ Use only enough pillows to keep your neck straight (and airway open).

■ Sleep on your side with a pillow behind you as a wedge. If you still tend to roll onto your back, sew a small ball or marble to the back of your nightwear.

■ Avoid alcohol or sleeping pills that may further relax the muscles. And stop smoking (*see* SMOKING). Try nasal strips and other anti-snoring devices.

■ Excercise regularly, which may strengthen your head and neck, and help you to lose weight – the main contributory factor to snoring.

get started at Snowboarding

A snowboard looks like a short fat ski, but snowboard technique is very different from skiing. It's an odd feeling to have your feet strapped to a board. Start by spending some time adjusting the bindings on your board, so that you feel comfortable, and your body can move freely.

■ Skating is the snowboarder's means of moving around on flat terrain. Keep your front foot strapped into the binding, and use your back foot to push yourself along with short kicks, as if on a scooter. As you gain momentum, you can place your pushing foot on the board, in front of the back binding – a move known as gliding.

■ Zigzag down slopes, across the steepest part of the hillside (called the fall line). You control the direction of your board and its speed by pressing on the left foot to go left and right foot to go right. This is also a good way of getting down a slope that's too steep to turn on.

■ Turning involves changing the balance of the body from one edge of the board to the other, from the toes to the heels, to create a curving line down the slope like a series of linked 'S' shapes.

■ As you move down a slope, keep your arms just slightly away from your sides so you can move them to aid balance.

build a Snowman

A snowman is a satisfying seasonal sculpture. Grab the chance to make one when you can.

1 Begin by making a large snowball in your hands. Place it on the ground and roll it so that it gathers more snow. Change the orientation of the ball frequently so that the ball remains spherical rather than barrel-shaped. Make three balls, of decreasing sizes, in this way.

2 Flatten the top of your largest ball to form a stable base. Place the second ball on top, taking care that it doesn't crumble. The head, being smaller, is easier to place.

3 Decorate the snowman. Be creative: the main thing is to ensure that your snowman (or snow-woman) has charm and character.

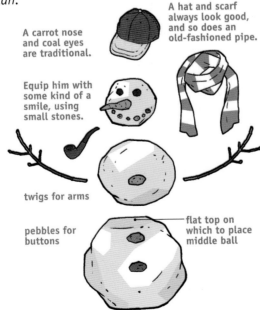

A carrot nose and coal eyes are traditional.

A hat and scarf always look good, and so does an old-fashioned pipe.

Equip him with some kind of a smile, using small stones.

twigs for arms

pebbles for buttons

flat top on which to place middle ball

A CLASSIC SNOWMAN consists primarily of three balls of snow sitting on top of each other. You can make a shorter, more rotund snowman out of two balls.

make Soda bread

This quick, simple bread made without yeast has a nutty taste thanks to the inclusion of wholemeal flour. If you don't have buttermilk to hand, use semi-skimmed milk and add it with a tablespoon of lemon juice.

MAKES 1 LARGE LOAF TO SERVE 6-8
225g plain white flour
225g plain wholemeal flour,
plus a little extra to sprinkle
1 tsp bicarbonate of soda
½ tsp salt
285ml buttermilk

1 Heat the oven to 200°C/gas 6. Sift the flours, bicarbonate of soda and salt into a bowl, tipping in any bran left in the sieve. Make a well in the centre, pour in the buttermilk and use a wooden spoon to mix. Bring together with your hands into a soft dough.

2 On a floured surface, knead lightly and briefly. Place on a greased baking sheet and flatten into a domed loaf shape. Use a sharp knife to cut a deep cross in the top, cutting about half way down into the dough. Sprinkle with a little wholemeal flour.

3 Bake for about 30 minutes or until well browned and the bread sounds hollow when tapped on the base. Leave to cool completely on a wire rack then serve at once.

S

Soldering

If you want to join together two pieces of metal, such as wires or plumbing pipes, soft soldering is a useful skill to have. Solder is a soft alloy, usually supplied in wire form, with a melting point lower than the metal it's joining. The solder is applied to the join, melted using a hand tool called a soldering iron, and then resets to create the join. Soldering irons should only be used in a well-ventilated space. Keep the iron in its stand, away from the edge of your workbench. Wear safety goggles.

YOU WILL NEED Soldering iron, damp sponge, solder, safety goggles

1 Turn on your soldering iron. When it reaches operating temperature, wipe the tip with the damp sponge to clean off any debris. Now touch a piece of solder to the tip, so that it melts and coats the tip completely. This is called 'tinning', and it helps the heat to flow to the joint.

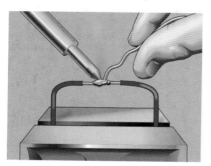

2 Hold the iron as if it were a pen. Touch it to the joint to be made, making sure that both items to be joined are in contact with each other. Feed a little solder onto the joint – not the iron. If you're soldering twisted wires together, the solder should flow freely into the twist.

3 Withdraw the solder, then the iron, and keep the join still until it cools.

prepare and dig Soil

Digging in late autumn or early spring is the best way of preparing most soils. For large areas you can use a rotovator, as long as there aren't a lot of perennial weeds (see WEEDS) whose roots will be chopped up and spread around.

Single digging

1 Dig the first trench to one spade's depth. Put the soil in a wheelbarrow and take it to the far end of the plot. Spread the remaining area with well-rotted manure or compost.

2 Dig the next trench alongside the first, throwing soil into the first one. Continue over the whole plot. Fill the final trench with the reserved soil, mixed with some manure or compost.

Double digging

1 Use for a newly cultivated patch or to improve clay and other firm soils. For the first trench, dig to two spade depths, and remove soil as for single digging. Fork over the base of each trench.

2 Add plenty of compost or well-rotted manure before starting the next trench. Finish by filling in with your reserved soil.

No-dig gardening On light soils such as chalk and sand, and in raised beds, avoid digging and cover in autumn with a thick layer of well-rotted compost, which worms will draw into the soil over the winter.

test and know your Soil

All soil is made up of sand, silt, clay and organic matter. Once you know what kind of soil you have, and its acidity level, you can work to improve it and will be able to choose the most appropriate plants.

Use a testing kit to measure the acidity of the soil on the pH scale. Follow the instructions and take samples of soil from different parts of the garden. A pH reading of 7 is neutral, lower than 6 very acid, above 8 very alkaline.

1 2 3 4 5 6	7 8 9	10 11 12 13 14
ACIDIC	NEUTRAL	ALKALINE

THE pH SCALE is usually shown as a strip of 14 colours. Test results may consist of the colour or number, or both.

Acid soils are good for heathers, azaleas, rhododendrons and blueberries, which won't tolerate alkaline conditions, although most vegetables and fruit prefer slightly acid soils. Neutralise them by adding lime as instructed on the packet.

Alkaline soils are good for daphnes, pinks, mulleins, sage, lilacs and laburnums. Organic matter will help to neutralise and acidify them.

Soil type Test your soil at different locations in your garden by scooping up a handful and trying to make it into a ball with your hands.

Soil type	Properties and treatment
SANDY – won't form a ball, very loose and gritty.	Free draining, lacks fertility, needs generous composting.
SILT OR LOAM – holds some shape, smooth but slightly gritty in texture.	Fertile, holds water well but also free draining. Compost annually.
CHALKY – will hold some shape, pale in colour often with white limestone visible.	Fertile but quick draining, alkaline. Compost well and never add lime.
CLAY – easily forms a firm ball, soapy in texture.	Tends to waterlog, bakes hard in hot weather and can be very fertile, usually acid. Add sand to help to break it up and compost generously.
PEATY OR ORGANIC – crumbly and fibrous, dark in colour.	Very fertile, retains water well. Can be acid or alkaline.

make a refreshing Sorbet

All kinds of fruit and fruit juices can be used for good sorbets. These easy-to-make frozen desserts are a refreshingly healthy alternative to ice cream.

Strawberry sorbet

SERVES 4

250g granulated sugar
250ml water
500g strawberries, hulled,
plus extra to decorate
2 tsp lemon juice
1 egg white, lightly whipped

1 Put the sugar and water into a pan over low heat and stir until the sugar dissolves. Bring to the boil and simmer for 2 minutes. Leave to cool.

2 Purée the strawberries in a food processor or liquidiser, then press through a sieve. Stir in the sugar syrup and lemon juice. Pour into a freezable container and freeze until half-set. Break up the mixture with a fork, then whizz in the processor or beat until smooth. Fold in the egg white then refreeze until completely frozen. Serve garnished with slices of strawberry.

S

relieve a
Sore throat

Make a honey gargle Soothing honey coats the throat and is mildly antibacterial. Stir a couple of teaspoons into a cup of warm water and gargle two to three times a day.

Try salt water To help to cleanse the throat of phlegm, dissolve ½ tsp of sea salt in a cup of warm water and gargle two to three times a day.

Drink plenty of fluids This helps to keep the mucous membrane moist and relieves a ticklish sore throat.

Take a mild painkiller You can help to dull the pain with paracetamol or aspirin (not for children under 16).

Avoid cigarettes Now is a good time to stop smoking (*see* SMOKING).

See a doctor If your sore throat is accompanied by a fever, severe pain or difficulty in breathing or swallowing, see your GP.

banish **Spam** emails

Spam is one of the irritations of the internet age. It's hard to avoid completely, but there are ways to stop it clogging up your inbox.

- Activate your email program's spam or 'junk' filter.
- Don't hit the 'unsubscribe' button on spam emails: this only confirms that your email address is active.
- Use a separate, free email address when buying online or subscribing to newsgroups; keep your main email address for friends and colleagues.
- Don't publish your email address on the web: a 'spambot' might find it and start to bombard you.

make individual cheese **Soufflé** pots

A soufflé is impressive and not as difficult as you might think. You can make this in one large dish if you wish (about 1.5 litres capacity), but increase the cooking time to 40-45 minutes.

SERVES 4

25g salted butter, plus extra for greasing
25g plain flour
225ml milk
½ tsp Dijon mustard
4 eggs, separated, plus 2 egg whites
120g Cheddar cheese, grated,
   plus extra for sprinkling
salt and freshly ground black pepper

1 Heat the oven to 180°C/gas 4, grease four individual soufflé dishes (each about 350ml) and put a baking sheet into the oven. Melt the remaining butter in a saucepan. Stir in the flour and cook gently for 1 to 2 minutes, stirring continuously. Remove from the heat and stir in the milk until completely smooth. Return to the heat, bring slowly to the boil and simmer for 10 minutes. Remove from the heat and beat in the mustard, egg yolks, cheese and seasonings.

2 In a large bowl, whisk the egg whites into stiff peaks. Fold 2 tbsp into the soufflé base followed by the remainder, using a chopping and folding action until just combined.

3 Pour into the prepared dishes, sprinkle with the extra cheese then put the dishes onto the hot baking sheet. Bake for 15-20 minutes, or until the soufflés are well risen and golden brown. Serve immediately.

choose the right **Spanner** or wrench

For many jobs, a simple combination spanner is the perfect tool, the open end making fast work of nuts

combination spanner

and bolts, with the ring end offering better grip. But there are more ingenious tools better suited to some jobs or situations.

adjustable spanner

ratchet-ring spanner

FITS ALL SIZES OF NUT An adjustable spanner is versatile, but doesn't grip as well as an open-ended spanner.

GREAT IN TIGHT SPACES A ratchet allows you to screw or unscrew a nut without removing the spanner from it. Available in different sizes.

pipe wrench

STRONG GRIP FOR PIPES Some plumbing jobs require a wrench, not a spanner. Their toothed jaws are also good for turning nuts with rounded-off edges.

ONE TOOL FITS ALL A collection of different sized sockets, with a variety of handles and flexible connectors, allows you to assemble exactly the right tool for the job in hand.

socket set

take care of your Spectacles

Clean the 'windows'
■ To wash plastic lenses, wet cleaning is best. Pass them under running water and dry with a clean microfibre cloth. Use specially formulated lens cleaner or a little diluted white-wine vinegar in a pump-action spray on oily smears.
■ Don't use tissues or paper towels – they will scratch the lenses.
■ To stop lenses steaming up, rub them over with a thin coating of soap then polish them until they're clear.

Clean the frames
■ Wash glasses from time to time in warm, soapy washing-up water – before you do the dishes.
■ Hold them by the frame not by an arm.

Everyday care
■ Avoid scratches by always resting spectacles on their folded arms, lenses uppermost, or – better still – keeping them in their case.
■ Take your spectacles off or shield them when using hairspray.
■ Always use two hands to put them on or take them off and don't push them up onto the top of your head, as this will strain the hinges.
■ Don't store your spectacles close to a source of heat.
■ Wash the cleaning cloth regularly in the washing machine in a normal load.

be a success at Speed-dating

In speed-dating, more so than in most normal social situations, first impressions really count.

■ You have just 3 or 4 minutes to make your mark, but don't fill that time with a monologue or string of ill-judged jokes. Make sure that you allow your date to speak as much as you do and take care to listen and respond.
■ Approach each person with a smile and warm greeting, and try to project confidence, even if you're a bit nervous. Create the impression that, for the short duration of your date, they are the only other person in the room.
■ Have in mind some questions that will allow your date to present their personality. *What do you do at the weekends?, What's your favourite film/song/cuisine?* Recent holidays and future plans are a rich and revealing topic.
■ Don't be afraid to broach the subject of dating – that's what you are both there for, after all. *What are you looking for in a partner?* is a fair thing to ask, but don't get too personal – and don't bring up past relationships!
■ Find a way to pay a compliment at some point: *Wow, you went to Siberia? That's really intrepid.*

make a good Speech

Public speaking needn't be terrifying if you approach it the right way and are well prepared.

Practise beforehand A speech is a visual performance as well as a talk, so it pays to know how you appear to your audience. Rehearse your speech in front of a mirror, then run it past a harsh but trusted critic: someone who will tell you when you're getting boring.

Know it off by heart It's dull to watch someone reading pages of notes out loud, because a person who's reading cannot make eye contact or engage emotionally with the audience. So learn your lines as if you were an actor. Your notes, if you need them, should be on unobtrusive index cards that you use as a prompt, at most.

Get off to a flying start Don't begin with thank-yous or a lengthy preamble. Make your first words a remark or a story that will grab the attention of your audience. A well-received anecdote will put everyone at ease, including you.

Use your body Your facial expression and your gestures can add warmth and meaning to what you're saying, so don't be too static. On the other hand, wild gesticulations will be distracting to everyone. Strike a balance.

Keep it brief Short speeches are nearly always preferable to long ones, however fascinating the subject matter.

S

remove Splinters

Use tweezers and pull out the way the splinter went in. If this fails, sterilise a needle with disinfectant and gently work along the line of the splinter to tease it out. Wash well and apply antiseptic.

Use adhesive if you can't get the splinter out. Soak the area in warm water, dry and dab on a spot of PVA adhesive. Peel off the glue when dry and the splinter should lift out.

Try a poultice to draw out a stubborn splinter. Make a paste with bicarbonate of soda and a little water and secure to the area overnight with a plaster. This makes the skin swell and push out the splinter.

See your doctor if you cannot remove the splinter, if it was dirty or an animal spine, or if the surrounding area becomes infected.

soothe itchy Spots and rashes

Resist the urge to scratch an itchy rash. Instead try these remedies.

Over-the-counter creams and lotions such as calamine. Antihistamine tablets may help, but they can make you drowsy. Ask the pharmacist for advice.

Aloe vera gel smoothed on the skin has a cooling effect.

A cup of oatmeal sprinkled in a warm bath is wonderfully calming to angry spots and rashes.

identify Spots and rashes

Your child has come out in an angry rash. Don't be alarmed, but read the symptoms and take appropriate action.

What to do?

Before you do anything else, test for meningitis (*see* MENINGITIS).

Eliminate obvious triggers Rashes can be caused by irritants such as stinging nettles, medication or polluted pool water. Also, try to identify anything eaten that could have caused an acute anaphylactic reaction (*see also* ALLERGIC EMERGENCY).

Check their temperature A child with an infectious disease may well have a fever. Keep your child at home, and wash your hands and theirs frequently to avoid the spread of infection (*see* HANDS).

Consult your GP If a rash doesn't fade overnight, see your doctor.

Call an ambulance if your child has difficulty breathing or swallowing or is abnormally drowsy.

Cause	What to look for and do
MEASLES 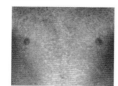 Acute, highly communicable viral disease.	**Incubation period** About 10 days. **Look for** Greyish-white 'Koplik's spots' on a red background inside the cheeks and on the throat. Two to four days after initial symptoms there will be a brown, spotty rash, usually starting behind the ears and around the hairline, spreading around the head and neck, then to the legs and over the body. The spots are initially small, but quickly increase in size and may join together to form angry blotches. The measles rash isn't intensely itchy. **Spread by** Contact with fluids from the respiratory tract, such as coughs and sneezes. **Exclude from school and child care** Keep your child at home for four days after the first rash appears.
RUBELLA 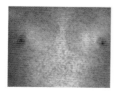 Also called German measles, often experienced as a milder illness than measles.	**Incubation period** 14-21 days. **Look for** Pink and flat rash, of very small spots, similar to a measles rash but less extensive. It starts at the hairline, face and neck, before spreading to the body, arms and legs. **Spread by** Contact with fluids in the respiratory tract, such as coughs and sneezes. **Exclude from school and child care** Isolate for seven days after onset of rash. **Pregnant women** Must not be exposed to rubella, which can seriously damage a developing foetus, especially in the early weeks.

Cause	What to look for and do
CHICKENPOX 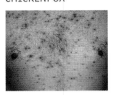 Highly communicable *Varicella zoster* virus is most infectious from a day or two before rash appears. *See also* SHINGLES.	**Incubation period** 14-16 days. **Look for** Small, flat red spots, which become raised, forming fluid-filled round blisters ('vesicles') against a red background. In the third stage the vesicles crust over. The rash is intensely itchy. It starts on the trunk before spreading to the face, arms and legs. Spots may also be found on the eyelids, and on the inside of the mouth and the vagina. **Spread by** Contact with fluids in the respiratory tract or by contact with fluid from an infected person's blisters. **Exclude from school and child care** From when spots first appear until all sores are crusted over (about five days after onset of blisters).
SLAPPED CHEEK SYNDROME 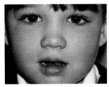 Viral illness also known as 'fifth disease'.	**Incubation period** 13-18 days. **Look for** Bright red and slightly raised rash on the cheek, developing a lacy appearance that lends a blotchy look, and spreading to the body, arms and legs. Other symptoms – temperature, sore throat and headache – appear up to a week before the rash. **Spread by** Contact with fluid in the respiratory tract. **Lasts for** Around five days, but the rash may return for a few weeks. Once the rash appears, the disease is no longer infectious, so there's no need to exclude from school or child care if the child feels well enough.
ECZEMA 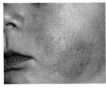 An inflammatory skin condition, also called atopic dermatitis.	**Look for** Itchy, dry and hot, or broken, raw and bleeding skin, most commonly on the face and neck, the inside of the elbows, and the knees and ankles. In infants, more typically found on the forehead, cheeks, scalp, neck, forearms and legs. Severity can vary. **Isn't contagious** No need to exclude from school.
RINGWORM 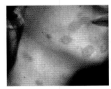 Caused by a fungus not a worm.	**Look for** Burning ring that expands outwards. **Spreads by** Skin contact with an infected person, through shared towels, bedding and facecloths; also passed on through pets. **Exclude from school or child care** There's no need for a child to stay off school, so long as they follow their treatment – usually an anitfungal cream – and take care with their hygiene.

treat Sprains and strains

A sprain is a stretched, twisted or torn ligament (or more than one). It can be more painful and slower to heal than a break.

A strain occurs when a muscle is stretched beyond its limit or forced to contract too abruptly.

Apply PRICE therapy in both cases to speed recovery.

PROTECT the injured area. For an ankle injury wear shoes that enclose and support the foot.

REST. Avoid activity in the first 48-72 hours. For a leg injury your doctor may offer crutches.

ICE. For the first two to three days apply an ice pack, wrapped in a towel, for 15-20 minutes every 2 or 3 hours during the daytime.

COMPRESS. Bandage the injury to reduce swelling and for support (*see* BANDAGE).

ELEVATE. Keep the injury raised and supported on a pillow (below) or chair to help to reduce swelling. This is especially important if your leg is injured: don't spend long periods without it raised.

S

use a Spray gun correctly

Spray guns are useful for painting large areas such as exterior masonry, rough surfaces and things like cane furniture that are awkward to paint with a brush. Traditionally, they have worked on compressed air, forcing paint through the nozzle of the 'gun'. More compact, electrically operated airless versions are now also available from DIY stores.

▪ Whichever gun you have, always prepare the equipment carefully. The gun should be scrupulously clean, and the paint should be thinned in accordance with the maker's instructions.
▪ If you have a spray gun that uses compressed air, adjust the airflow and compressor pressure, following the maker's recommendations.
▪ Adjust the fan pattern, then perform a test spray on a sheet of cardboard or somewhere away from the job you actually want to spray.
▪ When you're ready to start the job, spray in a wide, continuous sweeping motion that begins 15cm or so to one side of the object, and ends the same distance the other side. This overspraying ensures that the edges are properly painted.
▪ The gun should be 15-20cm away from the object to be painted, and you should move no faster than painting with an ordinary paintbrush.
▪ Each pass of the spray gun should overlap about half the area covered by the preceding one.
▪ Always wear safety goggles and a simple face mask when using a spray gun.
▪ Clean spray guns immediately after use, before the paint dries.

create a basic Spreadsheet

Computer spreadsheets are a great way to keep track of budgets and accounts. A spreadsheet is a grid of cells into which you put information in the form of words or numbers. Excel is the best-known spreadsheet program, but Microsoft Works is also perfectly suitable for most domestic purposes.

Imagine the grid as a set of columns in an old-fashioned ledger.
▪ To do a home budget, make a column for each month. In the example here (right), type the months of the year in row 3, beginning at column C.
▪ Next, type a heading 'Income' in column A, then add categories from all your various

incomes into column B. Now type a heading 'Expenses' and add your main categories of expenditure: mortgage, utilities, food and so on. It's easy to add categories as you go – holidays, perhaps, or Christmas presents. Try to be specific and avoid a huge 'miscellaneous' figure.
▪ Now type in all the figures from your bank statements, pay slips and receipts under the appropriate month.

You can now get the program to do all the tiresome arithmetic for you, and so analyse your finances. Using the **AutoSum** key, you can quickly see if your outgoings exceed your income and you can get an instant figure for all food costs throughout a year, for example, or for all your expenditure for any given month. To calculate your monthly balance, in cell C4 in the example above, type the calculation '(C10-C19)' and press enter on your keyboard.

plan a Spring clean

Spring cleaning is aptly named, as it's best done when bright light highlights dust and dirt that has accumulated over the winter. As well as cleaning, plan to declutter as much as possible.

Decluttering and tidying Tackle clutter room by room, including drawers and cupboards, and assess and deal with things in the following way.
▪ **Discard** Look out anything that can be thrown away, recycled, given to a charity shop or sold online or at a car boot sale, for example. Don't forget food cupboards, fridge and freezer (*see also* CUPBOARDS *and* FREEZER).
▪ **Keep** Includes papers to be filed and anything that needs to be put away. Replace all items to be kept neatly, in their correct place. Use storage boxes.
▪ **Action** Identify anything that needs cleaning, repairing or replacing; paperwork needing action; photos to put in albums and so on.

Assemble your cleaning kit Before you start work think about what you'll need to clean everything in the room you're tackling. Don't forget the windows, heavy-duty cleaners for any stains, something to reach cobwebs, such as a broom with its head wrapped in a clean, soft cloth, plenty of cloths and dusters, and stepladders for high places.

Your cleaning programme Start at the top of the house and work downwards. Work through each room in the following pattern, always finishing a room before starting the next.
- Take down curtains and launder or take for dry cleaning.
- Remove blinds and all pictures and other decorations from the walls.
- Think dry then wet – start with the dusting, sweeping and vacuuming, then move on to 'wet' cleaning such as windows and floors.
- Move all furniture to clean underneath it and blitz any neglected corners.
- Use the gentlest cleaning methods first, before moving on to something more aggressive for stubborn marks and stains.

understand the basics of Squash

Squash is a racket game played in an enclosed court. It's fast and furious, and gives you a high level of fitness.

Two players hit a small rubber ball against the front, back and side walls of the court, aiming to hit the front wall without bouncing. Either player can score points, and the first to 11 wins the game. Matches are usually the best of five games. When you return the ball, it must hit the front wall between the 'tin' at the bottom and the out line at the top. If it bouches, it's out. A rally happens when both players correctly return the ball to each other, and a point is won if your opponent doesn't serve or return the ball correctly.

out line

tin

service line

side wall line

short line

service box

back wall line

the 'T'

OUT LINE If the ball hits the front wall above this line it is 'out'. The side wall line marks the top edge of the side of the court.

SERVICE LINE On the serve, the ball must hit the front wall between the service line and out line.

BACK WALL LINE Balls can bounce off the back wall below this line.

TIN The lower section of the front wall is out of play.

SERVICE BOX The player must have at least one foot in the box when serving.

SHORT LINE The served ball must land behind this line after bouncing off the front wall. It must land on the opponent's side of the court.

THE 'T' Try to dominate the centre of the court and make your opponent do the running.

make a
Spun-sugar basket

Desserts served in spun-sugar baskets make an impressive display. They soften in a couple of hours, so don't make them too far ahead and only fill them just before serving.

YOU WILL NEED Granulated sugar, water, pastry brush, vegetable oil, ladle, baking tray, tablespoon, sugar thermometer (optional)

1 Put 150g granulated sugar and 150ml water in a pan. Heat gently to dissolve, then boil rapidly until light brown in colour, when a little syrup dropped into cold water immediately becomes hard and brittle; this is when the syrup reaches 150°C (*see* SUGAR THERMOMETER). Plunge the base of the pan into cold water for a few seconds to stop the caramel cooking. Leave to stand for 1-2 minutes.

2 Use a pastry brush to grease the outside of the ladle and a baking tray. With a tablespoon, trail thin threads of caramel over the ladle in a criss-cross pattern. Finish by trailing a ring of caramel around the edge to make a rim. Leave to cool until crisp then very gently ease off from the rim with the point of a sharp knife. Lift off with the other hand and carefully transfer to the baking tray to cool completely.

S

conquer
Stage fright

Actors aren't the only people who get stage fright. Anyone can get nervous when making a presentation or delivering a speech. A certain amount of nervousness is good, because it creates an adrenaline rush that makes you raise your game. But if you're crippled by stage fright, there are some things you can do that will help you to combat the fear.

■ Before you have to speak, find a quiet space and concentrate on breathing normally.
■ Mentally go over the first 5 minutes of your performance, whatever it may be. That is the crucial time, because your nerves will evaporate once you get going.
■ Practise, practise and practise some more. Practise in front of friends and family to familiarise yourself with an audience and practise in front of a mirror to build confidence and see how people will see you when you're on stage.
■ Sing or speak out loud before your performance to warm up your voice, and hum softly to keep it warm while you're waiting to speak.

apply Stain to wood

Staining is best done on light, undistinguished woods such as birch and new pine. Other, more distinctive woods – oak, beech, cherry, maple and mahogany – look best left in their natural colour.

■ Before you stain bare wood, be sure that the finish is as good as it can be. Sand the surface with a fine-grade sandpaper (*see* SAND), and use a soft brush to remove every speck of dust.
■ Test the woodstain on an offcut of the wood, or on a part of the object that will not generally be visible (the underside of a table, for example).

YOU WILL NEED Woodstain, paintbrush, sponge or cloth, fine abrasive paper

■ Apply stain with a brush, new washing-up sponge or non-fluffy cloth. Work quickly in the direction of the grain, spreading liberally over the whole surface. Use a clean, non-fluffy cloth to wipe off the excess.

■ When dry, you may find that the liquid stain has raised the grain of the wood. Sand smooth with fine abrasive paper. Re-apply a very light coat of stain to any exposed grain, and wipe with a cloth, as before.

clean Stainless steel

Unless deeply scratched to expose its untreated centre, stainless steel won't rust. But it needs a gentle touch to remove greasy marks.

Pots and cutlery Use hot water and washing-up liquid, removing stubborn food with a sponge or nylon-bristled brush. Polish with a clean dry cloth. Remove any stubborn grease spots with a cloth soaked in white vinegar or use a shop-bought stainless steel cleaner, following the maker's instructions.

Sinks and appliances Use warm water and a squirt of washing-up liquid on a sponge or soft cloth, working in the direction of the grain. Rinse with clear water and dry with paper towels or a soft cloth. If more cleaning is needed, scrub with a paste of bicarbonate of soda made with hot water, or with a solution of one part white vinegar in three parts of water. Baby oil or WD-40 wiped over the surface will also remove fingerprints and other marks.

remove Stains without leaving a trace

Prompt, correct action is the key to dealing with most stains. Always start with the gentlest cleaning tactics first and test any cleaning solution on an inconspicuous area before treating the stain. Remember that heat will almost always 'set' a stain, so get something really clean before you tumble dry or iron. For non-washable items, remove as much stain as possible, then take to the dry cleaners. For stains on carpets, *see* CARPET.

Stain	Action	Tips and hints
FOOD (milk, cream and cheese-based foods; also faeces and urine)	**Fresh stains on washable fabrics** Soak in cold water for 30 minutes. Put the stained area under running cold water and rub fabric gently against itself. Machine wash in warm water. **Dried-on stains on washable fabrics** Soak for 30 minutes in a solution of 1 tsp liquid biological detergent in 2 litres of cold water. Then machine wash in warm water. **Dried-on stains on upholstery** Lightly apply a solution of ½ tsp mild washing-up liquid in 1 litre cold water, blotting the stain with this using a cloth. Blot again with a paper towel then rinse with a cold water spray. Put a pad of paper towels over the spot, weight it down and allow to dry.	■ If stain persists after washing, don't dry. Soak for a further 30 minutes. ■ For persistent stains try using oxygen bleach in the next wash cycle.
GREASE (including hand lotion, salad dressings and suntan lotion)	**Washable fabrics** Pre-treat with liquid laundry detergent or a pre-wash stain-removing spray applied directly onto the stain. Machine wash immediately in hot water. **Satin** Dust with flour, leave for an hour then brush with a soft-bristled brush. Silk satin can be handwashed in ice-cold water with mild soap.	■ Blot up as much as possible with paper towels before treating. ■ Try ironing a fresh stain over blotting paper.
BLOOD	**Washable clothing** Blot with a clean rag wetted with cold water. Or mix a few drops of washing-up liquid with cold water in a bowl and dab onto the stain. Leave for 30 minutes. Or try an oxygen-based cleaner. Wash as usual. **Washable upholstery** Spray with cold water and blot with clean white towel. Repeat until clean. **Bedding** Rub in shampoo until fully absorbed. Lather with a stiff brush then rinse with cold water. Leave to dry naturally.	■ Always use cold water to prevent blood stains from 'setting'. ■ Be gentle. Work from the outside in to avoid spreading the stain. ■ Take non-washable items to be dry cleaned.
WINE (red and white)	**Washable fabrics** Soak for half an hour in a solution of 1 tsp biological detergent in 2 litres warm water. Machine wash in hottest possible water.	■ For stubborn stains try an oxygen-based cleaner.
GRASS (also 'dyes', such as blackcurrant, beetroot, mustard and ink)	**Washable fabrics** Pre-treat with pre-wash stain remover or apply liquid laundry detergent and rinse well. Soak in oxygen bleach solution, following the packet instructions, then launder as appropriate for the fabric. Hairspray is a great tool for removing ink stains. Simply spray the stained area, making sure the spray penetrates the fabric, and let it sit for a few minutes. Then put the item into the wash straight away.	■ If stain persists try soaking in chlorine bleach and water, but remember that this may cause irreparable damage to the fabric.

S

Stake plants

Without stakes, plants will flop and be prone to damage from wind and weather. Once beaten down by the rain they will never recover.

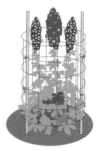

Slender stems
Push in a cane near the plant. Use string to gather the stems together near the crown and tie to the cane.

Tall perennials
Buy or make a cylinder of wide wire 'pig mesh' tied to a couple of canes and place it over flopping plants.

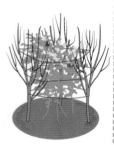

Short and medium perennials
As plants begin to grow, ring them with bamboo canes or twiggy stems of birch or hazel. Tie rings of green string at 15cm intervals to support the growing stems. You can buy plastic-coated metal kits that link together in a similar way.

Protect your eyes Use cane toppers to prevent accidental eye injuries when bending over in the garden. Buy rubber tops or improvise with plastic bottles or table tennis balls.

mend creaking Stairs

It's much easier to deal with a creak if you can get at the stairs from below, via an understairs cupboard, for example. To work from above, you'll need to lift the carpet and be sure you can replace it securely.

From under the staircase, ask someone to walk up and down the stairs, so that you can pinpoint the creaking step or steps.

■ Cut small blocks (right) from wood offcuts: two for each squeaky stair. Drill four holes in each block, one pair at right angles to the other.
■ Use PVA adhesive to glue the blocks into the angle between the tread (the step) and riser (the upright) then screw into place.
■ Take care that your screws are the right length and don't come through the stair.

Working from above, use a chisel to prise the tread away from the top of the riser slightly, and insert some PVA adhesive.

■ Drill clearance holes every 250mm along the tread edge and pilot holes into the top of the riser. Countersink the holes, and screw down the tread.
■ Fill the holes with wood filler, and smooth with abrasive paper.

start a Stamp collection

Stamps are tiny works of art, expressions of nationhood and markers of history. They are often worth far more than their face value.

To begin, tell everyone of your new hobby; ask them to save any overseas or commemorative stamps. Stamps are fragile and need to be handled with care, so ask friends and family to send you stamps still attached to the corners of their envelopes and not to try to remove them for you.

For serious collection you will need an album, stamp mounts or hinges; stamp tongs; scissors; magnifying glass; reference books on correct care and preservation, and a recognised catalogue of current stamp values.

To remove a stamp for collection cut the stamp corner from the envelope (not too close) and float it in tepid water or lay the stamp face up on damp blotting paper or newspaper until it peels off. Dry it face down on blotting paper and flatten it between the pages of a book before you mount it.

Decide how you want to sort your stamps – for example, geographically or on themes. There's a peculiar excitement in coming by stamps from countries that no longer exist – from Abyssinia to Zanzibar via Bechuanaland, Ceylon, Prussia, Rhodesia and many more. They all tell a tale.

Start to buy Dealers and hobby stores sell packets of used stamps. In the early stages of your collection go for packs containing a wide range, to lay down the basics of your album. Sell on any stamps that don't interest you.

Use the internet – with care Websites make it easy to research and buy stamps to add to your collection. The most reputable will show clear photographs, but it's not always possible to discern quality and condition.

Join a collectors' club Enthusiasts love to share their knowledge and experience. You can learn from them and take the opportunity to buy and sell or swap duplicates from your own and their collections.

cook a perfect Steak

The perfect steak is an individual thing – for one person it requires little more than a mere flash in the pan, for another, only meat that is on the verge of charring will do.

Cooking Fry steak in a heavy pan brushed with oil and heated until it's very hot. Lower the heat to medium after the first 3 minutes. For grilling, heat the grill to hot, brush the meat with oil and cook for 1 minute on each side, 7.5cm from the grill. Then turn down the grill to medium and use the timings given below. Turn halfway through cooking.

Testing The cooking times given here are per side for rump, fillet or sirloin steaks about 2.5cm thick. The best way to test is by pressing the steak gently with your finger. Match the feel of the fleshy part at the base of your thumb: touch your thumb to the tip of your first, middle, ring or little finger to emulate the feel of a rare to well-done steak.

Rare
- Fry: 2 minutes.
- Grill: 2½ minutes.
- Finger test: offers little resistance when pressed.

Medium rare
- Fry: 3 minutes.
- Grill: 3½ minutes.
- Finger test: feels slightly firmer when pressed.

Medium
- Fry: 4½ minutes.
- Grill: 5½ minutes.
- Finger test: feels firm when pressed.

Well done
- Fry: 5-7 minutes.
- Grill: 6-8 minutes.
- Finger test: feels quite firm when pressed.

use a Staple gun

A staple gun is often quicker and neater than a hammer and nails when you need to fix something thin to a solid base or backing. They are good for repairing upholstery, picture framing, fixing chicken wire to posts or hardboard on floors, and securing carpet underlay or insulation, for example, as well as for displaying papers on a noticeboard.

Staple guns can be manual or electrically powered, but all work by firing the staple into the materials to be joined together, so should always be used with care. Different grades and sizes of staple and stapler are available depending how heavy-duty the job in hand is.

- Hold the gun firmly and make sure it's in position before you fire the staple.
- Take great care to observe safety procedures: keep your fingers out of the way and never fire the gun towards anyone.

golden rules

STEAK SECRETS
- **Allow meat to come to room temperature before cooking.**
- **Time cooking accurately.**
- **Add salt after cooking, but pepper before cooking.**
- **Plan your timings so that all steaks are ready together, whether rare or well done.**

get to know
Star constellations
see pages 310-311

S

Star constellations

Man has been finding patterns and meanings in the stars for thousands of years, and we scour the night skies with the same fascination today. Here's a selection of heavenly wonders for the star-gazing beginner.

Looking up For city dwellers used to skies awash with light pollution, a star-spangled midnight-blue sky is a revelation. At first it looks like a blizzard of lights, but mentally filter out the fainter stars and you'll start to see the constellations. There are 88 of these groups of celestial bodies. They aren't scientific entities but form patterns that appeal to the human imagination.

THE SKY IS EVER CHANGING You'll see different constellations at different times of year and hours of the night, depending on your latitude, and the way the night side of the planet is facing. The moon, the planets and most constellations, including those of the zodiac, are visible all over the world, but constellations close to the poles stay above the horizon all night and are only visible from one hemisphere. In the deep, dark south you never see the Big Dipper (or Plough) – while benighted northerners don't know the glory of the Southern Cross, and the jewel-box cluster within it. The southern hemisphere has 11 such constellations, the northern only five. Star charts can be a bit baffling at first, but once you pick out the more familiar and distinctive constellations, everything begins to fall into place and you can start to spot some of the 'big names' up there in lights.

YOU WILL NEED Star chart for the month (available for free online), dim flashlight (preferably red) to read it, velvety darkness. You won't need binoculars or a telescope, at least at first. Even a galaxy 2.5 million light years away is visible to the naked eye.

KEY
- nebula
- star

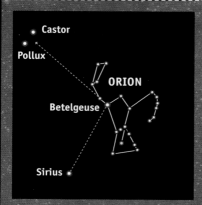

SCORPIUS The zodiacal constellation Scorpius rises in the sky as Orion sets – a nightly reminder that in Greek mythology the hunter Orion was killed by the sting of a scorpion. At the heart of the constellation lies Antares, the thirteenth brightest star in the night sky, with the body and tail of the scorpion arcing out below and the claws fanning out above. Every couple of years the planet Mars appears to travel closely past Antares, and their similarity in colour and brightness makes them easy to confuse. This is how Antares came by its name, which translates as 'rival to Mars'.

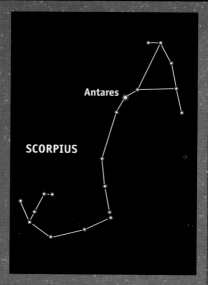

A HUNTER, THE TWINS AND A BIG DOG Orion, the celestial hunter, can be located in the winter months by the three bright stars that form his belt, from which hangs a sword. His left shoulder is represented by the bright star Betelgeuse. Move your eyes up and left from the belt to locate it, then onward and you find Castor and Pollux, a constellation dominated by two bright stars visualised as the heads of the Gemini twins. Trace the slanting line of Orion's belt leftwards and down to locate Sirius, the brightest star in the whole sky. It's known also as the Dog Star as it forms part of the constellation Canis Major (the Big Dog), Orion's faithful hound.

THE SEA SERPENT AND THE LITTLE DOG Another weird creature – best seen from the southern hemisphere although she rears her ugly heads in the north from January to May – is the Hydra, a giant beast of mythology with the body of a dog and 100 snake-like heads. This is the longest constellation in the sky and covers the largest area. It's so long that it takes more than six hours to rise completely. It resembles a snake twisting its way towards Canis Minor (Little Dog), which is visible in the northern hemisphere from December until April, and in the southern from November to April. It represents the smaller of Orion's two hunting dogs. Within Canis Minor, Procyon is the eighth brightest star in the night sky. The name means 'before the dog', and it's so called because it rises before Sirius.

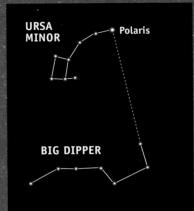

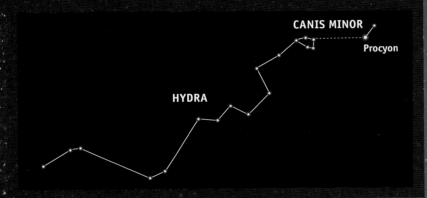

THE BIG DIPPER, DADDY BEAR AND BABY BEAR For star-spotters in the north the Big Dipper, part of the constellation Ursa Major (the Great Bear), is a constant presence, one of the most easily recognisable star groups in the sky. It has the shape of a saucepan – three stars for the handle, four for the bowl. The two stars farthest from the handle are known as 'pointer stars': follow the line of them and they draw your eye to Polaris, the North Star in the constellation Ursa Minor (Little Bear) and the tip of the bear's implausibly long tail. Ursa Minor consists of seven main stars and is also known as the Little Dipper for its resemblance to a scoop. Wherever you are in the northern hemisphere, if you're facing Polaris you're facing north.

A CROSS, A CENTAUR AND A WOLF Also known as Crux, the Southern Cross is one of the best-known groups of stars, thanks to its appearance on the flags of Australia and New Zealand. Despite its nation-defining status the constellation is quite small and

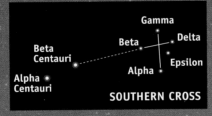

hard to spot. But once you have learnt to recognise it you can use the Southern Cross as a point of reference for sky-watching. It's a compact formation of four bright stars (one less bright star, Epsilon, is included on the Australian flag). Helpfully, two pointer stars, Beta Centauri and Alpha Centauri, are always nearby to show the viewer where to look. These are part of the constellation Centaurus (the Centaur). The mythical beast, half-man, half-horse, bears a lance, which he uses to kill Lupus, the wolf in front of him (visible from February to October). The dazzling Alpha Centauri is the third-brightest star in the southern sky and the closest to the Sun. Alpha Centauri in fact comprises a double star and a nearby red dwarf called Proxima Centauri.

S

Steam food
for maximum goodness

Steaming is an excellent way of preserving the flavour, goodness and colour of vegetables, and of cooking delicate ingredients such as fish. The technique also works well for sweet and savoury puddings cooked in a little liquid in a covered pan.

Equipment Purpose-made stacking steamer pans can be used on the hob, or you can buy stand-alone electric steamers. Alternatively, you can use a perforated basket with short legs placed over a little water in a pan with a tightly fitting lid.

Steaming vegetables
Typical steaming times are:
5-10 minutes: spinach, cabbage, courgettes.
10-15 minutes: broccoli, beans, cauliflower.
15-20 minutes: Brussels sprouts, new potatoes.
40-45 minutes: parsnips, beetroot, globe artichokes.

Fish and shellfish Wrap in baking parchment or foil before steaming, or place on a sheet of baking parchment in the steamer to make it easy to lift out without breaking.
5-10 minutes: thin fillets, scallops, prawns, mussels.
10-15 minutes: thick fillets.
20-25 minutes: whole trout or sea bass (longer for bigger fish).

Steamed puddings Use a heatproof bowl covered with a double layer of greaseproof paper, then a layer of foil, all tied on tightly to prevent water seeping in. Sit in a pan in a little water, topping up as necessary as it cooks. A suet or sponge pudding will take 1½ to 2 hours to cook, according to your recipe.

add a flourish with Stencils

Stencilled motifs lend a real touch of personality to your home. They can give new life to old furniture and transform a plain wall.

Before you start in earnest, practise on a piece of paper to perfect your technique. Working from the edges inward helps to prevent paint from running under the stencil and losing definition.

■ When you remove the stencil wipe off any excess paint. Make sure it is clean and dry before reusing on the next bit of wall or furniture.

YOU WILL NEED Stencil, masking tape, paint, stencilling brushes (with tightly packed, stiff bristles), synthetic sponge for a smooth finish or natural sponge for a more textured look

The brush method This is also known as 'pouncing', because of the jabbing, stippling action you use with the brush.
■ Wipe clean and prepare the surface to be stencilled. Sand it lightly, if necessary, to remove loose old paint or smooth out surface imperfections.

■ Position the stencil and secure it with masking tape.
■ Dip the brush into the paint and tap off any excess on a sheet of scrap paper. If you overload it you risk run-off, which spoils the effect.
■ Hold the brush at right angles to the surface and start to stipple – that is, apply colour with repeated light dabs of the bristle ends.
■ Aim to build colour gradually, blending shades rather than changing abruptly. Use a different brush for each shade.

The sponge method This gives you good control over the paint texture.
■ Fold or cut the sponge to make a small pad, dip it in the paint and dab it on an old rag or paper towel to remove any excess.
■ Apply with light dabs or gentle swirls.

Sterilise jars and baby bottles

Whether you're making strawberry jam or preparing a baby's bottle, wash containers thoroughly in soapy water before you sterilise them. Also, ensure that your hands and working area are clean (*see* HANDS).

Jam jars can be sterilised in the oven. Arrange the clean jars on a baking tray, open end up and making sure that they aren't touching. Put into a cold oven. Heat the oven to 110°C/gas ¼. Leave it on for 45 minutes, then turn off. Remove the jars when cool enough to handle, and place them upside-down on a clean cloth till needed.

Baby equipment can be sterilised by boiling in a pan – but check first that the bottles and teats are suitable for this. It's best to keep a pan specially for this purpose. Fill the pan with water and submerge all the feeding equipment. Check that there are no air pockets inside the bottles. Bring the pan to the boil at 100°C and keep it at that temperature for 10 minutes, with the lid on.

A specialised steam steriliser is the quickest and easiest way to sterilise baby bottles and feeding paraphernalia. You can buy microwave sterilisers or electric units. The equipment will remain sterile inside the steamer for 6 hours or until it's opened. *See also* BABY.

make the most of Sticky-back plastic

A staple of many craft projects, sticky-back plastic gives an easy but durable finish. It's usually sold as a roll and can be clear (colourless or tinted), or opaque in a range of colours. Cut the length you need and peel away the backing little by little, smoothing the plastic over the surface to prevent bubbles. Smooth out any bubbles that do occur with firm strokes using the edge of a ruler.

Covering books Sticky-back plastic makes a hard-wearing protective cover for books, though it's not possible to remove.

Adding decoration You don't need to cover an entire object. Sheets can be cut into self-adhesive shapes to decorate furniture, storage boxes and more.

Window frosting Clear or 'frosted' sticky-back plastic can be used as a film on windows for decoration, to obscure the view into a bathroom or toilet or to make a large, plate glass window more visible to avoid accidents.

relieve a Stiff neck

Your neck has to carry the 3-5kg weight of your head all day long and poor posture or support when sleeping can lead to strain. See your GP if the pain is sudden and severe or accompanied by other symptoms, such as high temperature, pins and needles or numbness in the arms or hands. Otherwise follow this simple advice to speed your recovery.

Keep moving Try to move as normally, but gently, as possible. Taking mild painkillers will help to make this more comfortable. Concentrate on not slumping or slouching to avoid further strain.

Warm it A gentle massage in a hot shower will help (*see* MASSAGE). Or try wrapping a hot water bottle and holding it to the centre of pain. A compress made by soaking a small towel in hot water is another way to bring relief.

Sleep on it A special neck pillow can make a real difference in the case of chronic pain, or it may be time to replace your regular pillows.

Stir-fry
a quick delicious meal

The key to a good stir-fry is fast cooking, allowing vegetables to keep their crunch and flavour.

Choosing a wok A round, not flat base is best for even cooking, though if you cook by electricity, you may have to compromise. For everyday use, stainless steel or non-stick woks are most practical.

Cooking tips There will be no time for chopping while you cook, so prepare all ingredients in small, even-sized pieces before you start.
■ Heat 2-3 tbsp of vegetable oil until very hot, swirling it to coat the whole surface of the wok.
■ Begin with the meat and set aside when almost cooked, ready to add back in near the end of cooking.
■ Add vegetables in batches, according to cooking time. Start with dense vegetables, like broccoli and carrots, and add leafy ones last.
■ Scoop, push and flip the pieces continuously, moving each piece of food over the entire surface of the wok. It should take no more than 5-10 minutes to cook a stir-fry.
■ Add any sauce at the end of the cooking time.

S

grow juicy
Strawberries

Fresh strawberries are hard to beat. They're easy to grow, as long as the soil is well drained and the site is sunny, and also do well in pots and hanging baskets.

Choosing varieties Single-crop strawberries produce one flush of fruit in summer. Perpetual varieties crop from early summer to autumn.

Planting For an early summer crop, plant in early autumn and protect plants with cloches over winter. Spring plantings will crop in late summer. Position plants 45cm apart.

Routine care Look out for slugs and snails that can devour your crop and use a layer of straw or a strawberry mat under each plant to keep the berries off the wet ground. Water plants regularly and well.

Propagating new plants In late summer, strawberries put out shoots, or runners, with new plants growing on them. Choose up to four of the strongest from each plant and use bent wire to peg them into the soil or pots of compost sunk into the bed. When the new plants are firmly rooted, cut them away from the parent plant to use next year.

keep stock of a Store cupboard

With a well-provisioned store cupboard you'll always have ingredients to hand to make impromptu meals on demand.

Keep an eye on use-by dates and always put newly bought food to the back of the cupboard. Airtight tins and jars with well-fitting lids are invaluable for storing dry goods once the packets have been opened, but note down the date and recommended storage times before you throw the packaging away. Clips and ties are useful for keeping open packets tightly sealed.

Keeping time	Typical food (unopened)
Less than 1 month	Cakes
1 month	Coffee beans, biscuits
2-3 months	Self-raising and wholemeal flour, ground coffee, breakfast cereals, cooking oil, stock cubes, mayonnaise, potato crisps
6 months	Plain flour, oats, fruit squash, icing sugar, jam, honey, nuts (whole and ground), dried yeast, dried herbs, baking powder, dried mushrooms, peanut butter, rich fruit cake, olive and vegetable oils
1 year	Cocoa, instant coffee, chocolate, tea, UHT milk, dried fruit, demerara and brown sugars, spices, ketchup, mustard, dried beans and peas, lentils
2 years	Pasta, pickles, sauces and chutneys, tomato paste, canned vegetables with low acidity (for example, sweetcorn), rice, gravy mixes, sauces, vinegar
5 years	Canned fish in oil, canned vegetables with high acidity (for example, tomatoes)
Indefinitely	Caster and granulated sugar

Food dating Apart from some tinned goods, foods are labelled in the following ways to give guidelines for safe storage.

Use by The last date recommended by the manufacturer for using the product. This is particularly important for yeasts and baby foods.

Best before The date after which food becomes stale, even if still edible. Applies to food such as cereals, UHT milk, jams, sauces and dried fruit.

Sell by The date before which a product should be sold to allow for some time before actual consumption – usually reserved for fresh foods.

practise basic Stretching exercises

Stretching can make you feel relaxed and help to keep you limber as well as preventing painful tight muscles after exercise.

Stretch slowly, feeling the muscles tense but stopping short of pain. Never 'bounce' to extend a stretch, but keep the pressure even as you gradually reach a little further. Alternate sides, repeating five times on each.

For chest and shoulders stand at right angles to a wall. Reach across to press against the wall. Make sure you're close enough to do this without leaning your body. Keeping your hips facing forwards, twist your torso towards the wall to feel a stretch in the back of your shoulder. Hold for 15 seconds then swap sides.

For a side stretch stand with feet shoulder-width apart and raise your right arm. Relax your left arm in front of you. Gently lean to the left, curving your right arm over your head, palm down. Stop when you feel a pull from hip to shoulder. Hold for 15 seconds then straighten. Repeat on the other side.

For calves stand arm's length from a wall and brace yourself with your palms flat against it. Step back with your left leg and lean gently in, bending the right leg at the knee, while keeping both heels firmly on the floor and making sure that your back and left leg remain straight. Press against the wall until you feel a stretch in your calf and hold for 15 seconds. Push yourself upright and repeat with the other leg.

combat Stress

A little stress can energise you for a while, but living with too much stress is wretched, emotionally sapping, and bad for your health. Deep relaxation, yoga or meditation (*see* MEDITATE, RELAXATION *and* YOGA) can help to relieve the symptoms, but to really conquer the problem you must take a practical approach to stress in everyday life.

Exercise releases tensions, burns off adrenaline and other stress hormones that the body generates, and releases mood-enhancing endorphins.

A long country walk can clear your head and put worries in perspective.

A heart to heart will often bring solace. Don't bottle up your anxieties: talk them through with friends and family or ask your doctor about counselling.

Try aromatherapy using essential oils that can affect your mood and calm you down when you're frazzled. Use them as bath oils and have a good soak in warm water or buy an aromatherapy diffuser. Good choices are cardamom, camomile roman, frankincense, lavender, rose, vetiver and ylang ylang.

Alcohol, tobacco and drugs aren't the answer. All bring worries of their own and are further threats to your good health.

Review your values Is it time to opt out of the rat race and stop pursuing ever-higher goals? Time to take up a creative hobby? Buy a smaller home? Identify the main cause of your stress and think about what you can do to eradicate it.

S

treat a Stye

A stye is an inflamed red lump on the eyelid, caused by a clogged eyelash follicle. It may cause the eye to water, and can take several days before it ruptures and heals.

- Apply a compress such as a clean, soft flannel soaked in warm water and wrung out.
- Or put 2 tsp of dried calendula flowers in a bowl, pour on two cups of boiling water and leave for 20 minutes. Strain the healing infusion and use it to soak the compress.

solve a Sudoku

The unalterable law of sudoku is that each number from 1 to 9 can appear only once in any row, column or box of nine squares. This means that the puzzle can be solved purely through logic and deduction.

Take the puzzle below. In the box of nine squares in the top left-hand corner, the number 2 can only go in the third row, because there's already a 2 in the top two rows of the grid. This kind of thinking, applied repeatedly to different parts of the puzzle, should take you to a solution for most sudokus.

recognise the symptoms of a Stroke

A stroke happens when a blood clot blocks the flow of blood to the brain, or a blood vessel in the brain bursts. The onset of symptoms is sudden and sometimes dramatic. Learn what to look for and prepare to act without delay.

Take FAST action A stroke causes numbness, weakness or paralysis on one side of the body. Speech may be slurred, and there may be blurred vision or loss of sight, unsteadiness and confusion or complete unconsciousness. If you suspect a stroke use the FAST test, and use it fast.

FACE. Look at the face. Do you notice any weakness? Ask the casualty to smile. A one-sided smile, while the other side of the face droops, suggests stroke.

ARMS. Ask the casualty to lift each arm in turn. If they cannot lift one of them, this is further evidence of stroke.

SPEAK. Ask the casualty to speak. If they have suffered a stroke they may not properly understand you or be able to respond.

TIME. Act fast and if the casualty fails any of these tests, call the ambulance. Offer reassurance. Check and make a note of levels of consciousness. Prepare to give CPR (*see* CPR).

Risk factors for a stroke include smoking, high blood pressure and heart disease, being overweight, raised cholesterol, diabetes, and excessive alcohol and caffeine consumption. It's not just an affliction of the elderly – even children may be affected. Alarming though a stroke is, if you recognise the warning signs and act quickly to get prompt medical help, a patient can make a good recovery.

1				2	8	3		
	8		1		4			2
7	2	6		8				
					7		5	
2	7		5				1	9
	3		9	4				6
	8		9			7		5
3			8		6		9	
	4	2	7					3

pack a Suitcase smartly

Be a clever traveller: pack only what you'll need for your trip. The secret is to plan ahead rather than to pack half your wardrobe at the last minute. Bon voyage!

▪ Make a list of everything you might want – then edit it.
▪ Lay out on the bed the items you mean to take. Edit again.
▪ Organise your items into four groups: smaller items such as underwear and swimwear; trousers that may crease; casual items such as jeans and T-shirts; other items that may crease, such as shirts, blouses and skirts. Follow the guide below to pack each group layer by layer.
▪ If you're taking casual jeans and T-shirts, the best way to save space is to pack them rolled into tight cylinders.

TOP LAYER
Clothes that will crease should be carefully folded and laid on top.

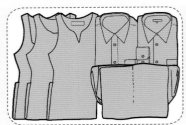

If items, such as jackets or dresses, can be laid flat rather than being folded, do so.

MIDDLE LAYER
Place a layer of jeans and T-shirts tightly rolled into cylinders. Pack any towels the same way.

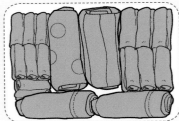

BOTTOM LAYER
Add washbag, swimwear, underwear, socks and tights.

AT THE SPINE
Put shoes and belts at the spine. Tuck rolled socks inside shoes to save space.

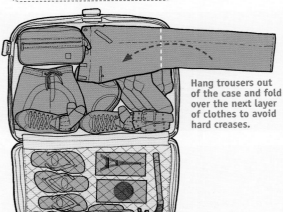

Hang trousers out of the case and fold over the next layer of clothes to avoid hard creases.

IN LID
Place flat items in the flaps of the lid.

---

use a Sugar thermometer

A sugar thermometer helps to take the guesswork out of making jam and marmalade, caramel and sweets of all kinds. It's a gadget no expert cook would be without.

Before use, put the thermometer into a bowl of hot water to make it react promptly. Then quickly wash and dry it and submerge its bulb in the pan, tilting the contents if necessary. After use, put it back into the hot water immediately to prevent sugar solidifying. *See also* JAM *and* MARMALADE.

These are the temperatures and descriptions of hot sugar commonly referred to in recipes.

103°C	Thread stage	Thin syrup, jam, marmalade
105°C	Pearl stage	Fondants and icings
110°C	Blow stage	Ice creams
115°C	Soft ball stage	Fondants and soft fudges
135°C	Crack stage	Soft toffee
150°C	Hard crack stage	Hard toffee and spun sugar
170°C	Caramel stage	Caramel coatings, praline

golden rules
SUGAR THERMOMETER
▪ **Always make sure the bulb is completely covered when testing temperatures.**
▪ **Don't let the thermometer touch the base or sides of the pan.**

S

avoid and soothe
Sunburn

Sunburn is caused by overexposure to the ultraviolet rays in sunlight. It's a risk factor for skin cancer as well as being known to age the skin.

Stay protected
■ Children and the fair-skinned in particular should keep covered up in strong sunlight, wear a wide-brimmed hat and stay in the shade.
■ Infants should be kept out of the sun entirely. Invest in sunshades for pushchairs and car windows, and consider buying a UV-protected tent for them to play in outside.
■ Use a sunscreen with a high protection factor. Apply a generous amount before you go out in the sun. Re-apply regularly – at least every 2 or 3 hours – and after going for a swim.

If you do get burned ...
■ Cool the area by sponging with lukewarm water or take a tepid shower.
■ Stay hydrated: drink plenty of fluids and avoid alcohol.
■ Apply aftersun lotion to moisturise the skin and prevent the sensation of tightening. Calamine lotion relieves the irritation.
■ More serious sunburn requires burn cream and dressings. Seek medical attention.
■ Always consult a doctor if a baby or small child has been sunburned.

Be aware that sunburn can occur even on overcast days, especially at high altitude.

get on board with Surfing

You don't have to be a total surfer dude to experience the thrill of catching a wave.

If you're a beginner, you should use a wide stable board, no less that 2.7m long. This kind of board is easier to balance on than the shorter variety used by many experienced surfers. At first, you should surf only in 'white water' – the part of the wave that has crested and broken, where the going is easier.

Before you can surf, you must first paddle out to the waves. To paddle, arch your back, keep your head up, and propel yourself with long, alternate strokes of the arms, as if doing the front crawl.

To catch a wave, turn your board toward the shore. As you feel a wave coming up behind you, paddle fast with your head low. If you pick up enough speed, the wave will carry you forwards.

To stand up, first place your hands on the outer edges of the board. When you feel the wave lifting the board behind you, bring your knees swiftly to your chest.

Get up on your feet, letting go of the board as you do so. Your feet should be shoulder-width apart, and at right angles to the direction of travel.

roll your own Sushi rolls

Sushi is made with special Japanese rice that's sticky when cooked and can include vegetables, raw or cooked fish or cooked shellfish.

YOU WILL NEED Sushi ingredients, large plate, rolling mat, sharp knife

MAKES ABOUT 20 ROLLS
- **125g sushi rice, rinsed and cooked**
- **25ml mirin (rice wine) or dry sherry**
- **1 tbsp sugar**
- **3 or 4 sheets of nori (dried seaweed)**
- **1½ tsp wasabi paste, plus extra to serve**
- **1 avocado, thinly sliced**

- **100g very fresh raw fish such as tuna, or smoked salmon, thinly sliced**
- **½ cucumber, deseeded and cut into strips**

TO SERVE
light soy sauce and pickled ginger

1 Spread the rice on a large plate to cool. Mix the mirin and sugar and heat gently until the sugar dissolves. Spread a sheet of nori onto the sushi mat, shiny side up and add the rice in a thin layer, leaving a 2.5cm gap at one end. Dab on a little wasabi paste. Add fish and vegetables in a single layer in the centre.

2 With the help of the mat, and working away from you, roll up tightly, then squeeze firmly. Unwrap and cut into 2.5cm rolls. Repeat with the remaining ingredients. Serve with the soy sauce, ginger and additional wasabi paste.

describe your Symptoms to a doctor

Visible symptoms such as a lump, rash, bruising or swelling speak for themselves. Underlying discomfort or malaise is harder to describe. Before you visit your doctor prepare to answer these questions to help with the diagnosis.

- What exactly are you experiencing?
- When did you first notice something wrong?
- Are symptoms constant? If not, when do they occur?
- Does anything make symptoms better – or worse?
- How do they affect your work and home life?
- Has anyone else in your household had the same symptoms?

Use plain and unambiguous language 'Dull ache', 'stabbing pain', 'nausea', 'weakness' – use a scale of 1-10 if it helps. Be ready with information about any medications, supplements or herbal remedies you take; your lifestyle, habits, and major life events that may have impacted on your health.

Swim the crawl

The crawl is the most useful swimming stroke – it's both fast and efficient.

1 Extend your left arm forward. Pull your right arm along your body, crooking your elbow so that your hand passes beneath your body. Keep your hand flat and your fingers together. Your right arm should exit the water by your thigh with elbow high and wrist low.

2 Roll to your left with your face in the water. Arc your right arm forward so the upper arm passes close to your ear. Anchor your left hand in the water and pull down and back beneath your body as in step 1.

3 As your left hand reaches your thigh, turn it so that the little finger leads. Lift your left elbow so that it leaves the water first. Spear your right arm into the water, fingers pointed.

4 As your left arm comes forward and your right back, roll to the right. Repeat steps 1-4 giving six strong scissor-style kicks during every cycle.

Breathing Your mouth clears the surface just before your hand exits on the same side. Take the chance to inhale deeply.

fix a wobbly leg on a **Table**

Evening up the legs on a wobbly table isn't hard – but don't do it yourself if the item is antique or valuable.

First, check the floor The problem may not be with the table, but an uneven floor. Place the table on a flat, level sheet of chipboard or plywood and check to see whether it still wobbles. Use a tape measure to see if all the legs are the same length.

If the table still wobbles, place thin squares of wood under the legs until the table is stable.

If just one leg is short, cut a piece of wood that fits the gap, and attach to the base of the leg with glue and a countersunk screw. Use a chisel to shape the wood to match the leg and smooth the edges with sandpaper, and stain or paint to match the leg. If the table has fancy feet, detach the short leg, if possible, and position your piece of wood at the top.

If more than one leg is short, trim all legs to match the shortest one.

- Identify the leg with the most wood packing.
- Set a pair of compasses so that the point is touching the chipboard or plywood sheet, and the pencil is touching the bottom of the leg.
- Mark the other three legs with the compass set at this distance. The compass point should always be in touch with the chipboard or plywood, while the pencil marks the leg at the point where it needs to be trimmed.
- Saw or chisel the excess from each leg, and smooth with sandpaper. The table should now be level.

lay a **Table** for dinner

A table set for a celebratory meal not only looks attractive, but serves a practical purpose for the diners – putting all the right tools to hand.

Flatware – knives, forks and spoons Always lay from the outside in, working in the order that implements will be used.
- Knives and spoons go on the right of the setting; forks on the left. Forks should be placed with tines upwards, knives with blades facing inwards.
- Lay a dessert spoon and fork horizontally above the setting, spoon above fork, with the bowl pointing to the left, the fork pointing to the right.
- Lay a butter knife on the side plate.

China – plates and bowls
- A side plate for bread should be laid on the left of the setting. The plate can sit next to the dinner fork is there's space, or above and to the left, if not.
- Other plates will usually be brought with the food, but a base plate, known as a service plate or charger, is often laid in the centre of the setting. The folded napkin (see NAPKIN) should be placed on this, unless the first course has already been served, in which case place the napkin next to the fork.

Glassware Lay a water glass above the knives. To the right of this lay a wine glass – or glasses, right to left in the order that wines will be served.

- -

have impeccable **Table manners**

Good table manners are mostly a matter of simple courtesy. Don't do anything to offend your hosts or spoil the meal for your fellow diners.

- Never start to eat until everyone at the table has been served.
- Conversing is as important as eating, so never take a mouthful larger than you can swallow quickly. You need to be able to reply if someone addresses a remark to you. Never speak with your mouth full.
- Talk to the diners on either side of you, giving them equal attention. Don't shout across the table or dominate the conversation, but listen attentively,

ask relevant leading questions and steer clear of controversial topics that could cause offence (*see* CONVERSATION).

▪ Be alert to the needs of fellow diners and offer to pass sauces, condiments or other dishes without being asked.

▪ Praise the host on the food in a meaningful way. *This is lovely* isn't much of a compliment. *Wonderful flavours – is that tarragon I can taste?* will please your host, and is a good conversational gambit.

▪ If you feel out of your depth at a formal dinner, follow the lead of the host, and if the port comes out at the end of the meal, remember the golden rule to pass it clockwise round the table – or to the left.

grasp the basics of Table tennis

As in other racket sports, the aim of table tennis is to prevent your opponent from returning the ball. It's fast, furious and lots of fun.

Hold your bat however it feels most comfortable: the shakehands grip or penhold (right).

At the start of a game, the serving player tosses up the ball and hits it so that it bounces once on their own side of the table and again beyond the net. The opponent attempts to return the ball to bounce in the server's court.

shakehands grip front

shakehands grip back

penhold grip front

penhold grip back

2.74m
1.52m
0.76m

A point is scored against a player who fails to place the ball in the opponent's court (that is, fails to hit the ball or hits a shot that misses the opposing half of the table). A game is won when a player reaches 11 points, and is two points clear of the opponent. A match usually consists of the best of five or seven sets. Service alternates every two points unless the score reaches 10-10, when it alternates on every point until one player wins.

In doubles, the ball must be served diagonally, so that it bounces first in the right-hand half of the server's court, then in the right-hand half of the receiver's. Thereafter, the four players must hit the ball in rotation.

learn shortcuts for times Tables

It can take hours of schooling to commit maths times tables to memory, but there are some quick tricks that will speed up those on-the-spot calculations.

One or nothing Any number multiplied by 1 equals itself. Multiply anything by 0 and it will make zero.

Multiples of 2 Anything multiplied by 2 will be that number simply added to itself, so 2 x 8 will be the same as 8 + 8, to get 16.

The law of 5 A number multiplied by 5 will always end in 5 or 0. If you multiply an even number by 5 the answer will be half that number with 0 after it: 6 x 5 = 30 (half of 6 is 3, add a zero and you have 30). When multiplying an odd number by 5, take one away from that number, halve it and add a 5: to work out 7 x 5, take one from 7 to get 6, halve 6 to get 3, then put a 5 after the 3 to reach 35.

To the power of 10 To multiply any number by 10, simply add a zero: 10 x 4 = 40.

Time for elevenses Single-digit numbers multiplied by 11 are simply that number repeated: 4 x 11 = 44. For double-digit numbers, separate the two digits, add them together and put the result in the middle: 11 x 26, for example, is 2_6; fill in the middle digit by adding 2 and 6 (2 + 6 = 8), so 11 x 26 = 286.

Tack fabric

Tacking or 'basting' is used to keep pieces of fabric in place before they're permanently sewn together, usually after pinning. Whatever you're sewing, accurate tacking is the key to a good result.

Starting off Thread a needle with thread of a contrasting colour to your fabric. Special tacking cotton is cheaper than sewing thread, as it isn't as strong, but you can use any thread you like. Knot one end and insert the needle.

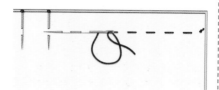

Even tacking Working from right to left, make stitches about 6mm long and the same distance apart. Use even tacking for smooth fabrics, on curved seams and all areas that need careful fitting.

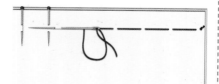

Uneven tacking Sew long stitches about 25mm long with about 5mm between each. Use for straight seams and for holding pieces in place when quilting (see QUILT).

Finishing End each piece of tacking with two or three stitches worked over each other. The tacking needs to hold firm but be easy to remove once the fabric is stitched.

master some Tai chi moves

This gentle form of exercise is often described as meditation in motion. It builds strength and agility and is suitable for all ages.

In tai chi, you perform a sequence of movements, called a 'form', based on the defensive and attacking actions of martial arts. Tai chi is, in effect, a stylised fight sequence, performed as gracefully as a slow-motion ballet. The moves look easy, but take many years to perfect, since they require mental focus, physical strength, balance, good posture and controlled breathing.

Perfecting a sequence Tai chi moves evolve from one set posture, such as 'bird's beak' (1) to another, such as 'strumming the lute' (7), below. A full routine of the 100 or so movements of other styles of tai chi would take up to 40 minutes or so, but start by mastering a simple sequence.

- Wear loose clothing that doesn't restrict your movements. Keep your feet bare, or wear thin-soled soft shoes.
- Learn a basic tai chi form. There are a certain number of moves in the basic form, and you need to memorise these as you would a choreographed dance. This stage is best done in a tai chi class.
- Be aware of your posture. Stand tall, then breathe out, relaxing any tension in your body before you start. Keep your knees slightly bent and imagine your weight dropping downwards, through your legs into the floor.
- Involve the whole body as you move. You never simply lift an arm in tai chi – the action unfolds from the abdominal region, and is coordinated with a turn of the waist. Each movement should flow seamlessly into the next.
- Keep your breathing slow and rhythmic, exhaling and inhaling through the nostrils. Allow your abdomen to rise and fall with each breath.
- Practise your tai chi every day – preferably first thing in the morning and again in the evening.

dance the Tango

It takes two to tango, but for this sensuous and dramatic dance, you also need a poker face – don't gaze longingly at your partner.

The music Tango was born in the working-class suburbs of Buenos Aires around the 1870s, and was banned in public places for being too voluptuous and improper. Start by thinking yourself into character. Dancer Isadora Duncan described the tango as, *Soft as a caress, toxic as love under the midday sun, cruel and dangerous as a tropical forest.*

The hold The man rests his right hand between the woman's shoulder blades and holds her right hand to the side. Her left hand tucks behind his right arm at the armpit. Torsos are angled slightly away from one another, with the woman to the man's right, and both dancers look to their left. Both hold their upper body straight and move from the hips in a haughty manner.

The movement is decisive, staccato (step and stop), and 'flat' with no obvious rise and fall. Although the dance is sexy, it isn't romantic, with graceful arcs or smooth rhythms.

- The tempo is about 120 beats a minute and the count is slow slow quick quick slow. That's eight counts of music – two for each slow step and one for each quick. The slow steps give a feeling of stalking – this dance is a game of cat and mouse, with the man pursuing the woman.
- Feet are planted and don't swivel. The heel should hit the floor first.
- The man faces out from the dance floor, and the dance progresses anticlockwise around the room. Steps should curve slightly to the left and can be tailored to the music, with a run of slow or quick steps that break the basic rhythm, or by adding rocking 'back and forth' steps when turning at corners.

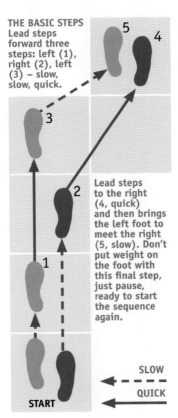

THE BASIC STEPS Lead steps forward three steps: left (1), right (2), left (3) – slow, slow, quick.

Lead steps to the right (4, quick) and then brings the left foot to meet the right (5, slow). Don't put weight on the foot with this final step, just pause, ready to start the sequence again.

SLOW

QUICK

START

deal with Tantrums

Tantrums are normal in toddlers when they feel thwarted. They are just part of your child learning to deal with their emotions.

- Stay calm. Don't pick up on the anger and reflect it back.
- Don't remonstrate; in the throes of a tantrum a child is beyond reasoning.
- Give neither bribe nor punishment. Send an unspoken message that tantrums are regrettable and serve no purpose.
- Don't give in to demands or you create a tiny tyrant who knows that tantrums get results.
- In public, tantrums are embarrassing, but the same rules apply. If you once pacify your child with a treat to keep them quiet they will learn that this is how to get the sweets. Move to another place if your child is disturbing others, and let the tantrum run its course. Remember, most other parents have been in the same situation.
- As the screams subside into sobs, offer cuddles, warmth and praise for the child calming down.
- Remember this is just a phase – and it's horrible for both for you and your child.

T

make the perfect cup of Tea

Top-quality tea – loose-leaf or bagged – and a simple routine are essential to the ideal cuppa.

■ Use fresh water from the cold tap, not water in the kettle that has been previously boiled, as minerals will be more concentrated and this can adversely affect the tea's flavour.

■ Boil the water and swirl a little of it in the pot to warm it.

■ Use a pot, and 1 bag or 1 rounded tsp of loose tea for each cup you're brewing. Add 'one for the pot' and top up with more boiling water after pouring the tea.

■ Bring the water back to the boil and pour it onto the tea in the pot.

■ Give tea time to brew. Start at about 2 minutes and increase gradually to reach the strength you want. For weak tea, 30 seconds might be enough.

■ It's down to your own taste whether you add milk first. If you want to avoid a caramel-like taste, pour in the milk before the tea.

■ Only bulk-buy tea if you can keep it in an airtight container and in a cool condition. Then it should be good for up to two years.

NAME OF TEA	BREWING TIME
Assam	3-4 minutes
Ceylon Dimbula	3-4 minutes
Ceylon Uva	3 minutes
Darjeeling	2-3 minutes
Genmaicha	3-4 minutes
Gunpowder	3-4 minutes
Jasmine	2-3 minutes
Kenya	2-3 minutes
Lapsang Souchong	4-5 minutes
Oolong	5-7 minutes
Sencha	2-2½ minutes

change the washer on a Tap

If water is dripping from the spout of your tap, then probably the washer needs replacing. You don't need a plumber – do it yourself!

There are two common types of tap: rising spindle, with a cross-shaped head; and shrouded head, which usually has a stubby wedge for a head. The procedure for changing a washer differs slightly between these two types, but in either case, the first step is to shut off the water supply at the main stoptap, at a gate valve by the cold water cistern or at a service valve in the pipework leading to the dripping tap. Open the tap to drain any water in the pipe.

Shrouded head tap

1 The washer in this kind of tap is within the body of the tap, beneath the handle or head. To get to the washer, first unscrew or lever off the cover – the part that's often labelled red or blue for hot and cold.

2 Unscrew the screw you find beneath, then take off the head.

3 Undo the headgear with a spanner – bracing the tap with your free hand, as above.

4 The inner section, along with the washer, can now be lifted out. Lever off the washer, replace and reassemble.

Rising spindle tap

1 Remove the handle (right), then use a wrench wrapped in a protective cloth to unscrew the bell-shaped shroud. Use an adjustable spanner, or open-ended spanner of the right size (*see* SPANNER), to unscrew the headgear nut just above the spout. Brace the tap with your free hand, or with a pipe wrench wrapped in cloth to prevent it turning and cracking the basin or distorting the pipework.

2 The top half of the tap can now be lifted out. The valve, with washer attached, will either be left in the lower half of the tap, or will come out with the top portion. It may be held in place with a small nut. Replace the washer, reassemble the tap, turn the tap off and turn the water supply back on.

Remove the screw to release the handle from the spindle. If any nuts or screws are seized, free them with a squirt of WD-40.

manage a Team

■ Be approachable: your subordinates should see you as an essential member of the group, not as a general commanding the troops from afar.
■ Acknowledge hard work, and give praise where it's due: nothing demoralises a team more quickly than feeling undervalued.
■ Never reprimand a member of your team publicly.
■ Learn the strengths of the individuals in your team, assign tasks accordingly, and allow people to do their tasks in their own way – don't just issue orders and insist on a particular way of working.
■ When building a team, resist the temptation to only pick people who are professional clones of yourself or share your temperament: the strength of any team lies in the diversity of its skills and ideas.

clean your Teeth properly

Flossing
■ Once every day, take a length of floss about 45cm and wind the ends around your middle fingers. Pinch between thumbs and forefingers to isolate around 2.5cm of it, draw taut and slide it up and down in the gaps between your teeth (don't 'saw' with it and risk cutting your gums but try a circular movement with your fingers).
■ As you move on to the next pair of teeth, wind the floss on a little to expose a fresh length.
■ Don't worry if your gums bleed a little at first. This should stop as dental hygiene improves.

Brushing
■ Brush morning and night for at least 2 minutes, getting into all the nooks and crannies; make the time to do a thorough job.
■ Use a pea-sized blob of toothpaste.
■ Use small, circular movements rather than a scrubbing motion and make sure you work on all surfaces; don't neglect the insides.
■ Brush along the gum line as well as the teeth, and clean the tongue.

ease the pain of Teething

When babies start teething, at about six months, it can make them fractious and tearful, but you can take the heat out of the situation.

■ Use a water-filled teething ring. Chill it in the fridge (not the freezer) and offer to your baby to chew on and cool the painful gums. Never tie a ring around a baby's neck. A clean, cold wet flannel can also help.
■ Offer a piece of chilled raw fruit or vegetable, such as an apple slice or carrot stick, to gnaw on. You can also use specific sugar-free teething rusks. Always supervise your child closely to avoid choking.
■ If your baby has a temperature, you could use a liquid painkiller, specifically for children, closely following the label instructions. Don't give aspirin – this isn't suitable for any child under 16.
■ Don't forget that a good, old-fashioned cuddle can soothe you both.

understand a Teenager

Teenagers are baffling – even to themselves. Keep the lines of communication open and ride the storm until your teenagers emerge as young adults.

Think back to your own youth. It will help you to cope with trying teenage behaviour if you recall that you were once a less-than-charming presence in your parents' home. It may amaze and intrigue your teenagers if you can talk about your own adolescent experiences in a way that makes it clear that you know what they are going through.

Keep abreast of your adolescent child's school and social life. Be interested without interfering. Know who their friends are, and allow them to come to your home. When friends visit, say a brief 'hello', then leave them alone. But set boundaries for, and talk openly about, unacceptable behaviour.

Make time for your teenagers and allow them into your world: involve them in your adult conversations and activities. Spend time with them, doing something you can share and enjoy: shopping, watching football, going for a pizza.

Don't mock them or their views. You may not like your teenager's taste in rock, clothes or interior decoration, but keep your opinions to yourself. Saying that the music was better in your day, or anything along those lines is the expressway to sullen, silent alienation. What do you know, anyway?

Above all, pay your teenagers the compliment of treating them like the grown-ups that they will soon become.

take someone's body
Temperature

A normal temperature under the tongue is around 37°C (98.6°F); under the arm it's about 0.5°C (1°F) lower. You can buy a digital thermometer from your pharmacy, which is easy to use and safer than an old-fashioned glass thermometer, which contains poisonous mercury.

■ Before you start, thoroughly wash your hands (see HANDS) and clean the thermometer tip with a soft, damp cloth using soap and water.

■ For children under 5, put the thermometer in either armpit and hold the arm against the body. This prevents a child from biting down on the thermometer. Otherwise, place it gently under the tongue (above). Follow the manufacturer's instructions for guidance on the length of time to hold the thermometer in place.
■ Don't take a temperature reading for at least 20 minutes after taking food or drink, or a bath.
■ A high temperature is anything above 38°C (100.4°F), or 37.5°C (99.5°F) in a child under 5 (see FEVER).

build a simple Telescope

You might not be able to see the stars, but this fun science project will entertain budding pirates and astronomers alike.

Using two lenses means the image you see through your telescope is upside down, but children will enjoy this topsy-turvy view of the world.

YOU WILL NEED Two sheets of card flexible enough to roll into a tube (or use corrugated card), scissors, two magnifying glasses (preferably the same size), sticky tape

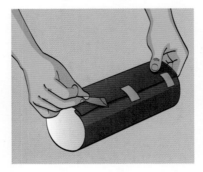

1 Roll one sheet of card into a tube the same diameter as your first magnifying glass and use sticky tape to hold it. The longer the tube, the more you'll be able to change the focus – but don't make it longer than you or your child can manage to hold.

2 Hold the magnifying glass tight to one end of the tube. Then tape the card around the frame of the magnifying glass to fix it firmly into place. A second pair of hands is useful here to do a really neat job.

3 Make another tube with the other sheet of card. This tube must be slightly narrower than the first, so that it can slide inside it. Fix the second magnifying glass to one end of the narrower tube then slide the narrower tube inside the other one.

4 If you wish, decorate the tubes with pens, paint or stickers. Your telescope is now ready to use. Move the lenses apart or closer together to focus the image, by sliding the tubes in and out.

get into the swing of Tennis

Tennis can be played indoors or out – on clay, grass or a synthetic surface, or simply for fun on a tarmac court at your local park or club.

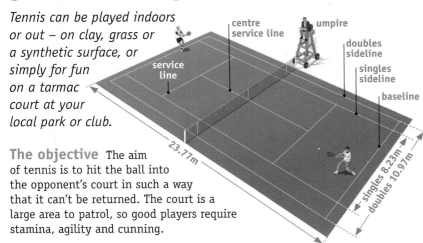

centre service line

umpire

service line

doubles sideline

singles sideline

baseline

23.77m

singles 8.23m
doubles 10.97m

The objective
The aim of tennis is to hit the ball into the opponent's court in such a way that it can't be returned. The court is a large area to patrol, so good players require stamina, agility and cunning.

Scoring A match is scored as a series of duels. Players must win four points (15, 30, 40 and 'game') to win a game. A 40:40 tie is called 'deuce' and a player must then win two consecutive points ('advantage' and 'game'). Service (below) alternates with each game and the first to six games or more, with a two-game advantage, takes the 'set'. Most matches are played to the best of three or five sets. If, in any set other than the decider, the score reaches six games each, a 'tie break' is played, which is won by the player who scores seven or more points with a two point advantage.

Playing tennis shots In a long rally, you'll use forehand and backhand, lob high balls over your opponent's head and fire back quick volleys. Practise the basic shots on the next page, then master the service, which must open each point. A good serve puts your opponent on the defensive.

1   2   3   4   5   6

How to serve Stand at the baseline with your body sideways on, and transfer some of your weight to your back foot (1). With a straight arm, toss the ball up and slightly forward (2), and bring your racket arm back into a 'throwing' position (3). As the ball reaches its highest point, bring your racket arm forwards, overhead (4). Aim to strike the ball at as high a point as possible (5), as this maximises power of the impact and the angle of the bounce, making the serve (6) harder for your opponent to reach and return.

continued overleaf ➔

relieve the pain of
Tennis elbow

This is an occupational as well as a recreational problem. Factory workers, carpenters, tennis players, golfers, even politicians at the end of a long campaign of hand-shaking can suffer as a result of repetitive strenuous arm movement while gripping with the hand. The tendon that anchors the muscles to the bottom of the upper arm bone becomes inflamed, causing an acute pain at the elbow and a dull ache down the forearm.

Self-help remedies
■ Rest the arm and change the activity that's causing the problem if you can. Speak to your employer or occupational health adviser if work is the cause.
■ Apply ice packs (*see* SPRAINS AND STRAINS) and take NSAIDs (non-steroidal anti-inflammatory drugs), such as ibuprofen, in cream or gel form, to ease the inflammation.
■ Try capsaicin (cayenne pepper) ointment, applied four times a day.
■ If the pain persists, consult your doctor, who may prescribe stronger anti-inflammatory drugs, give a shot of hydrocortisone into the tendon or suggest physiotherapy.

score a strike at
Tenpin bowling

To score strikes consistently you need to rotate the ball. A rotated ball takes a curved path as it rolls down the lane, and so strikes the pins at an angle, greatly increasing the chances that they will rattle into each other.

To throw a hook (as it's known), you approach the moment of release with your fingers beneath the ball, then turn your hand into a 'handshake' position as you release it. With practice, you can learn to rotate the ball so that it loops almost into the guter, and then curls in sharply as it aproaches the pins. And make sure you try to hit the headpin.

Forehand As the ball approaches you on your racket side (your right, if you're right-handed), bring the racket head back in a loop, so that it reaches head height. Turn your body away, so that you put all the muscle power of your legs and torso into the shot. Bring the racket round, aiming to make contact in front of the body as the ball bounces up to waist height. Follow through, so that your racket arm comes across your body, finishing high.

Backhand If the ball is coming to your non-racket side (your left, if you're right-handed) draw the racket across your body, so that it lies horizontally across your midriff. Step up to meet the ball in front of the body, and strike it (double-handed style above) as your weight comes onto your front foot, so that your forward momentum adds power to the shot. Push with your legs as well as your arm at the moment of impact, finishing high.

understand a Tenpin bowling scorecard

There's more to scoring a game of bowling than just adding up the pins you knock down. On a scorecard, each large box corresponds to a frame, a player's two throws of the ball, and gives a running total. The number of pins knocked over with each throw is recorded in the two smaller boxes.

FRAME 1 The player felled 5 pins with the first ball, and 3 with the second, making 8.

If a player knocks over all the pins with two throws (a spare), that's shown in the second of the small boxes as a diagonal slash.

When a spare is scored, the number of pins knocked over with the first ball of the following frame is added to a player's running total for the previous frame and then counted again in that next frame.

PLAYER NAME	1	2	3	4	5	6	7	8	9	10	TOTAL
	5 3	6 /	4 2	7 1	X	7 /	X	X	7 0	6 1	
Bella	8	22	28	36	56	76	103	120	127	134	134
	6 2	7 0	6 2	7 /	3 0	X	1 6	4 /	6 1	3 / 5	
Tilly	8	15	23	36	39	56	63	79	86	101	101

FRAME 2 The total of 22 equals 8 (frame 1) plus 10 (frame 2) plus 4 (first ball, frame 3).

If a player knocks over all ten pins at the first attempt (a strike), that's indicated by an X in the first smaller box. All the points made with the next two throws are added to the total.

FRAME 5 The total of 56 equals 36 (frame 4), plus 10 (the strike in frame 5), plus 10 (spare in frame 6).

If you score a strike with your first ball in frame 10, you get two more balls to complete your score. Throw a spare, and you get one more ball. The highest possible score is 300.

put up a dome Tent

Struggling to erect a tent on a wet and windy campsite is a sure way to spoil the start of your holiday. Follow some basic rules and always have a dry run in the garden with a new tent before you go away.

1 Lay out the 'footprint' groundsheet if you have one, to prevent stones damaging your integral groundsheet. Unfold and lay the tent on top. This tent is pitched inner first.

2 Fix poles together and lay them close to hand. Thread poles through tabs or clips on top of the inner tent and through central tab at top. Some tents are pitched flysheet (or outer) first and have long pockets through which you thread the poles.

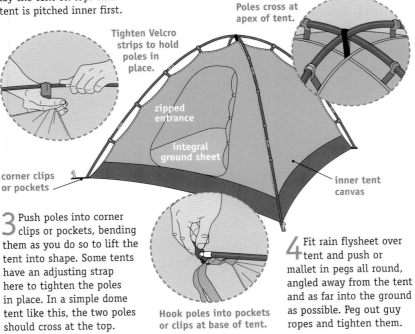

Poles cross at apex of tent.

Tighten Velcro strips to hold poles in place.

zipped entrance

integral ground sheet

corner clips or pockets

inner tent canvas

Hook poles into pockets or clips at base of tent.

3 Push poles into corner clips or pockets, bending them as you do so to lift the tent into shape. Some tents have an adjusting strap here to tighten the poles in place. In a simple dome tent like this, the two poles should cross at the top.

4 Fit rain flysheet over tent and push or mallet in pegs all round, angled away from the tent and as far into the ground as possible. Peg out guy ropes and tighten them.

examine your Testicles

Testicular cancer is almost always curable if detected early. Once a month, perform this simple check after a warm bath.

■ Use all your fingers and thumbs to feel around one testicle at a time. After a few times you'll know what is normal for you.
■ It's usual for one testicle to be a little larger and lower than the other.
■ The soft lump at the top towards the back of each is the sperm-carrying tube.

■ The testicles should be smooth and not swollen, with no ususual lumps or soreness.
■ They should be no harder or softer than usual and should not have changed noticeably in size or weight since your last check.
■ If you notice any change, talk to a doctor. Causes are usually benign.

say Thank you
in 12 languages

If you're going to learn a single word of any language – when going on holiday to a foreign country, say – then 'thank you' is the one that will be most useful, and make you the most friends. Here is the word for 'thank you' in 12 languages. The words are given below in their written form, then transcribed as an approximation of English pronunciation that should be close enough to make you understood. Capitals mean the stress falls on that part of the word.

LANGUAGE	PHRASE AND PRONUNCIATION
FRENCH	**Merci** *Mare-SEE*
GERMAN	**Danke** *DUN-ker*
ITALIAN	**Grazie** *GRAT-see*
SPANISH	**Gracias** *GRA-thee-ass*
RUSSIAN	**Spasibo** *Spah–SEE-bah*
TURKISH	**Teşekkür ederim** *Te-shi-KOOR e-DARE-im*
ICELANDIC	**Takk fyrir** *Tuck fear-EAR*
CROATIAN	**Hvala** *Hh-fa-LA*
JAPANESE	**Arigoto** *A-ree-gaw-TAW*
MANDARIN	**Xie xie** *SYEAR-syear*
ARABIC	**Shukran** *SHOO-krahn*
POLISH	**Dziękuje** *Jen-COO-yeah*

T

remove a Tick

Take precautions against being bitten by a tick in the first place. When out in woodland during the summer months, wear a long-sleeved shirt and long trousers, and tuck your trousers into your socks. Use DEET repellents, and check your skin carefully after a walk.

If you do get bitten, remove the tick as soon as you can. Wearing gloves, or covering the tick with a tissue to avoid contact with your fingers, grasp it with tweezers as close to your skin as possible. Pull straight upwards and don't squeeze the tick too hard, or you may force the contents of its stomach into the site of the bite. Pull gently, and it should come free. Make sure that its head and mouth parts haven't become detached.

After removing the tick, wash your hands and the bite with soap and water, and apply an antiseptic to the bite area. In rare cases, a tick bite can result in serious infection: if a rash appears around the bitten area, or you develop a fever, seek medical attention immediately.

write a sincere Thank you letter

Anyone who has made a gift or a gesture, offered hospitality or performed some kindness deserves a properly penned – yes, handwritten – note of gratitude.

Put pen to paper Take the trouble to show that a kindness has real meaning to you. In these days of texts and emails, it can be a lovely surprise to receive a letter or, perhaps even better, an attractively illustrated card. If you write a letter, make sure you use a good-quality paper and matching envelope – a piece of photocopy paper won't impress. And choose a pen that works – not one that's about to run out of ink or makes smudges. Don't wait too long to respond to a gift, treat or kindness. Send a letter or card within a few days. If you really haven't the time to send something in writing, an email is better than nothing, but should be sent as soon as possible.

Choose the right words The most important thing is to keep it personal. If you received 50 wedding gifts, that means 50 individual letters. Don't just change the name and address at the top; take time to craft each one. Do a few each day so you don't become jaded. Use the following basic framework.

1 Remember that it's a letter, not an email. Begin *Dear ...* name.

2 Say at once what it is that you're thankful for and why it's special. *The vase looks lovely filled with roses. I couldn't put the book down. How clever of you to pick just the right colour! What a treat to get up into the hills again!*

3 Close with the hope that you'll see one another or be in touch soon. If you already have a date in your diary, say how much you're looking forward to it.

4 Sign off on a warm note – *With love, With best wishes, Thanks again,* as appropriate. Avoid abbreviations – *LOL* or *xxxxxxx* will shriek of insincerity.

play Tiddlywinks

There's more to this traditional favourite than just popping counters into a cup. It's a game of strategy with complex rules. Have fun at home with this simplified version.

YOU WILL NEED **Six 'winks' (that is, four small and two large counters) of each colour (red, yellow, blue, green), felt mat measuring 1.8m by 0.9m, pot, 'squidgers' (small circular discs)**

To start Lay the mat on a hard surface such as a table or wooden floor. Four players form two pairs. Blue partners red; green partners yellow. The pot is placed at the centre of the mat, and colours occupy corners of the mat, in the order red, yellow, blue, green. Each player uses a squidger to press down on the edge of a wink and ping it towards the centre. The wink nearest to the pot gets to start. All winks are returned to the corners; play proceeds clockwise.

To play The basic aim is to flip all one's winks into the pot ('pot out'). Players have one shot per turn towards the centre and can play their winks in any order. If a player pots a wink they get another turn, meaning that it's feasible to pot all six in one go. If a wink lands off the mat it's returned to the edge and the player misses a go.

A wink is 'squopped' if it's overlapped even slightly by another wink, and cannot be played. If a player's last wink is squopped they are stymied until the covering wink is flipped away by the player to whom it belongs.

If nobody pots out within 25 minutes, the score of 'tiddlies' is counted thus:
3 for every potted wink
1 for each uncovered wink
0 for squopped and unplayed winks.

tie a Tie

There are many ways to tie a tie. The Windsor is particularly stylish, and the four-in-hand is easy to do.

Four-in-hand

1 Cross the tie on your shirtfront such that the wide end is about 30cm longer than the narrow end. Wrap the wide end round the back of the narrow end.

2 Bring the wide end back across the front of the narrow end, so that the front of the tie is facing outwards.

3 Take the wide end up through the gap between the tie and your collar button.

4 Pull the wide end down through the knot, and finish by sliding the knot up to your neck. The narrow end should come out fractionally shorter than the wide end.

continued overleaf ➜

Tie-dye successfully

It's easy to create colourful patterns on fabric, or on ready-made clothes such as T-shirts and skirts, by folding, crumpling or tying the fabric before dyeing it. The way you prepare the material will determine the finished result.

Marbled effect Crumple the fabric into a ball, then tie it in a criss-cross pattern with string.

Irregular stripes Fold the fabric like an accordion and tie it at intervals with thread.

Irregular spots Scrunch up small areas of fabric and tie them around with thread to enclose them.

Patterns Try sewing or folding objects such as buttons, small pebbles and dried beans into folds of the fabric.

Dyeing Use commercial hot and cold water dyes (*see* DYE) according to the manufacturer's instructions. Immerse the fabric in the dye as recommended, rinse, unfold and dry the fabric a little. Then iron it while it's still damp. For a second colour, allow the fabric to dry completely then repeat the process with a different dye.

☆ golden rules
TIE-DYE TIPS
- **Start with easy-to-dye fabric such as soft cotton.**
- **Dampen the fabric a little before you fold it.**
- **For deep colour areas mix dye and push it into creases and folds with a paintbrush or from a squeezable bottle.**

deal with Tinnitus

Many of us will at some time in our life experience mild tinnitus, a perception of buzzing or ringing in the ears when there's no external sound. If no underlying cause is found and treated, you can learn ways of coping with it.

- Don't worry. Anxiety is a major exacerbating factor (*see* RELAXATION *and* STRESS).
- Keep occupied. It really helps if you can take your mind off it.
- Use masking sound. In a quiet room, the brain will listen to random activity in the auditory pathway. Place a ticking clock in the room, or play some soft music, and the brain will filter out the unwanted buzzing or ringing.
- At bedtime try a 'sound therapy system'. This plays digital recordings of such soothing natural sounds as ocean waves and gentle rain, as you drift off to sleep.
- Herbal remedies ginkgo biloba or lesser periwinkle may help in some cases.
- Try a cup of fenugreek-seed tea morning, noon and night.
- Avoid exposure to loud noises and the build-up of ear wax.
- Try reflexology, acupuncture, acupressure or meditation (*see* MEDITATE). All have been known to help in some cases.
- Join a support group. It helps to share your experience and to know you're not alone.

Windsor

1 Cross the tie on your shirtfront such that the wide end is about 30cm longer than the narrow end.

2 Bring the wide end up behind the narrow end, then pull it down toward the front to make a loose twist at the neck.

3 Bring the wide end behind the narrow end to point out to the left, then take it through the loop from front to back.

4 Bring the wide end across the front of the narrow end from right to left, then take it behind and through the loop.

5 Now tuck the wide end through the inverted triangular knot that has formed at the top.

6 Pull down on the wide end to tighten the knot, and on the narrow end to slide the knot up to your collar.

Tile a floor

Ceramic tiles can be laid directly onto a concrete floor. Timber floors must be overlaid with 9mm exterior plywood, firmly screwed down.

1 Place a tile at the dead centre of the room. Dry lay single rows of tiles from this point to the walls to check that there will be no narrow slivers of tile at the edges. If there are, shift the rows so that you'll have half a tile or more at all edges.

Find the centre of the room by marking diagonal lines from corner to corner and seeing where they cross. In an irregular-shaped room, centre tiles on the largest area or align with a prominent feature.

2 Fix battens to the floor at one corner, where the outermost whole tile will go. Now dry-lay a square of nine tiles against the battens to check that they line up perfectly – if they don't, adjust the battens.

3 Spread enough adhesive on the floor for these tiles, lay them, with spacers between, and use a spirit level to check that they are level, measuring across each row and diagonal. Then lay the next set of nine.

4 Once the adhesive has set, remove the battens. Measure and cut each edge tile in turn (few rooms are exactly square), applying adhesive to the back of the tile. Leave for 24 hours, then apply a waterproof, stain-resistant grout.

Tile a wall

Take time to plan the positioning of tiles before you begin and you will achieve a far more professional result, with fewer awkward cuts.

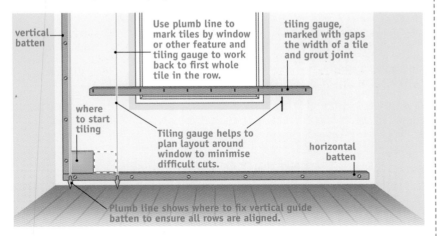

vertical batten

Use plumb line to mark tiles by window or other feature and tiling gauge to work back to first whole tile in the row.

tiling gauge, marked with gaps the width of a tile and grout joint

where to start tiling

Tiling gauge helps to plan layout around window to minimise difficult cuts.

horizontal batten

Plumb line shows where to fix vertical guide batten to ensure all rows are aligned.

Plan the layout Lay a row of tiles on the floor along the wall to be tiled, leaving gaps for spacers. Adjust the row so that the gap is even at either end. If there's a window, it may look better to centre tiles around it and live with unequal cuts at the edges of the wall. Use a plumb line to mark a vertical line at the point where the last whole tile goes, and nail a guide batten to the wall. Work out the vertical spacing in the same way and use a spirit level to mark a horizontal line under the lowest whole tile, and fix another batten. This creates a square corner that is the point from which you'll begin tiling.

continued overleaf →

make
Toffee apples

If you buy apples from a shop, you'll need to remove the preservative wax that covers them first, or else the toffee won't stick. If you use home-grown apples you can avoid this boiling water treatment (see step 1 below). A sugar thermometer makes it simple to judge the temperature.

MAKES 6

6 crisp eating apples
350g demerara sugar
140ml water
35g butter
2 tbsp golden syrup

1 Put the apples into a large bowl, cover with boiling water then remove and dry thoroughly. Spear each with a wooden skewer or lolly stick and place on baking parchment.

2 Dissolve the sugar in the water over medium heat, add the butter and syrup and cook until the mixture reaches 150°C – the hard crack stage (*see* SUGAR THERMOMETER). Remove from the heat and dip in each apple in turn, twisting it to get an even coating of toffee. Place upside down on the baking parchment to cool. If the toffee starts to harden before all the apples are dipped, reheat it gently.

unblock a Toilet

■ If the blockage isn't caused by something out of the ordinary, there's a quick and clean way to clear it. Part-fill a bucket with water – not so much that it would fill the toilet pan. With one swift movement, pour the water all in one go into the centre of the toilet pan, where the pipework curves out of sight. The weight and the force of the water will probably be enough to shift the blockage.

■ If that doesn't work, use a special WC plunger that's large enough to cover the whole of the toilet outlet.

■ For a really stubborn blockage, try a plumber's snake, or auger (above). Insert the cable end of the tool into the U-bend and turn the crank handle. This winds the cable through the toilet's trap and into the soil pipe. Its hooked spring tip allows you to grab the blockage and carefully pull it back out through the trap or to push and break up the clog.

■ If none of this works, call a plumber.

Fixing the tiles to the wall

1 Apply adhesive to the wall in a band a little more than one tile wide. Place a tile, then another, moving horizontally along the row, and fitting spacers between each tile. Push firmly and evenly into place, making sure tiles are well bedded into the adhesive and level with the adjacent tiles. Use waterproof adhesive (and grout) around sinks, baths and showers, and in other wet areas.

2 Carry on up the wall with all the whole tiles. Wait 24 hours, then remove the battens and fill in the edges with cut tiles. It's easier to apply adhesive to the back of cut tiles than to the wall. Wait another 24 hours before removing the spacers and applying grout. Use a sponge or grouting tool to push grout between tiles and smooth it. Wipe tiles clean before the grout sets hard.

Toilet train a child

It can take a while to teach an infant to use the lavatory. Be patient and relaxed about it. They all get there in the end.

Buy a large comfortable potty ahead of time When the day comes to use it, the potty will be a familiar sight.

Choose your moment When your child can understand basic commands and exercise some bladder control by staying dry for a couple of hours – usually at about two years old – you can make a start. Don't expect night-time dryness until much later. Avoid starting at times of stress, like moving house.

Get them used to the potty After you give food or drink, put your child on the potty. If nothing happens, don't worry, but give praise if something does.

Phase out nappies As potty time becomes part of the routine, let your child go without a nappy. Choose a time when you can be at home, or in the garden. Use trainer pants instead of nappies and put your child on the potty every hour. Always praise success; don't scold a child for failure.

Mark triumphs Make a chart and stick on gold stars when the potty is used.

Use picture books A fun story with lots of pictures helps toddlers to understand what's involved. Or there are free child-friendly images online.

Take a step up When your child can manage it, introduce a toddler step and trainer seat for the lavatory. Teach correct wiping (with girls, particularly, teach to wipe from front to back) and thorough hand washing (*see* HANDS).

grow a great Tomato

You don't need a greenhouse to grow flavour-packed tomatoes. The key is to choose a variety well suited to your space and situation.

There's a huge range of sizes and colours available, from big red beefsteak tomatoes to yellow cherry ones designed to tumble out of hanging baskets.

YOU WILL NEED **Seeds or plants, compost, seed trays, pots, bamboo canes, soft string, watering can, tomato food**

Start growing with seeds (*see* SEEDS AND SEEDLINGS) in trays or small pots, kept on a sunny windowsill if you don't have a greenhouse. Sow seed in mid spring for outdoor varieties and late winter for indoor ones. They will need a temperature of 18°C to germinate.

Transplant seedlings to 7.5cm pots as soon as two true leaves have formed, then into permanent positions in the garden or into deep 9-12cm pots once the first flowers begin to form.

Support growing plants with a bamboo cane pushed in alongside each plant. Tie the stem to the cane with soft string in several places.

Pinching out is essential for cordon tomatoes, but not for bush varieties. Remove sideshoots regularly to leave about seven good fruit trusses on indoor plants and four on outdoor ones. Remove the top of the main stem to stop any more growth and concentrate development into the fruits. Water regularly to keep compost moist. Once fruit on the second truss begins to form, feed every 7-14 days with a shop-bought tomato feed. Keep pinching out shoots that grow from the joint between the stem and other shoots.

make a fresh Tomato sauce

Tomato sauce is the base of many dishes, and the star of the show in a simple bowl of pasta. You can use fresh tomatoes when they are in season and full of flavour, or canned ones all year round. The sauce freezes well and can be supplemented with olives, tuna, chilli or any other ingredient you like.

MAKES ENOUGH FOR 4 SERVINGS OF PASTA

4 tbsp olive oil
1 medium onion, finely chopped
2 cloves garlic, chopped
500g fresh tomatoes, skinned, deseeded and chopped (see right), with juice, or 400g tin

Italian chopped plum tomatoes, with juice
salt and freshly ground black pepper
2 tsp dried marjoram
handful of fresh basil, chopped

1 Heat the oil in a heavy-based saucepan and cook the onion until soft. Add the garlic, tomatoes, seasonings and marjoram. Cover and simmer for 20-30 minutes.

2 Just before the end of cooking, check the seasonings and add the basil. The sauce can be used as it is or liquidised for a totally smooth version.

skin and deseed a Tomato

Skin tomatoes to prevent pieces of skin coming off during cooking and spoiling a dish such as a sauce or casserole. As well as tomatoes, peaches and apricots can be skinned using this method.

1 With a small sharp knife, lightly cut a small cross shape in the base of each tomato. Remove any stalks.

2 Fill a large bowl with boiling water then immerse each tomato for 30-60 seconds, or until the cut skin begins to curl up. Don't submerge the tomatoes for too long or they will get soggy.

3 Remove with a slotted spoon, drain and allow to cool a little, then peel away the skin with the knife.

To deseed, quarter the tomatoes and remove the cores and pips with a knife or a teaspoon.

golden rules
TOMATO SAUCE TIP
■ **If the sauce isn't thick enough, cook it uncovered on a high heat, stirring, until you have the right consistency.**

sharpen Tools

A blunt tool is less effective than a sharp one, but also more dangerous. It's likely to slip during use and cause injury or damage. Keeping chisels and plane blades sharp is simple, but worthwhile.

YOU WILL NEED Oilstone, honing guide, some light machine oil

1 Prepare the stone by smearing a teaspoon of oil over it. Let it soak in, and then repeat the process.

2 Clamp the blade in the honing guide so that it projects the correct distance. Pour a little more oil on the stone to coat the surface.

3 Now move the guide up and down the oilstone, pressing down so that the tip of the blade to be sharpened is flat against the stone.

4 Then take the blade out, and rub its flat edge against the stone to remove the 'burr' – the little curl of metal that will have formed on the cutting edge.

create simple Topiary shapes

Plants such as box and bay are ideal subjects for making topiary shapes such as pyramids, globes and 'lollipops'. It's easiest to start with large potted plants before tackling hedge topiary.

YOU WILL NEED Potted plant, shears, canes, wire rings, secateurs

Pyramid or globe box Use shears to trim the plant to roughly the desired shape. Leave it to grow for a year. Then use canes and wire to construct a cutting guide to place over the plant. Trim once or twice a year with secateurs, following the lines of the guide. To look effective, these shapes must be neat and geometrically accurate.

Lollipop bay tree When the young tree is a little taller than needed, use secateurs to prune off the growing tip and cut off the side shoots from the lower trunk. When they are about 15cm long, pinch or cut out the tips of side shoots in the 'head' to encourage them to bush out. Continue to trim in this way as the tree grows.

relieve Toothache

It's time to see a dentist, but you can manage the pain while you wait for an appointment.

At the first slight discomfort drink hot liquids. For a continuous ache, hold a cold pack to your jaw and take some painkillers.

Sluice your mouth every hour with warm salt water. Hold the strong brine in your mouth and swish it around your teeth before spitting out. Unrefined grey sea salt, which is rich in minerals, is the most effective.

Clove oil is a natural dental painkiller. Dab a little on a cotton swab and hold it to the affected tooth (avoid touching it to your tongue, if possible).

Tea tree oil has natural antibacterial and pain-relieving properties; apply in the same way as clove oil.

avoid the rot of Tooth decay

To keep teeth in top condition, you must banish the bacteria that feed on food particles left on the teeth and produce corrosive acid.

■ Keep teeth clean (*see* TEETH). Brush at least twice a day with a toothpaste that contains fluoride, and floss regularly between teeth.
■ Ban sugary and starchy snacks, and fizzy drinks laced with sugar. Combine sugary foods with a meal, as this can limit the damage.

■ Chewing gum that contains the sweetener xylitol may retard the growth of bacteria.
■ See your dentist every six months to catch problems early on.
■ Consider sealants, which apply a protective coating to the biting surfaces of the back teeth.

leave Travel sickness at home

Travel sickness pills are effective at quelling nausea, but can cause drowsiness. Try these simple strategies to minimise the problem instead.

■ Try closing your eyes or looking into the distance at something in a fixed position or at the horizon.
■ Try deep breathing.
■ Play music and sing along.
■ Ensure adequate ventilation.
■ Take a flask of ginger tea: ginger

is a tried-and-tested nausea relief.
■ Schedule regular stops – at least once an hour.
■ On arrival, lie down, close your eyes and keep your head still until the feeling of movement passes.
See also SEASICKNESS.

drive safely with a Trailer

Driving with a trailer can be hazardous. So make sure you follow certain rules – before you set off and while you're driving.

Load up correctly There should more weight ahead of the trailer's axle than behind it. Check the tyre pressures before every journey.

Go slowly and legally In the UK, a lower speed limit applies to cars towing trailers (50mph on single carriageways and 60mph on dual carriageways). On motorways you may not use the outermost overtaking lane. Don't brake sharply on bends, or the trailer may jack-knife.

Take special care when reversing This is best done with the help of a second person who can see what is behind you (*see* CARAVAN).

Know how to stop snaking A trailer can weave from side to side if poorly loaded, you're going too fast or you get buffeted by side winds. Don't try to accelerate or steer out of trouble. Keep straight, change down a gear, take your foot off the accelerator and the clutch and let the car slow down gradually. Don't brake unless you're going downhill, and then only gently.

organise a Treasure hunt

Treasure hunts are terrific fun, but they require thoughtful forward planning. Ambiguous clues mean dead ends and lost treasure hunters.

The idea of a treasure hunt is to make a trail of clues that leads from one location to the next, and finally to a finish line. There need not be any 'treasure' along the way, but there should be a prize for the person or team that completes the hunt and reaches the finish first.

■ If you're doing a treasure hunt for children, keep the clues simple, make the hunt brief, and be sure that the area in which the hunt is to take place is safe and enclosed.
■ If you're doing a hunt for adults, make use of the location – be it a country house, a historic town centre or high street, or your own home – with cryptic clues, historical hints, puns and local knowledge to make clues harder.
■ First work out the route of your hunt, then write clues to fit. Remember, each clue must refer to the next place the hunters must go, not where they are now.
■ On private property, you can attach or even conceal the clues about the place. For a hunt in a public place, issue a complete list of all clues to the teams – each one in a sealed envelope, perhaps.
■ Make your clues witty, baffling, intriguing – rhyming, if you like. A good clue is unfathomable on its own, but reasonably easy for a hunter who is in the right spot. If you need inspiration, search online for 'treasure hunt clues' to find a selection of riddles and cryptic clues.

T

stake a young Tree

Until their roots are firmly anchored, which can take three years or more, young trees need to be staked. This prevents their roots from rocking about, which impairs their growth. Choose cushioned ties to protect the trunk, or add it yourself with a wad of sacking.

Sturdy and short-stemmed bare-rooted trees Use a short vertical stake that comes a third of the way up the trunk. Attach with a tie.

Container-grown trees Drive in a short stake angled so as to miss the rootball. Attach it about 45cm above ground level.

For any tree Drive in two short upright stakes 60cm apart on either side of the trunk and join them with a horizontal batten. Attach the tree to the batten.

plant a Tree

Autumn is the best season for planting deciduous trees, but frost-vulnerable container-grown evergreens are best planted in spring.

Before planting, make up a planting mixture as for shrubs and soak bare rooted trees in a bucket of water for several hours. If they are container-grown, water them well.

1 Work out the size of hole, allowing several extra centimetres in width and depth. Dig the hole and add the planting mixture (*see* SHRUB).

2 Put in the tree to check for correct depth – use a length of wood put across the hole and mark the trunk at the right position. Sprinkle in some granules of mycorrhizal root-stimulating compound following the maker's instructions.

3 Add a stake (see left) then put in the tree and spread the roots out as much as possible. Back-fill with soil, pressing it in well as you go. Firm in the tree with your foot. Water well, firm in again and add a layer of mulch.

cut off a Tree branch

Trees seldom benefit from pruning, because the wounds are vulnerable to infection. But sometimes it's necessary to remove lower branches to raise the crown, or take out boughs to thin the crown to allow more light through.

- Don't prune when a tree is producing or dropping its leaves.
- Always leave large, high or difficult-to-reach branches to a professional. Don't try to remove any branch you cannot reach from the ground.
- Use a pruning saw and wear sturdy gloves and eye protection. Don't use a chainsaw for this job unless you have been trained to do so.
- Remove branches where they meet the trunk or shorten them to a lateral stem (one branching off) that is at least one-third of the diameter of the branch you're removing.

1 Make sure the area into which the branch will fall is clear. Begin by cutting a third of the way through the branch from below, 3-5cm from the trunk, using a pruning saw. Then repeat from above, 3-5cm further away from the trunk. This helps to prevent the branch from tearing from the tree.

2 Then cut through the branch, with an angled cut that is flush with the trunk at the top and slopes away slightly. If sap 'bleeds' from the cut, don't dress or bandage it, or you may inhibit the natural healing processes.

shorten a pair of Trousers

Trousers bought off the peg are often too long, but shortening them is easy with a little care. This method also works for unlined sleeves.

YOU WILL NEED Tape measure, pins, stitch remover, iron, full-length mirror, needle and thread, scissors

1 Measure the depth of the existing hems. Try on the trousers, turn up and mark the new length with pins on each leg (you may need to recruit a helper for this). Take them off, turn them inside out, undo the existing hems and press. Turn up to your pin marks, using the tape measure to make sure that both hems are equal. Try on, checking in the mirror that legs match exactly for length. Adjust as necessary.

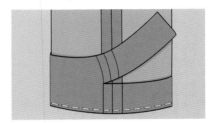

2 Tack new hems close to the turned-up edge, then cut off any excess fabric. If legs are tapered, open the side seams to make the fabric lie flat.

3 To neaten raw edges, make a small turning or finish as for seams (*see* SEAM). Pin, then hem using a hemming or blind hemming stitch (*see* SEWING).

get tweeting on Twitter

Anyone can say ('tweet') anything they like, and if it's interesting enough and anyone is reading ('following'), it may spark a conversation.

■ Once you have signed up at the Twitter website, identify some people to 'follow' – each tweet they write will then appear on your 'Home' page. Most people start by following friends and family or colleagues. Click on **Who To Follow**, type in people's names to find their accounts, then click **Follow**.
■ You also need followers of your own; otherwise your tweets will only be read if someone happens across them via the site's search engine. At first, you can start by hoping that the people you are following will reciprocate.
■ To tweet, click in the 'What's happening?' text box, type your message and click **Tweet**, but remember you only have 140 characters: every letter, comma and space counts. A space-saving Twitter and text language is evolving, with shortcuts such as TY for 'thank you' and IRL ('in real life').
■ Make your tweets as interesting as possible and one of your followers might 'retweet' (RT) one of your messages – that is forward it to their own followers, some of whom might then choose to follow you.
■ The hash tag (#readersdigest) before a name in your tweet will help users to search for more information about something you mention.
■ If you mention another twitter user, type '@' before their name and they will be more likely to see your tweet, as it will appear in a different place.

do a Tumble turn
in the pool

A tumble turn is an underwater somersault and twist. The aim is to change direction quickly at the end of a length.

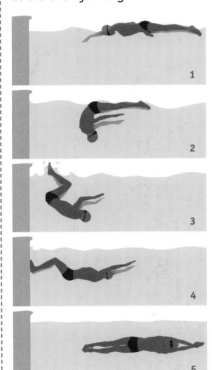

1 Make ready to turn when you see the 'T' on the bottom of the pool.

2 Turn your palms to face the pool floor. Push your hands down, tuck your chin to your chest, and give a dolphin kick.

3 Perfrom a front somersault, tucking chin and chest close to your knees, with your feet just above the surface. As you rotate into the face-up position, start pulling your hands towards your head.

4 Plant feet against the wall, under the water, and push off. Stretch out your arms and press them against your ears.

5 Turn on to your front. Glide with the momentum of your push-off, then kick your legs and aim for the surface.

deal with a Tyre blowout

If a front tyre bursts, don't brake since this will pull your car heavily to the side. Let the car slow naturally, if possible. Steer to counter the drag of the burst tyre, and pull over if it's safe to do so. Try to stop on firm ground where you can change the tyre.

If a back tyre bursts, brake very gently if you must – but not too hard, or you risk losing control of the car. Be prepared for the car to slide at the back. Keep a firm grip on the wheel to maintain a straight course. Change down a gear to slow the car, and pull over.

check the condition of your Tyres

Inspect your tyres regularly and thoroughly. Make sure the handbrake is firmly on before you begin.
■ Look for cuts, bulges and embedded objects such as nails or glass shards.
■ Check the tread depth. It must be more than 1.6mm in a continuous band around the centre over three-quarters of the tyre width. Any less and the tyre must be replaced. Manufacturers often mould 'tread bars' at 1.6mm. If the tread has worn as far as the bars, replace the tyre. If there are no bars, buy and use a tread depth gauge.

learn to Type

A QWERTY keyboard is ingeniously designed to facilitate touch typing. You'll soon have the skill at your fingertips.

This primer covers lower-case letters only. From here you can go on to learn numerals, unlock the mystery of the shift key and master punctuation marks and symbols.

LEARN THE HOME KEYS
■ Rest the fingers of the left hand on A S D F.
■ Rest the fingers of the right hand on J K L and semicolon.
■ These are your 'home keys' – that is, the default position for your fingers.
■ Each of your fingers is responsible for its home key and one or two keys above and below it (see below); the space bar is controlled by a thumb.

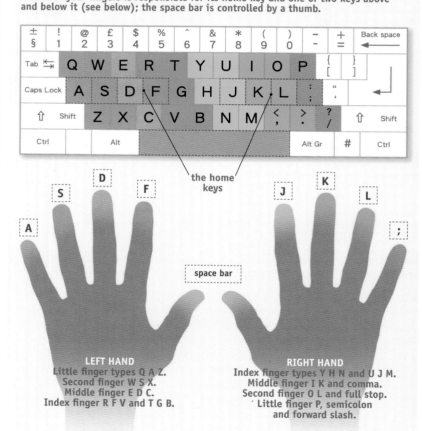

the home keys

LEFT HAND
Little finger types Q A Z.
Second finger W S X.
Middle finger E D C.
Index finger R F V and T G B.

RIGHT HAND
Index finger types Y H N and U J M.
Middle finger I K and comma.
Second finger O L and full stop.
Little finger P, semicolon and forward slash.

Look at the screen Use your fingers to press the keys for which they are responsible, working down in lines. Feel for the keys, don't look at them.

Pangrams make perfect Practise these phrases, which use every letter: *the quick brown fox jumps over a lazy dog; heavy boxes perform quick waltzes and jigs; the five boxing wizards jump quickly.*

Copy some written text Cover your hands with a scarf so you can't cheat.

relieve the pain of mouth Ulcers

Most people experience a painful sore, or ulcer, in their mouth at some time. It can be caused by damage to the mouth, such as an accidental bite to the cheek, or sharp teeth or food, and also by stress. If you suffer from recurrent mouth ulcers, seek advice from your doctor; you may have an underlying condition such as a vitamin deficiency or you may need to avoid certain foods or medications. Whether recurrent or not, most mouth ulcers will clear up without treatment, but there are actions you can take to help yourself.

For pain relief
- Put a dab of peppermint oil on the affected area, but don't overdo it or you could cause further irritation.
- Use a mouthwash of cooled camomile tea.
- Chew some fresh basil leaves.

To speed the healing process
- Avoid hard foods such as crisps or toast that may aggravate the ulcer.
- Use a soft toothbrush.
- Try relaxing activites such as yoga or meditation (*see* YOGA *and* MEDITATE) to reduce stress levels.

---

deal with Unconsciousness

A blow to the head, poisoning and shock are among the many reasons why someone might pass out (*see also* FAINTING). The cause may need medical attention, but first priority is to avert the risk that the casualty's tongue will fall back and block their windpipe, or that they will choke on saliva or vomit.

- Lie the person on their back and kneel by their shoulder. Place one hand on the forehead and tilt their head back so the mouth falls slightly open.
- Still holding the forehead, use two fingers of the other hand to lift the point of the chin, which moves the tongue away from the back of the mouth. Put your ear to the patient's mouth and nose and listen for breathing. Look to see if the chest is moving.

If no regular breaths
- Call the emergency services or send someone to do so. Ask them to confirm that the call has been made.
- Begin cardio-pulmonary resuscitation (*see* CPR).

If the casualty is breathing
Treat any conditions that affect blood circulation (*see* BLEEDING *and* BURNS AND SCALDS). Place the casualty in the recovery position (*see* RECOVERY POSITION) and call for emergency help. Monitor the patient's breathing and circulation closely.

repair an Umbrella

Not only is it raining, but a gust of wind catches your umbrella and tears the fabric from a spoke. Don't throw it away – take it home and make this simple repair, instead.

YOU WILL NEED Strong thick thread, needle

1 Check the corner seam of the umbrella where it's supposed to meet the spoke. If it's undone, repair with a few stitches.

2 Fold the seam corner about 6mm in towards the umbrella's centre, and add a few stitches to hold it in place.

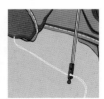

3 Insert your needle into the edge seam just to one side of the folded corner.

4 Pass the needle through the hole in the loose spoke of your umbrella.

5 Add a stitch in the seam on the opposite side of the folded corner. Then go back through the spoke hole again and repeat steps 4 and 5 once more.

6 Knot the end of your thread. Working close to the fabric, wrap the thread around the needle twice, then pull the needle through. Repeat for strength.

mark and record
Valuables

Take precautions to ensure that you can identify your property if it's stolen and found, or so that you can claim on contents insurance if you're the victim of theft.

■ Seek professional valuations of jewellery, antiques and rare objects, and keep a record. Have them revalued every few years, as valuations can quickly become out of date.
■ Certain objects can be indelibly marked with house number and postcode using invisible fluorescent ink pens. Or you can simply etch your postcode and house number on an object, such as a bicycle.
■ Make an inventory of all possessions of value, noting serial numbers, brand names and other identifying information.
■ Photograph important items against a plain background and next to a ruler to show scale. Note any distinguishing marks such as crests, initials, signatures, or chips or scratches.

make Vegetable stock

A well-flavoured vegetable stock makes the world of difference to soups, braised dishes, casseroles and sauces. You can use almost any vegetables – and it's a great way of using up oddments from the bottom of the fridge.

TO MAKE 2.5 LITRES OF STOCK

3 tbsp olive oil
750g onions, chopped
1 leek, chopped
1 clove garlic, chopped
350g carrots, chopped
2 sticks celery, chopped
8 mushrooms, quartered

small bunch parsley
sprig of thyme
a few sage leaves
salt and freshly ground
    black pepper
2.5 litres water

Heat the oil in a large saucepan and soften the onions, leek and garlic until the onions are golden. Add the remaining ingredients, bring to the boil and skim off any scum. Simmer, covered, for 2 hours before straining the stock through a fine sieve.

get started with a Vegetable garden

Freshly picked home-grown vegetables are full of flavour, nutritious and immensely satisfying to cultivate. You can grow them almost anywhere in the garden, in borders or in containers, but a traditional plot, if you have enough space, will give better results and be easier to maintain. Raised beds (*see* RAISED BED), which reduce the need for digging, are excellent for growing vegetables.

Site A sunny place is vital, ideally sheltered from the wind, which can impede plant growth. Vegetables prefer a well-drained soil, so you'll need to add generous amounts of organic matter if it's heavy clay or very light sand or chalk (*see* SOIL). Easy access to water is also essential.

Permanent features You'll need one or two compost bins (*see* COMPOST), a space to stack manure or other bulky materials like leaf mould, paths for easy access and gardening tools. In a small garden, go for tall compost bins that take up less ground space.

What to plant Begin with the vegetables you most like to eat, and match them to your space. Quick-growing salads, spinach and mangetout peas are good to start with. On a small plot, choose vegetables that can be grown close together such as lettuces, beans, garlic and onions. Plant in blocks rather than rows.

How to plant Divide the plot roughly into quarters and plan to rotate crops to avoid build-up of pests and diseases. Each year, alternate positions of the four main types of crops: legumes (peas and beans), brassicas (such as broccoli and cabbage), potatoes, and root vegetables and onions.

cook perfect Vegetables

The art of cooking vegetables is to retain maximum possible nutrients and to produce a pleasing taste and texture. Before cooking, vegetables need to be prepared by washing, peeling, slicing or podding to clean them and remove tough or inedible parts. All offcuts can be kept for composting or adding to a wormery (*see* COMPOST *and* WORMERY), and many are suitable for making stocks and soups.

Cut vegetables into even-sized pieces before cooking. Many vegetables are best cooked al dente; the exceptions are potatoes and root vegetables such as parsnips and swedes, which should be tender but firm. Test that vegetables are cooked through by pricking them with the point of a sharp knife or a skewer. Never overcook green vegetables – not only do they go mushy but brassicas such as cabbage and Brussels sprouts take on an unpleasant, sulphurous taste.

Method	Cooking instructions and tips
BOILING	**Leafy vegetables, beans and peas:** use a minimum amount of water with ½ tsp salt added per 300ml so that vegetables part steam. Plunge into boiling water, cover and simmer for about 5 minutes. Drain well. **Root vegetables:** add just enough cold salted water to cover, bring to the boil, then simmer for 10-20 minutes.
STEAMING	**Good for most vegetables.** Put into a steamer with a tightly fitting lid over a little rapidly boiling water. Allow 3-5 minutes longer cooking time than for boiling. Add salt before or after cooking, as desired.
SHALLOW FRYING	**Good for soft-fleshed vegetables** such as mushrooms, aubergines and tomatoes, and for courgettes, peppers and celery. Use olive or other vegetable oil, with a little butter added if desired, heated in a wide heavy-based pan. Root vegetables, whole french beans and thick-stemmed vegetables such as broccoli are best parboiled (partly cooked by boiling) before being shallow fried.
DEEP FRYING	**Best for potatoes, onions, courgettes, peppers and aubergines.** Vegetables, which may be coated in batter or egg and breadcrumbs, are immersed in hot vegetable oil and fried quickly. Fat should be at 190°C, or so hot that a cube of day-old bread browns in 1 minute.
GRILLING	**Best for aubergines, courgettes, mushrooms, asparagus and tomatoes.** Brush with a little oil and cook under a hot grill, turning once if necessary.
BRAISING	**Best for celery, leeks, lettuce, chicory, onions, carrots and celeriac.** Blanch vegetables for 2-3 minutes in boiling water, drain and cover with stock. Cover with a tightly fitting lid and cook in the oven at 180°C/gas 4 or on the stove top.
BAKING	**Best for potatoes, whole marrows or pumpkins, peppers or tomatoes.** Prick potatoes before baking to prevent them from exploding. Vegetables, which can be brushed with a little oil, are oven-cooked uncovered. Individual vegetables may be foil-wrapped and/or stuffed.
ROASTING	**Good for a wide range of vegetables, including root vegetables, onions, garlic, peppers, squashes and courgettes.** Vegetables are cooked in the oven in hot fat, either alone or around a joint of meat. Potatoes are best parboiled before roasting.

clean
Venetian blinds

They always look modern and stylish, but venetian blinds attract dust like a magnet and offer a real cleaning challenge. The trick is to maintain them regularly – it will avoid a much more difficult job later on.

Save yourself work by vacuuming venetian blinds regularly, ideally with the help of a purpose-made cleaning attachment, or use an old paintbrush to clean the slats.

Or put on an old pair of soft, absorbent gloves and run your hands along both sides of each slat. If you don't have an appropriate pair of gloves, use a couple of anti-static dusters. When the blind is pulled up, wipe the cords with a clean, dampened duster.

If washable blinds are really dirty, take them down and wash them in the bath with warm soapy water, using a small brush to work between the slats. Put a towel in the bottom of the bath to prevent damaging its surface. Rinse the blinds well and dry them with the help of a clean tea towel before re-hanging.

make the most of Velcro

Velcro, which comes in sew-on and adhesive-backed versions, is a handy substitute for zips or buttons on garments – especially useful for quick-change stage costumes – and for cushion closures. But it can be used in many other situations, too. Each piece consists of a rough 'hook' tape that joins tight to a softer 'loop' tape.

On fabric pin and tack (*see* TACK) the hook part of the tape into position, making it the underneath part of the closure. Sew into place using backstitch (*see* SEWING), or by machine. Position the loop part of the tape then sew into place. Machine stitch or work backstitch by hand from the right side of the fabric to ensure a neat finish.
■ Close Velcro fastenings before washing and ironing garments.

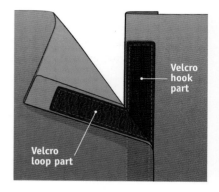

Velcro hook part

Velcro loop part

Hard surfaces Combine sew-on and stick-on types of Velcro for attaching fabric to hard surfaces, as when joining a curtain pelmet to a wooden support. Use adhesive-backed Velcro as a temporary closure for a door with a broken latch.

Other uses Use a hook strip of Velcro to remove fuzzy build-up from sweaters. Cut Velcro strips to create firm ties for securing plants to supports, or for holding electrical cables in neat bundles. Stick hook strips of Velcro on the wall of a child's room and use them to hold soft toys.

clean and restore Velvet

Velvet can be made from a variety of yarns, usually cotton or synthetics, but when high quality is made of silk. Dry cleaning, following the instructions given below, is always the safest cleaning method, and a must for crushed velvet, the surface of which will be ruined by water. Be sure to test an inconspicuous area of the fabric first. Specific stains should be removed with a dry cleaning solvent, following the manufacturer's instructions.

■ Brush the velvet gently against the nap to raise the pile or, for upholstery, use a vacuum cleaner.
■ Mix half a teaspoon of washing-up liquid with warm water to make a foam and use a sponge to apply the foam only. Be sure not to get the fabric wet or the backing may shrink.
■ Leave for 24 hours until the foam has completely dried out then brush, working against the pile. Never brush velvet while damp.

bake a Victoria sponge

The filling of this classic tea-time treat can be varied as you wish – use jam alone, fresh fruit or a butter icing. Although best eaten fresh, the cake will keep, undecorated, in an airtight tin for two to three days.

SERVES 6-8

175g butter or block margarine
175g caster sugar
3 eggs, lightly beaten
175g self-raising flour, sifted
a few drops vanilla essence
a little milk
4-6 tbsp raspberry jam
150ml double cream, whipped
2 tbsp icing sugar

1 Heat the oven to 180°C/gas 4. Grease two 20cm sandwich tins and line the bases with baking parchment. Beat the butter and sugar until really soft, ideally using a mixer. Gradually beat in the eggs, adding 1 tbsp of flour with each addition. Fold in the remaining flour with the vanilla and enough milk to make a soft mixture that will drop from a lifted spoon.

2 Divide between the tins, smooth level and bake for 30 minutes or until risen and golden. The sponge should spring back when lightly pressed in the centre. Cool in the tins for a few minutes then turn onto racks to cool completely.

3 Spread the jam over the top of one cake and the cream on the underside of the other. Sandwich together then dust the top with sifted icing sugar.

liven up food with flavoured Vinegars

Vinegars flavoured with herbs and spices add an extra dimension to salad dressings and marinades. They are best made with a mild vinegar and will keep for three to six months if stored in scrupulously clean containers in a cool dark place. Experiment with different flavour combinations as you wish.

YOU WILL NEED Large glass jar with coated metal lid, muslin, sieve, glass bowl, bottles, plastic funnel, corks or coated metal screw tops

Tarragon vinegar Makes 500ml. Pour 500ml white or cider vinegar into a glass jar. Add a bunch of fresh tarragon, setting aside one or two sprigs for later use. Put on the lid and leave to infuse for four weeks. Strain through muslin into a glass bowl. Put the reserved tarragon sprigs into one or two bottles, pour in the vinegar and seal.

Rosemary vinegar Cover five sprigs of the herb with boiling vinegar, cover and steep for three days before straining and bottling.

Chilli vinegar Split two chillis in half lengthwise, cover with cold vinegar and steep for four to six weeks before straining and bottling.

golden rules

PERFECT VICTORIA SPONGE
- **Measure out the butter, sugar and flour accurately.**
- **Sift the flour first to prevent lumps forming in the mixture.**
- **Use eggs at room temperature and add them gradually to prevent curdling.**
- **Don't open the oven door until after the first 20 minutes of cooking time.**

digitise your Video

The principles for digitising video are the same as for other 'analogue' media such as photos, vinyl records and music cassettes. You need:

- A device to read or play the analogue material (in this instance a VCR or camcorder).
- A physical connection with your computer (an audio-visual cable).
- Some software such as Windows Movie Maker to manipulate and replay the digital files.
- Somewhere to store the digitised material. Video files take up a great deal of computer memory, so it's best to store them on an external hard disk or transfer them to DVD rather than keep them on your hard drive.

Turn on your PC, then connect up your VCR or camcorder and turn it on. Your PC will respond by starting up the appropriate software, or by asking you to confirm which software you want to use. Follow the on-screen prompts or click on **Help** to see instructions on how to use your particular software package.

See also CASSETTES, PHOTOS *and* VINYL RECORDS.

V

convert
Vinyl records
to digital

The key requirement for digitising vinyl records is to have a turntable that you can connect to your PC.

Record player If you have a record player connected to a stereo system, look for two small round sockets labelled 'line out'. From here run a '3.5mm stereo plug to 2 phono leads' cable (available from specialist electronics retailers) to the 'line in' socket on your PC. Or buy a turntable designed specifically for digitising vinyl records. This comes with its own USB connection.

Software Download some free music-digitising software such as Audacity.

■ Clean your records thoroughly (see opposite), and buy a new stylus.
■ Connect your record player to your PC and activate your software.
■ Play your records through; in the process the music is converted into digital music files.
■ Save your files to CD (see CD) or load them on to your MP3 player.

grow Vines outdoors

With the many new varieties now available it's perfectly possible to grow your own grapes outdoors.

Soil and site You'll need free-draining soil that's not deep clay or chalk and a site such as a south or southwest-facing wall or fence that will provide plants with maximum sunlight and protection from spring frosts.

Erect supports Install four strong galvanised horizontal wires 30cm apart attached to the wall with 20cm 'vine eyes' (for a wall) or eye bolts (for a fence). Tie in a vertical cane support for each plant.

Preparation and planting Dig the soil, incorporating plenty of organic matter. Plant vines about 2m apart in late autumn or early spring as for shrubs (see SHRUB). Fill in with soil mixed with gravel to improve drainage.

YEAR 1, SUMMER Tie the strongest shoot to the support, pinch out others to one or two leaves.

YEAR 1, AUTUMN Cut back to three or four buds.

YEAR 2, SUMMER Train the three strongest shoots to the support wires. Pinch out all other unwanted shoots.

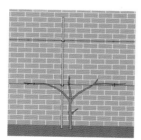
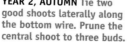
YEAR 2, AUTUMN Tie two good shoots laterally along the bottom wire. Prune the central shoot to three buds.

SUBSEQUENT SPRINGS AND SUMMERS Train the laterals along horizontal wires. Thin out side shoots to 20cm apart. Feed with a high potash fertiliser as fruit begins to form. Pinch out growing tips above the top wire.

SUBSEQUENT AUTUMNS
After harvesting, cut the centre shoot back to three buds and tie in new shoots to the bottom wire. Cut fruited stems back to the base.

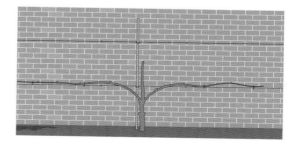

clean Vinyl records

Always clean a vinyl record before you play it; this prolongs the life of the record itself, and of the stylus. Neither are easy to replace.

■ Velvet record brushes are the best way to clean an LP. Once commonplace, they are now sold in specialist record shops.
■ If, say, you acquire a rare but grimy record from a car boot sale, it's acceptable to wash it with distilled water, but take care not to wet the label.
■ Let the record air-dry and then put it in a new, clean inner sleeve, discarding the old one. Always store your LPs upright on a shelf.

- -

get more Vitamins into your diet

Vitamins nourish the body, help to ward off chronic disease and prevent premature ageing. It's all about what you eat – and what you don't.

Vitamins are organic compounds vital to the normal function of the body. The vitamins you need to thrive are the water-soluble B vitamin complex and vitamin C, and the fat-soluble vitamins A, D, E and K. Fat-soluble vitamins are stored in the liver and fatty tissues. Water-soluble vitamins can't be stored; the body uses what it can and excretes the rest. A balanced diet (*see* DIET) usually supplies all the body's needs, but there are measures you can take to boost your supply.

Eat the rainbow Enjoy an abundance of fresh fruit and vegetables across the colour spectrum – especially dark-green leafy and orange vegetables and deep-hued berries. Super-fresh home-grown fruit and vegetables are more nutritious than produce that has been packaged, transported and stored.

Raw or cooked? A good intake of raw fruit and vegetables helps to provide nutrients destroyed by cooking, so eat salads and crudités, and choose fruit for dessert. However, studies show that overzealous 'raw foodists' can miss out. Tomato products when cooked, for instance, have more available lycopene, a powerful antioxidant. How you cook things can also make a difference – you'll lose fewer nutrients if you steam rather than boil vegetables.

Favour fresh foods 'Live' whole, natural foods are richer in vitamins than heavily processed ('dead') ones.

Eat plenty of oily fish for fat-soluble vitamins.

Scrub rather than peel vegetables, or remove as little of the skin as possible. Most peel is edible and rich in vitamins. The nutrients in a potato are mainly concentrated just under the skin. To avoid further vitamin loss, don't slice or cut fruit and vegetables into small pieces or prepare ahead of time.

Steam rather than boil Water-soluble vitamins leach into cooking water. Whether you boil or steam, save the liquid to make soup.

Avoid deep-frying, which is destructive, especially to vitamin E, and don't overcook meat – another sure way to break down vitamins.

know your Vitamins

A balanced diet should provide all the vitamins your body needs (left). Adjust your food intake where you can rather than turning to vitamin supplements.

Vitamin A
Good for: immune system, vision in dim light, skin
Found in: cheese, eggs, oily fish, milk, yoghurt

B Vitamins
Essential for: good general health
Found in: a varied, healthy diet (*see* DIET)

Vitamin C
Good for: general health
Found in: peppers, broccoli, brussels sprouts, sweet potatoes, oranges and other fruit

Vitamin D
Good for: bones and teeth
Found in: mainly formed in the skin on exposure to sunlight, but also in oily fish, eggs, fortified spreads and breakfast cereals

Vitamin E
Good for: protecting cell membranes
Found in: soya, corn and olive oil, nuts and seeds, wheat germ, cereals and cereal products

Vitamin K
Good for: blood clotting, bones
Found in: broccoli, spinach, vegetable oils

make
Vol-au-vents

MAKES 12-14 SMALL VOL-AU-VENT
CASES (BOUCHÉES)

450g puff pastry
plain flour
one beaten egg

1 Heat the oven to 220°C/gas 7. Roll out the pastry on a floured surface to 3mm thick and stamp out 24-28 rounds with a 5cm diameter pastry cutter. Place half of these on a dampened baking tray and brush with the beaten egg.

2 Use a 2.5cm diameter cutter to cut out the centres of the remaining rounds and place them on top of those on the baking tray, pressing gently to make them stick. Brush with beaten egg. Put the left-over circles onto a baking tray and brush with beaten egg. Bake rounds and circles for about 15 minutes until the rounds are well risen and golden. Transfer to a rack, cool, then use a teaspoon to remove any uncooked dough from the centres.

3 Fill as you wish, for example with prawns in a béchamel sauce; cream cheese with herbs; mushroom, liver or smoked salmon pâté (*see* PÂTÉ); chicken or egg mayonnaise (*see* MAYONNAISE). Top with the lids.

master the basics of Volleyball

Volleyball is a six-a-side game played over a high net. Two teams use their hands to get a ball over the net, trying to ground it inside the opposition's half of the court. If they are successful in doing this, they gain a point. The team that wins the point then serves, and the game continues until one team reaches 25 points, with at least a two-point lead.

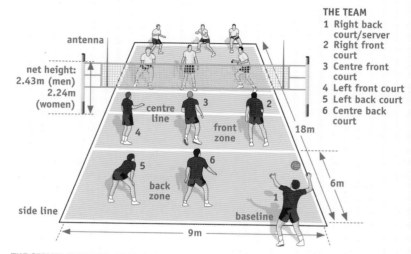

THE TEAM
1 Right back court/server
2 Right front court
3 Centre front court
4 Left front court
5 Left back court
6 Centre back court

antenna
net height: 2.43m (men) 2.24m (women)
centre line
front zone
back zone
side line
baseline
18m
6m
9m

THE SERVER STANDS behind the baseline, tosses the ball up and strikes it over the net with a flat hand (overhand) or a lightly clenched fist (underhand).

THE RECEIVING TEAM can touch the ball three times before returning it. Catching, carrying and throwing the ball aren't permitted and no player can have two touches in a row. Generally, teams use their three touches to set up the ball to be hit forcefully downwards from a position close to the net. This shot – the 'spike' – is the key attacking shot in volleyball, and the close 'block' is the most important defensive ploy.

WHEN THE RECEIVING TEAM WINS A RALLY, and therefore the right to serve, its players rotate clockwise, so each player plays in every position in the course of a match.

THE DIG Used to take a low ball and divert it upwards. Hold your hands together, the arms extended and wrists upwards, and meet the ball with the wrists.

THE SET Another technique to send the ball upwards to a position where it can be spiked. Played with palms upwards, using the fingers to direct the ball with precision.

THE SPIKE Used to hit the ball at speed towards an undefended part of the opponent's court. Jump up close to the net and strike the ball with your clenched fist.

take up Walking

Walking is the most accessible form of exercise, and it's a great way to enjoy town and country.

Planning If possible plan a circular route, chosen to suit your level of fitness You may want to avoid steep hills or very uneven surfaces. On average a four to five mile walk on easy terrain will take 1½ to 2 hours. If you're walking in an unfamiliar area use a detailed Ordnance Survey map and take it with you.

Footwear Wear substantial 'walking trainers' that give you good support or, for rough or wet ground, lightweight waterproof walking boots that protect your ankles if you turn over your foot. Wear boots one or two sizes bigger than your regular shoes to allow for a thicker pair of purpose-made walking socks. If possible, try to test boots on a slope before buying to check that your toes don't bang against the end of the boot when coming downhill. Always wear boots in before using them in earnest.

Other equipment Choose warm, loose, breathable clothing such as a fleece, an anorak or cagoule with pockets large enough for a map, and comfortable trousers or shorts. A hat is essential for protection from rain, wind and sun. Light, waterproof overtrousers are a good investment if you walk a lot. Favour layers of clothing. Avoid jeans – they're heavy and slow to dry if you get soaked through. In a rucksack pack water, and some food if you're going to be out for several hours, plus a small first-aid kit (*see* FIRST-AID KIT), including sunblock in summer, a map and a mobile phone.

How to walk Hold your head high and shoulders back but watch the ground to avoid obstacles. Push off with your back leg and swing your arms for power. To speed up, lengthen your stride rather than taking shorter, quicker steps.

paint a Wall

- Paint walls before you do the skirting and other wooden surfaces – but after you have done the ceiling (*see* CEILING).
- You can apply emulsion directly to new plaster, but it's best to cover old plaster with lining paper first (*see* WALLPAPER). You can paint over old wallpaper, but the results won't be the best. Test an area first to see that the paper doesn't bubble or come away from the wall.
- When using a roller to apply paint, work from top to bottom in horizontal bands about 50cm wide. When painting with a brush or a paint pad, work in areas about 50cm square, and use a combination of diagonal, vertical and horizontal strokes.

make Waffles

Waffles are fun to make but you do need a purpose-made non-stick waffle iron. Serve waffles piping hot with honey, maple or golden syrup and with grilled bacon on the side for an all-American breakfast.

MAKES ABOUT 12

175g self-raising flour
pinch of salt
3 tbsp caster sugar
3 eggs, separated
200ml milk
40g butter, melted
1 tsp vanilla essence
vegetable oil for greasing

1 Sift the flour and salt into a bowl and stir in the sugar. Make a well in the centre and add the egg yolks. Mix thoroughly then beat in the milk and butter alternately to make a batter. Stir in the vanilla essence. (For speed use a food processor to make the batter, then transfer the mixture to a bowl.)

2 Whisk the egg whites until stiff then fold into the batter with a large metal spoon. Grease the waffle iron and heat it as in the manufacturer's instructions. Pour in a little batter to cover about two-thirds of the iron and cook until golden brown on each side – about 3 minutes. The waffle is ready when it stops steaming and the iron opens easily.

prevent and treat
Warts and verrucas

Warts are benign growths of dead cells in the top layer of the skin caused by a virus, usually papilloma. A wart on the sole of the foot is called a 'verruca' or 'plantar wart'. Because of the weight of the body, they appear quite flat. Almost everyone will have a wart at some time.

To treat warts Most warts need no treatment. In children, 30-50 per cent of warts disappear this way within six months, although some may not go for up to two years.

Seek medical advice if a wart is unsightly, painful or itchy, if there are concerns about it spreading, if you have warts on the genital or rectal area, or if you're over 45.

Try covering the wart with duct tape Leave it covered for six days then remove the tape, soak the wart and rub it with an emery board or pumice. Leave it overnight and cover again in the morning. Continue the six day cycle for up to two months.

Paint the wart morning and evening with lemon juice, or a few drops of thuja or calendula tincture.

To guard against warts
■ Warts are contagious, so if someone has a wart, avoid contact with it.
■ Don't scratch or pick a wart; this may spread it.
■ Don't share a towel with anyone who has warts, or shoes and socks with anyone who has a verruca.
■ Wear flip-flops in communal shower areas and around swimming pools and dry your feet thoroughly.
■ Don't bite your nails (*see* NAILS); it can encourage warts around them.

dance the Waltz

One-two-three, one-two-three, around you go, light on your feet, gliding across the floor. This may be the simplest of the ballroom dances to learn, but few others match its grace and elegance.

The waltz is a romantic dance in 3/4 time characterised by a continuous series of turns (its name comes from the German *walzen* meaning 'to revolve'). It can be danced to the classical strains of composers such as Franz Schubert or the Strauss family, or to more modern popular songs such as 'Edelweiss' and 'Moon River'. Either way, it should be performed with fluidity of movement.

The hold The man puts his right hand on the woman's back just below her shoulder blade and clasps her right hand with his left, holding it in a curve with the elbow lifted. She places her left hand on his right shoulder.

The basic step Six steps, counted 'one-two-three, one-two-three', make up a basic 'box step'. The man continues to go forward, alternating the starting leg each time. The steps shown are for the man; the woman's are the mirror image.

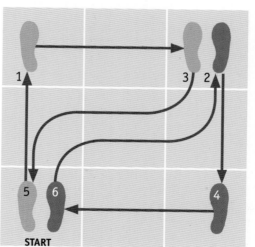

ONE-TWO-THREE The man steps forward with his left foot (1). He steps forward and to the right with his right foot (2). He closes his left foot to his right (3).

ONE-TWO-THREE He steps back with his right foot (4). He steps back and to the left with his left foot (5). He closes his right foot to his left (6).

Try adding some variation The leader dictates this by changing the direction or angle of the turns taken, and the length of each step. He can also add a 'rise and fall' movement to the dance, bending his legs slightly at the beginning of each three step sequence and extending up to his fullest height by the end. This helps to make the movement of the dance appear effortless.

deal with a Wasp sting

Unlike a honey bee, a wasp can sting more than once. Like a bee sting, in rare cases wasp venom can cause a serious allergic reaction (*see* ALLERGIC EMERGENCY). If you experience symptoms other than localised inflammation, swelling and itching, seek medical help. For a simple sting try the following.

- Wash with soap and water.
- Apply antihistamine cream.
- Apply an ice pack to cool the area and reduce swelling.

For additional relief, you can try the following:
- Apply a cotton wool pad soaked in apple cider vinegar.
- Tape a copper coin over the skin for 15 minutes.
- Press a slice of onion to the sting.

unblock a Washing machine

Always unplug the machine and turn off the water supply before you attempt to clear blockages.

Lint filter This coarse sieve catches bits of fluff, small coins and other objects as water drains from the machine. If it gets blocked, water can remain in the machine and leaks can occur. To check for blockages, open the access hatch on the front of the machine, undo the filter cap and pull out the filter assembly. Remove any fluff and other debris, then rinse and refit. It's worth doing this every six months or so as a precaution against future blockages.

Inlet filter If the machine takes a long time to fill, then it may be that the inlet filters are blocked. These filters are inside the screwed inlets to which the hot and cold hoses are attached (some machines only have one cold inlet hose). Pull the machine out from the wall. Unscrew one of the hoses, and put the washer to one side. Use long-nose pliers to remove the filter and its rubber seating. Clean the filter under a running tap and pick out any bits of grit with a pin. Reassemble and replace, then do the same with the other hose.

Outlet hose Check that there's no kink in the hose: if the machine fails to empty, this is often the cause. If not, disconnect the outlet hose from its exit point at the bottom on the back of the machine. You may have to remove a cover, or tip the machine on its side, to gain access to it. Loosen the clip, and remove the hose. Use a length of wire hanger bound in masking tape to fish out any blockage in the pipe. While the hose is off, feel inside the machine. The vanes of the pump should move freely. If not, and you can't free them yourself, call a repairer.

make a Wasp trap

Wasps are beneficial to the environment but unwelcome visitors at a picnic. A trap is easy to make – and they will live to sting another day!

YOU WILL NEED Plastic bottle (2 litre size), sharp scissors or scalpel (or similar), jam or molasses or similar sweet bait

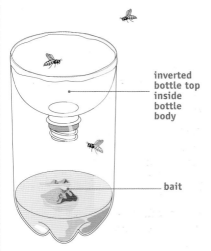

inverted bottle top inside bottle body

bait

1 Cut the top off the bottle at the point where the neck widens right out. Pour a little water into the bottom and add a teaspoon of the bait.

2 Invert the bottle top and push it down into the base; make sure it fits snugly. Tape it if necessary.

Wasps will be attracted down this funnel, and once they are in the bottom of the bottle they won't be able to find their way out again. From time to time dispose of them; set them free, away from your home. Do this at night or on a cold day as the wasps will be less active and so less agitated.

Wallpaper
a room
see pages 352-353

W

Wallpaper a room

Wallpapering requires a degree of precision, but need not be a difficult job if you equip yourself with the correct tools and are prepared to take your time – don't rush it. Work out how much paper you need, add a bit for spare and ensure that the rolls all have the same batch number to be sure that they match perfectly.

YOU WILL NEED Plumb line, paperhanger's scissors, plastic bucket, paste, wallpaper, paste table, paste brush, paperhanger's brush, trimming knife (optional), sponge and some clean rags, seam roller, small scissors

ESTIMATING QUANTITIES Measure the height of the walls to work out how many 'drops', or lengths of paper, you can get from one roll. Standard rolls are approximately 10m long. If your paper has a repeating pattern, add the length of one pattern repeat to each drop (this length is usually noted on the packaging) so that the pattern will align.

Measure around the room, including alcoves and chimney breasts, and divide the total length by the width of the wallpaper: this tells you the total number of drops you'll need.

Calculate how many rolls you require by dividing the total number of drops you need for the room by the number of drops you can get from one roll, rounded up to the nearest whole figure.

PASTING Tie a length of string tautly across the rim of your paste bucket, both to support the brush when not in use, and so that you can remove excess paste from the brush by drawing it across the string.

1 Cut several drops of wallpaper, remembering to allow for any pattern repeat (see above) plus an extra 100mm for trimming.

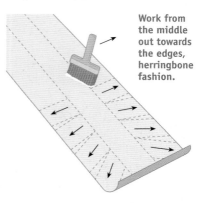

Work from the middle out towards the edges, herringbone fashion.

2 With the paper just overlapping the table edge, apply paste evenly to the back of the paper. Paste from the middle out (above).

3 Fold the ends into the middle, pasted sides together, but don't crease the paper. Number drops before you paste them and hang in that order.

HANGING Begin hanging on the wall next to the window wall (or the wall with the largest window) and work away from the light. This means that any slight overlaps won't cast shadows on the wall.

1 Use the plumb line to mark a vertical line on the wall at the starting point. This should be at most a paper's width minus 15mm from one corner of the room.

2 Unfold the top of your first length and align its right hand edge with the vertical line, allowing 50mm at the top for trimming. Smooth down with the paperhanger's brush.

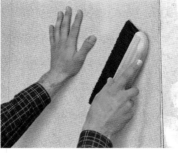

3 Smooth down the middle first, then outwards towards the edges in a kind of herringbone pattern, working out any bubbles. Unfold the bottom part of the drop, and smooth it down in the same way.

4 Use the back of your scissors to crease the paper where it meets the skirting and ceiling and trim to length. Butt the next length to the first, matching any pattern and pressing the join with a seam roller.

TURNING CORNERS Few corners are a perfect 90 degrees, but you can master the knack of papering them.

At an internal corner, cut the length to 15mm wider than the widest distance to the corner. Put it up in the normal way, using the brush to push right into the corner. Measure the offcut, add 15mm and hang the offcut this distance from the corner on the adjacent wall.

At an external corner, cut paper to wrap 25mm round the corner. If you try to turn more than this, the paper is likely to crease.

After the corner, if the turned-round edge is vertical, butt the next drop of paper to it. If not, you will need to overlap it onto the turned-round edge, matching any pattern as best you can.

WORKING ROUND OBSTACLES
It's not hard to do a tidy job around light switches and fittings.

Turn off the power and loosen the screws just enough to tuck some paper underneath. Cut a cross in the paper to the corners of the fitting and peel back the flaps. Trim to leave about 3mm of paper and gently push this behind the switch cover, using a lolly stick or just smooth the paper into place with the brush. Tighten the screws once the paper has dried and turn the power back on.

DECORATIVE EFFECTS You can do more than just cover all four walls with the same paper. Try doing just one 'feature' wall in a bold pattern or lavish paper: a large floral design, say, or something pictorial or typographical. For children's rooms you can buy wallpaper murals in a variety of designs. Keep the other walls plain to make a contrast (and to keep the cost down) and choose soft furnishings to coordinate.

Alternatively, use a single drop of patterned paper as a kind of stencilled motif – down the centre of a chimney breast, for example, or in the two alcoves either side. Pick a colour from the design of the paper, and paint the walls to match. Or try hanging a strong stripe pattern horizontally for a strikingly modern effect.

conserve Water

A frugal attitude to water is good for the environment – and it can save you money too.

■ If you have a leaky tap, fix it (*see* TAP). One dripping tap can waste more than 5,000 litres of water a year.

■ Take shorter showers and shallower baths. Have a timer in your bathroom, and set it when you get in the shower, so you know when it's time to get out. Knock a minute or two off your shower-time every so often.

■ Fit a water butt to your downpipe (see right).

■ Wash your car with a bucket and sponge rather than with a hose.

■ Use the half-flush option on your toilet if you have one. If not, place a large plastic bottle of water – with the lid on – inside the cistern, well clear of the flush mechanism. With each flush, you'll save as much water as there is in the bottle.

■ Turn off the tap while cleaning your teeth.

■ Rinse dishes in a sink of clean water rather than running them under the tap.

■ Don't run your dishwasher or washing machine unless you have a full load.

■ Only fill kettles with as much water as you need.

■ Keep a jug of cold water in the fridge, so you don't need to run the tap until the water is cold.

■ Water your garden in the evening or early morning, when less of the water will evaporate. If you must use a hosepipe, fit a trigger so that no water spills uselessly on the ground. Don't water your lawn, even if it looks parched: it will go green and lush again as soon as it rains.

unblock a Waste disposal unit

Minor blockages that slow the rotation of the blades inside a waste disposal unit are easy to clear.

■ Take out the drain trap (the little basket in the drain hole), and shake any debris trapped inside into the rubbish bin. Put it back in the drain, and twist it to the closed position.

■ Fill the sink with warm water to a depth of 10cm. Add 100g of bicarbonate of soda to the water.

■ Turn on the unit, and let it run for a second or two before twisting the drain trap to the open position. Let the soda solution sluice through the unit, then run the tap again until you can hear that the disposer is spinning freely.

install a Water butt

A butt conserves precious water – and rainwater is better for your plants than mains water.

Position your water butt next to a convenient downpipe, and on level ground. Place the butt next to the downpipe on its stand (you must have a stand, so that you can fit a watering can under the tap). There are two ways to divert water from the downpipe into the butt: you can fit a 'rain diverter', or you can direct the downpipe straight into the top of the butt.

Put the lid on your butt and lock it in place: this is primarily a child-safety measure, but it also serves to prevent mosquitoes laying eggs in the water.

Direct method Saw off the downpipe 20cm or so above the top of the butt, and use angled downpipe connectors and short straight sections to drop the pipe through a hole in the lid. Most butts have holes marked for this purpose; they can be drilled or knocked out.

■ With this method, you must also fit an overflow kit: a pipe that leads from a point high on the side of the butt to a drain.

Diverter method This is a hose that leads from the downpipe into a marked hole in the side of the butt (the hole will be marked on the butt). The design of diverters varies – follow the instructions with your kit.

■ Measure about 8cm down from the top of the butt, and cut out a section of the downpipe.

■ Insert the diverter, and re-attach the downpipe top and bottom.

■ With this method you don't need an overflow pipe.

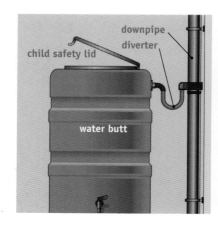

child safety lid
downpipe
diverter
water butt

paint a Watercolour scene

A broad horizon and changeable sky provide a perfect backdrop for a simple impressionistic watercolour landscape.

YOU WILL NEED Sheet of medium-weight art paper, a size 12 round brush, paint in tubes (more convenient than cakes), two big, clear water jars (one for washing the brush, one for mixing colours), palette with mixing wells

Keep it simple Break down the landscape into broad areas of colour, then work with a limited range of paints to create your mixes. Watercolour isn't the medium for fine detail, so simplify any shapes in the scene, such as trees and buildings. Work with dash and spontaneity.

Build up your scene

1 Start with the sky. Mix two washes to match your scene – one brighter, one darker. A blue-based mix and a gray-based one are often effective.

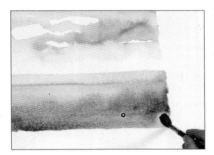

2 Lay a band of the brighter wash across the top of the paper. Then lay the darker wash below, working across and down to the horizon. Don't worry about gaps; they can serve as clouds. Vary the angle of the brush to modulate the colour. Lighten the area just above the horizon by laying a wash of clean water.

3 Prepare three mixes of a colour for the foreground, one light, one medium and one dark. Paint a band of the lightest across the horizon and work in the medium and then the dark mixes as you make your way down the paper. Allow the colours to flood into each other so that you lose the brush marks.

4 Now add in the details of the scene, using stronger colours and remembering to simplify the shapes. For trees, such as in the scene above, use a darker wash for the base of the foliage and pull the paint down to describe the tree trunks (no need for another colour). For crisply defined edges, leave puddles of stronger colour to dry.

Water plants
effectively

The plants that need most water are vegetables, container-grown plants and all newly planted annuals, perennials, shrubs and lawns.

Timing In spring and autumn, water in the morning to protect from frost damage. In hot weather, water in the early morning or in the evening to reduce evaporation and prevent leaf scorching.

Amount Water well, less often, rather than sprinkling plants daily. This prevents them from becoming stressed and from growing roots too near the surface.

How to water Water as near to the ground as possible. Use a watering can or a hose directed onto individual plants in turn.

For individual plants sink purpose-made watering tubes, or inverted plastic bottles with their bases cut off, next to plants and water into these direct.

Reduce your use of water by collecting rainwater (see opposite). Also, save water used in the kitchen for washing vegetables to water your plants.

golden rules
WATER PLANTS
- **Cut down watering by improving soil with organic matter and adding mulch.**
- **The smaller the plants the finer the spray should be.**
- **Add water-retaining gel to the compost of container-grown plants.**

remove
Watermarks
from furniture

Watermarks are hard to get out, and no single method works in every instance. The methods given below are for white water stains affecting only the surface of the wood. Black water stains (those which have penetrated the wood's finish) can only be treated by stripping off the finish and bleaching the wood.

If you have a white water stain on a wooden surface, try this method first.

■ Gently rub the stain with a cloth dipped in metal polish, car paint cleaner (not wax) or a special ring remover, working with the grain of the wood.
■ Buff the stained area with a clean cloth, and apply furniture polish to the whole surface.

If that doesn't work, try one of the following methods. They all do the trick – sometimes.
■ Rub on a half-and-half mix of bicarbonate of soda and plain white toothpaste (never coloured toothpaste or gel).
■ Apply a thin coating of shop-bought mayonnaise, and let it sit for an hour.
■ Apply petroleum jelly, and leave it for a day.
■ Make up a solution of equal parts of vinegar, boiled linseed oil and turpentine. Apply with a soft cloth.
■ Apply olive oil using superfine (0000 grade) steel wool.

If you baulk at trying some of these experiments on beloved or precious items of furniture, then your only option is to have the piece refinished by a professional.

stay on your feet when # Waterskiing

There are few more exhilarating experiences than skimming across a body of water behind a speedboat. Once you're up on the skis, it's largely a question of holding on and enjoying the ride.

1 To stay on your feet, you must first get on your feet. Bend your legs until you're almost sitting on the back of your skis and lean back so that the tips of your skis are slightly out of the water. Make sure that the tow rope is fed out between your ski tips.

2 Signal your readiness. The boat will now move forward slowly to take the slack out of the rope. Once the rope has tightened, shout 'Go boat!' As the boat slowly accelerates away, stay crouched and keep your weight over the back of the skis as they rise to the surface.

3 Once the skis have broken the surface, slowly push against them to come out of your crouch. Keep your knees bent to absorb any bumps and lean back to counter the pull of the boat. Lean into any turns that the boat makes so that you stay within its wake.

renovate a # Waxed jacket

Waxed cotton is a weather-resistant fabric made by weaving cotton yarn into canvas fabric, which is then treated with a mixture of waxes to create a barrier to wind and water, while maintaining the cotton's breathability. A waxed jacket, worn frequently, will need reproofing within a year.

■ Every time you take off your jacket, immediately remove any dried mud, grit and dirt by sponging, gently hosing or lightly brushing with a soft-bristle brush, and hang it to dry in a well-ventilated space. Don't leave it in direct sunlight.
■ The makers of high-quality waxed jackets such as Barbour caution against machine-washing, tumble-drying or dry-cleaning. Don't use soaps, detergents, solvents, bleach or starch. When the fabric starts to show shiny or dried-out areas, or when moisture no longer beads and runs off, apply reproofing dressing (available from a sportswear supplier or online) to the affected areas. Ensure the jacket is clean and dry and apply the cream sparingly, in a circular motion, with a lint-free cloth. Wipe off excess and hang to dry overnight.

set up a Webcam

It's easy to install a camera on your computer, and it opens up a new way to communicate with family, friends and colleagues.

■ Many laptops and other computers come with a camera already installed. Otherwise, a camera is inexpensive to buy, and a basic model will be adequate for making Skype calls (*see* SKYPE) and for most internet chat purposes.
■ Install the driver that was supplied on a CD along with your camera. When prompted, plug your camera into a USB port on your computer. Many webcams also have an inbuilt microphone, which makes it possible for you to chat with friends and family over the internet.
■ It's best to perch your camera on top of your screen if you can. That way the person you're chatting to will have a more-or-less natural view of your face (though it may appear that you're looking at each other's noses).

design a simple Website

Putting together a website is no harder than creating a document in a word-processing program.

Experienced web designers use versatile software such as Front Page or Dreamweaver. If you're a beginner, it's easiest to use a pre-designed template and build your website online. Many web companies will allow you to do this for free: take a look at Moonfruit, Google Sites or Mr Site.

Before you start, consider the content of your site. Gather together all the text you want to include, plus all the pictures, movies, soundfiles and so forth. Think about the structure and the links. Draw a rough diagram of the various pages, so you have a workable visual hierarchy for your intended site. Keep it simple so that users can easily find their way around the pages.

Go to a free web-design site – in this case Google Sites – and register if you haven't already done so. Choose a template that fits the kind of site you intend to make. You'll find various categories, and a number of differently themed designs within each category.

Choose a name for your project This will be the last part of your site's name, so if it's for a business, use the company name. Click on **Create site.**

You're now ready to begin adapting the template to your own needs Click on **Edit page** and write or cut and paste your text into the boxes that appear. Use the other buttons and links – such as the one saying **'How to change this sidebar'** – to alter the elements of the template so that it conforms to the plan that you have made. Each new page can be slotted into the hierarchy that you sketched out at the beginning.

Use the preview page to check how your site is shaping up. Once you're happy with it, click **Save** and your web pages will go live on the web. You can go back in and change your site at any time.

spot Weather signs

Changes in the weather are caused by rising or falling air pressure – which are visibly reflected in natural phenomena.

cumulonimbus cloud

Clouds are the best clue to incoming weather. Towering cumulonimbus clouds with a dark base are a sure sign of rain. Sometimes you can see the approaching rain at a distance – it appears as a wispy grey streak between the base of the cloud and the horizon. Pendulous blobs hanging from the underside of a cloud – a rare sight – indicate that a severe storm or even a tornado is on the way.

Low-flying swallows are a sign of impending rain. When air pressure is low and air is full of moisture, the insects that they live on aren't carried upwards on the air, so the swallows dive to catch them.

Dandelions and tulips close their flowers before rain. So too does the less common scarlet pimpernel. Not for nothing is it also known as the 'shepherd's sundial' or the 'poor man's weatherglass'. If you see it with its bright red petals closed in the morning, then it's sure to be raining by lunchtime.

Generally, there's always a good chance that tomorrow's weather will be much like today's.

determine your ideal
Weight

Your ideal weight depends mainly on how tall you are, but your build also makes a difference.

A simple way to get an idea of your build is to wrap a hand around your wrist. If your thumb overlaps with one of your fingers you have a small frame; if they just touch, you're medium; if they don't touch you have a large frame. Bear your frame size in mind when using the table below. If you're small-boned you should be towards the lower end of the weight range given for your height. If you're large-framed you should be towards the higher end. Very fit muscular people may weigh more than the stated ranges.

HEIGHT cm	MAN WEIGHT kg	WOMAN WEIGHT kg
147	55-66	45-59
150	56-67	45-60
152	57-68	46-62
155	58-70	47-63
157	59-72	49-65
160	60-74	50-67
162	61-75	51-69
165	62-77	53-70
170	63-79	54-72
172	64-81	55-74
175	65-83	57-75
177	66-85	58-77
180	69-89	60-78
182	71-91	66-85

control Weeds

Weeding is a regular chore necessary to keep a garden neat and to allow your chosen plants to thrive without unwanted competition. Above all you need to avoid spreading small pieces of the roots of perennial weeds, which quickly sprout into new plants.

Regular hoeing is the best way of removing small weeds, especially annuals. Leave uprooted weeds on the soil surface to dry out, then compost them.

Digging with a trowel or spade is essential for removing the roots of perennial weeds such as ground elder, convolvulus and couch grass, and for dandelions with long tap roots from which weeds can regrow.

Chemical treatment Kill both shoots and roots of persistent weeds with glyphosate, a systemic weedkiller, following the maker's instructions.

Cover up Help to clear areas of perennial weeds by covering them with old carpet or heavy-duty black polythene, weighted down and left for a full growing season. *See also* MULCH.

Wetshave your face

The art of shaving is regularly practised, so with the right materials and technique it can be easily perfected.

■ Shave after you shower, or apply a flannel soaked in hot water before you begin: wet, warm stubble is much easier to remove.
■ Apply an even layer of lather to the entire beard area.
■ Check your razor: blades grow dull after a few uses, and a blunt razor is more likely to cause nicks and irritation.
■ Shave in the direction of growth (you may get a closer shave by going against the grain, but there's more chance of razor burn if you do).
■ Rinse well with cold water, and apply a moisturiser rather than an alcohol-based aftershave.

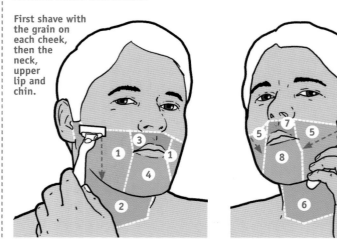

First shave with the grain on each cheek, then the neck, upper lip and chin.

Then shave each area again but across and at a slight angle to the grain to finish.

play Whist

Whist has long been one of the most popular card games the world over. It's simple and fun to play, and success depends on a pleasing combination of luck and judgment.

Whist is a game for four people who play in pairs to win the highest number of 'tricks'. Each player cuts the deck of 52 cards (ace ranks high), with the two highest scorers playing the lowest scorers. Partners sit opposite each other.

    The deck is cut again and the highest scorer is the first dealer. They then deal the cards one at a time until each player has 13. The last card dealt is shown before going into the dealer's hand and this determines which suit is trumps (the highest scoring).

The dealer turns up the last card dealt to determine which suit is trumps.

The play

■ Players may not comment on their hands, and partners may not signal to each other.
■ The player on the dealer's left starts by laying down any card.
■ Other players must follow suit if they can. If they can't, they can lay down a card from the trump suit or discard a low-scoring card of any suit. The highest of four same-suit cards wins the trick. If trumps are played, the highest trump wins the trick. Even low-ranking trump cards beat cards of a different suit. The winner of each trick starts the next.

The first five tricks are won by the highest-ranking card in the suit, but, with diamonds as trumps, the ace of clubs in the last trick is beaten by the three of diamonds.

■ When 13 tricks have been played the pair who won more tricks scores 1 point for each trick they won in excess of six. The first partners to score 5 win. If neither pair has reached 5, there's another deal. Conventionally, a second deck is waiting, ready shuffled.

Whistle

a happy tune

Whistling tunefully, like all musical skills, takes practice. Begin by learning to produce a single note.

■ Form your mouth as if to say 'oo'.
■ Keeping your mouth in this position, try to make an 'ee' sound. This will make you tauten your cheek muscles and force your tongue down in your mouth.
■ Blow a gentle but steady stream of air through your rounded lips.
■ If you don't get a note, try moving the tip of your tongue slightly – you should be able to feel it close to the point where your lower teeth meet your gums.
■ Keep experimenting – eventually you'll find the mouth position that produces a melodious whistle.

Whittle wood

Whittling soft wood with a sharp knife or chisel is a relaxing, satisfying and creative pastime.

Kits are available for beginners. These often contain a selection of knifes or blades, and other useful whittling tools such as 'palm chisels'.

For safety's sake, always wear a carving glove on the hand that holds your work, and use only sharp tools.

■ Draw a centreline on each side of the wood, then 'block out' – that is, draw the rough shape of your figure on each surface of your wood, so that you can see from any angle what needs paring away.
■ Work by making small cuts – so that you don't accidentally take off too much, and so as not to strain your hands. Pause at intervals to block out the next stage of your work, then continue whittling.

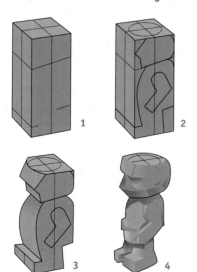

TO MAKE A SMALL MAN draw a centreline on each surface and other guidelines (1). Then draw on the basic body features and the circumference of the head (2). Whittle the wood down to create a block figure (3) then add further detail as you continue to carve (4).

care for a Wig

Synthetic fibre wigs are easier to manage than natural hair varieties, but they need the right care if they are to maintain their condition.

■ When you buy a wig, invest also in the correct accessories – a wig brush and comb, shampoo and conditioner, a proper stand for it, a wig cap, synthetic fibre spray and lustre.
■ Don't be tempted to leave your own hair unwashed beneath the wig. Always shampoo your hair before wearing your wig, and wear a nylon wig cap to protect your wig from oils.
■ Brush a wig lightly before washing it, then add a little wig shampoo to a basin of cold (never hot) water. Soak it for a minute until it's wet through then rinse lightly for a further minute. Squeeze the wig out gently – don't wring it. Blot off excess water with a towel. Place the wig back on its stand and wait for it to dry entirely before any styling. Condition the wig every few washes.
■ After wearing a wig, brush it through and always store it on its stand to help it to retain its form.
■ Make-up traces around the hairline can be removed by the gentle use of a soft toothbrush with soap and water.

contribute to Wikipedia

To write for Wikipedia, you must first register with the site. You'll find lots of guidance there, but you need to remember some key things.

■ Your article must be on a subject of encyclopaedic interest (don't write about your cat, your street or your grandfather).
■ Provide references to reliable sources (gather these before you begin) and write in links to other connected subjects.
■ Your article should be balanced, scholarly and original (there's no point in writing a piece on Elvis Presley; it's already there).
■ Hone your piece in your own 'user space' before you move it into the main area. And be flattered, rather than annoyed, if other users add to your entry or edit it. That is how Wikipedia works.

correct a Wikipedia article

You don't have to be a registered user to edit a Wikipedia article. Simply click on an **edit this page** link and make your changes in the box that comes up. Write a brief account of what you've done in the 'edit summary' box. If you want to change the meaning of an article or change the facts that it contains, this counts as a 'major edit'. If you're planning a major edit, consider making your intentions known to other interested editors via a 'discussion page'. When you incorporate the thoughts and opinions of other users, it's less likely that your changes will be disputed or deleted.

make a Window box

The advantage of making your own window boxes is that you can tailor them exactly to the space you have available. Before being filled, this box could be attached to a wall with strong metal brackets.

YOU WILL NEED Exterior grade plywood cut to size, drill with spade bit, length of 25mm x 25mm batten, tape measure, pencil, exterior wood adhesive, screws, screwdriver, clamps, cardboard, saw, wood preservative, paint

1 Determine the dimensions you require then buy the plywood for the sides, ends and base cut to size. Use the spade bit to drill holes in the base for drainage.

2 Measure and cut four short battens for the inside corners and two long ones to support the base. Use the adhesive and screws to attach the corner battens to the ends. Drill pilot and clearance holes and countersink the clearance holes so that the screw heads lie flush.

3 Fix battens along the bottom inside edges of the back and front sections. Clamp the back section into position, using cardboard to stop the clamps damaging the wood, and screw the two ends into place. Fix the front into place using the same method.

4 Saw a 25mm x 25mm notch into each corner of the base section and drop it into the box to rest on top of the two long battens. Treat inside and out with wood preservative then paint as you wish.

plant and maintain a Window box

Planting Add slow-release fertiliser and water-retaining gel granules to the compost before you plant. For full impact choose simple colour schemes such as red geraniums with ivy or pastel petunias with silver-leaved helichrysum. For north-facing windows choose ferns and busy lizzies. Plant generously.

Feeding Apply a measure of general liquid fertiliser every three or four weeks as plants mature.

Water regularly, as near to plant roots as possible. If you live above other people, or if your box overhangs a pavement, put a drip tray under the box so that passers-by don't get showered.

protect yourself in a Wildfire

Wildfires can spread incredibly fast, but there are ways to stay safe if you get caught up in one.

Do what you can to reduce the risk to the building where you're staying. Move combustible objects such as garden furniture and gas bottles away from the house. Turn off the mains gas supply. If possible, soak the walls and roof of the house with a hose. Do the same to fences, and nearby trees and grass. If the blaze comes close, don't stay to fight the fire.

Protect your home by creating a safety zone about 10m deep on all sides. Remove old cars, wood piles, felled trees and other debris. Make sure there's enough space for firefighters to protect the rear of your home. Make sure all fences have easily accessible gates. Keep lawns mown short (75mm or less), as grass cut short won't carry fire. Clear a 3m space around fuel tanks and fill this space with gravel, rock or short-mown grass.

Be ready to leave quickly Park your car near the exit with windows and vents closed. Have the keys on your person. Load up with drinking water. Plan several escape routes, so that you have options if you encounter a block in the road.

golden rules

MAINTAIN WINDOW BOXES
- Don't overdo the gel granules – they'll swell too much and push plants out of position.
- Replant as soon as plants are past their best.

clean Windows
without chemicals

It's inexpensive and effective to clean windows with plain water or a simple homemade solution. Always avoid sunny days for this job – quickly dried glass is more susceptible to streaking.

Plain water Apply water with a sponge or squeegee using just enough to prevent drenching the pane, working from side to side. Then wipe down with a wad of newspaper, paper towels, a chamois leather or a clean lint-free soft cloth.

Simple cleaner Mix 25ml white vinegar with 500ml water and use to fill a spray bottle. Spray on evenly, then buff off with a wad of newspaper, chamois or paper towels.

golden rules

CLEAN WINDOWS

- **Work from the top to the bottom of the pane.**
- **Wipe window corners with a rag before you begin.**
- **Protect indoor windowsills with old towels as you work.**

replace a broken Window pane

Before buying new glass, measure the window opening to the inside of the rebates (the recesses in which the pane sits). Subtract 3mm from the smallest height and width for an easy fit. Be careful: a wrongly sized pane is useless.

YOU WILL NEED New pane of glass, goggles, thick work gloves, hammer, old chisel or hacking knife, pliers, putty, glazing sprigs

1 Wearing goggles and gloves, remove the broken pane, using a hammer if necessary, and dispose carefully of the glass. Then, working on the outside of the window, use an old chisel or hacking knife to dig out fragments of glass and putty from the rebates. Pull out any remaining glazing sprigs with pliers.

2 Knead some putty until it's soft, then smooth a thin layer all around the frame. Place the new pane in the frame, and press the edges firmly into the bed of putty.

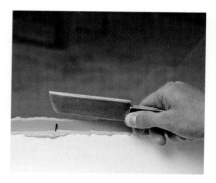

3 Using the back of your hacking knife, tap in new glazing sprigs about 250mm apart to hold the new pane in place. The heads of the sprigs should protrude about 5mm.

4 Apply more putty to the front of the glass to fill the rebate. Use your putty knife as shown right to compact the putty and to leave a level surface at 45 degrees to the glass. Draw the knife along the edge of the putty to smooth the putty into a neat bevel. It should cover the heads of the sprigs, and line up with the window frame on the inside edge. Make neat mitres at each corner and clean away excess putty from the inside of the window.

paint Windows

Start painting windows early in the day, so that they dry before you close them at night. Protect the glass with masking tape, or use a masking shield.

Casement windows These should be painted when open, and in the following order:

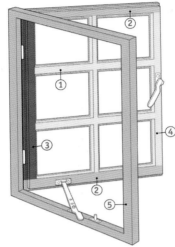

Crossbars and transoms (1), painting horizontal bars first then vertical ones. **Top and bottom rails** (2), including any rebates that fit around frame. **Hanging stile** (3), the vertical to which the hinges are attached. **Meeting stile** (4), the other vertical, to which the handle is attached. **Window frame** (5). If the inside and outside are painted in different colours or finishes, paint anything visible from inside, when the window is open, in the internal colour and vice versa.

Sash windows These should be opened so that the bottom window is as high as it will go, and the top window as low as it will go. Paint in the following order then reverse the sashes and paint the bits of each window that you couldn't reach on the first pass:

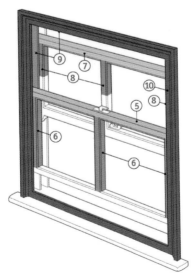

Meeting rail (1), the bottom horizontal of the top window. **Vertical bars** (2) as far as you can reach. **Bottom of the frame** (3), where the inner sash sits when closed, and a very thin coat on the sides or runners. **Bottom horizontal rail of the inner window** (4), including the underside. Swap the position of the sashes at this point, then paint **top horizontal of the inner window** (5) and **vertical bars** (6). **Top horizontal of the outer window** (7), including top edge and **remainder of the vertical bars** (8). Finish with upper inner side of frame and runners behind the cords (9), and the frame (10).

free stuck Windows

Sash windows can get stuck when the sashes are broken, but a more common reason is that they have been painted shut.

- Run a sharp trimming knife down the crack between the window and frame to break the seal of paint.
- Alternatively, apply paint stripper – but only if you're about to repaint, as this will ruin the paint finish on the window.
- Or insert the tip of a wide-bladed chisel at the bottom of the window from the outside – one sharp downwards push might break the old paint seal and free the window.

Casement windows can get stuck if they have been painted too often, or when the wood swells in damp or wet weather – a problem that may resolve itself once warmer weather comes. If not, plane the edge of the window that's causing the problem (most likely the bottom edge). Check that the putty around the glass is well covered with paint, as this will help to prevent the wood from swelling.

golden rules

SMOOTH, SMART WINDOWS
- **Metal windows tend to fit more snugly than wooden ones, so you may have to strip them back before you paint, or else they might not close properly.**
- **Rub down and clean wooden frames before painting to avoid a build-up of paint or a poor finish.**

deal with a broken car
Windscreen

The windscreen on most modern cars isn't prone to shatter. But even a small chip in the driver's sightline can obscure your vision, and will only get worse if you leave it and don't get it repaired.

- If your windscreen does shatter while you're driving, don't try to punch out the glass while you're still in motion.
- Slow down and, making use of whatever sight you have of the road, find a safe place to stop.
- Stuff rags or newspapers into any vents before firmly and steadily pushing the glass outwards onto the bonnet using a gloved hand, spanner or jack handle.
- If you must drive on, go slowly straight to the nearest garage.

de-ice a frozen
Windscreen

- Don't use a credit card to scrape off ice – it might not do the glass much harm, but could render the card useless.
- First turn on the ignition and put the car's de-mister on its highest setting, directed onto the screen.
- Keep a can of de-icer and a windscreen scraper in your car during winter. Use them to clear the windscreen and side windows completely before you set off: it's dangerous to drive with a partially obscured view of the road.
- Never pour hot water on your windscreen to melt the ice: it might cause the glass to crack.
See also DRIVE.

learn to Windsurf

Windsurfing is part-sailing, part-surfing. As a beginner, you should be prepared for some dunkings, but when you first catch the wind and move, you'll discover an altogether exhilarating watersport.

Climbing aboard

1 Stand in waist-high water with your board in front of you and the sail downwind of the board. Climb aboard on your knees and grasp the 'uphaul', the line attached to the middle of the mast.

2 Stand up, place one foot on either side of the mast, and start to raise the rig, keeping your back to the wind. Make sure your back is straight and your weight is over the centre of the board.

Moving off

1 Find your balance before attempting to move. Let the rig swing freely downwind of you, while keeping hold of the uphaul. Get the feel of the board and make sure you feel comfortable with your position and balance.

2 Hold the boom (the horizontal bar), and pull it across your body as you step back towards the tail of the board. Your front foot should be at the base of the mast. As the wind catches the sail, you'll begin to move off at right angles to the wind. Pull back with your back hand to speed up and relax your pressure to ease off the speed.

match Wine with food

Finding a wine to complement a meal is not so very difficult. The basic rule of white wine with fish and white meat and red wine with red meat is a reliable place to start.

Type of wine	Good with
Red wines	
CABERNET SAUVIGNON A grape prominent in Bordeaux and New World wines. Has a distinctive and emphatic taste, with high tannin levels and flavours of oak, that's too strong for delicate foods.	Poultry, roast beef, roast lamb, kidneys, mature hard cheeses
MERLOT The most widely used red wine grape in Bordeaux, now grown around the world. Ripe, smooth and more adaptable than cabernet sauvignon.	Calves' liver, grilled steaks, stews
SYRAH/SHIRAZ Widely used in the Rhône Valley, California and Australia. Has flavours of blackcurrant, black pepper and spice.	Steak, roast beef, wild game, meat stews, mushrooms, Mexican chilli, chargrilled food
PINOT NOIR An elegant grape, but challenging to grow and rarely used in blends. Has soft tannins, shades of cherry, strawberry plum and leaf tea.	Salmon, tuna, venison, duck, baked ham, goose
BARBERA Italy's third-most-planted red grape, also popular in California. Cheap and cheerful, juicy and fruity: perfect with Italian food.	Pizza, tomato and meat pasta, salami
GAMAY French grape used in Beaujolais, but also in parts of Burgundy and California. Best drunk as a young wine, which is light and summery.	Cold meats, mushrooms. charcuterie
White wines	
CHARDONNAY Originated in Burgundy and used in Chablis. The most widely planted white wine grape in the world. Dry, rich, honeyed, sometimes oaky, though unoaked wines are available. Pairs well with many foods.	Omelette, fish, chicken, shellfish, mild game, coconut curries
SÉMILLON The major white-wine grape of Bordeaux. Also grown in Chile, Argentina, California and Australia. Strong notes of date or fig. Often blended with Sauvignon. Sweet Sauternes and Barsac are made from overripe Sémillon.	Dry Sémillon: fish, shellfish, pork Sweet Sémillon: blue cheese, mature hard cheese, creamy puddings
SAUVIGNON BLANC Originated in the Loire valley. Popular around the world. Makes light-to-medium-bodied white that pairs with a ride range of flavours.	Goat's cheese, asparagus, seafood, Thai food
RIESLING Classic grape from the Rhine and Mosel in Germany, Alsace in France and also popular in Australia. Light, aromatic and with a steely acidity; very flexible for pairing with food.	Fish, pork, shellfish, omelette, duck, goose, sushi
PINOT GRIGIO Widely grown in the Venezia and Alto-Adige regions of Italy, and increasingly popular. Crisp and bone dry with an acidic bite, versatile for drinking on its own or with food.	Light and creamy pasta dishes, pork, vegetable ravioli, pâtés

detect and treat
Woodworm

The tell-tale signs of woodworm attack are the small (2mm) round holes in the surface made by the adult beetles as they leave. Bare dark holes indicate an old attack; white holes, with small piles of wood dust, indicate recent and possibly ongoing activity that needs to be dealt with immediately to prevent further weakening of the wood.

■ Paint all surfaces of an infected piece of furniture with two coats of a shop-bought woodworm killer.
■ Alternatively, inject the holes using a can of woodworm killer with a special nozzle.
■ Furniture beetles won't lay eggs in treated wood, so one application should solve the problem.

⭐ golden rules
KEEPING WINE
■ **If you have wine left over in an open bottle, it should keep for about two days in the fridge. Reseal the bottle with a screw cap or airtight stopper.**
■ **Dessert wines will keep for longer, like sherries and ports, but taste them to be sure before serving to your guests.**

taste Wine like an expert

When a wine waiter brings wine to your table you should be shown the label to ensure that it's the wine you ordered. When it's opened and you're offered a little to taste, the point is to check that the wine isn't 'off', and that it's as described on the wine list, not to see whether you like it.

■ Take a look at the colour. Red wine shouldn't be cloudy or brownish.
■ Smell it first. If it's vinegary that's a sign of oxidation. If it smells musty it suggests a mouldy cork, which will have tainted the wine.
■ If you want to taste the wine, take a small sip and swill it around your mouth to activate all your taste buds. Suck a little air into your mouth as you do this to release all the flavours and aromas.

At a wine tasting there should be a spittoon to hand for you to spit out the samples you taste. Try lots of different wines to get a feel for which sorts you prefer and to learn how to pick out different flavours.
■ The sweetness of the wine is the easiest to detect, and the more it makes your mouth water, the higher its acidity. A balanced acidity is usually the most pleasurable to drink.
■ The drier and earthier the taste of a red wine, the higher its tannin level. Young red wines are low in tannin and good for drinking on their own. Wines high in tannin offer more complex flavours and pair best with food.

---

store and serve Wine

Most white and rosé wines are sold ready for drinking now and don't need laying down. Good-quality red wines, except for the lightest, such as Beaujolais, can benefit from careful storage. Even cheaper wines will taste better if you serve them properly and at the right temperature.

To store Ideal conditions for wine storage are darkness and a temperature of around 12°C/54°F. An understairs cupboard or a garage will be fine, but watch it doesn't freeze in winter.
■ A consistent temperature is more important than coolness. If wine is kept in an area a little cooler or warmer than the ideal, it won't suffer so much as if it's subject to sudden temperature change.
■ Store bottles in a rack, on their side, so the cork doesn't dry out. Bottles with a screw cap can be stored upright.

To serve Very expensive red wine may benefit from decanting, but most wine is fine served from the bottle. Have a quick taste to make sure the wine is in good condition and at the right temperature.
■ White wine is best served chilled, and red (with rare exceptions) at just below room temperature. An hour or so in the fridge for white wine or three at room temperature for red wine should be just right.
■ Open red wine a little ahead of time to let it 'breathe'.
■ Choose glasses large enough to swill around a standard measure (one-sixth of a bottle), since part of the pleasure is to smell it and enjoy the 'nose'.
■ Keep white wine on ice or in a chiller.

set up a Wormery in your garden

A wormery is an enclosed bin in which worms churn and chew your kitchen waste to produce a rich liquid fertiliser and compost.

Establishing a wormery It will take a couple of months for a wormery to start producing fertiliser. Keep feeding kitchen scraps, a little and often.
■ You'll need to buy a starter kit of special tiger worms or red brandlings, as earthworms from the garden are not good composters.
■ Put a wide variety of scraps into your wormery for best results. Try to avoid onion skins and citrus peel, which are too acidic.
■ Wormery kits usually have several layers. When the bottom tray is full start filling the next – the worms will wriggle up through the perforations.

1 Cover the base of the bottom tray of your wormery with cardboard and crumble over a layer of coir or a wormery bedding block. Mix in a little compost to get the worms started.

2 Add your worms and cover them with a layer of shredded newspaper and a damp sheet of cardboard or hemp matting to keep out the light. Put the lid on and leave it for a month.

3 After a month, start adding your kitchen scraps. Bury meat beneath the surface to avoid attracting pests.

4 The worms will turn the waste into rich garden compost, but also produce an excellent liquid feed, which you should drain from the tap. Dilute this 1 part to 10 parts water and use it to fertilise your garden plants.

organise your Workstation

A day spent organising your workspace will pay dividends in helping to maximise your efficiency.

Tidy desk, tidy mind
■ On your desk you should have only the things you need for the task in hand. If there are books, letters and printouts that you have finished with, or don't intend to use today, put them somewhere else.
■ Have a shoebox, tray or file where you keep pending correspondence and remove it to a shelf: that way the chaos is at least contained.
■ Shun desk toys and too many photos – they will clutter your mind as much as your desk.
■ If possible, don't have your printer on your desk: it takes up far too much useful space.

Filing and organisation
■ Use your desk drawers wisely: one for pens, another for paper stationery, another still for personal items, phone chargers and the like.
■ Be organised with filing, creating separate hanging files in drawers for current projects, important paperwork, recently completed jobs and other things that you may need to access at short notice.
■ Move old paperwork into archive boxes until you can dispose of it.

Safe and comfortable working
■ Take care where you position your computer. Don't have your monitor where you are looking into a bright light behind it or where glare will dazzle off the screen.
■ Make sure that your chair is supportive and that you're sitting at the right height at the desk.
See also SIT.

tackle Worms in pets

Even healthy-looking animals can be carrying roundworms and tapeworms. In young pets, worms can cause a pot belly, poor growth and diarrhoea. A heavy infestation can even cause a fatal blockage of the intestines. In adult pets, worms can lead to poor coat condition, vomiting and diarrhoea. Worms also pose a risk to humans – roundworms in dogs and cats (toxocara), for example, can cause blindness in children, though this is rare. Regular worming is essential to protect pets and people alike. Worms aren't choosy, and will live happily inside you, too.

■ Ask your vet for advice on the most suitable worming treatment to use on a pet.
■ Tapeworms rely on fleas to survive, so regular flea prevention treatment is important. Ask your vet for advice.
■ Note clearly on your calendar when treatments are due.
■ Always observe strict hygiene. Dispose of faeces and cat litter every day and always wash your hands afterwards (see HANDS). Make sure children do the same and stop then playing with mud. Cover sandpits, too, to avoid cat contamination.

golden rules
GIFT WRAPPING
■ **Work on a firm, flat surface.**
■ **Use double-sided sticky tape fixed between two surfaces of the paper, so that no tape shows on the finished parcel.**
■ **Measure the appropriate amount of paper; too much paper looks untidy.**

Wrap a gift

YOU WILL NEED Strong wrapping paper that won't tear, tape measure, scissors, transparent double-sided sticky tape in a dispenser

Rectangular or square shape

The paper should be wide enough to wrap right round the package, plus 50mm. Its length should be the package length, plus the package depth, plus 25mm.

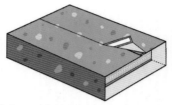

1 Centre the package, top down, on the paper and wrap the paper round it. Put tape beneath the top part of the overlap and press it down.

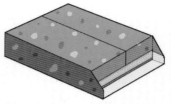

2 Fold the top of the paper over one end, pressing it in at the sides so that the side flaps slant down. Pinch the slants into sharp creases.

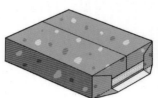

3 Fold the slanted sides inwards and press them in firmly at the base so the bottom flap slants in at the sides.

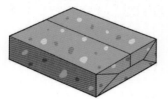

4 Fold the bottom flap of paper up and tape it into place. Repeat for the other end of the package.

Jar or bottle

Cut two squares of pliable paper, such as tissue or foil, with sides as long as twice the height of the jar or bottle plus three times its width. Lay one on the other with their corners alternating. Centre the jar or bottle, draw up the paper all round and tie it with a ribbon.

Tubular shape

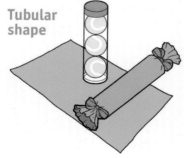

Cut a piece of paper 150mm longer than the tube and wide enough to wrap around the tube, plus 50mm. Use sticky tape to fix the paper in place lengthwise as for a box (above). At each end tie a ribbon to gather the paper. Spread the gathers evenly.

decorate a Wreath

Wreaths can be made from almost any plant material but work best with evergreens, buds and berries, or dried seed heads. Some of the foliage and the fir cones can be sprayed gold or silver.

YOU WILL NEED **Thick wire, vine wreath base (from florists' suppliers), evergreen stems such as holly, bay or ivy, secateurs, thin pliable wire, bunches of rosebuds or berries, fir cones, glue, ribbon, needle and thread. For spraying fir cones beforehand: spray paint, newspaper**

1 Use the thick wire to make a hanger across the back of the wreath base, inserting it between vine stems and winding the ends tightly to secure them. The wire should be short enough to be invisible when the wreath is hung up.

2 Strip the leaves from the bases of the evergreen stems and cut to uniform length with secateurs. Insert them firmly into the wreath so that they overlap and all point the same way. Bind them into place with thin wire until the wreath base is covered.

3 Wrap wire around the trimmed stems of the rosebuds to create small bunches, leaving a small length of wire for pinning to the wreath. Add to the wreath, pushing the wire around the vine stems at the back. Trim off any excess wire with secateurs.

4 Apply glue to the bases of the fir cones and add at different angles around the wreath. Allow to dry completely. You could also attach the cones using wire. Finally, wind ribbon around the wreath and sew or glue the ends together. Hang up.

prevent
Wrinkles

Wrinkles are inevitable and not all bad (think of laughter lines). Moisturising can help but a healthy lifestyle is more important.

■ Eat well (*see* DIET). Have more olive oil, fish, low-fat milk, fruit, vegetables, eggs, nuts and beans. Have less butter, red meat, cakes, pastries, soft drinks, full-fat milk, margarine, and chips and other fried foods.

■ Make sure there are plenty of vitamins in your diet (*see* VITAMINS). Foods rich in vitamin C, such as berries, red pepper and broccoli, can help to maintain skin elasticity.

■ Keep well hydrated by drinking water and not too much alcohol.

■ Cigarettes are ruinous to the complexion as well as to your general health, so try to give up (*see* SMOKING).

■ For 'glamorous sun tan' read 'solar damage'. Use a sun block. Wear sunglasses in bright light.

■ Don't drink through straws; they can cause wrinkles round the mouth.

■ Sleep on your back so your face isn't constantly crumpled at night. Use soft pillowcases.

■ Avoid frown lines; cultivate a positive state of mind. Don't worry, be happy!

play the
Xylophone

A xylophone is arranged like a piano keyboard (*see* PIANO). You strike the wooden bars with mallets to produce a note. Hold the mallets close to their midpoint, so that they are balanced, and orient them at a slight inward angle. The shorter the bar, the higher the note – hence the xylophone's distinctive wedge shape. Some xylophones have just one row of keys; professional instruments have a second row of bars for sharps and flats (like the black notes on a piano).

- If you're a beginner, try picking out a tune with one mallet: this will be easy to do if you're familiar with the piano.
- As you get better, play with a mallet in each hand to create harmonies, and to play phrases more quickly. Really skilled players can wield two mallets in each hand, and so play a maximum of four notes at a time.

master essential Yoga positions

Yoga improves your flexibility, strength and ability to relax. All you need are a yoga mat, clothes that let you move easily and a quiet space.

Practise at least three times a week, but never push yourself further than you can comfortably go. Breathe smoothly through the nostrils, and keep focused. Start with simple postures and always end a session with a few minutes of relaxed breathing, lying on your back. Avoid doing yoga after a meal, and take medical advice before starting if you have any health concerns or are pregnant. Here are some beginner's postures to try. Take between three to ten breaths in each position.

Triangle Stand tall, then bring your legs comfortably apart and your arms out. Point your right foot out, exhale and bend to the right, stretching your right hand down the leg and your left arm up, or folded behind your back. Look up at your hand and breathe, holding the pose. Then breathe in and come up. Repeat on the right.

Modified twist Sit with your left leg straight or folded to the left (as above). Cross your right foot over to the left side, foot flat. Place your left elbow inside the right knee and reach the hand towards the right ankle. Breathe in, sit up straight, exhale and turn to the right, with the right hand behind you. Repeat to the other side.

Downward dog Start on hands and knees. Tuck your toes under, exhale and raise hips to form an inverted 'V'. Lower your head, keep your arms and legs straight, with heels down. Push your chest towards your knees as you breathe out to flatten the curve in the upper back. Breathe, hold the position, then release. Hug your knees and rock from side to side.

Bridge Lie on your back, knees bent, legs hip-width apart, feet forward and arms to your sides. Bring your heels a little closer to the buttocks to make the shins vertical. Inhale and raise the middle of your body. Press arms and feet into the floor to lift yourself higher. Breathe, hold, then release. Hug your knees and rock from side to side.

post a video on YouTube

Posting a short piece of film on YouTube is simple to do – and it's a great way to share life events, opinions and know-how.

Whatever the subject of your video – highlights of your wedding or tips on playing blues guitar, for instance – spend some time making the film as good as you can (*see* FILM). Use the video-editing software on your computer to create something that's both slick and brief. Most YouTube users won't want to watch anything that's longer than a couple of minutes.

■ Before you can upload a finished video clip, you must first register with YouTube. Go to the site and follow the instructions for setting up an account. Once you're registered, you can post videos straight away.
■ Click on **Upload** and then **Upload video**, and specify the file that you want to make public on YouTube; double-click on it to begin the upload.
■ While the film is uploading, give it a title and description along with some keywords, so that your work can be found by people using search engines.

There will be a delay of half an hour or so before your film appears on the site. You'll receive an email notification with a link to its location. Pass the web address on to anyone you think might be interested.

---

learn basic Yo-yo moves

Playing with a yo-yo is addictive, fun and easy to learn. You'll be performing gravity-defying tricks in no time at all.

Basic throw Hold the yo-yo on your palm with the string loop around the middle finger. Curl your arm up beside your ear, palm to the rear. Unfurl your arm so that the yo-yo arcs out over your fingertips. When it reaches the end of the string flip your hand over – the yo-yo will run back up to your palm.

Sleeper For your first trick, perform the basic throw with extra speed. The yo-yo should spin ('sleep') at the end of the string until you jerk your hand to wake the yo-yo up and bring it spinning back to your hand.

Walk the dog

1 Throw the sleeper move as described above. As the yo-yo spins on the end of the string touch it lightly to the floor and it will scuttle forward.

2 Flip your hand palm down and give a slight upward jerk. The obedient yo-yo will leap back to your hand. Good doggy!

make perfect Yorkshire pudding

The secret of this traditional accompaniment to roast beef is piping hot fat and a very hot oven. It can be made as a single dish or as individual 'popovers', which can cook while the meat 'rests' before carving. With pepper omitted it can be enjoyed as a dessert, topped with maple or golden syrup or with poached fruit.

SERVES 4: MAKES 1 LARGE OR 12 INDIVIDUAL PUDDINGS

125g plain flour
2 eggs
300ml semi-skimmed milk
salt and freshly ground black pepper
25g dripping or lard,
   or 30ml vegetable oil

1 Heat the oven to 220°C/gas 7. Sift the flour into a bowl, make a well in the centre and add the eggs. Work into the flour, then beat in the milk and seasonings with an electric beater. Alternatively, mix all the ingredients in a food processor or liquidiser.

2 Put the dripping into a 28cm x 18cm roasting tin or use it to grease a 12 hole bun tin. Put your chosen container into the oven, placed on a baking sheet. When the fat is very hot, remove it and pour in the batter mixture. If the fat is at the right temperature, the batter should sizzle as you pour it in. Replace onto the baking sheet. Cook a single pudding for 25-30 minutes, individual ones for 15-20 minutes, or until crisp and well risen. Serve at once.

make Zabaglione

This rich, impressive Italian dessert is much easier to create than it looks. But it must be made immediately before serving as it will begin to separate in just 5 minutes. A key ingredient is Marsala, a fortified Italian wine available in most supermarkets.

SERVES 4

4 egg yolks
60g golden caster sugar
75ml Marsala
toasted flaked almonds, to garnish
almond biscuits, such as Italian biscotti, to serve

1 Put the egg yolks into a heatproof bowl, add the sugar and briskly whisk together for about a minute. Gradually add the Marsala and whisk in gently.

2 Place the bowl over a pan of simmering water and heat, whisking constantly, for about 10-15 minutes until the mixture is thick and creamy and stands in soft peaks. Spoon into individual glasses and top each with a few almonds. Serve at once accompanied by the almond biscuits.

■ While heating the mixture, don't let the bottom of the bowl touch the simmering water or the eggs may cook too quickly and scramble.

golden rules
ZIP STITCHING
■ **Use the marks made by the original stitching as a guide for tacking and sewing.**
■ **Sew as close to the zip teeth as possible.**

fix a Zip quick

Just running the tab up and down may be enough to cure a sticky zip, but if teeth are broken you may need to replace it. Or try these quick fixes.

Stuck teeth Apply a small amount of lip balm to the teeth and run the zip up and down. Or try rubbing the teeth with a candle or pencil lead.

Broken pull tab Replace the tab with a paperclip, then bind the clip with thread of a matching or contrasting colour.

Runner detached from the teeth at the bottom Pull the runner to the zip base, then make a cut into the zip tape between the teeth about 6mm above the runner on the unattached side. Work the teeth into the runner. Pull up the zip, then use a needle and thread to oversew the two sides of the zip together just above the cut to form a new stop for the runner.

replace a Zip

When a zip breaks on a favourite pair of trousers it pays to be able to replace it yourself – but it's essential to make sure that the new and old zips match exactly in length and as closely as possible in colour and weight. This easy technique can be adapted to replace zips on other garments.

YOU WILL NEED Stitch remover (ripper), small scissors, new zip, pins, thread, needle. Optional: sewing machine with zipper foot

1 Take out the old zip, using a stitch remover to release only the stitches that are holding it in place. Don't undo the waistband stitching but use small scissors to cut off the old zip at the top.

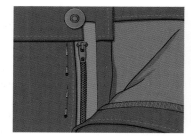

2 Pin one side of the new zip to the base of the crotch, then pin into place up to the waistband. Fold the top of the zip tape under so that the top teeth lie flush with the bottom of the waistband. Tack, then sew into position by hand, using small neat backstitch (*see* SEWING *and* TACK), or by machine using the zipper foot.

3 Close the zip and turn the trousers inside out, taking care to lie them flat. Pin, then tack, the second side of the zip into position, again folding under the top of the zip tape. Backstitch into position by hand, taking care to stitch through only one layer of fabric so that stitches don't show on the outside.

4 On the inside, make a 1cm row of small, tight overlapping stitches (a bar tack) below the bottom of the new zip to create a strong hold.

recognise signs of the Zodiac

The complex and arcane system of astrology takes as its starting point 12 signs determined by the position of the sun at the time of birth.

Birth sign	Symbol	Date and type	Characteristics
ARIES *the ram*		March 21-April 19. Cardinal. Element: fire	Impulsive, strong-minded, honest and trusting, dominant, short fuse
TAURUS *the bull*		April 20-May 20. Fixed. Element: earth	Patient, dependable, resolute, practical, loyal, won't budge
GEMINI *the twins*		May 21-June 21. Mutable. Element: air	Versatile, expressive, silver-tongued, changeful, easily bored
CANCER *the crab*		June 22-July 22. Cardinal. Element: water	Tenacious, intuitive, emotional, sensitive, empathetic, traditional, moody
LEO *the lion*		July 23-August 22. Fixed. Element: fire	Lion-hearted, idealistic, dignified, romantic, aspiring, overbearing
VIRGO *the virgin*		August 23-September 22. Mutable. Element: earth	Gentle, hard-working, reliable, sincere, methodical, worrier
LIBRA *the scales*		September 23-October 23. Cardinal. Element: air	Artistic, eloquent, diplomatic, logical, passion for justice, indecisive, fickle
SCORPIO *the scorpion*		October 24-November 21. Fixed. Element: water	Passionate, loyal, resourceful, driven, private, temperamental, doesn't suffer fools gladly
SAGITTARIUS *the archer*		November 22-December 21. Mutable. Element: fire	Friendly, open-handed, open-hearted, confident, honest, fractious, blunt
CAPRICORN *the goat*		December 22-January 19. Cardinal. Element: earth	Earnest, reliable, industrious, cautious, traditional, responsible, bears grudges
AQUARIUS *the water carrier*		January 20-February 18. Fixed. Element: air	Independent, broad-minded, curious, penetrating, progressive, wilful
PISCES *the fish*		February 19-March 20. Mutable. Element: water	Sensitive, humane, adaptable, idealistic, good intuition, vulnerable

Each birth sign is governed by a dominant element with symbolic meanings. **Fire** denotes creativity, intuition, a spirit of adventure, the visionary. **Earth** denotes practicality, objectivity, feet-on-the-ground stability – indeed, a sense of being 'earthed'. **Air** denotes the thinker, with high principles and impartiality, the conceiver of concepts. **Water** denotes a feeling and receptive soul, empathy, understanding and instinct. Additionally, the signs of the zodiac are divided into Cardinal, Fixed and Mutable signs. **Cardinal** signs are characterised by enterprise. **Fixed** signs are characterised by firmness and stability. **Mutable** signs are characterised by adaptability.

INDEX

INDEX

INDEX

Acknowledgments

The publishers would like to thank the following people and organisations for their help and advice:

Sophie Adwick, Wildlife Expert, RSPB; Mark Allen, Scottish Wildfire Forum; Association of British Insurers; Bernice Bass, The British Tenpin Bowling Association; Kate Beddington-Brown, CIFAS – The UK's Fraud Prevention Service; Dave Berriman, National Coaching Officer, English Table Tennis Association; Karen Bessant, Feline Advisory Bureau, International Society of Feline Medicine; The Boarding House, Exeter; British Airways; The British Darts Organisation; British Judo Association; British Veterinary Association; Paul Calland, Deputy Station Officer, Morecambe Search and Rescue; Simon Carter, The Scout Association; Liane Cowther, Training Manager, The Horse Trust; Tim Daniels, www.poultrykeeper.com; Mark Diggins, Sportscotland Avalanche Information Service; Dolphin Surf School, Newquay, Cornwall; Patrick Donovan, Chief Executive Officer, British Water Ski & Wakeboard; Nick Eden, Director, Arboricultural Association; Food Standards Agency; Karen Ford, Head of Trading Standards, Milton Keynes Council; Kay Gallagher, The National Bed Federation Ltd; William Gorman, The United Kingdom Tea Council Ltd; Christine Gray, The British Beekeepers Association; Neil Greig, Director of Policy and Research, Peter Rodger, Chief Examiner, and Caroline Homes, Communications Officer, IAM (Institute of Advanced Motorists); Jo Hampson, Smoky Jo's; Roy Henderson, British Association of Skiing Instructors; Phil Holden, Department of Earth Sciences, Open University, Milton Keynes; Keith Horton, Chief Executive, National Ice Skating Association; Pam Horton, British Wheel of Yoga; Alison Howard, Rounders England; Darren Jehan, Bedford Astronomical Society; Lucy Jessop, Architectural Investigator, English Heritage; Kelvin Jones, English Association of Snooker & Billiards; Ryan Jones, England Squash and Racketball; Andrew Kennedy, www.just-fish.co.uk; Elizabeth Larsson, The Croquet Association; Bob Leeds, Football Development Officer, Amateur Football Association; London Luton Airport; Annette Love, Creative Plus Publishing Ltd; Andrew McGrorey, Road Risk Advisory Team, Bedford Borough Council; Faith Mall, Fairtrade; Julian Marczak, President, Association of British Riding Schools; Rosie Mayglothling, Technical Co-ordinator, GB Rowing Team; Pet Owners Association; Pro Coach Cricket Academy, Yorkshire County Cricket Club; Miles Quest, British Hospitality Association; David Radford, www.taichifinder.co.uk; Andrew Reid, High Performance Coach, Swim Ulster; Royal College of Midwives; RYA (Royal Yachting Association); Lauren Sanderson, Amateur Swimming Association; Emma Scott, Professional Affairs Manager, The Textile Institute; Brian Seabright, British Karate Association; Simon Selmon, London Swing Dance Society; Duncan Sivell, Biodiversity Officer, Buglife – The Invertebrate Conservation Trust; Claire Small, Clinical Director, Pure Sports Medicine; David Smith, Performance Coach, Pure Sports Medicine; Karen Sparrow, Optometrist and Education Adviser at the Association of Optometrists (AOP); Richard Stacey-Chapman, Technical Administrator, Volleyball England; Rachelle Stretch, English Amateur Dancesport Association; Dan Thorp, Lawn Tennis Association; Greg Tilbury, PGA Professional, Wavendon Golf Centre; Danielle Waller, Events Manager, SpeedDater Ltd; Sean Wensley, PDSA Senior Veterinary Surgeon, The People's Dispensary for Sick Animals; Chris Whitehead, Chairman, Bristol Pool League; Richard Whitehouse, www.TheGoodGamblingGuide.co.uk; Michelle Whiteman, UK Payments Administration Ltd; Rosie Worrall, Milton Keynes Cats Rescue; Loo Yeo, CID UNESCO, Salsa & Merengue Society; www.hensforhomes.co.uk; www.thetropicaltank.co.uk

Picture credits

T = top; C = centre; B = bottom; A = above; L = left; R = right

Front Cover: ShutterStock, Inc, iStockphoto.com; **4 R** ShutterStock, Inc/Oorka; **7** iStockphoto.com/Troels Graugaard; **12 CL** Alamy Images/Robert Harding Picture Library Ltd, **BL** Alamy Images/Ben Ramos, **BR** Alamy Images/bluudaisy; **13** Alamy Images/GFC Collection, **TR** Alamy Images/Images Etc. Ltd, **BR** Alamy Images/Sandra Baker; **14** © RD; **15** ShutterStock, Inc/Anke van Wyk; **18** Getty Images/Gary Houlder; **19 T** Baby Archive, **B** iStockphoto.com; **20** ShutterStock, Inc/Lasse Kristensen; **22** Getty Images/Dorling Kindersley; **26** Getty Images/Tom Grill; **28-29** ShutterStock, Inc/Gravicapa; **30** © RD; **31** Getty Images/Dorling Kindersley; **32** iStockphoto.com/Okea; **33 TL** iStockphoto.com/4x6, **TC** iStockphoto.com/Francisco Romero, **TR** iStockphoto.com/Nicolas Hansen, **BL** iStockphoto.com/Angela Hawkey, **BC** iStockphoto.com/Zone Creative, **BR** Photolibrary.com/Daniel Ehrenworth; **34** Getty Images/Myles New; **40** iStockphoto.com/Olada; **42 T** ShutterStock, Inc/Audi Dela Cruz, **B** © RD; **43** © RD; **47 L** ShutterStock, Inc/bonchan, **C** ShutterStock, Inc/Victor1, **R** iStockphoto.com/Robert Anthony; **48** Photolibrary.com/Michael Powell; **50** iStockphoto.com/Edward O'Neil Photography Inc; **51 TL** Photolibrary.com/Joy Skipper, **TC** Photolibrary.com/Foodfolio, **TR** Photolibrary.com/Eaglemoss Consumer Publications, **CR** © RD, **BR** Photolibrary.com/More Images (Oceania); **52** iStockphoto.com/Brian Jackson; **56** iStockphoto.com/Travellinglight; **57** © RD; **58 T** ShutterStock, Inc/Anat-Oli, **B** Getty Images/National Geographic; **59 TL** ShutterStock, Inc/Aleksandra Duda, **TR** ShutterStock, Inc/Richard Peterson, **C** ShutterStock, Inc/Lantapix, **CB** ShutterStock, Inc/photo-master, **BRA** ShutterStock, Inc/z-art, **B** ShutterStock, Inc/Rocket 400 Studio, **BL** ShutterStock, Inc/Subbotina Anna; **61-62** © RD; **64** ShutterStock, Inc/Creatista; **65 T** ShutterStock, Inc/Carsten Reisinger; **66 & 67 T** © RD, **BL** ShutterStock, Inc/S_Oleg, **BR** ShutterStock, Inc/Ersin Kurtdal; **69** Getty Images/Ian O'Leary; **70** © RD; **71** www.garden-collection.com/Marie O'Hara; **72-73** Home Laundering Consultative Council/www.care-labelling.co.uk; **76** iStockphoto.com/Cameron Whitman; **77 TL** iStockphoto.com/okea, **TC** iStockphoto.com/Ergeny Karandaev, **TR** iStockphoto.com/Rebecca Ellis, **BL** iStockphoto.com/Ivan Mateev, **BC** iStockphoto.com/Rebecca Ellis, **BR** iStockphoto.com/Steve Cukrov; **79 L** Corbis/Ocean, **C** Pubilc Domain, **R** ShutterStock, Inc/Chrislofoto; **81** © RD; **82** ShutterStock, Inc/chrisbrignell; **83** © RD; **84** Getty Images/GAP Photos; **85-88** © RD; **89** Getty Images/Anna Williams; **94** Photolibrary.com/David Marsden; **99** ShutterStock, Inc/Tonn; **103** © RD; **105** Getty Images/Andy Crawford; **107** ShutterStock, Inc/homydesign; **108-109** © RD; **112 TL&BL** © RD; **112-113** Alamy Images/Alvey & Towers Picture Library; **113 L** Alamy Images/Mint Photography, **R** Getty Images/Andrew Bret Wallis; **119 L** © RD, **R** ShutterStock, Inc/mates; **126** © RD; **127 T** ShutterStock, Inc/niderlander, **B** ShutterStock, Inc/Dmitriy Shironosov; **128 TR, C&CR** © RD, **BL** Science Photo Library/Mark Sykes; **129** ShutterStock, Inc/Wiktor Bubriak; **132 T** Photolibrary.com/Maximilian Stock Ltd, **B** Dorling Kindersley/Jerry Young; **133** Photolibrary.com/Tony Robins; **134** ShutterStock, Inc/Woodsy; **135-137** © RD; **139** Getty Images/Matthew Ward; **142 L** ShutterStock, Inc/Rey Kamensky; **145** Photolibrary.com/Sian Irvine; **146** www.garden-collection.com/Neil Sutherland; **148 L** Photolibrary.com/Fresh Food Images, **C** Alamy Images/Bon Appetit, **R** Photolibrary.com/Photocuisine; **150** ShutterStock, Inc/Tischenko Irina; **151** © RD; **152** Phil Sheldon Picture Library/Phil Sheldon; **153 T** Golf Picture Library/Matthew Harris, **CL, C&CR** Phil Sheldon Picture Library/Phil Sheldon, **B** Phil Sheldon Picture Library/Hugh Routledge; **154** © RD; **157 T** Getty Images/Dorling Kindersley, **B** www.theassayoffice.co.uk/gem@theassayoffice.co.uk; **160 BL** Getty Images/Wire Image, **BR** Rex Features Ltd/Matt Baron/BEI; **161 TL** Rex Features Ltd/Startraks Photo; **163-164** © RD; **165** Getty Images/Peter Anderson; **168 T** Photolibrary.com/Imagebroker; **169** Getty Images/Ryan McVay; **173** ShutterStock, Inc/Oliver Hoffman; **175-176** © RD; **180 T** Getty Images/Jerry Young, **BL&BR** Dorling Kindersley/Dorling Kindersley; **181** © RD; **182 T** iStockphoto.com/AndersonAnderson, **B** © RD; **185 R** ShutterStock, Inc/Muellek Josef; **187** Photolibrary.com/Photodisc; **190** www.garden-collection.com/Derek St Romaine; **191** www.garden-collection.com/Liz Eddison; **194** Bloomberg via Getty Images; **195** Getty Images/Ivo Noppen; **198** ShutterStock, Inc/Chepko Danil Vitalevich; **200 L** Photolibrary.com/Norman Hollands, **R** Photolibrary.com/Fresh Food Images; **205 T** Photolibrary.com/Monkey Business Images Ltd, **B** Alamy Images/Medical-on-Line; **206** ShutterStock, Inc/Sergey Kamshylin; **210** Science Photo Library/Dr. John Brackenbury; **211** www.garden-collection.com/Jonathan Buckley; **213-219** © RD; **220 R** Eaglemoss Publications; **221** Photolibrary.com/Amanda Heywood; **222** ShutterStock, Inc/Ioannis Pantziaras; **223-225** © RD; **226** Photolibrary.com/Fresh Food Images; **228** © RD; **229 L** ShutterStock, Inc/Iwona Grodzka, **229 R & 231** © RD; **232 L** ShutterStock, Inc/barbaradudzinska, **R** ShutterStock, Inc/Subbotina Anna; **233** Getty Images/James Ross; **235** Photolibrary.com/Ingram Publishing; **236** Photolibrary.com/Fresh Food Images; **237** © RD; **238** Photolibrary.com/Fresh Food Images; **240** © RD; **241** ShutterStock, Inc/Monkey Business Images; **242-244** © RD; **245** ShutterStock, Inc/Terrace Studio; **246 L** ShutterStock, Inc/Miguel Andel Salinas Salinas; **248 TC** ShutterStock, Inc/pzAxe, **TR** © RD, **BR** ShutterStock, Inc/ER_09; **249-251** © RD; **252 TR** ShutterStock, Inc/Oorka; **254 L** © RD; **256 TL** Getty Images/Philip Wilkins, **C&BR** © RD; **257** © RD; **258** Alamy Images/David Gee 3; **259** ShutterStock, Inc/Sunnys; **260** Photolibrary.com/Datacraft; **261** Photolibrary.com/Fresh Food Images/Steve Lee; **264 T** www.garden-collection.com/Liz Eddison, **L** www.garden-collection.com/Nicola Stocken Tomkins, **BR** www.garden-collection.com/Jonathan Buckley; **265 R** www.garden-collection.com/Liz Eddison, **Inset** © RD; **266 TR** ShutterStock, Inc/Alhovik; **267 C** ShutterStock, Inc/Neda; **269** Getty Images/Annabelle Breakey; **271** Getty Images/Ann Stratton; **272** Photolibrary.com/Tony West; **273** Alamy Images/Philip Bird; **275-280 T** © RD; **282** www.garden-collection.com/Jonathan Buckley, **B** Gap Photos Ltd/Maxine Adcock; **282-283** Gap Photos Ltd/J S Sira; **283** Gap Photos Ltd/Friedrich Strauss; **287-289** © RD; **291** ShutterStock, Inc/Jorg Hackermann; **294 L** www.garden-collection.com/Torie Chugg, **TR** © RD; **296** ShutterStock, Inc/Leodor; **297** Photolibrary.com/Fresh Food Images/Philip Wilkins; **298 & 299 T** © RD, **299 B** Photolibrary.com/Blue Moon Images; **300 T** Photolibrary.com/Fresh Food Images/Huw Jones, **B** © RD; **301** © RD; **302-303** Science Photo Library/Dr. P. Marazzi; **305** Dorling Kindersley/Jerry Young; **308** © RD; **310-311** Science Photo Library/Babak Tafreshi; **312** © RD; **313** Photolibrary.com/Fresh Food Images/Martin Brigdate; **314-316 TC, TR, BC & BR** © RD, **BL** ShutterStock, Inc/Wendy Kaveney Photography; **319 L** Getty Images/Brand X/James & James; **324-326 L** © RD; **328 L** Photolibrary.com; **330** Alamy Images; **332-334** © RD; **335** Photolibrary.com/Imagebroker.net/Bodo Schiere; **336-338** © RD; **340** Photolibrary.com/Imagebroker.net/Jochen Jack; **341** © RD; **345** Photolibrary.com/Fresh Food Images/Tim Hill; **348** Photolibrary.com/Fresh Food Images/Philippe Desnerck; **349 L** ShutterStock, Inc/Auremar, **R** Photolibrary.com/Food Collection; **351** © RD; **352 T** www.gapinteriors.com/Clive Nichols, **C** www.gapinteriors.com/Costas Picadas, **BL** © RD, **BR** www.gapinteriors.com/Rachel Smith; **353** © RD; **355** Eaglemoss Publications; **357** ShutterStock, Inc/Sky Light Pictures; **359** ShutterStock, Inc/Francesco Abrignani; **361-362** © RD; **365 T** ShutterStock, Inc/DVARG, **B** iStockphoto.com/eAlisa; **366** SuperStock Ltd./NHPA; **367** www.garden-collection.com/Marie O'Hara; **370** SuperStock Ltd./fstop; **373** ShutterStock, Inc/Cihan Demirok/CIDEPIX

Project team

Project Manager John Andrews
Project Editor Alison Candlin
Editor Jonathan Asbury
Art Editor Julie Bennett
Designer Austin Taylor
Illustrations Commissioner Simon Webb
Assistant Designer Holly Jackman
Researcher Ollie McGhie
Proofreader Matthew Griffiths
Indexer Marie Lorimer

Writers Jonathan Bastable, Ruth Binney, Rose Shepherd

Illustrators Galia Bernstein/nb illustration, Maurizio De Angelis/Beehive Illustration, Jo Goodberry/nb illustration, Ben Hasler/nb illustration, Scott Jessop/nb illustration, John Ley/a3 studios, Ian Moores Graphics, Sylvie Pinsonneaux/Eye Candy Illustration, Martin Sanders/Beehive Illustration, Glyn Walton/linedesign, Graham White/nb illustration, Darren Whittington/PhosphorArt, John Woodcock, Lee Woodgate/Son of Alan

Authenticators Glynis Barnes-Mellish, Katharine Goddard, David Holloway, Franka Knight, Margaret Maino, Elizabeth Marsh, Sheena Meredith, Patsy North, Cheryl Owen, Tony Rilett, Angelika Romacker, Sara Withers, Rachel Yallop

FOR VIVAT DIRECT
Editorial Director Julian Browne
Art Director Anne-Marie Bulat
Managing Editor Nina Hathway
Trade Books Editor Penny Craig
Picture Resource Manager Sarah Stewart-Richardson
Pre-press Technical Manager Dean Russell
Product Production Manager Claudette Bramble
Senior Production Controller Jan Bucil

Colour origination FMG
Printed and bound in China

How To Do Just About Anything

This paperback edition published in 2012 in the United Kingdom by Vivat Direct Limited (t/a Reader's Digest), 157 Edgware Road, London W2 2HR.

First published in 2011

How To Do Just About Anything is owned and under licence from The Reader's Digest Association, Inc. All rights reserved.

Copyright © 2011 The Reader's Digest Association, Inc.
Copyright © 2011 The Reader's Digest Association Far East Limited
Philippines Copyright © 2011 Reader's Digest Association Far East Limited
Copyright © 2011 Reader's Digest (Australia) Pty Limited
Copyright © 2011 Reader's Digest India Pvt Limited
Copyright © 2011 Reader's Digest Asia Pvt Limited

We are committed both to the quality of our products and the service we provide to our customers. We value your comments, so please do contact us on **0871 351 1000** or via our website at **www.readersdigest.co.uk**

If you have any comments or suggestions about the content of our books, email us at **gbeditorial@readersdigest.co.uk**

While the creators of this work have made every effort to ensure safety and accuracy, the publishers cannot be held liable for injuries suffered or losses incurred as a result of following the instructions contained within the book. Readers should study the information carefully and make sure they understand it before undertaking any work. Always observe any warnings. Readers are also recommended to consult qualified professionals for advice.

ISBN 978 1 78020 123 8
Book code 400-594 UP0000-1